Astrology for All

Astrology without Calculations

by

Alan Leo

PRINTWORLD

Publishers of Indian Traditions

Cataloging in Publication Data — DK
[Courtesy: D.K. Agencies (P) Ltd. <docinfo@dkagencies.com>]

Leo, Alan, author.
Astrology for all : astrology without calculations / by Alan Leo.
pages cm
Reprint.
ISBN 9788124612156 (HB)
ISBN 9788124612163 (PB)

1. Astrology. 2. Zodiac. I. Title.

LCC BF1701.L45 2023 | DDC 133.5 23

ISBN 978-81-246-1215-6 (HB)
ISBN 978-81-246-1216-3 (PB)
First published by Modern Astrology Office, London, UK, in 1921
Reprinted in 2023
Author: Alan Leo (1860-1917)

Printed and published by:
D.K. Printworld (P) Ltd.
Regd. Office: "Vedaśrī", F-395, Sudarshan Park
ESI Hospital Metro Station, New Delhi - 110015
Phones: (011) 2545-3975; 2546-6019
e-mail: indology@dkprintworld.com
Website: www.dkprintworld.com

PREFACE TO THE FOURTH EDITION.

ASTROLOGY FOR ALL, the first of the "Astrology for All" Series of books, has now become a standard work.

As an introductory work to the science of Astrology the popularity of this book has been unrivalled. No calculations or mathematics of any description being necessary, the most simple-minded enquirer has been placed in a position to learn a great deal concerning a science that previously had been associated with abstruse mathematical formulæ, and copious rules for judgment that could only be acquired after many years of patient labour and perseverance.

The success of this work is due to its simplicity of expression and convenience of arrangement. It was written with the object of giving reliable information concerning Astrology in the initial stages of its study, and with the hope that the deeper side of its mysteries will be studied later.

The care exercised in revision and the orderly arrangement adopted in the two previous editions, have left little room for improvement in this, and the few alterations made, allow the paging for purposes of reference to remain as before. An Appendix has been added on "Astrology: Exoteric and Esoteric" (p. 290).

The work following this, and originally entitled *Astrology for All, Part II.*, contains a condensed Ephemeris of the Planets' Places for the past 60 years, and may be used in conjunction with the present work to advantage.

ALAN LEO.

EDITOR'S NOTE

Since Alan Leo wrote *Astrology for All* Maurice Wemyss put forward in 1917 the theory that there were still planets to be discovered, and repeated and elaborated the theory in *Wheel of Life*, Vol. III Appendix VII, published in December 1929. Among these was a group of planets ruling Virgo with rates of motion a little more or a little less than 1° per annum, and having orbits further from the Sun than that of Neptune. One of these was discovered on a photograph taken at Lowell Observatory on 21st January 1930, the so-called Lowell planet predicted by Professor Lowell (cf. MA. 1930. 151). It has since been misnamed Pluto, a name already assigned by Maurice Wemyss to another planet. The approximate position of Lowell-Pluto may be readily deduced from the table given in MA. 1930 p.375. It has a mean rate of motion of roughly 1°.44 per annum, though at certain portions of its orbit its rate is about 1° per annum. The researches of Maurice Wemyss indicate that there is little doubt that it is part ruler of Virgo and reflects the "influence" of that sign (though some writers regard it as ruler of Scorpio, and others as ruler of Aries). The view is also now gaining ground that Uranus is exalted in Aquarius, but ruler of Scorpio; and that Neptune is exalted in Pisces, but ruler of Libra, in accordance with the sign rulership theory of Maurice Wemyss.

The Rational Basis of Astrology.

As each copy of this book is likely to come into the hands of a great number of people who here find their first introduction to the subject of ASTROLOGY, *or at least their first incentive to a serious consideration thereof, it is thought well to devote this fly-leaf to a brief setting forth of the foundational principles upon which the science rests, and also of the claims of Astrology as a basis for character study. There will be many to whom the mere sublimity of the subject will at once appeal; but there are others whose attitude of mind is philosophical rather than devotional, and it is to these that we address ourselves here.*

The *first principle* upon which the science of astrology rests is, that the whole Universe is actually what the term implies—a unity; and that a law which is found in manifestation in one portion of the Universe must also be equally operative throughout the whole. The consequent to this major premise is, that our own solar system being in itself a complete whole, those laws which are operative among the major constituents of that system, *viz.*, the planetary bodies, are also in force among the lesser components of the same system—to wit, ourselves, and the other objects on this earth, whether solid, fluid, or gaseous, whether human, animal, vegetable or mineral.

The *second principle* is, that by a study of the motions and relative positions of the planets the operations of these laws may be observed, measured, and determined.

From these two first principles, aided by present-day observation and a mind capable of a metaphysical grasp of the metaphysical significance of phenomena, the whole science of Astrology as now expounded can be deduced. It is a mistake far too prevalent even among thoughtful and unprejudiced people to suppose that the present interest in Astrology is merely the decadent revival of an ancient superstition, based entirely on accepted tradition.

Nevertheless, since Truth is the same in all times, the learning of the ancients, transmitted to us by tradition—largely in the form of myth—is of the greatest value to the modern student. Indeed, the astrologer who had to depend entirely on the two first principles given above would certainly have a herculean task before him of observation, tabulation and induction before he would be even so well equipped as the reader who procures an elementary text-book such as this and intelligently applies its principles. For while the attributes of the various planets, Mars, Venus, Jupiter and Saturn for instance, are daily shown to be in entire accordance with the *dicta* of the ancients.—

this is a fact that is quite lost sight of by the ordinary critic,—yet the arrival at such conclusions by sheer experimental methods alone would be nearly as long deferred as some of the modern theories about matter and force, which are seen when understood to be after all mere corollaries of the elementary principles of mechanics, already centuries old.

Having thus considered the philosophical, or perhaps one should rather say the scientific grounds for this study, as a means of comprehending nature's laws, we will briefly enumerate the claims of astrology as regards its practical application to ordinary life. It will be noted that we have carefully avoided all reference to the grandeur of the subject and have treated the matter from the dispassionate standpoint of pure reason. And, if the principles here alluded to be not considered proven, it is at least impossible for the most ingenious casuist to demonstrate their impossibility, or reasonably to argue their *a priori* unlikelihood.

The Claims of Astrology then are, that it offers first and foremost a means of general character study entirely surpassing the combined advantages of ordinary anthropological methods, being at once more comprehensive and more subtle. Secondly, and this is pre-eminently its greatest, its divine use, a means for the unbiassed examination of one's own character, and the most effective means of strengthening it. Thirdly, a knowledge of times and seasons appropriate for certain works, and a means of *testing* one's development of character. Lastly and leastly, though unfortunately by many made firstly and solely, a means to some extent—indeed, with those specially fitted, to a very remarkable extent—of forecasting future events.

The utility of the study of this ancient, this *synthesised* wisdom is by no means exhausted in the above condensed statement, but these are the chief features which entitle the subject to claim the attention of every earnest and thoughtful person.

Finally we may add that, while in reality the profoundest of studies, it is so based upon simplicity that anyone can in a short while become sufficiently proficient, not only to " cast a horoscope " (in itself a mere question of reckoning), but also to some extent to " judge a nativity."

THE WORKS OF ALAN LEO

Astrology for All
Casting the Horoscope
How to Judge a Nativity
The Art of Synthesis
The Progressed Horoscope
The Key to Your Own Nativity
One Thousand and One Notable Nativities
Practical Astrology
The Horoscope in Detail
*Esoteric Astrology
*Mundane Astrology
*The Degrees of the Zodiac Symbolised
*The "Reason Why" in Astrology
*Directions and Directing
*What is a Horoscope and How Is It Cast
*Planetary Influences
*Everybody's Astrology
*What Do We Mean by Astrology

*Out of Print

CONTENTS.

CHAPTER XVII.

CHAPTER XVIII.

CHAPTER XIX.

CHAPTER XX.

CHAPTER XXL

CHAPTER XXII.

CHAPTER XXIII.

CHAPTER XXIV.

INTRODUCTION.

MANY attempts have been made to bring the study of ASTROLOGY within the reach of all persons endowed with a thinking mind, but owing to the magnitude of the subject and the great difficulty of reducing a metaphysical science into terms of natural philosophy, the object has hitherto been only partly achieved. In the present work a final attempt is made by the author to reach the multitude of earnest and thoughtful searchers after truth, whose numbers are day by day increasing; more especially to reach those who wish to have some practical demonstration of the widespread belief that a wise ruler is behind all manifestation of life, guiding and influencing humanity towards a definite end, that purpose being perfection—the Millennium.

The day is past for writing a defence of Astrology, and no amount of argument will ever convince the sceptic who is either too indolent or too perverse to investigate a science which claims to explain the law that governs all things. The best test that can be applied, to this as to all other subjects where first-hand knowledge is required, is that of experience.

Reason, thought, and experience, constitute the basis upon which the system adopted in this work is built. The ripened fruit of many years' toil and practice is here offered to those who are sufficiently thirsty for the knowledge that Astrology brings to mankind, the main object of the present publication being to satisfy the demand made by growing students for more light.

ASTROLOGY is the oldest of all sciences. Its history can be traced so far into the past that it becomes a hopeless task to actually discover when and where it had its origin. From Babylonia and Chaldea we find a belief in Astrology spreading throughout the whole world. Once the religion of a great and mighty race, it taught its people to lift their aspirations by faith, hope, and reverence, through the planetary spirits to the LOGOS of our solar system, the One Supreme and Universal Self.

Since the days of happy Chaldea, whose wise priests by the expansion of their consciousness could reach the shining ones, the star of Astrology appears to have waned, and for the multitude to have entirely disappeared. Its re-discovery is due to the spiritual activity that is again reviving the Wisdom Religion, as taught by Pythagoras and his earnest followers, and now once more we hope to see the star of stars slowly rising to shine again in all the splendour of its beneficent glory.

Bérósus, the Chaldean priest, to whom a statue with a gilt tongue was erected at Athens, translated the *Illumination of Bel*, an early Babylonian work, and introduced Astrology into Greece. The Greeks held to the old tradition for a time, but the study gradually became more of an art than a science with them, and had so far degenerated in its teachings that little trace of the original truths can be found in the Greek authors known to us, while it was left to the Romans finally to destroy the little life that was left in Astrology as an esoteric study. Nevertheless, in spite of strong governmental opposition it flourished in the early days of the Roman Empire, in its exoteric form, though through the pandering of its exponents to political exigencies it became corrupted and sank into what was known as judicial Astrology, finally becoming nothing more than a form of divination by which horoscopes were cast for the hour.* By this time the knowledge of Uranus, the astrologer's star, had entirely disappeared, and substitutes were used to supply the place of the mystic planet in 'horary' Astrology; the old traditions were either lost, or had become so corrupted and distorted that Astrology could no longer be called a science, but rather a mere mode of divination.

To restore the Astrology of the Chaldeans is the only hope that is left for all who would make this subject a practical and a beneficial study. With all due respect to modern exponents of the science, who have laboured hard in its defence, we are bound to admit that their study has been too much mixed up with considerations appertaining to 'horary' Astrology, a system which will not compare with the methods of astrological practice taught by the wise men of the East.

The discoveries of Egyptologists prove that the Egyptians had no claim to the invention of Astrology. They were taught by the Chaldean priests, who believe that "An affinity existed between the stars and the souls of men; that the ethereal essence is Divine; that the souls of men are taken from this reservoir, and return to it at death; and that the souls of the more eminent of mankind are converted into stars." With them, "the soul was a spark taken from the stellar essence," a belief held also by the great Pythagoras.

* Horary Astrology.

INTRODUCTION.

When we come to consider that Astrology was the beginning of nearly all that we hold valuable in art, literature, religion and science; that the constellations were our first pictures; and that astronomy, and also to a certain extent mathematics, sprang from Chaldean Astrology, we may judge of its value to humanity: nor shall we wonder at its survival amidst the fall of nations and the decline of mighty races.

THE TRUTH can never be destroyed, and when we recognise in Astrology the law of the Supreme Ruler we need some courage, as well as mental ability, before we commence the task of learning the harmony of that law. Yet the same energy that is expended in seeking to refute it, would, if turned in the direction of learning its first principles, unbar the gate that leads to its understanding.

For the first time since the glorious days of wise Chaldea an attempt is made in the present series to place before the world the true Chaldean system of Astrology. That truth has been preserved in its symbology, and so plain are its symbols that he who runs may read. The time has come to again reveal the hidden meaning concealed so long in circle, cross, and star. We shall commence the task by removing some of the débris that has fallen around the title during the past ages. One desire only prompts our writing, the desire to serve humanity and to give to those who possess an eager intellect and a pure love for truth some of the crumbs of wisdom that have fallen from the table of those whom the author is truly grateful to know as his teachers.

"THE UNREAL HATH NO BEING; THE REAL NEVER CEASETH TO BE."—*Bhagavad Gita*.

Astrology for All.

CHAPTER I.

First Steps.—Elements of Astronomy.

Before entering upon a study of Astrology it is advisable to have some clear ideas concerning the Solar System, and these may be obtained without going into all the elaborate details connected with Astronomy. A general understanding of its broad outlines is therefore all that is necessary, and without being proficient in mathematics anyone of ordinary education may follow quite easily all we shall have to say upon the subject.

Astronomy gives a knowledge of the celestial bodies, their magnitudes, motions, distances, periods, size, weight, order, etc., and generally takes us beyond the solar system far away into space, amid the fixed stars, which are now, by nearly all astronomers, believed to be central suns of other solar systems.

The Universe contains an infinite number of these solar systems, many very much greater than our own. As we *realise* this our vision will widen, our minds expand, and our hearts become filled with wonder and reverence for that Great Supreme and Unknowable Power that is the primary cause of all the glory that fills space. But no amount of speculation concerning other solar systems can reveal the true state of things in the broad expanse of the heavens. It therefore becomes more profitable to us at our present stage to confine our attention to the solar system of which we form a part, leaving the fixed stars with their immense distances and magnitude out of our consideration.

If we draw a circle, and place in the centre a single point, we shall have focussed our attention upon a miniature copy of ourselves in space. If we now expand our imagination and think of our Sun as being in the centre of an enormous circle, extending millions of miles into space and embracing the whole solar system, we might begin to realise what the circumference of a solar system means. It will be well to ponder over this wonderful system. In the days of old the Sun was recognised as the home and source of the primal energy from which came all life and light, it being in fact the centre or, as we would term it for practical purposes, the *body* of the LOGOS of the solar system. From this glorious body radiates the light which illuminates the whole, and there can be no grander conception of God than this idea of One who sustains the whole of His universe by His manifestation, the Sun: "In Him we live, and move, and have our being," truly.

All narrow and bigoted conceptions of religion must fade into insignificance as we realise that the Sun is the light and the life of ourselves and of the whole system.

Can we wonder at the sun-worship of the Chaldeans since they *knew* that the Father pours forth His spirit over the whole world. They worshipped that Spirit, seeking to become filled with it by such love and devotion as we now seem to be incapable of. Many thousands of years ago—for time is past our reckoning when dealing with the stars and with evolution—their civilisation reached its height.

It is now astronomically accepted that the whole solar system was a vast heated nebulous mass which, cooling down, threw off huge portions which finally became planets or worlds, forming a complete planetary system revolving round the Sun.

We cannot fully estimate what we owe to Pythagoras, who upheld the belief that the Sun was at rest at the centre of the universe, and that the heavenly bodies all moved round that centre. This knowledge he had gained from the Chaldeans, but it was not generally accepted, and that which is known as the Ptolemaic system became later on firmly established; and so strong a hold had this idea upon the people about the year 1500, that it was first folly, then madness, and finally impious heresy, to assert that the earth was not stationary!

About the year 1507 Copernicus began to restore the Pythagorean system, completing his work about thirty years later. But Europe was then under the bondage of prejudice and ignorance, so that the same fate awaited this genius as that accorded to other great philosophers, and the revived system met with nothing but opposition and ridicule. Later, Galileo, the champion of the Copernican doctrine, was, through religious bigotry, made to renounce his belief before the Inquisition. Nevertheless he persevered and wrote his celebrated *Dialogues*, which afterwards had their due effect, but at the time reawakened the anger of the Inquisitors. For at seventy years of age Galileo was brought before the dread tribunal, and escaped the death penalty only to be imprisoned in one of their loathsome dungeons, where, to save his life, at Rome in the Convent of Minerva on June 22nd, 1633, he signed a document in which he professes "with sincere heart and faith unfeigned to abjure, execrate and detest the error and heresy of believing and teaching that the Sun is the centre of the world and immovable, and that the earth is not the centre, and moves, a doctrine repugnant to Holy Scripture." Yet the good work had begun, and the reformation assisted it, and now in our own time we are returning to the truths taught thousands of years ago.

Astrology has always been based upon the fact that THE SUN is the centre of the solar system.* It could not be a solar system otherwise. Revolving round the Sun then, we have several planets. The first, not yet discovered by astronomers, is called *Vulcan*. Then *Mercury*, who performs a revolution round the Sun in 88 days, 23¼ hours, which makes the length of his year: his distance from the Sun is about thirty-six million miles. He is a small planet, shining with a pale bluish light; but as he is never more than about 30 degrees from the Sun he is rarely visible to the naked eye. This planet was typically known as Hermes, also as the winged messenger of the gods, by the mythologists, while the Chaldeans called him Nebo: he has always been the planet of warning. It is interesting to note that according to a certain body of occult teaching this planet is destined to become the future physical home for the majority of our humanity, and also that he belongs to our own chain of worlds. His symbol is made thus: ☿

Venus, next in order from the Sun, is nearly sixty-seven million miles distant from the centre, and makes one annual revolution in 224 days, 17 hours; the length of this planet's day almost coincides with that of our own. She is the bright Evening Star often seen about sunset, though at certain times during the year (when she rises before the Sun) she is the Morning Star. We learn, from those more advanced in knowledge than ourselves, that she is inhabited and that her humanity has reached a very

* This is not easily understood by those who have not carefully studied the subject, and it has caused a great deal of misapprehension in the minds of many fair-minded critics

high stage. For each planet, as we shall learn later, is a physical world for the purpose of evolution. Venus was known to the Greeks as Aphrodite, and to the Latins as Lucifer when the morning star and Vesper when as the evening star she shone after sunset. Her symbol is a circle surmounting the cross. ♀

The Earth is the next in order of the planets and its distance from the Sun is about ninety-two million miles. The earth moves once round the Sun in what we know in time as one year, and also rotates upon her own axis once in 24 hours; this is important to remember. (There is also another motion which arises from the precession of the equinoxes which is equal to about 50 seconds in a year, and there is the decrease in the obliquity of the ecliptic of about 52 seconds in a century; but neither of these concern us at our present stage of study.) The earth is surrounded by an envelope of mixed gases called the atmosphere, by which light is refracted and dispersed. This atmosphere, or air, from being dense at the surface becomes more rarefied as distance increases. In it we breathe, and in it do the phenomena of lightning, thunder, wind and rain arise. The Earth was known as Rhea, and the symbol is a cross within a circle. ⊕

The Moon is a satellite of the earth, and makes a revolution around it in an elliptical orbit in 29½ days; she also appears to revolve from one point in the heavens to the same point again in 27 days, 7 hours, 43 minutes; she is 240,000 miles from the earth. The Moon is an important body in Astrology, and should be very carefully studied astronomically. The Moon may be called the mother of the earth; for all life that once existed there, together with its water and atmosphere, has been drawn off by the earth, the Moon being the physical globe in a past chain of worlds connected with our evolution. She has been best known as Luna or Isis: her symbol is the half-circle or the crescent. ☽

Mars is the planet next to our earth and is about 139 million miles from the Sun, has a year of 687 of our days, and a day about 40 minutes longer than our own. He has been known as the god of war and hunting, by the names of Ares and Nimrod; his mission appears to be to dispel terror and fear. This planet also belongs to our chain of worlds. His symbol is the circle under the cross and is made thus, the arrow-head standing for the cross. ♂

The circles of the *Asteroids* come next, the principal planet, which is small, being Vesta. For present purposes they may be neglected.

In *Jupiter* we come to the largest orb (except the Sun) in our solar system. He is about 476 million miles from the centre, and takes twelve years in going round the Sun; his day consists of about ten hours. Jupiter is the next brightest planet to Venus, and is accompanied by four satellites: is in course of preparation for its humanity, being at present uninhabited. This planet has been known as Zeus. His symbol is the half circle over the cross but is generally made thus: ♃

Saturn, the next planet in order, is 872 million miles from the centre, and he takes nearly thirty years to revolve round the Sun; the length of his day is over ten hours; he is surrounded by three rings, and has nine Moons. Saturn was the son of Uranus, and was known as Chronos. His symbol is the half-circle under the cross, usually made in this way, however. ♄

Beyond Saturn is *Uranus*, commonly called Herschel, after his re-discoverer. His distance from the Sun is about 1,754 million miles; he revolves round the solar orb once in 84 of our years, and is accompanied by four satellites. He was known as Ouranos, his symbol being ♅

Next to Uranus comes *Neptune*, the most distant planet as yet discovered, who revolves round the Sun at a distance of about 2,746 millions of miles. His year is equal to 165 of our years, and his symbol is the trident. ♆

These symbols are most important and they should be thoroughly mastered.

ASTRONOMICAL TABLE.

Symbol	Name of Planet	Mean distance from the Sun	Diameter	Length of Year	Length of Day		Hourly motion in orbit	Moons
		Miles	*Miles*	*Days*	*Hrs.*	*Mins.*	*Miles*	
☿	Mercury -	35,392,000	3,058	88	24	5	105,000	0
♀	Venus -	66,134,000	7,510	225	23	21	77,050	0
⊕	The Earth	91,430,000	7,926	365¼	24	0	65,533	1
♂	Mars -	139,311,000	4,363	687	24	37	53,090	2
♃	Jupiter -	475,692,000	84,846	4,333	9	55	28,744	4
♄	Saturn -	872,137,000	70,136	10,759	10	29	21,221	9
♅	Uranus -	1,753,869,000	33,247	30,687	9	30	14,963	4
♆	Neptune -	2,745,998,000	37,276	60,127	—		11,958	1

CHAPTER II.

THE EARTH AND THE SUN.

THE Earth revolves around the Sun, making one complete circuit around that centre in a period which we term one year. In this revolution round the Sun, the solar orb is successively seen from the earth through each one of the twelve signs of the zodiac.

The astronomical and astrological year commences about the 21st of March, which is called the Vernal Equinox. At this time the Sun is said to enter the sign Aries, the first sign of the zodiac, and during the year he passes through the whole twelve signs or 360 degrees of the circle. This journey of the Sun (or rather of the earth around the Sun, causing that luminary to appear to pass through these signs) takes a little under 365¼ days. Each month marks off one distinct division so far as the zodiac is concerned, and by this we judge the internal or *individual* characteristics of the person born in that particular month. This gives us twelve kinds of people, twelve types that stand out very clearly and definitely, the characteristics being the more marked as the Sun's rays pass through the middle degrees of each sign (a sign consisting of exactly 30 degrees).

The earth also revolves once upon her own axis every 24 hours, and this causes the whole twelve signs of the zodiac in turn to pass over each portion of the earth once in each day of 24 hours, a fresh sign rising upon the ascendant at any place *about* every two hours, and one separate degree of the zodiac about every four minutes. Hence we may have two entirely different individuals born within five minutes of time. It should be remembered that every four minutes of time equals (approximately) 1 degree of the zodiac; thus every hour = 15 degrees (15°) *i.e.*, 30°, or one whole sign of the zodiac, equals *two* hours in time. From this it will be seen that a given point on the earth will be two hours, more or less, in passing through one sign of the zodiac. Thus the East point or Ascendant passes through the whole of the circle of the zodiac in one day, owing to the rotation of the earth on its axis; whereas by the earth's revolution in its orbit the Sun is made to appear to pass through the twelve signs in one year, or one sign for each month. The sign occupying the East point (or, as it is called, "on the ascendant") is known as the Rising Sign, *and it is very important to clearly distinguish between this and the sign occupied by the Sun.* Otherwise great confusion will arise. These two separate motions must be clearly thought out, and the astronomical fact of these two revolutions of the earth constantly borne in mind,—once round the Sun, and once upon its own axis; the former taking a year of twelve months, and the latter a day of 24 hours.

There is still another motion through the zodiac which we must consider, making three motions in all—and that is the motion of the Moon around the earth, once every lunar month of 28 days, whereby the Moon appears to pass through each sign in 2½ days, making the complete circuit in a 'moon-eth' or lunar month, a consideration that we will take up later on. These three motions form the elements, the "pounds, shillings and pence," as it were, of the astrologer's calculations, or, to vary the simile, the hour-band, minute-hand and second-hand of his watch.

It must, then, be learned that there are three very important considerations with regard to the signs of the zodiac. *First*, the position of the Sun each month, caused by the annual revolution of the earth round the Sun (given in detail at the end of this chapter). *Secondly*, the Moon's place in the zodiac each day; and *thirdly*, the position of the East point or 'ascendant,' caused by the earth's daily revolution upon its own axis.

The Zodiac is the most important element of Astrology to become thoroughly acquainted with. It is the track, or belt, through which all the planets pass; it is commonly known as the ecliptic, and cuts the equator at the spot that is called the first point of Aries, constituting the Vernal Equinox. The signs of the zodiac should never be confused with the twelve constellations bearing the same names; for though at certain periods of the world's evolution the signs and the constellations coincided, and will do so again, this is *not* now the case; but this will be thoroughly explained in its proper place. The following diagram, the signs of the zodiac, and the paragraph that follows should now be studied.

The twelve zodiacal signs and their symbols are :—

♈ Aries ♉ Taurus ♊ Gemini ♋ Cancer ♌ Leo ♍ Virgo	*Northern Signs* (spring and summer)	*Southern Signs* (autumn and winter)	Libra Scorpio Sagittarius Capricorn Aquarius Pisces	♎ ♏ ♐ ♑ ♒ ♓

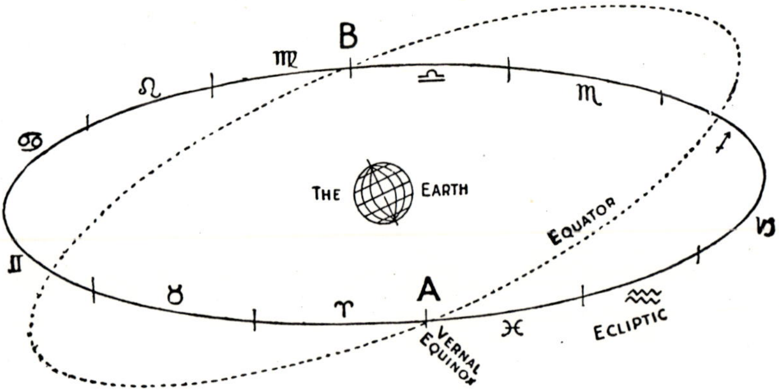

The measurement of this zone or belt called the Zodiac (which extends some 8 degrees on each side of the ecliptic)—or of *any* circle, in fact —is reckoned by seconds, minutes, degrees and signs, as follows :—

60 Seconds (″)	-	=	1 Minute (′)
60 Minutes	-	=	1 Degree (°)
30 Degrees	-	=	1 Sign (*s.*)
60 ,,	-	=	1 Sextant
90 ,,	-	=	1 Quadrant or Right Angle
360 ,,	-	=	1 Circle or Circumference

N.B.—The Signs are not bodies, but spaces of thirty degrees each, and divide the ecliptic, or apparent track of the Sun (and planets) round the earth, into twelve equal parts; and the measurement, both of the Ecliptic and of the Equator, begins where they cross each other as the Sun ascends northward. We measure the distance from this point (called the vernal equinox, or first point of Aries) on the Ecliptic, and call it (celestial) *longitude.* If a planet be a little north or south of the Ecliptic, or Sun's apparent track, we call that distance N. or S. of the Ecliptic, *latitude.* The longitude of a planet is measured on the Ecliptic by signs and degrees, but on the Equator by degrees only, and this is called its *right ascension*, or R.A.; while its distance N. or S. of the Equator is called *declination*, or decl. This will be gone into fully in part ii.

The Sun's (apparent) entry into the various signs of the zodiac takes place on the dates given in the following table, which should be committed to memory. The planetary 'ruler' of each sign is also given.

	SIGN OF THE ZODIAC	SUN APPEARS TO ENTER ON		RULING PLANET
♈	ARIES, the Ram	March 21	Spring Signs	♂
♉	TAURUS, the Bull	April 21		♀
♊	GEMINI, the Twins	May 21		☿
♋	CANCER, the Crab	June 21	Summer Signs	☽
♌	LEO, the Lion	July 22		☉
♍	VIRGO, the Virgin	Aug. 22		☿
♎	LIBRA, the Balance	Sept. 22	Autumn Signs	♀
♏	SCORPIO, the Scorpion	Oct. 23		♂
♐	SAGITTARIUS, the Archer	Nov. 22		♃
♑	CAPRICORNUS, the Goat	Dec. 21	Winter Signs	♄
♒	AQUARIUS, the Water-bearer	Jan. 20		♄
♓	PISCES, the Fishes	Feb. 18		♃

(It should be noted that these dates are approximate only, since owing to leap year the Sun does not always enter a sign on exactly the same day every year. See table of Sun's place at end of book.)

The following diagram shows the bodily parts under the rule of the various zodiacal signs, and it should be carefully studied.

Positive Signs.

Aries ♈ *(head)*

Gemini ♊ *(arms and lungs)*

Leo ♌ *(heart and back)*

Libra ♎ *(loins and kidneys)*

Sagittarius ♐ *(thighs)*

Aquarius ♒ *(legs and ankles)*

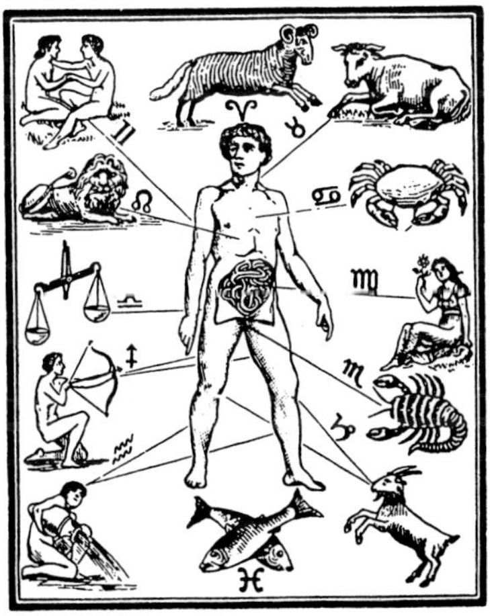

Negative Signs.

Taurus ♉ *(throat and neck)*

Cancer ♋ *(breasts and stomach)*

Virgo ♍ *(bowels)*

Scorpio ♏ *(secrets)*

Capricorn ♑ *(knees)*

Pisces ♓ *(feet)*

CHAPTER III.

The Sun and the Zodiac.

The Sun is the centre of all life, force or energy, and represents the Positive and primal fount of all existence. In the Sun are contained all the colours of the solar spectrum. Every form of existence manifesting in the solar system is bathed in these rays, from which is drawn the life that is at the centre of its existence, all of which may be summed up in the term "Positive Life."

The Moon represents the Negative influence, her light being that which is borrowed from the Sun, she having no light of her own except that which she collects as a reflector.

These two great principles of positive and negative are symbols of the spirit and the soul; father and mother. The former is the constructive, energising, and creative principle, the latter the preserving, moulding, and formative condition. The Sun is the root of all things in manifestation, for without the Sun there would be no life, light, heat nor motion in the physical world. In occultism the Sun is known as the vehicle or body of the Logos of the solar system, and is therefore the highest physical and mental influence that we can know, while using our brain consciousness as a means of cognition.

There is but one life, and that is the life of the Logos. We, as units, are bathed in that one life. The planetary spirits and the planetary bodies have their own specialised forms of this one life, and humanity in its turn holds this life in a separate form while moving in the great whole. The holding of this life or consciousness constitutes the individual, who individualises the special ray of the great All-consciousness, and thus knows himself as I, the Ego. It is this specialisation of the rays of consciousness, or solar life, that makes the Individuality. This work of building up the Individuality, as it is called, has taken vast cycles of time to accomplish, requiring many earth lives and physical embodiments to produce the wonderful results that we are familiar with to-day. Potentially we are all sons of God, sparks from the great flame, sent forth from the bosom of the Father to become like unto Him; each to acquire a definite self-consciousness and to maintain a separate centre from which the individual creative powers may become manifest. When this great truth is realised, we shall understand the true meaning of the word *sacrifice*, and turn our thoughts in adoration and devotion to those Great Ones who have guided us in this grand scheme of evolution to the point of self-consciousness.

The SUN may stand to us as a symbol of spirit, and the MOON as matter, the two acting in unison as spirit-matter, or life and form. If we can think of these two factors as positive and negative, we shall find it easier to understand all that follows with regard to planetary influence, as it is called.

The one great power and central principle is the Sun, and all other symbols are but representatives of the modifications of this universal principle. Each planetary system will be, so to speak, a modification of the consciousness of the Logos. Each is a centre of life and force in the solar system.

The zodiac, as explained in the last chapter, is divided into twelve equal parts called signs, each subdivided into thirty degrees. It is in reality an imaginary circle passing round the earth in the plane of the ecliptic, the first point being called Aries 0°. The twelve signs are in their nature alternately positive and negative, and each contains a certain specialised influence of its own, having a lord or ruler from which the nature of its influence is obtained.

We now come to a very important part of our study, in which we shall consider the Sun's apparent passage through the twelve signs of the zodiac, caused by the earth's movement round the Sun. From the Sun's position each month we may judge of the character of each individual, and we shall learn that, more or less, every person born during the period in which the Sun passes through a particular sign of the zodiac will exhibit its characteristics as delineated in the following chapters. This will indicate the character of the INDIVIDUAL then born, and by the same rule when the Moon is found in these signs at birth the PERSONALITY will be described. Later on we shall explain the planetary influence in each sign, and also extend the main features of this chapter.

IMPORTANT NOTE.

SUNRISE HOROSCOPES AND RECTIFICATION.

THE following delineations, based upon the Sun's position in the twelve signs of the zodiac, are the result of the author's first-hand experience during twenty years of an extensive practice, in the course of which some th usands of horoscopes have been delineated.

These delineations of the twelve types of character may, however, be either modified or expanded in individual cases; though in the main they will be found sufficiently accurate to serve all practical purposes. If further elaboration should be necessary the reader is referred to the second edition of *How to Judge a Nativity, Part I.*

If found desirable to discover the other modifying factors operating at birth, and the true time of birth be unknown, a skeleton horoscope may be erected for Sunrise at the birth-place. The sign in which the Sun appeared at birth should then be counted as the Rising Sign, or substituted ascendant, the remainder of the signs following in their respective order being considered as houses. For instance, on page 187 will be found the horoscope of the Czar of Russia. The Sun is in the sign Taurus: count this as the first sign or ascendant; Gemini will then be the second house, with ☿ in it; Cancer the third house, with ♅ and ♀ therein; and so on with the other signs and houses. The planets in the signs, with the delineations, will be found at the end of the book.

In this way a "sunrise," or approximate horoscope may be erected for anyone whose birthtime is unknown. It will, of course, be only a substitute for the real horoscope.

Persons not knowing their time of birth, and anxious to obtain a correct horoscope, will find the "Delineations based on the Rising Sign," commencing on page 164, very useful, and may, after reading them carefully, come to a conclusion as to the sign of the zodiac rising at birth. Many correct horoscopes have been discovered in this manner, and it is therefore a method to be recommended before going to the expense of "Rectification."

CHAPTER IV.

THE INDIVIDUAL AND PERSONAL CHARACTER OF THE SIGN ARIES.*

☉ *in* ♈. *Mar.* 21 *to Apr.* 20. ☉ *in* ♈.

THIS sign governs the head and face, and the consciousness making the character of the Aries individual will always express itself through the head ; this sign is the first of the *fiery* triplicity and of the *cardinal* cross. We find persons born under the rule of this sign always looking forward, they are leaders in ideals and pioneers of advanced thought. They have great mental energy, but are inclined to be very headstrong and impulsive. They incline towards prophecy, and love to predict things that will happen, for they can easily look ahead into the future, possessing remarkable foresight. When freed from other influences and not slaves to their personality, they become truly clairvoyant, being especially gifted in this direction. This sign gives extreme ideality, and those under its influence are more idealistic than practical. They are always full of new schemes and plans, ever exploring and originating. They are fond of constant change, loving novelty, romance and speculation, nearly always living in a world of ideas. They are very highly strung, sometimes hyper-sensitive, and are noted for their perception. They seem to live more in the perceptive region of the brain than the reflective, and are rarely deceived where perception is concerned. They are extremely sensitive persons, with all the senses fully alive, except one; for, the consciousness being more readily expressed in the head, they have keen sight, sense, taste and hearing, but from the fact of their being most alive in the head they do not *feel*, and are therefore less sensitive to touch in other parts of the body. They are very self-willed and often self-opinionated, so that it is exceedingly difficult to restrain them, as they are

* It is well to note that those born when the Sun is in any sign are here said to be born "in" and NOT "under" that sign : this latter phrase is commonly applied only to those born when the said sign is rising on the Eastern horizon—it is then called the "ascendant" (see chap. XIX). No confusion need arise if the distinction between Individuality and Personality is well borne in mind : for both the Ascendant and the Moon's place are included in the Personality, while the sign occupied by the Sun indicates the Individuality. The dates given are *approximate* : see table of Sun's place.

always inclined to act upon impulse without waiting to mature their plans. They are frank and outspoken, and impulsively generous, yet while they are fond of reason and argument they are often combative and assertive. They can be both sceptical and credulous, but the former mood most often sways them. Decidedly lacking in caution, being far too venturesome, they often run to great extremes, at times even being lacking in discretion—but never in zeal.

They are ambitious persons, who love to engage in great enterprises. With them the intellect is the main feature, but they always find it difficult to understand their own emotions and feelings, and they are too often inclined to fly off at a tangent. When not living up to the highest strength of their character, they have a tendency to jealousy; they expect great loyalty from others, and are somewhat exacting in this respect. When fully individualised these persons make very grand characters, especially in all pioneer work, their enthusiasm rarely being daunted by obstacles. When once the mind is made up they seek to overcome all opposition, more by their dominant will and masterful spirit than by simple perseverance. They are interested in all matters that are occult and metaphysical, and love to live in a world of ideas. Always intellectual, they make splendid companions, being affable, genial and witty. They are never at a loss for a word, and make excellent conversationalists; as hosts or hostesses they are full of little plans for making those around them happy, and they can always be relied upon to provide plenty of entertainment.

They love harmonious surroundings, and possessing artistic tastes they generally seek to make their environment as beautiful as possible. It is not easy to deceive those born during the period of influence of this sign, and were they to cultivate their clairvoyant powers they would be remarkable for their insight; or what is generally termed intuition. They sense others in a surprising way, going straight to the core with those in whom they are interested; for their mental sympathies are always quick to respond to the least good which they may find in others. They are sometimes too hopeful with regard to their enterprises, and are inclined to over-estimate their own abilities, but they are excellent at all work that does not require sustained effort, and where things are required quickly and promptly they are the people who can do them best; but their true mission in life is to inspire and lead, as they are natural prophets and teachers.

The head being the most sensitive part, this will be the first to give out; therefore when the health fails severe headaches result. As Aries governs the face also, the eyes suffer when the system is depleted, and there is liability to neuralgia. This being the head of the cardinal signs, the stomach and kidneys suffer by reflex action. It is essential for the physical well-being of the Aries character to have plenty of fresh air, also daily exercise. The best cure for all their physical ailments is peace, quiet, and rest; for amidst harmonious surroundings they can readily recuperate, and recover that which to them is essential—balance.

People of this type do best in life as organisers, leaders, architects, designers, company promoters, etc., they are also found among phrenologists, character readers, agents, brokers, appraisers, auctioneers, surveyors, salesmen, detectives, guides and couriers, travelling companions, house and estate agents, inspectors, foremen, managers, lecturers, novelists, writers of short stories, photographers, reformers, elocutionists.

The Aries type would marry well with Sagittarius individuals, born from November 22nd to December 20th (provided the planetary indications in the two horoscopes were harmonious); but the Aries person would benefit most by union with one born from July 22nd to August 21st (☉ in ♌), as the opportunity would then be offered of joining heart with head, and Leo being more practical than Aries a better blend would be obtained from this union. The fiery and airy triplicities being in sympathy, it is out of these that the best unions arise, for the Aries person would find those born in earthy or watery signs too matter-of-fact or too emotional to suit his idealistic tendencies: he really requires to unite with those who can draw out his CONJUGALITY, which is more *latent* in this sign than any of the others.

We may sum up those born in this sign of the zodiac as belonging to the intellectual trinity. Their aim in life always appears to be to live in the mind: this makes of them very independent characters, with clear and decided ideas, and a spirit that is dauntless, fearless and aspiring. When perverting their gifts their greatest fault is deception, and they are often clever enough to deceive successfully; but when strongly individualised, their independence enables them to rise above all mean and petty actions, while their pathway ever leads to clear thought, and finally to the perfected intuition; for the inner quality or *destiny* of this sign is TRUTH.

CHAPTER V.

THE INDIVIDUAL AND PERSONAL CHARACTER OF THE SIGN TAURUS.

☉ in ♉. *Apr.* 21 *to May* 20. ☉ in ♉.

THIS sign is the first of the *earthy* triplicity and the first of the *fixed* signs, and in this sign is concealed will and desire, both of which express themselves in the character of the Taureans more or less. This being the sign of solidity, it makes those born in it exceedingly solid, practical, and substantial. They are exactly the reverse of all that has been said of the foregoing sign, Aries being all that is idealistic, while Taurus is all that is practical.

The Taureans are slow, plodding, patient, enduring, persistent, executive and matter-of-fact persons. They are remarkable for their conservatism, and they never seem to waste their forces like the Aries types, who scatter them broadcast. Persons of the strongest wills are born in this sign, and when living exclusively for themselves, they become exceedingly obstinate. They can be very determined, persistent and dogmatic; they usually speak with a quiet, firm and authoritative tone. Possessing a great amount of physical vitality, the Taureans become very furious and violent when severely angered, though as they are usually slow and cautious it takes a very great deal to rouse them; when very excited, however, they are beside themselves with rage. They can do a great amount of good by their steady, building capacity, and are thoroughly capable of carrying out all plans entrusted to them.

They have much perseverance, are steady, patient and enduring. Secretive and very reserved, they yet make faithful friends. They are excellent companions to those possessing ideas, and as co-workers they are reliable, sincere and trustworthy. They seem to possess a great amount of pent-up energy, which makes them very tenacious, holding on till something comes to liberate their stored-up forces. As masseurs and healers they are unequalled. They always benefit persons deficient in vitality, having the power to magnetically heal and soothe those who are nervous and irritable.

The mental and physical vitality of the Taureans is tremendous, and persons born under this sign usually possess a splendid physique. They are fearless and generous, and when fully individualised they set no store on wealth except to do good with it.

When they concentrate their thoughts they have immense power, and WILL then has the ascendancy over desire; but when the latter is most in evidence they become very worldly and incline to take pleasure in the good things of this life, being fond of feasting and comfort. The Taureans make the best psychic mediums, and they may be contrasted with the Aries types by the fact that they are more inclined to live in their feelings than in their minds. The true Taurean may be said to be one great feeling ; but, as this sign belongs to the earthy triplicity, it is more often physical and objective than subjective feeling. Taurus governs the neck, and just as this is so constituted as to serve the head which turns upon it, it may be said that Taureans make better servants than masters. Being trustworthy, they make excellent public servants and officials, and they are often chosen by the public as their representatives.

Taurus governs the throat also, hence this may be said to be the most sensitive part of the organism, while as this sign is the first of the fixed group of signs, one of which (♌) governs the heart, the latter is often affected by sympathy; belonging to the earthy triplicity, moreover, dropsical and tumorous afflictions are indicated.

The *throat*, however, should always have the first attention, exhaustion through speech or singing being avoided. Taureans are more inclined to suffer from too much physical strength than too little, and when giving way to what is often their greatest fault, laziness, they nurse many disorders that produce rapid, fatal results. When the Venus side of the nature is in excess, they are liable to apoplexy and sudden death. It would seem as though they were benefited most by those things that also assist the Aries types, and it would be better for them to exchange magnetism with others and so obtain a more equal distribution of the life forces. They often pass out of their bodies earlier than might be expected through a kind of magnetic stagnation ; so that if they were to energise their minds a little more, and live less in the feelings, they would be greatly benefited in health. All morbid tendencies should be strenuously resisted, as if indulged in they tend to 'grow upon' the Taurean.

These persons possess the ability to get money for others, and Taurus being the second sign of the zodiac, governing finance, they are best suited for all callings in which the handling of money is concerned. They therefore make good bankers, stockbrokers, treasurers, cashiers and speculators. When living more in the personal nature they are best adapted for mechanical and laborious pursuits, where they are required to work slowly and patiently. They are good at all executive work, and are, as a rule, excellent singers and sometimes capable actors. They also succeed as magnetic healers, doctors, and nurses; and in agricultural pursuits as farmers, fruit-growers, or gardeners, also as builders, etc.; they are found amongst bill-discounters, financial agents, book-binders, manufacturing chemists, compositors, dressmakers, florists, French-polishers, house painters and decorators, japanners, collectors, insurance agents, taxidermists, etc.

It would be well for these persons to marry those born in one of the other earthy or in one of the watery signs, to ensure mental and physical sympathy.

Finally, we may say of the Taureans that they possess more vitality than any other of the twelve types, in fact, they appear to suffer from an over-abundance of life rather than a deficit of it. The words "to him that hath shall be given" seem to be applicable to these persons, as their leading characteristic is acquisitiveness, and it is quite natural for them to be conservative, reserved, and secretive. It would be difficult without a knowledge of the planetary configurations at the time of birth to say whether they would be actuated chiefly by Will or Desire. Either one or the other would tend to predominate, but in all cases they would lean more to the objective and concrete than the subjective and ideal; owing to this they often pass through a period of extreme materialistic thought which leaves a strong impress on their future actions. They appear to be born to realise the practical demonstration of the law, for the inner quality or *aestiny* of this sign is OBEDIENCE.

CHAPTER VI.

The Individual and Personal Character of the Sign Gemini.

☉ *in* ♊. *May* 21 *to June* 20. ☉ *in* ♊.

This is the first of the *airy* triplicity, and the first of the *mutable* signs. The airy triplicity governs the mental conditions of humanity, hence we find those born in this sign living chiefly in the mind; owing to this sign belonging to the mutable group, however, they are 'dualistic' —this being the main feature of the mutable signs, causing a tendency to express two conditions and an inclination to be very easily influenced one way or the other. This sign governs the lungs and arms, which have both dual functions, and Gemini persons are rarely content with a single occupation or pursuit, seeming to delight in having two things in hand at the same time. They can very quickly adapt themselves to their surroundings and are hence remarkable for their versatility, while they are very sensitive, having, nevertheless, the ability to reason upon and analyse their sensations. They love change and diversity, and are always the best persons to rely upon in an emergency, as they can instantly respond to the requirements of the moment. They love variety of thought and delight in all mental pursuits, which they sometimes carry to extremes; they seem to take an especial pleasure in leaving their work unfinished. They will take up one thing, partly finish it, and then go on to another, which they are also apt to leave unfinished; therefore their best work is done when co-operating with others, for when working in unity with those who understand their peculiarities they are capable of great attainments: nevertheless, the spirit of diversity often makes them experience two extremes during life.

They can be generous and also niggardly: can present a bold front and assertive attitude, and yet be highly timid and nervous: are conservative and progressive; altogether quite dualistic subjects, very difficult for others to understand. We have known persons born in this sign who have expressed a desire to be in two places at the same moment.

On the whole, however, Gemini persons are rather given to impulse, which generally decides the line they take. They appear to be unable to stand any worry or anxiety, which quite unnerves them; yet when left alone to work out their own designs, in accordance with their own peculiar methods, they can do a great amount of useful work: they must, however, first realise that they consist of many compartments, so to speak. When they can change their times for working and thinking, and, in fact, live in a life of change, they succeed very well; but they must have diversity. This may make them appear to their friends fickle and indecisive, but it is their particular way of working and therefore perfectly legitimate for them. Throughout the whole of their life they must expect dual impressions and many contradictory states of consciousness. Being very sensitive, nervous, and highly strung, it would be well for them to analyse each particular mood they find themselves in, and endeavour not to be too much swayed by the thought-spheres of others. They are ambitious, but it is chiefly a mental ambition for refinement and better conditions.

The sign Gemini governs the lungs, shoulders, arms and hands, and disease or ill-health is mostly caused by excess of activity, or worry; this brings on nervous disorders (which belong to the airy triplicity), and consumptive tendencies (belonging to the mutable signs); therefore the chief concern should be to avoid too much excitement, and keep free from anxiety and worry. It is sometimes necessary to study the laws of hygiene with regard to diet, and plenty of sleep is always required.

These persons succeed best in all work where the hands are employed; they make excellent book-keepers, clerks and commercial travellers; they love variety of employment or posts where the mind can be engaged in two pursuits at the same time. Their best outlet is in the literary world, and as editors, reporters and newspaper men they succeed well, for they have the ability to come into touch with the public mind, and can therefore cater well for the public literary taste. They make good accountants, solicitors, attendants, post office officials, clerks, decorative artists, school-masters, guides, journalists, lecturers, milliners, photographers, postmen, railway employees, secretaries and translators.

These persons would do well to marry those born in some sign of the airy or fiery triplicities.

We may sum up the Gemini type of person born between May 22nd and June 20th as dualistic and restless, intellectual and sensational, nervous and irritable; like the air to which they belong they must ever be moving from place to place or from thought to thought. Forming as they do the last of the intellectual trinity, they seem to be able to express the two foregoing signs in themselves (thus, if we think of Aries as father and Taurus as mother, Gemini may be regarded as the child of these twain). Indeed, it would seem as if they were ever trying to blend the ideal with the practical, the life with the form; for all that is contained in the spirit-matter of the positive and negative union of Aries with Taurus is seeking expression in their consciousness. They are, as it were, placed between two poles, and are ever being called upon to decide towards which side they shall lean, so that their experience of life is ever obtained from duality.

They all possess fine organic quality, and the ability to become very clever: quick-witted and mentally impulsive, they seem to draw a great deal on what is really an inspirational nature. Their chief characteristics are force and motive, and when they seek to discover the motives for their actions they may be considered very progressive, but when they live the unbalanced personal life they become diffusive and unreliable. The inner nature or *destiny* of this sign is MOTIVE.

CHAPTER VII.

The Individual and Personal Character of the sign Cancer.

☉ in ♋. *Jun.* 21 *to Jul.* 21. ☉ in ♋.

The sign Cancer begins the maternal trinity. It is the first of the *watery* and the second of the *cardinal* signs, and governs the breast and stomach: it is one of the most sensitive signs of the zodiac, and being the first of the *maternal* trinity, it governs all home and domestic affairs in which the feelings play a prominent part. Persons born in this sign are characterised as slow but sure: they are best described by the crab, whose tenacity is proverbial, for it will lose its claw sooner than release its hold. The main feature of this sign is the power of retentive memory. Cancer persons have the most remarkable memory of any given by the twelve signs, and find no difficulty in recalling minute incidents of the past. This makes them somewhat antiquated, as they love to dwell on past events, or to go over in their memory past occurrences: through this they often become somewhat limited and hindered, particularly where attachment to family is prominent in the life. Their highly sensitive nature makes them feel very keenly everything that affects the other members of the family, and for them domestic affairs become a kind of brake on their own individual progress. They are highly approbative, and always yearn for the sympathy of others; are timid, reserved and shy, fearing ridicule or disapproval very much, which makes them somewhat conventional, and binds them closely to clan or sect. When attached to the Catholic faith they are very sincere and earnest in all ritualistic observances. They are also fond of banding together into sects, and when moving along the higher lines, men become freemasons and members of occult and secret communities, and women are drawn to mystical and occult meetings. When fully individualised these persons are remarkable for their imagination, but when inclining to the personal side of life, they are fanciful, romantic and superstitious. From sensation they work through feeling to the highest emotion. It is difficult to find harmonious persons born in this sign, though in matters of feeling they are truly wonderful people; this feeling may carry them into the worst forms of sensationalism or upward into the plane of the emotions. Being exceedingly sensitive, their feelings are very easily wounded. In their feelings they possess a psychic gift, being able easily to feel the impressions around them. They are economical and very fond of saving, which trait runs into almost all the details of their life, as they are very fond of saving letters, books, and all kind of curios. They hoard up curios to a remarkable extent, being extremely fond of all that is antique. They greatly respect age and custom, and tend to become very conservative. They are persistent and exceedingly tenacious; they are apt, however, to live more in the personal side of their nature than is good for their well-being and that of those around them, but they have a certain amount of tact, which assists them considerably. When fully individualised these persons possess a great love of power, and once having gained it they seem to have the ability to hold it. They are not ambitious, in fact, but rather lovers of fame and public recognition; this they ardently desire, as they seek a world-wide approval. They can rake up from the past things that others have long forgotten. When acting along personal lines only, they are inactive and inclined to be somewhat grasping.

As this sign governs the stomach, this organ will be a sensitive part of the system, and when the personal element is strong we shall find these persons suffering from weak digestion and gastric troubles. They require to be careful in diet, there being a tendency to suffer from fermentation in the stomach. Worry and anxiety with them are frequent causes of indigestion, which produces a defective circulation, and brings in its train constipation, congestion, rheumatism and chronic disorders. They are liable also to suffer from fancied ailments, inclining to hypochondria.

They are always nervous when ailing, and generally fear the worst results of any functional disorders; in this respect they become so morbid that they actually produce the illness they imagine themselves suffering from. Their cure is a healthy imagination and freedom from all anxiety, especially with regard to domestic affairs.

Cancer persons are best adapted for those pursuits which embrace catering for the masses, or any business or profession in which the general public is largely concerned. They make splendid historians, being able to write up the past with considerable accuracy. As the Aries types would do well as leaders in the military world, as captains, generals, etc., so will the Cancer types do well as naval captains and in all professions connected with the sea. They make good nurses, caterers, and hotel keepers, barmaids, confectioners, actors and actresses, companions, cooks, laundresses, dealers in second-hand clothing, second-hand booksellers, dressmakers, matrons, midwives, mineral water manufacturers, researchers, stewardesses, etc., succeeding best, in all matters of a fluctuating and public nature, in commodities that change hands often, and in matters of small profits and quick returns.

In summarising the character of the Cancer portion of humanity, we may best illustrate the character of this type by saying that they are seeking to become perfectly individualised, and for this purpose *tenacity* is one of their chief characteristics. They are very reserved and sensitive, sympathetic, persistent and impatient, impressionable and emotional. It is at times necessary for them to become what the world calls selfish that they may protect their individuality; but when this has been attained they are strong, self-possessed and also self-reliant characters. This sign completes the first four signs in the zodiac, in which the four triplicities, fire, earth, air and water, commingle, as it were; it is symbolic of the film or auric egg that contains the whole. The inner nature or *destiny* of this sign is Power.

CHAPTER VIII.

The Individual and Personal Character of the Sign Leo.

☉ *in* ♌. *Jul.* 22 *to Aug.* 21. ☉ *in* ♌.

Leo is the middle sign of the *maternal* trinity, the second of the *fiery* triplicity, and the second of the *fixed* signs; therefore it may be said to hold the central point in the zodiac, and when joined with the next sign it certainly contains the essence of the whole twelve signs. Leo governs the heart, therefore it will be from this centre that the character of those born in this sign must be judged.

Standing, as this sign does, in the centre, we shall find the forces of the heart running either upward or downward; but only in those who are fully individualised, or, as it is termed, self-conscious, shall we find the consciousness centred in the heart. Generally speaking, the emotions are fully active in the Leo characters. They are forceful and highly magnetic, and, possessing an abundance of vitality, they carry with them an aura that is beneficial to all. They are genuinely kind, warm-hearted and loving, but usually like to express their love in action, their emotional nature being of the heart. They can be impulsive and diffusive, but it is usually the impulse of a generous nature. They possess a very attractive individuality and are always decided characters. They are usually very practical with regard to their ideals, as they prefer to live them rather than talk of them. While the Aries nature usually spins wonderful ideals in thought and ever seems to be straining after the unattainable, the Leo types are silently and quietly seeking to make them realities. This comes from the wonderful faith which they inherently possess, their motto being "Whatever is, is best"; this comes, however, only when the Leo nature is awakened and the desire has been sent out to unify the individual will with the Supreme Will. Being the centre of the fiery triplicity they possess a very strong love nature, which makes them very ardent and sincere in their affections. As the second of the fixed signs, and in contrast with the Taureans, they have more unity of will and desire, acting more on the side of will than that of desire. The Leos love to rule, but it is a rule rather of the heart than of the head. They are philanthropic, and always obey the impulses of the heart where sympathy is concerned. This sign produces individuals who are more thorough than any of the other signs, for they seem to combine the practical with the philosophical and the ideal with the real. When self-controlled they are wonderful individuals, being able to influence great numbers. They have the power to send their thoughts to any distance, and when conserving their energies, heal through sympathy. They seem to radiate from their centre a beautiful warmth, like the Sun, which is ruler of their sign. But when turning their forces downward and living to the personal side of life they are very amative, with very strong passions. It is found that the weakest and the strongest individuals come out of this sign. The weakest are those who are too easily led through their feelings, though this is often caused by associating with those who take advantage of their Leo nature; they then fall into dissipation and may become dissolute characters. But the true spiritual fire is ever burning within, and phœnix-like they will rise from the dead ashes of themselves to greater and nobler things; for this sign is known by astrologers as the house of the Sun, and it is through this sign that the rays of the Sun become most powerfully charged with spiritual life and energy. When Leo persons seek to become self-conscious they seem to make more rapid progress than those born under other signs, and possessing as they do such very sensitive natures, they are able to readily respond to spiritual influences; their faith then becomes marvellous, and the whole of their life seems to be devoted to doing good to others.

Leo governing the heart causes this part of the system to be the centre and most easily affected when the character is inharmonious and the life running to discord and disorder instead of peace and progress; the circulation then suffers, setting up many troubles of a more or less feverish nature, which in turn react upon the mind, bringing gloom and despondency. It is essential for the well-being and perfect health of all Leo persons that they have a certain time, if only a few minutes each day, when they can be quite alone and perfectly at rest. This enables them to 'start the machinery from the heart' at an even and harmonious rate of vibration. Their best medicine is love, peace and harmony.

All Leo persons succeed best where they have authority, or hold some high and responsible position, but in trades or professions they will do best as jewellers or goldsmiths, as writers of love stories or dramatic sketches. They also make excellent musicians and poets. Although they possess great strength and vitality they are not fond of laborious work, and they can only be really happy in positions of trust and management.

We may sum up the Leo persons as firm and self-controlling individuals, ever aiming at high and noble things. They are all born with a nobility of character which can only be counteracted by contradictory planetary influences.

They are generous to a fault, faithful, sincere, earnest and persevering, and although ambitious their ambition is nearly always turned in the direction of self-perfection. This sign gives the intuitions of the heart, and as the centre of the maternal trinity, it holds and binds all the others by the power of love; its inner nature or *destiny* is HARMONY.

CHAPTER IX.

THE INDIVIDUAL AND PERSONAL CHARACTER OF THE SIGN VIRGO.

☉ *in* ♍. *Aug.* 22 *to Sep.* 21. ☉ *in* ♍.

THE sign Virgo is the second of the *earthy* and the second of the *mutable* signs; it is the third of the *maternal* trinity and the turning-point from the northern to the southern signs: it is specially characterised by its self-containing qualities. Out of this sign, for the majority of individualities, wisdom is to be born; for, although belonging to the earthy triplicity (from which we might suppose that too much of the earthy element would come into their make-up), this sign represents the virgin soil, the spirit-matter, as it were, which yields the most readily to vibrations passing through it from the other signs. The individuals born in this sign are constructive and able to make the most of their conditions they are more generally found in the business world, particularly in pursuits which provide for the general welfare of the whole of the community. As characters they are philosophical, though they seem to blend the ideal with the practical in a marvellous manner. This makes them very discriminative, giving them large reasoning powers and very ingenious methods of working. They are the most critical of all individuals, but they usually turn this criticism upon themselves as well as others, for they seem to be always taking themselves to pieces. They are careful and cautious, and usually act methodically, with much apparent forethought. They are very industrious and persistent, tending more toward the practical than the ideal. They are precise in details, and can readily put right any errors and defects in their own character; but they are also extremely sensitive, not from a sympathetic standpoint, but more from a mental attitude, for they are very introspective, and may be said to know themselves better than those born under other signs. They possess that keen intellect which comes from experience more than from education, and they have remarkable tact and ingenuity; but they are usually fully aware of all their attainments, and are inclined to be somewhat proud of them, so that when running along personal lines, these persons become more selfish than those of other signs, since they are always alive to their own interests. They then become rather materialistic, and tend to carry the practical too far into scepticism and doubt, while they expect from others what they themselves are not willing to give; they thus seek all the good things in life for themselves, and may attain great worldly success, as they possess all the ability to enable them to attain their desired altitude. They may be said to have many faults when running to the personal side of their nature; and they become very domineering, using their good intellectual abilities to the detriment of others, and a certain hardness takes possession of them, which causes them to identify themselves almost exclusively with the external world. But when living more in their individuality, or becoming what is termed more self-conscious, they are really very splendid characters, being discriminative and wise, and often possessing the power to psychometrise and sense psychic conditions from the higher standpoint. They are capable of making wonderful progress in spiritual development and usually seek to live the most chaste lives, becoming like their symbol, a virgin in purity. This sign acts to the maternal trinity in exactly the same way as Gemini does to the intellectual, seeking to express in itself the union of Cancer and Leo.

Those born in this sign possess great recuperative powers. They are rarely sick or ill, and may attribute much, if not all, of any ill-health they may suffer from to their own habits of life. Being natural students of the laws of hygiene, they usually know how to live properly; they should always avoid drugs of every kind, as, being very sensitive physically, they readily absorb the poisons of drugs into their system, speedily affecting the circulation. They are more sensitive to the vibrations around them than persons of other signs; they feel the changes in atmospheric conditions almost directly they begin, and their bodies act like barometers, expressing to the sensitive soul within every change that takes place in their surroundings. Their best medicine for all disease is to be alone with Nature and to have around them harmonious conditions. They will do well to study diet and to be particular in food and with regard to the magnetisms surrounding them.

The Virgo type may be summed up as retiring, ingenious, discriminative, active and mercurial. They always seem to have their wits about them, and are generally self-possessed; they seem, however, to be capable of extremes of good and so-called evil, being much 'smarter' than the majority of those around them; and when living only for themselves they are capable of outwitting others for the sake of personal gain; they generally act, however, with a full consciousness of what they are doing. This arises from their inventive genius, and being thoroughly alive to all advantages and disadvantages, they can so readily adapt themselves to the requirements of those around them that they make excellent entertainers and splendid social companions; and when they succeed in letting go the personal element they are truly beautiful characters.

Persons born in this sign can readily adapt themselves to almost any environment, but they have their best success in life in the business world. All commercial affairs succeed under their ingenious management. They are good providers, and do remarkably well in all matters connected with food stuffs. They are natural chemists, therefore succeed in all matters connected with chemistry. They have also a fondness for general literature, and have success in literary pursuits from author to printer. They make excellent agents, and in fact are quite ready to follow any avocation in which activity and general mental ability help them to succeed in life; but their greatest success is to be found rather in the business than the professional world. They like to handle solid materials; and to deal in merchandise allows their mental ability full scope. The inner nature or *destiny* of this sign is DISCRIMINATION.

CHAPTER X.

THE INDIVIDUAL AND PERSONAL CHARACTER OF THE SIGN LIBRA.

☉ *in* ♎. *Sep.* 22 *to Oct.* 22. ☉ *in* ♎

LIBRA, the sign of the balance, the equalising sign of the zodiac, is the second of the *airy* triplicity, and the third of the *cardinal* signs. It is the first sign of the *reproductive* trinity. The individuality of this sign is expressed in justice, equilibrium, balance, order, and dispassionate judgment. Those born in this sign are remarkable for their powers of comparison; they seem to be able to weigh and balance all things mentally, as though they were inspired. Extremes will be found in this as in all the cardinal signs; but sooner or later opportunities come into the life to take an impartial and dispassionate view. It is the aim of the individuality working through this sign to seek equilibrium; and this causes Libra persons to love harmony so much, that they feel exceedingly sensitive until the whole of the organism is in a state of balance. They have always a kind and amiable disposition, expressing the Venus side of their nature more than any other, and this makes them courteous, agreeable and very pleasant persons. They are remarkable for their perceptive faculties, and there is, moreover, a great amount of inspiration in this sign, so that sooner or later the Libra individuals come to realise that there is an unseen as well as a seen world; this makes them remarkably intuitive, as they are thus able to draw from both sources. They possess the most perfect forms produced by any of the signs, forms through which the soul is able to express itself better than through any other medium. Each Sign of the Zodiac is best studied by knowing its opposite, and in Libra we get the balance of Aries, which makes the spiritual perceptions the keenest and the most manifest, seeming to have the ability of getting occult knowledge through inner perception. These psychic gifts are obtained from the thought-realms, and not from the emotional planes; this enables them, when fully individualised, to temperately expound the hidden knowledge contained in the one great

World-religion. They seem to accept fate in a way that others are not capable of, and to realise the justice of all things. When working along personal lines these persons live more in the form aspect of life: they then become exceedingly approbative and very sensitive, are rather impatient, and inclined to be somewhat careless; but their personal faults and failings are such as may be easily forgiven, for they are usually very even-tempered and amenable to all the good influences that surround them.

When unbalanced these persons suffer from the complaints common to the cardinal signs. The reins and kidneys are the most sensitive parts; the best medicine is music, harmony and retirement, but Libra persons usually possess the intuition exactly how to bring their physical conditions into a state of equilibrium.

They would do best in life as overseers, or in positions of refinement where, through their large perceptives, they can quietly and calmly manage affairs. They make excellent librarians and secretaries. They would also be good stage managers, and musical directors, and successful in any profession where they could preserve harmony or bring it about in others. They would be proficient in all artistic arrangements and would succeed as decorators, arrangers, housekeepers and such like.

To sum up the individuality of the Librans we may consider them as inspirational and perceptive characters, always leaning more to the spiritual side of life than the purely physical. They are sensitive so far as the personality is concerned, when not fully self-conscious, but they are always just and generous. They seem to be ever striving to manifest that which must be attained by all humanity—compassion. These persons possess knowledge which seems to be the cream of all the mental characteristics of the preceding sign, and with them it may be said that the balance of their individuality brings them into real touch with the highest form of mind that we have any conception of, which can only be expressed as a refined mental condition which is not dependent upon the brain for its physical manifestation. The inner nature or *destiny* of this sign is BALANCE.

CHAPTER XI.

The Individual and Personal Character of the Sign Scorpio.

⊙ *in* ♏. *Oct.* 23 *to Nov.* 21. ⊙ *in* ♏.

Scorpio is the third of the *fixed* signs and the second or middle of the *watery* triplicity, also the second of the *reproductive* trinity. Its symbol is the scorpion, whose sting is its most prominent feature. Evolving through this sign we may find all characters, from the lowest and most degraded to the highest and most exalted, for there appears to be more scope for extremes of character in this sign than in any other. The Scorpio character is decided and unmistakable, being rarely, if ever, vacillating or feeble. It would seem as though there were two types, the evil and the good, evolving within this sign. It is the eighth sign of the zodiac and marks the higher octave, as it were, *after* the balance has been turned. It would seem as though the worst products of Scorpio were the failures from the preceding seven signs, whereas the strongly individualised types would be those who had succeeded in learning the mystery of this sign. The 'sting of the scorpion' must be extracted before real progress onward through the other signs can be successfully accomplished. When living the purel personal life, living only for the self, the Scorpio types of humanity are very uncompromising and exacting beings, and their vindictiveness and fault-finding tendencies may be carried to an abnormal degree. Ignorance and lust mark the character of the undeveloped Scorpio nature.

This sign governs the generative system, and when the life forces are scattered and wasted through the excesses of sensuality, these characters become like devils, working mischief far and wide, regardless of the suffering which they cause to others. When evil they are unmistakably evil, and with the thoroughness characteristic of the fixed signs they plunge into sin with a delight that those born under other signs are incapable of; yet when they become regenerate, and fully self-conscious, they reach great heights, the generative force within them, the "vril" with which they abound, being turned into psychic faculties, endowing them with peculiar penetration, and they then become the true mystics whose awakening vision quickly senses the future possibilities that lie before the soul. Gifted with what is called second sight, or clairvoyance, they enter into occultism with a zeal and earnestness that is unequalled.

Those individualised in Scorpio are remarkable for their keen judgment; they can criticise perfectly and impartially, and they are able to give their judgment in a decisive and clear manner; they are very quick in thought, and can at once see the purpose and meaning of the things they are criticising. When awakened there are no better types of humanity than those born in this sign, for they then realise what they may become: when unawakened, however, they criticise for the sake of criticism, and thus become the most exacting and undesirable persons; and when running along the lower levels they are always mixed up in some tragedy or disastrous affair, for they are then jealous, severe, hard and cruel; but when all this force is turned upward and the passions have been conquered and temperance learned, they are of great benefit to others through their magnetic healing power. A great deal might be said of this sign that would be extremely difficult for the majority to understand; the few that are awakened can alone appreciate its wonderful possibilities. Scorpio people have a very remarkable power of attachment, and seem to contain in themselves the silence of Pisces and the tenacity of Cancer, the companion watery signs. They are generally marked by their very dignified manner, and though often affable and courteous, they are ready at any moment to stand upon their dignity. They can be very abrupt and brusque when they wish, but they are always amenable to approval. They have the power of self-control to a very great extent, even to the power of controlling the whole of the sex nature, turning it into the highest spiritual development; they are then (as it were) a huge engine with steam up, all ready to start upon a very long journey. But these persons are powerless to move or make any progress until they have overcome their very tiresome and trying personality, which is always very much to the front in this sign.

Their ill-health arises out of the nature of the fixed and watery signs, giving rise to inflammatory complaints. They suffer from peculiar and uncommon disorders, which usually affect them in some secret part; they are also liable to gout and affections of the heart. But the whole of their disorders may be corrected by conserving the life forces, since, possessing unbounded vitality, they have the power of recuperation to a very marked degree.

As magnetic healers and doctors they find their best outlets to gain success. They have a peculiar knowledge of chemicals, and readily succeed as dyers and chemists, or in any business connected with oils. They make good surgeons and dentists, also detectives, being well fitted for employment where nerve and pluck are required. When living the personal life they have success as butchers, smiths, and those who work in metals. They possess the dramatic ability common to the fixed signs.

We might sum up those persons born in the sign Scorpio as very determined, reserved, tenacious and secretive. They are firm and somewhat proud, and capable of unmistakable traits of character that cause them to be either very much liked or very much disliked. Their somewhat suspicious nature causes them to be distrustful, but amidst all their apparent evil traits they have that grit and backbone which enables them to make higher attainments than those born in the other signs; for the 'wisdom of the serpent' lies concealed in this sign, and they may become so discreet, wise and prudent as to display extraordinary genius. It has been said "the greater the animal the greater the man," and it may be that in the animal passions there lie the germs of that spiritual force which when sent upwards may achieve great and mighty things. That which was *latent* will and desire in the sign Taurus becomes in this sign energy *expressed*. The Scorpio man's desires are potent, and charged with the power to attain, and when the desires are subservient to the *Will*, there are none more powerful or determined. As stated, more could be said on this sign, but that is reserved for another chapter; in conclusion, it may be said of the Scorpio individuals that they have reached the point that decides their future progress. The inner nature or *destiny* of this sign is REGENERATION.

CHAPTER XII.

THE INDIVIDUAL AND PERSONAL CHARACTER OF THE SIGN SAGITTARIUS.

☉ *in* ♐. *Nov.* 22 *to Dec.* 20. ☉ *in* ♐.

SAGITTARIUS is the sign of the archer, who stands ready to shoot from his bow the arrow which is said to never fail in hitting the mark; this alludes to the power of prophecy. There is an idea of freedom conveyed in this symbol of the archer, and of Sagittarius individuals it may be said that they always aim for the highest. If we can judge of the individualised Scorpio character now standing prepared to shoot forth his self-generated thoughts, we can imagine that this sign will fulfil all the mysticism contained in the preceding sign. Sagittarius is the last of the *fiery* triplicity and of the *reproductive* trinity, and the third of the *mutable* signs; it therefore represents the union of the qualities of head and heart, now sent upward in devotion to the Heart of all things. When fully individualised, those born in this sign are great lovers of law and order; they are very intuitive, and prophetic, possessing the power of sending their thoughts to any distance that they wish. The seer and the prophet are born in this sign, and we find those born in this sign, when awakened, to be the most self-confident and self-reliant of any of the signs. They are always looking forward with a bright and happy disposition, full of joy and hope for the future. They know intuitively that the future state is far better than any that have preceded it, and this lends them the power of inspiration, making them always enterprising, progressive and prophetic. They seem to possess only one thought at a time and this thought carries them on to the goal they wish to reach. They have a decisive way of expressing themselves which can never be mistaken, for behind it is the intuition that *knows*. It may be said of those born in this sign that their failings are such as can be easily forgiven, since the worst evils have been left for the sign Scorpio to work out. When personal, they are very personal; for they are then restless and inclined to over-activity, are nervous and highly strung, displaying a tendency to become petulant and irritable. The personal Sagittarian is a bluff and outspoken character, somewhat exacting, and very apt to domineer. When perverted, the nature is exceedingly rebellious, unwilling to submit to the least restraint, and when angered knowing exactly where to hurt. This last characteristic arises from the ability to sense the weak spots in others.

There are very few at our present stage who can express all that lies concealed in this sign ; for it is the 'ninth house' of the Zodiac, the house of the *guru* or teacher, and it leads through science to philosophy and thence to the true religion of law and love. Hence we find the tastes of Sagittarius always inclining toward one or other of these pursuits ; though the scientist may remain in the region of experimental science, unconscious of the higher claims of philosophy and religion to which his science should point him ; and the philosopher may continue immersed in learned disquisitions, or profound study, without attempting to turn his energies into devotion, which is the spirit of real religion, and the true nature of this sign. Nevertheless, the philosophic spirit is always strong within them, even after devotion has been awakened.

As the third of the mutable signs, we find at our present stage many undecided characters born in this sign, quite uninteresting and often very indolent persons. Indeed, many of them are quite content to let others shoot their mental arrows for them. Generally, however, they have clear conceptions of what they wish to achieve, and they set to work to put into practice their ideals. For this ninth sign is the sign of the future, the promise of the coming humanity whose thoughts shall no longer be scattered but undeviatingly directed to the goal which all are destined to reach.

Sagittarius being a mutable sign, and having sympathy with Gemini, its opposite, the lungs are the first part of the system to show weakness. This weakness is generally caused by over-activity, causing depletion of vitality by the scattering of the life forces. Walking exercise in the open air is the best cure for Sagittarians, as they are thus enabled to draw into themselves the vitality needed: moderation should be observed, however, as even in this direction they tend to over-exert themselves. Being naturally fond of sports and out-door exercise they usually live healthy lives, though they are more liable than others to accident, and in this way more often suffer from disease.

In common with those born in the other fiery signs Sagittarians make good military men. We may think of Aries as representing the common soldier, Leo as the captain, and Sagittarius as the general or commander. The common soldier would rush headlong into the fight with the impulse and impetuosity characteristic of his nature; the captain with his determination, decision, and thoroughness would be able to weld the heterogeneous elements into a co-ordinate whole; while the commander (Sagittarius), with his admirable foresight and ability to plan, would see how to direct and manipulate his various corps. Other vocations favoured by those born in this sign comprise teaching, the ministry, law, astronomy, photography, designing, etc.: as inspectors, equestrians, horse-dealers, sportsmen, and advance agents they excel.

To sum up their character generally, Sagittarians may be described as impressionable, active and enterprising individuals, somewhat introspective, but always frank, honest, generous and sincere; loyal to those to whom they become attached, and generally wise in their love expression. Although not so demonstrative as Aries, nor so fixed as Leo, Sagittarius yet gives expressive feelings and an affectionate nature. Being lovers of liberty, those born in this sign can recognise the law of order and harmony, and they make splendid characters when allowed perfect freedom: but when bound or placed under any restraint they become fretful, irritable and rebellious, until it is difficult to pacify them. They never willingly hurt, but when pushed to extremes they are apt to say more than they mean, and sometimes inflict great pain in this way. They like always to do one thing at a time, and in this particular are quite different to people in Gemini, the opposite sign, who like to leave things unfinished, or to do them in scraps; the Sagittarians, however, being of one mind like to accomplish that which they have conceived. Persons born in this sign are capable of reaching to great heights of prophecy, and they may make great progress in the world on spiritual lines. The inner nature or *destiny* of this sign is LAW.

CHAPTER XIII.

THE INDIVIDUAL AND PERSONAL CHARACTER OF THE SIGN CAPRICORN.

☉ *in* ♑. *Dec.* 21 *to Jan.* 19. ☉ *in* ♑.

CAPRICORN is the last of the *cardinal* signs, and also the last of the *earthy* triplicity and the first of the *serving* trinity.

In this, the tenth, sign is contained the perfect number, and all the attributes of the perfect man are to be found concealed in this sign, which in a few words is conveyed in the expression "And whosoever will be chief among you let him be your servant." The symbol represents a high mountain, on which a goat is seen to be steadily climbing towards the top; but many symbols could be used to pourtray the wonderful power that is concealed in this, the strongest of all the signs. If we trace the Sun in his journey from the first point of Aries (spring) to Capricorn (winter) and consider the gradual unfolding of the life forces until maturity is reached, we shall see how in Capricorn a consummation of character well-nigh perfect is attained. The Capricornians, when individualised, are impartial, just and accurate, aiming to be precise, exact and constant, fulfilling all things through persistent, industrious and persevering endeavour. They are assiduous, arduous and careful, zealous and diligent, ever enduring with a calm, earnest patience and grave reflective demeanour.

They seem to have brought the economy of Cancer to a kind of perfection, and they know how to be frugal and thrifty without being mean; when fully individualised they are very contemplative, reserved, deep and profound. They are always independent characters, possessing quiet self-reliance and steady determination, and when living up to their highest ideal are the true servants of humanity; but when not awakened, and living to the personal side of their nature, they pass through the opposite extremes of all these virtues. They are always more or less self-conscious, and seem to know the state of consciousness they are in more readily than those born in the other signs. When personal they are melancholic, doubtful and sceptical, and inclined to be very indifferent and perverse; and when working on the lower levels they are constantly repining and expressing a heavy, morose, cold and distant nature, their despondency and gloom carrying them into an obscurity that is painful to themselves and all who are connected with them. When very backward in their development they become miserly, avaricious, deceptive and dishonourable. Capricornian individuals are capable of attaining great heights, as they possess both ambition and endurance, and with their punctual attention to details, and their thrifty and acquisitive methods, they can build while others are dreaming of the work. They make the most of all their opportunities, and being self-reliant they accomplish their ends. With their practical conception of things, they know how to produce in the concrete the ideal that is in their minds, for it would seem as though all the ideals conceived of in the preceding sign become actual beautiful crystals in Capricorn.

All their ill-health appears to arise from despondency and melancholia, and they may gradually sink into a morbid condition from which spring numerous complaints which would appear to have their seat in the sympathetic disarrangement of the digestive system. Their counteracting medicine is hope and cheerful society; a change of scenery and surroundings becomes essential when they have given way to their greatest enemy, despondency.

Many of those born in the sign Capricorn rise in life through their own efforts and personal merit, and they acquire riches by a steady and patient industry: indeed, great wealth is often found associated with this sign, and some of the greatest aristocrats have been born between the above-mentioned dates. They are successful in all land and building speculations, and are best adapted for general and practical work connected with the earth, agriculture for instance. They make good scientific researchers and writers; and in any avocation where steady application and industry are required, they are the persons to succeed. They have great ambitions and are able to undertake very large contracts with success; they are best suited for builders, upholsterers, designers and decorators. Large speculations, elaborate enterprises, and huge undertakings, are best conducted by the Capricornians.

We may sum up the character of persons born in this sign by considering them as truly Saturnian individuals; they range from all that is icy-cold, limited and barren, up to the calm, cool, contemplative meditator on things divine. A great number of persons born in this sign favour a concrete or ceremonial religion, and they are always more or less ambitious, ever seeking in some way or other to display their independence There are many who 'ape' humility born in this sign, it is true, but it nevertheless gives us some of the strongest characters, able and willing to serve the world to its great advantage.

In studying Capricorn we may learn much from the race which is said to be chiefly under its influence—the Hindus. Among these people we find great learning, great wealth, great power, and great rank; but we have also great servility and, amongst the lower castes, a cringing humility which is truly distressing to those who can realise from what lofty heights they have fallen. In common with the other earthy signs, those born in Capricorn can be extremely selfish; but their virtue lies in patience, contemplation, and reflection. The inner nature or *destiny* of this sign is SERVICE.

CHAPTER XIV.

THE INDIVIDUAL AND PERSONAL CHARACTER OF THE SIGN AQUARIUS.

☉ *in* ♒. *Jan.* 20 *to Feb.* 18. ☉ *in* ♒.

AQUARIUS is the last of the *airy* triplicity, also the last of the *fixed* signs and the centre of the *serving* trinity. Nothing that might be said of this sign at our present stage of evolution could possibly convey the idea of the state to be reached when the whole of humanity advances to the condition of this sign. Its symbol is the man, commonly known as the water-bearer, and that which the perfected man will be in the concrete or the objective world (Capricorn) will also be attained in the subjective world by the Aquarian. If we combine the idea of fixity with that of air, we have the idea of fixed air, from which we may deduce the fact that the thoughts will be fixed and concentrated, and thus become *real.* Aquarian individuals are determined, patient, quiet, unobtrusive and faithful. They have the power of concentrating their thoughts, and are generally philosophic and scientific. They incline toward the unconventional, and thus make excellent reformers; they have bright and clear intellects, and persevere patiently with all their pursuits. They are persons one feels one can depend upon, and they inspire trust by their equable dispositions. They are always kind, humane, and retiring in disposition. They are exceedingly fond of art, music and literature, but seem to have more ability for scientific studies; in these they are helped considerably by their intuitive and penetrating nature. When fully individualised, they have a great love for all humanitarian undertakings and concerns that produce harmony for the many; this gives them marked social tendencies, and makes them delight in giving pleasure to others; they are moreover patient in devotion and careful in thought, and they develop excellent memories for subjective ideas.

The main, indeed the characteristic, feature of this sign is the remarkable ability that it gives for the study of human nature; for the Aquarian individuals are born character-readers, and they are rarely mistaken in their judgment. They seem to contain the essence of the airy triplicity, possessing a mentality of the highest and most refined quality, which makes them natural clairvoyants, clear reasoners, and careful students. When living along the purely personal lines, they are chaotic, diffusive, deceptive, tricky and clever for their own ends; egotistical, and apt to use their inflexible wills in the direction of sclfisb mental desires; or inclined to be vacillating and capricious, often boasting of things they cannot perform. There are very few true Aquarians amongst us as yet. Their day is, however, approaching, and we may catch a glimpse of what we may expect in the lives of Dickens, Edison, Ruskin, and George Peabody, in the clairvoyance of Swedenborg, and in the science of Darwin; all of whom were born in this sign. We may thus gain some idea of what the future humanity will be.

Defective circulation is the chief cause of the troubles common to the Aquarians when not living healthy and progressive lives, for they have more mental vitality, as it were, than physical; therefore exercise and fresh air constitute their finest medicine. Beautiful scenery and harmonious surroundings, and the concentration of their thoughts upon good health and perfect circulation, will do much to benefit them physically.

The Aquarians succeed best in life in all pursuits where steady application of the mind and the concentration of thought are necessary; they make good artists, designers, and musicians. They have inventive genius, and are responsible for more inventions for the benefit of humanity than any of the other signs. They would have success in all employments connected with electricity; or as writers; or in connection with railways.

The Aquarians may be summed up as honest, steady, discriminative, truly intelligent individuals. They are noted for the integrity and sincerity they possess, having the intense and fixed love nature of the fixed signs combined with the refined mental quality of the airy signs; so that they are faithful in their love until the end, the love generally living in the higher mind. They succeed in life where others would fail, having clear conceptions of all they undertake. They are studious and thoughtful, and at the same time versatile. They can retain whatever knowledge they acquire, and are discriminative enough to turn all their forces in the best direction. They are acquisitive without being miserly, and are inclined to leave their possessions for the benefit of bumanity. They seem to readily take to strangers, and rarely consider that others are in any way strange to them, while through their excellent ability to read and judge human character they rarely make mistakes in their estimates. They all possess the latent ability to become "the MAN" that their sign symbolises, and when they have united their grand mentality with their polar sign Leo, in which are contained all the feelings, love, and emotions of the heart, they are then able, like the water-bearer, to pour out upon the earth the living waters of life which nourish and sustain all around them. Light and life await those who break away from the personality and live in the individuality of this sign. The inner nature and *destiny* of this sign is expressed in the one word HUMANITY.

CHAPTER XV.

The Individual and Personal Character of the Sign Pisces.

☉ *in* ♓. *Feb.* 19. *to Mar.* 20. ☉ *in* ♓.

This is the last sign of the zodiac, the sign of the fishes. It is the last of the *watery* and *mutable* signs, and of the *serving* trinity. Its symbol represents two fishes tied together, one swimming in one direction and the other in the opposite. In some respects this sign represents the failures of humanity, and for this reason it is somewhat difficult to express all that is conveyed in the symbol of this sign.

There can be no such thing as a real failure; but if we were to think of a progression through all the signs, and then think of the sign Pisces as representing, on the one hand, those who had succeeded in extracting the virtue from each, and, on the other hand, those who had *failed* to accomplish this entirely, we might obtain some idea of what is meant by the term often applied hereto—" the sign of self-undoing." We do get apparent failures in life indicated by this sign; and these are the persons who may be said to live an entirely personal life, to the total exclusion of the individual; their consciousness, as it were, functioning only on the very lowest levels of manifested life. They are then over-restless and over-anxious, lacking life and energy, apparently undecided how to act, and always waiting for an opportunity. It is exceedingly difficult to interpret this sign with any degree of clearness, for not one in fifty born in it will ever admit his own character. They nearly always pretend to be something different from what they really are, and as they are usually hampered with an over-abundance of self-esteem and approbativeness combined, it becomes very difficult for them to admit their failings. A considerable amount of the Pisces personal character appears to arise from a lack of decision; being very receptive to all the conditions that are around them, they find it very difficult to become fully individualised, and therefore are often merely "a bundle of inconsistencies tied with the cord of discontent." There are more 'mediums' born in this sign than in all the others put together; in fact, many are so mediumistic that they rarely know themselves from other people, and are ever ready to attribute their failings to the conditions that are around them. They are more easily obsessed than any of the other types, and are so psychic and receptive as to draw many spirits around them, who live quite peacefully in their floating aura. Possessing very strong emotions they become much attached to their friends, quietly accepting their advice and opinion and endeavouring to act upon it whenever possible. They are very changeable and imaginative, or, more correctly, fanciful. They love to live in a world of romance, and are fond of sensational novels, greedily devouring everything of a highly exciting nature. Some of the lowest types are apt to take to drink under any severe anxiety and worry, and to give way to the worst forms of temptation. When becoming individualised and more self-controlled, they are very patient, gentle and submissive persons, possessing a quiet yet deep understanding; and as they awaken and unfold, they become deeply interested in occult phenomena.

Their character, as it grows, becomes more confiding and more trustful, but rarely self-reliant; although they are capable of being very honest, amiable, loving and kind, having an abundance of sympathy, especially with all dumb animals. They are ever apt to be too timid rather than over bold, and it will usually be found that where self-esteem is lacking, approbativeness will take its place, and *vice versa*. It is essential that they live pure and clean lives, for they are very magnetic and more liable to absorb evil influences than those born in any of the other signs; the dualistic nature of Pisces makes it very difficult to extract the good from that which appears bad. They love roaming about; are rather fastidious, and sometimes too fond of detail; they are, however, very hospitable, and seek to do all in their power to make those dependent on them comfortable and happy. As caterers, hotel proprietors, nurses, and those who minister to the welfare of others generally, they find their *forte* in life.

The Pisces individuals seem to be more liable to consumption than the other mutable signs; but they seem to cause this themselves, by despondency and melancholy. When worried their digestive conditions become disordered, and this produces many other troubles. Through being over-anxious and worrying they often weaken the system and cause it to suffer from functional disorders. To preserve their health they should be very cleanly in their habits, avoiding all impure magnetisms and infection.

The Piscurians are generally fond of the sea, and they succeed best in life in all pursuits connected with the sea, or water; as captains or naval men they are in their right vocation. They are good travellers and advance agents; they make good novelists, book-keepers and accountants; and are successful as painters, and in any employment that brings some kind of change, or where attention to details is necessary, or where they may complete the work of others.

It would be difficult to find the word that would express the Pisces individuals, except it be that they are excellent *mediums*, and are able to receive some of the impressions coming from the preceding signs. They are emotional and secretive, patient and meditative, kind and generous, imitative, receptive and peaceful when living up to the best of their nature. They love to investigate phenomena, and seem to possess a peculiar understanding of their own. They are nearly all more or less drawn to spiritualism, or the investigation of the unseen. If it be true that they come under the planet Neptune, which is supposed to govern Pisces to a considerable extent, then it is not to be wondered at that the sign is difficult to express; but as there are extremes in all the signs, we may expect in this, as in the others, some very good, and also some weak characters. The inner nature and final *destiny* of this sign is SPIRITUALITY.

In the foregoing chapters the nature of the Sun's influence while vitalising each sign of the Zodiac has been given for each of the twelve months of the year; and the same delineations, when suitably modified, will also give a description of the personality when the Moon is located therein, as will be detailed in the succeeding chapters.

NOTE:—A word of explanation with regard to the term Individuality, to those who have not yet distinguished between the individual part of man's nature and that which we recognise as the Personality.

The Individuality, shown by the sign in which the Sun is placed, represents to us the pure mind, or what is termed in Sanskrit, Manas: it is the human portion, as distinct from the animal—the MAN. The Personality, represented by the Moon (together with the Ascendant), is what is known in the Eastern Philosophy as Kâma-Manas, or the mind linked with desire—generally known as the ANIMAL MAN.

CHAPTER XVI.

THE NATURE OF THE TWELVE SIGNS OF THE ZODIAC.

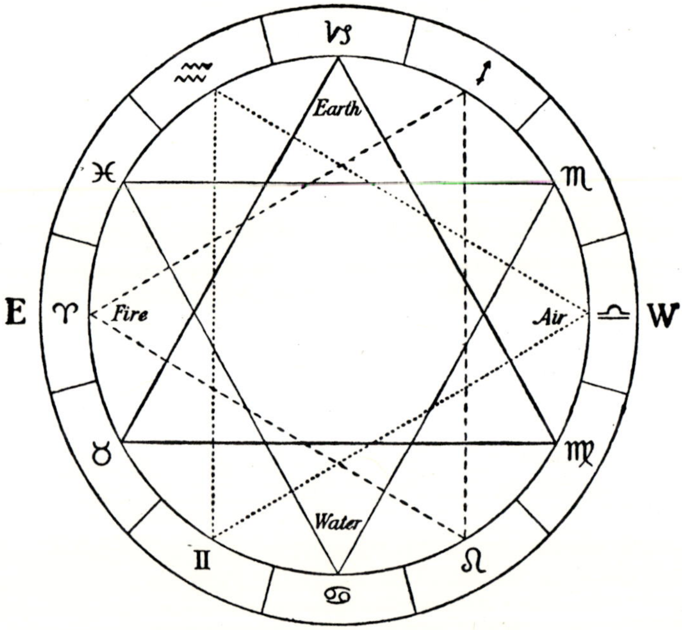

This diagram should be well studied.

WE may now examine the Zodiac as a whole, and also in its various divisions, a correct knowledge thereof being absolutely essential before proceeding further. The Twelve Signs of the Zodiac play a most important part in the delineation of nativities, and unless the true nature of each sign is thoroughly understood a correct judgment cannot be given; therefore it is necessary to study the twelve signs as exhaustively as possible. It is impossible to understand the twelve signs as one whole, without perfect knowledge; but we may know a great deal of the whole by studying the signs in part. Taken in their entirety, the signs of the zodiac represent: (i.) the desire-nature, composed of the feelings, passions and emotions of the world's humanity; (ii.) the whole of the personal consciousness that is dependent upon the senses for its experiences, generally spoken of as "common-sense."

We shall now begin to study the parts, separating the twelve signs into pairs of positive and negative; then into four groups, known as triplicities; finally into three distinct divisions, known as qualities, which we may arrange as in the table on pp. 50 and 51.

The IDEOGRAPHS and *symbols* of the signs are of paramount importance. Indeed, it is not too much to say that in them is contained the whole sublimated Wisdom of Astrology; for they form the alphabet of its language, and may almost be said to be the "signs manual" of the great Spiritual Rulers of the twelve-fold division of the Cosmos. And similar remarks would also apply to the planetary ideographs, in relation to our own solar system.

A careful study of the 'primal forms' out of which each ideograph is constructed, and meditation upon the metaphysical significance thereof, will teach the true student, through his inner perception, far more than could ever be imparted through tongue or pen.* These ideographs, therefore, convey in the simplest way the notion of the true inner nature of each sign, far better than any word could do.

Hence we can see how necessary it is that the student should not merely memorise them, but that he should moreover learn to *think* of each sign by its ideograph, and not by the name ordinarily given to it. Thus, Aries should be thought of as ♈ and not as ARIES or *The Ram*, notwithstanding that the animal we call the ram shows this symbol distinctly in its facial contour.

By examining and carefully studying this table, we shall gradually become better acquainted with the meaning of each sign, until we are finally able to apprehend its true value.

* For instance, Taurus (♉) consists of a circle and a semi-circle of equal radius touching one another externally; while Aries (♈) is constructed out of two quadrants in contact, taken from two equal circles touching each other externally—the horizon passing through their centres and point of contact; and so on with the rest of the signs.

NORTHERN SIGNS.

Ideograph	♈	♉	♊	
Sign	ARIES	TAURUS	GEMINI	
Polarity	Positive	Negative	Positive	
Quality	Cardinal	Fixed	Mutable	SPRING
Power	Angular	Suceedent	Cadent	
Nature	Fiery	Earthy	Airy	
Symbol	Ram	Bull	Twins	
Part of Body	HEAD	THROAT	LUNGS	
No. of Sign	i.	ii.	iii.	

Ideograph	♋	♌	♍	
Sign	CANCER	LEO	VIRGO	
Polarity	Negative	Positive	Negative	
Quality	Cardinal	Fixed	Mutable	SUMMER
Power	Angular	Succedent	Cadent	
Nature	Watery	Fiery	Earthy	
Symbol	Crab	Lion	Virgin	
Part of Body	STOMACH	HEART	BOWELS	
No. of Sign	iv.	v.	vi.	

NORTHERN SIGNS.

SOUTHERN SIGNS,

	Ideograph	♎	♏	♐
	Sign	Libra	Scorpio	Sagittarius
Autumn	*Polarity*	Positive	Negative	Positive
	Quality	Cardinal	Fixed	Mutable
	Power	Angular	Succedent	Cadent
	Nature	Airy	Watery	Fiery
	Symbol	Balance	Scorpion	Archer
	Part of Body	Reins	Secrets	Thighs
	No. of Sign	vii.	viii.	ix.

	Ideograph	♑	♒	♓
	Sign	Capricorn	Aouarius	Pisces
Winter	*Polarity*	Negative	Positive	Negative
	Quality	Cardinal	Fixed	Mutable
	Power	Angular	Succedent	Cadent
	Nature	Earthy	Airy	Watery
	Symbol	Goat	The Man	The Fishes
	Part of Body	Knees	Ankles	Feet
	No. of Sign	x.	xi.	xii.

SOUTHERN SIGNS.

The following two groupings will greatly assist us :—

Triplicities.

Fiery	♈ ♌ ♐
Earthy	♉ ♍ ♑
Airy	♊ ♎ ♒
Watery	♋ ♏ ♓

Groups of Qualities.

Cardinal	♈ ♋ ♎ ♑
Fixed	♉ ♌ ♏ ♒
Mutable	♊ ♍ ♐ ♓

[Readers who are not fond of metaphysical thought may omit this and the two following paragraphs, without prejudice to the continuity of the subject.]

It is to be specially remarked that these are not arbitrary or casual arrangements. A "triplicity" of signs of like nature consists of three signs representing a three-fold manifestation of ONE nature—fiery, for example; and its differentiation into three modes of manifestation is due to the fact that *spirit in manifestation* necessarily possesses three attributes. This idea is familiar to all as the religious idea of the trinity of Deity, who possesses the three attributes of Activity, Power, and Wisdom; this necessity of a triune manifestation being reflected in man, who expresses himself as *body*, *spirit* and *soul.* The three dimensions of space—length, breadth, and depth—are but examples of the inherent tri-unity of all our conceptions. This "triune" nature is a *spiritual* characteristic, it is to be remembered: and this latter consideration will throw light on the reason why the 'trine' aspect (which will claim our attention later on) should be always found to be a harmonious one.

The four "natures"—fiery, earthy, airy and watery—on the other hand, are divisions arising purely out of the necessities of *material* manifestation and they are limited solely to the plane of matter, corresponding to the 'square' aspect and being concerned with physical manifestation. Just as the division treated of in the last paragraph results from the relation of the △ to the ○ (see diagram at commencement of chapter), so is the present one founded on the relation of the + to the ○. This division results from the essential duality of life and form, *life* being represented by the horizontal, and *form* by the vertical; both, of course, being essential to evolution. Each of these having two 'poles' as it were, centrifugal and centripetal in their nature, we have thus a four-fold differentiation.

We have then (1) a four-fold division (⊕), appertaining only to the plane of physical manifestation, and consisting of signs of fiery, earthy, airy and watery natures respectively; and (2) a three-fold division ((△)) appertaining primarily to the spiritual condition, but nevertheless reflected into material manifestation, and consisting of those "qualities" named by astrologers 'cardinal' 'fixed' and 'mutable,' and corresponding to the divine attributes ot Activity, Power, and Wisdom (or to the human being's *body*, *spirit* and *soul*), respectively. These are the essential facts to be grasped, and the important distinctions to be borne in mind.

We may now discover the meaning of *the triplicities* by separating them into pairs, as follows:

Positive Group	♈ ♌ ♐ ARIES, LEO, SAGITTARIUS	Fiery and ardent	The ideal and intuitive world
Negative Group	♏ ♋ ♓ SCORPIO, CANCER, PISCES	Watery and plastic	The astral and psychic world

The FIERY signs represent energy, force and life, and govern the passions and higher emotions, the highest feelings in which warmth and activity are expressed. They have a tendency to expand, to burn up and refine all the dross out of the nature, and expend in force the best part of the emotions: the direction of the energy depends upon the strength of the will behind, and is seen by the planetary indications.

The WATERY signs represent the receptive part of the nature, which, unless moved by desire or impulse from without, is inactive: they govern the personal feelings and the sensitive part of the nature. In undeveloped types sensation is needed to enable those under their influence to realise that they are attached to their personality; but in the more evolved, the feelings are instinctive, giving rise to intuition, and the psychic nature is more active. The watery signs govern the negative and more dependent side of the desire nature; they *seek* affection, while the fiery signs prefer to *give* it—the latter are the pursuers, the former the receivers.

The next pair are composed of AIRY and EARTHY signs, and their nature may be learned by comparison.

Positive Group	♊ ♎ ♒ GEMINI, LIBRA, AQUARIUS	Airy and intellectual	The mental and artistic world
Negative Group	♍ ♉ ♑ VIRGO, TAURUS, CAPRICORN	Earthy and solid	The physical and objective world

This group is composed of the signs that have to do with the mind rather than the feelings, more particularly the positive signs of this group, belonging to the airy triplicity. We may analyse this group in the same way as the former, the airy signs representing the intellectual, educational, mental, artistic or professional characteristics, and the earthy the practical, business and politic side of life. Those individuals born in the former signs live more in the intellectual world and think out the plans for the future; the latter carry them out in detail by practical, solid, matter-of-fact methods.

These remarks might be extended to a great length, but we must pass on to the method of learning the exact value of each sign apart from these groups: this is obtained by studying the *qualities*, which are CARDINAL, FIXED and MUTABLE, as follows:

Quality.	*Signs.*	*Expression.*
CARDINAL	♈ ♋ ♎ ♑	Intellect, Ambition, Ideality.
FIXED	♉ ♌ ♏ ♒	Will, Power, Purpose.
MUTABLE	♊ ♍ ♐ ♓	Emotion, Flexibility, Restlessness.

There is furthermore a division of the twelve signs into four *trinities*, consisting of groups of three signs taken in zodiacal order: thus,

(1) INTELLECTUAL TRINITY		♈ ♉ ♊
(2) MATERNAL	"	♋ ♌ ♍
(3) GENERATIVE	"	♎ ♏ ♐
(4) SERVING	"	♑ ♒ ♓

Again, the first four signs of the zodiac, ♈ ♉ ♊ ♋, are *physical* signs. The four middle signs, ♌ ♍ ♎ ♏, are *psychic* signs, and the last four signs, ♐ ♑ ♒ ♓, are *spiritual* signs; but until the true nature of each sign is fully understood these must be considered so in a general sense only. Following the type of nomenclature just adopted these might be well termed QUATERNARIES.

In this way, by dividing the circle into three and into four (i) superficially and (ii) circumferentially, we have four distinct classes into which the signs fall—no two signs occupying the same position in any two classes,—and which we have termed *triplicities* and *qualities*, *trinities* and *quaternaries* respectively.

We must here warn the reader against taking the words used in describing these 'trinities' and 'quaternaries' ("intellectual," "serving," etc.), too literally, or they will be liable to misconceptions—to suppose that for instance a person born in the early months of the year (March to May) is necessarily more intellectual than one born later. Nothing could be a greater mistake. Nevertheless, the fundamental tendency of the first three signs is *in the direction of* intellect, and this, whether the native be a prizeman or a blockhead. And in a similar way the other terms used denote the inherent tendency of the nature.

♈ Examining the signs separately, we find ARIES belongs to the positive, cardinal and fiery groups. We have thus at once a clue to the nature of the sign Aries. In its positive condition we see that it is an expressive sign; and we gather from its fiery nature that it gives an inclination to act independently and to assert its force; and, from its cardinal nature, we may judge that it is an acute sign, giving prominence to all that it indicates. In making a distinction between positive and negative signs, we may consider the former as more directly concerned with the *life* side of evolution, and the latter with the *form* aspect. The energies and life-giving properties are represented by the positive signs, and the medium or form through which the life works by the negative signs. We find in the table that the sign Aries governs the head, and that its nature is ram-like; from this we may judge that the activities are more easily expressed through the head. The ram butts his way through obstacles, and those in whom the Aries nature is the leading characteristic are known as pioneers of dauntless courage and fiery enthusiasm. On reference to the group of triplicities we find that Aries is grouped with those signs governing the positive emotions. Passing now to the table of qualities, we find Aries a cardinal sign, giving ambition, progress and ideality. It does not now require much judgment to obtain a final idea regarding this sign. As it governs the head, we shall naturally expect to find the mental emotions prominent in the character. The life forces working through the head will stimulate the higher emotions, producing ideality and clear thought. It may be that in undeveloped cases (indicated by the planetary aspects) this nature, being perverted, will be passionate, combative and deceptive; but in any case this sign endows those who come under its influence with the higher aspirations, either for external betterment or for internal development.

♉ We may now study the second sign of the zodiac, TAURUS, the first of the earthy triplicity in the order of the signs. This is a negative sign, and we have classed it under the group of "Negative-mind" signs concerned with the objective and lower mind. Being earthy in nature it is dependent upon physical objects for expression. Its triplicity and quality give us the idea of fixed earth, and bull-like character. In the body it governs the neck and throat, that part of the physical anatomy upon which the head rests and turns. It is easy, then, to associate either great will-power or obstinacy with this sign, and one or the other is sure to be expressed by the Taurus nature. Slow to move, these people move to purpose when aroused; quiet and inoffensive, patient and enduring, always acting with deliberation and rigid movement, the idea of OBEDIENCE as the main characteristic of this sign is readily arrived at. Duty and obedience are the high keynotes of the Taurus nature; but when undeveloped, obstinacy and a surly, slothful indifference may be expected. Nevertheless, in any case we may consider that Taurus is the sign of solidarity.

♊ GEMINI, the third sign of the zodiac, is the first of the airy triplicity, and is mutable in quality. All the mutable signs are generally termed common signs by astrologers, there being nothing definite or fixed about them. They are each composed of two characters: ♊, the twins; ♍, the virgin with the ears of corn; ♐, the archer, half man, half horse; and ♓, the fishes. Some idea of this duality may be gathered from the study of Gemini. This is a positive sign of the airy triplicity, and we have placed it with those governing the positive, or the subjective, and higher, mind. The Hindus symbolise this sign by a beautiful woman, amorous and fond of ornaments, also a man clad in armour, thus indicating the double nature of the sign. The key to its nature is obtained from the knowledge that, although an airy sign, it belongs to the mutable group of signs, all of which belong to change, indecision and mutability. We may associate this sign with education and higher mental conditions, but it is still indecisive and impermanent. Using comparison to help us we may compare it with the other airy signs for a moment. Libra is of the cardinal quality, and is thus more pronounced and active in expression, so that from the following illustration we may at once learn to distinguish between these two. The Libra type of mind loves chiefly colour and expression; for instance, an artist in whom the Libra quality is active would paint in colours, while the Gemini artist would prefer plain line drawing, pen-and-ink sketches, or crayon work. The mind of the Gemini nature is plain, but decidedly more professional than business-like; the work, however, although refined, would always be mechanical.

There are two distinct natures in the Gemini person, so that it would seem as though the mind had not completely severed itself from the lower senses; but we can endorse the remark of one astrological writer that Gemini people reason from their sensations. To understand the nature of the sign Gemini, two clear ideas are necessary: first, that it is a positive airy sign ; second, that it is also a common or mutable sign. From these two factors we know that it must be a sign that causes restlessness, and a constant desire for change. It gives quickness in movement, and when governing those who are developed, it gives aptitude in abstract things; but when those who are undeveloped come under its influence, it produces a highly impressionable nature, showing irritability and indecision. We find many literary persons who cater for the public taste, such as newspaper men, reporters, news-collectors, etc., born in this sign. The sign Gemini seems to lack concentration, and the worst trait of character with which it endows its children is diffusiveness ; but there is usually motive behind all their actions. Yet though they are subject to many extremes and moods, they never lack versatility, and they are the best persons to call upon in an emergency, for they readily respond to their environment.

♋ We now come to the fourth sign of the zodiac, CANCER, the first of the watery triplicity, and the second of the cardinal signs. This sign we have placed with those concerned with the negative emotions. The sign Cancer is the most receptive and sensitive sign of the zodiac, and may be likened to a limpid lake, its ripples being caused either by movement from within or vibration from without. It is first negative and then acute, nearly always requiring action to come from without to stimulate and awaken its latency. From this we may judge that it is the sign which has precedence in all personal matters. The Moon has the greatest affinity with this sign, and it is the most plastic, so that all the personal feelings and emotions that spring out of sensation, fancy, and the highest imagination arise from the conditions given by this sign. Like the lake, it reflects and gives back an image of all that is reflected into it, and by this simile we can perceive that the Cancer person has a most retentive memory. But it is only when the lake is clear and free from disturbance that images can be correctly reflected, and similarly it is only when the feelings are impersonal and unbiased that they reflect the true conditions of the soul. If not taken in too literal a sense, the three watery signs may be considered as representing the three aspects of the soul, animal, human and spiritual. Cancer in a general sense is the negative half of Leo, and represents the sensitive human soul ; but this is not to be taken as a hard and fast rule, for the sign is one of form, and represents the film or shell only. There is, however, one feature about this sign that may be learned from the crab, its physical representative, and that is, *tenacity*. The Cancer persons hold on, crab-like, with grim determination, and they will suffer extremely before they will let go. When undeveloped, they retain feelings connected with the lower emotions, and are then often peevish, morose and sour-tempered persons; but when advanced, receptive to the very best influences, they make excellent providers, for they know how to economise, and from their nourishing, succouring and sustaining instincts they contrive to be always at the disposal of those who require their protection; for weakness and strength are combined in this sign, as we can see by the illustration. The crab, so easily crushed, is yet so tenacious that it is extremely difficult to release oneself from the nip of its claw. Cancer gives in place of ambition a love of fame. The negative cardinal signs prefer greatness to descend upon them rather than to achieve it. When pure, the Cancer types of humanity are very psychic, as from their receptive condition they absorb the conditions of others, readily sensing the psychic atmosphere around them. Their greatest fault when undeveloped is their inactivity, for they need a stimulus from without to move them to action. The first feeling in the savage is hunger, which awakens the dormant feelings that are eventually to make the growing ego hungry for mental as well as physical food. A centre has to be formed, and the first centre is that which is formed in the breast, where all the finest feelings reside, to be eventually expressed by the true Cancer nature, in the maternal principle. If sensitive and easily wounded, they are also conservative and loyal in regard to their ties and duties.

♌ The fifth sign of the zodiac, LEO, is a fiery, positive sign, ruling the heart. This is the central sign of the fiery triplicity, and from its fixed nature we may judge that the higher emotions are the chief centre of activity. In all the fixed signs we may expect either indifference and obstinacy, or firmness and fixity of purpose. Power and austerity are the marked characteristics of the Leo nature, and the will usually is rather internal than external. It is a sign of strength and magnanimity. From its position as centre it is more potent and full of meaning than the other fiery signs (this applies also to the central sign of each triplicity). Love of power and command are the prevailing characteristics of Leo people; they live in a world of their own creation, and nothing seems too great for their ideality. Being full of faith they accomplish and achieve by persistent determination; to them their will is law. When developed they carry with them the most harmonious vibrations of the twelve signs, and have the power to soothe and heal. This sign prompts the higher emotions and gives love of honesty and the higher morality. The passional nature is keen and ardent, all the feelings coming direct from the heart. When undeveloped, the characteristics are pride, arrogance and extreme passion.

♍ In dealing with VIRGO, the sixth sign of the zodiac, we first note that it is a negative, earthy, mutable sign, governing the objective mind. It is the central sign of the earthy triplicity, and, in common with the earthy signs, it governs the practical and solid side of formative life. It is a sign conferring upon its subjects industry, and the ability to follow many different pursuits, having great adaptability to circumstance and environment. In this sign are provided all the requirements of the business nature. The mind is full of feeling of the objective type, and the whole nature is very psychic, pliable and instinctive.

This completes the general description of the first six signs of the zodiac. The remaining six may be briefly dealt with, a repetition of the method of judgment being unnecessary.

♎ LIBRA is the centre of the airy signs, and cardinal in quality. It denotes balance, justice and equilibrium. It is an ambitious and aspiring sign, refined, harmonious, and expansive in nature. Intellectually, it gives wonderful powers of perception and comparison, and when developed those who are under its influence are compassionate, and lovers of unity and equality. This sign represents the state of consciousness that is between the higher and the lower emotions, the dispassionate and equalised state of the intellect, the pure mind, freed from the senses: it represents the point in human evolution in which the mind is weighed in the balance, Libra being the central sign of the zodiac.

♏ SCORPIO is a fixed sign, and the centre of the negative watery signs. It is the sign of reserved force and power, and may be termed a formative sign. Moulded by feeling, the character is of the strongest type, the worst as well as the best characters being formed under the influences of this sign. In the undeveloped we find pride, jealousy, and secretiveness, the power for evil working in the direction of hatred and vindictiveness; but in the developed we find the powers of the magician concealed, Scorpio being the sign of regeneration and purification.

♐ SAGITTARIUS is the ninth sign of the zodiac. It is a mutable fiery, positive sign. In common with all the mutable signs, two natures are often expressed, and those under these influences are impressionable, and very sensitive through the emotions. This sign is half human and half animal, the first half tending to religion and the higher emotions, while the latter half inclines to sports and external pleasures. In the undeveloped we find carelessness, restlessness and extremes.

♑ CAPRICORN, a cardinal, earthy and negative sign, is the tenth sign of the zodiac. The ambitious nature of this sign is symbolised by the goat, who reaches the highest summit of the mountain. This is the most formative of the earthy signs; it gives perseverance, industry, prudence, patience and thoughtfulness, but renders the undeveloped capricious, crafty, suspicious and exacting.

♒ AQUARIUS, the eleventh sign of the zodiac, is a fixed, airy, positive sign, of the nature of fixed air; it gives concentration and firmness. The symbol of this sign is the man, denoting it to be the most humane of the twelve signs. It gives intuition, faithfulness, and marked artistic tendencies, with very catholic tastes.

♓ PISCES is the twelfth and last sign of the Zodiac. It is watery, mutable, negative, and the most dual of all the signs. The emotions are deep and silent, and a marked feature of this sign is the love for dumb animals that its natives possess. They are always kind and hospitable, and often very mediumistic and psychic.

It is essential to memorise the symbols of the signs of the zodiac in their numerical order as follows:

Aries	Taurus	Gemini	Cancer	Leo	Virgo
♈	♉	♊	♋	♌	♍
I.	II.	III.	IV.	V.	VI.
Libra	**Scorpio**	**Sagittarius**	**Capricorn**	**Aquarius**	**Pisces**
♎	♏	♐	♑	♒	♓
VII.	VIII.	IX.	X.	XI.	XII.

Harmony, happiness and success in marriage or in business will be more likely to prevail by marrying or trading with persons born in the sign mentioned in the last column of the following table, in which are also given the gems* for each month of the year, and the ruling planet of each sign :—

	Name of the sign.	Planet ruling the sign.	Birth stone or mystical gem.	Harmonious signs for business, marriage or companionship.
1.	ARIES	Mars	Amethyst, diamond	Sagittarius or Leo.
2.	TAURUS	Venus	Moss agate, emerald	Capricorn, Virgo, Cancer.
3.	GEMINI	Mercury	Beryl, aquamarine	Aquarius or Libra.
4.	CANCER	Moon	Emerald, black onyx	Pisces, Scorpio, Taurus.
5.	LEO	Sun	Ruby, diamond	Sagittarius or Aries.
6.	VIRGO	Mercury	Pink jasper, hyacinth	Capricorn or Taurus.
7.	LIBRA	Venus	Diamond and opal	Aquarius, Gemini.
8.	SCORPIO	Mars	Topaz, malachite	Cancer or Pisces.
9.	SAGITTARIUS	Jupiter	Carbuncle, turquoise	Aries, Leo, Sagittarius.
10.	CAPRICORN	Saturn	Wh. onyx, moonstone	Taurus, Virgo, Libra.
11.	AQUARIUS	Uranus	Sapphire, opal	Libra, Gemini, Aries.
12.	PISCES	Jupiter	Chrysolite, moonstone	Cancer, Scorpio, Virgo.

The first column contains the twelve signs of the zodiac. The second column contains the planet ruling each sign, and the third the two birth stones belonging to the sign occupied by the Sun during the month in which you were born. For instance, if you were born on June 26th (any year) your zodiacal sign will be Cancer, its ruler the Moon, and your birth stones the Emerald and Black Onyx. Where one stone only is chosen the first one should be worn, but you may wear either or both. This table will apply equally well in regard to the Rising Sign (chap. xix.).

In this chapter we have gained a deeper insight into the nature of the zodiac; but there is much more to learn, and this will require other chapters. All that has been said here should be well studied, for it will save much labour and difficulty in connection with the judgment of nativities. We may now pass on to a consideration of the positive and negative centres of life and of the characteristics bestowed by the Moon when in each of the signs.

* It is probable that gems are governed by the *planets* rather than by the *signs*, and hence will be in harmony with more than one sign.

ASPECTS.

Throughout this work there will occasionally be found references to "aspects." The complete consideration of these must be reserved for a later volume; they need not be explained here, further than to say that by this term we understand that the Sun (or Moon, as the case may be) is so situated as to be at, or very nearly at, a *definite zodiacal distance* from some particular planet or planets, which distance is called an *aspect.* These "aspects" correspond to the division formed in a circle by the sides of equal-sided figures, or polygons, inscribed therein; these polygons having respectively 12, 10, 8, 6, 5, 4, 3, ($2\frac{2}{3}$), ($2\frac{1}{2}$), ($2\frac{2}{5}$), (2) and (0) sides, thus forming a complete series, as follows:—

Name of aspect	*Semi-sextile*	*Semi-quintile*	*Semi-square*	*Sextile*	*Quintile*	*Square*	*Trine*	*Sesquiquadrate*	*Bi-quintile*	*Inconjunct*	*Opposition*	*Conjunction*
No. of degrees	30)	(36)	(45)	60	(72)	90	120	(135)	(144)	(150)	180	360
Ideograph	⊻	s-Q.	∠	✱	Q.	□	△	⚼	Bq.	⚻	☍	☌

With regard to this somewhat formidable list, which is thus given only for the sake of *completeness*, including every aspect practically recognised, it will here suffice to say that those in brackets are comparatively weak, if not inconsiderable, and at least do not need to enter into present considerations.

Of the remaining five, ✱ and △ are always *good* ("benefic"), □ and ☍ always *evil* ("malefic"), while ☌ is variable, being good with ♃, ♀ or ☿, and bad with ♅, ♄ or ♂.

When the Sun or Moon (or any planet) is in bad aspect to another planet, especially any one of the three last mentioned, it is then said to be "afflicted by" or "in affliction with" that planet, and these expressions must herefore be understood in that sense when employed hereafter in this book.

CHAPTER XVII.

The Moon and the Zodiac.

The Sun rules by day and the Moon by night. The Sun represents the positive life-giving principle, and the Moon the negative or receptive. A great portion of humanity is at the present time preparing to emerge from the illusive fascination of the Moon's influence, but it will be many centuries ere the majority are free from its limitations. We have said in a previous chapter that the delineations given for the Sun's (apparent) passage through the various signs of the Zodiac would also indicate the character of the *personality* when the Moon was posited in that sign at birth: with certain modifications, this is true. The Sun represents the heart, the higher emotions, the purer part of our nature, and the character which is at the root of our being; whilst the Moon represents the brain, the senses, and the part of our nature which cognises and gains experiences from the physical and objective world. The distinction between the two luminaries is very marked and definite, although in the truest sense they represent but two halves of one whole. Objectively, we see the light from the Moon when she is above the earth and the Sun below; subjectively, we know that when the personality is strong, and the individuality weak, the lunar nature is in evidence. Strong personalities are full of desire and self-hood, whilst strong individuals are more expansive, broad, liberal, and magnanimous. The former cling to form, perception, and objects, the senses are more sensitive, keen, and active; whilst the latter are not so bound by the senses, living more in the mind and the higher emotions, the subjective world being of more importance to them than the objective; reflection, thoughtfulness, and will-power are stronger than desire and impulse.

Until the student of human nature has learned to distinguish between the character as severally expressed by the *heart* and by the *brain*, he will find it difficult to discover how much individual character there is apart from the personal, or how much is personal and how much individual; particularly at the present time, when, comparatively speaking, there are so few who know themselves. As a general rule, the Moon placed higher in the heavens than the Sun is an indication that the personality is the stronger. When both Sun and Moon are above the earth, both characters may be strong. In nocturnal horoscopes (that is, when the birth takes place after sunset), the Moon is usually above the earth; but it may also happen that both luminaries are below, and both may therefore be weak and the life correspondingly unfortunate. All this, however, will be explained later on when we treat of the judgment of horoscopes.

We will now give a few hints as to the nature of the personality when the Moon is passing through any one of the twelve signs. The term "native" used here and elsewhere applies to the subject of the horoscope. This usage is common in astrological writings, and the term is convenient; but it has, of course, no bearing on *nationality*, such as is implied in the every-day meaning.

☽ *in* ♈. THE MOON IN ARIES. ☽ *in* ♈.

This makes the person an enthusiast in some direction; impulsive, aggressive and militant in manner, sometimes irritable and liable to fits of anger. Insists on having his own way; disobedient to superiors; independent and self-reliant. Somewhat volatile or changeable, and dependent upon impulse; disliking conventionality or discipline. He will achieve popularity or notoriety in some form, and may be placed in some position in which he exercises authority over a number of people. He will be at the head of some undertaking, or will be in some way prominent in his sphere of life, and will go more by intellect than intuition. The mother will play a prominent part in the life in some way, often not a sympathetic or fortunate one; and there is likelihood of differences between the native and his parents, or the latter may die early or be separated from him. He will strike out a path for himself or at least attempt to do so; and much that he does, both wrong and right, will be unexpected by his friends and contrary to their advice. Mysticism or occultism of some kind will show in his life; or the tendency may take the form of a necessity for secrecy in some of his affairs; his occupation may sometimes involve secrecy or mystery, or be of a low class, though this is very contrary to his nature. He will meet with unpopularity or be threatened with scandal of some kind. This position favours military pursuits, and independent or original ventures.

☽ *in* ♉. THE MOON IN TAURUS. ☽ *in* ♉.

This person is quiet and unimpulsive; persistent, determined, and not to be thwarted in his aims. Somewhat hopeful, ambitious, and desirous of excelling. Follows established customs and is conservative by nature, resisting change and outside influences. This lunar position gains friends and favours the acquisition of money, houses, or land. It also favours occupations of the nature of the earthy element; dealing in land, houses, heavy goods, old established businesses; succeeding to the father's business; gain or inheritance from a parent. Sometimes the occupation may be one considered low-class, plebeian, or unpopular, involving secrecy or mystery; but it will generally be remunerative, and the native will prosper financially. This position is favourable for occupations dealing with water and liquids, and for living near rivers or on the coast; also slightly good for money derived from companies, wholesale trading, associations, societies, etc. It is favourable for singing, music, painting; for gaining friends and for joining societies. The native is somewhat sensuous and materialistic, though sociable and of good disposition.

☽ *in* ♊. THE MOON IN GEMINI. ☽ *in* ♊.

This lunar position strengthens the intellect, and makes the native a lover of study, of books, and of scientific and literary pursuits; it inclines him to some occupation of a mental nature. He is active in mind and body; likely to change his residence frequently, or to have more than one house; often goes on short journeys; travels, or is out and about a good deal; is often out of doors, walking or riding, etc., or calling on other people. He is skilful and dexterous with his hands and arms. Is able to live by his wits, and may gain a livelihood as messenger, traveller, salesman, speaker, clerk, writer, designer, journalist, engraver, artist, sculptor; or by study and literature. Is likely to have more than one occupation, or to change his occupation. The mind is very prone to change, and there may be irresolution, or lack of perseverance ; In a 'bad' horoscope, that is to say when the other planets are not well placed, this may show as subtlety and underhandedness, or a lack of straightforwardness and honesty.

☽ *in* ♋. THE MOON IN CANCER. ☽ *in* ♋.

This indicates a personality fond of ease and comfort, homely in his habits, and attached to his family, especially to his mother, whom he will much resemble. He is friendly and sociable in manner, imaginative, emotional and changeable. He is influenced greatly by his surroundings, being very sensitive to outside influences, and so falls in readily with the ways and methods of others, adopts their suggestions, sympathises with their joys and sorrows, and generally takes his colouring from outside to some extent. He is most fortunate when acting under the direction of, or in accordance with the advice of, someone else. But this may be greatly modified if positive signs or planets are prominent in the nativity ; under the influence of Mars or martial signs, especially, he will show much positiveness and independence. There is some ability for mimicking, acting, or expressing the thoughts and emotions of others ; also for music, painting or poetry. This position relates somewhat to mediumship, psychism, and the astral plane generally. The native is drawn to the watery element ; lives near water or travels by water ; deals in liquids ; and is fortunate with house or land property and shipping.

☽ *in* ♌. THE MOON IN LEO. ☽ *in* ♌.

This lunar position tends to uplift the native, to put him in positions of responsibility or prominence, and to give him authority over others as head, manager, or director. He is ambitious, desirous of occupying a prominent place, and does not hesitate to come before the public. He is honourable, generous in money matters, high-minded, candid, warm-hearted. He is susceptible in affairs of the heart, a favourite with the opposite sex, and a sincere lover. This position favours intuition and genius ; it gives a love of music, poetry, or painting, also some love of luxuries, pleasures, perfumes, jewels, fine clothes, etc. It inclines to the favour of those in higher ranks of life than the native.

☽ *in* ♍. THE MOON IN VIRGO. ☽ *in* ♍.

The native has excellent mental powers and is capable of following some intellectual pursuit; he has a good memory, learns easily, and is suited for a great variety of occupations: such as servant, manager, agent, or subordinate in any capacity; any occupation connected with grain or food-stuffs, such as farmer, miller, grocer, maltster, confectioner; or with drugs or medicine, such as chemist, druggist, herbalist, analyst, doctor, dispenser, etc. He makes a trustworthy and fortunate servant and is himself fortunate through servants or those under him. This position, taken alone, tends to a quiet and easy-going, somewhat irresolute, unambitious and unpretentious life. Many friends, especially female friends, are shown. There is likelihood of many short journeys and work as secretary, messenger, clerk, traveller, schoolmaster, etc., also of belonging to some company, firm, society, or association.

☽ *in* ♎. THE MOON IN LIBRA. ☽ *in* ♎.

This position favours general popularity. It gives fondness for music, poetry, and the fine arts generally, with some ability in this direction. This person is affectionate and good-natured, kind in manner and gains friends easily. The native is fond of company, society and friends. Much of his fate and many events of his life will come about through his association with other people, for he will be greatly swayed and influenced by other people; generally by some one person. He works with another person in nearly all undertakings; and without necessarily being irresolute depends largely upon someone else, and can get along best in almost all things when associated with someone. The same may be said of the occupation, for this position tends strongly to partnership, not merely in business, but in almost all affairs of life.

☽ *in* ♏. THE MOON IN SCORPIO. ☽ *in* ♏.

This lunar position makes those born under it very firm and determined, self-reliant and assured, well able to stand alone and fight their own battles. Abrupt and plain-spoken, positive, energetic and capable of hard work, they are yet fond of the good things of this world. Somewhat conservative and averse to change, especially if forced upon them from without, they are difficult to influence and may be very obstinate; yet for their own purposes they will sometimes appear changeable, and will advocate or carry out great and revolutionary changes. They are sometimes irritable, angry and revengeful; this being a very bad position if backed up by other evil influences, for it by no means favours morality, and may give habits of drinking. It often causes a coarseness in speech or manner, and threatens some scandal to the native; moreover, it rather tends against fineness of feeling and refined instincts, though it inclines to psychism, occultism and mediumship. A death occurs in the family, or in the ranks of their close associates, shortly before or soon after his birth or early in his life, and they have in some way much to do with death, as executors, or are frequently brought into relation with the dead, often following some occupation connected with the dead. Attraction towards the opposite sex is strongly felt, and this position favours marriage in a male horoscope, but to females threatens disharmony in the married state or in any relations with the opposite sex.

☽ *in* ♐. THE MOON IN SAGITTARIUS. ☽ *in* ♐.

This gives a quick, restless and unsettled manner, either of body or mind; the native is active in body and fond of physical exercise and sports, is inclined to travel, and is a quick walker and worker. He changes his abode frequently, and his disposition is candid and honourable, kindly and good-humoured, while he is sincere in his religious belief even if it be unorthodox. There is some inclination for mysticism, psychism, and the occult; he is a natural teacher or preacher, and has something of the prophet in his nature. The intuition is active, and there may be some psychic gift, such as clairvoyance, though there is a tendency to dreaming and somnambulism. There will be talent or even genius for religion, philosophy, music, or poetry. In the lower type of horoscope the animal nature of the sign will be to the fore, and then occupations and amusements connected with shipping and horses will be prominent in the life. A faithful worker or servant, he himself benefits by servants or those under him. He is likely to have two occupations, or to change his occupation.

☽ *in* ♑. THE MOON IN CAPRICORN. ☽ *in* ♑.

This tends to bring the native before the public for good or evil, causing popularity or notoriety, though it usually has some drawback attaching to it. He will achieve relative fame, and will move in some sphere that brings him before many people. If the Moon is well aspected at birth, he will be popular as the head of some undertaking, or will attract attention as a prominent or responsible person in some way, for something he has done or with which he is associated; but if badly aspected in the nativity, the publicity signified by this position is likely to be of an unpleasant nature. This position gives some degree of generalship and administrative ability, which is intensified if the sun is in a cardinal sign, or if a cardinal sign is rising. There is, nevertheless, always some drawback or difficulty attaching to the occupation, or to the fame or position the native gains; he may raise up enemies, open or secret, or his reputation will suffer, with or without his having deserved it. The native is somewhat fond of show, rather selfish, careful with money matters, cautious and calculating; knows how to influence others, but is often cold by nature and thinks too little of the feelings of others. If other influences assist, he may attain very considerable fame or prominence. If the horoscope* as a whole is a good one, the more undesirable characteristics of this position will be obviated.

☽ *in* ♒. THE MOON IN AQUARIUS. ☽ *in* ♒.

This lunar position gives some inclination for Astrology, fortune telling, dreaming, visions, mediumship, mysticism, and the occult generally. Subjects that are unusual, original, eccentric, and novel, attract the native. He may become a freemason, or join some secret or mystical society, association or brotherhood. He is broad and humanitarian in his sympathies; fraternises readily with those who are congenial to him, is easily drawn into the company of such, and will be found in some club, society, association, or group of those similarly minded. He has an inclination for political, educational, and scientific work, and may join any movement or public body relating to these; has

* *See* Preliminary Notes on p. 72.

some inclination for local politics and municipal affairs. He is sociable and sympathetic in manner, and desirous of the good opinion of others; yet he may be very independent, unorthodox, and unconventional at times. This position increases the imagination and the intuition and mental sensitiveness generally. It is slightly unfavourable for the constitution, especially the nervous system, while if the Moon is "afflicted"* the eyesight may suffer.

☽ *in* ♓. THE MOON IN PISCES. ☽ *in* ♓.

The native is quiet, retiring, and easy-going, restless and fond of variety, changes his mind easily, is irresolute and not always to be depended upon, is rather easily discouraged, and meets with obstacles, misfortune and opposition in life. This position gives a liking for reading of a romantic or emotional kind, for poetry and music that appeals to the emotions and feelings. As speaker, writer, or composer the native is fluent, copious and imaginative, but diffuse. He inclines to be religious, but is in this respect more emotional than intellectual, and prone to feel rather than to reason out. Somewhat wanting in buoyancy and hope, he is too serious or too easily depressed, and may even lack matter-of-fact common-sense and humour. There is sometimes a tendency to intemperance, dissipation, or laudanum drinking, while on the other hand mediumship, clear dreaming, and various psychic powers may manifest themselves. This lunar position softens the frame and increases the fleshy and glandular structures; is therefore not favourable for robust health. There is danger from secret enemies; or the native may himself be not quite straightforward. There is some liability to detention in a hospital, poor-house, or prison; but these bad effects will not ensue unless there are accompanying bad aspects or other indications in the nativity.*

We may now definitely establish in our minds the idea that the Sun represents the *positive* centre, from which the true life is flowing; whereas the Moon is representative of the receiver, or the *negative* and magnetic point. It is necessary to thoroughly grasp this idea before proceeding to the next chapter, in which the soli-lunar combinations or "polarities" are presented.

* *See* Preliminary Notes, p. 73

CHAPTER XVIII.

THE SOLI-LUNAR COMBINATIONS OR POLARITIES.

IT often happens that the birth-time is not accurately known, perhaps no nearer than the day of the month and year, thus rendering it impossible to actually cast the horoscope.* When this is the case, the Sun in the signs, as delineated in Chapter IV., will give us an indication of the individual character, though it is often found that these individual characteristics have to be considerably modified; it then becomes necessary to know what sign the Moon occupied on the day of birth. For this purpose an Ephemeris of the Moon's position from 1850 to 1905 is given at the end of the book.

It is quite true that the Sun's position considerably influences the permanent or *moral* character of the native, while the Moon exercises a considerable amount of influence, according to the sign she is in, over the *personal* character, or that part of the consciousness that is expressed through the brain; so that when the foregoing chapters have been carefully studied so as to know the exact value of these solar and lunar positions, it becomes a simple matter of blending these two influences to discover the characteristics of those born on certain days. The following delineations of the Sun and Moon in the various signs, which may be called soli-lunar combinations, will apply in general to *all* persons born on those days, irrespective of the other planetary positions, though influenced thereby, also (and to a much greater extent) by the rising sign: these will be dealt with separately in succeeding chapters.

The principle upon which these soli-lunar combinations is based is the one given above; that the SUN is the positive, primary, and life-giving element, and the MOON the negative or secondary and formative element. So that when the nature of the sign is thoroughly understood, it

* That is, unless the birth-time is determined from the events of life. This, however, involves much study and elaborate calculation, such as we are not here concerned with.

can easily be seen on the one hand how far the life side, represented by the Sun, influences the *character*; and on the other, how far the form side, represented by the Moon, affects the *personality*. It will save much confusion if the student clearly impresses this fact on his mind :—that the Sun represents the life side, governing the Individual, and the Moon the form side, governing the whole of the Personal (and physical) characteristics. These two symbols blended together represent spirit-matter, each dependent on the other for expression.

The following blendings of the 'life' and 'form' principles, or as we have called them " Polarities," should now be carefully studied.

PRELIMINARY NOTES.

At this stage of our study, before proceeding further into the modifications produced by the blending of the Individual and Personal characteristics in a nativity, it is important to pause a moment and consider the essential elements of which a horoscope consists.

Without going into details for which the reader is not yet prepared, it may be said that a " horoscope " roughly consists of:

(1) The *Solar position*. (3) The *Ascendant*.
(2) The *Lunar position*. (4) The *Planetary aspects*.

The importance of these four factors is indicated by their order, the solar position being paramount.

To revert to a previous simile, if (1), (2) and (3) be likened to the *pounds*, *shillings* and *pence* of ordinary currency, the planetary aspects* may be considered as analogous to those commercial or political considerations which modify the "rate of exchange" or other financial conditions controlling the actual value of gold, silver or copper as the case may be. This analogy is really more close than might be supposed, and it forms a very apt illustration of the way in which the "ascendant"† or planetary aspects may modify the expression of a character that is really *there*, but latent.

For, to continue the illustration, small articles can only be purchased by a copper or a silver coin; and unlimited wealth in gold is of little value for ordinary retail trading, if it is unaccompanied with an ample supply of small cash. Again, commercial operations cannot be carried on by a company, however wealthy, in a country where the requisite governmental concessions cannot be obtained. Yet in each case the wealth and the business ability may both be there, but unable to manifest owing to lack of suitable *conditions*. These two instances illustrate by

* P. 62. † *See* Chapter XIX.

analogy how the qualities 'latent' in a polarity may lack the means of expression. The first one corresponds to a polarity which is only badly expressed through the ascendant; while the second is analogous to the case in which a polarity is hampered or restricted in its expression through unfavourable "aspects."

It is, then, important to understand, and in studying the following "polarities" it is necessary constantly to bear in mind, that the Solar and Lunar positions by which these "polarities" are established furnish only *two*—albeit the most important—of the nine planetary positions, to say nothing of the influence of the "rising sign" (to which a special chapter is devoted later on) and the other factors which comprise the "horoscope."

It must therefore not be expected that *every* detail given will be exactly represented in each case; for the modifying influences of the other planets may greatly accentuate, or, on the other hand, even succeed in entirely suppressing some characteristics. Nevertheless—and this is the essential point—the polarities here given represent the two *chief* factors of the horoscope, so that the salient characteristics described will in most cases be found on investigation to exist in the nature in a latent state, if not in actual active manifestation. This matter has, however, been already treated of in our first manual (*Everybody's Astrology*, second edition, p. 7), and it is hardly necessary to repeat the illustration there given.

When the word 'afflicted' is used, it indicates that one or other of the luminaries (Sun or Moon, that is) is placed in what is known as a "bad aspect"* to some planet (usually ♄ or ♂) in the horoscope. This, as will be readily understood, considerably modifies the native's character, individual or personal as the case may be,—that is to say, it modifies the *expression* of that Individual or Personal character.

Whether 'afflicted' or no, the character will be in its inner nature much as is here described; but the 'affliction,' if saturnine, will have the effect of cramping and hindering, or, if martial, of distorting and over-stimulating the full and harmonious expression of the true nature.

Whether the luminaries *are* so "afflicted" or not can only be determined by consulting the *Ephemeris*† for the year of birth or the *Condensed Ephemeris for the last fifty-five years* published with part ii. of this work. It would be quite impossible to include such data in the present volume, which is expressly designed to deal only with the most general and comprehensive presentment of the principles of Astrology: the details must be studied later.

In the ensuing delineations the term "native" is employed, as has been said before, to denote the individual under discussion. It has of course no relation to *nationality*, as is the case when used in its ordinary sense.

* *See* p. 62. † 1s. per year.

THE SUN IN ARIES.

☉ *in* ♈. **I.** ☉ *in* ♈.

The Sun's (apparent) passage through the celestial sign Aries has been thoroughly described in Chapter IV., so that it is only necessary now to observe that the primary characteristics of the Sun in this sign are force and energy, and that the fundamental basis of the character will consist of an ambitious, aspiring, and enthusiastic nature. During the month that the Sun remains in this sign, the twelve lunar positions will either considerably modify this primary influence, or accentuate it and increase its manifestation. But without the Moon to focus the rays of the Sun and to collect the influences that are constantly being distributed, the individual character would be always flying off at a tangent, having no medium through which it could be rendered definite. In studying each one of these combinations, however, it is important to remember that the solar force is the primary and energising influence, the lunar centre being always secondary, negative, and expressive.

THE SUN AND MOON IN ARIES.

☉ *in* ♈. **I.—i.** ☽ *in* ♈.

This is equivalent to the Sun and the Moon being in conjunction in the first house of the horoscope, and will act in a similar manner with regard to character. This position of Sun and Moon will accentuate the consciousness in the brain, giving great activity of thought and quickness of perception, with strong inclinations to excitement, endowing those born under this combination with an intense desire to be at the head of all things, and to be intellectual pioneers. This position gives, in fact, abundance of energy and vitality, thus favouring health and long life. It shows masterfulness, independence and self-reliance, making a forceful and original personality ; one certain to attract attention in his sphere of life and possibly gain considerable prominence therein. With a suitable horoscope, he will rise in the world. He is fitted for positions of authority and responsibility, and these will usually seem to fall naturally to his lot. In some cases he will be militant in disposition and manner, domineering, irritable, intolerant of opposition or contradiction, hard and unyielding. With the softening influence of Venus or Jupiter, the more unpleasant phases of this influence may be removed; otherwise he will be a tyrant or a rebel. There is danger to the head, brain, or nervous system at some period of life. The Sun will in this case be stronger than the Moon, the sign Aries being of a fiery nature, whereas the Moon partakes more of the nature of water. Over-work, excessive worry, intense excitement, and too much activity (mental or physical) would tend to produce disease of the brain, and if persisted in, would finally result in mental derangement. This combination increases self-esteem and approbativeness, and brings changes in life through too great independence, with many troubles following on impulsive action and rash conduct. This person needs the steadying influence of Saturn, otherwise he may be a slave to impulse. There is a tendency to live too much in the mind, to make intellect too prominent ; and there is, moreover, some danger of becoming too self-centred or conceited.

THE SUN IN ARIES AND MOON IN TAURUS.

☉ *in* ♈. I.—ii. ☽ *in* ♉.

The Sun is exalted in Aries, and the Moon in Taurus, so that this combination strengthens both the positive and negative elements, producing a very strong character. The physical side of the nature is practical; but with the force of the Sun in Aries behind it, the ideal and practical are well blended, while the disposition becomes a very determined one. The result is a fairly all-round character. There is the will and energy to originate and the steadiness and practical ability to execute. Such an one shapes his ideal, or forms his plan of campaign, and does not rest until he has carried it out, no matter at what expense of time or trouble. He can both plan and perform, preach and practise, direct others and do the work himself. He is likely to come to the front, to occupy some position of responsibility or trust. The disposition is composed of the Martial and Venusian elements, the senses being called into full activity. The intellect and intuition are both alike marked, but there is usually a great tendency to be self-willed and dogmatic. The magnetic forces are very powerful, and the affections are warm ; the native makes friends readily and is faithful to them. There is a tendency to be too positive, self-willed, and dogmatic. The intellect and intuitional sides of the nature are both strong, especially if favourable planetary positions bring them out. It is thus a splendid combination for mental expression, and the nature tends to become harmonious, though there is sometimes a great degree of sensitiveness. Those born under this combination may become mental and physical healers, especially along hygienic lines, for this sign gives a superabundance of vitality. This is a good position for financial success in life, also for positions of trust and authority, and it tends in general to make the life fortunate, the personality being able to carry out the ideals of the Aries individuality.

THE SUN IN ARIES AND MOON IN GEMINI.

☉ *in* ♈. I.—iii. ☽ *in* ♊.

This combination gives a considerable amount of mental activity and manual dexterity, but there is apt to be a great deal of restlessness and over-exertion ; for the nature is a very changeable one, loving variety and expression, while there is a lack of determination and tenacity of purpose. This combination gives refinement and artistic tendencies, and makes those under its influence good novelists and clever writers of fiction, though the dualistic tendencies of Gemini cause much of the qualities of Aries to be wasted, so that there is frequently less done than is talked about. The native is witty, lively in mind and speech, prone to exaggeration, of great mental ingenuity, and good at all forms of mental work, study, education, speaking. In a bad horoscope, a tendency to deceit or dishonesty, or nervous or mental trouble is shown. It is not a very reliable combination until some degree of thought-control has been practised; but it decidedly favours mechanical ability, and is good for travel and all literary undertakings, promising some success in life in this direction. Over-activity and excitement will tend to produce nervous troubles, and rest will often be required to restore harmony to the system.

THE SUN IN ARIES AND MOON IN CANCER.

☉ *in* ♈. I.—iv. ☽ *in* ♋.

This is an exceedingly sensitive combination, giving a considerable amount of ambition and love of fame; and the Moon, being receptive in nature and here placed in the executive sign Cancer, will add the power of achievement to the splendid idealism of Aries, greatly adding to the strength of the combination, which, moreover, increases the intuitive and psychic faculties, expands the imagination, improves the memory and strengthens the brain. There are two somewhat contradictory sides to the character; one enterprising, active, bold, and domineering, and the other sensitive, domestic and homely. Under cross influences this may cause irritation or bad temper, and may affect the nerves or even the mind: it gives more caution and acquisitiveness than Aries alone. The sensitiveness of this position causes those born under it to feel very keenly the surrounding conditions, and to suffer from them occasionally, though when not too approbative they are easily able to reason and arrive at correct conclusions; there is generally a great deal of anxiety, especially in regard to domestic affairs or matters connected with home life. Care in diet is necessary for the successful expression of this combination, as the health is often marred by worry and anxiety. It promises success in life through matters connected with horticulture, and gives ability to design and plan, especially in architecture.

THE SUN IN ARIES AND MOON IN LEO.

☉ *in* ♈. I.—v. ☽ *in* ♌.

This combination gives remarkable intuition and a very affectionate and warm heart, with an innate sensitiveness to the surrounding thought sphere. It is a harmonious blend and acts chiefly upon the feelings, stimulating the heart into greater activity; the brain feeding the heart, as it were, and rendering the intuitions and spiritual aspirations very keen. This combination gives correct mental impressions, and the power of clear thinking, with a tendency to religious thought. The metaphysical is easily encouraged, and there is a certain amount of originality of thought and action. Extremes in affairs of the heart would act injuriously and the health would be seriously impaired through disappointments in the love life. This position brings success through ambition and favours all matters connected with music and the drama. It endows with good vitality, and makes a strong, positive, forceful personality, displaying firmness and, when aroused, energy and enterprise, ambition and self-reliance. The native is good-humoured, honest and candid, having some fondness for show and ceremony, fine clothes, decorated rooms, large houses: generally possesses a very good opinion of himself, and likes the good opinion of others, even their flattery.

THE SUN IN ARIES AND MOON IN VIRGO.

☉ *in* ♈. I.—vi. ☽ *in* ♍.

This combination stimulates the critical and discriminative tendency of the Moon in Virgo. It exalts the practical nature and brings out all the scientific characteristics. The solar position considerably improves the lunar characteristics and makes the mind more logical and more accurate in its judgments. It gives a considerable amount of ability in all literary pursuits, but also awakens all the exacting tendencies, although it dispels some of the melancholic attributes, of Virgo. It intensifies the love of study and also gives a considerable amount of musical ability, especially in regard to expression. It often gives greater ability than there is opportunity to use profitably, so that success comes through holding some relatively subordinate position, such as a servant of an employer yet occupying a position of trust, private secretary, agent, etc.

THE SUN IN ARIES AND MOON IN LIBRA.

☉ *in* ♈. I.—vii. ☽ *in* ♎.

We have now reached what is practically the opposition of the Sun and Moon; therefore all that is contained in the Aries nature may find its expression in the equilibrium and balance of the sign Libra. This is a good position for all who have developed the faculty of comparison, as it tends to bring reflection and perception to a state of *balance*. It causes a keenly sensitive nature, one that is very receptive to the surrounding mental atmosphere. It brings out all matters related to music and the fine arts; gives a lovc of recognition, and benefits the life when it co-operates with others. It makes those born under it observant, alert, of keen perceptions; may have the air of being all on the surface, but are not necessarily superficial. Sociable, companionable, amorous, disliking to live or work alone. Mental abilities fairly good, but adapted to outward use in the world rather than to philosophical thinking. Fairly good practical workers but rather of the quick, original, independent kind than of the slow, plodding type. They are good counsellers and advisers, and fitted for the legal profession, or all matters where arbitration and judgment are required; for the judgment is usually unbiassed and carefully weighed. This position tends to bring out the clairvoyant faculties. It will bring some fame or recognition, or place those under its influence in prominent positions.

THE SUN IN ARIES AND MOON IN SCORPIO.

☉ *in* ♈. I.—viii. ☽ *in* ♏.

This is not a good combination, the martial element being very strongly marked, increasing the passions and disposing the nature to be hard, dogmatic, positive, and jealous. It causes the life principle of Aries to be expressed on physical lines, giving revolutionary tendencies, and making those under its influence easily excited, irritable, angry, and revengeful. They are sometimes proud and conventional, matter-of-fact and materialistic; but they can be very destructive when it suits their ends. In cases where the rising sign indicates it and the planetary positions are favourable, it inclines to mysticism and the occult; but there is a danger of the psychic faculties being somewhat abused. Children born under this combination need a good education and should be taught to be less combative and forceful, and also to live pure lives. This is not a good position for the health. It favours success by assertion and aggressiveness. Self-control is essential to progress.

THE SUN IN ARIES AND MOON IN SAGITTARIUS.

☉ *in* ♈. I.—ix. ☽ *in* ♐.

This is a very good combination, the fiery triplicity being well represented. It gives a very quick, sympathetic and inspirational nature, with a tendency to go to extremes, especially in physical matters, while there is always a certain amount of restlessness and hastiness, especially in speech. It intensifies the religious inclinations, it strengthens the sincerity and straightforwardness of the personality, and gives very strong tendencies to prophesy or speak accurately, yet unconsciously so, in regard to the future. It gives impulsiveness and some exaggeration, also a tendency to chatter. The native is changeable, irresolute, given to enthusiasms that do not last; though he has plenty of energy and determination while he is in the mood. Is generous and humanitarian; can feel for others, and will help them if he can. A natural tendency to religion of some kind, but this may easily take an unorthodox direction if planets incline thereto. More vital energy than stamina; the tendency to go to excess may weaken the health, but with a strong horoscope and good aspects there may be a long and full life. This combination gives some skill in musical performance, and fits those under its influence to become good teachers or preachers: it is also good for travelling and exploration. It brings benefit through religious matters and the Church.

THE SUN IN ARIES AND MOON IN CAPRICORN.

☉ *in* ♈. I.—x. ☽ *in* ♑.

This combination gives an intense love of fame. The naturally saturnine qualities of the Moon are accentuated, and the personality made exacting and inclined to fluctuating moods. It gives remarkable imagination and splendid ability in all practical methods concerned with gaining popularity. This combination increases the inquisitiveness of the personality, and gives a very determined and positive nature. Cleverness is much appreciated, and persons in a higher rank of Society are sometimes worshipped. This is a very sensitive combination, and the brain is a very receptive one, especially to the mental conditions of others. It is a good business polarity, also for all pursuits depending upon energy and force of character, being masterful and ambitious, sometimes also worldly and materialistic. It inclines to a public career, but tact and diplomacy are often over-ridden by impulse and self-assertiveness, for this position weakens the self-esteem while it increases the love of approbation. It causes those under its influence to aim for leadership, and to domineer rather than to rule over others. They love wealth for the power it gives. It favours uncommon pursuits, and brings success through force of character. In a bad horoscope, a hard, selfish, ill-tempered, gloomy nature. There is a tendency to weakness of digestion or bowels.

THE SUN IN ARIES AND MOON IN AQUARIUS.

☉ *in* ♈. I.—xi. ☽ *in* ♒.

This combination gives ability to study human nature. It brings out all the pleasing characteristics of the Moon in Aquarius, giving an original mind, mentally positive and combative; the personality is somewhat original and at times eccentric, in speech sometimes hasty, erratic, brusque, or without consideration. It intensifies the artistic faculties, and gives some ability in literary matters, with a bright, clear mind, well able to express itself. The imagination, intuition and mental sensitiveness are much increased, and there is a love of educational and scientific work. It increases the feeling of independence, but gives the ability to deal with others successfully. The native lives largely in the mind, and influences others through the mind; is witty and can be very sarcastic. Determination and enterprise are combined, the Aries nature being steadied and its influence made very reliable. This is a fortunate influence in all matters connected with associations, public bodies, local governments; it also brings help and assistance from friends and acquaintances.

THE SUN IN ARIES AND MOON IN PISCES.

☉ *in* ♈. I.—xii. ☽ *in* ♓.

This combination is not altogether a harmonious one, the action of the Sun being too strong for the lunar position, producing a discontented, restless, and often worrying nature. But it tones down considerably the impulsiveness of Aries, and when the two are working harmoniously, it increases the kindliness of the nature, and gives a love of the occult, the profound and mysterious. Usually, however, much sorrow comes into the life, which causes those born under it to think more deeply than those under most of the Aries combinations. Under bad aspects they may suffer from scandal or slander and from secret enmity; but they must guard themselves against behaving in the same way to other people. There is a danger, in a bad horoscope, of untruthfulness, dishonesty, want of candour. Otherwise, in this combination the personality is charitable, sympathetic and philanthropic, being very receptive to all the impressions coming from the higher nature; but it must be peaceful and harmonious, or the Solar force will be too strong and cause the Moon to receive too many evil impressions. This position gives success in connection with public institutions, asylums, etc., and confers some authority of a quiet and unobtrusive kind; it is favourable for veterinary work.

See Preliminary Notes on pp. 72, 73.

THE SUN IN TAURUS.

☉ *in* ♉. II. ☉ *in* ♉.

The Sun in Taurus makes the individual character behind each lunar expression more firm, plodding, enduring and determined; but there will be a tendency to move more slowly and act more cautiously, quietly and practically than with the Sun in Aries. We have here the expression of the Sun from a sign that is the 'exaltation' of the Moon; each combination will therefore tend to strengthen the personality more than the individuality which lies behind the personal expression.

THE SUN IN TAURUS AND MOON IN ARIES.

☉ *in* ♉. II.—i. ☽ *in* ♈.

This combination gives a very strong personality. There is a tendency to be impulsive, headstrong and rather too dogmatic. There is a considerable amount of persistency, tenacity and exactitude, and the abilities are by no means under-rated. There is plenty of reserve power behind all the force that is expended, and when those born under this combination make up their minds to carry out any purpose in life, they nearly always succeed; but they expect a great deal from others and manifest a stubborn desire to make others conform to their requirements. They prefer their own methods to those of other people, being enterprising and independent, sometimes wilful and wrong-headed. Fitted for positions of some prominence and responsibility. Under affliction, or when the system is run down, the head or nervous system will suffer. This is a combination which gives success in life through energy and the desire to excel. It is fairly fortunate in worldly matters, and favours enterprise, the spirit of daring, and all matters where a determined will is required. It gives good constructive power and the ability to organise. Prosperity is obtained through perseverance. The moral nature is usually very strong.

THE SUN IN TAURUS AND MOON IN TAURUS.

☉ *in* ♉. II.—ii. ☽ *in* ♉

This combination gives a considerable amount of determination, and those born under its influence are not easily thwarted in their purposes. Equable, friendly, companionable, cheerful and maybe musical or artistic, they possess a great amount of self-control, but are rather too self-contained, too reserved, and often secretive; are nevertheless remarkably strong characters, fearless, persistent and hopeful, possessing much feeling and an affectionate nature. They easily attain to great success in the financial world; yet they appear to have a disregard for finance although they cannot help being often very much mixed up with it. This combination is the most solid and practical of influences, but there is a danger of becoming too obstinate. When obedience has been developed they make very fine characters. There is a tendency, however, to become too self-centred, too determined or too secretive. There is a predisposition to apoplexy, and to suffering from the eyes if the Moon is afflicted.

THE SUN IN TAURUS AND MOON IN GEMINI.

☉ *in* ♉. II.—iii. ☽ *in* ♊.

The restlessness of Gemini is here considerably steadied by the Taurus quality, and owing to this there is less diffusion, and more initiative force; yet there is an inclination towards both despondency and self-esteem, due to certain superficial tendencies that have not been eradicated. Those under this combination are inclined to be somewhat selfish, and apt to be assertive; but the intellectual tendencies give them ability to write and speak, and in some cases the powers of language and musical expression are easily developed. It is, however, not a very harmonious combination, and the acquisitive tendencies are usually very large. There is a love of the beautiful in nature and art, with some instinctive neatness. While somewhat unenterprising the native has yet good intellectual abilities. Temperance is advisable, and nervous disorders will have to be guarded against.

THE SUN IN TAURUS AND MOON IN CANCER.

☉ *in* ♉. II.—iv. ☽ *in* ♋.

This is a rather negative combination, since the sensitiveness of Cancer is somewhat accentuated, so that the emotional nature is very easily excited, especially in matters connected with the home life. This combination not only increases timidity and reserve, but also produces much economy, with some anxiety in regard to the future welfare. The imagination is very keen, and there is some tendency to go to extremes, especially when influenced by others. There is sometimes a tendency to inactivity, and the desire for sensation is increased; but on the whole it is a fortunate combination, giving gain through property and probably by inheritance also. There is large caution, unless Mars is prominent, and good business ability, with extreme carefulness in money matters.

THE SUN IN TAURUS AND MOON IN LEO.

☉ *in* ♉. II.—v. ☽ *in* ♌.

The emotional and sensational nature is much increased under this combination; there is a great tendency to exaggerate or to go to extremes, also to be very easily influenced in all matters connected with speculation; probably towards gambling and sensational pleasures. The affections may be easily drawn into unfortunate channels, and there is often a great tendency to express keen likes and dislikes. The native has a good constitution and sound health, unless planetary positions contradict. He is self-confident and fond of show, and hence may be popular or cut something of a figure socially; very fond of pleasure and of society. Care will be necessary to avoid over-indulgence, especially in the appetites, which may become abnormal unless checked. The moral nature may be strengthened considerably towards the close of the life; but the early portion is often one in which either psychic tendencies or sensations play a very prominent part. The lower nature is ardent and at times passionate: there is moreover some poetic ability, the imagination being very vivid. Excesses should be avoided.

THE SUN IN TAURUS AND MOON IN VIRGO.

☉ *in* ♉. II.—vi. ☽ *in* ♍.

The critical faculties are accentuated by the practical Taurean nature behind the personality, so that this combination gives us some of the very best commercial types of men. In all business pursuits they are precise, persistent, and very pronounced in their judgments, yet have abilities in several different directions; they can manage more than one type of business and are eminently adaptable. While sometimes lacking in enterprise, they can quickly apply and develope the suggestions of others. Make good servants or subordinates, and do well with someone to lead or work with them. This is a very successful combination, being a harmonious blend of two signs of the earthy triplicity, bringing out all the practical tendencies. Virgo being the ruler of the business world, the personality has here the best facilities for expression. The moral nature is firm, giving much conscientiousness to assist the personal character, so that behind much apparent pliability there is a fixed determination which gives success.

THE SUN IN TAURUS AND MOON IN LIBRA.

☉ *in* ♉. II.—vii. ☽ *in* ♎.

This is an inharmonious combination, there being usually a considerable amount of bias in the nature. For the blending of an earthy individuality and an airy personality is not very favourable; it tends to increase the separative element, and usually causes the personality to arrive at faulty decisions, often the result of another's influence in the life. This combination gives a certain amount of determination, usually of a stubborn nature, and those born under this influence are apt to be guided by their feelings rather than by reason. They have ability for music or art, and outwardly seem to be observant and intellectual, but at heart they are emotional and devotional, or sensuous. The personality is apt to be very affable, agreeable and more refined and polished than the individual character, but the determination that is behind the personality will often carry the point where neither merit nor persuasion has succeeded. There is likely to be much individual jealousy and vindictiveness displayed, especially towards strangers and opponents. This combination depends very much on the planetary positions.

THE SUN IN TAURUS AND MOON IN SCORPIO.

☉ *in* ♉. II.—viii. ☽ *in* ♏.

This position gives a certain amount of vanity and self-esteem, the feelings being very strong and intense. There is much reserve and concentrated force, with a good deal of secretiveness. A good education is very necessary with this combination, otherwise there is a tendency for those born with it to be far too easily influenced by environment and surrounding conditions, so that they get in a groove; hence are very conservative, except when opposed or angered. Jealousy and pride may cause the downfall of those who are born under this combination, since there is always a considerable amount of determination for good or evil; and unless the latter is restrained the nature will become a very selfish one. Good vitality; under bad aspects there is a danger of accidents, fits, apoplexy, etc. A fairly good polarity for martial occupations, and some kinds of business; fond of money, sensuous. Appetites and passions need curbing. Success in life will come through persistent determination and dogged self-reliance and stubbornness.

THE SUN IN TAURUS AND MOON IN SAGITTARIUS.

☉ *in* ♉. II.—ix. ☽ *in* ♐.

The determination behind the Sagittarius personality will very greatly incline those born under this influence to go to extremes in all things. It gives a tendency to impulsive action and hasty speech, and when provoked a very great deal more is said than is probably thought or meant; while there may be a tendency to be very disputatious when annoyed. This is not a good combination unless planetary positions assist, the personality being far too impulsive for the individual nature; there is, however, aspiration, and a love of science, also a tendency toward philosophy and religion, which somewhat improves the nature, which is generous, charitable and sympathetic; but the aspirations being higher than the inherent abilities, promise usually outruns performance. Good for occupations connected with athletics and horses, imaginative pursuits, the higher cultivation of the mind, or the church. Hopeful, optimistic, and of good vitality, the native yet loses energy through fits of overwork, undertaking more than he can accomplish.

THE SUN IN TAURUS AND MOON IN CAPRICORN.

☉ *in* ♉. II.—x. ☽ *in* ♑.

This is a very practical combination, giving economy and caution, with an aptitude for making very carefully thought-out plans and schemes, which are generally carried to a successful issue. The whole character is very independent and determined, and the ambitions are high, but chiefly concerned with conventional ideals and pertaining to physical objects and personal surroundings. This is the most successful combination of the earthy triplicity, making those born under it extremely practical and well able to build up a fortune. They are especially adapted for a public life, or where the energies are put to good uses in carving out a prosperous career; they have great attainments and aspire to reach great heights, being filled with ambition and well able to exert the personality for the purpose of achieving success. They have ability to deal with big schemes, to organise, and to carry out huge plans. They have good vitality and live long.

THE SUN IN TAURUS AND MOON IN AQUARIUS.

☉ *in* ♉. II.—xi. ☽ *in* ♒.

This is a practical combination, giving thoroughness, carefulness, prudence and caution, with a considerable amount of reserve; it gives honesty of purpose, sincerity and refinement. Those born under this combination are well able to concentrate their thoughts, and are industrious, persevering and successful. This combination causes those born under it to become very self-centred, and tends towards eccentricity. It is suitable for public life, for holding public offices or appointments, and for working through companies, associations, factories, or large bodies of people. Tolerably fortunate for acquiring money and possessions.

THE SUN IN TAURUS AND MOON IN PISCES.

☉ *in* ♉. II.—xii. ☽ *in* ♓.

This is not quite so unfortunate as the combination of Sun in Aries and Moon in Pisces. It steadies the mind and gives less inclination to restlessness; but in some respects it increases the combativeness. Those born under this combination are very hospitable, very receptive to the wants and requirements of others, kind and pliable, and very well disposed: they have plenty of friends and acquaintances, but if Moon is much afflicted may suffer through them. Fortunate socially; rather less so in business or public life; but may benefit through occupations connected with water. It is on the whole a fortunate combination; it increases the mediumistic tendencies and gives receptivity to psychic influences. The disposition is kindly but is easily affected, and inclines towards good living, peace and harmony. There is increase of prosperity towards the latter part of life. If the Moon is afflicted there is some liability to diseases of the bladder or lower bowel.

See PRELIMINARY NOTES ON pp. 72, 73.

THE SUN IN GEMINI.

☉ *in* ♊. III. ☉ *in* ♊.

The Sun in Gemini as the motive force behind the lunar expression gives a dualistic, restless and irritable tendency, the desires always running on intellectual lines. The individual character will be dual in expression, so that there is less permanency than in either of the foregoing solar positions. Nevertheless, the will power is strong, and there is some pride or love of pedigree.

THE SUN IN GEMINI AND MOON IN ARIES.

☉ *in* ♊. III.—i. ☽ *in* ♈.

This combination gives a very mental nature, making those born under it given to intellectual pursuits, studious and fond of expressing their thoughts; yet there is a danger of the personality going to extremes and becoming too independent, also somewhat too changeable. But in all intellectual matters it is a very powerful combination. It gives a very ambitious spirit and strengthens the assertiveness. The nature is a very positive one, somewhat lacking in sympathy and feeling, and there is a liability to live too much in the head, thus giving danger of brain troubles. There is also a tendency to become erratic, and to be too self-willed. The nature is lacking in calmness, steadiness, self-control and perseverance, is combative, and disobedient. Witty, and sharp-tongued with a talent for drawing and sculpture. Likely to travel.

THE SUN IN GEMINI AND MOON IN TAURUS.

☉ *in* ♊. III.—ii. ☽ *in* ♉.

This combination gives a considerable amount of sensitiveness, with much determination and firmness. It causes the feelings and ambitions to be prominent and powerful, owing to the intellect that is mixed up with the sensational nature. There is generally a considerable amount of energy, perseverance and determination. It is fairly fortunate for popularity, friends, acquaintances, and general success. There is good business ability for organising, planning, acting as agent, manager lecturer, etc. The Gemini characteristics are very much strengthened by this combination, and there is not so much changeableness, restlessness, and irritability; but it is not altogether a favourable one, nevertheless. It indicates gain through relatives, or by literary pursuits.

THE SUN IN GEMINI AND MOON IN GEMINI.

☉ *in* ♊. III.—iii. ☽ *in* ♊.

This combination indicates a considerable amount of wilfulness, activity and restlessness, and a tendency to measure all things from an intellectual standpoint. There is a certain amount of self-esteem and independence, and the feelings are not so active in this polarity as in the other combinations. The motive temperament will dominate, and there is much dexterity in all matters where the hands are employed. With suitable planetary positions considerable popularity may be enjoyed, while there is ability amounting to genius in some intellectual direction. Docile in temperament and impartial in judgment. The Moon expresses the Sun very clearly in this combination, giving artistic tendencies, refinement, and literary ability.

THE SUN IN GEMINI AND MOON IN CANCER.

☉ *in* ♊. III.—iv. ☽ *in* ♋.

This combination gives a strong inclination towards economy and thrift in the home life, also in all matters concerned with the welfare of others, coupled with a sensitive and anxious disposition. There is likely to be a great deal of travelling, also much restlessness and a longing for sympathy from others, but the artistic and imaginative faculties are well developed. The receptive nature is very easily affected and upset by surrounding conditions, but there is a good memory and a well-stored and comprehensive mind, intuitional, versatile, agreeable and plausible. This position gives success in all matters relating to public affairs.

THE SUN IN GEMINI AND MOON IN LEO.

☉ *in* ♊. III.—v. ☽ *in* ♌.

In this combination the personality suffers somewhat, as there is not sufficient firmness in the background to support the Leo inclinations; so that there is likely to be too much impulse, the affections being very easily moved. The native therefore fluctuates; is at times very self-confident and hopeful, works well and achieves much; but often he feels that he has greater powers than he can express outwardly; he understands, but is slow at working out. The imagination is active, and there is poetical and dramatic ability. This combination gives a kind of weird tendency, and there is at times a liability to hypochondria. The affections are keen, but there is some love of display, though abundant sympathy. There is literary ability in the direction of fiction, etc.

THE SUN IN GEMINI AND MOON IN VIRGO.

☉ *in* ♊. III.—vi. ☽ *in* ♍.

This is a good combination, the Mercurial elements coming out forcibly and inclining the mind to be studious, critical and analytical. It gives a great love for chemistry, with humanitarian views; inclines to a study of the laws of hygiene. With regard to the mind, however, it is a very sensitive combination; there is apt to be mistrustfulness and a melancholic tendency, so that if worry or anxiety be given way to, the nervous system suffers considerably. Persons born under this combination may obtain great benefit through nursing and serving others; also by their critical talent; but should avoid irritability, which is apt to mar the finer qualities. They can be very impartial and judicial, seeing equally both sides of a question, hence make good lawyers. Are apt to be changeable, undecided, and lacking in perseverance, so that they do not always get credit for all the abilities they possess. They do well when working for others, and both good and bad fortune comes to them largely through relatives. This position gives a strong will, and some subtlety when perverted there is a liability to indecision or duplicity.

THE SUN IN GEMINI AND MOON IN LIBRA.

☉ *in* ♊. III.—vii. ☽ *in* ♎.

This is a very good combination, built up on the airy triplicity: it increases the intuitions, and bestows much refinement, with a sympathetic nature; gives a great amount of foresight, sharpens the perceptive faculties, inclines to study, and gives a great amount of imitativeness, with ability for public writing. It is necessary for those born under this combination to live purely. The faculty of comparison is well developed, and there is some probability of becoming popular. It gives success in artistic pursuits, and a cheerful, sociable, humane nature. The native lives sympathetically with family and relatives; and may marry a relative.

THE SUN IN GEMINI AND MOON IN SCORPIO.

☉. *in* ♊. III.—viii. ☽ *in* ♏.

This is by no means a good combination, there being very little harmony between the common and fixed signs. It accentuates the critical faculties, which become hard and severe, while there is a tendency to combativeness, and a desire to pull down without rebuilding; it gives much determination, argumentiveness, assertiveness, over-sensitiveness, jealousy, pride, and self-esteem. There is sarcasm, liveliness and wit, with some practical business ability and power of management; but the usual cheerful self-confidence sometimes gives way to irritable, jealous, and quarrelsome moods.

THE SUN IN GEMINI AND MOON IN SAGITTARIUS.

☉ *in* ♊. III.—ix. ☽ *in* ♐.

This is not always a good combination, owing to these two signs giving too much activity and restlessness, too much force, resulting in lack of continuity and nervousness. There is an instinctive love of travelling with considerable mental capacity, both intellectual and intuitive. Under favourable conditions the native is humane, generous, charitable and benevolent, with an inclination to philosophy or religion, genial, companionable, and of quick and good judgment. There is apt to be waste of mental energy, much enthusiasm, exceptional force of character and a great deal of excitement; the personal character appears to be far in excess of the individual, but the higher and lower minds are both active, and may benefit each other, the lower aspiring for light by devotion.

THE SUN IN GEMINI AND MOON IN CAPRICORN.

☉ *in* ♊. III.—x. ☽ *in* ♑.

This is a very good business combination, as it gives Saturnine ballast and steadiness to the Mercurial tendency. The individuality is quick, the personality often slow; there may therefore be a considerable lack of harmony, but by labour, patience, and perseverance, a great deal of good work may be done by the personal character for the building up of the individuality. There is good memory, with mental abilities of the solid kind (not showy): suitable for Civil Service, professorships, governmental positions, public appointments. Too serious and despondent at times. This combination gives a highly mental temperament, a love of science, some tact and diplomacy, and often much ingenuity.

THE SUN IN GEMINI AND MOON IN AQUARIUS.

☉ *in* ♊. III.—xi. ☽ *in* ♒.

This is a good combination of the airy signs, giving a great deal of mental and physical activity. Those born under this combination are very good character-readers, also good students of metaphysics; can receive a good education; make acquaintances easily, but are somewhat reserved nevertheless, also very independent; and though they are able to get along very well with strangers, they should always avoid excitement. At times erratic, always inventive and original. There is some inclination for psychic or occult matters and the artistic faculty may be cultivated.

Success will come through co-operation with others, also through science and art.

THE SUN IN GEMINI AND MOON IN PISCES.

☉ *in* ♊. III.—xii. ☽ *in* ♓

This intensifies the restlessness and causes a great deal of irritability; but it gives a great desire for knowledge, which often comes psychically. There is frequently a great deal of dissatisfaction, a yearning for the unattainable, discontent and peevishness; but under favourable planetary positions the native is charitable, benevolent, social and sympathetic, has common-sense and good judgment. There is some likelihood of travelling, and some ability for medicine or nursing. This is a psychic combination, producing great receptivity, and an inclination to dip into hidden mysteries, the mind becoming very receptive to the mysterious and weird; it also gives success in writing strange and *outré* novels, and in uncommon pursuits.

See PRELIMINARY NOTES on pp. 72, 73.

THE SUN IN CANCER.

☉ *in* ♋. IV. ☉ *in* ♋.

This is not a strong position for the individuality; therefore the personal characteristics may considerably pull away from the higher qualities: tenacity, attachment and clinging desire for objects are very marked. This position makes the individual character exceedingly sensitive, impressionable and highly emotional, often lacking in self-reliance, with a yearning for sensation. There is power to psychometrise and sense the general conditions of others. It gives a very tenacious moral character, and the signs of awakening will be shown in *activity* and *power*.

THE SUN IN CANCER AND MOON IN ARIES.

☉ *in* ♋. IV.—i. ☽ *in* ♈.

This combination gives a great deal of activity and much persistency; a liability to become headstrong and go to extremes, a love of fame and a desire to lead and be at the head of things. The native is independent, disliking control, rebellious, discontented, a disobedient servant; and will change his occupation more than once. The parents will affect the life very considerably: he may not get on with them, or may lose them early. There is a great deal of impulse in the personal character, which will bring many sorrows into the life. The head and stomach are likely to be affected. Success will come through public affairs, and fame will be steadfastly sought.

THE SUN IN CANCER AND MOON IN TAURUS.

☉ *in* ♋. IV.—ii. ☽ *in* ♉.

This gives a considerable amount of sensitiveness, but all the higher faculties are stimulated. At its best this polarity gives a share of both energy (♋) and perseverance (♉), activity and practical ability. There is a fair amount of independence and resolution; the native inclines to run in a groove for a time, but changes come, perhaps suddenly, which quite alter the life, and a different groove is lived in. There are some morbid tendencies in this combination, and self-control must be practised before success can be obtained, for this gives a very psychic nature, with keen intuitions, but great receptivity. The nature is imaginative, impressionable, and very easily affected by others. Good company should always be chosen. This combination makes good mediums, giving the ability to psychometrise. There is a certain amount of fortune attached to this combination. It favours the sympathetic temperament, but unless contradicted by planets, there may be a good deal of self and acquisitiveness. Fairly good for health. Some success in business or with houses or land.

THE SUN IN CANCER AND MOON IN GEMINI.

☉ *in* ♋. IV.—iii. ☽ *in* ♊.

This gives a personality very susceptible to education, and makes the brain exceedingly sensitive and receptive to the higher part of the nature. The nature is somewhat irresolute, and liable to change, being wanting in patient perseverance. A versatile mind, familiar with several subjects. There is a great love of knowledge and a great deal of activity and energy, especially in literary matters and travel. Artistic tendencies in the home life may be displayed. Success will come through the help and assistance of relatives.

THE SUN IN CANCER AND MOON IN CANCER.

☉ *in* ♋. IV.—iv. ☽ *in* ♋.

Fancy and imagination will be manifest in this combination, and there is a great liability to go to extremes. It gives independence, with conservatism or a clinging to ancient customs and habits; yet there is also much changeableness. Inertia will produce laziness, but when other planetary influences allow, the tenacity and motive power will be great. The characteristics of ☉ in ♋ will show out strongly. A good parental influence in early life, with possible inheritance from parents. The native is acquisitive and careful in money matters; and there is some good fortune through property, houses or land. May have psychic inclinations or abilities, dreaming, intuition, etc.

THE SUN IN CANCER AND MOON IN LEO.

☉ *in* ♋ IV.—v. ☽ *in* ♌.

This combination gives very keen and sensitive feelings. It awakens the animal side of the nature, and there is a liability to go to extremes, causing restlessness, especially where love is concerned. It gives a great love of the drama, and sometimes a craving for ardent feelings and sensation; the affectional nature is very strong and romantic. On the whole good for health and worldly success.

THE SUN IN CANCER AND MOON IN VIRGO.

☉ *in* ♋. IV.—vi. ☽ *in* ♍.

This gives a very sensitive and passive nature, with a certain amount of discrimination in all matters where the feelings and emotions are concerned. This is a good business polarity, either as manager or employée, there being both adaptability and agreeableness. There is a liability to go to extremes and to worry, especially where business matters are concerned. The nature is receptive, and mediumistic; at times there is a liability to obsession, the nature being very receptive to psychic influences. This polarity is good for digestion, nutrition, and bodily strength.

THE SUN IN CANCER AND MOON IN LIBRA.

☉ *in* ♋. IV.—vii. ☽ *in* ♎.

This gives balance to the sensitive, emotional nature of Cancer and increases the perception and affections, particularly in matters connected with the home life; it stimulates the ideality, giving harmony and balance to the internal feelings. It also gives ability for writing, and a love of fame and recognition. The native is emotional or sensational, and displays some ability for music or art, with a love of the beautiful and harmonious in sights, colours and sounds. Observant and very conscious of what goes on. The fullest growth and widest life occur after marriage. There are many changes in the life; very likely a change of occupation, and certainly changes of residence. May leave the parental family while young.

THE SUN IN CANCER AND MOON IN SCORPIO.

☉ *in* ♋. IV.—viii. ☽ *in* ♏.

This combination enables the personality to have a solidifying effect upon the sensitive nature of Cancer, making it harder (and sometimes selfish); there is apt to be pride and vindictiveness, especially in matters connected with the feelings. It gives a love of display and attracts towards the opposite sex, with success in magical and psychic affairs: but the magnetism is easily stimulated towards sensation. There is early death of, or separation from, a parent. In some cases the native follows closely on parental lines, both in character and occupation; in others a great change occurs, and an entirely new environment and occupation is taken up.

THE SUN IN CANCER AND MOON IN SAGITTARIUS.

☉ *in* ♋. IV.—ix. ☽ *in* ♐.

This is a very inharmonious combination, the personality being far too active for the individuality; but it stimulates the emotional and devotional nature, giving much activity with regard to speech, coupled with a restless nature and a constant yearning for the unattainable. There are also some psychic gifts, inspirational speaking, the ability to prophesy, or to bring through into the brain dreams, etc. The native has a changeable, companionable and kind nature; is generally a quick worker and can accomplish much in a short time. Fond of travelling, exploring, new scenes, new thoughts and ideas, so that success is found in foreign affairs and in religious matters.

THE SUN IN CANCER AND MOON IN CAPRICORN.

☉ *in* ♋. IV.—x. ☽ *in* ♑.

This makes the individual character more practical and more ambitious, giving aptitude for business pursuits. The native is very acquisitive, and is likely to accumulate money or property; is desirous of wealth. Is suited for a public or commercial life rather than one in the family: likely to inherit from parents (unless 'afflicted'). The parents' heredity and family influences play a very important part in the native's life, more so than usual; sometimes he wishes to be independent of them but finds it impossible. If afflicted (that is to say if either Sun or Moon is badly 'aspected' by the major planets), he will not get on with them or there will be separation. If much afflicted he is unfortunate, having long periods of misfortune. There is, too, an inability to express the internal feelings. Many obstacles will come into the life, but the ambitions will be keen and there will be a great love of fame and a desire to lead and govern.

THE SUN IN CANCER AND MOON IN AQUARIUS.

☉ *in* ♋. IV.—xi. ☽ *in* ♒.

This is not a very harmonious combination; but it gives ability in all matters connected with associations, and some degree of success in public life. Persons born under this combination are tactful, careful and diplomatic; it fits for externalities rather than for the interior life. It gives ability for painting and general artistic faculties. The native is rather reserved, quiet and self-contained. Has some inclination for mystical or psychic pursuits; and is more sociable and companionable within than he appears to be on the surface. One of the parents dies early. The eyesight may need protection.

THE SUN IN CANCER AND MOON IN PISCES.

☉ *in* ♋. IV.—xii. ☽ *in* ♓.

This is a very harmonious combination of watery signs, awakening the emotional nature. and making the mind very receptive; it gives mediumistic tendencies, much fancy, and a desire to obtain knowledge, with some liability to hysteria. Psychic faculties may be developed, and there will be an interior knowledge of the public mind and its requirements. The native is domesticated, good-natured and sociable; shows to more advantage in the family circle than in public life; is changeable, fond of sensation and novelty. The position tends to success, business connected with liquids being specially favoured.

See PRELIMINARY NOTES ON pp. 72, 73.

THE SUN IN LEO.

☉ *in* ♌. V. ☉ *in* ♌.

The Sun in Leo gives a good moral nature; it makes the individuality very sincere and ardent in all matters of affection, firm, self-reliant, sincere, magnanimous, sometimes austere, and determined. All combinations from this solar centre will be strengthened by the individuality. Many of the experiences of the life will be in connection with love affairs, matters of the heart and the inner feelings.

THE SUN IN LEO AND MOON IN ARIES.

☉ *in* ♌. V.—i. ☽ *in* ♈.

This is a harmonious combination belonging to the fiery triplicity, and there is a love of philosophy, and a tendency towards religious thought; determination and love of leadership are marked characteristics. It gives a very persistent, dominant, enthusiastic, and energetic nature, with much combativeness, though the combativeness of Aries is subdued by the Leo influence; but there is a necessity for restraint where feeling is concerned. It gives success in life, for the native is independent, and can make his own way, being self-reliant, firm and positive (though generous and good humoured); so that he will form his own opinions and not be led by others. He will travel for pleasure, if circumstances permit.

THE SUN IN LEO AND MOON IN TAURUS.

☉ *in* ♌. V.—ii. ☽ *in* ♉.

This gives a very determined nature, with an Inclination to put the heart into physical things. It strengthens the business intuitions, and gives fortune in finance, making a good banker or stockbroker; it gives a strongly vitalised constitution and also a love of hygiene. There is much strength in this combination; the character is very firm and at times obstinate, but much depends on the aspects. The native is likely to be popular and to come before the public, being very sociable, companionable, good natured and agreeable. He is fond of pleasure, sensation and emotion. If the Moon is afflicted, the eyes may be affected.

THE SUN IN LEO AND MOON IN GEMINI.

☉ *in* ♌. V.—iii. ☽ *in* ♊.

This gives energy to the personal nature, with much determination behind it, thus urging the lunar tendencies to greater activity, so that restraint will be needed. It inclines towards music and the drama, and gives ability for writing and poetry, the hands being ever ready to express the heart. This combination makes gifted and clever persons, enthusiastic and lovable; their abilities may amount to genius in some intellectual direction. The mind is broad, comprehensive, and fertile. Many acquaintances and friends among worthy people; good family influence in early life; harmony with brethren.

THE SUN IN LEO AND MOON IN CANCER.

☉ *in* ♌. V.—iv. ☽ *in* ♋.

This causes great sensitiveness, and much sorrow in love affairs: it gives a tendency to go to extremes, and some restraint will be necessary. It is, however, a good combination for the mind, the brain being receptive to influences from the heart; it stimulates the love emotions and makes the feelings very keen and sensitive, ardent and rather too attached to the object of affection; the sex nature is strong, sociable and affectionate, loving companionship and the family circle, very fond of children, also of pleasure and sensation, and of living in fine houses and ornamented rooms. This combination gives good financial success, especially when associated with other members of the family. All the senses are keenly sensitive but under bad aspects the sight or some other sense will suffer —most probably the sight.

THE SUN IN LEO AND MOON IN LEO.

☉ *in* ♌. V.—v. ☽ *in* ♌.

This gives a very independent nature, making those born under it rather self-centred and somewhat proud, but very kind-hearted and generous; they are capable of holding their own under great difficulties, though they are apt to go to extremes. It often gives reserve, yet with a great desire for affection from others. This combination gives much intuition, and great ability as teachers or for work in connection with schools, concerts, pleasure parties and amusements. There is plenty of vitality, energy and resource, with some fondness for show, either in position or appearance. The native, if a public speaker, will be rhetorical and poetical or high flown, and in writing, much the same; there is in fact some ostentation in the character. He has plenty of friends, by whom he may benefit; and he is a person of some note in his sphere: he will rise in life, or will make the acquaintance of those in superior positions.

THE SUN IN LEO AND MOON IN VIRGO.

☉ *in* ♌. V.—vi. ☽ *in* ♍.

The Moon is in the first sign from the Sun. This gives good business instincts, ideality and chastity, with a tendency, however, to be very critical, restless and anxious. There is ability either for music and literature, or chemistry, hygiene, etc., in fact for many subjects where the ideal and practical are blended. It also fits those under its influence to hold responsible subordinate posts as head servants either in public or private life. It is a combination that achieves success, yet is sometimes lacking in practical enterprise, although always fertile in resource. May succeed better through other people than when working on their own account. Fairly fortunate, but if Moon is afflicted will find themselves constantly thwarted. Are apt to think their work somewhat beneath them, that they do not get their deserts, that they are fitted for better positions than they occupy. With a favourable horoscope, at their best they are good practical workers and can accomplish much. They fraternise readily with others.

THE SUN IN LEO AND MOON IN LIBRA.

☉ *in* ♌. V.—vii. ☽ *in* ♎.

This gives spiritual inclinations, with a love of classifying and harmonising, while there is ability to foresee the future by the strong intuitional impressions which come from the individuality. It strengthens the affections, gives compassion and a desire to do some public good. There is a love of poetry, music or art, and the native may have considerable ability in one of these directions; moreover the mind is strong and active. He associates readily with other people, and is friendly and companionable, disliking loneliness. This polarity tends to marriage or partnership, to popularity, and to friendship. A very harmonious and successful combination.

THE SUN IN LEO AND MOON IN SCORPIO.

☉ *in* ♌. V.—viii. ☽ *in* ♏.

This combination gives some austerity, with an inclination to be rather hard, and at times proud and arrogant; there is much love of show. Persons born under this influence very often have their internal Leo nature quite hidden under this hard exterior. The native is much attracted by the senses; this may take a high or a low form, passional, emotional, or mental, according to the general condition of the whole horoscope. In love affairs or where sensation is concerned there is danger of going to excesses, and this should be guarded against, for a reckless or careless life would injure or disease the heart. Not fortunate for the mother or the wife; there is liability to separation from or death of one of them. Very fixed and determined nature; ardent, but at times too positive, worldly, and sensual. The native would make a good magnetic healer.

THE SUN IN LEO AND MOON IN SAGITTARIUS.

☉ *in* ♌. V.—ix. ☽ *in* ♐.

This is a very good combination, belonging to the fiery triplicity, but it gives restlessness, and a great inclination to go to extremes especially in religious matters or affairs of the heart. A benevolent and good-hearted disposition, with sometimes too much impulse, and a lack of caution or self-restraint. Active sympathies. Intuitive foresight, in some cases. Will show much activity in religion or some humanitarian or philanthropic work; but in lower natures this may show as the pursuit of pleasure, love of sports, athletics, etc. The Moon is in the fifth sign from the Sun, and therefore in perfect harmony with it. There is much hope and joy in the nature, and a great love of pleasure, this being a hopeful and successful combination, and a good polarity for health if native does not ov erdo it: he will travel for pleasure.

THE SUN IN LEO AND MOON IN CAPRICORN.

☉ *in* ♌. V.—x. ☽ *in* ♑.

This tends to harden the interior nature, giving much ambition and exactitude. The personality is inclined to be rather grasping, selfish, and worldly externally; but in its inner life, the heart is always pulling away from externals. This combination gives a love of power and leadership, and ability to organise, govern and rule others: it is good for either a business or political career. The ambitions are very keen and determined, and the native is likely to occupy a prominent position in his sphere, or to hold a responsible public post. Generally speaking, it is good for length of life and also fairly fortunate for money or property. There is a liability to rheumatic, heart or stomach troubles.

THE SUN IN LEO AND MOON IN AQUARIUS.

☉ *in* ♌. V.—xi. ☽ *in* ♒.

This combination is equiv alent to the Moon being in opposition to the Sun. It acts as a 'seventh house' influence, causing the personality to go out to many indiscriminately; yet it gives intuition and ability to judge human nature quickly, together with some very marked occult tendencies, refinement, much determination and will-power. The native is independent and good-natured, and sociable too, but with some exterior reserve. Adapted to a public career, or to occupy some position in connection with local or general political or ruling bodies, and if the horoscope is a fortunate one, he will rise in life; for this combination is good for marriage and friendship, as well as popularity. The health is good unless the Sun is 'afflicted' by bad aspects of planets, in which case rheumatic, heart or kidney troubles may result. The circulation is apt to suffer.

THE SUN IN LEO AND MOON IN PISCES.

☉ *in* ♌. V.—xii. ☽ *in* ♓.

There is very little harmony in this combination, as the brain is often negative to the internal feelings; there is therefore often discontent and dissatisfaction. There is some tendency to occultism, mediumship, and inspirational speaking, poetry and strange writing. The native is inclined to become dreamy, being at times too passive. Nevertheless, with a good horoscope, he will be very generous, kind and charitable, and will benefit from these qualities in others, also through institutions, hospitals, etc., either directly or indirectly. But if the Moon is "afflicted," there will be danger of deception, fraud, duplicity or slander, deserved or otherwise; danger also on water or through drink in some way.

See PRELIMINARY NOTES on pp. 72. 73.

THE SUN IN VIRGO.

☉ *in* ♍. VI. ☉ *in* ♍.

This gives an innately practical nature, with a highly discriminative individuality. It tends to lead the whole of the lunar expression into practical methods, the discriminative faculties being called out as fully as possible. It connects the personality with maternal and family affairs, the home instincts being strongly marked.

THE SUN IN VIRGO AND MOON IN ARIES.

☉ *in* ♍. VI.—i. ☽ *in* ♈.

This gives very keen mental abilities, and tends to fit one to take the lead in any business affairs. The personality is mirthful, witty, active, sharp, impulsive and quick to foresee, while the solid nature of the solar influence behind it enables the whole combination to work harmoniously. The native is good at debate, argument and controversy; but is apt to be too independent and pugnacious mentally, and hence a little difficult to get on with. He is too unyielding, and exaggerates either his own importance or his abilities: if well educated he will have a good deal of pride in his own accomplishments, for there is some tendency to live too much in the head, and the nature may be lacking in sympathy, so that selfishness will express itself when the will is thwarted; this will manifest itself in sarcastic and bitter speeches.

THE SUN IN VIRGO AND MOON IN TAURUS.

☉ *in* ♍. VI.—ii. ☽ *in* ♉.

This combination from the earthy triplicity, while bringing out all the intuitive faculties, strengthens the scientific or practical ability, giving keen perceptions and rendering those under its influence very capable in the business world. It gives much receptivity to the surrounding thought-sphere and some poetic instinct, together with some reserve and secretiveness; and there will be a tendency to be over-cautious. Unless the luminaries are "afflicted," the native is fortunate in business and money matters, practical, methodical, and persevering. He makes a capable and successful employee, or executant along his own line, whatever it may be; and he gets on well with those in his own employ. He appears more obstinate than he really is at heart; for though he is not easily influenced by others he often has doubts in his own mind, though he may not admit this. Born probably into a prosperous environment, he inherits money; or else he rises in life and earns a good stipend. Generally speaking, the health is very good under this combination: under bad aspects, the eyes will suffer.

THE SUN IN VIRGO AND MOON IN GEMINI.

☉ *in* ♍. VI.—iii. ☽ *in* ♊.

This quickens the intellect and speech, giving general ability, and bringing into activity all the mental expressions; but there is often loss of opportunity in the life, arising from irresolution. It will, however, bring those born under this combination into eminent position, which nevertheless may not be retained: it fits the native for receiving a good education and following some scientific or professional career, in which intellect is more important than practical business ability. He may gain public success and become a person of some note along these lines. Would do well as clerk, reporter, editor, or in any literary capacity; in educational pursuits, or as secretary, agent or traveller. Is much concerned with relatives, especially brothers and sisters, uncles and aunts or cousins. He displays some reserve and also some lack of enterprise, but he has good critical and judicial ability. Will change his occupation, or follow two at once. Friendship and hospitality are marked features in this combination.

THE SUN IN VIRGO AND MOON IN CANCER

☉ *in* ♍. VI.—iv. ☽ *in* ♋.

This quickens the sensitive nature of the Moon in Cancer, though it also awakens the anxious side of the nature, stimulating the activities on domestic lines. This is a very receptive combination and somewhat over-sensitive. It gives an economical, persevering and industrious nature, with very strong leanings to everything pertaining to the home life and family affairs, together with some tendency towards conservatism or sectarianism. There is adaptability and agreeableness, with some degree of subtlety of mind and quick appreciation of the motives of other people. Gives a smooth and pursuasive tongue and fluent speech, if Mercury is prominent. There is more in the native than appears on the surface; yet though sometimes reserved he makes acquaintances easily. This combination increases the economical tendencies of Cancer.

THE SUN IN VIRGO AND MOON IN LEO.

☉ *in* ♍. VI.—v. ☽ *in* ♌.

This stimulates the affectional and emotional nature of the Moon in Leo, but behind the personality there is not much fixity; therefore there is anxiety for fresh loves and there will be many love episodes in the life. This combination softens the critical side of the Virgo nature, and stimulates the psychic side of the solar position. The native is proud of his own attainments and accomplishments, and exhibits some love of show and ceremony, and a liking for fine clothes; if an author he displays grandeur of style. There is a keen love of beauty in nature and art, with poetic feeling and a generous, warm-hearted, humanitarian disposition. Excess of feeling in religious matters would here be very harmful, the imagination being vivid.

THE SUN IN VIRGO AND MOON IN VIRGO.

☉ *in* ♍. VI.—vi. ☽ *in* ♍

This quickens the whole of the Virgo nature, giving great love of everything of a maternal character, or where kindred and the home life are concerned. This combination increases the impressional nature, also the discrimination, independence, self-reliance, and foresight; but there is a tendency to be too self-contained and somewhat self-centred. It is on the whole a harmonious blend, but both luminaries being in a common sign there is a tendency to be, although refined and polished, too methodical and precise; but it is a fairly good business polarity, inclining to accuracy in the most minute details. The native is a hard worker, frugal and persevering, but somewhat apt to repine. Regular work with due exercise and immunity from worry are essential to health. All tendencies to melancholy should be actively combated.

THE SUN IN VIRGO AND MOON IN LIBRA.

☉ *in* ♍. VI.—vii. ☽ *in* ♎.

This combination gives independence of thought, together with talent for writing, either philosophic or scientific. It quickens all the perceptive faculties of Libra, and gives great ability in all matters where fine judgment and perception are required. It strengthens the intuition, imagination, and ambition, while it gives a very clear mentality. The native, however, is not sufficiently patient or plodding, and is liable to change and fluctuate in opinion. If well educated, he will have a wide range of reading and be "well up" in many subjects. There is some inclination towards travel, and much artistic ability.

THE SUN IN VIRGO AND MOON IN SCORPIO.

☉ *in* ♍. VI.—viii. ☽ *in* ♏.

This is a rather selfish combination, inclining the native to be hard and somewhat careless as to the feelings of others, excepting those of his own family or those who minister to his personal comfort. The sympathies are slight, and jealousy is easily aroused, while there is a tendency to be rather unforgiving and severe with wrong-doers. Criticism and judgment are keenly developed, and this combination is good for all matters connected with industry; the Scorpio persistency of character and self-reliance strengthen the Virgo nature in this respect. A very fortunate combination for either nursing or doctoring, as the two influences harmonise well in these matters. But if either luminary is much "afflicted" it is not good for health.

THE SUN IN VIRGO AND MOON IN SAGITTARIUS.

☉ *in* ♍. VI.—ix. ☽ *in* ♐.

The Moon in Sagittarius tends to make the personality inclined towards philosophy, very intuitive, with a strong desire to teach others. Hence it is suited for occupations connected with religion, learning or science; or with travelling. But there is a tendency to be too impulsive and too apt to make hasty judgments. Dual tendencies are often found in this sign, such as religious instincts and commercial enterprise, philosophy and love of power. Nevertheless, this is a successful combination, especially where the acquistion of wealth is concerned, though the native is rather lacking in steady persistency.

THE SUN IN VIRGO AND MOON IN CAPRICORN.

☉ *in* ♍. VI.—x. ☽ *in* ♑.

This is the most practical of all combinations; and while there is much independence, and a tendency to lean towards materialistic and selfish lines of thought, there is splendid ability and a desire to accumulate wealth either in the professional or business world. This combination acts similarly to the conjunction of Mercury and Saturn in nativities, giving shrewdness and a calculating mind. It is good for government occupations, or those connected with public authorities, all official appointments, managerships, etc.; also for stocks, shares and investments, unless the Moon is afflicted. The mind is serious and somewhat gloomy at times, but determined, and the memory is often very retentive. The bowels and the digestive organs will be affected by weakness.

THE SUN IN VIRGO AND MOON IN AQUARIUS.

☉ *in* ♍. VI.—xi. ☽ *in* ♒.

This intensifies the intuitive faculties and quickens the psychic impressions, though it oftens acts along practical lines and gives ability for business pursuits, especially in trading with large companies, associations and huge concerns. The discriminative faculties are well developed, and there is much ability to judge human nature; an original mind, ingenious and inventive, which has opinions and adheres to them, and is not easily pursuaded differently. Fond of the company of a few, if Moon is well aspected he has faithful friends. and is fortunate in his friends and acquaintances. Apt to be despondent at times. Unconventional, and yet sometimes lacking in enterprise, "go," and self-assertion. This combination also gives reserve and some scientific ability, and an inclination to investigate psychic matters; there is a strong impulse to all the peculiarities, occupations, characteristics, and diseases that have been described as appertaining to Virgo, but the higher nature of this sign is also quickened.

THE SUN IN VIRGO AND MOON IN PISCES.

☉ *in* ♍. VI.—xii. ☽ *in* ♓.

This makes the personality mediumistic and receptive to the requirements of the individuality; but it gives restlessness and a great love of change and novelty, and there is therefore apt to be much dissatisfaction, and some irritability. The native is a very good servant, subordinate or employee, and is a good worker, very correct in details, though at times lazy. Is sympathetic and charitable, and receives sympathy and charity from others. With a bad horoscope the native is liable to be deceitful or not straightforward, or to suffer from this in others: he follows obscure occupations, and finds it difficult to rise out of them. This combination is not favourable for the health; it also gives a lack of self-reliance, and there is a danger of being somewhat superficial, although there is always a hospitable nature displayed.

See PRELIMINARY NOTES on pp. 72, 73.

THE SUN IN LIBRA.

☉ *in* ♎. VII. ☉ *in* ♎.

This gives a very harmonious individuality, with a tendency to act through perception more than through reflection. The spiritual qualities of the sign are called out, and the higher mind seeks to equalise all the various combinations of the Moon. There is a keen love of justice and great power of comparison, but there is also a certain sensitiveness in this sign, with very ambitious desires, especially on intellectual lines.

THE SUN IN LIBRA AND MOON IN ARIES.

☉ *in* ♎. VII.—i. ☽ *in* ♈.

Reason and perception are well blended in this combination and there should be a great amount of mental refinement, with much ability in all mental pursuits. The personality is active, and the individuality quiet: the will power is fairly strong, hence the native is active, independent, and at times aggressive on the surface, but at heart more quiet, harmonious and affectionate; he is fond of change, and quick to appreciate new ideas. Unless the "ascendant" or the planetary positions contradict, he will have little or nothing of the slow, plodding virtues and will be at times impatient and lacking in perseverance. An inharmonious marriage is probable, few being able to respond to the ideals of this combination; but there is much power in this blend, and those possessing it can obtain much influence over others. Physically this combination is very good for all who love athletics. It brings success in all gymnastic affairs, the spine and muscular system being very supple: but there is some liability to head troubles.

THE SUN IN LIBRA AND MOON IN TAURUS.

☉ *in* ♎. VII.—ii. ☽ *in* ♉.

The Venus nature is well harmonised in this sign; perseverance, endurance, patience and caution will be manifested. There is also some psychic power and inventive ability, but the personality is apt to be somewhat too receptive to physical surroundings and conditions. The combination gives gain through partners or through marriage: it fits those under its influence to undertake huge building schemes, and is fairly fortunate for money generally, also for friends and popularity. There may be aptitude for music or acting, while practical ability is shown in the domestic sphere, together with power to retain conjugal affection.

THE SUN IN LIBRA AND MOON IN GEMINI.

☉ *in* ♎. VII.—iii. ☽ *in* ♊.

This is a harmonious combination in the airy triplicity, giving refinement, artistic tastes and oratorical ability. It gives a great love of knowledge and intensifies the intellectual aspirations, but also gives a liability to go to extremes, especially in mental pursuits. The native is easily adaptable to different occupations, conditions or careers in life, their nature varying with the influence of the "ascendant" (or Rising Sign), —if the latter tends to domesticity, there will be much affection, emotion, and faithfulness; if to study or intellectual pursuits, there will be great ability in some such direction. Lives very harmoniously with brethren and the family, and is fortunate in travelling. Observant, versatile, and with many interests; letter-writing will be a favourite occupation, or will in some way occupy a considerable amount of attention. Some indecision may be displayed, and a want of stability, but this may easily be overcome; thought and feeling are blended in this combination, which gives great influence over others, especially through power of speech.

THE SUN IN LIBRA AND MOON IN CANCER.

☉ *in* ♎ VII.—iv. ☽ *in* ♋.

This combination in the cardinal group intensifies the sensitiveness and the emotional nature; it inclines to anxiety, especially with regard to home affairs. It also gives some changeableness, but with desires for progress; there is some psychic ability and inspiration, which may, however, remain latent owing to the ambitious tendency of the cardinal signs. Hence this is to some extent a contradictory combination, for there is at the same time a sympathetic domesticated disposition, and yet a good deal of ability for a public life. The outer nature will be quite different from the inner; and this polarity, like the last, varies a great deal with the strongest planet and the ascendant of the nativity. The parental nature, the attraction to family and relatives, is strong; and, unless the Moon is "afflicted," there are considerable possessions. Moderately fortunate in other respects.

THE SUN IN LIBRA AND MOON IN LEO.

☉ *in* ♎. VII.—v. ☽ *in* ♌.

This is a very good combination with regard to the feelings of the personality, as it intensifies the spiritual and refining influences. It tends to balance the individual and personal nature and bring harmony. It gives a strong inclination towards spiritual things, and sometimes makes the nature rather too idealistic. The feelings and impulses are strong; there is an intense love of beauty, and great enthusiasm in pursuit of an ideal. The native is popular and has many friends, as he is hopeful, sociable and generous. The love nature is very intense and sincere. It is difficult for such a person to remain single, so that he or she is apt to marry too much in haste and repent afterwards. There is poetic and musical ability, and either the artistic or moral nature will have many opportunities for development.

THE SUN IN LIBRA AND MOON IN VIRGO.

☉ *in* ♎. VII.—vi. ☽ *in* ♍.

This combination gives a critical personality, which is softened considerably by the great power of comparison. It bestows much receptivity, but tends to lead the mind into physical, practical matters, giving intuition in business affairs. It is a refined combination and produces an attractive personality. There is good general mental ability with, in some cases, special aptitude in some one direction (determined by the ascendant, or the strongest planet). A companionable nature, but sometimes lacking in determination or strength of will.

THE SUN IN LIBRA AND MOON IN LIBRA

☉ *in* ♎. VII.—vii. ☽ *in* ♎.

Although this gives a clear perception, there is apt to be too much reliance upon others, and inability to move forward spontaneously. This combination brings dreams and the power to see visions; it is good for the character, making it affable, courteous, obliging and well-disposed. There is much foresight and mental sensitiveness, coupled with humanitarian views and a desire to do good; which are, however, very often spoilt by a self-centring inclination that makes the idealism of the 'dreamy' order, and fails to accomplish that which it regards as ideal. Much depends upon the planetary influences as to how this combination will act. The fate will be largely influenced by other people, either through marriage, partnership, or general association. At its best, this polarity may give a very harmonious mind, hopeful, practical along its own lines, popular and contented; artistic or musical also, with an ardent love of beauty.

THE SUN IN LIBRA AND MOON IN SCORPIO.

☉ *in* ♎. VII.—viii. ☽ *in* ♏.

This gives a love of approbation and an ambitious nature, the native being fully aware of his own abilities and inclined to be somewhat combative,—although not as assertive as would seem, owing to the individuality seeking to harmonise and soften the hard positiveness of Scorpio. Outwardly he will be positive, matter-of-fact, worldly, hard and sometimes a little coarse; but when intimately known, he will seem much more companionable, genial and yielding. When the personality has the greater power there will be great energy, industry, and ambition displayed. If the planetary positions are favourable, the native may be very practical and executive. There is danger of trouble connected with marriage or partnership; also of death of own parent (or of marriage partner's) early. If well "aspected" he may benefit much by marriage or partnership.

THE SUN IN LIBRA AND MOON IN SAGITTARIUS.

☉ *in* ♎. VII.—ix. ☽ *in* ♐.

This is a very good combination, although the personality is inclined to be rather reckless and careless, and too over-active and excitable. It intensifies the activity of the brain and also increases the rapidity of speech. This combination gives prophetic talents, with ability for preaching and public speaking; and in many pursuits it brings success in life. The native has a rich and well-stored mind, fruitful, imaginative and emotional, his abilities in connection with religion or law being specially marked. Social and benevolent, of good disposition, he will be a universal favourite.

THE SUN IN LIBRA AND MOON IN CAPRICORN.

☉ *in* ♎. VII.—x. ☽ *in* ♑.

This gives some musical ability, and inclines also to neatness, orderliness and method, which will show out in the habits of the mind if not of the outward life. It gives some amount of caution, prudence, worldly wisdom, and sometimes also selfishness. This latter mainly in the lower type of character; in a higher type it will show as self-control. The emotions and impulses are disciplined and well regulated. It is a good combination, but the mind is apt to be too material for the solar influence, leading it out into the external world. It is favourable for popularity and public recognition. The ambitions will be achieved, and there will be considerable prominence in some sphere, but there is danger of downfall or reversal. There is likely to be some misfortune or inharmony connected with the parents.

THE SUN IN LIBRA AND MOON IN AQUARIUS

☉ *in* ♎. VII.—xi. ☽ *in* ♒.

This is a very harmonious combination from the airy triplicity. It gives splendid foresight, especially in all matters connected with humanitarian principles, large businesses, associations, and public companies; also the power to psychometrise, with ability to judge human nature; moreover it enables the mind to concentrate. The disposition is kind, gentle and humane; sometimes too unresisting, though never where principles are at stake. The mind is original, inventive and intuitional, the memory usually good, the nature reserved and controlled but sociable and friendly (also popular, if supported by the planetary positions).

THE SUN IN LIBRA AND MOON IN PISCES.

☉ *in* ♎. VII.—xii. ☽ *in* ♓.

This gives a great deal of restlessness, together with some industry and perseverance, though there is apt to be a tendency to dream rather than to be practical. It inclines towards mediumship, which, however, is always *dangerous* with this combination: when the mind is busily occupied in practical and physical occupations the nature is improved. The disposition is gentle, sociable and affectionate, charitable and humanitarian; but it will be lacking in positiveness and strength of will, unless this is supplied by ascendant or planets.

See Preliminary Notes on pp. 72, 73.

THE SUN IN SCORPIO.

VIII.

☉ *in* ♏. ☉ *in* ♏.

The Sun in the sign Scorpio gives a very firm, determined, and reserved individuality, with an inclination to be very dignified, secretive and full of desire. It gives pride to the individuality, and tends towards much self-control with regard to each of the lunar indications; the individuality may be either very well disposed or very selfish, according to progress. Scorpio is a sign of strength, independence and industry.

THE SUN IN SCORPIO AND MOON IN ARIES.

☉ *in* ♏. VIII.—i. ☽ *in* ♈.

This gives stubbornness, and a liability to go to extremes of anger; also much positiveness, impulse, and jealousy. It makes strong characters, dogmatic, self-assertive, and full of very keen likes and dislikes. The passional nature is often very strong, and there is a liability to become rather tyrannical, owing to the forcefulness of the nature. Hence the native has courage, resolution, resource and independence, and is sure to make his mark in life in some way, for good or evil: will probably be a person widely known for strength of character and will. In most cases he will be very practical, and desirous of bringing all theories to the test of action; but if the planetary positions are singificant of it, the feelings and the intellect may be either of them well developed. There is a liability of injuries to the head; or the native may suffer from over-work or excitement. The worst defect of the character is a lack of coolness, calmness, humility; and the native should ponder on the text, "Blessed are the meek, for they shall inherit the earth." For the race is not always to the swift, nor the battle to the strong.

THE SUN IN SCORPIO AND MOON IN TAURUS.

☉ *in* ♏. VIII.—ii. ☽ *in* ♉.

This is not a very good combination, although the lunar tendencies will reduce some of the positiveness of the Scorpio nature. It makes good medical men, however, giving remarkable intuition or instinct with regard to disease. It increases the approbativeness and love of display of the Scorpio nature (without which the combination would not be so good), and gives success in business pursuits, the nature being very firm and determined. Indeed, the native will have considerable practical business ability, especially if associated with other people, either by partnership or in companies, etc. In this and other directions he will have a fixed course of life, and will be very persistent and persevering in following it out. Will be very unchanging and conservative in most habits and customs, both good and bad, and hence is apt to live in a groove nearly all his life. The domestic and social side of the nature is well developed; and if planetary positions accord, music, art, etc., may be cultivated. Cheerful and generally good-natured, the native is fairly fortunate (except when "cross-aspects" occur); but if undeveloped is apt to be very inert and slothful.

THE SUN IN SCORPIO AND MOON IN GEMINI.

☉ *in* ♏. VIII.—iii. ☽ *n* ♊.

This is by no means a good combination as a rule, as the personality is inclined to great extremes and is easily drawn into reckless habits. It gives a love of cleverness, smartness, and shrewdness; and therefore makes good writers, reviewers, and literary critics. There is great ability for outward expression by tongue or pen; invention and wit, pungent sarcasm, and capacity for sustained intellectual effort. The native could subsist by literature, clerical work or travelling; or by organising and superintending others in one of these directions: has also abilities for scientific work. The lungs may suffer at some time of life, for it is not a good combination for the health.

THE SUN IN SCORPIO AND MOON IN CANCER.

☉ *in* ♏. VIII.—iv. ☽ *in* ♋.

This is a harmonious combination in the watery triplicity; but there is a great liability to be easily drawn into mistakes through the feelings and sensations, and those under this combination are very easily led by others into acts of folly. Early marriage is thus to be recommended, for, the powers of attachment being very strong, the life may thus be influenced for good. The native has a rather hard and practical nature in things that necessitate his going out into the world and mixing with men, but a kinder and softer side in social matters or family life. If planetary positions harmonise, he will have considerable business ability; will earn or inherit money or property, and manage it economically. There are sometimes psychic or occult tendencies. This position is good for health, both as regards nutrition and digestion, if not "afflicted." In some cases may increase the size of the body and cause stoutness.

THE SUN IN SCORPIO AND MOON IN LEO.

☉ *in* ♏. VIII.—v. ☽ *in* ♌.

This is as a rule, though not necessarily, a decidedly inharmonious combination, inclining the mind to romance and love affairs of an intense, emotional nature, and increasing all the passions and desires, making the feelings very intense and very acute. It gives pride, some arrogance, and much love of power, coupled with ardour, imagination, emotion, energy and ambition, which latter may take a variety of directions according to general type of horoscope. There is some love of grandeur, pomp, show and ostentation, and considerable dramatic feeling. With suitable planetary positions, such persons might make a very decided figure in the direction of the drama or music. The nature is strong and commanding, firm and self-directed, even when most emotional; well able to influence others to a very great extent, and to control, direct and organise.

THE SUN IN SCORPIO AND MOON IN VIRGO.

☉ *in* ♏. VIII.—vi. ☽ *in* ♍.

This is the most critical of all the twelve lunar positions. It gives literary ability, with a great deal of pride, much passion, and a liability to become very sarcastic and bitter in speech. Those born under this combination are apt to criticise themselves severely, and to be very dissatisfied with their own achievements, not from diffidence but from a desire for a perfection that is never achieved. They make friends among those in humbler positions than themselves, and are greatly affected through the death of some particular friend or a subordinate. It is a good combination for a doctor or chemist, or one who is inclined toward scientific discoveries, and females make good nurses. There is a tendency to become very worldly.

THE SUN IN SCORPIO AND MOON IN LIBRA.

☉ *in* ♏. VIII.—vii. ☽ *in* ♎.

This gives a tendency to "second sight," some inclination towards the occult and mystical, and a love for all that is psychic, romantic and wonderful, with leanings towards metaphysics, and higher thought. A great deal depends upon planetary influences as to the working of this combination: in some cases there will be no occult ability, but business foresight instead. There is a disposition to join some mystical brotherhood. Under affliction this position causes an inharmonious marriage or in some cases death of marriage partner. Charitable and benevolent disposition: under bad aspects may suffer from enmity, treachery, deceit. A good and well-meaning nature that is sometimes apt to take the wrong path in life. There may be some inharmony or misfortune, through one of the parents (depending upon which luminary is most afflicted). If both are well aspected the native has an affectionate nature and is a well-disposed person, likely to have many friends and to marry well; will gain by marriage or partnership.

THE SUN IN SCORPIO AND MOON IN SCORPIO.

☉ *in* ♏. VIII.—viii. ☽ *in* ♏.

This combination gives much independence and self-reliance, and an inclination towards materialism with ability to govern others, though there is always a tendency to over-ride domineer and master. It gives much pride and a great amount of reserve, yet there is a tendency to be inquisitive and search into hidden secrets. These characteristics may vary greatly according to the planetary positions and aspects. If Mars or Saturn are strongest, the native is very capable and practical but too hard, matter-of-fact and unyielding. If Jupiter or Venus, there will be a lively imagination, active emotions and warm feelings. Unless well aspected, not good for health; may cause stoutness, and lymphatic temperament. But there is generally much energy and activity, with a capable executive nature, in some cases a very strong, firm, decided character, with an iron will. Under "affliction" liable to very heavy buffets of fate; but with good aspects will accomplish and acquire much. Parents either die early or prove unsympathetic.

THE SUN IN SCORPIO AND MOON IN SAGITTARIUS.

☉ *in* ♏. VIII.—ix. ☽ *in* ♐.

This combination gives much combativeness, with a tendency to sarcasm, or indiscreet and explosive speech. Impulse is strong, and there is an inclination towards rash conduct. There is a tendency to combine occultism and religion. There is an innate conservatism combined with progressive ideas. Terrible in anger, on occasion. Busy and practical workers, enthusiastic and ardent for any cause they espouse or anything that interests them. Sometimes liable to "overdo it," either mentally or physically, although this polarity tends to give very good vitality. They follow occupations connected with the church or religious movements, or according to station make good soldiers or sailors; they have ability for law or medicine, these tendencies depending upon planetary positions to bring them into prominence.

THE SUN IN SCORPIO AND MOON IN CAPRICORN.

☉ *in* ♏. VIII.—x. ☽ *in* ♑.

This intensifies the pride of Scorpio, and gives strong inclinations towards self-indulgence, but with a great amount of patience, perseverance and endurance. It is apt to give a rather hard nature, with great self-will and fixedness of opinion and habit, somewhat combative and aggres.

sive, and alternating at times between extremes of rashness and caution, liberality and thrift. Supported by suitable planetary positions, it may give considerable business ability, with great financial acuteness and prudence in investments or in buying and selling. Suitable occupations are soldier, engineer, worker in metals: or some official position may be held in some public body. The harder qualities of the combination may be softened down if there are beneficial aspects to the luminaries.* Under bad aspects the native may easily find himself at variance with brethren, the family, and the public, or separated from the former. He has much practical executive ability, and would make a good overseer or superintendent, or could fill any position necessitating control of others. There is ambition with great determination behind it, and very high attainments are possible. The tendency of this combination however, is toward materialistic thought. It makes capital dramatic critics.

THE SUN IN SCORPIO AND MOON IN AQUARIUS.

☉ *in* ♏. VIII.—xi. ☽ *in* ♒.

This gives ability for Government employments; a tendency to mix in large concerns; much conservatism, with pride, and a keen desire-nature. There is a love of external appearances, wealth and grandeur, but also some love of the occult and mysterious, nevertheless. This position tends somewhat to mental activity, which may take a variety of directions according to the type of horoscope and predominant planet; if Mercury is strong, intellectual activity will be increased; if Venus, the feelings; and so on. It gives some smartness, liveliness, acuteness, inventiveness and originality; which, under affliction, may become irritability, nervous worry, or aggressiveness. Sometimes opinionative and dogmatic. A little lacking in pliability and adaptability; must do things in his own way or not at all. Apt to have keen likes and dislikes with regard to his acquaintances. A faithful friend and unchanging enemy. If benefics† are strong may be very popular; if the reverse, may be more disliked than he deserves. Has some natural dramatic power. Is much attached to home life, and, except under contrary aspects, does not easily

* *i.e.* Sun and Moon. † The 'benefics' are Jupiter and Venus.

forsake it. Will have much strength of will, mental concentration, mesmeric power. Death may be comparatively sudden.

THE SUN IN SCORPIO AND MOON IN PISCES.

☉ *in* ♏. VIII.—xii. ☽ *in* ♓.

This combination gives a very restless and anxious nature; it makes mediumship easy, but in many respects is rather a weak combination for the morals. The mind is somewhat mathematically inclined, but there is a tendency towards deception and duplicity. If other planets permit, the native is very affectionate, warm-hearted, sympathetic, charitable, benevolent; and he may benefit from these qualities in others. Under affliction he is apt to be very unlucky and constantly thwarted; there is more promise than performance: he may benefit by children and friends. This position tends to mysticism, but sometimes to a very dogmatic and sectarian religion. It increases offspring: but there is ambition ungratified and a difficulty in rising into one's proper sphere.

See PRELIMINARY NOTES ON pp. 72, 73.

THE SUN IN SAGITTARIUS.

☉ *in* ♐. IX. ☉ *in* ♐.

The Sun in the sign Sagittarius inclines the individual towards science, philosophy and religion. It gives much activity, and a restless spirit, but a nature frank, honest, sincere, loyal, and liberty-loving. It gives a tendency to prophecy, which will manifest itself according to the particular sign that the Moon may be placed in. In undeveloped egos there will be a rebellious and dominative spirit, but in the advanced souls a love of law and order.

THE SUN IN SAGITTARIUS AND MOON IN ARIES.

☉ *in* ♐. IX.—i. ☽ *in* ♈.

This is a combination of the fiery triplicity. It intensifies the activity, but inclines the mind to be always rushing out impulsively; this is apt to give a somewhat exacting nature and a tendency towards discontent. Considerable restraint is therefore needed, otherwise too much mental energy will be expressed, resulting in considerable changeableness and excitability. There will be great desire to excel, and sometimes to over-reach, others; the passional nature is often active, and the personality is very strong and tends to over-ride restraint. Impulse, energy, and activity predominate, and may be expressed through almost any channel, according to the strongest planet in the horoscope. Unless aspects contradict, the native will be generous, ardent, enthusiastic, wilful and sometimes rebellious; espousing causes or movements zealously, and defending his friends as himself. There is an activity and vigour which may manifest either physically in muscular strength and bodily restlessness, or socially through the feelings and emotions, or mentally in intensity of purpose. In a good horoscope, can accomplish much for good by pioneering, bringing about reforms, originating and improving. Under cross aspects may be too militant, aggressive, detructive, and lacking in judicious restraint and calmness. Likely to travel and to change his residence and perhaps his occupation.

THE SUN IN SAGITTARIUS AND MOON IN TAURUS.

☉ *in* ♐. IX.—ii. ☽ *in* ♉.

This is a sympathetic combination ; while the solar position expands the sympathies, the reserve of Taurus lessens the impulsiveness of Sagittarius and also gives more stability to the foresight, which is nearly always reliable. The native possesses warm affections, geniality, and sympathy ; also imagination, and some qualification for artistic, musical or allied pursuits. Makes a faithful servant, conscientious and honourable (unless afflicted). It is a fortunate combination for worldly success, the foresight of Sagittarius being used for practical ends.

THE SUN IN SAGITTARIUS AND MOON IN GEMINI.

☉ *in* ♐. IX.—iii. ☽ *in* ♊.

This combination quickens the activities of Sagittarius. It gives a liability to become hasty in speech, over-excited, and too active. There are many obstacles in the life to overcome, though there is always a great love of education. It inclines to a highly nervous condition, which may induce nervous disorders or consumptive tendencies. It favours the motive temperament and gives a love of travel, while there is considerable journalistic ability. Judgment and memory should both be good unless contra-indicated by bad aspects. The nature is active and often a little abrupt, but is yet somewhat liable to vacillation, change and irresolution. The native benefits through relatives, and may marry one.

THE SUN IN SAGITTARIUS AND MOON IN CANCER.

☉ *in* ♐. IX.—iv. ☽ *in* ♋.

This is not a very harmonious combination, fire and water not being agreeable companions ; many mistakes are apt to be made in life through the sympathetic impulsiveness of the individuality, which is easily expressed through the personal, emotional, psychic and imaginative characteristics of Cancer. This combination gives intuition and confers the gift of prophecy and true dreaming, but inclines somewhat towards sensation, increasing the imagination and the emotional and affectional nature. Appreciation of the beautiful in nature and art is intense, and with suitable planetary positions the native may show considerable ability for painting, music, or allied pursuits; also religious tendencies of a mystical or imaginative kind. This position tends to voyages, and is, moreover, somewhat favourable for money and property. Unless afflicted, good parental heredity and congenial family influence are indicated.

THE SUN IN SAGITTARIUS AND MOON IN LEO.

☉ *in* ♐. IX.—v. ☽ *in* ♌.

This is a splendid combination from the fiery triplicity; it awakens either the passional or the spiritual side of the nature, the latter giving great ability to foresee the future and hence to prophesy. It tends to make the mind very proud, but quick and alert, with the ability to sense other minds. This is the most affectional combination of this group, the heart being very active. The love nature can go out to many, and there is apt to be some confusion in this respect. There is some ability for the drama, either as author or interpreter, and a love of grand surroundings, whether natural or social. With suitable planetary positions, the native may accomplish much in life and perhaps make a great figure. In itself this combination may sometimes make a nature more imaginative than practical; but the practical qualities may be supplied by the Rising Sign or planetary positions. If born in a suitable sphere of life, will have considerable adaptability for the higher mental activities, religion, philosophy, politics, etc.

THE SUN IN SAGITTARIUS AND MOON IN VIRGO.

☉ *in* ♐. IX.—vi. ☽ *in* ♍.

This gives excellent discriminative powers; there is intuition and refinement, power of language, a love of harmony, and ability to intellectually foresee with regard to material things. The higher mind is active and tends to make the personality bright and clear in thought and speech, though very critical. There is good intellectual ability, suitable for literature, law, the ministry, and a variety of pursuits in which the higher educational endowments can be utilised. The native may occupy some public appointment of a legal, medical, or other official kind. This combination tends somewhat towards love of home life and a domesticated nature; under affliction, however, may show irritability or despondency. This position generally shows common sense, sober judgment, and quiet dignity.

THE SUN IN SAGITTARIUS AND MOON IN LIBRA.

☉ *in* ♐. IX.—vii. ☽ *in* ♎.

In this combination the personal characteristics tend to equalise and modify the impulse of Sagittarius. It awakens the ambitions, and gives a fairly strong personality, with very quick and accurate perception, added to great powers of comparison. There is also refinement, and some artistic or musical ability. This combination gives some popularity, and attracts to friends and acquaintances of fairly good social standing who will be congenial to the native and may benefit him, and amongst whom he may marry. Gives good-nature, sincerity and hopefulness, unless afflicted, and is a generally harmonious polarity. If supported by good planetary positions there will be considerable mental power and imagination.

THE SUN IN SAGITTARIUS AND MOON IN SCORPIO.

☉ *in* ♐. IX.—viii. ☽ *in* ♏.

This is a good combination, the Martial-Jupiterian influence predominating. There is apt to be much sarcasm in speech, while pride and considerable temper, combativeness, and impetuosity mark the disposition; but where the mind is led into the occult great attainments may be made. It gives much perseverance and persistence, with plenty of energy and a strong desire for independence. It is good for health and strength of constitution, and bestows both endurance and working power, either physical or otherwise according to planetary position. Marked muscular strength is probable, with some tendency to fleshiness. Under affliction, there is some danger of the passional nature being too active, but there is a fair amount of practical executive ability. The native will be free and generous, and if aspects are favourable will earn (or inherit) considerable wealth.

THE SUN IN SAGITTARIUS AND MOON IN SAGITTARIUS.

☉ *in* ♐. IX.—ix. ☽ *in* ♐.

This combination gives too much independence, and a too great love of freedom, inducing a tendency to become reckless and rebellious; while at the same time there are some inclinations towards conservatism: it quickens the mental and physical powers. Sagittarius is well expressed by this combination, the love of travel, science, philosophy, and religion being very strongly marked. If "benefics" (♃ and ♀) are prominent there is much generosity, with strong social and benevolent feelings, and a fairly harmonious and all-round nature. The duality of Sagittarius will probably show out strongly, causing occasional indecision of mind as well as changes in occupation or mode of life (as described under *The Moon in Sagittarius*).

THE SUN IN SAGITTARIUS AND MOON IN CAPRICORN.

☉ *in* ♐. IX.—x. ☽ *in* ♑.

Here the personal characteristics steady the individuality, which on its side awakens the personal nature into greater activity, giving keen ambition in the direction of higher thought, etc. There is decided musical ability, or at least great love for music, and though there is some liability to changeableness, the mind is industrious and practical, though somewhat sensual. There is good executive ability and sound common sense. The native is suited for a variety of pursuits, business, church, law, some public office, or for political life, and has some ability for successful financial speculation, if planets co-operate. This combination gives influence in religious matters, and tends to orderliness and method.

THE SUN IN SAGITTARIUS AND MOON IN AQUARIUS.

☉ *in* ♐. IX.—xi. ☽ *in* ♒.

This quickens the intuitions, and enlarges the views; it gives ability to deal with the multitude, and with associations and public bodies: but there is a liability to over-exertion. It increases the qualities of imagination, wonder and sublimity, and gives some attraction to the occult side of life. It will co-operate with any planetary positions that tend towards higher education and mental cultivation, or to religion, philosophy, metaphysics, or any form of original thought or scientific investigation. It is also a good combination for commercial life, or any calling where the personality comes prominently before others.

THE SUN IN SAGITTARIUS AND MOON IN PISCES.

☉ *in* ♐. IX.—xii. ☽ *in* ♓.

This combination gives much anxiety, restlessness and inclination to worry; but the prophetic nature can easily express itself through the personality when the latter is restful and mediumistically inclined. There is a strong religious tendency, and an inclination to be charitable, sympathetic and benevolent; but this is weakened by a lack of initiative, so that work is best carried out when under the direction of others. This is not a good combination for the health. This polarity is good for family life, for good relations with parents and children, and harmony of the home (unless "afflicted"). It tends somewhat to travelling, and unless afflicted is moderately good for property and possessions; those in the lower ranks of life may benefit through almshouses, charitable institutions, etc., while the well-to-do will be philanthropically disposed.

See PRELIMINARY NOTES ON pp. 72, 73.

THE SUN IN CAPRICORN.

☉ *in* ♑. X. ☉ *in* ♑

This gives a very ambitious individuality, possessing much independence, much strength of character, a keen love of justice and a desire to attain to the highest position possible. There is much self-reliance and determination expressed through this sign, which considerably strengthens the various personalities attached to it.

THE SUN IN CAPRICORN AND MOON IN ARIES.

☉ *in* ♑. X.—i. ☽ *in* ♈.

This gives much ambition, a keen desire to be at the head of everything, much determination, extreme independence and self-assertion, with very egotistical tendencies. It quickens all the Aries vibrations, giving an intense love of music. It brings the native into prominence, especially in governmental affairs or where there is great responsibility. The native is of a capable executive nature, has strong will and much force of character; can work hard and accomplish much. Suited for the army, for engineering or mining, for large business undertakings, or for public life. If the influence of Mercury is strong in the horoscope he will be suitable for literary pursuits or for philosophical or scientific occupations, having an intellect keenly critical, but not destructively so; not devotional in any way, but tending to bring everything to the test of practical life in outward action. If badly aspected, there may be some harshness or hardness, great irritability, and an undisciplined nature, causing family jars and public conflict.

THE SUN IN CAPRICORN AND MOON IN TAURUS.

☉ *in* ♑. X—ii. ☽ *in* ♉.

This gives a very persistent mind, much firmness and self-control, a desire to elevate and improve others, yet with a certain amount of conservatism. It is the most practical of this set of combinations, giving the ability to acquire wealth and the power to do good with it. With good aspects, it is very fortunate for possessions, legacies, worldly prosperity, and social and family life. It gives a strong but harmonious nature, with good feelings, patience, and faithfulness. These characteristics will vary a good deal according to aspects.

THE SUN IN CAPRICORN AND MOON IN GEMINI.

☉ *in* ♑. X.—iii. ☽ *in* ♊.

The steady carefulness of Capricorn behind the activity of Gemini causes this combination to be studious, yet very much inclined to give expression to the thoughts, especially those concerning the higher life behind the personality. This combination is good for occupations connected with travel, or with intellectual work of various kinds, and may give eminence therein. It produces commercial travellers, messengers, whether business or state, consuls, ambassadors, literary men, accountants, scientists, public speakers, and professors. It gives an orderly, methodical mind, ingenious and sometimes if not generally profound, coupled with a good memory. The native will make a good and faithful servant.

THE SUN IN CAPRICORN AND MOON IN CANCER.

☉ *in* ♑. X.—iv. ☽ *in* ♋.

This increases the sensitiveness of Cancer, and gives a strong inclination towards economy, thrift, and prudence, but also a certain amount of selfishness. There is a love of change and a desire for high attainments in the physical world. It gives a love of economy, and much tenacity, yet with the desire to travel. With good aspects, there will be gain through parents or marriage. This polarity is good also for the home life, possessions, estate, honour, and reputation. The native will occupy some public position, more or less notable according to the sphere of his birth, or will hold some official post. But with bad aspects, all these indications tend to be more or less reversed, and to entail *misfortune* in the same direction. In a good horoscope success comes towards middle age; the parents are of good position and honourable.

THE SUN IN CAPRICORN AND MOON IN LEO.

☉ *in* ♑. X.—v. ☽ *in* ♌.

This is not a very harmonious combination, the personal tendencies being towards affection, and hence conflicting with the internal ambitious instincts; nevertheless conjugality can be well expressed by this combination. There is some love of ostentation and display, and the ideals are very high as regards the surroundings, whether artistic, social, or political. At its best, however, this polarity gives a dignified, self-reliant nature, ambitious of power and distinction, firm, strong-willed, and with much force of character, honourable, and kindly. There will probably be some dramatic power, and ability for occupations connected with public life, theatres, concerts, music, public amusements, etc. The native is fitted for occupying a prominent position, and, with suitable aspects, is likely to rise in life and gain both in dignity and authority. He is ambitious of social distinction, and has some capacity for financial speculations and large business enterprises; with probable success through them, if aspects are favourable. There will be gain by legacy or marriage. The native has good vitality and may expect to live long, unless the luminaries are afflicted. There is some likelihood of an accidental or rather sudden death; but not unless seriously afflicted.

THE SUN IN CAPRICORN AND MOON IN VIRGO.

☉ *in* ♑. X.—vi. ☽ *in* ♍.

This is an excellent combination of the earthy triplicity, the critical and analytical tendencies of Virgo being considerably softened by the meditative and contemplative Capricorn nature. It gives splendid ability to judge and criticise, and intensifies the discriminative faculties, giving ability for literary and scientific employments, especially the latter. The native has an orderly and methodical mind, logical, analytical and clear-headed. A little lacking in enterprise, reliance or initiative, perhaps; but this may be supplied by the planetary positions or the ascendant (Rising Sign). This polarity is good for appointments held under authority, public or private, pertaining to medicine, law or science. The native has good business ability, but is at his best either when associated with some one else, or in employ of others. Bad aspects tend to make the native unsettled and changeable.

THE SUN IN CAPRICORN AND MOON IN LIBRA.

☉ *in* ♑. X.—vii. ☽ *in* ♎.

The well-balanced brain of Libra will have behind it the careful thoughtfulness of Capricorn, which will give splendid intuition, comparison, careful foresight and an inclination towards the metaphysical. This combination gives a love of popularity and the desire for fame. It is good for partnership, marriage, and friendship, also for gain by these, unless the Moon is seriously afflicted by malefics (♂, ♄, or ♅); in which case trouble may come through these, and the popularity and fame be in danger of reversal. In a good horoscope it is good for parental and family life, and will give an equable, methodical, law-abiding nature, of good disposition, dignified though ambitious, and humane.

THE SUN IN CAPRICORN AND MOON IN SCORPIO.

☉ *in* ♑. X.—viii. ☽ *in* ♏.

This gives positiveness and determination, strength of will, masterfulness, with some hardness and selfishness. A nature apt to be very self-centred and difficult to influence. It tends towards materialistic thought, and gives some revolutionary tendencies, the feeling of independence being strong and the desire for revenge, when thwarted, keen. In a good horoscope, this polarity shows one who can control others, organise, plot, plan, scheme, exert tact and diplomacy, and exhibit qualities useful in a master or leader, whether in business or politics. If supported by benefics (♃, ♀) there will be good fortune in money, legacy, property, or honours and dignities. But if much afflicted by malefics (♂, ♄, ♅) the polarity may bring loss in any of these directions and danger of accident, injury, or even sudden death.

THE SUN IN CAPRICORN AND MOON IN SAGITTARIUS.

☉ *in* ♑. X.—ix. ☽ *in* ♐.

This is not altogether a harmonious combination, but the practical nature of Capricorn will steady down the recklessness and impulsiveness of Sagittarius and improve the executive ability. It is, however, good for explorers; and also for the church, as it gives much religious ambition. There is decided business and financial ability; but its outcome, whether successful or the reverse, depends greatly on aspects: if these are good, there will be considerable gain through investments, speculative or otherwise, also through travel and commerce, or in occupations connected with the church, law or religious bodies. Under evil aspects, however, there may be serious loss through any of these, as well as by fraud or deception.

THE SUN IN CAPRICORN AND MOON IN CAPRICORN.

☉ *in* ♑. X.—x. ☽ *in* ♑.

This gives a very thoughtful character, with some inclination to despondency. There is apt to be too much independence at times, resulting in isolation, or a desire to live a life of loneliness. The feelings are not expansive, and there is a tendency to retire inward more than is good for the character. It gives good business ability, making the nature acquisitive and somewhat self-centred. The native is usually steady, quiet and thoughtful, persistent in purpose, and both plodding and thorough in his methods. Planetary positions will vary the type a good deal. Strong aspects from Mars or Jupiter will give more vigour, energy and ambition, which may be turned to various ends, whether in business, politics or science. If Mercury is strong he will possess considerable intellectual power. Bad aspects may cause persistent misfortune, however. Orderly and methodical, the native can both use tact and keep a secret; he does not show his whole nature on the surface, but is self-controlled and reserved.

THE SUN IN CAPRICORN AND MOON IN AQUARIUS.

☉ *in* ♑. X.—xi. ☽ *in* ♒.

This gives splendid organising ability, with success in large undertakings, such as public companies, etc. It quickens the perceptions and gives considerable intuition, with the ability to read character accurately. Much progress is made in life through careful forethought and steady persistence. A great deal depends on the aspects, however, in the combination. If supported by suitable planetary indications, this polarity gives a strong tendency to the psychic or occult; with a prominent Uranus or Mercury, for instance, intellectual or metaphysical ability and an original and inventive mind. The social and domestic nature and the inclination to marriage are more easily manifested than with the last polarity; but even this depends a good deal upon the ascendant and planets; with support from Venus or Jupiter, there may be a fair amount of geniality and popularity. Money may be gained through governmental or other official positions; and, unless contra-indicated by adverse planetary positions, there will be good business ability, with success in financial operations and investments, etc.

THE SUN IN CAPRICORN AND MOON IN PISCES.

☉ *in* ♑. X.—xii. ☽ *in* ♓.

This polarity tends to produce a quiet, undemonstrative, easy-going nature, moderately sociable and home-loving. Sometimes rather retiring, self-distrustful; possessing better abilities than people suppose, but lacking the energy or opportunity to use them to advantage. Some will be careful and frugal, anxious about the future; but others rather indolent, easy-going, and careless, or indifferent. Charitable and sympathetic, according to their means: or, if circumstances necessitate it, they may benefit by the charity and philanthropy of others, public or private. Suited for occupations connected with liquids, with hospitals, nursing, charitable movements and institutions, or prisons. If intellect is supplied by the planetary positions, or the "ascendant" is a mercurial sign (♊ or ♍), they may make writers, speakers or preachers; but they usually lean more to the imaginative and emotional or speculative than to the purely intellectual, and hence make novelists, poets or musicians, rather than mathematicians or scientists. Mediumship or psychic ability of some kind is easily called out. These persons possess some considerable amount of tact, diplomacy, secrecy, and reserve; they do not show their whole nature on the surface, by any means. If badly afflicted by malefics (especially ♂) they may suffer seriously through other people, or may not be quite straightforward themselves (shown by the general configuration of the horoscope).

See PRELIMINARY NOTES on pp 72, 73.

THE SUN IN AQUARIUS.

☉ *in* ♒. XI. ☉ *in* ♒.

The Sun in Aquarius gives a very refined individuality, loving everything of a humanitarian nature, very faithful, sincere, humane and just, with very broad sympathies and a desire to embrace the whole of humanity. The individuality will be active in awakened souls, but in the younger members of the race it will not be manifest, and the personality will act as though no individuality were behind it; that is to say the position of the Moon alone will have to be considered.

THE SUN IN AQUARIUS AND MOON IN ARIES.

☉ *in* ♒. XI.—i. ☽ *in* ♈.

This gives a very firm character, quiet, and not very expressive, but with real perceptive ability, and capable of judging human character; persevering in nature, but liable at times to go to extremes in action. There is a very strong will, with great determination and persistence of purpose. Such characters cannot endure being controlled or thwarted, and will go to great lengths and be very unreasonable through their desire to have their own way. In a suitable horoscope, there may be considerable mental power, and ability for occupations connected with writing, study, literature, travelling or science, with some adaptability for political or other official positions. They are fond of imposing their will upon others, leading, or controlling. And yet they are not always most fortunate when in sole control, or when the whole responsibility for any affair is theirs. They *must* learn to submit to association with others; if not as subordinates, then as partners or companions, and they will then usually obtain the best results. If malefics afflict, their personal desires and passions are apt to get very much out of control, and make them licentious, cunning and revengeful ; but in a good horoscope an energetic and hard-working character is shown, able and executive.

THE SUN IN AQUARIUS AND MOON IN TAURUS.

☉ *in* ♒. XI.—ii. ☽ *in* ♉.

This makes an excellent character reader, true insight into human nature being well developed. It inclines to the practical in all its manifestations, and is faithful, sincere, firm, just and reliable. The native possesses, in short, a steady, quiet and practical character which may find its outlet in many departments of life, according to circumstances. Nevertheless, when such persons have once found a congenial channel to work in they do not easily forsake it unless compelled to do so ; for change of any kind is foreign to their nature, and whatever their mode of life may be, whether commercial, professional, political or otherwise, they tend to continue faithfully and ploddingly in it, for a lifetime maybe, and only vary or alter their course under extreme necessity. They are sincere, just and faithful in family life, unless aspects are very adverse. In business or profession they usually accumulate either honours, money or possessions, whichever they may have set their minds upon, because of this very persistency ; although these may not come until middle or old age. If the ascendant supplies enthusiasm and energy they may accomplish much in the world. If seriously afflicted, especially by Mars, their misfortunes may be sudden and violent ; which applies to most fixed sign polarities. The influence is good for friends, acquaintances, and social and public relations generally.

THE SUN IN AQUARIUS AND MOON IN GEMINI.

☉ *in* ♒. XI.—iii. ☽ *in* ♊.

This combination belongs to the airy triplicity. It intensifies all the intellectual qualities, giving oratorical power and a studious mind, well adapted for all literary pursuits ; there is also displayed considerable industry, neatness, and perfection in regard to details. With a good education these persons may be fitted for almost any occupation calling for intellectual ability, acuteness and originality of mind, or mental resource. In political or educational matters they would succeed well, also as speakers, preachers, professors, writers, teachers, etc. Unless the ascendant supplies energy and initiative, they succeed better when in partnership or association with others than when relying upon their own resources solely. They are sometimes a little retiring, liking reserve and seclusion, but this may easily be counteracted if Jupiter or Venus is prominent, as it does not arise from an unsociable nature. They are kind and good-hearted, and have many acquaintances if few intimate friends. They often have a good memory and well stored minds.

THE SUN IN AQUARIUS AND MOON IN CANCER.

☉ *in* ♒. XI.—iv. ☽ *in* ♋

This is not a very harmonious combination. It intensifies the economical tendencies of Cancer, and gives firmness with regard to all matters of a domestic nature. It awakens the sensitiveness of Cancer and gives great intuition with regard to persons where there is much attachment. If the horoscope is, on the whole, a fairly harmonious one, these persons have a strong attraction to home life, marriage, friendship, social and domestic matters, and to the emotional side of the nature generally, and they will prosper in such matters. If aspects are adverse, their greatest misfortunes will come through these channels,—parentage, marriage, or family. They have good mental abilities, but usually of an emotional or imaginative type rather than the purely intellectual. Psychic or occult experiences may be met with.

THE SUN IN AQUARIUS AND MOON IN LEO.

☉ *in* ♒. XI.—v. ☽ *in* ♌

This intensifies the love nature and gives a strong desire to become devoted to one; there is an inclination to worship those who are loved. It is rather a peculiar combination, giving considerable psychic ability and the power to psychometrise. The nature will tend towards either the intellect or the feelings, according to the balance of influences in the horoscope. There is an active mind and a lively imagination, which in a high type of person may achieve great things: there is also a sense of dignity and proper pride, coupled with a liking for society, a love of approbation, and a desire for distinction and honour, for "cutting a figure" or taking the lead. Leo adds warmth, ardour, and imagination to the Aquarius nature, which will express itself in a variety of ways according to the kind of horoscope, and perhaps confer distinction through whatever may be the strongest planet There is ability for occupying public or prominent positions, according to the sphere of life. Unless afflicted, it is good for marriage and friendship.

THE SUN IN AQUARIUS AND MOON IN VIRGO

☉ *in* ♒. XI.—vi. ☽ *in* ♍.

This considerably improves the characteristics, intensifying the love of hygiene, giving neatness, precision, carefulness, and awakening all the critical faculties. It gives prudence, practicalness and business ability, with a love of science and intellectual pursuits in general; but unless the influence is supplied elsewhere by the ascendant or planets, there may be some lack of demonstrativeness, initiative, activity, or hopefulness. Such a person would prosper best when in association with another or under the control of another who would supply the initiative or enterprise; in this way he is both able and willing to work very thoroughly, and might occupy an official or other post in some company, public or private association or organisation, or large business undertaking.

THE SUN IN AQUARIUS AND MOON IN LIBRA.

☉ *in* ♒. XI.—vii. ☽ *in* ♎.

This is a very fine combination, of the airy triplicity. It gives splendid powers of judgment, remarkable perception, and a very intuitive mind, with much foresight. It awakens the spiritual side of the nature, giving balance and equilibrium to the internal perceptions. Success in marriage is indicated in this combination. It gives considerable imagination and love of the beautiful, with a keen appreciation of art, music, etc., all of which will be very active if Venus is strong. It conduces to sociability, popularity, partnership and friendship; also to love of company, and harmonising or humanising influences generally.

THE SUN IN AQUARIUS AND MOON IN SCORPIO.

☉ *in* ♒. XI.—viii. ☽ *in* ♏.

This is a less harmonious combination, the Scorpio nature not being in harmony with the Aquarian : it inclines to make the nature somewhat worldly and selfish. There is great ability displayed in playing upon the nature of others. The chief undesirable features of this polarity are, that it is apt to make the nature somewhat too positive, self-reliant, sometimes self-assertive, and proud; very strong-willed, and not easily influenced or turned aside. Sometimes there is irritability, abruptness, or aggressiveness. The less desirable characteristics may easily be toned down if "benefics" (♀, ♃) are prominent, and then the nature becomes extremely useful in the world, practical, executive, business-like, firm, steady, and hard-working; suitable for positions of prominence or responsibility, and likely to gain money, property, power, or dignity. If there are strong afflictions from malefics (♂, ♄, ♅), there is some danger of rather sudden and serious trouble at times. There may be trouble or sorrow through either of the parents.

THE SUN IN AQUARIUS AND MOON IN SAGITTARIUS.

☉ *in* ♒. XI.—ix. ☽ *in* ♐.

This combination makes the personality rather too quick for the slow, steady individuality; but it adds more concentrativeness to the impulsive nature of Sagittarius. There is apt to be much impulse in speech and inclination to be rather abrupt. It gives religious or psychic tendencies, and considerable literary ability, increasing the higher mind and calling out imagination, love of beauty, and those faculties that work through music, acting, painting and the emotions and feelings generally whether artistic, religious, or humanitarian. It tends to increase the number of acquaintances and friends, also the popularity and social sympathies in general. There is some fitness for a public career in connection with religion, philosophy, law, or one of the fine arts.

THE SUN IN AQUARIUS AND MOON IN CAPRICORN.

☉ *in* ♒. XI.—x. ☽ *in* ♑.

This combination makes the personality very shrewd, tactful and ambitious; eager to attain to great heights, which are often reached through favouritism and the help of friends. There is much solidity of thought and ability for political matters, the ideas being broad and the mind subtle. A somewhat serious, grave and thoughtful nature, with a good deal of firmness, patience, perseverance, and continuity of thought, in whatever sphere of life the native may move. There is a good deal of fitness for a public career of some sort, or the holding of some public office or appointment, in which (if planetary aspects are favourable) much success may be gained. There is ambition, tact, the power to face adverse circumstances unmoved, ability to control other people, and suitability for positions of prominence and responsibility. There is a likelihood of much mental power, depth of thought, a comprehensive mind, and a good memory; and the native will be able to deal with difficult, profound and complex subjects and with important undertakings, whether in public or private life, and whether in practical affairs or in the sphere of the mind. The favour of the public, of acquaintances, and of superiors is likely to be gained; but if the Moon is much afflicted criticism, opposition, or worse troubles may be encountered in these directions. There is a tendency to reserve; the nature is not all shown on the surface. Hence there is considerable ability for matters involving secrecy and diplomacy ; in a bad horoscope this may manifest as lack of candour and straightforwardness, from which the native will himself suffer on the part of others if the horoscope is otherwise good. There may be in some cases gloom, despondency, a want of buoyancy, or lack of energy ; but this may be overcome by prominent benefics (♃, ♀), by a suitable ascendant, or by a strong aspect (△ or ⚹) from Mars. If supported by planetary positions, there will be remarkable business and financial ability.

THE SUN IN AQUARIUS AND MOON IN AQUARIUS.

☉ *in* ♒. XI.—xi. ☽ *in* ♒.

This combination is good for the individuality, giving much refinement, a great deal of discretion, discrimination, and careful thought. It intensifies the clearness and brightness of the Aquarian intellect, and tones down the self-centring of the luminaries in the same sign. It is not altogether fortunate in a worldly sense, but, nevertheless, makes the mind positive, self-reliant, original, fairly active, humane, well-disposed and well-balanced ; if the mental significators (☿, ♃) are well placed, the native will be capable of assimilating unlimited education and mental culture. This polarity is well suited for a public career, or for holding office or appointment in connection with some public body. With fairly good aspects the native is likely to be very popular, and to have many acquaintances and a pleasant home life ; but with adverse aspects these indications will be more or less reversed, and trouble or opposition will ensue. Marriage is extremely probable.

THE SUN IN AQUARIUS AND MOON IN PISCES.

☉ *in* ♒. XI.—xii. ☽ *in* ♓.

This is a more favourable Pisces combination than those previously given, as it gives much perseverance and carefulness, awakening the studious side of the Pisces nature. But with regard to this, much will depend upon planetary influences and the aspects to Sun and Moon. There is some amount of imagination, love of beauty, musical or artistic ability, refinement, and sentiment; much charitable feeling and sympathy. Some psychic or occult tendencies exist, and mediumship is easily developed. Unless very positive tendencies are given by the ascendant or planetary positions, the nature is unassuming, a little retiring, agreeable and sociable; more suited for some relatively quiet and unambitious occupation than for one involving publicity, responsibility, or conflict. Will benefit by friends and patrons,—or even by charity, if the planetary positions indicate any need of this.

See Preliminary Notes pp. 72, 73.

THE SUN IN PISCES.

☉ *in* ♓. XII. ☉ *in* ♓.

The Sun in the sign Pisces tends to make the individual nature emotional and receptive, meditative and imitative. This is not the strongest of the twelve signs, but it gives a very deep internal nature, with strong inclinations towards occult development. There are two types of individuals under the sign Pisces, the undeveloped and the developed. The latter are extremely altruistic characters, filled with an inexhaustible love for all created beings. The former are weaklings.

THE SUN IN PISCES AND MOON IN ARIES.

☉ *in* ♓. XII.—i. ☽ *in* ♈.

This combination considerably strengthens the individual character, adds more force and energy to the Pisces sign, and gives more self-reliance; but at the same time there is considerable wilfulness, though with a tendency to be easily led if not easily driven. There is positiveness, force, energy and activity, though of a rather restless and unsettled kind. The native is busy and brisk, interested in details, prolific of ideas or words or enthusiasms, and a copious worker. There is likely to be hopefulness and ardour, an active fancy, and a many-sided nature. New causes, pursuits, or studies, are taken up eagerly, though sometimes with too much haste, so that they are incontinently dropped again; too much having been expected of them, they are apt to be abandoned. There is sometimes over-much tendency to change, novelty and variety; too little steady persistency and sober self-control. There is too often a good deal of wilfulness; and though generous and kind-hearted, the native may be difficult to get on with or to work with, and may sometimes be his own worst enemy. If there is much affliction there is a little danger of the personal desires, impulses and passions getting out of control; while, on the otherhand, if the benefics (♀, ♃) are weak he will be somewhat fussy, meddlesome, and fault-finding: but if the latter are prominent, these characteristics will be toned down, so as not to be noticeable.

THE SUN IN PISCES AND MOON IN TAURUS.

⊙ *in* ♓. XII.—ii. ☽ *in* ♉.

This intensifies the negative nature of this combination; it gives a considerable amount of sensitiveness, and a great love of the occult. The firmness of Taurus strengthens the vacillation of Pisces, and makes a kind, quiet and pleasant nature. There is some love of money indicated, yet with a very hospitable disposition, quiet, sociable, genial, and agreeable; the native is one that is attracted towards home, brethren and friends; he is somewhat fortunate in money matters, and displays carefulness, some economy, and a tendency to slow and patient accumulation. There is also some practical business ability, and he makes a good servant or under-manager. Sympathy and benevolence may be easily called out by prominent benefics: also musical or artistic ability. With Mars or the Sun strong, there will be firmness and positiveness, or even obstinacy. Unless otherwise indicated, there will be little ambition or likelihood of rising to a lofty position in the world, and quieter or relatively subordinate positions are more fortunate. If the Moon is "angular"* or Mercury strong, money may readily be earned by writing or travelling. This polarity tends towards steadiness, conscientiousness, and some seriousness. If ever in a position to need it, the native will benefit considerably by charity, friends, or brethren.

THE SUN IN PISCES AND MOON IN GEMINI.

⊙ *in* ♓. XII.—iii. ☽ *in* ♊.

This combination gives vacillation and a tendency to worry, with a lack of continuity or fixity of purpose; there is a great deal of indecision

* *I.e.*, rising, setting, or culminating.

and an inclination to restless over-activity as regards all mental matters. The native is easily affected by the moods of others, and becomes rather fanciful. While this polarity makes the mind active, yet with the activity there is ever likely to be some irresolution, vacillation or indecision; or at least lack of continuity or fixity of purpose. This may be partly counteracted, however, if the ascendant* or important planets are in fixed signs. There is sometimes diffidence or reserve, and lack of enterprise, initiative, or ambition; but this will be overcome if positive planets or signs are prominent. The native learns readily, and can usually take a good education, sometimes showing decided precocity. There is always a love of reading or writing, and there will also be ability for speaking if Mercury is strong. Among the lower middle classes, this polarity makes good servants, agents, messengers or clerks; while those in better circumstances would be suited for any occupation involving book-work, study, examinations, writing, clerical labour, etc. A love of teaching or preaching is often found associated with this influence, and nearly always a love of travelling. In some cases there are changes of occupation or unnecessary changes of residence, two occupations are followed or two residences kept. In a bad horoscope some tendency to duplicity or lack of candour is shown, and danger of inharmony in the family; but prominent benefics (♀, ♃) or good aspects will override this, giving a subtle and acute mind, critical and judicious, capable of embracing many subjects and going into much detail.

THE SUN IN PISCES AND MOON IN CANCER.

☉ *in* ♓. XII.—iv. ☽ *in* ♋.

This intensifies the imaginative and sensitive nature of Cancer, and increases the economy, also the receptivity. It is one of the psychical combinations, awakening the psychic faculties. The emotional nature is very keen, but not lacking in reflection, and the whole nature is harmonious, though sensitive, and very hospitable. The feelings and emotions are active, love of home and family, affection, sympathy, kindness, and companionship are marked. There will be a strong attraction

* See chap. XIX., also under heading "The soli-lunar combinations extended," at end of present chapter.

to the mother, and a resemblance to her; also long association with her. or benefit through her or her side of the family. Unless positive planets (☉, ♂, ♃, ♅) or the *odd* signs are prominent, the nature will be rather too negative and receptive of the thoughts, feelings, and influences of others; this may even extend to the catching of infectious diseases, and should be combated by a steadfast will. Psychic experiences will be met with, and mediumship would be readily developed. There will be much sensitiveness and imagination, which might be utilised in the direction of music, painting, or poetry, if Venus is sufficiently strong. Religious and charitable influences will be congenial; and either directly or indirectly the native will benefit through hospitals, charitable organisations, etc. There is a tendency to economy and carefulness, in small matters especially: with good aspects there will be considerable gain through house-property, land or investments.

THE SUN IN PISCES AND MOON IN LEO.

☉ *in* ♓. XII.—V. ☽ *in* ♌.

This is an inharmonious combination, so far as the physical world is concerned, as it gives a continual yearning for the unattainable, or for something that seems far beyond physical realisation. It inclines very much to the occult and metaphysical, giving a love of everything that is romantic, weird and mysterious. It is rather unfortunate than otherwise, often placing those under its influence in positions they cannot maintain, making them erratic and liable to varying moods. Under favourable planetary aspects there will be considerable ability as imaginative writers. There is a generous disposition, much warmth of heart, sympathy, and charitable feelings. There is some love of outward show, much social ambition, a sense of dignity and personal worth, and a considerable regard for appearances, with a love of fine surroundings, whether in furniture, clothes, house, locality, or scenery. There is apt to be some little ostentation and self-importance, but there is really a homely and quiet nature behind it. There may be artistic, poetic or musical ability, and there will in any case be imagination and emotion, which may be adapted to the higher pursuits and occupations if adequately supported by the ascendant or by Mercury. The influence of planets and of the ascendant is extremely important in this polarity, according as to which of the two polar positions receives most support, the solar or the lunar. Under affliction or "cross aspects," there is apt to be more promise than performance, a higher ambition than the nature can sustain, and hence a failure to realise apparent possibilities. In some cases there may be lack of practical ability and worldly knowledge, in others too free a rein is given to sensations, feelings and passions; but both these can be altered by the ascendant or planetary positions. The native is suited for the position of an under-manager and succeeds as a worker associated with another; but is apt to aim beyond this and fail. The influence is good generally for home, family, and children. It is not so good for health as it might be, unless supported by favourable planetary positions.

THE SUN IN PISCES AND MOON IN VIRGO.

☉ *in* ♓. XII.—vi. ☽ *in* ♍.

Pisces is considerably improved by this combination. The intuition is active, and the critical nature of Virgo has behind it much inspiration. There is good ability, and the native is a good worker in a variety of directions, and possesses fairly all-round abilities. The mental side of the nature is well developed, and intuition and intellect blend very well. A good education will make the native suitable for any of the higher pursuits, literary, legal, or medical, for instance; or he would be adapted for business, according to the predominant influence in the horoscope. In some cases there will be a receptive, self-distrustful disposition, showing reserve, diffidence and coldness; but a positive and quietly affectionate nature can easily be called out. Prudence, steadiness, and common-sense are virtues well to the fore, and much may be done in a quiet way. This is a polarity giving a steady and useful disposition, and one that is likely to be greatly esteemed, though rarely fortunate in a worldly sense.

THE SUN IN PISCES AND MOON IN LIBRA.

☉ *in* ♓. XII.—vii. ☽ *in* ♎.

This gives an equable tendency to the personality, and inclines one to all inspirational and spiritual things, giving the ability to weigh up and balance the internal sense of things possessed by Pisces. It strengthens the perceptions of the Pisces nature, and gives a great love of music, with usually some executive ability therein. This polarity may vary greatly according as to whether the total influence in the horoscope is fortunate or unfortunate. In the former case there will be a benevolent, sympathetic, kindly nature, popular, and easily making friends; hopeful, cheerful, sociable and well disposed. There is much imagination, and frequently some special artistic faculty, together with a great appreciation of religion. The native will be inclined to associate with others, whether as friend, partner, or companion; there will be no liking for a lonely or isolated life, and this will strongly tend towards marriage. The mind will have much refinement, and, if other positions agree, may be susceptible of a high degree of cultivation. If the planetary aspects are very adverse, a good deal of rather persistent "bad luck" may be experienced, of which hostile criticism, lack of sympathy, a sense of frustration, opposition and rivalry, and misfortunes brought about by other people, or resulting from association with others, will be notable features.

THE SUN IN PISCES AND MOON IN SCORPIO.

☉ *in* ♓. XII.—viii. ☽ *in* ♏.

This is not so good a combination as might be thought, although both belong to the watery triplicity, for the Scorpio nature is rather too hard and selfish. It brings misfortunes into the life, and it makes those under its influence inclined to be decidedly jealous, as it is a polarity very easily affected by the conduct of others. In a bad horoscope it indicates treachery. Where the benefics (♃, ♀) are weak or afflicted by bad aspects, there will be some morbid inclinations and many acts of indiscretion. In any case there is a good deal of energy working out through these two watery signs, with practical and executive business ability; and unless afflicted there may be a fortune (acquired or inherited) derived from occupations associated with the water or with liquids generally, also from people who follow such occupations. Sailors, fishermen, publicans aerated-water dealers, wine or spirit merchants, sometimes also surgeons chemists, nurses, and frequently officials connected with hospitals, prisons, almshouses, workhouses, and asylums, also coroners are found under this polarity. Very considerable business ability, or even commercial genius may be manifested if supported by planetary positions, coupled with some amount of worldliness or even hardness of disposition, however. The native will sometimes find himself in a calling that does not wholly accord with his real nature, and yet will be quite unable to change it; and the same often with regard to adopted habits and customs, from which he finds he cannot free himself. He is often misjudged by the world, and may seem too positive, hard, conventional, or unyielding; for the real inner nature is much more kindly and sympathetic than it seems outwardly. The character will vary a good deal, according to the planetary positions, from generosity to selfishness, from a hard-working self-sacrificing disposition to self-indulgence or sloth, and from active kindly emotions to jealousy and vindictiveness. In some cases there will be too much positiveness and self-assertion, and the native will be misled into doing or saying things he cannot justify, or occupying positions he cannot maintain, giving rise to failure or reversal; but he will contend aggressively for rights and privileges, and may display considerable power of regaining his prestige. Some travelling, especially by water, is likely.

THE SUN IN PISCES AND MOON IN SAGITTARIUS.

☉ *in* ♓. XII.—ix. ☽ *in* ♐.

This is a somewhat excitable and irritable combination, belonging to the common signs. It gives over-activity to the personality, but reduces the impulsiveness of Sagittarius, although it often gives a very talkative disposition, with a propensity for tittle-tattle that sometimes verges on scandal-mongering. There is much sympathy in the nature, and strong feelings of charity and religious sentiment. In a good horoscope, this polarity gives warmth, activity and expansiveness to the feelings and emotions, which will work out in various directions according to the type of horoscope: in religion; in some philanthropic or humanitarian direction; in philosophy or the higher cultivation of the mind; in social and family life; or in the world of the imagination as shown in painting, music, poetry, etc. In any one of these directions the native may make considerable attainments, and rise high in his sphere of life, and probably attract notice. He will be a busy worker and accomplish much; and yet, if the planetary positions lend themselves to it, he will have a full appreciation of ease, comfort, luxury, elegance and refinement, and the "good things" of life generally. There is some ability for public speaking or a public career; and the polarity lends itself well to an active business life if suitable influence is supplied from elsewhere, either by the ascendant or an aspect from Saturn,—as it is decidedly more scattering than acquisitive if taken alone. There is a great love of change, some likelihood of a change of occupation, and many changes of residence, coupled with a general love of travel, especially by sea: two pursuits or occupations may be carried on simultaneously. A busy nature, and, if the intellect is active, covering many subjects, seeing both sides of a question, acute and penetrating. There are great possibilities in this polarity if suitably supported by the rest of the horoscope. Otherwise, the well-intentioned internal nature will fritter its energies away in a multitude of useless or superficial projects, or even in mere dissipation.

THE SUN IN PISCES AND MOON IN CAPRICORN.

☉ *in* ♓. XII.—x. ☉ *in* ♑.

Here the personality is apt to lead the individuality captive to the materialistic desires of the Capricorn nature, which is ever seeking to be practical rather than dreamy. An active life is best for those under this combination, and they should be placed in positions of responsibility where they can take the lead. It gives a good deal of business ability in some cases, with special inclination for large undertakings or responsible positions. There will be carefulness, prudence, economy, and forethought, which may be utilised in private or public life according to circumstances. The native will display financial ability in the matter of property and investments, or the power of organising, managing, arranging, planning, and scheming; and he is hence well fitted to fill some position, official or otherwise, demanding the exercise of these qualities, unless adverse aspects militate against this. He may hold an appointment connected with some local or national public body, or may be himself a member of some such body. He has as a rule more inclination for public than private life, but the possibilities here vary greatly according to circumstances. In the lower ranks of life he may become connected with, or follow, some occupation having to do with hospitals, prisons, asylums, the police and poor-law or other officials; and, in a higher position, with town councils, or other public bodies, parliament, and movements of public importance. Which of these are most likely will be shown by the horoscope as a whole. There is usually quietness, sobriety, and self-control. The planetary aspects and other positions will produce several varieties of character and fortune in this polarity. In some cases there will be lack of initiative, and a tendency to gloom or despondency; in others, the personality will seem hard, selfish, reserved, lacking in candour, and secretive; or, again, the native will be placed by circumstances in some position he cannot maintain, and which will therefore result in failure of some sort. Under serious affliction (especially from Mars), there will be public or private hostility, a conflict with the law, with the "powers that be," or with established customs. But with favourable aspects there is very great power for good here.

THE SUN IN PISCES AND MOON IN AQUARIUS.

☉ *in* ♓. XII.—xi. ☽ *in* ♒.

This gives ability for business, and pursuits on a large scale where the intuition may be used. It gives a quiet, retiring, and harmless disposition and in many respects it is an excellent combination. The native makes friends easily, has many acquaintances, may in some cases be a rather popular person, and it is often better suited for some more or less public pursuit than for a purely domestic one; although the homely and social virtues may all be brought out by suitable planetary positions. There will be considerable power of imagination and a love of the mysterious or weird, with decided intuition, especially as regards religious matters; and one of these influences according to prominence will incline to artistic or musical tastes, to psychic or occult experiences, or to a religious career as the case may be. Good mental abilities will be possessed, with sound judgment, and memory; these will be called out by appropriate circumstances. There will be impulses towards philanthropic and humanitarian movements, also to a higher thought, education or science. Local or national public interests will attract the native's attention, and in some cases enlist his services also, at least his sympathies and enthusiasm. Good business ability may be possessed if not contradicted by adverse aspects. Under affliction, the native will suffer from criticism, opposition, or something still more serious on the part of friends and acquaintances or the public; but with good aspects he will gain either in reputation or popularity.

THE SUN IN PISCES AND MOON IN PISCES.

☉ *in* ♓. XII.—xii. ☽ *in* ♓.

This combination gives a hospitable nature, but there is a tendency to be over-anxious and somewhat too restless. It gives an inclination towards spiritualistic phenomena. The imagination is very active, and sometimes rather morbid, so that there is a tendency to give way to melancholia. This brings out fully the Pisces nature, which has been elsewhere described. The native is sympathetic, emotional, imaginative, good-natured, easy-going, romantic, and affectionate. The ascendant largely determines the direction of the activities and the general trend of the character. There is some inclination to religion, also to charity and benevolence if the position in life allows; native may be associated with charitable or similar institutions, or may himself benefit through them in some way. Psychic experiences and mediumship rather easily manifest themselves. There is sufficient religious tendency to determine the native to a career in this direction if the horoscope supports it; and the same may be said of the imaginative faculty and its operation, whether through music, painting, or literature, novel-writing, etc. Under serious affliction from Saturn there may be a tendency to gloom, or lack of self-reliance, and the native may suffer in reputation; but if this planet is well placed there will be worldly success and good fortune. With affliction from Mars, may suffer from deceit, treachery, and the enmity of apparent friends; with a good aspect, however, will be enterprising, resourceful, and able to overcome obstacles. There is some love of travelling, of change, and novelty: this tendency may also show as vacillation, irresolution, lack of promptness and decision, unless harmonious aspects or rising planets strengthen the character. With benefics fairly strong the native has a hopeful, buoyant, sociable and thoroughly good-natured disposition.

IMPORTANT NOTE.

When both luminaries are in the same sign, the ascendant* largely determines the polarity. Examples: Cecil Rhodes, Sun and Moon in Cancer, and Sagittarius rising; Sir Humphrey Davy, Sun and Moon in Sagittarius, and Scorpio rising. These are practically equivalent to Cancer-Sagittarius, and to Sagittarius-Scorpio polarities.

When the luminaries are one in a positive and the other in a negative sign, the Ascendant will determine the "balance of power."

When Sun, Moon, and Ascendant are all in the same sign, the ruler of the ascendant or the strongest planet will determine the polarity.

See PRELIMINARY NOTES, pp. 72, 73.

---

* See p. 7, also Chap. xix.

THE SOLI-LUNAR COMBINATIONS EXTENDED.

To the student of Astrology these polarities are especially interesting, for they may be extended very considerably by an understanding of the law upon which they are based, which I will now endeavour to explain.

There are three FUNDAMENTAL QUALITIES in Nature, known as *Inertia*, *Activity*, and *Harmony*.* These qualities are latent in all things, as well as in every human being ; but, in any given individual, one (or perhaps two) of these qualities will be the most prominent while the others are comparatively inactive, or even in some cases entirely latent, according to the growth, desire and environment of the Ego. They give respectively 'stability,' 'movement,' and 'perfection,' according to the development of the Individual.

In the foregoing combinations of the ☉ and ☽ only *two* of these qualities are treated of, want of space and the complicated nature of the triple expressions preventing† their delineation in this work.

It has been before pointed out (pp. 7, 72) that there are *three* points of chief significance in any horoscope, *viz.*, the *Sun*, *Moon*, and *Ascendant*, their relative importance being indicated by comparing them to pounds, shillings and pence respectively. For the reasons just stated, only the soli-lunar combinations (corresponding to the 'pounds' and 'shillings' in the above simile) have been given in the body of this work, but students who are sufficiently interested may elaborate the idea according to their

* Known in Eastern philosophy as *Tamas*, *Rajas*, and *Sattva*. See p. 52, also, where these qualities are alluded to under the terms Power, Activity, Wisdom.

† Of which there would of course be 12 × 12 × 12=1728.

ability by adding as the third factor ('pence') the Ascendant or Rising Sign, when that has been determined.* This may then be interpreted as follows:—

Fixed Signs denote *inertia*,—bulk, weight, mass and stability; they give reserve, resistance, power and rigidity. The fixed quality corresponds to mind-force, moral stamina, or what may be termed *Spirit* or Will, the self-generated, self-sustained Alpha and Omega of Manifestation.

Cardinal Signs denote *activity*,—motion, expression, changeableness; they give alertness, restlessness, flexibility and suppleness. The cardinal quality corresponds to *Soul* in its various conditions, animal, human or spiritual; *i.e.*, the modifying influence operating in the world of form.

Mutable Signs denote *harmony*,—vibration, rhythm and symmetry; they give plasticity and adaptability, and usually more or less instability. The mutable quality corresponds to *Body*, *i.e.*, the vehicle of the Spirit and Soul, or the plastic medium upon which Spirit exerts its power of transmutation through the interplay of Soul, but not necessarily the physical body alone.

It must be clearly understood that this allocation of the signs to the three fundamental modes of manifestation termed *Inertia*, *Activity*, and *Harmony* (spirit, soul, body), has reference to the greater *prominence* of one of these attributes, as manifested in each group of signs, 'fixed, 'cardinal' and 'mutable respectively. But each group of necessity possesses all three of these attributes, though one of the three is "on top" as it were,—that is, most in evidence.

The idea it is intended to convey may perhaps be made clearer by an illustration. Every solid body must possess the "three dimensions" of length, breadth and thickness; for although any one or two of these may be of such slight magnitude in comparison with the rest as to be almost unnoticeable (as in a piece of gold leaf or a length of fine steel wire), yet all three dimensions *must* be represented or the object cannot exist. It is just the same with regard to the signs, and hence it would be absurd to suppose, for instance, that anyone born with no planets in fixed signs had therefore no spirituality or no will, though it would be a safe assumption in the majority of cases that neither of these attributes would be so prominent as to be remarkable.

Spirit, Soul and Body have before been said to bear relation to the Sun, Moon and Earth (Ascendant) respectively (*Everybody's Astrology*, p. 4, second edition). It will therefore be seen that the fixed, cardinal and mutable signs are themselves duly related to Sun, Moon and Ascendant. Hence the following characterisation may be taken as

* See chap. xix.

typical of the "normal" or most natural expression, while other arrangements with any or all of the factors changed will bring about modifications such as will naturally suggest themselves to the mind,—the Sun in a cardinal and Moon in a fixed sign, for instance, bestowing a personality too rigid and too little impressible by the solar force of the individuality behind; and so on.

The SUN in a Fixed Sign gives individual power, reserve force, restraint, stability and reliance to the character; if abused this will show as pride, arrogance, over-determination and dogmatism.

The MOON in a Cardinal Sign gives a changeable, flexible and ambitious personality, which if abused will lead to insincerity, love of fame or notoriety, exaggeration, untruthfulness, and recklessness of conduct.

The ASCENDANT in a Mutable Sign gives adaptability, graceful movements, and a delicate expression of the nature, free from either stolidity or over-assertiveness.

From this it will be seen that a careful judgment of these factors in their various combinations will bring a flood of light to bear upon the three inherent expressions of humanity, Spirit, Soul and Body.

The 'triplicities' involved will, of course, modify to a great extent the above brief illustration; for if the Sun is in an *airy* sign the mental attitude will predominate, while if in a *fiery* sign the higher emotions will have the greatest influence, whereas when in a *watery* sign the feelings and sensations, and when in an *earthy* sign the physical and practical side of the nature, will be most in evidence.

The part of the nature most free is that represented by the ☉, which embraces the whole of the mind, *as* mind (contra-distinguished from 'intellect'), or "intelligence." The ☽ will represent the whole of the feelings, sensations and instincts, while the body is represented by the ascendant, the most limiting and restricting of the three, through which alone can the spirit and the soul find expression. The more ductile and expansive the sign upon the ascendant, the more expression will be obtained from the body.

As space is limited the following illustration must suffice :—

Suppose the RISING SIGN is Libra : the native is very expressive and inclined to make *comparisons* (♎, opposite to ♈, sign of 'balance') ; sees clearly from the *mental* standpoint (cardinal sign), and loves refinement and all that pertains to beauty (♀ ruler).

The feelings as expressed by Libra will, however, be modified by the MOON, her mundane position and aspects, as well as by the sign she occupies (more especially the latter). If in Capricorn, say, the feelings will be definite, practical and *material* (earthy sign), yet refined and steadied by the nature of Capricorn (house of ♄) ; nevertheless, they will be both flexible and changeable, while much *activity* will be expressed (cardinal sign).

The SUN will then modify or accentuate this physical and psychical expression of the Ascendant and Moon. Suppose the Sun to be in Aries; this will *increase* the flexibility and changeableness conferred by the Ascendant and Lunar position, and will add to the expressiveness and *activity* (cardinal sign), the only restraint coming from the Moon (in the house of ♄). The general tendency will therefore be in the direction of external activities of a more or less public character, tinctured with the mental element and strongly flavoured with emotionalism ; the whole being marked by intense enthusiasm and ideality.

The intuition of the student will perceive the great advantage this method of judgment gives over the mere knowledge of the "signs," considered apart from their inherent qualities of *inertia*, *activity*, or *harmony*.

Suffice it to add that each sign (and similarly also *each degree of a sign*) has a triple expression of 'inertia,' 'activity' and 'harmony' through its third part or "decanate" (space of 10°).* Further illustration of this idea will be found in a later part of this series, entitled *How to Judge a Nativity*.†

---

* *Everybody's Astrology*, p. 6 (second edition).

† Uniform with this volume : part i., dealing with the Horoscope, 16s. ; part ii., giving in great detail the characteristics of the Planets, 16s.

CHAPTER XIX.

To Find the Rising Sign.

When the *time* of birth is also known as well as the day and year, the Rising Sign may be readily found as follows :—

(1) To the Sidereal Time* *at noon* on day of birth add or subtract as the case may be the required number of hours according as the time of birth was a.m. or p.m. : this is *the sidereal time of birth.* (If more than 24, *subtract* 24 · if less than 0, *add* 24).

(2) Look in the Table of Houses, in the column at the left hand side marked " Sidereal Time," till you come to the given *sidereal time of birth.* The middle column, marked " Asc.," will then give the sign and the number of degrees thereof ascending at the time of birth—which is, of course, the Rising Sign.

[Important Note.—The table here given is for London. Nevertheless (since the time of birth is rarely known with great accuracy), it is practically serviceable in this respect for *the whole of the British Isles.* The birth time must however be given in *local time* and not in Greenwich mean time—unless the birth-place be London or near it.]

Example :— We take as an example the case of the Duke of York referred to later (the present Prince of Wales). This royal personage

* The *Sidereal Time at noon* on any day of any year is (approximately) as follows :—

Mar. 22— 0h. 0m.	Apr. 22— 2h. 0m.	May 22— 4h. 0m.	*For each succeeding day, add 4 minutes.*
June 22— 6h. 0m	July 22— 8h. 0m.	Aug. 22—10h. 0m.	
Sep. 21—12h. 0m.	Oct. 21—14h. 0m.	Nov. 21—16h. 0m.	
Dec. 22—18h. 0m.	Jan. 21—20h. 0m.	Feb. 20—22h. 0m.	

was born in London, June 3rd, 1865, at 1.18 a.m. (For the complete horoscope, with a discussion of the nativity, the reader is referred to *Modern Astrology*, Vol. VIII., p. 126.)

Sidereal time at noon, May 22nd	4h. 0m.
Add twelve days, at 4 minutes per day	0h. 48m.
Gives sidereal time at noon, June 3rd, day of birth	4h. 48m.
(Add 24 hours)	24h. 0m.
	28h. 48m.
Less the number of hours before noon	10h. 42m.
Gives sidereal time at moment of birth (1.18 a.m., 3/6/'65)	18h. 6m.

If we refer to the Table of Houses we shall see that this time gives ♈ on the ascendant, and this is therefore the Prince's "*Rising Sign.*"

If now the paragraphs relating to the sign Aries be again read, the reader will then have, in addition to the individual and personal characteristics already enumerated, a clue to the general outlook on life natural to those who are born under the ascendancy of the sign ARIES.

In a similar way anyone who knows his or her time of birth may find the Rising Sign.

It is perhaps well at this point, even at the risk of appearing tedious, once more to insist on the distinction to be observed between the Sun, Moon, and Ascendant, as representing the three centres of life, Individual, Personal, and Physical; since it is often found that in reference thereto considerable confusion exists among those who are just taking up this study for the first time.

(1) The SUN represents the Individuality, the prime cause of all manifestation as regards any particular human being:—the true *Will.*

(2) The MOON signifies the Personality (Lat. *persona*, a mask),—which is the vehicle of the individuality, the means whereby its purposes are carried out:—the *Desires.*

(3) The ASCENDANT indicates the physical body, which is the instrument or tool which is used by the personality to carry into effect the purposes of the individuality as interpreted by and through the personality:—the *Agent.*

It will then be readily understood that by 'a backward Ego' we mean one in whom the individuality is scarcely manifesting, the personality alone actuating the body merely for the gratification of its ephemeral desires : while by 'a progressive soul' we mean one in whose life the main controlling factor is the individuality, typified by the Sign in which the Sun was placed at birth.

The respective importance of these three centres of energy may be clearly rendered by our homely analogy of *£ s. d.*,—Pounds representing the Sun and individual characteristics, Silver the Moon and fluctuating personality, and Copper (bronze) the 'corruptible body.' For it will be perceived that silver and copper owe their value as currency entirely to the degree in which they represent the standard gold coinage of the country.

Following this chapter, there is given a complete series of delineations of the character and fortune, in a general sense, of all persons born under each one of the Twelve Signs, also an account of the general influence of each planet in each of the Twelve Signs; after which, tables of the signs occupied by the four superior planets during the last fifty-five years, and of the Moon's Place for every day from January 1st, 1850, to December 31st, 1905, inclusive, with a brief explanation of the method of casting a horoscope, bring this volume of the series to a close. Further on we give a Table of Houses for London, by the aid of which the British-born reader who knows the hour of his birth may find his Rising Sign.

In regard to the Delineations Based on the Rising Sign,—which are adapted from a series contributed to *The Astrologer's Magazine** (copies no longer obtainable), during the year 1893, by a well-known astrological writer, and of which a subsequent re-issue in pamphlet form is now also out of print—it must be borne in mind that the characteristics there given are *general* in their application ; and therefore there will necessarily be many statements which will hardly be literally true of *each* person born under the sign concerned. Nevertheless, the delineations as given will be found in the main surprisingly accurate as regards the general scope of the life and the broad outlines of the character.

See PRELIMINARY NOTES, pp. 72, 73.

---

* Subsequently re named *Modern Astrology*

CHAPTER XX.

Delineations Based on the Rising Sign.

ARIES.

The subjects of this sign are of a simple, frank and outspoken nature, well-disposed, and capable of holding command in executive positions, though they are not good in originating schemes. They are brave and venturesome, generous even to extravagance, and likely to be fooled into giving undeserved charities. Having strong inclinations they are sometimes quarrelsome and petulant, while if touched with the religious spirit they will prove fanatical or very zealous. They are well-informed, very busy, ingenious, rather deficient in knowledge of human character, eclectic and free in their opinions, much moved by politics, and apt to enforce their opinions. The natives of Aries are very destructive, and are apt to run a crusade against existing institutions and bodies. They see things only as they desire them to be, and have a tendency to self-imposition. They often change their views and opinions, but are very sure of their beliefs as long as they last. They are remarkable for sudden changes and quick action: often bigoted, but generally progressive in tendency, they are, though liable to change, at all times enthusiastic in the pursuit of a prevailing idea. The Aries man is ambitious of honours and position but will have difficulties to meet with which will employ all his courage and will. In religion and politics he is ardent, often having some peculiar crank, and he can go almost into *violence* in his expression of feeling, but it is only a fire of straw and is soon over, leaving no sense of resentment. The fortunes are variable and there is gain through property, and in rural industries, sometimes also by marriage. Strifes and legal processes are likely to occur in connection with money and property, and in this women are apt to be much involved: in industrial arts and in cultivation he will succeed. The native is frequently the only child, or may become such by the death of brothers or sisters; moreover, during childhood there are many obstacles arising through the affairs of the parents; frequently the father dies early and leaves him unprovided for. Travelling is likely to occur in connection with family affairs, on account of health, or to avoid troubles: there is a love of high positions and mountain climbing. Relatives are not favourable, and the family ties are sometimes strained.

There is frequent change of residence, the Aries people seldom remaining long in the same place; and they go long voyages and visit distant countries as agents or missionaries, or hold some command there. They are unfruitful, having few children, frequently none at all. In temperament they are hot and dry, and not fond of water or much bathing; they are liable to flatulence, colic, pains in the bowels, internal disorders of an inflammatory nature, also accidents to the eyes, hands and feet. It is not uncommon for them to be exiled to a foreign country, or to be restrained therein by some forced seclusion; sometimes this is necessary in order to escape from enemies. The position of the subject is usually honourable, and high positions are attained, often followed by reversal; any position is held only with much strife. They marry early, or in a hurry, and there is occasion for repentance in most cases; frequently there are legal processes leading to divorce or separation.

The Aries person is essentially a *pioneer*, whether in the intellectual, civic, or military world, and may gain some celebrity by deeds of daring or on account of long travels and voyages. The military and legal professions are favoured, though there is also an inclination to mining and exploration. Friends give him much support and frequently bring him into high positions; they are numerous and faithful, and much renowned for their humane character and kind spirit. Enemies are found in the religious, legal and publishing worlds and are very numerous though not formidable. The worst enemies are in foreign countries, and frequently molest the native. The Aries person may be the cause of his own death, for he aspires to martyrdom in some form or other.

TAURUS.

The subjects of this sign are self-possessed, dogmatic and obstinate, requiring no counsel and suffering no contradiction, difficult to know, and desiring strife for the sake of conquest. Slow to anger and equally hard to appease, they often harbour ill-feeling and resentment for a long time. These are the chief instincts of the Taurean, though they may be modified by prevailing planetary influences. He is full of diplomacy, and is apt to be selfish and self-centred. The temper is usually quiet, but is capable of strong passions, while the mind is apt to be bigoted and stubborn. He is fond of his own opinions, silent and inflexible, of firm will, much steady perseverance and quiet decision; hence he is good at governing, and may rise to a very high position. Fond of natural history, gardening or horticulture, he is a patient worker, very exact and precise in method, and tediously attentive to small details, yet nevertheless fond of comfort and repose.

Those born with this ascendant are very careful of their possessions and have much desire for honours of all kinds. In love they are usually jealous, but inconstant. There is often strife, of which the subject himself will be the cause, also illness due to excess of work or pleasure. A certain degree of wealth is shown, though losses either total or partial may happen through legal disputes, loss of employment, or attachments after marriage. Unforeseen windfalls come to them; and they also gain by some person's devoted affection, also from friends. The sign Taurus gives a good parentage, especially on the father's side; usually the father is a man of some consequence in his sphere of life. Sorrows arise through relatives, especially brothers or sisters. The native gains by speculation, also through children, but is likely to lose by strifes and in legal affairs. Death of the eldest child is likely, if it be a boy; otherwise danger of loss among the progeny during infancy. The children will be a source of gain and satisfaction to the native, and usually make good progress in scholastic and artistic studies. There are, however, some quarrels to be feared at one time or another.

On the whole the life is calm and peaceful, though hurts are likely to occur through the subject's misguided resistance to obstacles and through his stubborn opinions. The health is affected by maladies incident to the spleen, liver, and kidneys, and in the case of females the ovarian vesicles; gravel, stone, and diabetes also are complaints incident to this sign; sore throat, quinsy and tonsilitis being of frequent occurrence. Troubles in the marriage state are denoted, generally strife, or the death of the wife. The fortunes and position of the native are insecure during youth, but are advanced during adult age through fortunate associations, and through the sciences, arts, literature, or some scholastic vocation. He has many friends, some of whom are in high positions, and he may gain by legacy from a friend; but will be sure to experience loss and sorrow through some of his associations. Moreover, he will have open enemies who are capable of causing losses and troubles, and some of these may be violently slanderous. Enemies affect his married life also, and thus interfere with his happiness, while the wife (or husband) is sometimes forced into retirement or seclusion from one cause or another, seldom appearing in connection with her partner. The Taurus person usually lives long and passes through many perils. He has a full sense of the comforts of life and frequently studies diet and hygiene. Death often transpires at sea or in a foreign land.

GEMINI.

The native of this sign is endowed with a kind, willing, flexible and upright nature, humane in its tendencies, but easily worried and irritated though as quickly calmed; sometimes excessive in anger but readily repenting of it. He is capable of obtaining celebrity in literature, art or science, or even by travel. The Gemini person is inventive and original in ideas, fond of science, literature and the arts; he is clever in legal matters, in negotiations and in trade, well-informed, subtle, flexible and business-like; vigilant and communicative, especially when drawn out upon a favourite subject, but otherwise somewhat self-contained and frequently nervous if suddenly called upon to speak or act. Gemini gives a love of command, without pride or tyranny, and a firm and strong will, though this is often so nicely balanced, and the nature so adaptable, that it is considered weak and irresolute.

The fortunes are subject to many changes and are usually much affected for good or ill by the influence of women. The native generally experiences both privation and affluence during his life, and there are some family secrets or much strife, though the relatives are usually well connected and prosperous, while a brother of the native holds a government position or high office. There are many causes for family disputes, and the native does not agree altogether with the father; yet he himself is the cause of his own downfall, or ill-luck. The members of his family are well-favoured, of moderate number, and disposed to excellence in the fine arts. There are secrets connected with love affairs and attachments, and losses and troubles occur through the progeny, or in consequence of the native's love intrigues. The complaints incident to Gemini are: strangury, piles, fistula, affections of the bladder and excretory system; fevers, and poisoning of the system. Nervous affections and lung complaints are also to be feared in some cases, especially in the *dark* types of Gemini men and women. Servants give trouble and open enemies are found among foreigners or in foreign lands.

The native usually marries twice or has two simultaneous attachments—generally one in a foreign country or to a foreigner. Many troubles are caused by women, while there is a danger of accidents through horses. Death happens in a foreign country or through some person in power, and when natural is the result of cold taken while travelling or in the execution of professional duties. The subject usually holds a good position and follows two occupations at the same time. Friends are many and varied, and are frequently the cause of strife and loss, associations generally lead to hostilities. There are many obstacles to the attainment of position, these being largely caused by clergymen or lawyers; moreover, the native is sometimes apt to come to grief "between two stools," or from want of decision in professional or business matters, while secret enemies injure the position, though the marriage partner benefits it. Treachery occurs and losses take place through women and secret love affairs, and the subject is in general often liable to many accidents, from which, however, he is providentially protected. This sign favours the legal and clerical professions and promises eventual success, which may, however, be wholly ruined by the native himself. Inheritance of land or houses is usually given by this sign. It is productive of a high order of intellect, giving much power in professional circles.

CANCER.

The subjects of this sign are remarkable for a changeful life, with many ups and downs in fortune and position, while in most cases, moreover, a certain degree of notoriety and power is attained. They have a quiet reserved nature, quick and short temper, and impatient disposition, being sometimes very autocratic and severe. They are gifted with a fertile imagination, delighting in strange scenes and adventures, while the power of adaptation to the nature of others and the faculty of absorbing other people's ideas is very great. This often leads to a species of morbid vanity or to the assumption of the *rôle* of hero or martyr, a condition inspired into them by reading or by example. They are remarkably gifted with the dramatic faculty, and though sometimes original, they are frequently copyists or even plagiarists, being clever at compiling and otherwise 'dishing up' old material. The temper is changeful and capricious, and although disillusion follows each new association, the imperative need of friendship and attachment impels towards new and other scenes and relationships continually.

The natives of this sign are discreet and independent in many things, and very capable in a variety of ways, the faculty of adaptation being enormous, though there is a high degree of nervous irritability, the result of extreme sensitiveness, this being a concomitant of the lunar and fluidic nature. In negotiations and public movements they are very capable, and there is a love of position and wealth and honours. This sign makes women born under it to be very laborious though somewhat exacting; but to all it gives great versatility coupled with a spirit of eclecticism. According to circumstances the subject is either courageous or timid, generally timid as to physical dangers but brave in his mental and moral attitude. At times distrustful, cautious and prudent, there is a sudden reversion to gaiety, inconstancy and fanciful romance, while anger comes and goes in quick alternation, the temper being as changeful as the ocean. Difficulty in acquiring wealth is shown and frequently the inheritance is lost through relatives or by speculation and affairs connected with children, or by love attachments. But although there are dangers of losses in this way, the latter part of life is on the whole more successful and prosperous. The subjects of Cancer frequently inherit money and property, but it comes to them only with great tardiness or in spite of many obstacles. Premature death of a brother or sister is shown and troubles through relatives, with whom the native disagrees. He has usually a second family, or may become adopted. Children give trouble and cause many discords in the life, but the eldest succeeds in the medical, chemical or military profession, and achieves honours: in advanced years the children are oftentimes a source of protection.

This sign exposes to many dangers, both mysterious and public, but a providence seems to protect and deliver the native. It is opposed to marriage or gives little happiness therein, while inheritance comes through marriage only after legal difficulties. Voyages are certain to be frequent and long and generally successful; while some may bring honours. There are many dangers, especially of captivity and secret enemies, ambushes and so forth, to be feared in foreign lands, but nothing serious comes of them. The position is acquired by strife or is much debated, and slander may be experienced. The sign gives success through one's own enterprise and daring. Before thirty-five the position is uncertain, but after that age it becomes more assured. Friends, women especially, will help and support the native of this sign, and financial help will proceed from them; one of them, however, will cause a reversal of position. There is much danger of secret and violent enemies, and of cabals formed against the native; these are often found among near relatives or neighbours, and even among servants: frequently some publications or slanderous letters are put forth against the native by secret enemies.

The maladies incident to this sign are affections of the chest and stomach, also rheumatism and sciatica. There are signs of danger by falls, or hurts from horses during residence in foreign countries or while travelling. Wounds by human hands are also to be feared.

LEO.

Persons born under this sign rise to position and honour through their own merits. They are frequently associated with individuals in high life, titled ladies especially. Leo gives an elevated nature, a strong will, an open, frank and noble spirit, and an ambitious, persevering will: the mind is just, firm, confident, generous, and often highly gifted. At times presumptuous and proud, but always self-possessed and masterful, the Leo man scorns small and puny actions: he loves the things of the daylight and all that is big and noble in life. He has a quick temper when provoked, but his anger does not last long, and though seldom foregoing his revenge, he takes it in a generous and open way. He is constant in his affections and loves truly. He is patient in his work and achieves his ends by solid endurance.

The capabilities are diverse, but frequently favour the fine arts and public offices, and there is some love of display at times: the poetical instinct is strong, and also love of the drama. Whatever the Leo man does he tries to do well, and is very thorough in his intentions, so that honours come to the native without his seeking them. The passions are strong, but under control: the opinions are fixed and often dogmatic;

and undertakings are carried to their end even at great personal risk. Wealth comes by personal merit and by work, and also by relations in good position, or by favour of rich patrons, while losses are likely to occur through servants and by bad health or family troubles. The native gains by friends and by trading in the commodities of life, such as food and clothing. The father is inimical to the position, and frequently dies while the native is young, producing a reversal of fortune; otherwise he is a source of strife at times. There are often legal disputes in regard to inheritance or in regard to long voyages and life in a foreign country. Accidents while travelling are encountered, but no serious hurt is done Children are usually numerous, but the death of the eldest is very likely to happen in its childhood: there may be twins, especially if the native is a female or if the husband is born under the sign Aquarius, and differences arise between the children when they grow up. Frequently there are two marriages and children by both wives (or husbands, as the case may be).

The chief ailments of this sign are heart affections, spinal complaints, rheumatism, and chronic ailments of the bones and blood: in many cases the wife or husband suffers from long-standing complaints. Not infrequently, during some period of their life, Leo men have to go through a good deal of hardship and want of food and comfort, and marital life is crossed with discord, caused frequently by servants or by friends or associates. Legacies are likely to come to the native or to his children. There are few or no voyages, and such as take place are not advantageous and seriously affect the position and interest: there are many journeys on land, however, and prosperity is brought about thereby. The occupation is honourable and profitable and generally necessitates much travelling by rail or coach. Persons in high positions prosper the business or profession of the native, especially women of rank and wealth, and the native does well to rely on their patronage. Friends among literary and artistic people are numerous. There may arise quarrels through friends which yet lead to gain in the end. Secret enemies are chiefly found among women whose power to hurt is really slight.

VIRGO.

The subjects of this sign acquire honours and position by their own personal merits, and by the use of their inherent faculties. They are endowed with a cool, clear intellect, and have a great sense of justice, but are often impassively cold and harsh in their treatment of others: they make good faithful friends, but very hard masters. There is a want of proportion in the mind, which tends to give undue importance to small things. The nature is pious and honest, and very careful of ways and means in the affairs of life. Kind, modest, retiring and yet agreeable in company, the subjects of Virgo are often difficult to know, though very confiding where affection or trust is given. Generally good-tempered, slow to anger, but also very slow to forgive, they hold those long in displeasure who have hurt them; but under adequate inducement they will repent their anger. The will is firm and strong, though capable of sudden changes under persuasion. The mind is highly endowed, intelligent and ingenious, holding its opinions with great tenacity.

This sign conduces to a love of the liberal arts, literature, history, the drama, and divinity; it renders the native eloquent, persuasive, sometimes a great talker, but generally of quiet tone and demeanour. There is frequently a love of horticulture, gardening, farming, etc., but the mind is equally capable of mastering the theoretical and practical sciences, and frequently inclines to more recondite and abstruse studies. The young life is fraught with dangers of sickness or accident while in the cradle. The degree of wealth shown is not very considerable, and is frequently acquired only by dint of hard labour; even then there remains a menace of loss, especially during the earlier part of life, the close being more fortunate. There is generally some inheritance, and the native gains property through the wife or partner; also by science or teaching: yet although there is success in connection with some art or science by the work and intelligence of the native, there is still a menace of reversal, but wealth will be acquired in foreign lands. Virgo people make successful bankers and business men generally, though there is danger for them in speculation. Relatives and neighbours do not favour the fortunes of the subject, and the death of an elder brother or sister is likely: but there is generally little or no sympathy between the members of the family There is some danger of accidental death, especially by animals. There are usually some family secrets; the father marries twice, or some illegal attachment lies behind the native's life. The first child of the native seldom lives to maturity, and his family is small and difficult to manage, while the children do not marry early or readily.

Disappointment and tardiness in love affairs is shown, and the native usually marries twice or has a second attachment during the life of his legal wife. Strifes will occur in the marital state, while there is some secret touching the wife (or husband) which renders seclusion necessary. After many difficulties the native is usually successful in achieving a position in life, but there are generally many changes of occupation, while much travelling and many short journeys are shown in connection with business affairs.

The occupation will generally be of a clerical, literary, or artistic nature; frequently the native has many things in hand at the same time. "Between two stools" he often comes to the ground, but in the end success is attained. Long voyages in search of wealth, or in connection with property in foreign countries, are indicated by this sign, and frequently the native has a commission to fulfil in foreign lands: there are frequent changes of residence, and often at the end of life the native has two homes or property in two places. Friends will be changeable, or many changes in life will cause frequent breaks in the circle of friends, new associations being frequently formed. Women of position favour the native. Friends in the native town or country, and friendships formed while upon the high seas, are likely to influence the life very much; but frequent changes are certain to effect a degree of instability in these relations. The native has powerful enemies among men of position belonging to the world of art, or engaged in speculation, and frequently some permanent hatred is directed against the native on account of some love affair, while the death or sequestration of a child is likely to happen.

The complaints incident to Virgo are, colic and flatulent pains in the bowels, dysentery, diarrhœa, and uterine affections; dyspeptic action arising from debility, want of tone or blood impurity. Eczema also is a common complaint with subjects of this sign.

LIBRA.

Libra confers upon its subject a sweet and gentle nature, very flexible and sensitive, and easily influenced by prevailing conditions. It gives courtesy, honesty, and a sense of justice which controls all the actions of life, with kindness, compassion and deep affection. The nature is upright and frank, at times very hopeful and anon very me ancholy; liable to extremes of temper and mood, and easily angered but as readily pacified. In the affairs of life there is a certain lack of decision observed in this subject, who generally waits "to see what will be done" by others before moving himself. The mind is inventive and shows ability in constructive and decorative work, and may show inclination for maritime arts and navigation. The will is strong, but does not always endure.

The native of this sign is quick in learning, has a taste for the arts, and also for business affairs generally: yet the appetites are keen and the love of pleasure great, while the passions are fervent and sincere. The subject is apt to ride a hobby and to pursue a "fad" to extreme length, and while engaged on anything is very intense; but he is liable to change his views at any moment and to take up some new pursuit. Generally speaking, success is the result of some occupation connected with navigation, or fluids: many of those born under this sign become wine or spirit merchants, chemists, doctors and surgeons, or even sailors in the marines; wherever water is the motive power there is a prospect of success. But there are signs of disputes and losses in connection therewith, caused by death or by disagreement with the business partner; while in contracts there is much danger of loss. Brothers and sisters are generally numerous, or become so after marriage by the wife (or husband) being member of a large family: but there are strifes and disputes among the relatives, and some legal processes may follow. The father is a source of trouble or loss to the native and frequently has fallen from a high position: in some cases the father dies when the native is quite young; in all other cases there are disputes, hindrances and restraints brought about by the father. Few children are born to the native, but they are fortunate and give satisfaction. Among the relatives there is likely to be a double tie through adopted parents or by a second marriage of the father or mother (usually the father).

The maladies to which Libra people are subject are, affections of the liver, kidneys and veins, humid affections of the feet, and danger of intestinal complaints. The marriage is apt to be sterile, and trouble is threatened in married life, with separation or death of the partner. The wife (or husband) is usually well off and even wealthy; and the native is likely to gain by unexpected legacies from females. There are many voyages to and journeys in distant countries, and some dangers therein. In the middle of life a reversal is to be feared, the mother of the native being frequently the direct or indirect cause of it: there are, however, signs of popularity and of securing a good position at the close of life. The native will have much to do with the public, and in connection with the occupation he will make many changes of residence and some long voyages. Instability marks the position, and honours are likely to be impermanent, though the family sometimes assist the native in this particular; while dealing in land and houses will lead to honour as well as profit. Success is shown in the native land and even in the native town. The friends and supporters of the native are frequently persons of high birth or lineage, and among artists and professional people he will find many an unexpected friend: there is, however, some danger of his harming one or more of them involuntarily. There are secret enemies among servants and members of the family on the father's side; moreover, family affairs will cause enmity. The children of the native are frequently his best supporters in old age.

SCORPIO.

The native of this sign is bold and warlike, inclined to rush into quarrels and to be involved in disputes which are likely to be harmful to him. The nature is excessive, and goes to extremes both in work and pleasures, thus bringing both sickness and trouble; for there is a strong tendency to play the critic, so that the native is apt to be sarcastic and severe to his opponents. The will is very strong and fights to the end. The executive and destructive faculties are large, the Scorpio man representing the function of dissolution in Nature: he pulls down and destroys existing theories, institutions and beliefs, and this is frequently effected by the acute penetration of the Scorpio mind, which is endowed with the "eagle eye" and which has moreover an insatiable thirst for finding out the secret nature of things. The occult researcher, the chemist, the inductive philosopher and even the detective, owe their faculty to this sign.

The imagination is fertile and the nature very resourceful: the temper is uncertain and petulant, very fiery, but not necessarily of long malice, though the loves and hates are keen and absorbing. The manners are frequently brusque and rude, but direct spoken and fearless; the native keeps his own counsel and is wary and watchful of his interests: there is much pride in the mental disposition. In anger the native is oftimes irresistible; and a naturally quarrelsome disposition may, under the influence of education and training, express itself in fiery debates and wordy warfare. The native is ambitious of honour and frequently attains high positions. There is a taste for arms and for maritime pursuits; and also for government and leadership. The monetary affairs of the native are fraught with uncertainty: the early part of life is not fortunate, but the second half is frequently very prosperous, and the native gains by exploits in foreign lands, by marriage relatives, legal affairs, and also directly by marriage. Generally there are two distinct sources of income to the native and often two occupations quite dissimilar; but Scorpio is a sign which produces eventual wealth. There are few brothers and sisters and frequently the native is the only son or daughter; while if others are born there is danger of death to them by falls from high places or from natural causes induced by maternal evils and cold. The father is friendly to the native, but is in danger of reversals. This sign gives many children, and sometimes twins are born: the children marry early: there is some secret trouble, however, in connection with them. Many secret love affairs are likely to enter into the native's life.

The ailments incident to Scorpio are affections of the excretory system, piles, fistula, diseases of the bladder and anus; inflammatory and poisonous complaints of the generative system; affections of the head and brain, fevers, etc.: and some violent accidents by fire or steel are shown. The right arm is in danger of being hurt or even lost, and the head is in danger of cuts and wounds: the eyes are sometimes affected by disease or accident. The native himself is frequently the cause of his own illnesses, due to excess in several directions.

The native is likely to marry more than once, and the premature loss of the first partner is to be feared, for the partner is in danger of long illness, or accident or hurts by animals or secret enemies, especially rivals in love: the premature death of a dear friend moreover will cause trouble to the native. Fortunate and long voyages are shown which lead to honours, and many exploits on the high seas in foreign lands may be expected. A series of difficulties in the early part of life will eventually lead on to good position and even honours, and success will at last crown the efforts of the native. There will be a serious heart trouble, disappointment or loss of one beloved before the age of thirty-five years. The native has many friends and supporters among persons in high life or in the artistic or dramatic world; and some love affair of the native will injure or advance the position, affecting the honour one way or another very much. The family and relations of the native are friendly to his interests and welfare, but there is frequently a loss of friends about the thirtieth year. Enemies will be found chiefly among his own associates, while the love affairs and marriage of the native are likely to lead to some serious contests: in foreign countries the native will be in danger of secret violence, from which he will be providentially protected.

SAGITTARIUS.

The native of this sign is frank, open, honest and generous, and has more regard to actions than to their results, being ever ambitious of doing and achieving, though not so much in respect to the fruits of such action as in obedience to the imperative demands of a sympathetic nature. It is possible for the native to show two very different characters, one external and another internal, being both bold, reckless and daring yet at the same time very sensitive, impressionable and reticent. Hence the subjects of this sign are difficult to know. They are usually ingenious and versatile and master many branches of learning. They are ardent and rather petulant but seldom bear malice. The sense of justice is very keen, and harshness to others amounts almost to a personal injury.

The mind is clear and quick at apprehending things, very readily assimilating new ideas and new modes of life. There is a certain irritability often shown, which results from no apparent cause; but which in reality is the result of restraint, and is caused by the double nature of the sign coming into play at one and the same time. The manners are naturally gentle, only becoming brusque or defiant in the presence of enemies or when stirred to self-defence, while the nature is hopeful, joyous and youthful even in advanced years, and the disposition although sometimes disturbed is generally calm. The native is simple in his mode of living and above all things delights in his independence, sacrificing everything rather than bear restraint, and fretting exceedingly in unsympathetic surroundings. There is also a certain watchfulness and distrust of others (and also of himself), which leads to deception while trying to avoid it. He is a friend of peace, truth and justice, and is seldom engaged in strife without good cause, and though at times timid he will on occasion show extreme courage and daring. The Sagittarius man is complex and difficult to gauge, usually very apt, clever in conversation, eloquent and sometimes visionary, fond of theology and spiritual subjects, and frequently reclusive and devoted to study and research. The passions are numerous and ardent, but controlled by the reason; the opinions changeful, ponderable and often heterodox.

The early part of life is not very fortunate owing to the premature death of the father or to some reversal of the fortunes of the parents. The native succeeds at length in the acquirement of good fortune by personal application to his calling or profession, sometimes moreover coming into an inheritance. This sign gives few brothers, and some troubles through those that the native has; nevertheless, the relations generally are friendly. There is usually some secret trouble with the parent, the father or father-in-law; and this may lead to the native's downfall or to a restraint which is almost worse than imprisonment. He has few children and there is not much sympathy between him and them; it is often the case that the native is separated from his children, or from one of them. There are usually two or more marriages or long associations, of which one will be inimical to the welfare and position of the native. There are many obstacles in the first part of life, but fortune comes in the end; and the occupation is likely to be of a double nature. At about thirty years of age the native is liable to reversals, falls from high places, nervous affections, or some serious calamity. There are few or no voyages, but many journeys; there being danger in the case of sea-voyages, while death usually takes place in a foreign country.

The chief ailments are affections of the throat, ears and bronchial tubes; sciatica and rheumatism; varicose veins and swellings in the legs; but generally the health is very good. A parent dies while the native is in a foreign country or away from home; sometimes a parent is lost while travelling. Friends are illustrious and useful, and the support of friends is very useful and effective in the native's life; the services of a lady of rank will prove timely and fortunate, but a false friend seeks to injure the honour, though without success. Enemies are numerous and violent and sometimes are led to acts of violence; the family affairs and home life of the native, as well as his married life, may be at the mercy of these snake-like enemies. Usually the career is long and useful.

CAPRICORNUS.

The native of this sign is endowed with a quiet yet ambitious, persevering and persistent spirit, capable of enormous efforts towards the attainment of a desired object : at times melancholic, and frequently malicious and revengeful, he is in some respects martial and warlike, yet always self-possessed, and of firm will. The native frequently has some marked peculiarity in his step or in manner of action, while the body is oftentimes angular and awkward in carriage; he may be deformed from the cradle or meet with bodily hurts through accidents. The speech is brusque and direct and the native though often eloquent has generally an impediment or peculiarity in the speech. The temper is strong, forceful, and enduring, the mind suspicious and melancholic; and in spite of inordinate ambition and much courage, frequently resulting in great achievements, the life is often unhappy. The desire for power is strong, and the native is, though quiet and reticent in the presence of strangers, yet forcible and eloquent among friends: there is more force than persuasion in the disposition. The will is liable to change but generally effects its object at all hazards. The native may forgive but never forgets an injury; he makes a good friend and an unrelenting enemy.

Caution and prudence mark the actions and policy of the man of Capricorn, but when a course is decided upon he is very persistent: he has a good sense of ways and means, and is apt in the use of them. The affections are sincere but frequently subject to change, due more to destiny than inclination. The wealth is due to personal merit, to the assistance of friends, and to the support of the family, but speculations may enrich the native : most frequently, however, the native gains by his own enterprise and work. The brothers and sisters are usually numerous and frequently cause great enmities and sorrows in the native's life, while rivalries and secret troubles arise among the relations. Journeys are both numerous and dangerous, and frequently for some secret purpose. In land journeys the native may fall into the ambush of his enemies. The father and the family generally are hostile and may cause strifes and obstacles, especially in regard to marriage. During infancy, the native is liable to danger by fire, or wounds by steel, etc., and the father is in danger of early death. The children are few and the ambitions of the native are likely to be closely connected with the first-born or heir: sometimes moreover they are harmful to the position and sometimes the position is dangerous to them. There are many strifes and contests, and some serious trouble among relatives, while there is a liability to strife and illness during travels.

Capricorn tends to produce affections due to cold and obstructions, rheumatism (especially in the knees, arms, and hands), nervous affections of the stomach, colic pains due to flatulence, and sometimes paralysis or epilepsy; falls and hurts by human hands are also to be feared, especially during travels: often the native is afflicted with melancholic fancies and hypochondriac affections. The marital relationship is very uncertain and much affects the life. Some Capricorn men are much opposed to marriage, while others marry early and more than once: in all cases the affairs of the heart are liable to great and fateful changes, while the wife will be the obstacle to some main ambition. In the case of a plural marriage one wife will die, and another is likely to confer wealth. The ambitions and position are subject very largely to the wife or wives, who will influence the career to a wonderful extent. In all cases the position gives rise to grave contests and creates many enemies. The voyages of the native are dangerous and will cause losses, privations and sickness, if they are not indeed the effect of these evils. Friends will be of the martial type, soldiers, marines, doctors, surgeons, chemists, etc., and there will be many surprises and sudden losses among them: death will count them out one by one. Among them will be found one traitor who will influence the last days of the native's career and will overthrow his greatest ambitions, bringing his name into obloquy. Enemies will be found in foreign lands and among foreigners, and generally speaking the relatives of the native will be inimical to his success and safety, or relatives by marriage will injure his position. Oftentimes it is found that there is a combination of enemies, some of whom are in high position and some in common service. The native of Capricorn is subject to a great reversal of fortune in mature life.

AQUARIUS.

Those born under Aquarius have some degree of literary and artistic faculty, and are usually advocates of the liberal arts and of scientific research. Not infrequently they are given to occult research and secret methods of experimental science. They are good orators and writers and have a taste for eclectic philosophy, music and the drama. They have strong affections and can love with exceeding constancy: they generally remain the ardent lover of their wives till old age, and always play "Darby" to the wife's "Joan." Sometimes they live in seclusion or are of very retiring habits. Their nature is frank, open, perfectly ingenuous, and very humane.

The natives of Aquarius make good enduring friends: they have strong forceful tempers, but do not bear malice, and the disposition generally is kind and sweet. The will is firm and inflexible, and continues to the end of any proposed achievement in spite of obstacles. The native although inclined to solitude is not misanthropic, and the spirits are usually buoyant, cheerful, and full of geniality. The native is not averse to honours and to wealth, though he is frequently unsuccessful in reaching either, though patient in labour and enduring. What he achieves is due to devotion and personal merit, but the monetary success is likely to be of an uncertain nature, subject to great mutations and to serious obstacles, due chiefly to hidden enemies, secret conspiracies, and deaths among the business circle. He may and probably will receive valuable assistance from friends, especially men of letters, the clergy, lawyers, etc. He may gain an inheritance or receive assistance from the family, but it is more than likely that this will be a source of trouble to him. Long voyages are taken in respect to the getting of money, and in connection with the occupation, there are many journeys by land. Sometimes a relation, especially a brother, is the cause of trouble in business, and the relatives generally are inimical to the honour and position of the subject.

The sign Aquarius produces two or more sources of income, and usually the occupation has something of a secret nature about it: it may be chemical research; a secret commission from military or governmental heads; or even detective work or something of like nature, in which secrecy is required. Aquarius gives few brothers and sisters and not much agreement among them; frequently the native is involved in quarrels thereby. Dangers in travelling by land or rail are indicated, especially in connection with business or the affairs of the relatives; but the native of Aquarius is fond of travelling backwards and forwards, and often journeys for small causes. The father is engaged in farming, speculative buying and selling, or stock-rearing: he is in danger of dying early. The native has few children (sometimes twins), and incurs dangers through them: they are subject to violence, especially the first-born, while the native has to travel much on their account.

This sign gives certain ailments such as, blood affections, eczema, spasmodic action, indigestion, stomach complaints, neuralgic affections of the head, and sometimes gout. Marriage is pretty certain, and usually takes place at an early age. The wife is likely to be of high birth or following some artistic occupation, such as artist, actress, or musician: the same applies to the husband, *mutatis mutandis*. The marital life is generally enduring and very happy so far as regards the continued affection of the partners. The native may gain by legacy from relatives, and the wife (or husband) has money in chancery, or so tied up in some way or other that it scarcely benefits him in any way, while the children are likely to receive inheritance or legacy from relatives of the native. Voyages cause strife, and open enemies are found in foreign lands or are made during a voyage, and sometimes in regard to religious or legal affairs. The native takes long voyages in connection with property, or in regard to the family or the father (who may live in a foreign country), and the native is likely to end his days abroad. The native's position is fraught with dangers, martial people being able to influence it to a large extent. Relatives, and especially a brother, have much influence on the credit and position, and a death will seriously affect his business fortunes.

The subject of this sign not infrequently meets his death in the commission of his business, or in a public place: he may be exiled, or imprisoned, being liable to some forced seclusion, and having enemies among men of power who can harm him, though he has friends who will help him financially among the clerical and legal professions. He frequently has access to the best society and the association of people in good position, but is yet capable of being his own enemy in many ways, especially by associations of a secret nature. Generally, however, the subject of Aquarius is a man of good counsel and capable of commanding public esteem and of securing very many friends.

NOTE.—The last two signs, Aquarius and Pisces, are so complex in their nature, and humanity at its present stage is so little capable of fully interpreting their true inner qualities, that but few of the foregoing characteristics will be found completely expressed in any ordinary person, while the lower types who are born under these two signs will chiefly display respectively erratic 'contrariness' and fatuous indecision.

PISCES.

The subject of this sign is capable of lifting himself by his own merits to a position of considerable celebrity and honour, and generally it happens that literature or the arts and sciences form the chief means of his support. Many popular authors and writers will be found to be natives of this sign, the mind being restless and creative, always on the search for new ideas. The native is impressionable, romantic, imaginative and flexible, and easily torments itself with curious fancies: for the nature is in itself difficult to know, being very imitative and readily moved by the proximity or association of others. The mind is upright, just, kind, benevolent and powerful, and the spirit contemplative, studious and poetical. The native likes to taste the good things of life and has a capital idea of enjoying himself; the disposition is, however, generous, and he does not willingly allow his pleasures to hurt others. The will, though changeful, is strong, can exercise authority without harshness, and be firm with a pleasantness of manner.

The nature is full, rich and prudent, and while inclining to agreement out of good-will, does not readily bind itself, so that the native can be very critical though without prejudice. Slow to anger, but hard to appease, the native is yet often content with a noble vengeance. He is much occupied and undertakes many pursuits, in which success may be achieved in two out of every three, the disposition being cordial and delighting in society and good company, and the native being moreover gifted with eloquence or literary ability. The mind is very broad on many subjects, the tendency being entirely eclectic and unorthodox, while the passions are strong but changeful. The wealth of the native will be largely due to his own efforts and works; frequently his writings are successful, or he gains by much travelling and has the goodwill and assistance of relatives; but losses will come through long voyages to foreign lands, and by the death of some near associate. The native follows a double occupation, and has a capacity for many things. The brothers and sisters are numerous, and the relatives are able to be of much help to him: in some cases there is the premature loss of a brother or sister. The parents are not conducive to the native's welfare, and it is often the case that the father dies prematurely, while the parents generally are subject to accidents and violence. The family estate becomes split up and does not enrich the native to any extent: frequently the mother marries twice. The children of the native are numerous and fortunate, will go long voyages, and will be subject to frequent changes.

The maladies to which the sign predisposes are, affections of the feet and ankles, colic pains in the bowels, affections of the heart and eyes, and dangers of wounds by fire or iron. There is frequently a renal affection and, in the case of females, danger of ovarian disease or irregularities of the system. This sign confers two marriages in many cases and generally a good deal of trouble in the marital state, for the wife is a great invalid or afflicted in some way, or the relatives of the native are able to affect the married life detrimentally. Servants also may cause confusion and trouble. The wife generally dies before the native, who then inclines to a second marriage: she sometimes has property by legacy or inheritance. Long sea voyages are attended with dangers in foreign countries or on the high seas. The native has friends in high circles, and his occupation is advanced by their means. Long journeys are taken in connection with the occupation, two distinct professions being often followed by the native at the same time. There will be a treacherous friend of a saturnine nature, who will become a secret enemy; and although friends are powerful, changes are shown—chiefly due to the varied occupation. An open enemy may be the cause of the native's death: he has some enemies who will become friends, and yet others who will do much to injure his friendships. This sign is capable of conferring well-merited honours and also considerable wealth.

(See note on p 182*).*

CHAPTER XXI.

WHAT IS A HOROSCOPE AND HOW IS IT CAST?

FULL details as to casting the horoscope will be found in the second volume of this series*, and therefore it is unnecessary here to do more than merely explain in general terms (1) what is meant by the word "horoscope" and (2) the method of calculation.

A "horoscope," then, is a diagram or map of the heavens for any given moment,—in the sense in which we are here using it, the moment of birth. This map of the heavens at birth, or 'nativity,' constitutes a *chart*, as it were, of the life-voyage of the person then born, and, if rightly interpreted, is as indispensable to the wayfarer on earth as are nautical charts to the seaman who desires to make the surest and the safest journey. *No one can make the fullest possible use of his opportunities, material or spiritual, in this world without a close and deep study of his nativity.* This is not the mere hyperbole of an enthusiast, but a cold fact. For Character is Destiny, and in no other way can a man gain that clear and *unbiased* insight into his own character that is required for the most effective development and improvement thereof, than by a study of those positions of the celestial bodies which have conferred upon him the qualities of disposition and temperament that he finds himself endowed with.

The horoscope or map of the heavens is erected in the following manner:—

Suppose that at the moment of birth an observer stands facing due south, quite upright, with arms extended: and let an imaginary line be extended in both directions, first through his body, and next through his arms, so that each line cuts the heavenly sphere in two points. These will then constitute the cardinal points or 'angles,' as they are called, of the horoscope; known respectively as the Zenith, Nadir, Ascendant and Descendant: if the Signs of the Zodiac were *visible*, the Rising Sign or Ascendant would be seen on the left just peeping above the horizon.* The sphere will then be divided into four quadrants, and the easiest way of representing this on paper is to draw a circle, with vertical and horizontal diameters in some such way as shown in the following illustration.

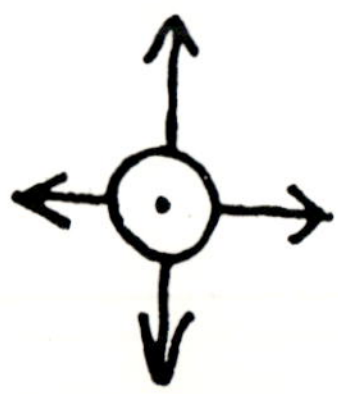

This is the framework or skeleton of the horoscope, the four arms or radii dividing the circle into four quadrants. Each quadrant is further divided into three "houses," each consisting of 30° of the circle (something like the sections of an orange), making twelve in all. These are numbered in rotation, beginning with the Ascendant (left hand, east point when looking south), and continuing under the earth (*i.e.*, in a contrary direction to the hands of a watch) till the Descendant is reached and then through the visible heavens till the Ascendant is arrived at once more.

(A useful way to remember the divisions of a horoscope is to think of a watch-face; begin at 9 o'clock and count backwards.)

* Suppose, for instance, a man to stand on the top of St. Paul's looking over the Thames in the direction of the Elephant and Castle. The "Ascendant" wlll lie on his left in the direction of the Bank, and the Descendant in the opposite direction, Feet Street way; while the Zenith or M.C. (*medium coeli*) will be immediatelv overhead and the Nadir (I.C., *imum coeli*) directly beneath his feet.

A HOROSCOPE.

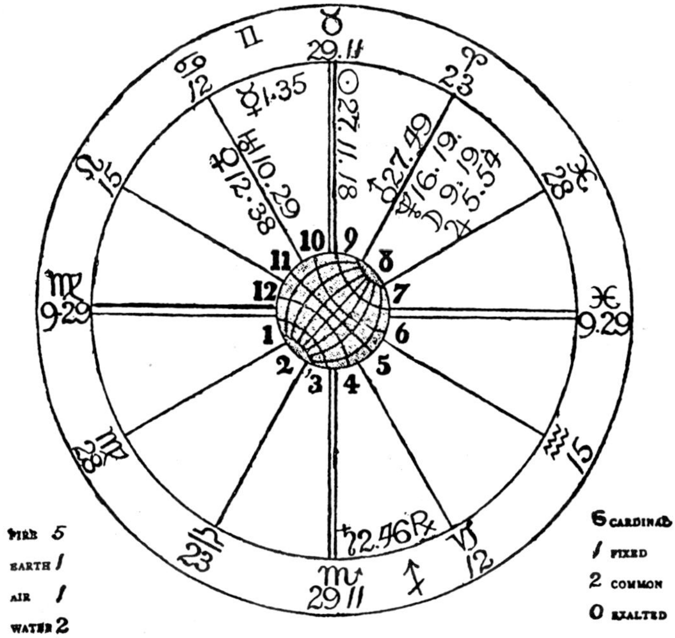

CZAR NICHOLAS II. OF RUSSIA.

Born May 15th, 1868, 0h. 2m. p.m. St. Petersburg.

These twelve "houses" as they are called, and which are very important, have affinity with the Twelve Signs of the Zodiac; thus the first house is in affinity with *Aries* and rules the head, the second with *Taurus* ruling the throat; and so on.

It is clear that in thus dividing the heavens into twelve equal sectors, since the belt of the Zodiac runs across the sky from East to West, we shall have some one particular degree on the edge or "cusp" of each house. When these have been inserted, the positions of the planets, according to the "houses" and also according to the "signs" that they occupy are then added, and the horoscope is complete.

Such, in brief, is the method of casting a horoscope. In ancient times the planets' places, cusps of the houses, etc., were no doubt determined by direct observation; but no such labour is now necessary, for the *Astronomical Ephemeris** supplies us with the zodiacal places of the planets for noon each day, so that it is merely a matter of simple proportion to find them for any given moment.

Similarly also there are "Tables of Houses" (*see* table for London, at end) published for nearly all places in the world, so that the actual calculations required in erecting the map are reduced to a minimum: on all points connected therewith the next treatise of this series gives full information, in addition to containing time and labour-saving tables, ready reckoner, proportional logarithms, etc.

There are few, we think, who having read thus far will rest content without working out their own nativities.

This is perhaps a fitting point at which to take leave of our readers, since with this chapter the expository portion of the present Volume comes to an end, the remaining two chapters and the tables which follow being intended chiefly for reference.

In concluding this book, then, the first of a series which is designed to cover the whole ground of Astrological Study, we would impress upon readers the necessity of giving patient and careful thought to the principles here enunciated, if they wish to achieve a thoroughly comprehensive grasp of the subject. And we would further urge them to remember that while the special aim of this book has been to present the fundamental principles of Astrology in such a simple and clear manner as to be readily comprehended by any intelligent person, yet we have been able to give only the broad outlines of the subject, as it were; and therefore exception should not be taken to general statements simply because they are not literally accurate in every detail.

CHAPTER XXII.

The Planets and their Positions.

It is not within the scope of the present treatise, which is primarily intended for the beginner who is entirely unacquainted with the subject of Astrology, to deal separately with the nature of the planets. This subject has been reserved for "How to Judge a Nativity" (Part ii.) in which book each planet is severally treated in great detail.*

However, it has been thought well to include a description of the general influence of each planet according to the sign it occupies at birth, and the following pages are accordingly devoted to these delineations. These will apply, in a general sense, to *all* people born under the respective influences, but will be applicable in a more particular sense (1) when the planet in question is *rising* (*i.e.*, in the "Ascendant"), or *culminating* (in the "tenth house"); (2) when the given planet is ruler of the sign on the Ascendant or Rising Sign: (to find the planetary ruler of each sign see table on p. 9.) In fact, the descriptions are most appropriate only in the latter case, for the reason that since *some* planet must be ruler of the ascending sign, while all cannot be, the influence of that 'ruling planet' will necessarily predominate over that of the others. The order in which they are given is that of relative motion, the slowest moving planets being given first, as follows—♆ ♅ ♄ ♃ ♂ ♀ ☿.

The planet Saturn having the greatest influence over the fate of man, the readings given of his influence when in each sign will be found to have the widest application.

Owing to the rapidity of motion of the inferior planets, Mercury and Venus, and their great (apparent) irregularity of movement, it is not feasible to include a table of their positions during the last fifty-five years; but those of the *superior* planets, *i.e.*, those whose orbits lie outside of that of our earth (♆, ♅, ♄, ♃, and ♂), are included with the solar and lunar positions at the end of the book. The Sun's zodiacal position is (approximately) the same each year on any given day, as has been before explained, and the Moon's position is separately given for (Greenwich) noon every day, from 1850 to 1905.

The student is therefore now in a position to ascertain with a quite sufficient degree of precision for his present state of knowledge the signs occupied by seven of the nine planets that rule the fate of man; and since Venus is never more than 45° and Mercury never more than 29° distant from the Sun, it will not be difficult to guess which of the two or three possible signs they may occupy. For exact particulars, however, an Ephemeris must be consulted.

* A short account of each planet's influence may be found in chap xiv. of *Everybody's Astrology* (Astrological Manuals, No. 1, price 1s., post free).

SPECIAL NOTE.

In regard to the ensuing delineations of the influences of each planet in the various signs, it must be pointed out (and this should constantly be kept in mind), that this influence will be prominent according to the prominence of the planet concerned in the scheme of the nativity; *i.e.*, whether rising, culminating, or setting, etc. This depends upon the *time of day* at which birth occurred. Hence the following readings must be taken in their most comprehensive and general sense only, or they may lead to erroneous conclusions.*

Saturn and Jupiter have most relation to the general fate, *i.e.*, environment and opportunity; while Mars and Venus chiefly apply to the disposition, energetic or pleasure-loving, etc.: Mercury represents the general capabilities.

* They will be susceptible of the most literal application when the planet is ruler" (*see* p. 9) of the sign rising at birth—*see* Rising Sign.

♆

NEPTUNE.

♆ *in* ♈. NEPTUNE IN ARIES. ♆ *in* ♈.

(*Positive House of Mars.*)

Is likely to intensify the senses, feelings, and emotions, which may show out either for good or evil, largely depending upon the rising sign. The native has mystical experiences or beliefs. A love of travelling for its own sake, sympathy, charity and benevolence of disposition, and also considerable intuition in regard to spiritual matters, are prominent characteristics.

♆ *in* ♉. NEPTUNE IN TAURUS. ♆ *in* ♉

(*Negative House of Venus.*)

This position, well aspected and supported by favourable planetary aspects, is very good for money and business; but the reverse if afflicted. It increases the æsthetic taste and also any tendencies to sensuousness, conferring, moreover, good-nature, companionability, patience and good humour. It is favourable for both friendship and marriage, unless seriously afflicted, in which case it threatens a tragedy.

♆ *in* ♊. NEPTUNE IN GEMINI. ♆ *in* ♊.

(*Positive House of Mercury.*)

This strengthens the intuition and imagination, and gives many often prophetic or symbolical dreams. It inclines towards travelling

It confers musical taste and great mental sensitiveness. Conduces to sympathy with brethren.

♆ *in* ♋. NEPTUNE IN CANCER. ♆ *in* ♋.

(*House of the Moon.*)

Bestows either mediumship or some psychical faculty. Conduces to close association with the mother, and promises some benefits through her. The native is fond of home and home comforts, is sympathetic and impressionable. There are many changes of residence, and if afflicted some psychic experiences in connection therewith; *e.g.*, haunted houses, etc.

♆ *in* ♌. NEPTUNE IN LEO. ♆ *in* ♌

(*House of the Sun.*)

Bestows warm affections; the senses and feelings are active and powerful; there is a love of company, society, sport and pleasure. The native possesses a good heart and benevolent disposition, and in general displays lavish generosity. Music, poetry, painting and the drama are keenly followed and intensely appreciated, if planetary positions permit.

♆ *in* ♍. NEPTUNE IN VIRGO. ♆ *in* ♍.

(*Negative House of Mercury.*)

The planet is not strong in this sign but, if well aspected, promises remarkable success through such employments as clerical work, nursing, medicine, etc. In a very favourable horoscope conduces to genius in art or poetry.

♆ *in* ♎. NEPTUNE IN LIBRA. ♆ *in* ♎.

(*Positive House oj Venus.*)

This position gives an intense and poetical love of beauty and artistic elegance, with a fervent imagination, coupled with a taste for music or painting; great attraction is felt for the opposite sex; love, friendship, and marriage, also general popularity, are favoured, and good fortune in general is indicated unless afflicted.

♆ *in* ♏. NEPTUNE IN SCORPIO. ♆ *in* ♏.

(*Negative House of Mars.*)

This intensifies the feelings and emotions, giving in a high degree the love of sensation and luxury. Unless afflicted is good for money by marriage, partnership, or legacy. In a favourable horoscope it may contribute to give practical occult experiences.

♆ *in* ♐. NEPTUNE IN SAGITTARIUS. ♆ *in* ♐.

(*Positive House of Jupiter.*)

The native is given to travelling, either for pleasure or of necessity. There is considerable religious, mystical, or poetical feeling. Dreams, visions, or other psychical experiences form a prominent feature of the life; and under favourable conditions there may be inspiration of a prophetic order, either in relation to religion, art or science.

♆ *in* ♑. NEPTUNE IN CAPRICORN. ♆ *in* ♑.

(*Negative House of Saturn.*)

Unless well aspected, trouble through the family in early life and sorrow through the father are indicated. If well aspected, this position is good for financial affairs and money making generally. Favourable for art, music, etc., and for occupations bordering upon the psychical, or for business of a distributive character on a large scale, *e.g.*, catering, etc.

♆ *in* ♒. NEPTUNE IN AQUARIUS. ♆ *in* ♒.

(*Positive House of Saturn.*)

Good for friendship, popularity, love and marriage. If afflicted, sorrow or scandal through these. Buoyancy and expansiveness of mind, sympathy, sociability, humanity, and frequently great intuition, are prominent characteristics.

♆ *in* ♓. NEPTUNE IN PISCES. ♆ *in* ♓.

(*Negative House of Jupiter.*)

This inclines the native to be broad-minded, charitable, homely, sympathetic. If well aspected, he may benefit through the help or charity of others, or on the other hand may endow charitable institutions, etc. If afflicted, it is bad for health and fortune; the native meets with bad luck, his schemes are thwarted, and serious losses are experienced.

In these, as in all other cases, much depends upon the position of the planet in the horoscope. For an unfavourable *position*, by 'house,' will negative much of the good promised by a favourable *sign*, and *vice versâ*.

See note on p. 190.

♅

URANUS.

(URANUS IN ARIES.) ♅ *in* ♈.

(*Positive House of Mars.*)

Gives positiveness, force and impulse to the mind, and is apt to make the manner or speech hasty and brusque at times; the native may give offence without intending it, being very outspoken and sometimes lacking in tact and restraint. This position increases mental vigour, and supplies energy, resource and inventiveness. It gives great independence and love of freedom, and hence sometimes causes disputes and estrangements.

♅ *in* ♉. URANUS IN TAURUS. ♅ *in* ♉.

(*Negative House of Venus.*)

Is not altogether good for money matters unless very well aspected. It is apt to cause ups and downs, sudden losses or an involved state of the affairs. But if well aspected, the native, although confronted by obstacles, will extricate himself by his own ingenuity and resource. This position sometimes indicates money through partnership, marriage or associations.

♅ *in* ♊. URANUS IN GEMINI. ♅ *in* ♊.

(*Positive House of Mercury.*)

Increases mental power and activity; gives originality and ingenuity, some eccentricity of mind or fondness for occult or out-of-the-way subjects. If other planetary positions permit its full expression, it gives depth of thought, scientific, literary or metaphysical ability, with considerable inventive faculty and some intuition; in any case great fondness for travelling, and many friends among literary people. The native may espouse unpopular causes; or, if afflicted, will have trouble through education, letters, examinations, etc., and may disagree with his brethren.

♅ *in* ♋. URANUS IN CANCER. ♅ *in* ♋.

(*House of the Moon.*)

Makes the emotions and feelings sensitive, easily touched and quickly moved. May cause trouble or estrangement in domestic affairs and the home life; if afflicted, loss through houses or land, trouble through the house or dwelling place, and obstacles connected with the occupation, especially when just entering upon it in early life. This position inclines slightly to mediumship, dreaming or occult experiences, also to travelling.

♅ *in* ♌. URANUS IN LEO. ♅ *in* ♌.

(*House of the Sun.*)

Trouble and obstacles in the family life, especially in youth; loss or difficulty through the father in some way. The native displays a disregard for conventionality, a great love of freedom and independence, with sometimes a rebellious disposition, thereby incurring the disfavour of superiors. He is fickle and changeable in love matters, or on the other hand suffers greatly from this in others. Well aspected, it is good for a public or professional career and may give much success through it, though there are likely to be hindrances or annoyances socially and also through children.

♅ *in* ♍. URANUS IN VIRGO. ♅ *in* ♍.

(*Negative House of Mercury.*)

There are apt to be hindrances or restrictions connected with the occupation; insurmountable difficulties, thwarted ambition, and much trouble through servants. If well supported by the general planetary indications, the intellectual ability is increased, and the native may succeed well in partnership or associated with others; or in the employment of others, especially in chemistry, science or art. He gains through public occupations or those connected with the state (or perhaps some local authority): but if badly aspected he will on the other hand incur the hostility of such, and must beware of public enmity and criticism. The mind is subtle and penetrating, independent and original.

♅ *in* ♎. URANUS IN LIBRA. ♅ *in* ♎.

(Positive House of Venus.)

Apt to cause enmity, rivalry, opposition, criticism, broken friendships; estrangement of sympathy in matters relating to marriage, partnership, or friendship. This may be due to impulsiveness, stubbornness, or some peculiarity of temperament or isolation of manner in the native. There is sometimes a hasty engagement and marriage, with danger of separation, divorce, or death of partner. It is good for artistic or literary occupations, and tends somewhat to bring these into the life; and in cases where the marriage or partnership is based upon such interests the risks involved are lessened. This position increases the imagination, taste, and æsthetic faculties, and if the planetary positions permit will give remarkable intuition.

♅ *in* ♏. URANUS IN SCORPIO. ♅ *in* ♏.

(Negative House of Mars.)

The native possesses great strength of will, determination, and power of concentration, and generally much self-will; may be broken but not bent. If other positions show intellect, this will co-operate in giving strength of mind, acuteness, incisiveness, wit, mental grasp, and comprehensiveness. In some cases it shows an aggressive rebellious nature, one who frequently finds himself at variance with other people, and rather delights in being at war with the world. If malefic influences are strong, there is some danger of sudden accidents, falls, gun-shots, explosions, etc. (especially the latter), and in extreme cases liability to a sudden end: this last only when afflicted. There is mesmeric power, strong will-power, and in general considerable ability for practical occult investigation.

♅ *in* ♐. URANUS IN SAGITTARIUS. ♅ *in* ♐.

(*Positive House of Jupiter.*)

This position increases the imagination and inventiveness; often also the religious sentiments and the higher emotions: there is some tendency to religious mysticism, ritualism, etc., or to very advanced religious views. It favours dreams or visions, and inclines strongly towards travelling, while it co-operates with other influences to develop the higher side of the mind in almost every direction in which wide cultivation and higher education afford scope. If much afflicted, on the other hand, troubles will come from any or all of these sources and also through the marriage partner.

♅ *in* ♑. URANUS IN CAPRICORN. ♅ *in* ♑.

(*Negative House of Saturn.*)

This helps to cause thoughtfulness, seriousness, and reserve, but it also assists in intensifying ambition, steadfastness, and perseverance. If well supported by the other planetary positions, it gives success in public occupations, those connected with municipalities, or governing bodies; it helps to lift the native up and put him in some position of authority or responsibility; but is better for the special occupations connected with this planet (such as electrical or manufacturing machinery, etc.), than for ordinary pursuits. There is some danger of family discord or trouble, especially in early life, loss of father or separation from him. If afflicted, the disfavour of superiors, opposition from those in authority and severe public criticism will be met with, while there is a danger of sudden reversals and difficulties in the occupation, with many changes of locality.

♅ *in* ♒. URANUS IN AQUARIUS. ♅ *in* ♒.

(*Positive House of Saturn.*)

This position increases the mental power and gives originality, ingenuity, independence of mind, inventiveness and resourcefulness; it strengthens the memory and gives comprehensiveness of mind, and great aptitude for receiving education. Often the native can follow more than one pursuit or line of study simultaneously; he can work well in association with others, and hence is suited for large undertakings, factories, companies, large businesses, public life, municipal appointments Any inclination that may exist towards physical matters or out-of-the-way pursuits is increased by this position and the native is attracted to friends having similar tastes. If well supported by favourable planetary positions the native benefits through friends, partners or marriage; but if much afflicted, there will be trouble and inharmony therefrom.

♅ *in* ♓. URANUS IN PISCES. ♅ *in* ♓.

(Negative House of Jupiter.)

This tends towards mysticism; inner religious feeling; occult experiences; many dreams, keen interest in all psychical matters, and association with people concerned in them. If afflicted there will be trouble through these, also estrangement from friends and the public, while a lack of sociability or sympathy may be displayed in ordinary matters and hostility encountered from others. There is some liability to reverses and unexpected misfortunes; the reputation may be in danger.

NOTE ON THE SIGN POSITION OF URANUS AND NEPTUNE.

These two planets remain for so long a time in each sign, Uranus for more than *seven years*, and Neptune nearly *fourteen*, that great caution is necessary in drawing conclusions based upon their sign position; more so, indeed, than with any other of the heavenly bodies. It is clearly impossible that all persons born during these periods should possess the accompanying characteristics and fortune to an exactly equal extent. The reader, therefore, should take these delineations in their most general sense only, and he is advised not to base any prognostications upon the position of either of these planets unless the characteristics mentioned are supported by sympathetic planetary positions. For instance, if Uranus is in a sign indicating an active intellect, and this influence is accompanied by a like influence from the Sun, Moon, or Mercury, its full effect may be expected; but if not, the influence is greatly weakened, and the unfavourable side of the planet's nature is more likely to be marked.

These remarks apply with more or less force to all the planetary positions here given, since Saturn remains two and a half years, Jupiter one year, and even Mars sometimes as much as six months, in one sign.

Nevertheless, while as has been before hinted the actual position at birth, whether rising, culminating, etc., has much to do—indeed, everything almost—with the *prominence* of any planet's influence in the nativity (irrespective of the zodiacal sign occupied), yet the general tendencies are as described and can be traced in any life according to the prominence of the planet in question. That this is so can be seen, in the case of Uranus and Neptune especially, by studying contemporary history during the time of their occupancy of any given sign.

In these, as in all other cases, much depends upon the position of the planet in the horoscope. For an unfavourable *position*, by 'house,' will negative much of the good promised by a favourable *sign*, and *vice versâ*.

♄

SATURN.

♄ *in* ♈. SATURN IN ARIES. ♄ *in* ♈.

(*Positive House of Mars.*)

The native is likely to come to the front more or less in his sphere of life; he has ambition, love of power and high position, and can exercise authority over others, can influence and manage others. He is somewhat of an organiser, can plan and arrange, and is highly diplomatic though somewhat distrustful. He has self-confidence and assurance, but sometimes may show austerity, gloominess and love of retirement. He has many acquaintances, but few intimates; he makes friends at a distance from his home, also through letters, writings, journeys, and largely through the father, brethren or superiors rather than through personal effort. It gives a touch of selfishness, and somewhat coarsens the finer side of the nature. It may give some degree of irritability, or even bad temper when aroused. The native's fate in life, especially his public career or occupation, is largely of his own choosing, and his misfortunes are often his own fault or due to his own action, directly or indirectly. He will succeed through connection with companies, associations, societies, large firms, etc. The position is not very fortunate for the parents; in many cases the relation of the father to the native is very close, and he may exercise considerable control over the native, but the position is rather critical and the influence is more often unfortunate than otherwise. In some cases there may be positive ill-will between the father and the native, but this only where Saturn is badly aspected.

♄ *in* ♉. SATURN IN TAURUS. ♄ *in* ♉.

(*Negative House of Venus.*)

This tends to make the native strong-willed, very firm and persistent in pursuing his purposes; of a quiet, slow, kind nature, unless afflicted, but easily roused to anger and passion. It is not good for money matters, and (unless very well aspected) money comes but slowly or wastes away. There is a possibility of inheritance, especially through a parent—probably father—and the native may gain money (or lose it, if afflicted) through public ventures, investments, stocks, shares, banks, companies, or speculations in these matters. The good aspects of Jupiter, the Moon and Venus to Saturn are the best for pecuniary purposes. As Saturn has more power in the latter half of life than in the earlier years, its influence often developes and changes after the expiration of its first period (twenty-eight to thirty years). This is equally true whatever sign Saturn may occupy. The native is usually careful and saving in money matters, either from inclination or necessity, and is sometimes even miserly. In any case there is a tendency to selfishness.

♄ *in* ♊. SATURN IN GEMINI. ♄ *in* ♊.

(*Positive House of Mercury.*)

This will bring trouble and difficulties, especially in early life, these being connected with education, clerical and literary work, brethren, and short journeys. But there may be considerable intellectual ability, strength of character, subtlety of purpose, depth of thought, ability for scientific work or for invention and discovery. If well aspected, the native gains some little success or renown through matters ruled by Gemini (*q.v.*), and may follow an occupation governed by that sign. But if the planet is afflicted there will be trouble through all such matters. There will be some irritability, lack of candour, a hard intellectual nature, cynicism and bitterness. The position is not very good for the father.

♄ *in* ♋. SATURN IN CANCER. ♄ *in* ♋.

(*House of the Moon.*)

This is unfortunate for worldly position, honour, wealth, possessions, and general success in life. It brings many troubles in business, occupation, and profession. It threatens downfall, loss of repute, financial troubles and poverty, especially if afflicted by the Moon, Venus, or Jupiter. It is not good for the parents (especially the father); one either dies prematurely, or there is estrangement or separation in some way. It may conduce towards mediumship or occultism of some kind. It is unfavourable for the dwelling house and house property. To a slight extent it is bad for marriage. The occupation may be relatively unpopular, of low class or disreputable.

♄ *in* ♌. SATURN IN LEO. ♄ *in* ♌.

(*House of the Sun.*)

This helps to lift the native up in life and give him power, authority, or responsibility; in great things or small he will, to some extent, stand outside the crowd of ordinary people. It brings favour from superiors and those in higher ranks of life, and there may be gifts or legacies from the father or superiors: if much afflicted, however, these significations will be checked or reversed, according to the nature of the afflicting planet or planets. It slightly diminishes the vitality, and may affect the heart. It gives some tinge of selfishness; the native may be somewhat cold and self-contained. Scandal may arise through love-affairs or through the passions. It is not good for the children, and diminishes the number of them. It may indicate premature death of the father or separation from him. The father will interfere with a love affair, or (if well aspected) may, on the other hand, bring it about.

♄ *in* ♍. SATURN IN VIRGO. ♄ *in* ♍

(*Negative House of Mercury.*)

Gives an orderly, critical, and analytical mind, and of a very serious cast if Saturn is prominent in the horoscope. It tends to an original and capable intellect, one that is fitted to deal with profound subjects. This will very likely not show to advantage during early life, and as a child the native may therefore be considered dull, unless there is assistance elsewhere in the horoscope. The serious tendency will increase to gloom or melancholy at times; or there will be diffidence and reserve. There is some likelihood of disappointment or reversal in the profession, occupation or career; thus there will be thwarted ambition, a desire to rise which is frustrated, or the native will be kept back by an unpopular occupation, by ill-health, or he may be hampered in his projects by his father. It is not a good position for the father, who may be a drag upon the native in some way, or perhaps unsympathetic to him. Unless well aspected, the native suffers through servants, subordinates, and employés, and is not very fortunate himself in any such capacity; but if the planet receives assistance from Venus, Jupiter, or the luminaries, he succeeds as a superior servant or a manager, and benefits in association with the father. The native will travel chiefly for business or health, if at all.

♄ *in* ♎. SATURN IN LIBRA. ♄ *in* ♎.

(*Positive House of Venus.*)

If free from affliction this is on the whole good. There will be some difference in age, worldly position, or wealth, between the native and the marriage or business partner; one of the two benefits by the marriage (or partnership), or both may gain by it; *e.g.*, one will gain wealth and the other position. One of the two may be actuated by desire for wealth or position in marrying, or at least will "go where money is," or where worldly position is, and gain either or both. One will be colder, more austere, or more desirous of wealth or position than the other. This is generally the marriage partner; and the one who gains (wealth or position) is generally the marriage partner; sometimes, however, it may be the native, or, as remarked, both may gain. The father of the native (or of the marriage partner) will greatly influence the marriage and may do something towards bringing it about; but if there is affliction, one of the fathers will hinder, or try to hinder, the marriage. This is more likely to be the father of the native, but it may be either. All that is here said of marriage is also true, *mutatus mutandis*, of partnership and of associations generally. This position is favourable for partnerships, especially with persons older or of better position than the native, or with the father. Position, power, or dignity is gained or money earned through partnership, companies, or association with others. It diminishes somewhat the selfishness, austerity, and isolation of Saturn, widens the sympathies, and disposes to more consideration for others. It is slightly favourable for religion and for the mystical side of it. Any affliction will diminish the good and bring about the opposite evil, according to the nature of the afflicting planet, and the tendency of friendship and partnership will then turn into inharmony, opposition, enmity, jealousy, etc.

♄ *in* ♏. SATURN IN SCORPIO. ♄ *in* ♏.

(*Negative House of Mars.*)

This increases the force of character, strength of will, love of power and authority, ability to control others, and dislike of opposition and restraint. It may produce a very forceful, strong, even turbulent character, unless counteracted by good influence from benefics. Its tendency is rather critical, and unless well aspected or accompanied by prominent benefics, it is more likely to be productive of evil than good. It imperils the honour and reputation, may cause unpopularity or scandal, and unless well aspected threatens overthrow, reverse, collapse, or downfall. If well aspected, or benefics are strong, it produces a character both masterful and subtle, one that will excel through plot and counterplot, and influence men through ways they do not understand; or it may give eminence and power in things that are secret, hidden, occult, mystical, or that are on the other hand merely unpopular and of low degree; or sometimes, in an unfavourable horoscope, notoriety in crime or shame. It is not very favourable for the occupation or for any public pursuit, as it tends to break up, disrupt, disintegrate, dissociate. The same applies to the father; he either dies early in the native's life, or there will be inharmony or separation; he may bring trouble to the native, or even death in extreme cases. In the absence of bad aspects, it is good for occupations concerned with death and the affairs or goods of the dead, also chemicals, sanitation, etc. Its influence upon the health is rather perilous in early life, but if that be overpast it then tends to long life, especially if well aspected. Dangers come from diseases of the parts signified by Scorpio; from accidents, poisons, or surgical operations; from infectious or "filth" diseases; and there is some likelihood of death occurring in some public place or in a more or less public manner. It is favourable for joining mystical, occult, or secret societies or associations.

♄ *in* ♐. SATURN IN SAGITTARIUS. ♄ *in* ♐.

(*Positive House of Jupiter.*)

This position enables the native to earn money or gain position through some occupation or affair described under Sagittarius (*q.v.*). Its precise influence upon religion seems to vary with the other influences that co-operate with or antagonise it in any horoscope. It tends to give some degree of power, prominence, authority, or responsibility in religious matters, according to the native's sphere in life. In some cases the inclination may be to philosophy of some kind, or to politics, but generally to the grave and serious side of the subject. If the native is orthodox in religion, this position will tend to the serious, earnest and devout; but if unorthodox, it will bring philosophical or original thinking and an enquiring mind, together with a disposition to oppose religion or to embrace new views, yet with equal gravity and seriousness. It tends to lift up and give prominence or power through some activity in the religious or legal world, and money or possessions may come through the same channel, or, if afflicted, be lost; religion, philosophy, the deeper affairs of the mind, science, travelling, voyaging, shipping, matters connected with horses, all these will afford scope for the influence according to the native's station in life; and if suitably supported by other indications in the horoscope the native may become a great divine, a distinguished philosopher, a renowned explorer, an eminent financier, etc. If badly aspected, there will be loss instead of gain in these matters, and unpopularity, or even notoriety. The native will follow two occupations at once, or be interested in two subjects at once and divide his time between them, or he may change his occupation after a time. Money comes through the father, from whom the native may be early separated through some cause arising out of travelling, religion, philosophy, politics, etc. He gains friends among people of a religious and philosophical nature, and may join some society, association, or group of such.

♄ *in* ♑. SATURN IN CAPRICORN. ♄ *in* ♑.

(Negative House of Saturn.)

This tends to lift up the native, or to give power, authority, mastery, rulership, independence, ambition, sometimes great selfishness, or loneliness and isolation. Its influence is of course modified according to the native's sphere of life. This is its general influence, and it may manifest to the extent of its opportunity in any walk of life, commercial, political, military, legal, financial, etc. It is usually considered to give much misfortune in occupation and financial affairs, with ultimate reversal or collapse; but it seems open to doubt whether the planet's influence has been sufficiently separated from that of any unfortunate combination that may be present in the horoscope. Taken alone, its influence seems to be of the nature given above, and this may be fortunate with a good combination and unfortunate with a bad one. Saturn in Capricorn receiving evil aspects, especially from the Moon, is very unfortunate, and any influence received here will manifest through the father, the occupation, worldly position, power, fame, etc.* In this position, Saturn seems to render the native very self-centred. In a weak or unfortunate personality this will show as melancholy, despondency, gloom, seriousness, and perhaps bring loneliness or isolation, which may or may not be of the native's own seeking. In a strong personality, it brings ambition, love of power and responsibility, and, unless Jupiter, Venus, or the Sun prevent, much selfish indifference to other people's interests.

Saturn in this sign has an interesting significance. If the first point of Aries (commencement of spring) be taken as representing conception the first point of Capricorn (winter solstice) will stand for birth: Capricorn and Saturn, its ruler, will then be the symbols of Man and the

* An aspect from Venus will affect money and marriage; from the Moon, worldly position, general prosperity, the parents, health; from Mars, the will, actions originating in the native himself, death, the money of the marriage or business partner; and so on according to the nature of the planet aspecting Saturn.

human soul in general—the strong, clearly-marked, well-defined individuality, with power over himself and over the world. This is the astronomical reason why so many of the world heroes and saviours have been symbolised as being born at the time of the year signified by Capricorn (Christmas time).

♄ *in* ♒. SATURN IN AQUARIUS. ♄ *in* ♒

(*Positive House of Saturn.*)

In this position, if fairly free from affliction, Saturn gives power and good fortune to any or all the activities signified by this sign (*q.v.*). It brings success to the native through societies, associations, companies, or groups of people having some common object. It lifts him up and brings either general success or else prominence, position and authority through these matters. It is good for members of Parliament, Town or County Councillors and all who hold similar official positions in any bodies, imperial, municipal or democratic, also trade unions, secret societies, etc. It is good for those who are the heads of large movements, or who are prominent persons therein. Its influence is rather more democratic than that of Capricorn, although this fact may not prevent the native being conservative, reserved and autocratic. But where their inclinations are not democratic, fate often throws these natives into popular movements, and sometimes puts them into positions of more or less antagonism or opposition to higher powers. If receiving help from Venus or Jupiter by good aspect, this position favours acquisition of wealth through stocks, shares, companies, speculation, etc.; or through the father, Government or municipal employ, or official positions in connection with public bodies. If badly aspected it may bring much misfortune through any of these matters, according to the nature of the afflicting planet. There is the instinct for mysticism or occultism. The native is usually widely known, and will have many acquaintances even if few friends; while, if afflicted, he may suffer through friends and become the victim of false charges, deceit or scandal.

♄ *in* ♓. SATURN IN PISCES. ♄ *in* ♓.

(*Negative House of Jupiter.*)

This position is not fortunate, and very little good can be expected from it unless well aspected. It is unfavourable for the occupation, public position, reputation and popularity. The native will suffer severely through any of these, and may incur opprobrium or disrepute in connection therewith. Superiors, authorities and those in high position are apt to be hostile to him or unsympathetic in some way; he has many critics, also enemies and false friends. If himself a person of position, he is liable to attacks from his inferiors, and may suffer some downfall or exposure. Trouble through the father is sometimes experienced, lack of sympathy, hostility, separation, financial troubles; or the father may be brought down in the world and himself experience misfortunes. If well-aspected, benefit may come or money be earned through any affairs, occupations or persons signified by Pisces, such as hospitals, workhouses, charitable institutions, asylums, secret or private occupations, secret societies, or pursuits that are unpopular or considered of low caste, or even in some cases those that are unlawful. If afflicted the native will suffer through any of these channels, meeting with many undeserved misfortunes and being the subject of much unaccountable secret enmity and persecution.

In these, as in all other cases, much depends upon the position of the planet in the horoscope. For an unfavourable *position*, by 'house,' will negative much of the good promised by a favourable *sign*, and *vice versa*.

♃

JUPITER.

♃ *in* ♈. JUPITER IN ARIES. ♃ *in* ♈.

(*Positive House of Mars.*)

A generous, candid, ardent and high-minded disposition. There is a strong inclination to science, literature, religion, study, travelling, the higher cultivation of the mind, or to any of the subjects dear to those born in Sagittarius (*q.v.*); any of these may become prominent in the life history: ships and voyaging, horses and races may be to the fore with others; and amusements, occupations and hobbies founded upon any of these will attract attention. Pecuniary success is indicated in matters signified by Aries, while success is largely owing to personal merit and the native's own exertions; he carves out his own fate, though he may meet with reverses at times. This position indicates one who is to some extent a pioneer or innovator, not very conservative by nature, who is generally fortunate and well respected, and is ambitious of advancement. In religion he is usually active and sincere, whatever his views, orthodox or otherwise, and they may be of either type; but he is pretty sure to oppose received opinions in some degree and to advocate new ones, either in religion or in some department of the activities ruled by Jupiter and consequently represented by Sagittarius. He may have two occupations, or will change his pursuit at some time in life. Few children, but of good disposition. If badly afflicted by Mars, Saturn or Venus he may lose money in various ways or find it very difficult to earn a living, and may come to want; in any case it will be partly his own fault.

♃ *in* ♉. JUPITER IN TAURUS. ♃ *in* ♉.

(Negative House of Venus.)

This gives gain of money through occupations connected in some way with the church, religion, philosophy, learning, the higher faculties of the mind, shipping, voyages, horses. The native is fixed in religion and in his opinions generally, devout and not prone to change. He is fond of home, and does not travel much except for some definite end such as health, business, or the profession. He will gain through land, farming and the products of the land, food stuffs, etc., but there may be loss through these channels if the planet is afflicted. Fortunate in money matters as a rule, and often the recipient of legacies and gifts, the native, though usually generous, is apt to be too fond of money for its own sake in some instances. There is some degree of pride, but also a very warm-hearted, affectionate nature.

♃ *in* ♊. JUPITER IN GEMINI. ♃ *in* ♊.

(Positive House of Mercury.)

This gives a good disposition, courteous, truthful and trustworthy. The native is changeable and restless mentally, and often physically as well; is fond of novelty, also of travelling, and somewhat wanting in perseverance. This position is favourable for education and mental culture, literature or study. The tendency is to the intellectual side of religion, sometimes to mysticism or an eclectic religion; but the native may be changeable and uncertain in his views or even appear indifferent. There is a strong probability of marriage with a relative or someone closely associated, or perhaps even two marriages. But there will be trouble in marriage through fickleness, or in connection with letters, travel or relatives. To a slight extent it brings trouble to or from the mother, brothers or sisters—differences, or separation,—also danger while travelling; but none of this will be serious unless the planet is afflicted. The better occupations and affairs coming under the rulership of Jupiter (as related under the headings of Sagittarius and Pisces) will be prominent in the life, but to a slight extent it is unfavourable for land or house property. There is sympathy, charity. benevolence and brotherly feeling.

♃ *in* ♋. JUPITER IN CANCER. ♃ *in* ♋.

(*House of the Moon.*)

The native is good-humoured, charitable, benevolent, humane, religious, and to some extent yielding in disposition and changeable in opinions. He may change his religion or hold it loosely, and yet be thoroughly sincere and devout. The emotional side of the nature and the imagination and intuition are strengthened, and may show themselves in various ways; in poetry, music or the fine arts, in a inclination to the poetical or mystical in religion, in a fondness for mysteries and the marvellous, the investigation of psychism, etc. The native is fond of home and the parents, especially the mother, and there is likely to be some special link between the native and the mother. There will be voyages and travels by water, for pleasure, health, etc.; the native may travel with a parent (or because of parents). If much afflicted there will be trouble connected with travels and the watery element generally, but it is improbable that this will be serious. It promises offspring, unless afflicted; and there will be money or legacy from the mother or her side of the family. There is some probability of death at a distance from home.

♃ *in* ♌. JUPITER IN LEO. ♃ *in* ♌.

(*House of the Sun.*)

The native is sincere, generous, magnanimous; somewhat ambitious and fond of power, dignity, pomp, display. Is fitted for some public work or pursuit, where he can be at the head of some undertaking, and can direct or control others. There is something of the dramatic in him and a liking for grandeur and ceremony, or great undertakings: he does well in government employ, or in some prominent position. There is a very strong attraction to religion, philosophy, the higher sciences, the fine arts, and the higher cultivation of the mind in general; so that he may gain eminence in one of these directions. The tendency to travel is not great; there may be one long voyage, but travelling is generally for some definite end rather than for the love of travelling. This position favours intuition, and the manifestation of genius and the higher faculties generally. It increases the vitality, strengthens the constitution, and favours the birth of children. The native has a deep and sincere love-nature, is easily moved through love, is compassionate, benevolent, and high-minded.

♃ *in* ♍. JUPITER IN VIRGO. ♃ *in* ♍.

(*Negative House of Mercury.*)

With this position the native is rather matter-of-fact in religious views, taking the intellectual or even somewhat materialistic view of things rather than the devotional and spiritual. This tends to permeate the higher side of the mind in all directions, philosophical, poetical, religious, etc.; he is practical, matter-of-fact, analytical in mind, doubting and hesitating. Ability for scientific study and investigation of facts is marked, as he possesses a mind that classifies, analyses, studies and draws conclusions; doubting until it has reasons for believing, and always requiring reasons for all things,—"a why and a wherefore": there is some ability for teaching, when a good education has been received. A faithful servant himself, he also benefits through servants as a rule; but if afflicted he may suffer severely, either through or as a servant, and treachery or deceit will be manifested, indolence and misfortunes of various kinds. This position tends somewhat to occupations of Virgo or Sagittarius, and it inclines slightly to travelling, principally by land. It is not good for liver, digestion or bowels. The influence upon marriage is very slight but is not good, especially if afflicted. The native is sometimes lacking in method, wanting in application, or absent-minded.

♃ *in* ♎. JUPITER IN LIBRA. ♃ *in* ♎.

(*Positive House of Venus.*)

This position favours sincerity and religious feeling, and gives an imaginative or mystical disposition, with an inclination to poetry, music, etc., and for partnership, comradeship and association with others; the native will gain some degree of popularity among his friends and associates. It is fortunate for marriage and friendship. It is rather favourable for both long and short journeys, and there will be some liking for travelling. There will be gain through the marriage or business partner or associate; or, if much afflicted, trouble from open or secret enemies, loss of money through a woman, through brethren or friends; opposition and treachery from friends or associates. It is a favourable position for charitable gifts, compassion and help; both from and to the native, according to circumstances. The native retains the affection of brethren and friends. He may arouse opposition or incur enmity from the clergy.

♃ *in* ♏. JUPITER IN SCORPIO. ♃ *in* ♏.

(*Negative House of Mars.*)

An active, self-confident, fruitful mind. firmly set on its object. There is ardour and perseverance, generosity and enthusiasm. This positionde notes one who is fond of mysteries, secret and occult things; analytical, and both constructive and destructive: in religion positive, sometimes aggressive; inclining to some unpopular, sceptical or mystical religion or philosophy. It is slightly good for the birth of children, but the death of one is probable. There is danger and misfortune from the water and voyages; liability to death through water or while travelling. Money will be gained through occupations signified by Scorpio (*q.v.*). It strengthens the imaginative and emotional side of the nature, and gives love of pleasure, amusement and show.

♃ *in* ♐. JUPITER IN SAGITTARIUS. ♃ *in* ♐.

(*Positive House of Jupiter.*)

This being the house and 'joy' of Jupiter it strengthens the best characteristics of Jupiter, and endows the native with them strongly. It gives good humour, tolerance, kindness, liberality, a broad mind and a noble nature, humanity, love of justice, mercy and compassion. It is favourable for literature, voyages, travels, dealings with horses or shipping, for success and preferment in religious, philosophical and learned bodies. It contributes to general good fortune and success. As a rule the native is religious and sincere, and the better qualities of the mind are sure to be displayed.

♃ in ♑. JUPITER IN CAPRICORN. ♃ in ♑.

(*Negative House of Saturn.*)

This detracts from the buoyancy, cheerfulness and good humour of Jupiter ; the mind is graver, more serious, less hopeful. It is fortunate for the occupation, generally speaking, especially a public career or one in which the native is head over others, or has others under him. It is good for money or legacy from the father or superiors, and for the favour and assistance of superiors. It gives some measure of power, popularity and esteem; and success in any public or governmental career. It inclines somewhat to travelling, a voyage or long journey at some time of life; and (if born in a suitable station in life) it may incline the native to philosophy, learning, and contemplation, also to religion of a thoughtful character, not always orthodox. There is as a rule frugality and carefulness in money matters, although this may be easily counteracted elsewhere in the horoscope.

♃ in ♒. JUPITER IN AQUARIUS. ♃ in ♒.

(*Positive House of Saturn.*)

This gives good and sincere friends, with pleasure and benefit from them. It sometimes inclines to curious beliefs and superstitions, to fondness for out-of-the-way subjects of study or investigation, and to uncommon religious views, sometimes deep, mystical or occult. It strengthens the intuition, refines and spiritualises the mind somewhat (especially when supported elsewhere in the horoscope), it inclines to original and independent views, and favours the manifestation or acquirement of almost any of the higher qualities of the mind, religious, philanthropic, philosophic, scientific, musical, poetic, etc. Good fortune or pleasure comes through societies, associations, etc. The native may have uncommon psychical or spiritual experiences.

♃ in ♓. JUPITER IN PISCES. ♃ in ♓.

(*Negative House of Jupiter.*)

This brings good fortune to the native from persons and affairs signified by Pisces (*q.v.*). It inclines the disposition to be kind, charitable, quiet and unassuming, unambitious, sociable, rather changeable and easily influenced, ease-loving, sometimes indolent and lacking in energy and "go," at others restless, unsettled and undecided. It disposes somewhat to travelling, especially by water. In religion it indicates sincere belief, often with something mystical, occult, or secret about it, and it increases the emotional and imaginative side of the nature generally. There is some fondness for secrets and mysteries, and there may be some ability for any occupation involving these, *e.g.*, detective, lawyer, policeman, writer of fiction, etc. It is slightly good for the parents. If the planet is much afflicted by malefics, however—especially Mars—it will not be productive of much good.

In these, as in all other cases, much depends upon the position of the planet in the horoscope. For an unfavourable *position*, by 'house,' will negative much of the good promised by a favourable *sign*, and *vice versâ*.

♂

MARS.

♂ *in* ♈. MARS IN ARIES. ♂ *in* ♈.

(*Positive House of Mars.*)

This strengthens all the martial elements in the nature, and they are sure to be prominent in the life history. It gives energy, activity, forcefulness, combativeness, positiveness, enterprise, originality, self-assurance, desire to be at the head of things. It increases the vitality, but gives liability to fevers, accidents, wounds, danger by fire, and surgical operations. It helps to fit the native for any of the occupations of Aries (*q.v.*). There is some likelihood of the native's illnesses, and even his death, being due, directly or indirectly, to his own action, his own fault. To a slighter extent (unless afflicted) he is fortunate with servants and those under him, or when he himself is servant or subordinate to another (although the tendency of the position is the opposite to that of subserviency, as it gives love of independence, candour, openness, dislike of bonds, and, if afflicted, a rebellious disposition). He is often impulsive, imprudent, acts in haste, dislikes secrecy or restrictions, and is generally found out if he tells a lie or does wrong or tries to conceal anything. He is fitted for cutting out his own way in life, whether there is any need for him to do so or not; and he may win some measure of popularity, public success, and good fortune through his own exertions. Some of the most important events in his life, will be due to his own act. Whether for good or evil, he acts, and does not merely drift through life or require to be pushed on by others. As a rule it greatly increases vitality and probable length of life, and gives magnetic and healing power and superfluous vital force, which can be radiated to others. But the native lives, generates and uses up force rapidly, and is more likely to "wear out" than "rust out."

♂ *in* ♉. MARS IN TAURUS. ♂ *in* ♉.

(*Negative House of Venus.*)

The native is firm and obstinately set on his own ends; he will encounter any obstacle, and feels able to overcome any difficulty. He is practical, a good worker and manager, can carry plans and ideas into practical execution, and is a man of the world. If much afflicted there will be irritability and bad temper, and, if the horoscope is bad, the anger will be sudden and violent. He may earn much money, especially if well aspected, but seldom keeps it, spending money freely, either from inclination or necessity. His expenses will be high, and he may have to work hard all his life; will be almost certain to lose money or property or be in straitened circumstances at some period. Generally earns his own living; but even if born to wealth, will do something which will bring him money. There is a likelihood of a legacy: if Mars is afflicted it may fail to be realised, however. This position inclines to marriage, but brings trouble with it. It threatens some scandal in connection with marriage or the opposite sex.

♂ *in* ♊. MARS IN GEMINI. ♂ *in* ♊.

(*Positive House of Mercury.*)

The native is quick and sharp in mind and speech; the wit is nimble and active, though it may not be always, agreeable: sometimes too plain spoken, more forcible than smooth; mentally combative and positive. May be given to satire, irony, fault-finding, criticism of others is practical, apt, and ready, and comes to conclusions quickly. If well aspected native will speak or write well, and be fond of writing, reading, or speaking; will travel a good deal. There is some likelihood of trouble through education, letters, writings and travelling, also brothers or sisters; sometimes estrangement or separation from the latter, especially if afflicted. This position may sometimes accompany an impediment in the speech. In some cases the mind is restless, wanting in fixedness and concentration, given to wandering and indecision. Death may occur while on a journey or at a distance from home.

♂ *in* ♋. MARS IN CANCER. ♂ *in* ♋.

(*House of the Moon.*)

The native will be rather uncertain in temper, irritable, sometimes nursing ill-feeling, and (if afflicted) capable of much malevolence or given to sudden outbursts of temper; he may not be altogether candid or straightforward. This position tends to sensuousness and fondness for luxury. There will be early death of the mother, or else some kind of separation from or disagreement with her. If well aspected, the native may inherit from the mother or her side of the family; or may otherwise inherit houses or land; but if at all afflicted he will suffer or have much annoyance through houses, land, or legacy, and may lose them; will change his abode frequently, or may have accidents to oi in a house, such as fire, theft, storm, flood, earthquake, etc. There is danger from the watery element indicated; and when death occurs, it may be occasioned thereby. The native is original, independent, and rebels against authority. There is some liability to diseases of the nerves and stomach.

♂ *in* ♌. MARS IN LEO. ♂ *in* ♌.

(*House oj the Sun.*)

The native is generous, candid, and sincere; above anything mean or petty; independent in manner, enthusiastic, active, capable of quick and hard work. He is warm hearted and affectionate; sociable and fond of company; but at times has a quick temper and a militant aggressive manner, and so may arouse opposition and open enmity. He has some amount of authority in his manner; is capable of directing and controlling others; and may rise to a position of responsibility or authority. Unless afflicted, good fortune through people in authority or in higher ranks is shown. He is ardent and often hasty in love; sometimes too unrestrained in his emotions and passions; if at all afflicted, liable to disappointment in love, death of a loved one, or separation, or some irregularity in the union. There may be one son, but if at all afflicted this position of Mars threatens death of a child, disaster or separation. It increases the vitality but gives liability to martial diseases and accidents, and, when afflicted or afflicting, affects the heart and back; although as Mars is strong in this position nothing very evil need be expected except in a bad horoscope. The native may receive money or legacy through the father or superiors.

♂ *in* ♍. MARS IN VIRGO. ♂ *in* ♍.

(*Negative House of Mercury.*)

The native is a good worker in a subordinate capacity. Unless indications of rulership and mastery are supplied elsewhere in the horoscope, he succeeds best and is most fortunate when directed by, or associated with someone else. He is not good at commanding others; and however independent he may appear, he is seldom so in reality so far as this position is concerned. Sometimes the native is very ambitious and desirous of power and fame, but this position puts difficulties in the way and helps to bring reversal, downfall, and continual difficulties and opposition. He is never so open nor so devoid of concealment as the best type of Mars men usually are; he often has something he keeps in reserve; inclines more to secrecy; he follows his own will, if not openly, then quietly and in secret, and is capable of working in the dark and in secret; whether for good or evil depends upon the horoscope as a whole. If the horoscope is a good one, he may be of a quiet retiring nature; if an evil one, he will be deceitful or work ill deeds in secret. He is likely to suffer from servants, subordinates, co-workers, and false friends. The position relates somewhat to medicine, surgery, drugs, hygiene, food products; adapts for science, and gives shrewdness and mental activity. The bowels or nervous system will suffer from some complaint brought on or aggravated by Mars. There may be disorders of the parts signified by Virgo, and diseases are likely to be complicated or inborn and incurable. The native may lose friends or servants by death, or be parted from them through quarrels or misunderstanding.

♂ *in* ♎. MARS IN LIBRA. ♂ *in* ♎.

(*Positive House of Venus.*)

This inclines to a rash and ardent love, sometimes to an early or hasty marriage. Occasionally marriage is very much delayed through an early disappointment. The native is passionate and quick in love, and may suffer through his affections, or be entangled detrimentally with the opposite sex. The marriage partner and the opposite sex have great attractions for him, exercise much control over him, and he is sure to meet with grief or trouble of some kind through this. Trouble comes upon him through other people, although it may be indirectly due to some fault or weakness in himself. He meets with criticism, enmity, rivalry and opposition, open or secret. There is severing of bonds through disagreement or death between the native and partner (marriage or otherwise), friends, associates and relatives, unless there are strong good aspects to the planet.

♂ *in* ♏. MARS IN SCORPIO. ♂ *in* ♏.

(*Negative House of Mars.*)

Mars is strong here and its influence is on the whole fortunate. The martial side of the nature is rendered powerful, and the native is firm, positive and determined. There is executive power, a practical nature, the ability to work hard and accomplish much. There is a worldly, matter-of-fact, materialistic tendency, selfishness, pride and disregard of the feelings of others. There is some liability to weakness of health in early life, some accident, fever, surgical operation, (or even premature death, but this chiefly when afflicted). This position increases strength and vitality in adults and old people, but the intensity of the martial influence may be too much in childhood. If afflicted there will be anger and bad temper. It favours legacies and gain of money through association with others.

♂ *in* ♐. MARS IN SAGITTARIUS. ♂ *in* ♐.

(*Positive House of Jupiter.*)

An active mind seldom in agreement with others, fixed and positive in its own ideas, and frequently at variance with accepted opinions. In religion militant, aggressive, unorthodox or sceptical, enthusiastic and active. Because he resists the influence of others and thinks for himself, he will probably change his opinions in important particulars, perhaps more than once in his life: will leave one religion, philosophy, or mode of thought and take up with another. He is mentally and morally brave, daring and fearless of the opinions of others. The position makes him somewhat of a traveller, walker, rider, sailor or athlete, and there will be danger through journeys and travelling. Money may be earned best in partnership or associated in some way with someone else. If afflicted, possible loss of a legacy. It is not good for brothers, sisters, and cousins ; one or more will die, or there may be disagreement.

♂ *in* ♑. MARS IN CAPRICORN. ♂ *in* ♑.

(*Negative House of Saturn.*)

The native is ambitious, and fond of a public life, one bringing him before the multitude rather than confining him to a narrow scope. He is energetic, and wins prominence or authority thereby ; is willing to take much responsibility upon his shoulders ; is fond of exercising authority, and will probably hold some more or less responsible or prominent position. Mars is strong in this sign and generally for good, although there is often a good deal of quick temper, irritability, and passion. The native sometimes comes into conflict with people in authority, superiors, those in higher ranks, and is unfortunate through them. He may arouse opposition, enmity, rivalry, criticism. It is rather unfortunate for a parent (probably father), either of the native or the marriage partner ; one may die prematurely, or there will be separation or disagreement, either between the native and a parent or between the parents themselves. To a less extent it is similarly unfortunate for brothers and sisters, writings, letters and short journeys. There will be money or a legacy from the father, brothers or sisters.

♂ *in* ♒. MARS IN AQUARIUS. ♂ *in* ♒.

(*Positive House of Saturn.*)

This causes some degree of impulsiveness and abruptness in manner or speech. The native may do things quickly and unexpectedly, either because he makes up his mind quickly or because he does not fully realise the consequences. He often sums up facts or opinions and comes to a conclusion very quickly. He is ready and prompt ; knows what to do in an emergency; has all his wits about him. As a speaker, he is a ready and incisive debater, forcible and determined. His opinions are fixed and not easily changed from outside; but when he does change, it often happens so suddenly and abruptly as to surprise everyone. He alienates his friends by his actions, suffers from their opposition and hostility. He loses some friend by death and others by separation or estrangement, and may be in danger from a false friend. This position is not favourable for societies, associations, companies or firms, and trouble occurs to him in connection with them, unless the planet is well aspected. He is somewhat ambitious and aspiring, and is independent in manner, too much so to associate on an equal footing with others for any length of time; such links are broken either through his ambition or his love of independence. Sometimes he seems to be a democrat, but there is a good deal of the autocrat in him; he has a love of leading and guiding others. He may meet his death directly or indirectly through a friend. To a slight extent it is unfavourable for the parents; there may be estrangement from, or the comparatively early death of, one of them.

♂ *in* ♓. MARS IN PISCES. ♂ *in* ♓.

(*Negative House of Jupiter.*)

This is not a fortunate position, but the nature of the troubles indicated differs a good deal according to the kind of horoscope, the prominence or otherwise of the benefics, and the aspects the planet receives. Its influence may be considered under two heads, the good and the bad.

In its bad influence, the native often proves to be his own worst enemy; he is prone to indolence, vacillation, irresolution and indecision; he drifts too much, and is too open to the influence of others. He is also sometimes lacking in candour, truthfulness and honesty. He is often involved in almost irremediable troubles and misfortunes, which are usually more or less his own fault, due directly or indirectly to his own action. He may suffer from secret enmity in various forms, theft, scandal, false reports, slander, etc., with or without deserving it; but he may also himself act wrongly in this way, and play the secret enemy to others. When the influence bears upon health, it is apt to cause lingering illnesses and such as are incurable or nearly so. There is danger from water and liquids generally, drowning, scalding, poisons, or foods in liquid form. To a slight extent there is likelihood of the death of children. There will be some tendency to dissipation, while the native may be easily depressed, gloomy or pessimistic. In its better influence, the native is quiet and retiring, avoiding open rupture or conflict; changeable in opinion, however, and lacking in promptness and decision; perhaps changing his occupation or following two occupations; meeting with many heavy misfortunes and difficulties, but honestly trying to surmount them. It gives ability for a detective, lawyer, magistrate, and inspector: and the native may be instrumental in bringing injustice and evil-doing to light. He does good work quietly and is perhaps desirous of popularity, but unable to gain it. The idea of detention or restraint belongs to the twelfth sign and may accompany this position, manifesting through ill-health, enmity, crime, or poverty.

In these, as in all other cases, much depends upon the position of the planet in the horoscope. For an unfavourable *position*, by 'house,' will negative much of the good promised by a favourable *sign*, and *vice versa*.

♀

VENUS.

♀ *in* ♈. VENUS IN ARIES. ♀ *in* ♈.

(Positive House of Mars.)

Shows a nature ardent in love; one that finds it difficult to restrain the affections when they are once bestowed; fond of love and admiration, and too easily influenced by the attraction of the opposite sex. This position gives some degree of popularity, and ability to make friends easily. It inclines to early love and marriage, and sometimes to a hasty marriage. There is some danger (if ♀ is afflicted by ♂) that the native may think too lightly of the necessary restrictions on the emotions and passions. There will be some ability for music, poetry or painting, and much enthusiasm though little application in their study; love of show and fine clothes and ornaments. Venus in this sign is rather favourable for money, but the disposition is free and generous, and there may be consequent pecuniary losses, free expenditure, and loss of money through the native's own action or fault.

♀ *in* ♉. VENUS IN TAURUS. ♀ *in* ♉.

(Negative House of Venus.)

An affectionate nature, faithful in love, and generally fixed, determined, decided, positive and tenacious in opinion. Marriage is likely but is sometimes delayed. Some trouble will be introduced in connection with the marriage, either through money or because of a death (possibly of marriage partner), or separation from the loved one; there may be incompatibility of temper or an unyielding disposition on one side or the other. The worst of these troubles will not follow unless there are bad aspects, however, though the marriage is likely to be for money on one side. The position is generally favourable for money and possessions; money by legacy, partnership, or marriage is likely, and there is good fortune in business and trading generally. The native is fond of money, but generous with it, nevertheless, and gains money through some occupation signified by Venus.

♀ *in* ♊. VENUS IN GEMINI. ♀ *in* ♊.

(*Positive House of Mercury.*)

The native is sociable in manner, good-humoured and friendly, clear in ideas and intuitional. He is original and inventive and should receive a good education. Is inclined to religion, especially of a poetic or mystical kind. The native may accomplish much as a writer, speaker, musician, or artist, as this position refines the mind and feelings, and tends in one of these directions (the position sometimes goes with neat handwriting). Harmony is preserved between the native and his brethren and cousins. He will earn money through matters signified by Gemini, and will have more than one occupation or receive money from more than one source. There will be pleasure and profit from journeys and travelling. The position is favourable for marriage and for social popularity, and there is a likelihood of more than one love affair or marriage. The native will marry or have a love affair with a relative; or the wife may come from a considerable distance. There is some tendency to flirting and inconstancy in love.

♀ *in* ♋. VENUS IN CANCER. ♀ *in* ♋.

(*House of the Moon.*)

Associates the native closely with one of the parents, probably the mother, and inclines him to family life; he is emotional, affectionate, kind-hearted and imaginative. The position is not wholly fortunate either for marriage or money, and introduces obstacles to both. There will be considerable difference in age or position between the native and the marriage partner, and the marriage may be delayed for various reasons, sometimes on account of money or occupation; a parent (either of the native or marriage partner) will in some special way help or hinder the marriage. Money or property is gained from the parents of the native or the marriage partner, also through some occupation connected either with the watery element, or with houses and property: some unpopular, humble, or relatively plebeian occupation offers sources of gain also.

♀ *in* ♌. VENUS IN LEO. ♀ *in* ♌.

(*House of the Sun.*)

Kind-hearted; the affections and sympathies are easily moved, while the love is ardent and constant, and very set on its object. Marriage is likely to be a love match, and the attraction "love at first sight." The native is popular and is fond of society, company, friends, show, gaiety, pleasures and amusements of all sorts; it is difficult for him to live alone, or a retired life; he must mix with the world and enjoy the company of others. He will attract the attention of his superiors or those in higher ranks of life, and benefit through them socially and pecuniarily. The position may exist with considerable talent or genius for something signified by Venus—poetry, painting, music, the drama, etc. The native gains money, either by speculation, or some occupation connected with the young. Marriage and the birth and prosperity of children are indicated.

♀ *in* ♍. VENUS IN VIRGO. ♀ *in* ♍.

(*Negative House of Mercury.*)

This causes delay or disappointment in love, partnership or marriage. The native may marry one in a different station of life from his own, probably lower. He gains money through servants or subordinates, or by himself occupying such a position; also through occupations of the earthy element and those connected with medicine, drugs, food, nursing, farming, or gardening. This position contributes to sustain the health, and gives a good digestion and appetite.

♀ *in* ♎. VENUS IN LIBRA. ♀ *in* ♎.

(*Positive House of Venus.*)

This strengthens the better part of the Venus element in the nature. It increases sympathy and kindliness of manner; contributes to sociability and popularity, and gives love of poetry, music or the fine arts. It is favourable for friendship, love and marriage. The native earns money through things signified by Venus, and benefits under the direction of another, or in association with another, whether as friend, partner or superior. Money by marriage is likely.

♀ *in* ♏. VENUS IN SCORPIO. ♀ *in* ♏.

(*Negative House of Mars.*)

This increases the passions, emotions, and appetites of the body; and gives love of luxury, pleasure and sensation. The native is ardent in love and passionate in the affections. It sometimes gives undue freedom or forwardness of manner in men, and a lack of restraint and modesty in women, and *may* weaken the moral sense in matters of sex. These results need not follow if the horoscope is otherwise good. Much depends upon the rising sign. The native will be attracted to the opposite sex, and is sure to be unfortunate through them, more or less. There will be trouble of some kind in courtship, love and marriage, though it will differ much in different horoscopes; disappointment in love, delay in love or marriage, loss by separation or death of the loved one or the marriage partner, disagreement or jealousy are forms it may assume. Money by legacy, gift, partnership, or marriage is probable, but there is always delay or trouble connected with it and bad aspects may prevent it altogether. Money will be gained also through occupations of the watery element, or things connected with the dead. There is likely to be either an extravagant nature, too free expenditure, or for some reason no opportunity of saving.

♀ *in* ♐. VENUS IN SAGITTARIUS. ♀ *in* ♐.

(*Positive House of Jupiter.*)

Strengthens the imagination and sense of the romantic and beautiful.

In a very refined nature will give much love of beauty in poetry, painting, music, etc.; also inclination to religion of an elevated or mystical nature, much intuition, and love of all things noble, beautiful, good and harmonious. In a less highly developed individual these idealistic tendencies will probably show out in a highly susceptible love nature. The native will marry amongst his own kin, or else someone from a considerable distance, probably a foreigner. The native will be attracted to more than one of the opposite sex, and may prove fickle in his affections. Money will be earned by the Sagittarius occupations: religion, the church, the higher kinds of literary and intellectual work, and those involving the higher faculties of the mind; also those connected with the animal side of the sign, horses, shipping, voyaging, travelling, athletics. Money may be gained from two different sources at the same time. This position favours travelling and voyaging, especially for pleasure. It slightly favours money by legacy or partnership, and inclines to more than one marriage or serious love-affair.

♀ *in* ♑. VENUS IN CAPRICORN. ♀ *in* ♑.

(Negative House of Saturn.)

This contributes to popularity, and the favour of elders, superiors, employers, masters, and those in higher ranks of life. It helps to lift the native up into some position of responsibility and profit. It brings many friends or acquaintances, and social and general popularity. The position is rather good for business, commerce, investments, banking, stocks and shares. The native gains through these and through enterprises that are public rather than private, through such things as bring him before the many rather than the few, and through occupations that place him over others to direct or control. He gains also through the earthy element, either directly or indirectly: this is a favourable position for a dealer in precious stones, for instance. Marriage is delayed through reasons arising out of age, money, occupation or parents. The marriage partner is likely to be older than the native, and may be wealthier or of higher position; though sometimes this may be reversed. The native is strongly attached to one parent, probably the father, and benefits more through that parent.

♀ *in* ♒. VENUS IN AQUARIUS. ♀ *in* ♒.

(*Positive House of Saturn.*)

This position gives many friends and acquaintances, some wealthier than the native, and financial benefit from some of them. Many friends among the opposite sex. It brings about many and remarkable love affairs, difference in age, and probably trouble in connection therewith, also danger of intrigues, and sometimes marriage towards middle life or old age. Occult affairs or matters signified by Uranus will play some part in the love or marriage, and strange and unexpected events will occur: a love affair may be suddenly entered upon or suddenly broken off, or there may be union without marriage, or a platonic marriage. This position of Venus gives ability for music, poetry or painting, and love of the beautiful. There will be fondness for pleasure and social life, and the native is likely to join some society or association for pleasure or profit. The position favours money through partnership, association with others, companies, societies, firms, and to some extent through investments or banking. It is good for gaining money by public enterprises and by occupations that bring the native before the multitude, and by the assistance of friends and associates. It gives some intuition and predisposes to cultivation of the mind.

♀ *in* ♓. VENUS IN PISCES. ♀ *in* ♓.

(*Negative House of Jupiter.*)

This increases the emotional side of the nature, and gives an intense love of the beautiful, which may find expression in music, painting, or any of the Venus occupations. The native is cheerful, fond of company, society, and friendly intercourse, peaceful, easy-going, charitable, and sometimes indolent. He is likely to follow more than one pursuit or occupation at the same time, or may change from one to another. He may gain money by charity or gift, from friends and acquaintances, or by painting, music, etc; or from some obscure or subordinate pursuit. If much afflicted he may lose money heavily, or find it almost impossible to gain it; and loss may occur through deception, fraud, or his own action. In a bad horoscope the native will be not too scrupulous in his methods of acquiring. There is likelihood of more than one marriage or love affair, and the native may be fickle and careless in matters of affection; or there will be a secret marriage or engagement. He will marry beneath him, or suffer pecuniarily through a woman. If afflicted he may be entangled to his detriment with the opposite sex, and there will be delays and obstacles to the marriage.

In these, as in all other cases, much depends upon the position of the planet in the horoscope. For an unfavourable *position*, by 'house,' will negative much of the good promised by a favourable *sign*, and *vice versâ*.

☿

MERCURY.

☿ *in* ♈. MERCURY IN ARIES. ☿ *in* ♈.

(*Positive House of Mars.*)

The native will be quick-witted, apt at writing or speaking, quick at retort, witty, observant, and sharp; sometimes given to exaggeration, sarcastic, enthusiastic or excitable. He may write or publish, and will make friends among writers, readers or literary people. This position favours short writings rather than elaborate works, but the native may be a quick and very prolific writer, with a fertile mind, original and inventive. It is good for the occupations of Gemini and Virgo (*q.v.*) and may co-operate with other influences in bringing any of them forward. The native will be the cleverest of his family or the most celebrated in matters governed by the planet. If afflicted,* it threatens some trouble to the head or bowels, giving also a liability to feverish complaints or to accidents affecting the above parts. There is likelihood of many short journeys.

☿ *in* ♉. MERCURY IN TAURUS. ☿ *in* ♉.

(*Negative House of Venus.*)

The native is slow to make up his mind, but is fixed and determined when it is made up, and will exercise much patience and perseverance in all matters and pursuits where the acquirement of knowledge is con-

* *See* preliminary note, p. 73.

cerned. He is rather fond of money and possessions, and may make money by any occupations signified by Gemini or Virgo (*q.v.*). This position does not incline to travelling except for money matters, or on behalf of some one else or for health. It gives a sociable, friendly, and affectionate disposition, with some inclination to religion, and to art, music or poetry; capable of much endurance in mental work, and probably possessing a good memory. If afflicted, will show much irritation and anger at times.

☿ *in* ♊. MERCURY IN GEMINI. ☿ *in* ♊.

(*Positive House of Mercury.*)

This brings prominently to the front in the life history all things signified by Gemini, of which ☿ is ruler. It inclines the native to travelling, and to reading and study, though perhaps of a desultory description, embracing many subjects, carrying on two different occupations or studies at the same time, or quickly changing from one to another. It helps to make him suited for any occupation signified by Gemini or Virgo and he may rise to some distinction in Virgo matters or occupations (*q.v.*).

☿ *in* ♋. MERCURY IN CANCER. ☿ *in* ♋.

(*House of the Moon.*)

The native is quiet, good-humoured, easy-going and sociable in disposition and speech. He is sometimes changeable; his mind grasps many subjects, and he takes a wide, comprehensive view of things. His memory is good, and his mind sound and strong, if not always quick or alert. There is a sense of rhythm and motion which will show either physically in dancing or athletics, or mentally in music or poetry. He will gain money through occupations and affairs connected with land or property, through the watery element, and through brothers, sisters, cousins, and the mother or her side of the family. He is fond of the water and will travel by it, especially on short journeys; is in general somewhat inclined to travelling. There is some likelihood of his investigating occult subjects; and he may be a somnambulist or dreamer, or possess some kind of occult gift. This position may exist with intuition and some amount of genius, especially if other influences harmonise. The native is the servant of many; he makes friends among people signified by Virgo and Cancer (*q.v.*), also among those in a lower rank of life than himself, and sometimes among those investigating mystical or occult subjects. It is a very favourable position for joining societies, associations and companies; and the native works better with a firm or in association with partners or co-workers than when alone. It is good for the digestion, but the state of the mind and the stomach act and react on each other to a greater degree than is usually the case.

☿ *in* ♌. MERCURY IN LEO. ☿ *in* ♌.

(*House of the Sun.*)

The native is strong-minded and positive, but kind-hearted, easy-going, fond of pleasure, and self-indulgent. He generally rises to some more or less prominent or responsible position in matters signified by the third and sixth houses, and is capable of directing, managing for, or controlling others in these matters. He may make money through art or business enterprise, designing, etc.; and there will be many short journeys on account of such things. He will be fond of children, of music, singing, poetry or the fine arts. He may give up too much of his time to mental pursuits, and so neglect other duties; in such pursuits or occupations, however, he will show perseverance and mental concentration. It is not quite so fortunate for Virgo matters as for those of Gemini, and if afflicted trouble may ensue; treachery or slander of servants or employees, or trouble to himself through superiors; danger from drugs, weakness of the heart or bowels.

☿ *in* ♍. MERCURY IN VIRGO. ☿ *in* ♍.

(*Negative House of Mercury.*)

The intellect is active and comprehensive; the native learns readily, is fond of science and speculative philosophy, and of study and reading generally, has a good memory, and can turn his studies to account in everyday life. He is practical and utilitarian; makes a good secretary, clerk, or servant in any capacity where intellect or mental affairs generally are of importance; but he is apt to study too many subjects, and to have too many irons in the fire. He has natural inclination to the occupations and affairs of Virgo and may contract a habit of taking drugs. He may have to travel for health. This position is slightly opposed to public success or much popularity in writings, study, and speaking, though the native may achieve much in these directions in a quiet way, or in a sphere that does not bring him forward as a leader or head: the serving influence will always be detected. He may write upon or study occult or psychic subjects; or the influence may take the form of his dealing with comparatively unpopular or neglected subjects, and matters that do not bring wide publicity or fame. If Mercury is afflicted he is likely to suffer from bowel complaints.

☿ *in* ♎. MERCURY IN LIBRA. ☿ *in* ♎.

(Positive House of Venus.)

This is favourable for carrying on studies, writing, reading, and educational pursuits generally, in conjunction with some other person; there may or may not be any technical partnership in the matter, but the native, in carrying out these affairs, is sure to associate with some other person, generally by his own desire, but sometimes from necessity. He may earn money through some one of the various Virgo occupations, and here the idea of partnership or association will again be forward. The marriage will be one of intellectual comradeship, of the mind rather than the emotions. There may be marriage with a cousin or relative, or with one inferior to native in respect of money, or relatively a subordinate. There will be harmonious relations with brethren, cousins, nephews and nieces. If afflicted there will be many and great obstacles to the marriage; and happiness in marriage or success in love affairs is very doubtful. The position is favourable for education and intellect, and to some respect for poetry, music, art, etc. It strengthens the intuition. It gives love of society and comradeship; fondness for intellectual pleasures and amusements, and for children.

☿ *in* ♏. MERCURY IN SCORPIO. ☿ *in* ♏.

(Negative House of Mars.)

The native is positive in his opinions, obstinate, and difficult to convince; will be moved to much enthusiasm for any cause he espouses, and to great indignation or hate by a real or imaginary wrong. He can pursue a train of thought with great mental concentration. He is lively and active in mind, witty and sarcastic, and will have a great flow of words and command of language (unless Saturn afflicts): he has manual dexterity, is ingenious and fertile of resource mentally, and may invent or discover something of great practical utility. He is fond of looking beneath the surface for the causes of things, of searching into mysteries, and solving problems. According to his station in life he may be alchemist, practical occultist, chemist, surgeon, detective, soldier, worker in metals; but mental ingenuity will show in each case. He may make a powerful mesmerist; a healer or controller by the will. Danger will be met with while travelling, chiefly short journeys by water; and there will be death of a brother, sister, or cousin in close association with native or affecting the native. If afflicted, the temper will be very uncertain.

☿ *in* ♐. MERCURY IN SAGITTARIUS. ☿ *in* ♐.

(*Positive House of Jupiter.*)

The mind is just, generous, and sincere; the native inclines to some earnest kind of religion, even if unorthodox, and has aptitude for medicine, science and literature. The native is very active mentally, and perhaps also physically, but very changeable. He will study more than one subject at once, or carry on more than one occupation at once, and will quickly pass from one subject to another. As a writer, his inclination is to deal with religion, philosophy or science, and to write books (or pamphlets, for he is an enthusiastic propagandist as a rule) rather than short articles or ephemeral literature. He seldom deals with simple and popular subjects, and either his style or the subjects dealt with will seldom be simple and straightforward, but either involved or lacking in clearness. He can take a good education, solid rather than superficial or brilliant, and his mental abilities do not show to good advantage during youth or early life. He may write or publish in partnership, or be helped or instigated in some way to write. He is fond of walking, travelling, or riding; there is likely to be illness while travelling, or he may travel for health. He is attracted to drugs, medicine, foods, and may follow some occupation connected with Virgo There will be some trouble connected with education, writings, brothers and sisters, and short journeys; there is a likelihood of many journeys.

☿ *in* ♑. MERCURY IN CAPRICORN. ☿ *in* ♑.

(*Negative House of Saturn.*)

The native will gain prominence, and perhaps fame, through some occupation ruled by Gemini and Virgo. He will be cautious, diplomatic, subtle and profound, his whole nature seldom or never seen on the surface. He can influence other people through the mind. There is always a serious side to his character, and, with a fair education, he will incline to serious and profound studies, or to mysticism of some kind. If afflicted or unbalanced by good, there will be bad temper, secrecy, cunning, and want of candour, or duplicity. This position is favourable for winning honours and prizes at school, or by force of character. The native will be cleverer or better educated than his brothers and sisters, and makes something of a show in all matters governed by Mercury, is ambitious in these things, and keeps an eye on his own advancement. May hold a Government post, or occupy an important position as manager or agent under the authority of another. The occupation will necessitate many short journeys.

☿ *in* ♒. MERCURY IN AQUARIUS. ☿ *in* ♒.

(*Positive House of Saturn.*)

This strengthens the intellect, gives a good memory and a strong and comprehensive mind. It increases any tendency to the cultivation of the mind, to science, literature, or religion. The native is of fixed opinions, averse to change, and not easily influenced in his ideas. He is capable of hard work mentally, is original, and is deserving of a good education. He has friends and acquaintances among people signified by Gemini and Virgo, and following occupations agreeable to these signs. He is likely to join some society or association signified by these signs, or to follow one of the corresponding occupations. The native will travel for some definite object, not often for the mere sake of travelling. Mercury is strong in this sign, the scientific and critical influence particularly so. To a slight extent it inclines to an intellectual form of religion and perhaps to mysticism of some kind, and it strengthens the intuition.

☿ *in* ♓. MERCURY IN PISCES. ☿ *in* ♓.

(*Negative House of Jupiter.*)

The native is just, magnanimous and good-humoured. Affairs signified by the signs Gemini and Virgo are likely to suffer through deceit, treachery and underhand acts; there may be trouble of this nature from servants, subordinates, or employees; or the native, when occupying such a position himself, may cause or be accused of causing these troubles to others. He has detective and analytical skill, and an inclination for such work; can work quietly, subtly, and in the dark; can either discover mysteries or plan them; can speak, write, and act diplomatically and cautiously, and if Mercury is well 'aspected' he will have much ability as an imaginative writer. He has talent for amusements or occupations that give scope for these tendencies, and may gain considerable success or fame through speaking, singing, music, writing, clerical and secretarial work, and whatever depends upon ingenuity and manual dexterity. So far as this position is concerned, he occupies himself with many subjects rather than with one; and he is prone to carry on two lines of study or work at once. He may have to do with nursing, medicine, prison, hospitals; but there is generally some drawback or unpleasantness connected with such work, which is lessened if he can work in partnership, or in association with some one. This position threatens some weakness connected with the regions governed by Virgo or Pisces, and there is trouble in connection with education, travelling by water, or brothers and sisters.

In these, as in all other cases, much depends upon the position of the planet in the horoscope. For an unfavourable *position*, by 'house,' will negative much of the good promised by a favourable *sign*, and *vice versâ*.

CHAPTER XXIII.

THE CHARACTER AND DESTINY OF EACH DEGREE OF THE ZODIAC.

THE following brief delineation of the influence of each separate degree of the zodiac will be found of great interest in connection with the Table of the Sun's Place given later.

The readings here given will apply in general to the whole of the *Individuality* represented by the Sun, forming, in fact, an epitome of the individual character and destiny; and in a similar way, when the time of birth is known,* they will also apply in the case of the Moon, referring, however, then to the *Personality*, it will be understood.† It is perhaps hardly necessary to point out that these significations, being condensed into the fewest possible words in order to save space, should be interpreted in the widest possible sense, and not restricted to their most literal application. For instance, "brethren" implies sisters as well as brethren; and so on. Both character and destiny, or fate, are hinted at in most cases, and the *higher* side of the influence is generally described.

THE DEGREE OCCUPIED BY THE SUN is found as follows:—The approximate time of birth being known, add or subtract at the rate of $2\frac{1}{2}'$ per hour, according as the time is after or before noon, to or from the place of the Sun as given in the table.

Thus, suppose the given time is 6 p.m., December 7th, 1868: this being a leap year we find the Sun's place to be ♐ 15°37′, to which we *add* $2\frac{1}{2}' \times 6 = 15'$, giving ♐ 15°52′, *i.e., the sixteenth degree of Sagittarius.* Similarly in any other case.

In the case of THE MOON, her position is similarly found by simple

* When the time of birth is *not* known, it will, of course, be impossible to find the degree of the Moon. In this case, take the degree of the Sun only, for *noon* at the place of birth: the tables being computed for Greenwich, if born abroad the equivalent Greenwich time must be used—for instance, noon at New York is equivalent to 4.56 p.m. at Greenwich.

† And also, of course, to the ascendant (*Body*), when the exact degree of the latter is known.

proportion, the daily motion being *divided by twelve* and *multiplied by* HALF *the number of hours.* Thus, to take the same date, the Moon moves between noon on the 7th and noon on the 8th (♎7°30′ − ♍23°33′ =) 13°57′; this divided by 12 = 1°10′ (nearly), which, multiplied by *three*, is 3°30′; giving ♍27°3′ as the position at 6 p.m.

It is to be noted that the sphere of influence of any degree extends on either side to an equal amount; thus the influence culminating at, say, ♐ 16°0′ extends backwards to 15°31′ and forwards to 16°29′. Hence the Moon in the above instance is to be counted as in *the twenty-seventh degree* of ♍, and NOT *in the twenty-eighth* degree, which would generally be considered its position according to common acceptance.

The use of these "nut-shell" delineations need by no means be limited to the Sun and Moon positions as above described, and at a later stage of his studies the reader may return to them for many useful hints. Thus, if the time of birth is accurately known, so that the exact degree on the cusp of the Ascendant can be ascertained as explained in Chapter XXI., the reading will have a particular application to the native and will have a general bearing on his character and destiny (taken with the Sun and Moon positions as previously described), in a way that cannot fail to be interesting. In some cases it may be helpful in deciding the ascending degree when the exact time is not known with certainty

Again, on p. 61 each sign is shown to have a ruling planet, and the degree occupied by the "lord" or ruler of the Rising Sign is very important. For instance, on p. 204 of *Practical Astrology* (second edition) is given a horoscope with Cancer rising and the Moon (ruler) in 6°59′ of Taurus. This is followed by a detailed delineation and an account of the native's life, and both will be found epitomised in the description here given of the seventh degree of Taurus.

These uses of the delineations which follow will best be left till the student has obtained *Part II.* of this work and is able to cast his own horoscope, but are mentioned here in order that they may be borne in mind so as to be of greater service later on.

♈ Aries. ♈

Aries decanate

1° Positive, forceful, uncontrollable: creates own destiny.
2° Enterprising, fertile and practical: an organiser.
3° Ardent, refined and subtle, with literary and poetic ability: ambitious strivings.
4° Impulsive and sensuous, yet capable of great attachments.
5° Magnanimous yet imperious: creative ability in art.
6° Unsatisfied longings: a cramped life and distasteful tasks.
7° A spiritual nature, with lofty ideals: an ideal marriage.
8° A rash and ungovernable spirit, turbulent and revengeful.
9° A philosophic mind and a sympathetic nature: many travels.
10° Can rise to great heights, ambitious of prestige: friends in high places.

Leo decanate

11° A student, given to sciences: hopes realised.
12° Aspirations quenched, trials endured: spiritual intuitions.
13° Aggressive and destructive, lustful: abandonment of plans.
14° Violent in temper, yet of a brooding nature: vehement in desires.
15° Timid and irresolute, yet well-disposed: a capable writer.
16° A public man and an orator of persuasive tongue: yet fond of his family.
17° Transcendental inclinations: fond of children, and happy with them.
18° An acute experimentalist, devoted to science: a querulous disposition.
19° A fertile mind and a noble disposition: a passionate lover.
20° Resource and executiveness, with a somewhat unscrupulous character.

Sagittarius decanate

21° Active and impressionable: meets adventures by sea.
22° Profound, yet somewhat melancholy: ambitions realised.
23° A seeker after strange things: many wanderings.
24° A silent nature, philosophical in temperament and patient in affliction.
25° A restless spirit, prone to travel: fate in foreign lands.
26° Subject to inspirations, and possessing creative genius: artistic.
27° The high-priest of some *cultus* or other: powerful and commanding.
28° Gloomy and meditative, thoughtful and tenacious of purpose: a recluse.
29° Lofty ideals, great powers of realising them: famous children and successful enterprises.
30° Initiation into the mysteries: a prophet of some new order.

♉ Taurus. ♉

Taurus decanate

1° Masterful and victorious: great power of combination.
2° A deep student of the recondite sciences, uxorious: magical ability.
3° A generous disposition, a philosophical mind: many travels.
4° One accustomed to authority, a disciplinarian: lofty station.
5° The founder of a sect: into his keeping is given the law.
6° A degree of double nature: a hermit, or a glutton.
7° Resolute yet enterprising, an initiator of new systems: many enemies.
8° A stubborn nature, resourceful and determined: influential positions.
9° Profound in thought and expressive in speech: gain by relatives.
10° Firm yet persuasive, domesticated: home with relatives.

Virgo decanate

11° A rich nature, ardent and generous: genius in art.
12° Painstaking and laborious, precise: an experimental scientist.
13° Refined and artistic, capable in business: well served by inferiors.
14° An influential character, mystically inclined: unfortunate marriage.
15° Ready sympathies, religious nature: death abroad.
16° Subtle and retentive of purpose: friends at court.
17° Acute and powerful mind, original conceptions: influence in societies.
18° Broad sympathies and wide tolerance: a patron of charities.
19° Resourceful and able in execution: leader of a party.
20° Self-reliant and redoubtable: source of own fortunes.

Capricorn decanate

21° A versatile nature, fecund of resource: oratorical abilities.
22° Established in the home and in the affections: many travels by water.
23° Aspiring and passionate: will carry out plans at all costs.
24° Chaste and humble in spirit: a patient worker.
25° Great intuition and poetic ability: a recluse.
26° Power and authority, firm and often unscrupulous: death of partner.
27° Eloquent and persuasive: good fortune by marriage.
28° Steadfast and persevering: a fortune through the employment.
29° A powerful will and great organising ability: success in land.
30° A favourite of fortune: wide influence and a beneficient sway.

♊ Gemini. ♊

Gemini decanate

1° Original and enterprising mind: friends among workers.
2° Practical and somewhat materialistic: trouble caused by possessions.
3° Ready and fluent, capable in emergency: an ambassador.
4° Magnetic and fanciful, some talent: fortune by water.
5° Artistic and literary, skilful in expression: distinguished brethren.
6° Sensitive and retiring, liable to be misunderstood: quiet fortunes.
7° Courteous and affable, suave and obliging: a love marriage.
8° A cantankerous disposition, irritable yet alert: executorships.
9° Refined and agreeable, candid and free: marriage to a foreigner.
10° Lofty ideals: elevation of rank through marriage or partnership.

Libra decanate

11° Commanding intellect, affable demeanour: long journeys through friends.
12° Hesitating and mistrustful: honour through charities.
13° Restless and domineering, active and strong: hopes realised.
14° Inharmonious and doubtful nature: benefits through charities.
15° Active and alert, ingenious: probably has a twin brother or sister.
16° Emotional and sensuous: inherits a home.
17° Powerful and commanding, energetic and able: artistic brethren.
18° Dual temperament and woman-like nature: business at home.
19° Artistic sympathies, humane disposition: popular enterprises
20° Mystical notions, sensuous nature: many disagreeable tasks.

Aquarius decanate

21° Aspiring mind and love of travel: a spiritual union.
22° Public recognition through literary abilities: death of father.
23° Comprehensive ideas, impracticable in many cases: awakening through associations.
24° Ready sympathies, silent yearnings: subordinate to partner.
25° One who sees a new light, fired by ideas: achievement of hopes.
26° Compassion and intellect blended: inspiration and insight.
27° Genius, either in art or diplomacy: sympathy of relatives.
28° Impressionable: gain by the mother, fluctuating fortunes.
29° Positive yet impulsive, kind yet domineering: gifted.
30° Capable and executive: a hard worker, but given to worry.

♋ Cancer. ♋

Cancer decanate

1° Sensuous but refined, one who is at home with the public: trading by sea.
2° Subtle and acute, enterprising in mysteries: death of children.
3° Emotionally religious, active and lethargic by turns: education abroad.
4° Contemplative and profound, penetrating intellect: marriage to an elder.
5° Fanciful and imaginative, quaint conceits: death of friends.
6° Sympathetic and receptive, inclined to indulgence: enlightenment by sea voyages.
7° Intellectual and ingenious, full of expedients: creates his own prestige.
8° Astute and practical, acquisitive: friends among the labouring classes.
9° Sensitive and irresolute, timid yet eloquent: enemies among brethren.
10° Reclusive and domesticated, horizon bounded by home ties: secures own competency.

Scorpio decanate

11° Impulsive and ardent, inherited artistic gifts: gain by speculation.
12° Capable in business, yet fond of science and inclined to the mystical: many compulsory journeys.
13° Somewhat uxorious and indolent: opposition in the home.
14° Senses keen and emotions vivid, turbulent desires: disastrous enterprises.
15° Aspiring nature, good disposition, kind to servants: enlightenment through work.
16° Designing nature, apt in executing plans: exceptional parentage, fame through marriage.
17° Plastic and versatile, a student of humanity: many friends at school.
18° Fond of the sea, a rover: companionable and jovial: hampered by uncles.
19° Restless and domineering, not to be controlled: usurps position of elders.
20° Fortunate and prosperous, somewhat sensual: hopes realised.

Pisces decanate

21° Of enquiring mind and agreeable disposition: given to worry: difficulties through literary matters.
22° Sensitive and secretive, sympathetic and fond of home: extremely attached to mother.
23° Shy, but impulsive, very generous withal: benefits through enterprise.
24° Studious and discriminative: a good critical writer.
25° Somewhat lazy, no early riser: mother dies at native's own home.
26° Innately mystical, or inordinately given to pleasure: luckless in love affairs.
27° Generally fortunate: compulsory journeys on business.
28° A public character, politically inclined: disagreement with father.
29° A reclusive nature: hopes and wishes realised through partner's wealth.
30° Profound and silent nature: difficulties through long journeys.

♌ Leo. ♌

Leo decanate

1° Ardent, enterprising, forceful and illuminated: passionate love.
2° Artistic, sensuous, gifted and subject to inspiration: inheritance from father.
3° Enthusiastic yet diffident, ability in speech and letters: friends among brethren.
4° Powerful will and strong attachments, sensitive disposition: enmity in the home.
5° Self-moved and self-sustained, a strong character: retired life.
6° Energy and enterprise in business concerns: worry concerning patrimony.
7° Generous, courteous and obliging, ever hospitable: devotion to brethren.
8° Strong passions, and keen love of sensation: treachery in the home.
9° Magnanimous and open-handed, candid and free: journeys due to own enterprise.
10° Firm, steadfast and sure, calculating and diplomatic: worry through the profession.

Sagittarius decanate

11° Broad views and wide sympathies: devotion to friends, yet opposition therefrom.
12° Warm-hearted and open-minded, yet shy and sensitive: troubles turned to blessings.
13° Over-impetuous and rash, restless and ever on the move: fortunate on the whole.
14° Impulsive and ingenuous, idealistic and mystical: strong link to parents.
15° Easily kindled and readily appeased, too apprehensive: journeys through friends.
16° Affectionate and demonstrative, yet prone to repine: troubles at sea.
17° Self-inspired and capable of great undertakings: an occultist.
18° Sympathetic and kind, studious and diligent: riches acquired.
19° Gentle yet powerful, æsthetic in tastes: opposition from relatives.
20° Forceful and rebellious, subtle and scheming: regeneration at end of life.

Aries decanate

21° Frank and outspoken, apt to be too diffusive and forceful: enjoys love of kindred.
22° A good organiser, especially in military matters: disagreement with parents.
23° Enthusiastic in propaganda work: many friends among women.
24° Hardworking in charitable projects: trouble in connection with occupation.
25° An initiator of schemes and commercial enterprises: prophetic insight.
26° Practical use made of innate enthusiasm, fortune by the profession: well-to-do parents.
27° Ever ready to seize opportunities, capable in emergencies: intellectual friendships.
28° Practical methods of achieving success: home life contributes to fortune.
29° A ruler and a man, enterprising and courageous, yet steadfast: a free path.
30° A promising experimentalist and acute critic: success in literature.

♍ Virgo. ♍

Virgo decanate

1° Shy, reserved, studious and scientific, yet apt to lean on others: wealth by marriage.
2° Shrewd and penetrating, a delver into mysteries, literary tastes: treachery among brethren.
3° A writer and a dreamer, prolific in production and mystical in aims: death abroad.
4° Profound and metaphysical in thought, and devoted to profession: love towards father.
5° Acute, practical, and inclined towards commercial enterprises of a co-operative character.
6° Ready sympathiser, fond of ministering to others: trouble through marriage.
7° Eager intellect, shrewd insight, fecundity of ideas: brings about own regeneration.
8° Cautious and practical, with decided financial ability: good fortune through travel.
9° Literary abilities of a high order: reverence for brethren.
10° Frugal and economical, psychic inclinations: friends in the home.

Capricorn decanate

11° Sensitive and impulsive, inclined towards serious art: difficulties through love affairs.
12° Self-contained and somewhat self-sufficient: decides own employment.
13° Spiritual intuitions and lofty ideas, a poet: loss of heritage.
14° Inclinations towards oriental customs, reserved in speech: danger on short journeys.
15° Philosophic and artistic, well-disposed and genial: a foreign home.
16° Tendency to metaphysical thought, strong love of principles: devotion to profession.
17° Many curious ideas, a somewhat cantankerous mind: friends among servants.
18° Thoughtful but practical, devoted to service of fellow creatures: sorrow through separation.
19° Persistent in philosophic studies, keen insight and enterprising mind: brings about wealth of partner.
20° Commercial ability, with considerable intuition in mathematics: wealth abroad.

Taurus decanate

21° Resourceful in ideas and able in execution, ready with tongue or pen: dominated by relatives.
22° Capable of powerful attachments to friends: feelings of a very objective type.
23° Enthusiastic and impulsive, somewhat sensational: trouble in speculations.
24° Steadfast, self-controlled, and often not a little selfish: cures himself, or causes own ill-health.
25° Refined and lovable, with keen perception of sensuous beauty: spiritual inspirations.
26° Profound in thought and subtle in speech, keenly alive to art: danger by road.
27° Alert and aspiring in mind, having much business intuition and "go": fortunate in the home.
28° Deep and reserved, seldom shows inner nature: reverential disposition.
29° Kindly and expansive nature, but uncertain manner: worry through friends.
30° Occult tendencies and devotion to the spiritual side of life: restraint through marriage.

♎ Libra. ♎

Libra decanate

1° Forceful mentality and progressive spirit, desire for celibacy : creative power in art.
2° Intuition and inspiration well blended ; purification of the emotions : source of partner's wealth.
3° Active and enquiring mind, just and sympathetic : enlightenment through desultory reading.
4° Loving disposition, greatly attached to the object of affection : tenacious regarding profession.
5° An ardent nature, highly artistic, yet full of wild hopes : friendship turning to love.
6° Mentality more critical and less balanced than most in this sign, very sensitive : troubles regarding health.
7° A nature essentially self-sacrificing, highly idealistic and romantic : entire devotion to partner.
8° Highly sensuous temperament, keen delight in colour, taste and smell : danger through or loss of inheritance.
9° Devotion and love of science well blended, a frank nature : extensive foreign correspondence.
10° A student of mythology and kindred subjects : pursues a vocation at home.

Aquarius decanate

11° Comprehensive mind, broad sympathies, love of art : makes friends of children.
12° A gentle and retiring nature, full of sympathy : confinement through ill-health.
13° Strong desires, eager mind, progressive disposition : unlikely to marry.
14° Receptive nature and psychic temperament : wealth with marriage partner.
15° Highly susceptible to mental impressions, quick mind : hopes realised through brethren.
16° Mediumistic nature, prone to be too sensitive : influence of mother paramount.
17° Energy devoted to promoting large industrial combinations : platonic love.
18° Quiet unassuming nature, chaste and contented : trouble through servants.
19° A transcendentalist and a mystic, a deep student of scripture : austere life.
20° A pleasure-loving nature, somewhat self-indulgent : disbursement of patrimony.

Gemini decanate

21° Open, free and ingenuous, having a great gift of language : many little excursions.
22° Thoughtful, grave and reflective nature, with strong attachment to father : an ancient home.
23° An all-round mentality, comprehensive and well-balanced : platonic love affairs.
24° Negative temperament, prone to self-indulgence and given to many amours : health troubles.
25° Complaisant, yet impulsive, at the mercy of desires and rather weak in will.
26° Refined and artistic temperament, delicately poised and slightly sensuous : loss of patrimony.
27° Sensitive, dualistic temperament, contradictory motives : friends among children.
28° Sympathetic and somewhat sensational : vicissitudes in profession, suited to the stage.
29° Devotional temperament, literary tastes, and enthusiasm for society work.
30° Steadfastly devoted to the purification of the soul : meditative and chaste.

♏ Scorpio. ♏

Scorpio decanate

1° Strong individuality, passionate and sensuous nature : trouble through partner.
2° Reserved, studious, self-contained, mystical : effects own regeneration.
3° Powerful will and generous nature, scientific inspirations : successful journeys.
4° Shrewd and capable intellect : a political pamphleteer of broad views and deep insight.
5° Active and forcible, many ideas, inclined towards reform : friends in the home.
6° Dualistic, emotional temperament : alternately inclined to spirituality and sensualism.
7° Active and thorough, a hard worker : ability for chemistry and manufactures.
8° Strong sense nature, powerful emotions, great executive ability : fortunate in marriage.
9° A restless and critical disposition, ever trying new experiments : death of brethren.
10° Affectionate and clinging disposition, somewhat fickle : long voyages.

Pisces decanate

11° Passionate nature, with a taste for the magnificent : grand surroundings.
12° An experimental scientist, methodical and precise : servants become friends.
13° An emotional nature, given to many amours : troubles in partnership.
14° A resolute character, inclined to a seafaring life : creates own destiny.
15° Enthusiastic disposition, somewhat restless : inspiration in dreams.
16° A steady and constant mind, capable of profound study : mind fixed on profession.
17° A thirster after strange delights, steadfast in search thereof : hidden friendship.
18° A yielding and voluptuous nature, prone to sin, yet well-disposed : trouble in love.
19° Subtle in conception and bold in execution : a dangerous schemer, who ever serves himself.
20° A well-balanced character, of strong affections : inherited obstacles.

Cancer decanate

21° A sensitive nature and intensely critical mind : danger from brethren.
22° Strong attachment to the home, and great sympathy with mother.
23° Lofty ambitions and proud nature, gifted in many ways : good parentage and honourable profession.
24° Practical executive ability in commercial matters : friends among nurses.
25° Highly emotional temperament : marriage brings misfortune.
26° A powerful character, founder of a dynasty : dies by own hand or causes own death.
27° Sympathetic and genial disposition, philosophically inclined : fortunate heritage.
28° Subtle intellect, imaginative yet profound : elder brethren.
29° Comprehensive mind and wide interests : attached to friends.
30° Great sympathy with the destitute, harmonious nature : love affairs unfortunate

♐ Sagittarius. ♐

Sagittarius decanate

1° An intuitive and prophetic nature, gifted with keen insight: an explorer.
2° A practical visionary, carrying ideals into execution: success in subordinate positions.
3° Sensitive and poetical, with literary talent: marriage to a cousin or some relative.
4° Affectionate and demonstrative, fond of home: danger by water.
5° Creative ability, artistic inspiration and prophetic insight: love for a foreigner.
6° Refined and chaste, scientific ambitions: somewhat ruled by inferiors.
7° Agreeable and harmonious nature: opponents turn to friends.
8° Strong love of sensuous pleasure and recklessness in gratifying same: troubles through wife's patrimony.
9° Intense concentrativeness or extreme diffusiveness, as the case may be: a traveller.
10° Keen ambitions and good executive capacity: inherited rank.

Aries decanate

11° Loyal, fearless and humane, of broad views: friends made on short excursions.
12° Sensitive and somewhat restless, compassionate: invalids in the home.
13° Daring enterprises and risky ventures: an active life.
14° Sagacious and capable, efficient and hard-working: old family servants.
15° A well-balanced nature, inclined to an intellectual view of life: marriage twice.
16° A sensation-loving disposition, reckless in the pursuit of pleasure: danger in mines.
17° A rich nature, prodigal of gifts, joyous and inspired: children abroad.
18° Philosophic and critical, adaptable and ingenious: an able journalist.
19° Ingenious and approbative nature, of artistic tastes: friends among women.
20° Inspiration regarding bodily ailments, fearless nature: enemies among doctors.

Leo decanate

21° True insight in all enterprise, favour of superiors: generally fortunate, achieves success.
22° Political tendencies and a gift for polemics: hereditary honour.
23° Chiefly devoted to art, with socialistic sympathies: much friendly correspondence.
24° Sympathetic disposition, psychic temperament: residence in some charitable institution.
25° An enthusiastic nature, boundless vitality, all-round capacity: lives hard.
26° A poetic and sensuous temperament, craving physical delights: open to lofty inspirations.
27° Literary abilities of a high order, a novelist or imaginative writer: youthful partner.
28° A highly emotional disposition, sensitive, disposed to repine: danger of violent death.
29° Royal disposition and somewhat lavish nature: success in travel or the stage.
30° Enterprise in art or commerce, with adequate capacity: in rank lightly esteemed.

♑ Capricorn. ♑

Capricorn decanate

1° An ambitious and forceful nature, apt in commercial matters: rank through wife.
2° Subtle and designing, resourceful and capable, sensual: danger through friends.
3° A profound mind, alternately swayed by principle and ambition: troubles abroad.
4° Intense concentration of purpose, whether in good or evil: ambitious of perfection.
5° Ready and capable, apt at organising and controlling others: hopes centred on wealth.
6° Tactful and sympathetic, facile with tongue or pen, astute: trouble through brethren.
7° Powerful and domineering nature, of great forcefulness: rules in the home.
8° Steady, capable and practical, somewhat gross: good fortune in enterprises.
9° Sensitive and highly strung, given to experimentation: an able *litterateur*.
10° A highly parental temperament, watchful over others' welfare: devoted to mother.

Taurus decanate

11° Hard and grasping nature, astute and selfish: purification through love.
12° A well-balanced, but somewhat earthy and sensuous nature: enlightenment through work.
13° Somewhat of a voluptuary, artistic in tastes: women rule the life.
14° Skill in matters medical, powerful recuperative nature: blasted hopes.
15° Business aptitude and commercial foresight: trouble through relatives.
16° Steady carrying out of well-matured plans: of independent rank.
17° Determined yet flexible, capable of dealing with masses: wealth through associations.
18° Refined and artistic, sensuous temperament: charitable errands.
19° Enterprise in acquirement, and force in retention: cause of own end.
20° Great fixity of purpose and skill in performance: good fortune in love.

Virgo decanate

21° A mercurial disposition, enquiring mind and delicate conceptions: dual occupation.
22° Senses or sympathies paramount: a popular novelist or author.
23° A student of philosophy, mystical in thought: love in death.
24° Occult and scientific tendencies, given to the study of magic or medicine.
25° Strong inclinations towards deliberate self-indulgence, voluptuous nature.
26° A profound and mystical mind, coupled with a very sensual nature: power.
27° An enlightened mind and aspiring disposition: misfortunes in travel.
28° Absorbed either in ambition or in contemplation: continent and chaste.
29° Agreeable yet retiring, thoughtful and studious: hopes inherited.
30° A somewhat gloomy mind, prone to regard the darker side of life: death.

♒ Aquarius.* ♒

Aquarius decanate

1° A bold innovator, hating convention and despising society: no brethren.
2° A steady and reflective disposition, displaying independence of thought: fixity of residence.
3° Intellectual, and inclined to the artistic in literature: dual enterprises.
4° A sensitive and changeable disposition, rather weak: health greatly affected by home conditions.
5° Strong will and commanding nature, business instincts: aristocratic partner.
6° Gentle and retiring disposition, chaste: worry in connection with partner's goods.
7° A docile nature, harmonious, and contented with little: marriage abroad.
8° Original, daring and masterful, not to be taken alive in battle: dangerous pursuits.
9° Large views, wide sympathies, fearless nature: enlightenment through friendship.
10° Resourceful and of great organising ability, for either good or bad: elevation through enmity.

Gemini decanate

11° Erratic and incomprehensible, moved by strange impulses: isolation from all.
12° Psychic disposition, moved by the higher sympathies: misfortune through inheritance.
13° A ready and fertile mind, full of expedients, somewhat lacking in concentration.
14° Practical disposition and competent financial ability: strong attachment to money.
15° Fluent tongue and ready pen, considerable powers of mind: twin children.
16° Fanciful and sensitive disposition, somewhat inharmonious: strongly attached to occupation.
17° A powerful nature, fixed and centred, broad views: love in marriage. In lower natures deliberate lust.
18° Sensitive, impressionable, and somewhat querulous: celibate.
19° An all-round person, widely read and keenly intellectual: enlightenment by intuition.
20° Astute, practical, and either humanitarian or artistic: medical profession.

Libra decanate

21° Expansive and genial, kindly disposed to all: many foreign friends.
22° Political in tastes, able in plot and counter-plot: designs furthered by enemies.
23° Humanitarian views, artistic tastes, general culture: a platonic union and segregation from fellows.
24° Charitable and benevolent, deep sympathies: misfortunes are a source of inspiration.
25° Intellectual, scientific, eager to experiment: fluency of expression.
26° Skill in execution and persistency in accomplishment: fortune at home.
27° Enquiring mind, instinctively intellectual: love of brethren.
28° Intuitive and sensitive to occult impressions, whether psychic or spiritual.
29° A royal nature, a lover of the public and a doer of good works: love in union.
30° Reclusive and retiring, studious and chaste: deep intuitions.

♓ Pisces.* ♓

Pisces decanate

1° Artistic and sensuous, somewhat mystical in tastes: regeneration through marriage.
2° Highly emotional and sensuous, with some occult abilities: mental enlightenment through perils.
3° Able and intuitive, diplomatic, very plastic and versatile: idealism in profession.
4° Subtlety of ideas, with great power of accomplishment: friends of high rank.
5° Over sympathetic and plastic, unstable, yet with good abilities: suffering through friends.
6° Inscrutable and profound, difficult to comprehend: troubles turned to good account.
7° Restless and inharmonious, lacking balance: source and disposer of own wealth.
8° Tactful and resourceful, powerful in combination and mastery of others: fortunate in brethren.
9° Very discontinuous, sensitive, versatile and impressionable: two homes or residences.
10° Emotional and sensitive, yet practical and tenacious of desires: strong love of home.

Cancer decanate

11° Sympathetic and sensitive, impulsive and affectionate: occupation in art.
12° Occult sympathies, sensitive and somewhat retiring disposition: devoted to work.
13° Highly impressionable and artistic, with an inclination to science: danger through partner.
14° Powerful emotions, and ability to sway others by them: creative ability in plastic art.
15° Sensitive and responsive disposition, highly strung and irritable: aspirations toward travel.
16° Ambitious disposition, looking for perfection in details, lofty hopes: friendly relationship to parents.
17° Wavering temperament, receptive to great ideas, but incapable of effectively carrying them out: unfortunate.
18° Changeable and vacillating, inclined to be querulous, negatively sympathetic and receptive to others' woes.
19° Considerable enthusiasm and some practical ability for public work: an agitator, carves his own fortune.
20° Hospitable nature, with some capacity for organisation: fecund in ideas, finding inspiration in writing.

Scorpio decanate

21° A mixed nature, the feelings and intellect conflicting: foster parents, or two homes.
22° Powerful emotions, magnetic and hypnotic power, broad and catholic sympathies: strong love of mother.
23° Erratic and impulsive nature, hot and cold by turns: fiery occupations, enthusiasm in work.
24° Mystical temperament, with a turn for philosophic study: chastity in marriage, or a platonic union.
25° Strong sensuous nature, with a tendency to licentiousness: danger in partnerships.
26° Inclination for practical occultism, keen intuition in spiritual things: dangerous journeys.
27° Expressive nature, ready to form friendships: either rather superficial or very philosophical and profound.
28° Emotional and mental faculties well balanced: hopes of an ambitious character and influential friends.
29° A visionary: one having strong socialistic learnings, with a tendency to militant democracy.
30° A critical degree, the turning point of destiny: power to turn adversity to triumph, or else the source of own downfall.

* It should be remarked that at the present stage of human development the higher influences here spoken of are, in the case of these two signs, less likely to be actively manifested than in the previous ones; and the characteristics indicated will therefore in the majority of cases work out on the *lower* levels of action—originality becoming waywardness and sympathy instability, and so forth.

CHAPTER XXIV.

The Lunar and Planetary Positions from 1850 to 1905.

With this chapter we conclude the first part of "Astrology for All," and in the second part we shall take up the more complicated details connected with casting the horoscope, etc.; while in later treatises we shall give a complete course of instruction on how to judge a nativity when the horoscope has been cast,* as well as more extended remarks on the nature of the various planets, treating them in a manner never before attempted. For those who are not sure of the hour of birth, reference to the following tables will enable them by means of the foregoing description of the polarities to gain some general and fairly accurate idea as to their character, while further study will assist them in obtaining a greater knowledge of themselves, as indicated by the solar, lunar and planetary positions.

We will now illustrate the method of obtaining knowledge of the character.

Example: We will suppose A. B. to have been born January 1st, 1850. Reference to Chapter XIII., p. 39, will show us the *Individual Character* of persons born between December 21st and January 20th of any year, described by the Sun in the sign Capricorn. After noting all these characteristics we turn to the table giving the place of the Moon for 1850, and we find the Moon is in the sign ♌ (Leo), and in Chapter VIII., p. 25, we have an outline of the Leo characteristics in general; a more detailed description will be found on p. 66, under the heading of "The Moon in Leo," showing the Personal Disposition; then, if we would blend these two influences, we may refer to the soli-lunar combinations on p. 135, under the heading of "The Sun in Capricorn and Moon in Leo."

In the tables of "The Place of the Moon" the degrees of the Moon's place are given for each day at noon, Greenwich mean-time. There are 30° (*degrees*) in each sign and 60′ (*minutes*) in each degree; by simple

* Uniform with this volume, 16*s*.

proportion the Moon's place may be found for any hour in the day, *e.g.* on the 16th of January, 1850, the Moon is in 29° of ♒ (Aquarius) at noon therefore at 2 p.m. the Moon has changed her sign into ♓ (Pisces).

In general, the ☽ (Moon) moves about 1° in two hours.

It should always be remembered that the sign rising at birth and the planetary positions will always greatly modify, and sometimes almost entirely alter, the influence of the Sun and Moon; thus, although the Luminaries symbolise the consciousness and its expression, fate and the environment (the planets and their aspects) will form a prominent feature in many lives. Nevertheless, the main feature of each life will be the individual, permanent mood or *character*, represented by the Sun, which "rules by day"; and the personal, sensitive and changeable mood or *disposition*, signified by the Moon which "rules by night," constituting the vehicle of expression for the solar individual. The Rising Sign will indicate as it were the window through which the soul looks out on the world, and the Planets and their aspects will show the environment in which the individual will have to work, and the difficulties which are to be overcome. This it is true has been stated several times already, but in view of its importance it can scarcely be repeated too often; for experience shows that the judgment of students is more frequently at fault from neglect of these considerations than from any other single cause.

To make our meaning clear, we will look up the individual and personal character, and the polarity produced by the combination of the two, of the Prince of Wales, who was born June 3rd, 1865, at 1.18 a.m., London. Reference to the table of the place of the Moon, 1865, shows that on June 3rd, 1865, the Moon was in ♎ (Libra). The following is an extract from Chapter VI., representing:—

THE INDIVIDUAL AND PERSONAL CHARACTER OF THE SIGN GEMINI.

♊. *May* 21 *to June* 20. ♊.

This is the first of the *airy* triplicity, also the first of the *mutable* signs. The airy triplicity governs the mental conditions of humanity, hence we find those born in this sign living chiefly in the mind; owing to the sign belonging to the mutable group, however, they are 'dualistic'—this being the main feature of the mutable signs, causing a tendency to express two conditions and an inclination to be very easily influenced one way or the other. This sign governs the lungs and arms, which have both dual functions, and Gemini persons are rarely content with a single occupation or pursuit, seeming to delight in having two things in hand at the same time. They can very quickly adapt themselves to their surroundings and are hence remarkable for their versatility, while they are very sensitive, having, nevertheless, the ability to reason upon and analyse their sensations. They love change and diversity, and are always the best persons to rely upon in an emergency, as they can instantly respond to the requirements of the moment. They love variety of thought, and delight in all mental pursuits, which they sometimes carry to extremes; they seem to take an especial pleasure in leaving their work unfinished. They will take up one thing, partly finish it, and then go on to another, which they are also apt to leave unfinished ; therefore their best work is done when co-operating with others, for when working in unity with those who understand their peculiarities they are capable of great attainments: nevertheless, the spirit of diversity often makes them experience two extremes during life.

They can be generous and also niggardly : can present a bold front and assertive attitude, and yet be highly timid and nervous: are conservative and progressive; altogether quite dualistic subjects, very difficult for others to understand. We have known persons born in this sign who have expressed a desire to be in two places at the same moment, etc., etc.

We may then read what has been said about the Moon in the Zodiac, Chapter XVII., afterwards referring to page 67 and the paragraph lescribing the personal characteristics :—

THE MOON IN LIBRA.

This position favours general popularity. It gives fondness for music, poetry, and the fine arts generally, with some ability in this direction. This person is affectionate and good-natured, kind in manner and gains friends easily. The native is fond of company, society and friends. Much of his fate and many events of his life will come about through his association with other people, for he will be greatly swayed and influenced by other people; generally by some one person. He works with another person in nearly all undertakings; and without necessarily being irresolute depends largely upon someone else, and can get along best in almost all things when associated with someone. The same may be said of the occupation, for this position tends strongly to partnership not merely in business, but in almost all affairs of life.

By combining these two influences we obtain the polarity, as described on p. 93 :

THE SUN IN GEMINI AND MOON IN LIBRA.

This is a very good combination, built up on the airy triplicity : it increases the intuitions and bestows much refinement, with a sympathetic nature ; gives a great amount of foresight, sharpens the perceptive faculties, inclines to study, and gives a great amount of imitativeness, with ability for public writing. It is necessary for those born under this combination to live purely. The faculty of comparison is well developed, and there is some probability of becoming popular. It gives success in artistic pursuits, and a cheerful, sociable humane nature. The native lives sympathetically with family and relatives, and may marry a relative.

It is now necessary to know the environment into which the subject was born to judge as to the future. Much information may be gathered from a study of Chapter XVI., which describes "The nature of the twelve signs of the zodiac." Reference to this chapter and page 53, shows us that the Prince of Wales was born in the positive group of the *airy* triplicity, in *cardinal* and *mutable* signs. The last paragraph describes the airy signs, etc., etc. A careful study of this chapter will reveal a great deal of the character without knowing the actual birthtime, and without any elaborate system of mathematics; in fact, without any figures whatever.

In this way we have arrived at the two most vital factors in the life of the person described, namely, the INDIVIDUALITY (permanent), and the PERSONALITY (transitory).

We have now to find the next most important factor, namely, the PHYSICAL VEHICLE, or body (perishable), represented by the Ascendant. In Chapter XIX. we learnt that the Sidereal Time at noon on the 21st of June in any year is 6h. 0m. 0s. (approximately), and that it increases at the rate of (about) 4m. per day. As the present date, June 3rd, is 18 days earlier, we therefore subtract (18×4=) 72m., giving us 4h. 48m. as the Sidereal Time *at noon* on the 3rd of June: hence the Sidereal Time at 1.18 a.m., was 10h. 42m. *less*. Adding 24 hours, in order to perform the subtraction, we find, by the following simple sum,

	h.	*m.*
Sidereal Time, noon, 3/6/'65 - -	4	48
Add one day of 24 *hours* - - -	24	0
	28	48
Subtract time before noon that birth occurred -	10	42
RESULT: SIDEREAL TIME AT BIRTH -	18	6

that at the time of the Prince's birth the Sidereal Time was 18 hours and 6 minutes, as was demonstrated on p. 162.

Reference to the "Table of Houses" at the end of the book shows that Aries was then rising at London, and that is therefore the Prince's ASCENDANT, Rising or Ruling Sign.

It now only remains to turn to the general descriptions of Aries on p. 55, where the influence of this sign is described in reference to its own inherent nature, and we have, as it were spread out before us, the three primary elements of *spirit* (☉), *soul* (☽) and *body* (⊕), which constitute the trinity Man in the particular case we are studying.

Further light will be thrown upon the subject by a perusal of chapter XX. under the heading of Aries, where an outline of the main events of life is given.

Again, the table on p. 9 informs us that the planetary ruler of Aries is *Mars* (♂) which is therefore in this instance the ruling planet. Turning to the tables of planetary positions, p. 253, we find ♂ was in ♌, and this influence is described on p. 219. In this way a complete examination has been made of all the *inner activities*, spiritual, psychical and physical.

The planetary environment may now be separately studied, this constituting the NOT-SELF, the limitations and restrictions which the Ego has to cope with and subdue. These limitations are represented *typically* by the position of Saturn (♄) here placed in Libra (see p. 204,) while Jupiter (in this case in ♐, p. 214) indicates the amount of possible growth and expansion.

A further hint may here be given to the eager student. The planet ruling the signs occupied respectively by the Moon and Sun will have chief sway over the Personality and Individuality respectively, and therefore their zodiacal position should also be studied, just as that of the ruler of the Ascendant has been.

The *planetary aspects*, briefly referred to on p. 62, will receive detailed consideration in a later volume.*

In this way it will easily be seen that it is possible to analytically examine and lay bare each detail of the inner and the outer nature, just as the surgeon demonstrates anatomy on the operating table.

Just as in the latter case, however, we must beware of mistaking the *structure* for the *man*,—the muscular system is not the athlete, nor is the brain the mind.

And similarly the Horoscope is not the MAN, nor is its Fate his Destiny, for MAN IS MASTER OF HIS FATE, since, to reverse the usual phrase

DESTINY IS CHARACTER.

* *How to Judge a Nativity*, 16s.

THE SIGNS OCCUPIED BY THE MAJOR PLANETS,

Neptune, Uranus, Saturn, Jupiter, Mars,

From 1850 *to* 1905.

Owing to the phenomenon known as 'retrogradation,' due to the motion of the Earth, the planets at times appear to *quit* a sign after entering it, passing backwards into the preceding sign. In the following tables the dates given are those on which the planet in question *enters* the sign concerned, whether by direct or retrograde motion. Hence a glance will serve to show what sign was occupied by any one of the above planets on any given date.

It is perhaps well to remind the reader that these times are necessarily more or less approximate; but the actual time of entry or regression into each sign will, however, be found to be *within twelve hours of Greenwich mean noon on the dates given.*

It will be seen that in certain cases the stay of a planet in a sign greatly exceeds its average period of transit; thus for instance, ♂ remains in ♍ from November 8, 1885, till July 1, 1886, although its *mean* rate of progress is about ene sign in two months. For the explanation of this apparent irregularity of movement (which, like 'retrogradation,' is due to the motion of the earth in its orbit) the reader is referred to any elementary text-book on astronomy.

♆. NEPTUNE. ♆.

Note:—6.12.48 means *the sixth day of the twelfth month of the year* 1848, *i.e.*, December 6, 1848; and so on.

♆ *enters* ♓ 6.12.48: ♈ 14.4.61: ♓ 30.9.61: ♈ 14.2.62: ♉ 8.6.74: ♈ 30.9.74: ♉ 7.4.75: ♊ 16.8.87: ♉ 20.9.87: ♊ 26.5.88: ♉ 27.12.88: ♊ 21.3.89: ♋ 19.7.1901: ♊ 25.12.01: ♋ 21.5.02: *and continues in* ♋ *till about* 1915.

♅. URANUS. ♅

♅ *enters* ♉ 6.7.50: ♈ 4.9.50: ♉ 14.4.51: ♊ 1.6.58: ♉ 3.1.59; ♊ 12.3.59: ♋ 26.6.65: ♊ 21.2.66: ♋ 23.3.66: ♌ 13.9.71: ♋ 1.1.72: ♌ 28.6.72: ♍ 25.8.78: ♎ 14.10.84: ♍ 11.4.85: ♎ 28.7.85: ♏ 10.12.90: ♎ 5.4.91: ♏ 26.9.91: ♐ 2.12.97: ♏ 3.7.98: ♐ 10.9.98: ♑ 20.12.04: *and continues in* ♑ *till about* 1911.

♄. SATURN. ♄

♄ *enters* ♈ 3.4.49: ♉ 3.6.51: ♈ 4.11.51: ♉ 22.2.52: ♊ 29.7.53: ♉ 30 10.53: ♊ 14.4.54: ♋ 5.10.55: ♊ 20.10.55: ♋ 27.5.56: ♌ 9.7.58: ♍ 26.8.60 ♎ 22.10.62: ♍ 22.4.63: ♎ 10.7.63: ♏ 20.1.65: ♎ 27.2.65: ♏ 29.9.65: ♐ 17.12.67: ♏ 28.6.68: ♐ 6.9.68: ♑ 15.12.70: ♒ 13.3.73: ♑ 13.7.73: ♒ 10.12.73: ♓ 29.2.76: ♈ 14.5.78: ♓ 15.9.78: ♈ 5.2.79: ♉ 5.4.81: ♊ 24.5.83: ♋ 6.7.85: ♌ 18.8.87: ♋ 9.3.88: ♌ 21.4.88: ♍ 7.10.89: ♌ 25.2.90: ♍ 28.6.90: ♎ 27.12.91: ♍ 22.1.92: ♎ 29.8.92: ♏ 6.11.94: ♐ 7.2.97: ♏ 9.4.97: ♐ 27.10.97: ♑ 21.1.00: ♐ 18.7.00: ♑ 17.10.00: ♒ 19.1.03: ♓ 13.4.05: ♒ 16.8.05: *and continues in* ♒ *throughout remainder of year.*

♃. JUPITER. ♃.

♃ *enters* ♍ 11.8.49: ♎ 10.9.50: ♏ 11.10.51: ♐ 8.11.52: ♑ 1.12.53 ♒ 19.12.54: ♓ 11.5.55: ♒ 2.8.55: ♓ 28.12.55: ♈ 8.5.56: ♓ 3.11.56: ♈ 14.12.56: ♉ 15.5.57: ♊ 25.5.58: ♋ 10.6.59: ♌ 29.6.60: ♍ 26.7.61: ♎ 25.8.62: ♏ 25.9.63: ♐ 22.10.64: ♑ 15.11.65: ♒ 11.4.66: ♑ 28.6.66: ♒ 30.11.66: ♓ 14.4.67: ♒ 15.9.67: ♓ 1.12.67: ♈ 20.4.68: ♉ 28.4.69: ♊ 9.5.70: ♋ 24.5.71: ♌ 12.6.72: ♍ 16.11.72: ♌ 16.1.73: ♍ 7.7.73: ♎ 13.12.73: ♍ 19.2.74: ♎ 7.8.74: ♏ 13.1.75: ♎ 20.3.75: ♏ 7.9.75: ♐ 10.2.76: ♏ 23.4.76: ♐ 4.10.76: ♑ 1.3.77: ♐ 10.6.77: ♑ 26.10.77: ♒ 15.3.78: ♑ 12.8.78: ♒ 4.11.78: ♓ 25.3.79: ♈ 2.4.80: ♉ 11.4.81: ♊ 22.4.82: ♋ 20.9.82: ♊ 18.11.82: ♋ 5.5.83: ♌ 26.9.83: ♋ 16.1.84: ♌ 21.5.84: ♍ 18.10.84: ♌ 26 2.85: ♍ 15.6.85 ♎ 16.11.85: ♍ 30.3.86: ♎ 15.7.86: ♏ 17.12.86: ♎ 29.4.87: ♏ 16.8.87 ♐ 14.1.88: ♏ 3.6.88: ♐ 11.9.88 ♑ 6.2.89: ♐ 24.7.89: ♑ 26.9.89: ♒ 23.2.90: ♓ 8.3.91: ♈ 16.3.92: ♉ 25.3.93: ♊ 20.8.93: ♉ 19.10.93: ♊ 2.4 94: ♋ 19.8.94: ♊ 1.1.95: ♋ 10.4.95: ♌ 4.9.95: ♋ 1.3.96: ♌ 18.4.96: ♍ 28.9.96: ♎ 27.10.97: ♏ 27.11.98: ♐ 26.12.99: ♑ 19.1.01: ♒ 6.2.02: ♓ 20.2.03: ♈ 1.3.04: ♉ 12.3.05: ♊ 21.7.05: ♉ 4.12.05

♂. MARS. ♂.

NOTE:—Mars being so much more rapid in movement than the four foregoing planets, a slightly different arrangement has been necessary, and the dates are given as 15.3, meaning *the fifteenth day of the third month, i.e.*, March 15; and so on. MARS *enters*,

1850	♋15.3:	♌15.5:	♍6.7:	♎23.8:	♏7.10:	♐19.11:	♑30.12.		
1851	♒7.2:	♓18.3:	♈25.4:	♉4.6:	♊15.7:	♋30.8:	♌23.10.		
1852	♋4.2:	♌5.4:	♍11.6:	♎2.8:	♏17.9:	♐30.10:	♑10.12.		
1853	♒18.1:	♓25.2:	♈4.4:	♉13.5:	♊23.6:	♋6.8:	♌22.9:	♍16.11.	
1854	♌22.3:	♍27.4:	♎9.7:	♏27.8:	♐10.10:	♑20.11:	♒29.12.		
1855	♓5.2:	♈15.3:	♉23.4:	♊3.6:	♋17.7:	♌1.9:	♍20.10:	♎14.12.	
1856	♏31.7:	♐17.9:	♑29.10:	♒7.12.					
1857	♓14.1:	♈22.2:	♉3.4:	♊14.5:	♋27.6:	♌11.8:	♍28.9:	♎16.11.	
1858	♏8.1:	♐22.3:	♏29.4:	♐13.8:	♑2.10:	♒13.11:	♓23.12.		
1859	♈31.1:	♉13.3:	♊25.4:	♋8.6:	♌24.7:	♍9.9:	♎26.10:	♏13.12.	
1860	♐31.1:	♑23.3:	♒10.6:	♑23.6:	♒29.9:	♓21.11.			
1861	♈4.1:	♉17.2:	♊3.4:	♋19.5:	♌4.7:	♍21.8:	♎7.10:	♏22.11.	
1862	♐6.1:	♑19.2:	♒4.4:	♓18.5:	♈5.7.				
1863	♉15.1:	♊9.3:	♋27.4:	♌15.6:	♍2.8:	♎18.9:	♏3.11:	♐16.12.	
1864	♑28.1:	♒8.3:	♓17.4:	♈27.5:	♉8.7:	♊26.8.			
1865	♋31.3:	♌24.5:	♍13.7:	♎30.8:	♏14.10:	♐26.11.			
1866	♑6.1:	♒15.2:	♓26.3:	♈4.5:	♉12.6:	♊24.7:	♋10.9:	♌25.11:	♋7.12.
1867	♌26.4:	♍22.6:	♎11.8:	♏26.9:	♐7.11:	♑18.12.			
1868	♒26.1:	♓4.3:	♈12.4:	♉21.5:	♊1.7:	♋14.8:	♌2.10:	♍6.12.	
1869	♌31.1:	♍22.5:	♎19.7:	♏5.9:	♐18.10:	♑28.11.			
1870	♒5.1:	♓12.2:	♈23.3:	♉1.5:	♊11.6:	♋24.7:	♌8.9:	♍29.10:	♎30.12.
1871	♍17.3:	♎16.6:	♏12.8:	♐27.9:	♑7.11:	♒16.12.			
1872	♓23.1:	♈2.3:	♉10.4:	♊21.5:	♋4.7:	♌18.8:	♍5.10:	♎25.11.	
1873	♏22.1:	♎19.5:	♏25.6:	♐30.8:	♑13.10:	♒23.11.			
1874	♓1.1:	♈9.2:	♉21.3:	♊2.5:	♋15.6:	♌31.7:	♍16.9:	♎3.11:	♏22.12.
1875	♐12.2:	♑20.4:	♐15.6:	♑31.8:	♒23.10:	♓6.12.			
1876	♈16.1:	♉27.2:	♊11.4:	♋26.5:	♌11.7:	♍27.8:	♎13.10:	♏29.11.	
1877	♐14.1:	♑1.3:	♒17.4:	♓7.6:	♈10.12.				
1878	♉1.30:	♊19.3:	♋6.5:	♌23.6:	♍9.8:	♎25.9:	♏10.11:	♐24.12.	
1879	♑5.2:	♒18.3:	♓28.4:	♈8.6:	♉23.7.				
1880	♊14.2:	♋11.4:	♌1.6:	♍20.7:	♎6.9:	♏21.10:	♐3.12.		
1881	♑14.1:	♒23.2:	♓3.4:	♈12.5:	♉21.6:	♊3.8:	♋24.9.		
1882	♊12.1:	♋26.2:	♌8.5:	♍30.6:	♎18.8:	♏3.10:	♐15.11:	♑25.12.	
1883	♒3.2:	♓13.3:	♈20.4:	♉30.5:	♊10.7:	♋24.8:	♌14.10.		
1884	♍4.6:	♎27.7:	♏12.9:	♐25.10:	♑5.12.				
1885	♒13.1:	♓20.2:	♈30.3:	♉8.5:	♊18.6:	♋1.8:	♌16.9:	♍8.11.	
1886	♎1.7:	♏22.8:	♐5.10:	♑15.11:	♒24.12.				
1887	♓31.1:	♈10.3:	♉19.4:	♊30.5:	♋12.7:	♌27.8:	♍14.10:	♎6.12.	
1888	♏27.2:	♎10.3:	♏22.7:	♐10.9:	♑23.10:	♒2.12.			
1889	♓9.1:	♈17.2:	♉29.3:	♊9.5:	♋22.6:	♌7.8:	♍23.9:	♎10.11.	
1890	♏1.1:	♐1.3:	♏17.6:	♐22.7:	♑23.9:	♒6.11:	♓17.12.		
1891	♈26.1:	♉8.3:	♊20.4:	♋3.6:	♌19.7:	♍4.9:	♎21.10:	♏8.12.	
1892	♐24.1:	♑13.2:	♒6.5:	♓9.11:	♈27.12.				
1893	♉11.2:	♊28.3:	♋14.5:	♌30.6:	♍16.8:	♎2.10:	♏17.11.		
1894	♐1.1:	♑13.2:	♒28.3:	♓9.5:	♈23.6:	♉19.8:	♈13.10:	♉31.12.	
1895	♊1.3:	♋22.4:	♌10.6:	♍29.7:	♎14.9:	♏29.10:	♐12.12.		
1896	♑23.1:	♒3.3:	♓12.4:	♈21.5:	♉1.7:	♊16.8.			
1897	♋22.3:	♌18.5:	♍8.7:	♎25.8:	♏10.10:	♐22.11.			
1898	♑2.1:	♒10.2:	♓21.3:	♈28.4:	♉7.6:	♊19.7:	♋2.9:	♌30.10.	
1899	♋15.1:	♌15.4:	♍16.6:	♎5.8:	♏21.9:	♐3.11:	♑13.12.		
1900	♒21.1:	♓28.2:	♈8.4:	♉17.5:	♊27.6:	♋10.8:	♌26.9:	♍23.11.	
1901	♌1.3:	♍11.5:	♎13.7:	♏31.8:	♐14.10:	♑24.11.			
1902	♒1.1:	♓8.2:	♈19.3:	♉27.4:	♊7.6:	♋20.7:	♌4.9:	♍23.10:	♎20.12.
1903	♍19.4:	♎31.5:	♏6.8:	♐22.9:	♑3.11:	♒12.12.			
1904	♓19.1:	♈27.2:	♉6.4:	♊18.5:	♋30.6:	♌15.8:	♍1.10:	♎20.11.	
1905	♏13.1:	♐21.8:	♑8.10:	♒18.11:	♓27.12.				

THE SUN'S PLACE FOR EVERY DAY OF THE YEAR*

DM	Jan.	Feb.	Mar.	Apr.	May.	June.	July	Aug.	Sep.	Oct.	Nov.	Dec.
	° ′	° ′	° ′	° ′	° ′	° ′	° ′	° ′	° ′	° ′	° ′	° ′
1	10 ♑ 49	12 ♒ 22	10 ♓ 37	11 ♈ 26	10 ♉ 45	10 ♊ 37	9 ♋ 15	8 ♌ 51	8 ♍ 41	7 ♎ 58	8 ♏ 46	9 ♐ 2
2	11 51	13 23	11 38	12 26	11 44	11 34	10 13	9 48	9 39	8 58	9 46	10 2
3	12 52	14 24	12 38	13 25	12 42	12 32	11 10	10 46	10 37	9 57	10 46	11 3
4	13 53	15 25	13 38	14 24	13 40	13 29	12 7	11 43	11 35	10 56	11 46	12 4
5	14 54	16 26	14 38	15 23	14 38	14 26	13 4	12 41	12 34	11 55	12 47	13 5
6	15 55	17 27	15 38	16 22	15 36	15 24	14 1	13 38	13 32	12 54	13 47	14 6
7	16 57	18 27	16 38	17 21	16 34	16 21	14 58	14 36	14 30	13 53	14 47	15 7
8	17 58	19 28	17 38	18 20	17 32	17 18	15 56	15 33	15 28	14 53	15 47	16 8
9	18 59	20 29	18 38	19 18	18 30	18 16	16 53	16 31	16 27	15 52	16 48	17 9
10	20 0	21 29	19 37	20 17	19 28	19 13	17 50	17 28	17 25	16 51	17 48	18 10
11	21 1	22 30	20 37	21 16	20 26	20 10	18 47	18 26	18 23	17 51	18 48	19 11
12	22 2	23 31	21 37	22 15	21 24	21 8	19 44	19 23	19 22	18 50	19 49	20 12
13	23 3	24 31	22 37	23 13	22 21	22 5	20 42	20 21	20 20	19 50	20 49	21 13
14	24 4	25 32	23 37	24 12	23 19	23 2	21 39	21 19	21 19	20 49	21 50	22 14
15	25 5	26 32	24 36	25 11	24 17	23 59	22 36	22 16	22 17	21 49	22 50	23 15
16	26 7	27 33	25 36	26 9	25 15	24 57	23 33	23 14	23 16	22 48	23 51	24 16
17	27 8	28 33	26 36	27 8	26 12	25 54	24 31	24 12	24 14	23 48	24 51	25 17
18	28 9	29 34	27 35	28 7	27 10	26 51	25 28	25 10	25 13	24 47	25 52	26 18
19	29 10	0 ♓ 34	28 35	29 5	28 8	27 48	26 25	26 7	26 12	25 47	26 53	27 20
20	0 ♒ 11	1 35	29 34	0 ♉ 4	29 6	28 46	27 22	27 5	27 11	26 47	27 53	28 21
21	1 12	2 35	0 ♈ 34	1 2	0 ♊ 3	29 43	28 20	28 3	28 9	27 47	28 54	29 22
22	2 13	3 35	1 33	2 1	1 1	0 ♋ 40	29 17	29 1	29 8	28 46	29 55	0 ♑ 23
23	3 14	4 36	2 33	2 59	1 59	1 37	0 ♌ 14	29 59	0 ♎ 7	29 46	0 ♐ 55	1 24
24	4 15	5 36	3 32	3 57	2 56	2 35	1 12	0 ♍ 57	1 6	0 ♏ 46	1 56	2 25
25	5 16	6 36	4 32	4 56	3 54	3 32	2 9	1 55	2 5	1 46	2 57	3 26
26	6 17	7 37	5 31	5 54	4 51	4 29	3 6	2 53	3 3	2 46	3 57	4 28
27	7 18	8 37	6 30	6 52	5 49	5 26	4 4	3 51	4 2	3 46	4 58	5 29
28	8 19	9 37	7 30	7 51	6 47	6 24	5 1	4 49	5 1	4 46	5 59	6 30
29	9 20		8 29	8 49	7 44	7 21	5 59	5 47	6 0	5 46	7 0	7 31
30	10 21		9 28	9 47	8 42	8 18	6 56	6 45	6 59	6 46	8 1	8 32
31	11 22		10 27		9 39		7 53	7 43		7 46		9 33

DM	Jan.	Feb.	Mar.	Apr.	May	June	July	Aug.	Sep.	Oct.	Nov.	Dec.
	° ′	° ′	° ′	° ′	° ′	° ′	° ′	° ′	° ′	° ′	° ′	° ′
1	10 ♑ 18	11 ♒ 51	11 ♓ 6	11 ♈ 55	11 ♉ 14	11 ♊ 4	9 ♋ 43	9 ♌ 18	9 ♍ 9	8 ♎ 27	9 ♏ 15	9 ♐ 31
2	11 19	12 52	12 7	12 54	12 12	12 2	10 40	10 16	10 7	9 26	10 15	10 32
3	12 20	13 53	13 7	13 53	13 10	12 59	11 37	11 13	11 5	10 25	11 15	11 33
4	13 21	14 53	14 7	14 52	14 8	13 57	12 34	12 11	12 3	11 24	12 15	12 34
5	14 23	15 54	15 7	15 51	15 6	14 54	13 31	13 8	13 1	12 23	13 16	13 35
6	15 24	16 55	16 7	16 50	16 4	15 51	14 29	14 6	14 0	13 23	14 16	14 36
7	16 25	17 56	17 7	17 49	17 2	16 49	15 26	15 3	14 58	14 22	15 16	15 37
8	17 26	18 56	18 7	18 48	18 0	17 46	16 23	16 1	15 56	15 21	16 17	16 38
9	18 27	19 57	19 6	19 47	18 58	18 43	17 20	16 58	16 55	16 21	17 17	17 39
10	19 28	20 58	20 6	20 46	19 56	19 41	18 17	17 56	17 53	17 20	18 17	18 40
11	20 29	21 59	21 6	21 44	20 54	20 38	19 15	18 53	18 51	18 19	19 18	19 41
12	21 31	22 59	22 6	22 43	21 51	21 35	20 12	19 51	19 50	19 19	20 18	20 42
13	22 32	24 0	23 6	23 42	22 49	22 33	21 9	20 49	20 48	20 18	21 19	21 43
14	23 33	25 0	24 5	24 41	23 47	23 30	22 6	21 46	21 47	21 18	22 19	22 44
15	24 34	26 1	25 5	25 39	24 45	24 27	23 4	22 44	22 46	22 17	23 20	23 45
16	25 35	27 2	26 5	26 38	25 43	25 24	24 1	23 42	23 44	23 17	24 20	24 46
17	26 36	28 2	27 4	27 36	26 41	26 22	24 58	24 40	24 43	24 17	25 21	25 47
18	27 37	29 3	28 4	28 35	27 38	27 19	25 55	25 37	25 41	25 16	26 21	26 48
19	28 38	0 ♓ 3	29 4	29 34	28 36	28 16	26 53	26 35	26 40	26 16	27 22	27 50
20	29 39	1 4	0 ♈ 3	0 ♉ 32	29 34	29 14	27 50	27 33	27 39	27 16	28 23	28 51
21	0 ♒ 40	2 4	1 3	1 31	0 ♊ 31	0 ♋ 11	28 47	28 31	28 38	28 16	29 23	29 52
22	1 41	3 4	2 2	2 29	1 29	1 8	29 45	29 29	29 36	29 15	0 ♐ 24	0 ♑ 53
23	2 43	4 5	3 2	3 27	2 27	2 5	0 ♌ 42	0 ♍ 27	0 ♎ 35	0 ♏ 15	1 25	1 54
24	3 44	5 5	4 1	4 26	3 24	3 2	1 39	1 24	1 34	1 15	2 25	2 55
25	4 45	6 5	5 1	5 24	4 22	4 0	2 37	2 22	2 33	2 15	3 26	3 56
26	5 46	7 6	6 0	6 23	5 19	4 57	3 34	3 20	3 32	3 15	4 27	4 57
27	6 47	8 6	6 59	7 21	6 17	5 54	4 31	4 18	4 31	4 15	5 28	5 59
28	7 47	9 6	7 58	8 19	7 14	6 51	5 29	5 16	5 30	5 15	6 29	7 0
29	8 48	10 6	8 58	9 17	8 12	7 48	6 26	6 14	6 29	6 15	7 29	8 1
30	9 49		9 57	10 15	9 9	8 46	7 23	7 12	7 28	7 15	8 30	9 2
31	10 50		10 56		10 7		8 21	8 10		8 15		10 3

* The first table gives the Sun's (approximate) position every day *for the second year after leap year*: for the first year after leap year SUBTRACT, and for the third year after ADD, fifteen minutes (15′). The lower table is for leap year: leap years, of course, are those divisible by four, without remainder, (except 1800, 1900).

THE PLACE OF THE MOON FOR THE YEARS 1850–1851

D M	Jan.	Feb.	March	April	May	June	July	August	Sept.	Oct.	Nov.	Dec.
	° ′	° ′	° ′	° ′	° ′	° ′	° ′	° ′	° ′	° ′	° ′	° ′
1	21♌45	11♎58	19♎49	6♐26	8♑40	22♒17	24♓52	12♉15	3♋23	12♌9	5♎7	12♏15
2	6♍8	25 11	3♏8	18 44	20 32	4♓13	7♈16	25 45	17 49	26 39	19 9	25 27
3	20 2	7♏59	16 3	0♑47	2♒21	16 21	20 1	9♊41	2♌31	11♍14	3♏0	8♐26
4	3♎30	20 27	28 36	12 40	14 11	28 46	3♉11	24 2	17 24	25 48	16 37	21 10
5	16 33	2♐39	10♐52	24 30	26 8	11♈33	16 48	8♋45	2♍22	10♎15	29 56	3♑38
6	29 15	14 38	22 53	6♒20	8♓17	24 46	0♊54	23 45	17 16	24 29	12♐55	15 53
7	11♏40	26 31	4♑46	18 16	20 42	8♉27	15 25	8♌54	1♎58	8♏22	25 35	27 55
8	23 51	8♑20	16 34	0♓24	3♈29	22 35	0♋17	24 3	16 21	21 53	7♑55	9♒47
9	5♐53	20 8	28 24	12 47	16 40	7♊6	15 23	9♍3	0♏20	5♐0	20 1	21 35
10	17 49	2♒0	10♒19	25 27	0♉16	21 54	0♌34	23 45	13 52	17 43	1♒55	3♓22
11	29 40	13 57	22 22	8♈28	14 14	6♋51	15 39	8♎5	26 58	0♑5	13 44	15 14
12	11♑30	26 2	4♓37	21 48	28 31	21 47	0♍30	21 57	9♐40	12 12	25 32	27 16
13	23 20	8♓16	17 3	5♉27	13♊1	6♌36	15 1	5♏25	22 1	24 6	7♓25	9♈33
14	5♒11	20 41	29 49	19 20	27 37	21 10	29 10	18 26	4♑7	5♒55	19 28	22 10
15	17 7	3♈17	12♈48	3♊23	12♋11	5♍27	12♎53	1♐5	16 1	17 43	1♈47	5♉11
16	29 8	16 7	26 1	17 33	26 39	19 24	26 14	13 26	27 50	29 36	14 25	18 37
17	11♓17	29 12	9♉27	1♋45	10♌57	3♎1	9♏13	25 33	9♒37	11♓38	27 24	2♊29
18	23 38	12♉32	23 5	15 57	25 2	16 21	21 53	7♑29	21 28	23 53	10♉44	16 43
19	6♈13	26 10	6♊53	0♌5	8♍55	29 25	4♐18	19 20	3♓25	6♈22	24 24	1♋14
20	19 7	10♊5	20 51	14 10	22 35	12♏13	16 31	1♒8	15 31	19 9	8♊21	15 56
21	2♉23	24 17	4♋56	28 9	6♎4	24 49	28 34	12 56	27 48	2♉13	22 30	0♌42
22	16 3	8♋45	19 8	12♍3	19 21	7♐14	10♑29	24 47	10♈18	15 31	6♋46	15 24
23	0♊8	23 24	3♌24	25 51	2♏26	19 28	22 20	6♓44	23 0	29 2	21 4	29 58
24	14 38	8♌10	17 43	9♎29	15 19	1♑33	4♒8	18 48	5♉55	12♊44	5♌20	14♍18
25	29 28	22 56	2♍1	22 57	28 1	13 30	15 56	1♈1	19 2	26 34	19 32	28 22
26	14♋32	7♍35	16 14	6♏12	10♐30	25 21	27 46	13 25	2♊23	10♋29	3♍38	12♎11
27	29 42	22 0	0♎19	19 12	22 47	7♒9	9♓41	26 3	15 55	24 29	17 38	25 44
28	14♌48	6♎6	14 10	1♐57	4♑53	18 57	21 43	8♉54	29 40	8♌33	1♎30	9♏1
29	29 41		27 44	14 25	16 49	0♓47	3♈56	22 3	13♋38	22 40	15 14	22 4
30	14♍12		10♏58	26 38	28 40	12 44	16 23	5♊30	27 48	6♍50	28 50	4♐54
31	28 19		23 52		10♒27		29 9	19 17		20 59		17 30

D M	Jan.	Feb.	March	April	May	June	July	August	Sept.	Oct.	Nov.	Dec.
	° ′	° ′	° ′	° ′	° ′	° ′	° ′	° ′	° ′	° ′	° ′	° ′
1	29♐55	14♒47	23♒34	8♈7	11♉58	1♋8	8♌59	2♎41	24♏59	0♑36	16♒13	18♓3
2	12♑9	26 35	5♓22	20 23	24 54	15 3	23 32	17 9	8♐25	13 16	28 9	29 54
3	24 13	8♓23	17 13	2♉49	8♊4	29 5	8♍2	1♏18	21 27	25 37	10♓0	11♈49
4	6♒9	20 13	29 10	15 27	21 24	13♌13	22 27	15 6	4♑8	7♒43	21 50	23 51
5	17 59	2♈8	11♈14	28 16	4♋55	27 23	6♎42	28 33	16 32	19 39	3♈43	6♉5
6	29 46	14 11	23 26	11♊16	18 36	11♍35	20 45	11♐40	28 42	1♓30	15 43	18 31
7	11♓33	26 26	5♉49	24 30	2♌26	25 45	4♏36	24 30	10♒44	13 20	27 50	1♊12
8	23 25	8♉55	18 23	7♋58	16 25	9♎52	18 12	7♑4	22 39	25 11	10♉7	14 7
9	5♈25	21 44	1♊13	21 42	0♍33	23 55	1♐34	19 26	4♓31	7♈6	22 34	27 17
10	17 39	4♊55	14 20	5♌42	14 50	7♏50	14 14	1♒38	16 22	19 6	5♊12	10♋40
11	0♉12	18 32	27 47	20 0	29 12	21 35	27 35	13 42	28 13	1♉12	18 0	24 15
12	13 7	2♋35	11♋37	4♍32	13♎36	5♐8	10♑15	25 40	10♈7	13 25	0♋59	8♌0
13	26 27	17 5	25 50	19 16	27 57	18 25	22 42	7♓33	22 4	25 46	14 10	21 53
14	10♊16	1♌56	10♌25	4♎6	12♏9	1♑25	4♒57	19 24	4♉8	8♊17	27 32	5♍54
15	24 31	17 5	25 18	18 52	26 7	14 8	17 3	1♈14	16 19	21 0	11♌9	20 0
16	9♋9	2♍21	10♍24	3♏28	9♐47	26 35	29 0	13 7	28 41	3♋57	25 0	4♎11
17	24 6	17 34	25 33	17 46	23 5	8♒48	10♓52	25 6	11♊18	17 11	9♍6	18 25
18	9♌12	2♎34	10♎36	1♐39	6♑1	20 50	22 43	7♉14	24 12	0♌44	23 26	2♏38
19	24 18	17 14	25 22	15 6	18 36	2♓44	4♈35	19 35	7♋28	14 39	7♎56	16 47
20	9♍17	1♏28	9♏45	28 7	0♒52	14 34	16 33	2♊13	21 9	28 57	22 37	0♐49
21	23 59	15 13	23 40	10♑43	12 56	26 27	28 42	15 13	5♌17	13♍36	7♏16	14 39
22	8♎21	28 30	7♐5	23 0	24 49	8♈25	11♉5	28 37	19 50	28 32	21 47	28 16
23	22 19	11♐22	20 2	5♒1	6♓40	20 35	23 48	12♋27	4♍46	13♎36	6♐5	18♑35
24	5♏54	23 52	2♑35	16 53	18 31	3♉0	6♊53	26 45	19 58	28 39	20 3	24 36
25	19 6	6♑6	14 49	28 41	0♈29	15 44	20 22	11♌28	5♎16	13♏31	3♑38	7♒18
26	1♐58	18 7	26 48	10♓30	12 37	28 49	4♋17	26 29	20 28	28 4	16 48	19 44
27	14 32	29 59	8♒39	22 25	25 0	12♊16	18 35	11♍42	5♏24	12♐11	29 35	1♓55
28	26 53	11♒47	20 25	4♈29	7♉39	26 4	3♌13	26 55	19 56	25 49	12♒1	13 56
29	9♑2		2♓12	16 45	20 37	10♋10	18 4	11♎59	3♐59	8♑58	24 11	25 50
30	21 3		14 3	29 14	3♊32	24 30	3♍1	26 44	17 31	21 42	6♓10	7♈42
31	2♒57		26 0		17 23		17 56	11♏5		4♒5		19 37

THE PLACE OF THE MOON FOR THE YEARS 1852–1853

D M	Jan.	Feb.	March	April	May	June	July	August	Sept.	Oct.	Nov	Dec.
	° ′	° ′	° ′	° ′	° ′	° ′	° ′	° ′	° ′	° ′	° ′	° ′
1	1♉39	16♊52	7♋56	28♌9	6♎43	0♐36	7♑52	26♒5	11♈25	13♉44	28♊26	2♌48
2	13 53	0♋2	21 27	12♍57	21 51	15 10	21 31	8♓40	23 21	25 34	10♋39	15 41
3	26 22	13 37	5♌27	28 6	7♏2	29 26	4♒51	21 1	5♉13	7♊26	23 7	28 51
4	9♊10	27 37	19 56	13♎26	22 7	13♑20	17 53	3♈10	17 3	19 25	5♌53	12♍22
5	22 18	12♌1	4♍49	28 47	6♐56	26 50	0♓35	15 9	28 56	1♋36	19 3	26 14
6	5♋46	26 42	19 58	13♏55	21 21	9♒55	13 0	27 3	10♊56	14 3	2♍38	10♎27
7	19 33	11♍33	5♎13	28 43	5♑18	22 39	25 11	8♉55	23 9	26 52	16 41	25 0
8	3♌36	26 26	20 24	13♐4	18 48	5♓3	7♈12	20 51	5♋40	10♌7	1♎11	9♏48
9	17 50	11♎13	5♏20	26 54	1♒50	17 13	19 7	2♊54	18 34	23 51	16 5	24 45
10	2♍12	25 48	19 54	10♑17	14 30	29 13	1♉0	15 9	1♌54	8♍6	1♏15	9♐42
11	16 36	10♏5	4♐2	23 13	26 51	11♈6	12 56	27 43	15 42	22 48	16 31	24 32
12	0♎58	24 2	17 43	5♒48	8♓57	22 59	25 0	10♋37	29 59	7♎52	1♐43	9♑7
13	15 [illegible]	7♐39	0♑59	18 6	20 55	4♉54	7♊15	23 54	14♍38	23 9	16 41	23 20
14	29 22	20 58	13 53	0♓13	2♈47	16 55	19 45	7♌35	29 35	8♏26	1♑16	7♒8
15	13♏20	3♑39	26 29	12 10	14 38	29 6	2♋32	21 39	14♎39	23 33	15 25	20 31
16	27 7	16 47	8♒51	24 4	26 31	11♊27	15 37	6♍1	29 40	8♐21	29 6	3♓28
17	10♐41	29 22	21 3	5♈55	8♉28	24 1	29 1	20 35	14♏29	22 45	12♒20	16 4
18	24 3	11♒47	3♓7	17 47	20 31	6♋49	12♌42	5♎15	29 1	6♑42	25 10	28 22
19	7♑13	24 3	15 5	29 40	2♊42	19 50	26 37	19 52	13♐11	20 12	7♓41	10♈26
20	20 9	6♓11	27 0	11♉37	15 2	3♌6	10♍43	4♏22	26 58	3♒19	19 55	22 21
21	2♒53	18 13	8♈53	23 38	27 31	16 34	24 57	18 40	10♑25	16 6	1♈59	4♉12
22	15 24	0♈9	20 45	5♊45	10♋12	0♍16	9♎13	2♐43	23 33	28 36	13 55	16 2
23	27 42	12 2	2♉38	18 1	23 6	14 9	23 30	16 31	6♒24	10♓53	25 47	27 55
24	9♓50	23 53	14 33	0♋27	6♌14	28 12	7♏43	0♑5	19 3	23 1	7♉37	9♊55
25	21 50	5♉45	26 32	13 7	19 39	12♎25	21 50	13 25	1♓31	5♈2	19 29	22 4
26	3♈44	17 43	8♊40	26 5	3♍22	26 44	5♐51	26 32	13 49	16 59	1♊24	4♋24
27	15 35	29 50	21 0	9♌24	17 23	11♏17	19 43	9♒27	26 0	28 52	13 24	16 56
28	27 28	12♊12	3♋37	23 8	1♎43	25 30	3♑24	22 12	8♈4	10♉43	25 30	29 41
29	9♉28	24 52	16 34	7♍16	16 17	9♐47	16 55	4♓45	20 1	22 34	7♋45	12♌39
30	21 39		29 57	21 50	1♏2	23 56	0♒12	17 8	1♉54	4♊26	20 10	25 50
31	4♊5		13♌49		15 51		13 16	29 21		16 23		9♍15

D M	Jan.	Feb.	March	April	May	June	July	August	Sept.	Oct.	Nov.	Dec.
	° ′	° ′	° ′	° ′	° ′	° ′	° ′	° ′	° ′	° ′	° ′	° ′
1	22♍53	15♏53	26♏51	19♑13	25♒46	12♈38	15♉14	29♊4	14♌29	19♍28	10♏57	19♐12
2	6♎44	0♐1	10♐58	2♒38	8♓33	24 40	27 2	11♋9	27 35	3♎30	25 55	4♑22
3	20 47	14 6	24 54	15 48	21 6	6♉34	8♊50	23 27	11♍0	17 49	10♐52	19 19
4	5♏2	28 8	8♑39	28 44	3♈25	18 23	20 21	6♌0	24 43	2♏20	25 42	3♒56
5	19 24	12♑6	22 14	11♓27	15 34	0♊10	2♋39	18 49	8♎38	16 54	10♑18	18 9
6	3♐53	25 55	5♒38	24 0	27 35	11 59	14 46	1♍52	22 42	1♐27	24 36	1♓55
7	18 23	9♒35	18 53	6♈22	9♉30	23 50	27 3	15 9	6♏51	15 54	8♒34	15 17
8	2♑49	23 1	1♓57	18 35	21 20	5♋46	9♌32	28 39	21 2	0♑10	22 12	28 14
9	17 6	6♓13	14 48	0♉39	3♊8	17 50	22 14	12♎20	5♐11	14 15	5♓31	10♈52
10	1♒9	19 7	27 28	12 35	14 55	0♌4	5♍10	26 9	19 19	28 7	18 32	23 12
11	14 53	1♈44	9♈54	24 25	26 45	12 30	18 20	10♏7	3♑22	11♒48	1♈17	5♉20
12	28 15	14 4	22 8	6♊12	8♋40	25 11	1♎44	24 11	17 22	25 15	13 49	17 15
13	11♓16	26 10	4♉10	18 0	20 45	8♍9	15 25	8♐22	1♒17	8♓31	26 9	29 11
14	23 56	8♉7	16 4	29 51	3♌2	21 28	29 20	22 37	15 4	21 34	8♉19	11♊0
15	6♈17	19 57	27 53	11♋52	15 36	5♎8	13♏31	6♑55	28 43	4♈25	20 21	22 48
16	18 24	1♊46	9♊41	24 8	28 32	19 12	27 56	21 13	12♓10	17 3	2♊15	4♋37
17	0♉20	13 40	21 33	6♌43	11♍53	3♏37	12♐31	5♒26	25 23	29 28	14 5	16 29
18	12 10	25 44	3♋35	19 41	25 41	18 20	27 13	19 30	8♈20	11♉41	25 52	28 26
19	24 0	8♋3	15 52	3♍8	9♎56	3♐17	11♑55	3♓20	21 0	23 43	7♋39	10♌30
20	5♊55	20 41	28 30	17 4	24 36	18 20	26 32	16 52	3♉24	5♊37	19 30	22 44
21	17 59	3♌41	11♌32	1♎28	9♏36	3♑21	10♒55	0♈3	15 33	17 25	1♌28	5♍11
22	0♋15	17 4	25 2	16 16	24 47	18 11	25 0	12 54	27 30	29 12	13 37	17 55
23	12 47	0♍50	8♍59	1♏20	10♐0	2♒43	8♓43	25 24	9♊20	11♋1	26 2	0♎57
24	25 36	14 56	23 21	16 31	25 6	16 51	22 1	7♉37	21 8	22 58	8♍47	14 21
25	8♌43	29 15	8♎1	1♐38	9♑55	0♓34	4♈54	19 36	2♋58	5♌8	21 55	28 9
26	22 7	13♎42	22 54	16 33	24 22	13 50	17 26	1♊28	14 56	17 36	5♎30	12♏22
27	5♍45	28 10	7♏48	1♑10	8♒24	26 42	29 40	13 16	27 8	0♍26	19 33	26 59
28	19 35	12♏35	22 36	15 24	21 59	9♈11	11♉39	25 7	9♌39	13 42	4♏2	11♐55
29	3♎34		7♐12	29 13	5♓9	21 24	23 31	7♋5	22 31	27 25	18 53	27 4
30	17 38		21 31	12♒40	17 56	3♉23	5♊19	19 16	5♍47	11♎35	3♐59	12♑16
31	1♏45		5♑31		0♈25		17 8	1♌43		26 8		27 22

THE PLACE OF THE MOON FOR THE YEARS 1854 1855

D M	Jan.	Feb.	March	April	May	June	July	August	Sept.	Oct.	Nov.	Dec.
	° ′	° ′	° ′	° ′	° ′	° ′	° ′	° ′	° ′	° ′	° ′	° ′
1	12 ♒ 13	2 ♈ 15	10 ♈ 5	26 ♉ 9	28 ♊ 11	12 ♌ 9	15 ♍ 24	3 ♏ 6	24 ♐ 56	4 ♒ 9	26 ♓ 58	3 ♉ 31
2	26 40	15 25	23 13	8 ♊ 16	10 ♋ 1	24 12	27 55	6 54	9 ♑ 17	18 32	10 ♈ 37	16 16
3	10 ♓ 39	28 8	5 ♉ 58	20 12	21 51	6 ♍ 27	10 ♎ 44	0 ♐ 45	23 53	2 ♓ 55	24 4	28 55
4	24 10	10 ♉ 30	18 21	2 ♋ 2	3 ♌ 45	18 59	23 54	14 59	8 ♒ 39	17 13	7 ♉ 15	11 ♊ 20
5	7 ♈ 13	22 34	0 ♊ 28	13 51	15 48	1 ♎ 52	7 ♏ 28	29 36	23 29	1 ♈ 22	20 12	23 35
6	19 51	4 ♊ 28	12 24	25 45	28 5	15 8	21 29	14 ♑ 31	8 ♓ 14	15 14	2 ♊ 52	5 ♋ 41
7	2 ♉ 10	16 15	24 13	7 ♌ 49	10 ♍ 40	28 51	5 ♐ 56	29 38	22 46	28 48	15 18	17 40
8	14 13	28 2	6 ♋ 1	20 7	23 37	13 ♏ 0	20 46	14 ♒ 48	6 ♈ 58	12 ♉ 1	27 30	29 33
9	26 7	9 ♋ 53	17 54	2 ♍ 43	6 ♎ 58	27 34	5 ♑ 54	29 49	20 46	24 52	9 ♋ 32	11 ♌ 24
10	7 ♊ 54	21 51	29 57	15 39	20 43	12 ♐ 27	21 10	14 ♓ 32	4 ♉ 6	7 ♊ 24	21 27	23 16
11	19 41	4 ♌ 0	12 ♌ 12	28 57	4 ♏ 52	27 33	6 ♒ 25	28 51	17 2	19 40	3 ♌ 19	5 ♍ 13
12	1 ♋ 29	16 20	24 43	12 ♎ 35	19 22	12 ♑ 43	21 27	12 ♈ 41	29 34	1 ♋ 42	15 11	17 19
13	13 22	28 54	7 ♍ 31	26 31	4 ♐ 3	27 46	6 ♓ 7	26 1	11 ♊ 49	13 37	27 10	29 38
14	25 22	11 ♍ 41	20 36	10 ♏ 42	18 52	12 ♒ 35	20 21	8 ♉ 54	23 50	25 28	9 ♍ 20	12 ♎ 16
15	7 ♌ 30	24 39	3 ♎ 57	25 1	3 ♑ 42	27 3	4 ♈ 5	21 25	5 ♋ 43	7 ♌ 22	21 44	25 17
16	19 47	7 ♎ 49	17 32	9 ♐ 25	18 24	11 ♓ 7	17 21	3 ♊ 37	17 33	19 21	4 ♎ 27	8 ♏ 43
17	2 ♍ 15	21 10	1 ♏ 17	23 49	2 ♒ 54	24 45	0 ♉ 12	15 36	29 25	1 ♍ 32	17 31	22 36
18	14 54	4 ♏ 41	15 9	8 ♑ 9	17 8	7 ♈ 58	12 41	27 27	11 ♌ 23	13 57	0 ♏ 59	6 ♐ 57
19	27 45	18 23	29 8	22 23	1 ♓ 3	20 50	24 53	9 ♋ 16	23 30	26 38	14 49	21 40
20	10 ♎ 51	2 ♐ 16	13 ♐ 11	6 ♒ 28	14 40	3 ♉ 23	6 ♊ 54	21 6	5 ♍ 49	9 ♎ 37	28 59	6 ♑ 39
21	24 12	16 20	27 16	20 24	27 58	15 42	18 46	3 ♌ 0	18 20	22 52	13 ♐ 24	21 45
22	7 ♏ 50	0 ♑ 35	11 ♑ 24	4 ♓ 9	10 ♈ 59	27 49	0 ♋ 35	15 0	1 ♎ 5	6 ♏ 26	28 0	6 ♒ 48
23	21 48	14 59	25 32	17 42	23 45	9 ♊ 48	12 24	27 9	14 3	20 13	12 ♑ 39	21 40
24	6 ♐ 5	29 29	9 ♒ 40	1 ♈ 2	6 ♉ 17	21 41	24 14	9 ♍ 28	27 12	4 ♐ 11	27 15	6 ♓ 12
25	20 39	14 ♒ 0	23 44	14 8	18 37	3 ♋ 31	6 ♌ 9	21 56	10 ♏ 33	18 16	11 ♒ 43	20 22
26	5 ♑ 27	28 25	7 ♓ 41	27 1	0 ♊ 47	15 21	18 8	4 ♎ 34	24 4	2 ♑ 27	25 59	4 ♈ 8
27	20 23	12 ♓ 38	21 27	9 ♉ 39	12 49	27 11	0 ♍ 14	17 23	7 ♐ 46	16 40	10 ♓ 0	17 30
28	5 ♒ 19	26 33	4 ♈ 59	22 4	24 44	9 ♌ 4	12 29	0 ♏ 24	21 38	0 ♒ 53	23 45	0 ♉ 32
29	20 5		18 14	4 ♊ 16	6 ♋ 35	21 2	24 52	13 38	5 ♑ 40	15 3	7 ♈ 15	13 17
30	4 ♓ 34		1 ♉ 11	16 18	18 24	3 ♍ 8	7 ♎ 28	27 7	19 51	29 9	20 39	25 47
31	18 38		13 49		0 ♌ 14		20 19	10 ♐ 53		13 ♓ 8		8 ♊ 5

D M	Jan.	Feb.	March	April	May	June	July	August	Sept.	Oct.	Nov.	Dec.
	° ′	° ′	° ′	° ′	° ′	° ′	° ′	° ′	° ′	° ′	° ′	° ′
1	20 ♊ 15	5 ♌ 1	13 ♌ 47	28 ♍ 33	2 ♏ 23	22 ♐ 1	0 ♒ 22	24 ♓ 25	15 ♉ 53	20 ♊ 47	6 ♌ 6	7 ♍ 48
2	2 ♋ 19	16 54	25 42	11 ♎ 0	15 34	6 ♑ 23	15 19	8 ♈ 55	29 13	3 ♋ 26	18 4	19 38
3	14 18	28 49	7 ♍ 42	23 38	29 1	20 52	0 ♓ 10	23 0	12 ♊ 19	15 47	29 57	1 ♎ 31
4	26 12	10 ♍ 47	19 49	6 ♏ 28	12 ♐ 42	5 ♒ 25	14 46	6 ♉ 39	24 45	27 55	11 ♍ 48	13 33
5	8 ♌ 5	22 50	2 ♎ 2	19 31	26 35	19 54	29 3	19 53	7 ♋ 4	9 ♌ 52	23 41	25 47
6	19 57	5 ♎ 0	14 24	2 ♐ 46	10 ♑ 37	4 ♓ 15	13 ♈ 0	2 ♊ 48	19 12	21 45	5 ♎ 42	8 ♏ 17
7	1 ♍ 50	17 19	26 56	16 14	24 46	18 25	26 37	15 25	1 ♌ 11	3 ♍ 35	17 52	21 7
8	13 47	29 51	9 ♏ 38	29 55	8 ♒ 59	2 ♈ 23	9 ♉ 55	27 49	13 5	15 28	0 ♏ 15	4 ♐ 17
9	25 52	12 ♏ 40	22 35	13 ♑ 50	23 14	16 7	22 56	10 ♋ 2	24 57	27 24	12 52	17 48
10	8 ♎ 8	25 50	5 ♐ 48	27 57	7 ♓ 26	29 38	5 ♊ 43	22 7	6 ♍ 48	9 ♎ 27	25 44	1 ♑ 37
11	20 39	9 ♐ 25	19 19	12 ♒ 16	21 35	12 ♉ 56	18 18	4 ♌ 7	18 40	21 38	8 ♐ 51	15 39
12	3 ♏ 32	23 26	3 ♑ 12	26 42	5 ♈ 38	26 1	0 ♋ 43	16 2	0 ♎ 36	3 ♏ 59	22 11	29 52
13	16 49	7 ♑ 55	17 25	11 ♓ 13	19 32	8 ♊ 55	12 17	27 54	12 36	16 30	5 ♑ 45	14 ♒ 9
14	0 ♐ 34	22 48	1 ♒ 58	25 42	3 ♉ 15	21 36	25 8	9 ♍ 45	24 43	29 14	19 30	28 26
15	14 49	7 ♒ 58	16 47	10 ♈ 5	16 45	4 ♋ 6	7 ♌ 9	21 36	6 ♏ 59	12 ♐ 11	3 ♒ 25	12 ♓ 39
16	29 31	23 16	1 ♓ 44	24 15	29 59	16 25	19 5	3 ♎ 29	19 26	25 23	17 27	26 47
17	14 ♑ 36	8 ♓ 30	16 41	8 ♉ 8	12 ♊ 58	28 34	0 ♍ 56	15 28	2 ♐ 9	8 ♑ 51	1 ♓ 36	10 ♈ 48
18	29 55	23 29	1 ♈ 29	21 41	25 41	10 ♌ 34	12 47	27 36	15 11	22 36	15 50	24 41
19	15 ♒ 15	8 ♈ 5	16 0	4 ♊ 53	8 ♋ 9	22 28	24 38	9 ♏ 57	28 34	6 ♒ 38	0 ♈ 6	8 ♉ 26
20	0 ♓ 27	22 12	0 ♉ 7	17 43	20 23	4 ♍ 20	6 ♎ 35	22 36	12 ♑ 22	20 57	14 21	22 2
21	15 18	5 ♉ 49	13 48	0 ♋ 14	2 ♌ 27	16 13	18 42	5 ♐ 38	26 35	5 ♓ 29	28 33	5 ♊ 30
22	29 44	18 57	27 3	12 30	14 23	28 11	1 ♏ 3	19 5	11 ♒ 11	20 9	12 ♉ 37	18 46
23	13 ♈ 40	1 ♊ 41	9 ♊ 52	24 33	26 16	10 ♎ 21	13 45	3 ♑ 2	26 5	4 ♈ 53	26 31	1 ♋ 50
24	27 7	14 5	22 21	6 ♌ 29	8 ♍ 10	22 45	26 51	17 28	11 ♓ 11	19 34	10 ♊ 10	14 40
25	10 ♉ 9	26 13	4 ♋ 33	18 22	20 11	5 ♏ 30	10 ♐ 25	2 ♒ 19	26 19	4 ♉ 4	23 31	27 16
26	22 48	8 ♋ 12	16 34	0 ♍ 17	2 ♎ 22	18 39	24 28	17 29	11 ♈ 19	18 18	6 ♋ 34	9 ♌ 38
27	5 ♊ 11	20 4	28 28	12 17	14 48	2 ♐ 14	9 ♑ 0	2 ♓ 48	26 2	2 ♊ 11	19 18	21 47
28	17 20	1 ♌ 55	10 ♌ 19	24 27	27 33	16 16	23 56	18 5	10 ♉ 23	15 41	1 ♌ 44	3 ♍ 45
29	29 21		22 13	6 ♎ 51	10 ♏ 38	0 ♑ 42	9 ♒ 7	3 ♈ 9	24 18	28 47	13 55	15 36
30	11 ♋ 16		4 ♍ 11	19 29	24 6	15 27	24 22	17 51	7 ♊ 45	11 ♋ 31	25 55	27 25
31	23 9		16 17		7 ♐ 54		9 ♓ 31	2 ♉ 6		23 56		9 ♎ 17

THE PLACE OF THE MOON FOR THE YEARS 1856–1857

D M	Jan.	Feb	March	April	May	June	July	August	Sept.	Oct.	Nov.	Dec
	° ′	° ′	° ′	° ′	° ′	° ′	° ′	° ′	° ′	° ′	° ′	° ′
1	21 ♎ 16	6 ♐ 48	28 ♐ 25	19 ♒ 31	28 ♓ 17	21 ♉ 28	28 ♊ 35	16 ♌ 31	1 ♎ 29	3 ♏ 47	19 ♐ 4	24 ♑ 16
2	3 ♏ 29	20 3	12 ♑ 4	4 ♓ 14	13 ♈ 4	5 ♊ 42	11 ♋ 59	28 53	13 17	15 38	1 ♑ 33	7 ♒ 25
3	16 0	3 ♑ 50	26 13	19 14	27 53	19 42	25 8	11 ♍ 3	25 2	27 35	14 15	20 47
4	28 54	18 6	10 ♒ 49	4 ♈ 22	12 ♉ 38	3 ♋ 26	7 ♌ 59	23 1	6 ♏ 50	9 ♐ 42	27 13	4 ♓ 23
5	12 ♐ 13	2 ♒ 47	25 48	19 29	27 11	16 49	20 33	4 ♎ 52	18 43	22 2	10 ♒ 30	18 13
6	25 59	17 46	11 ♓ 0	4 ♉ 27	11 ♊ 26	29 50	2 ♍ 50	16 39	0 ♐ 47	4 ♑ 39	24 7	2 ♈ 17
7	10 ♑ 9	2 ♓ 54	26 16	19 6	25 19	12 ♌ 30	14 54	28 27	13 7	17 37	8 ♓ 6	16 35
8	24 38	18 0	11 ♈ 26	3 ♊ 23	8 ♋ 47	24 52	26 46	10 ♏ 21	25 46	0 ♒ 59	22 27	1 ♉ 6
9	9 ♒ 19	2 ♈ 54	26 19	17 13	21 50	6 ♍ 58	8 ♎ 37	22 26	8 ♑ 49	14 47	7 ♈ 7	15 45
10	24 5	17 30	10 ♉ 51	0 ♋ 36	4 ♌ 30	18 53	20 26	4 ♐ 47	22 20	29 2	22 2	0 ♊ 27
11	8 ♓ 46	1 ♉ 44	24 56	13 34	16 51	0 ♎ 43	2 ♏ 21	17 29	6 ♒ 18	13 ♓ 40	7 ♉ 5	15 5
12	23 17	15 36	8 ♊ 35	26 11	28 57	12 32	14 26	0 ♑ 36	20 43	28 39	22 8	29 31
13	7 ♈ 35	29 5	21 50	8 ♌ 29	10 ♍ 52	24 26	26 48	14 10	5 ♓ 31	13 ♈ 49	7 ♊ 1	13 ♋ 39
14	21 36	12 ♊ 15	4 ♋ 42	20 34	22 41	6 ♏ 30	9 ♐ 30	28 10	20 34	29 3	21 37	27 23
15	5 ♉ 21	25 8	17 16	2 ♍ 29	4 ♎ 30	18 48	22 33	12 ♒ 33	5 ♈ 43	14 ♉ 10	5 ♋ 48	10 ♌ 42
16	18 51	7 ♋ 47	29 35	14 19	16 22	1 ♐ 22	6 ♑ 0	27 14	20 49	29 1	19 32	23 35
17	2 ♊ 8	20 14	11 ♌ 43	26 8	28 21	14 14	19 49	12 ♓ 5	5 ♉ 43	13 ♊ 30	2 ♌ 48	6 ♍ 5
18	15 12	2 ♌ 31	23 42	7 ♎ 57	10 ♏ 31	27 25	3 ♒ 57	26 57	20 19	27 33	15 37	18 17
19	28 6	14 39	5 ♍ 35	19 51	22 53	10 ♑ 54	18 17	11 ♈ 43	4 ♊ 33	11 ♋ 8	28 4	0 ♎ 14
20	10 ♋ 49	26 41	17 26	1 ♏ 51	5 ♐ 29	24 37	2 ♓ 45	26 17	18 24	24 16	10 ♍ 13	12 4
21	23 22	8 ♍ 36	29 15	13 59	18 19	8 ♒ 32	17 13	10 ♉ 36	1 ♋ 51	7 ♌ 1	22 9	23 50
22	5 ♌ 44	20 28	11 ♎ 4	26 19	1 ♑ 24	22 34	1 ♈ 38	24 38	14 56	19 26	3 ♎ 58	5 ♏ 40
23	17 56	2 ♎ 16	22 5	8 ♐ 49	14 42	6 ♓ 41	15 55	8 ♊ 21	27 42	1 ♍ 36	15 44	17 37
24	29 59	14 4	4 ♏ 55	21 33	28 13	20 50	0 ♉ 2	21 48	10 ♌ 12	13 34	27 31	29 45
25	11 ♍ 54	25 56	17 0	4 ♑ 31	11 ♒ 55	4 ♈ 56	14 0	4 ♋ 59	22 28	25 25	9 ♏ 24	12 ♐ 7
26	23 44	7 ♏ 54	29 16	17 46	25 48	19 6	27 47	17 55	4 ♍ 34	7 ♎ 12	21 25	24 44
27	5 ♎ 31	20 3	11 ♐ 46	1 ♒ 17	9 ♓ 51	3 ♉ 11	11 ♊ 24	0 ♌ 37	16 32	18 59	3 ♐ 36	7 ♑ 38
28	17 21	2 ♐ 28	24 33	15 7	24 2	17 12	24 50	13 8	28 24	0 ♏ 48	15 59	20 46
29	29 18	15 14	7 ♑ 42	29 15	8 ♈ 20	1 ♊ 8	8 ♋ 4	25 27	10 ♎ 12	12 41	28 32	4 ♒ 7
30	11 ♏ 27		21 13	13 ♓ 39	22 43	14 57	21 6	7 ♍ 36	21 59	24 40	11 ♑ 18	17 39
31	23 55		5 ♒ 10		7 ♉ 7		3 ♌ 56	19 36		6 ♐ 47		1 ♓ 19

D M	Jan.	Feb.	March	April	May	June	July	August	Sept.	Oct.	Nov.	Dec.
	° ′	° ′	° ′	° ′	° ′	° ′	° ′	° ′	° ′	° ′	° ′	° ′
1	15 ♓ 7	8 ♉ 6	18 ♉ 46	10 ♋ 54	16 ♌ 51	2 ♎ 47	4 ♏ 54	18 ♐ 50	4 ♒ 42	9 ♓ 43	1 ♉ 24	9 ♊ 56
2	29 1	22 10	2 ♊ 58	24 16	29 30	14 41	16 43	1 ♑ 0	18 1	23 54	16 36	25 15
3	13 ♈ 1	6 ♊ 9	16 55	7 ♌ 18	11 ♍ 50	26 30	28 37	13 42	1 ♓ 39	8 ♈ 25	1 ♊ 52	10 ♋ 21
4	27 7	20 1	0 ♋ 38	20 1	23 57	8 ♏ 18	10 ♐ 38	26 31	15 36	23 12	17 0	25 3
5	11 ♉ 17	3 ♋ 45	14 5	2 ♍ 30	5 ♎ 54	20 8	22 50	9 ♒ 37	29 48	8 ♉ 6	1 ♋ 52	9 ♌ 17
6	25 31	17 19	27 17	14 45	17 45	2 ♐ 4	5 ♑ 13	22 58	14 ♈ 10	23 0	16 19	23 0
7	9 ♊ 46	0 ♌ 41	10 ♌ 15	26 51	29 34	14 7	17 49	6 ♓ 33	28 37	7 ♊ 46	0 ♌ 20	6 ♍ 13
8	23 56	13 50	23 0	8 ♎ 50	11 ♏ 23	26 18	0 ♒ 37	20 18	13 ♉ 4	22 17	13 54	19 1
9	7 ♋ 59	26 43	5 ♍ 33	20 43	23 14	8 ♑ 38	13 36	4 ♈ 13	27 28	6 ♋ 30	27 2	1 ♎ 28
10	21 47	9 ♍ 20	17 55	2 ♏ 34	5 ♐ 9	21 9	26 48	18 15	11 ♊ 44	20 23	9 ♍ 49	13 38
11	5 ♌ 19	21 42	0 ♎ 3	14 23	17 9	3 ♒ 50	10 ♓ 10	2 ♉ 21	25 51	3 ♌ 55	22 17	25 38
12	18 30	3 ♎ 51	12 4	26 13	29 18	16 43	23 43	16 31	9 ♋ 45	17 7	4 ♎ 32	7 ♏ 31
13	1 ♍ 19	15 48	23 58	8 ♐ 7	11 ♑ 35	29 50	7 ♈ 28	0 ♊ 43	23 28	0 ♍ 3	16 37	19 21
14	13 49	27 39	5 ♍ 48	20 8	24 4	13 ♓ 12	21 24	14 55	6 ♌ 57	12 44	28 36	1 ♐ 11
15	26 1	9 ♏ 27	17 37	2 ♑ 18	6 ♒ 48	26 50	5 ♉ 32	29 3	20 12	25 12	10 ♏ 30	13 4
16	8 ♎ 0	21 18	29 28	14 43	19 48	10 ♈ 48	19 50	13 ♋ 6	3 ♍ 13	7 ♎ 29	22 22	25 0
17	19 51	3 ♐ 16	11 ♐ 26	27 24	3 ♓ 8	25 4	4 ♊ 17	27 0	16 1	19 38	4 ♐ 13	7 ♑ 1
18	1 ♏ 38	15 27	23 35	10 ♒ 27	16 51	9 ♉ 37	18 48	10 ♌ 41	28 35	1 ♏ 40	16 5	19 8
19	13 29	27 55	6 ♑ 0	23 54	0 ♈ 58	24 24	3 ♋ 17	24 7	10 ♎ 57	13 35	27 59	1 ♒ 22
20	25 27	10 ♑ 44	18 46	7 ♓ 47	15 28	9 ♊ 18	17 38	7 ♍ 16	23 7	25 28	9 ♑ 57	13 44
21	7 ♐ 39	23 57	1 ♒ 55	22 6	0 ♉ 19	24 11	1 ♌ 45	20 7	5 ♏ 8	7 ♐ 18	22 2	26 18
22	20 7	7 ♒ 35	15 30	6 ♈ 49	15 24	8 ♋ 54	15 33	2 ♎ 40	17 2	19 9	4 ♒ 16	9 ♓ 4
23	2 ♑ 55	21 35	29 31	21 51	0 ♊ 35	23 19	28 58	14 58	28 53	1 ♑ 4	16 43	22 8
24	16 3	5 ♓ 54	13 ♓ 57	7 ♉ 4	15 42	7 ♌ 20	12 ♍ 1	27 3	10 ♐ 44	13 6	29 27	5 ♈ 31
25	29 31	20 27	28 43	22 17	0 ♋ 34	20 54	24 41	8 ♏ 59	22 40	25 20	12 ♓ 33	19 18
26	13 ♒ 16	5 ♈ 6	13 ♈ 42	7 ♊ 22	15 4	4 ♍ 1	7 ♎ 3	20 51	4 ♑ 44	7 ♒ 50	26 4	3 ♉ 29
27	27 14	19 46	28 45	22 8	29 6	16 42	19 9	2 ♐ 43	17 2	20 40	10 ♈ 3	18 3
28	11 ♓ 21	4 ♉ 21	13 ♉ 44	6 ♋ 30	12 ♌ 39	29 4	1 ♏ 5	14 39	29 38	3 ♓ 55	24 30	2 ♊ 57
29	25 33		28 32	20 24	25 44	11 ♎ 9	12 57	26 46	12 ♒ 35	17 37	9 ♉ 23	18 4
30	9 ♈ 47		13 ♊ 1	3 ♌ 50	8 ♍ 23	23 4	24 48	9 ♑ 7	25 56	1 ♈ 48	24 35	3 ♋ 13
31	23 58		27 9		20 43		6 ♐ 45	21 44		16 25		18 15

THE PLACE OF THE MOON FOR THE YEARS 1858–1859

D M	Jan.	Feb.	March	April	May	June	July	August	Sept.	Oct.	Nov.	Dec.
	° ′	° ′	° ′	° ′	° ′	° ′	° ′	° ′	° ′	° ′	° ′	° ′
1	2♌59	22♍15	0♎4	15♏50	18♐10	2♒34	6♓12	24♈57	17♊23	26♋45	18♍36	24♎36
2	17 19	5♎14	12 57	27 55	0♑3	14 38	18 47	8♉35	1♋41	10♌48	1♎51	7♏10
3	1♍9	17 51	25 33	9♐53	11 55	26 54	1♈39	22 32	16 6	24 46	14 55	19 34
4	14 31	0♏9	7♏53	21 46	23 50	9♓25	14 53	6♊49	0♌32	8♍35	27 48	1♐50
5	27 26	12 14	20 0	3♑39	5♒54	22 16	28 31	21 24	14 57	22 15	10♏30	13 58
6	9♎57	24 9	1♐58	15 36	18 10	5♈33	12♉35	6♋10	29 14	5♎42	23 0	25 58
7	22 11	6♐1	13 51	27 41	0♓43	19 17	27 6	21 3	13♍19	18 56	5♐19	7♑53
8	4♏11	17 54	25 45	10♒0	13 38	3♉31	11♊58	5♌54	27 8	1♏55	17 27	19 42
9	16 4	29 51	7♑43	22 37	27 0	18 13	27 5	20 35	10♎39	14 38	29 26	1♒30
10	27 54	11♑57	19 50	5♓35	10♈50	3♊16	12♋18	4♍59	23 49	27 5	11♑18	13 19
11	9♐45	24 14	2♒10	18 58	25 8	18 33	27 25	19 1	6♏38	9♐19	23 6	25 13
12	21 40	6♒45	14 47	2♈46	9♉51	3♋51	12♌18	2♎38	19 9	21 21	4♒56	7♓16
13	3♑42	19 29	27 42	16 57	24 52	19 1	26 48	15 51	1♐25	3♑15	16 51	19 35
14	15 52	2♓28	10♓57	1♉27	10♊2	3♌51	10♍52	28 41	13 28	15 6	28 58	2♈15
15	28 11	15 41	24 32	16 10	25 10	18 16	24 28	11♏11	25 23	26 59	11♓22	15 20
16	10♒40	29 6	8♈23	0♊59	10♋7	2♍13	7♎37	23 24	7♑16	8♒57	24 7	28 54
17	23 19	12♈43	22 29	15 45	24 44	15 42	20 23	5♐27	19 10	21 8	7♈18	12♉59
18	6♓8	26 30	6♉44	0♋21	8♌57	28 46	2♏49	17 22	1♒10	3♓34	20 58	27 32
19	19 9	10♉36	21 5	14 43	22 46	11♎29	15 1	29 14	13 20	16 21	5♉6	12♊30
20	2♈23	24 30	5♊26	28 47	6♍10	23 54	27 2	11♑8	25 44	29 31	19 38	27 43
21	15 51	8♊41	19 44	12♌33	19 14	6♏7	8♐57	23 6	8♓24	13♈4	4♊29	13♋1
22	29 36	22 56	3♋57	26 1	1♎59	18 10	20 49	5♒12	21 22	27 0	19 30	28 12
23	13♉36	7♋12	18 0	9♍12	14 30	0♐8	2♑42	17 28	4♈37	11♉14	4♋30	13♌8
24	27 53	21 27	1♌54	22 10	26 50	12 2	14 37	29 55	18 9	25 42	19 21	27 40
25	12♊24	5♌36	15 37	4♎55	9♏1	23 54	26 36	12♓35	1♉56	10♊16	3♌56	11♍47
26	27 4	19 35	29 9	17 28	21 5	5♑47	8♒42	25 28	15 54	24 50	18 10	25 27
27	11♋48	3♍22	12♍28	29 52	3♐4	17 41	20 55	8♈34	0♊1	9♋17	2♍4	8♎43
28	26 28	16 51	25 34	12♏7	14 59	29 39	3♓18	21 54	14 12	23 35	15 37	21 38
29	10♌55		8♎27	24 15	26 52	11♒42	15 51	5♉28	28 24	7♌40	28 51	4♏16
30	25 5		21 7	6♐15	8♑44	23 52	28 37	19 14	12♋36	21 31	11♎50	16 39
31	8♍52		3♏34		20 37		11♈39	2♊13		5♍10		28 52

D M	Jan.	Feb.	March	April	May	June	July	August	Sept.	Oct.	Nov.	Dec.
	° ′	° ′	° ′	° ′	° ′	° ′	° ′	° ′	° ′	° ′	° ′	° ′
1	10♐56	25♑24	3♒53	18♓29	22♈35	13♊10	21♋36	15♍11	6♏17	10♐53	25♑45	27♒12
2	22 54	7♒15	15 47	1♈8	6♉9	27 51	6♌39	29 43	19 40	23 30	7♒37	9♓0
3	4♑47	19 10	27 50	14 4	20 2	12♋37	21 33	13♎50	2♐37	5♑47	19 25	20 55
4	16 38	1♓10	10♓2	27 17	4♊9	27 21	6♍10	27 31	15 11	17 50	1♓14	3♈2
5	28 27	13 19	22 26	10♉46	18 27	11♌55	20 28	10♏48	27 27	29 42	13 9	15 25
6	10♒17	25 37	5♈2	24 26	2♋48	26 15	4♎23	23 41	9♑30	11♒30	25 16	28 9
7	22 9	8♈7	17 51	8♊17	17 9	10♍20	17 58	6♐16	21 23	23 18	7♈37	11♉15
8	4♓7	20 52	0♉54	22 16	1♌25	24 10	1♏12	18 34	3♒11	5♓11	20 16	24 46
9	16 13	3♉54	14 11	6♋20	15 35	7♎44	14 8	0♑40	14 59	17 13	3♉14	8♊38
10	28 33	17 15	27 42	20 27	29 36	21 4	26 48	12 38	26 49	29 27	16 31	22 48
11	11♈10	0♊58	11♊26	4♌36	13♍29	4♏11	9♐15	24 29	8♓44	11♈54	0♊4	7♋11
12	24 10	15 4	25 24	18 45	27 14	17 5	21 30	6♒18	20 47	24 35	13 50	21 40
13	7♉34	29 29	9♋35	2♍54	10♎49	29 47	3♑36	18 6	2♈59	7♉30	27 45	6♌10
14	21 27	14♋13	23 56	16 59	24 15	12♐17	15 35	29 55	15 22	20 38	11♋47	20 36
15	5♊47	29 9	8♌26	0♎59	7♏30	24 36	27 28	11♓49	27 57	3♊59	25 52	4♍54
16	20 33	14♌9	22 59	14 49	20 32	6♑45	9♒16	23 49	10♉44	17 30	9♌57	19 3
17	5♋39	29 6	7♍32	28 27	3♐20	18 45	21 4	5♈58	23 46	1♋11	24 3	3♎0
18	20 55	13♍51	21 58	11♏49	15 54	0♒37	2♓52	18 19	7♊2	15 1	8♍7	16 46
19	6♌10	28 17	6♎12	24 54	28 14	12 25	14 45	0♉53	20 34	29 0	22 10	0♏21
20	21 16	12♎19	20 9	7♐40	10♑21	24 13	26 47	13 45	4♋22	13♌7	6♎9	13 44
21	6♍2	25 55	3♏44	20 7	22 18	6♓3	9♈0	26 57	18 28	27 23	20 4	26 55
22	20 24	9♏5	16 56	2♑20	4♒9	18 2	21 30	10♊30	2♌50	11♍44	3♏52	9♐53
23	4♎18	21 51	29 47	14 19	15 57	0♈14	4♉20	24 28	17 26	26 7	17 28	22 38
24	17 45	4♐7	12♐16	26 11	27 48	12 44	17 35	8♋48	2♍11	10♎29	0♐51	5♑10
25	0♏46	16 27	24 29	8♒0	9♓47	25 37	1♊16	23 29	17 0	24 43	13 57	17 29
26	13 25	28 24	6♑28	19 52	21 59	8♉56	15 25	8♌25	1♎45	8♏44	26 46	29 36
27	25 47	10♑15	18 20	1♓51	4♈31	22 44	29 58	23 30	16 19	22 27	9♑17	11♒33
28	7♐55	22 3	0♒9	14 3	17 25	6♊58	14♋53	8♍35	0♏35	5♐49	21 31	23 23
29	19 53		11 59	26 33	0♉45	21 37	0♌1	23 32	14 27	18 48	3♒32	5♓10
30	1♑45		23 57	9♈23	14 31	6♋32	15 12	8♎11	27 53	1♑24	15 24	16 58
31	13 35		6♓6		28 41		0♍19	22 27		13 42		28 51

THE PLACE OF THE MOON FOR THE YEARS 1860–1861

D M	Jan.	Feb.	March	April	May	June	July	August	Sept.	Oct.	Nov.	Dec.
	° ′	° ′	° ′	° ′	° ′	° ′	° ′	° ′	° ′	° ′	° ′	° ′
1	10 ♈ 55	27 ♉ 11	19 ♊ 25	10 ♌ 46	19 ♍ 44	12 ♏ 54	19 ♐ 44	6 ♒ 47	21 ♓ 29	24 ♈ 11	10 ♊ 13	15 ♋ 45
2	23 16	10 ♊ 34	3 ♋ 2	25 7	4 ♎ 20	26 51	2 ♑ 46	18 54	3 ♈ 20	6 ♉ 14	22 53	29 8
3	5 ♉ 56	24 24	17 5	10 ♍ 5	18 59	10 ♐ 34	15 33	0 ♓ 54	15 12	18 22	5 ♋ 45	12 ♌ 42
4	19 1	8 ♋ 41	1 ♌ 33	25 4	3 ♏ 33	23 59	28 6	12 49	27 8	0 ♊ 39	18 49	26 27
5	2 ♊ 33	23 23	16 24	10 ♎ 6	17 56	7 ♑ 4	10 ♒ 24	24 40	9 ♉ 10	13 7	2 ♌ 9	10 ♍ 23
6	16 31	8 ♌ 23	1 ♍ 30	25 1	2 ♐ 0	19 50	22 31	6 ♈ 30	21 21	25 49	15 47	24 30
7	0 ♋ 52	23 34	16 45	9 ♏ 39	15 43	2 ♒ 18	4 ♓ 29	18 24	3 ♊ 46	8 ♋ 48	29 44	8 ♎ 47
8	15 33	8 ♍ 47	1 ♎ 57	23 55	29 0	14 29	16 21	0 ♉ 24	16 27	22 7	14 ♍ 0	23 11
9	0 ♌ 26	23 51	16 57	7 ♐ 44	11 ♑ 54	26 30	28 12	12 35	29 29	5 ♌ 50	28 35	7 ♏ 37
10	15 23	8 ♎ 38	1 ♏ 36	21 3	24 25	8 ♓ 22	10 ♈ 6	25 2	12 ♋ 56	19 58	13 ♎ 23	22 1
11	0 ♍ 16	23 3	15 48	3 ♑ 56	6 ♒ 37	20 13	22 7	7 ♊ 48	26 50	4 ♍ 31	28 17	6 ♐ 18
12	14 57	7 ♏ 2	29 31	16 25	18 37	2 ♈ 6	4 ♉ 20	20 57	11 ♌ 11	19 26	13 ♏ 10	20 20
13	29 23	20 34	12 ♐ 45	28 36	0 ♓ 29	14 7	16 49	4 ♋ 31	25 57	4 ♎ 35	27 51	4 ♑ 5
14	13 ♎ 30	3 ♐ 42	25 33	10 ♒ 33	12 18	26 21	29 39	18 32	11 ♍ 3	19 49	12 ♐ 13	17 28
15	27 17	16 27	7 ♑ 59	22 23	24 9	8 ♉ 49	12 ♊ 50	2 ♌ 58	26 20	4 ♏ 57	26 11	0 ♒ 30
16	10 ♏ 44	28 55	20 7	4 ♓ 10	6 ♈ 8	21 37	26 26	17 45	11 ♎ 36	19 49	9 ♑ 42	13 11
17	23 53	11 ♑ 7	2 ♒ 4	15 58	18 17	4 ♊ 44	10 ♋ 24	2 ♍ 46	26 42	4 ♐ 16	22 47	25 34
18	6 ♐ 46	23 9	13 54	27 53	0 ♉ 41	18 10	24 41	17 52	11 ♏ 27	18 14	5 ♒ 27	7 ♓ 42
19	19 24	5 ♒ 4	25 40	9 ♈ 56	13 19	1 ♋ 53	9 ♌ 14	2 ♎ 54	25 46	1 ♑ 42	17 47	19 40
20	1 ♑ 49	16 54	7 ♓ 27	22 9	26 13	15 51	23 56	17 44	9 ♐ 37	14 42	29 53	1 ♈ 33
21	14 3	28 42	19 17	4 ♉ 35	9 ♊ 22	0 ♌ 0	8 ♍ 40	2 ♏ 15	22 58	27 18	11 ♓ 48	13 25
22	26 9	10 ♓ 30	1 ♈ 13	17 12	22 44	14 16	23 19	16 22	5 ♑ 54	9 ♒ 35	23 39	25 21
23	8 ♒ 6	22 20	13 16	0 ♊ 0	6 ♋ 18	28 34	7 ♎ 49	0 ♐ 5	18 28	21 38	5 ♈ 30	7 ♉ 26
24	19 58	4 ♈ 14	25 27	13 1	20 1	12 ♍ 52	22 6	13 25	0 ♒ 46	3 ♓ 32	17 26	19 44
25	1 ♓ 46	16 14	7 ♉ 48	26 12	3 ♌ 53	27 7	6 ♏ 6	26 23	12 50	15 22	29 29	2 ♊ 16
26	13 33	28 23	20 19	9 ♋ 35	17 51	11 ♎ 17	19 49	9 ♑ 3	24 47	27 12	11 ♉ 42	15 6
27	25 22	10 ♉ 43	3 ♊ 2	23 11	1 ♍ 55	25 20	3 ♐ 16	21 28	6 ♓ 39	9 ♈ 5	24 7	28 12
28	7 ♈ 17	23 18	15 59	6 ♌ 59	16 5	9 ♏ 13	16 26	3 ♒ 41	18 30	21 3	6 ♊ 44	11 ♋ 35
29	19 21	6 ♊ 11	29 12	21 1	0 ♎ 18	22 56	29 20	15 46	0 ♈ 21	3 ♉ 8	19 32	25 13
30	1 ♉ 38		12 ♋ 43	5 ♍ 17	14 33	6 ♐ 27	12 ♑ 1	27 44	12 14	15 21	2 ♋ 33	9 ♌ 3
31	14 13		26 34		28 46		24 29	9 ♓ 38		27 43		23 3

D M	Jan.	Feb.	March	April	May	June	July	August	Sept.	Oct.	Nov.	Dec.
	° ′	° ′	° ′	° ′	° ′	° ′	° ′	° ′	° ′	° ′	° ′	° ′
1	7 ♍ 10	0 ♏ 40	10 ♏ 53	2 ♑ 21	7 ♒ 24	22 ♓ 47	24 ♈ 45	8 ♊ 39	24 ♋ 31	29 ♌ 54	22 ♎ 22	0 ♐ 57
2	21 21	14 47	25 11	15 33	19 56	4 ♈ 43	6 ♉ 39	20 59	7 ♌ 58	14 ♍ 19	7 ♏ 39	16 2
3	5 ♎ 33	28 39	9 ♐ 6	28 27	2 ♓ 11	16 35	18 36	3 ♋ 35	21 51	29 8	22 58	0 ♑ 55
4	19 44	12 ♐ 16	22 39	10 ♒ 52	14 14	28 27	0 ♊ 41	16 32	6 ♍ 8	14 ♎ 14	8 ♐ 6	15 26
5	3 ♏ 52	25 38	5 ♑ 49	23 8	26 10	10 ♉ 22	12 57	29 49	20 44	29 26	22 54	29 32
6	17 55	8 ♑ 46	18 41	5 ♓ 15	8 ♈ 2	22 23	25 26	13 ♌ 27	5 ♎ 32	14 ♏ 33	7 ♑ 17	13 ♒ 11
7	1 ♐ 50	21 41	1 ♒ 19	17 14	19 53	4 ♊ 31	8 ♋ 10	27 24	20 23	29 27	21 12	26 23
8	15 36	4 ♒ 25	13 45	29 9	1 ♉ 46	16 50	21 10	11 ♍ 35	5 ♏ 9	14 ♐ 0	4 ♒ 41	9 ♓ 11
9	29 10	16 57	26 1	11 ♈ 1	13 41	29 18	4 ♌ 26	25 55	19 43	28 9	17 44	21 39
10	12 ♑ 31	29 19	8 ♓ 9	22 53	25 42	11 ♋ 59	17 56	10 ♎ 21	4 ♐ 1	11 ♑ 54	0 ♓ 27	3 ♈ 51
11	25 36	11 ♓ 31	20 11	4 ♉ 46	7 ♊ 49	24 51	1 ♍ 39	24 45	18 1	25 15	12 52	15 52
12	8 ♒ 26	23 34	2 ♈ 9	16 41	20 3	7 ♌ 57	15 34	9 ♏ 4	1 ♑ 43	8 ♒ 16	25 5	27 46
13	21 0	5 ♈ 31	14 2	28 39	2 ♋ 26	21 17	29 37	23 15	15 7	21 0	7 ♈ 8	9 ♉ 36
14	3 ♓ 20	17 23	25 54	10 ♊ 43	15 1	4 ♍ 52	13 ♎ 46	7 ♐ 17	28 17	3 ♓ 31	19 5	21 26
15	15 28	29 15	7 ♉ 46	22 56	27 50	18 43	28 0	21 7	11 ♒ 13	15 51	0 ♉ 58	3 ♊ 20
16	27 27	11 ♉ 8	19 40	5 ♋ 21	10 ♌ 57	2 ♎ 48	12 ♏ 15	4 ♑ 47	23 57	28 2	12 49	15 18
17	9 ♈ 20	23 9	1 ♊ 40	18 3	24 23	17 6	26 30	18 15	6 ♓ 31	10 ♈ 6	24 40	27 24
18	21 12	5 ♊ 21	13 49	1 ♌ 5	8 ♍ 10	1 ♏ 36	10 ♐ 40	1 ♒ 31	18 55	22 4	6 ♊ 33	9 ♋ 39
19	3 ♉ 7	17 50	26 13	14 33	22 21	16 12	24 44	14 36	1 ♈ 10	3 ♉ 59	18 29	22 3
20	15 11	0 ♋ 39	8 ♋ 57	28 27	6 ♎ 53	0 ♐ 48	8 ♑ 37	27 28	13 17	15 50	0 ♋ 31	4 ♌ 40
21	27 27	13 53	22 4	12 ♍ 50	21 43	15 20	22 19	10 ♓ 7	25 16	27 40	12 41	17 29
22	10 ♊ 0	27 35	5 ♌ 39	27 38	6 ♏ 43	29 39	5 ♒ 44	22 34	7 ♉ 9	9 ♊ 31	25 1	0 ♍ 33
23	22 54	11 ♌ 43	19 43	12 ♎ 45	21 45	13 ♑ 43	18 54	4 ♈ 48	18 59	21 25	7 ♌ 36	13 52
24	6 ♋ 9	26 17	4 ♍ 16	28 3	6 ♐ 39	27 26	1 ♓ 46	16 53	0 ♊ 49	3 ♋ 28	20 29	27 29
25	19 48	11 ♍ 9	19 14	13 ♏ 20	21 18	10 ♒ 47	14 22	28 49	12 42	15 42	3 ♍ 43	11 ♎ 23
26	3 ♌ 47	26 13	4 ♎ 29	28 25	5 ♑ 34	23 46	26 42	10 ♉ 41	24 44	28 13	17 21	25 34
27	18 5	11 ♒ 17	19 49	13 ♐ 9	19 24	6 ♓ 25	8 ♈ 49	22 33	7 ♋ 0	11 ♌ 6	1 ♎ 25	10 ♏ 1
28	2 ♍ 35	26 13	5 ♏ 4	27 25	2 ♒ 48	18 46	20 48	4 ♊ 28	19 34	24 25	15 53	24 39
29	17 12		20 2	11 ♑ 12	15 47	0 ♈ 54	2 ♉ 42	16 33	2 ♌ 33	8 ♍ 13	0 ♏ 43	9 ♐ 25
30	1 ♎ 49		4 ♐ 37	24 31	28 23	12 52	14 35	28 52	15 59	22 31	15 47	24 10
31	16 20		18 43		10 ♓ 41		26 32	11 ♋ 30		7 ♎ 16		8 ♑ 48

THE PLACE OF THE MOON FOR THE YEARS 1862–1863

D M	Jan.	Feb.	March	April	May	June	July	August	Sept.	Oct.	Nov.	Dec.
	° ′	° ′	° ′	° ′	° ′	° ′	° ′	° ′	° ′	° ′	° ′	° ′
1	23♑12	12♓ 4	20♓15	5♉57	8♊17	22♋49	27♌ 4	16♎57	9♐41	18♑48	10♓13	15♈47
2	7♒18	24 58	2♈59	17 54	20 4	4♌59	9♍55	0♏43	23 49	2♒41	23 18	28 10
3	21 0	7♈33	15 28	29 45	1♋52	17 24	23 2	14 41	7♑58	16 26	6♈ 9	10♉21
4	4♓19	19 51	27 42	11♊32	13 47	0♍ 5	6♎27	28 50	22 7	0♓ 1	18 47	22 23
5	17 13	1♉55	9♉45	23 20	25 52	13 7	20 11	13♐10	6♒13	13 26	1♉13	4♊18
6	29 47	13 49	21 38	5♋14	8♌12	26 33	4♏15	27 38	20 13	26 39	13 29	16 8
7	12♈ 2	25 39	3♊27	17 19	20 52	10♎24	18 38	12♑ 9	4♓ 3	9♈38	25 34	27 57
8	24 4	7♊29	15 16	29 40	3♍56	24 40	3♐17	26 41	17 39	22 23	7♊30	9♋44
9	5♉58	19 25	27 11	12♌22	17 28	9♏19	18 7	11♒ 6	0♈59	4♉53	19 21	21 34
10	17 48	1♋33	9♋18	25 31	1♎28	24 17	3♑ 2	25 18	14 0	17 9	1♋ 8	3♌29
11	29 38	13 55	21 41	9♍ 7	15 56	9♐25	17 55	9♓13	26 41	29 12	12 55	15 31
12	11♊34	26 35	4♌25	23 12	0♏47	24 35	2♒37	22 46	9♉ 5	11♊ 6	24 46	27 45
13	23 38	9♌35	17 34	7♎43	15 54	9♑37	17 2	5♈56	21 13	22 54	6♌45	10♍14
14	5♋54	22 56	1♍ 8	22 33	1♐ 7	24 24	1♓ 5	18 44	3♊ 9	4♋41	18 58	23 2
15	18 24	6♍35	15 7	7♏34	16 17	8♒48	14 42	1♉10	14 59	16 32	1♍29	6♎12
16	1♌ 7	20 30	29 25	22 36	1♑14	22 47	27 53	13 19	26 47	28 33	14 23	19 48
17	14 6	4♎36	13♎59	7♐31	15 52	6♓19	10♈39	25 16	8♋39	10♌49	27 43	3♏51
18	27 19	18 48	28 39	22 12	0♒ 6	19 26	23 5	7♊ 6	20 41	23 24	11♎30	18 20
19	10♍45	3♏ 2	13♏18	6♑33	13 55	2♈ 9	5♉14	18 54	2♌57	6♍22	25 45	3♐11
20	24 24	17 15	27 51	20 34	27 19	14 33	17 10	0♋46	15 31	19 46	10♏23	18 18
21	8♎12	1♐24	12♐12	4♒13	10♓20	26 42	29 0	12 46	28 27	3♎36	25 19	3♑33
22	22 9	15 28	26 19	17 33	23 2	8♉40	10♊47	24 58	11♍44	17 49	10♐24	18 44
23	6♏14	29 26	10♑12	0♓36	5♈28	20 30	22 37	7♌25	25 23	2♏20	25 30	3♒44
24	20 25	13♑17	23 51	13 24	17 41	2♊18	4♋32	20 9	9♎19	17 2	10♑28	18 24
25	4♐40	27 1	7♒17	25 58	29 44	14 5	16 36	3♍10	23 29	1♐49	25 9	2♓37
26	18 57	10♒37	20 31	8♈22	11♉39	25 56	28 51	16 27	7♏46	16 32	9♒31	16 23
27	3♑13	24 2	3♓33	20 35	23 30	7♋51	11♌19	29 59	22 6	1♑ 6	23 29	29 42
28	17 24	7♓15	16 25	2♉40	5♊18	19 54	24 0	13♎42	6♐25	15 26	7♓ 4	12♈35
29	1♒27		29 5	14 37	17 5	2♌ 6	6♍54	27 35	20 40	29 32	20 17	25 7
30	15 17		11♈33	26 29	28 55	14 29	20 2	11♏33	4♑48	13♒21	3♈11	7♉22
31	28 50		23 50		10♋48		3♎23	25 36		26 55		19 24

D M	Jan	Feb.	March	April	May	June	July	August	Sept.	Oct.	Nov.	Dec.
	° ′	° ′	° ′	° ′	° ′	° ′	° ′	° ′	° ′	° ′	° ′	° ′
1	1♊17	15♋17	23♋32	8♍34	13♎ 1	3♐49	12♑13	6♓ 3	26♈47	0♊46	15♋13	16♌53
2	13 6	27 15	5♌35	21 32	26 49	18 41	27 27	20 39	10♉ 2	13 14	27 7	28 46
3	24 53	9♌21	17 51	4♎48	10♏57	3♑40	12♒34	4♈49	22 50	25 25	8♌59	10♍46
4	6♋42	21 38	0♍20	18 22	25 19	18 39	27 25	18 28	5♊16	7♋25	20 53	22 57
5	18 33	4♍ 5	13 5	2♏10	9♐52	3♒28	11♓53	1♉39	17 25	19 17	2♍55	5♎23
6	0♌30	16 44	26 4	16 9	24 28	18 2	25 54	14 24	29 22	1♌ 8	15 9	18 10
7	12 33	29 33	9♎15	0♐15	9♑ 2	2♓17	9♈27	26 48	11♋13	13 2	27 38	1♏19
8	24 45	12♎35	22 39	14 25	23 30	16 9	22 34	8♊56	23 2	25 4	10♎26	14 54
9	7♍ 7	25 49	6♏12	28 36	7♒47	29 40	5♉19	20 52	4♌54	7♍16	23 34	28 53
10	19 42	9♏16	19 53	12♑46	21 52	12♈50	17 45	2♋43	16 52	19 42	7♏ 1	13♐15
11	2♎31	22 58	3♐43	26 55	5♓43	25 41	29 56	14 31	28 58	2♎22	20 47	27 54
12	15 38	6♐56	17 41	11♒ 0	19 19	8♉16	11♊57	26 21	11♍14	15 17	4♐49	12♑44
13	29 4	21 10	1♑46	24 59	2♈41	20 38	23 51	8♌14	23 41	28 27	19 2	27 36
14	12♏52	5♑38	15 58	8♓52	15 47	2♊49	5♋42	20 12	6♎19	11♏51	3♑23	12♒23
15	27 3	20 18	0♒15	22 35	28 40	14 51	17 31	2♍18	19 8	25 25	17 46	26 58
16	11♐36	5♒ 3	14 34	6♈ 5	11♉20	26 48	29 20	14 31	2♏ 8	9♐10	2♒ 8	11♓16
17	26 26	19 48	28 52	19 22	23 46	8♋39	11♌13	26 53	15 20	23 4	16 24	25 15
18	11♑30	4♓23	13♓ 3	2♉23	6♊ 1	20 29	23 10	9♎25	28 43	7♑ 4	0♓33	8♈53
19	26 37	18 42	27 0	15 7	18 6	2♌18	5♍13	22 8	12♐20	21 11	14 32	22 13
20	11♒39	2♈38	10♈41	27 35	0♋ 3	14 10	17 24	5♏ 6	26 10	5♒22	28 21	5♉17
21	26 25	16 7	24 1	9♊49	11 55	26 8	29 46	18 19	10♑15	19 35	11♈57	18 5
22	10♓49	29 11	6♉59	21 51	23 44	8♍14	12♎22	1♐51	24 34	3♓49	25 21	0♊41
23	24 46	11♉50	19 36	3♋46	5♌34	20 33	25 15	15 44	9♒ 4	17 59	8♉31	13 6
24	8♈13	24 8	1♊55	15 34	17 30	3♎ 9	8♏29	29 58	23 41	2♈ 2	21 29	25 22
25	21 12	6♊10	13 59	27 25	29 36	16 5	22 6	14♑33	8♓19	15 54	4♊13	7♋29
26	3♉47	18 2	25 53	9♌21	11♍57	29 25	6♐ 9	29 24	22 51	29 31	16 43	19 31
27	16 2	29 50	7♋42	21 28	24 36	13♏11	20 37	14♒25	7♈ 9	12♉52	29 2	1♌27
28	28 2	11♋38	19 32	3♍50	7♎37	27 24	5♑28	29 27	21 9	25 53	11♋ 9	13 19
29	9♊53		1♌28	16 32	21 3	12♐ 3	20 36	14♓20	4♉45	8♊36	23 8	25 10
30	21 40		13 34	29 35	4 55	27 1	5♒51	28 55	17 57	21 2	5♌ 2	7♍ 3
31	3♋27		25 56		19 11		21 3	13♈ 5		3♋13		19 1

THE PLACE OF THE MOON FOR THE YEARS 1864–1865

D M	Jan.	Feb.	March	April	May	June	July	August	Sept.	Oct.	Nov.	Dec
	° ′	° ′	° ′	° ′	° ′	° ′	° ′	° ′	° ′	° ′	° ′	° ′
1	1 ♎ 8	17 ♏ 48	10 ♐ 35	2 ♒ 41	12 ♓ 6	4 ♉ 28	10 ♊ 36	27 ♋ 9	11 ♍ 54	14 ♎ 39	0 ♐ 56	6 ♑ 58
2	13 29	1 ♐ 8	24 13	17 10	26 25	17 56	23 18	9 ♌ 11	23 46	26 45	13 53	20 47
3	26 9	14 55	8 ♑ 16	1 ♓ 51	10 ♈ 41	1 ♊ 11	5 ♋ 49	21 8	5 ♎ 39	9 ♏ 0	27 3	4 ♒ 46
4	9 ♏ 12	29 11	22 44	16 37	24 48	14 13	18 10	3 ♍ 1	17 35	21 24	10 ♑ 27	18 50
5	22 41	13 ♑ 55	7 ♒ 33	1 ♈ 21	8 ♉ 42	27 1	0 ♌ 22	14 52	29 39	4 ♐ 1	24 5	2 ♓ 58
6	6 ♐ 39	29 1	22 37	15 55	22 21	9 ♋ 35	12 25	26 42	11 ♏ 52	16 53	7 ♒ 56	17 7
7	21 5	14 ♒ 21	7 ♓ 48	0 ♉ 13	5 ♊ 42	21 56	24 22	8 ♎ 35	24 19	0 ♑ 3	21 59	1 ♈ 16
8	5 ♑ 56	29 42	22 54	14 10	18 44	4 ♌ 5	6 ♍ 14	20 34	7 ♐ 4	13 32	6 ♓ 15	15 22
9	21 4	14 ♓ 53	7 ♈ 46	27 42	1 ♋ 27	16 5	18 5	2 ♏ 43	20 10	27 23	20 39	29 25
10	6 ♒ 19	29 44	22 15	10 ♊ 50	13 54	28 0	29 58	15 9	3 ♑ 42	11 ♒ 36	5 ♈ 8	13 ♉ 22
11	21 30	14 ♈ 9	6 ♉ 16	23 36	26 6	9 ♍ 52	11 ♎ 58	27 54	17 42	26 8	19 39	27 11
12	6 ♓ 28	28 3	19 49	6 ♋ 2	8 ♌ 7	21 47	24 9	11 ♐ 5	2 ♒ 9	10 ♓ 56	4 ♉ 5	10 ♊ 50
13	21 4	11 ♉ 28	2 ♊ 54	18 13	20 3	3 ♎ 49	6 ♏ 37	24 44	17 0	25 53	18 . 22	24 16
14	5 ♈ 14	24 26	15 35	0 ♌ 12	1 ♍ 56	16 3	19 27	8 ♑ 54	2 ♓ 9	10 ♈ 51	2 ♊ 24	7 ♋ 27
15	18 57	7 ♊ 1	27 57	12 6	13 52	28 34	2 ♐ 42	23 32	17 25	25 41	16 8	20 21
16	2 ♉ 14	19 19	10 ♋ 4	23 59	25 55	11 ♏ 25	16 25	8 ♒ 33	2 ♈ 38	10 ♉ 16	29 30	2 ♌ 59
17	15 9	1 ♋ 25	22 1	5 ♍ 54	8 ♎ 9	24 39	0 ♑ 37	23 48	17 37	24 30	12 ♋ 31	15 20
18	27 45	13 22	3 ♌ 53	17 55	20 38	8 ♐ 18	15 13	9 ♓ 7	2 ♉ 16	8 ♊ 19	25 11	27 28
19	10 ♊ 7	25 15	15 44	0 ♎ 6	3 ♏ 25	22 19	0 ♒ 9	24 18	16 28	21 42	7 ♌ 33	9 ♍ 25
20	22 19	7 ♌ 7	27 38	12 29	16 30	6 ♑ 41	15 15	9 ♈ 12	0 ♊ 12	4 ♋ 41	19 40	21 16
21	4 ♋ 22	18 59	9 ♍ 36	25 4	29 54	21 17	0 ♓ 20	23 42	13 29	17 18	1 ♍ 37	3 ♎ 5
22	16 21	0 ♍ 53	21 40	7 ♏ 53	13 ♐ 35	6 ♒ 0	15 16	7 ♉ 44	26 21	29 36	13 29	14 59
23	28 16	12 51	3 ♎ 53	20 56	27 32	20 43	29 55	21 19	8 ♋ 53	11 ♌ 41	25 20	27 3
24	10 ♌ 9	24 54	16 14	4 ♐ 13	11 ♑ 40	5 ♓ 18	14 ♈ 12	4 ♊ 29	21 9	23 57	7 ♎ 15	9 ♏ 21
25	22 1	7 ♎ 3	28 46	17 43	25 56	19 42	28 5	17 18	3 ♌ 13	5 ♍ 29	19 19	21 -57
26	3 ♍ 54	19 19	11 ♏ 28	1 ♑ 24	10 ♒ 15	3 ♈ 50	11 ♉ 36	29 49	15 9	17 19	1 ♏ 34	4 ♐ 56
27	15 50	1 ♏ 45	24 22	15 17	24 34	17 41	24 46	12 ♋ 7	27 2	29 13	14 5	18 18
28	27 50	14 25	7 ♐ 29	29 19	8 ♓ 49	1 ♉ 16	7 ♊ 39	24 15	8 ♍ 52	11 ♎ 14	26 53	2 ♑ 2
29	9 ♎ 59	27 20	20 51	13 ♒ 29	22 57	14 36	20 17	6 ♌ 15	20 44	23 22	9 ♐ 59	16 6
30	22 18		4 ♑ 30	27 46	6 ♈ 58	27 42	2 ♋ 43	18 11	2 ♎ 39	5 ♏ 42	23 21	0 ♒ 25
31	4 ♏ 53		18 27		20 48		15 0	0 ♍ 3		18 13		14 53

D M	Jan.	Feb.	March	April	May	June	July	August	Sept.	Oct.	Nov.	Dec.
	° ′	° ′	° ′	° ′	° ′	° ′	° ′	° ′	° ′	° ′	° ′	° ′
1	29 ♒ 22	22 ♈ 44	2 ♉ 14	22 ♊ 57	27 ♋ 35	12 ♍ 37	14 ♎ 15	28 ♏ 7	14 ♑ 39	20 ♒ 37	13 ♈ 7	21 ♉ 35
2	13 ♓ 48	6 ♉ 45	16 30	6 ♋ 9	10 ♌ 8	24 30	26 6	10 ♐ 34	28 20	5 ♓ 5	28 15	6 ♊ 30
3	28 6	20 27	0 ♊ 21	18 59	22 23	6 ♎ 19	8 ♏ 3	23 22	12 ♒ 27	19 56	13 ♉ 27	21 16
4	12 ♈ 13	3 ♊ 51	13 49	1 ♌ 29	4 ♍ 25	18 9	20 11	6 ♑ 35	26 59	5 ♈ 2	28 32	5 ♋ 45
5	26 9	16 59	26 55	13 43	16 18	0 ♏ 4	2 ♐ 36	20 13	11 ♓ 48	20 15	13 ♊ 22	19 50
6	9 ♉ 54	29 54	9 ♋ 42	25 46	28 7	12 8	15 19	4 ♒ 15	26 48	5 ♉ 25	27 50	3 ♌ 29
7	23 28	12 ♋ 37	22 14	7 ♍ 42	9 ♎ 55	24 25	28 23	18 35	11 ♈ 48	20 22	11 ♋ 50	16 41
8	6 ♊ 52	25 10	4 ♌ 34	19 32	21 47	6 ♐ 57	11 ♑ 48	3 ♓ 8	26 41	5 ♊ 1	25 23	29 26
9	20 5	7 ♌ 33	16 43	1 ♎ 21	3 ♏ 45	19 45	25 31	17 47	11 ♉ 21	19 16	8 ♌ 28	11 ♍ 49
10	3 ♋ 8	19 46	28 45	13 10	15 52	2 ♑ 49	9 ♒ 29	2 ♈ 25	25 42	3 ♋ 5	21 8	23 55
11	16 0	1 ♍ 51	10 ♍ 41	25 2	28 9	16 8	23 37	16 57	9 ♊ 43	16 28	3 ♍ 29	5 ♎ 49
12	28 40	13 49	22 33	6 ♏ 59	10 ♐ 39	29 40	7 ♓ 51	1 ♉ 17	23 23	29 29	15 34	17 37
13	11 ♌ 7	25 41	4 ♎ 22	19 3	23 21	13 ♒ 23	22 6	15 25	6 ♋ 44	12 ♌ 8	27 28	29 23
14	23 22	7 ♎ 29	16 11	1 ♐ 17	6 ♑ 17	27 16	6 ♈ 20	29 20	19 46	24 31	9 ♎ 16	11 ♏ 13
15	5 ♍ 26	19 17	28 1	13 42	19 27	11 ♓ 15	20 30	13 ♊ 0	2 ♌ 33	6 ♍ 40	21 2	23 10
16	17 21	1 ♏ 8	9 ♏ 56	26 21	2 ♒ 52	25 20	4 ♉ 34	26 28	15 5	18 39	2 ♏ 50	5 ♐ 17
17	29 10	13 7	21 59	9 ♑ 17	16 31	9 ♈ 30	18 33	9 ♋ 43	27 26	0 ♎ 32	14 42	17 37
18	10 ♎ 59	25 20	4 ♐ 14	22 32	0 ♓ 24	23 43	2 ♊ 25	22 45	9 ♍ 36	12 20	26 40	0 ♑ 9
19	22 50	7 ♐ 51	16 45	6 ♒ 8	14 32	7 ♉ 57	16 10	5 ♌ 35	21 37	24 7	8 ♐ 47	12 55
20	4 ♏ 51	20 45	29 37	20 7	28 58	22 10	29 46	18 12	3 ♎ 31	5 ♏ 55	21 3	25 54
21	17 6	4 ♑ 8	12 ♑ 52	4 ♓ 26	13 ♈ 23	6 ♊ 19	13 ♋ 10	0 ♍ 57	15 21	17 46	3 ♑ 29	9 ♒ 4
22	29 41	17 59	26 35	19 5	28 0	20 19	26 21	12 50	27 7	29 41	16 8	22 25
23	12 ♐ 41	2 ♒ 21	10 ♒ 45	3 ♈ 58	12 ♉ 38	4 ♋ 6	9 ♌ 17	24 53	8 ♏ 54	11 ♐ 44	28 59	5 ♓ 57
24	26 8	17 7	25 21	18 59	27 12	17 38	21 58	6 ♎ 46	20 44	23 58	12 ♒ 4	19 38
25	10 ♑ 3	2 ♓ 11	10 ♓ 18	3 ♉ 59	11 ♊ 34	0 ♌ 50	4 ♍ 22	18 35	2 ♐ 40	6 ♑ 24	25 26	3 ♈ 30
26	24 23	17 24	25 29	18 49	25 39	13 42	16 33	0 ♏ 21	14 48	19 7	9 ♓ 5	17 33
27	9 ♒ 4	2 ♈ 35	10 ♈ 43	3 ♊ 23	9 ♋ 23	26 15	28 32	12 9	27 11	2 ♒ 9	23 3	1 ♉ 47
28	23 58	17 34	25 51	17 34	22 44	8 ♍ 31	10 ♎ 23	24 5	9 ♑ 54	15 33	7 ♈ 19	16 9
29	8 ♓ 55		10 ♉ 44	1 ♋ 20	5 ♌ 42	20 33	22 11	6 ♐ 13	23 2	29 22	21 53	0 ♊ 38
30	23 45		25 14	14 40	18 17	2 ♎ 26	4 ♏ 0	18 38	6 ♒ 36	13 ♓ 35	6 ♉ 40	15 8
31	8 ♈ 23		9 ♊ 19		0 ♍ 34		15 57	1 ♑ 26		28 12		29 32

THE PLACE OF THE MOON FOR THE YEARS 1866–1867

D M	Jan.	Feb	March	April	May	June	July	August	Sept.	Oct.	Nov.	Dec.
	° ′	° ′	° ′	° ′	° ′	° ′	° ′	° ′	° ′	° ′	° ′	° ′
1	13 ♋ 46	2 ♍ 21	10 ♍ 47	25 ♎ 55	28 ♏ 20	13 ♑ 37	18 ♒ 31	8 ♈ 58	2 ♊ 5	11 ♋ 14	1 ♍ 54	6 ♎ 34
2	27 42	15 1	23 13	7 ♏ 46	10 ♐ 13	26 2	1 ♓ 35	22 51	16 16	25 2	14 39	18 43
3	11 ♌ 16	27 23	5 ♎ 27	19 35	22 11	8 ♒ 39	14 50	6 ♉ 52	0 ♋ 22	8 ♌ 34	27 10	0 ♏ 43
4	24 27	9 ♎ 31	17 30	1 ♐ 25	4 ♄ 17	21 29	28 19	21 2	14 22	21 50	9 ♎ 28	12 37
5	7 ♍ 14	21 28	29 24	13 18	16 33	4 ♓ 35	12 ♈ 3	5 ♊ 18	28 12	4 ♍ 52	21 37	24 28
6	19 39	3 ♏ 17	11 ♏ 14	25 20	29 2	18 0	26 3	19 37	11 ♌ 50	17 39	3 ♏ 39	6 ♐ 19
7	1 ♎ 48	15 6	23 2	7 ♑ 32	11 ♒ 48	1 ♈ 46	10 ♉ 19	3 ♋ 57	25 16	0 ♎ 14	15 36	18 11
8	13 43	26 58	4 ♐ 55	20 1	24 55	15 54	24 49	18 13	8 ♍ 27	12 38	27 29	0 ♑ 6
9	25 32	8 ♐ 59	16 55	2 ♒ 50	8 ♓ 24	0 ♉ 23	9 ♊ 29	2 ♌ 19	21 22	24 51	9 ♐ 20	12 3
10	7 ♏ 20	21 15	29 9	16 2	22 19	15 11	24 14	16 11	4 ♎ 2	6 ♏ 56	21 11	24 6
11	19 11	3 ♑ 49	11 ♑ 41	29 41	6 ♈ 40	0 ♊ 12	8 ♋ 56	29 45	16 27	18 53	3 ♑ 4	6 ♒ 16
12	1 ♐ 12	16 44	24 35	13 ♓ 46	21 24	15 17	23 26	12 ♍ 58	28 39	0 ♐ 46	15 1	18 35
13	13 26	0 ♒ 1	7 ♒ 53	28 16	6 ♉ 29	0 ♋ 17	7 ♌ 39	25 51	10 ♏ 40	12 36	27 6	1 ♓ 7
14	25 56	13 39	21 37	13 ♈ 7	21 39	15 3	21 29	8 ♎ 24	22 34	24 27	9 ♒ 22	13 55
15	8 ♑ 43	27 37	5 ♓ 45	28 12	6 ♊ 53	29 25	4 ♍ 54	20 40	4 ♐ 25	6 ♑ 24	21 54	27 4
16	21 48	11 ♓ 48	20 13	13 ♉ 22	21 57	13 ♌ 20	17 53	2 ♏ 44	16 18	18 30	4 ♓ 47	10 ♈ 37
17	5 ♒ 10	26 10	4 ♈ 57	28 27	6 ♋ 42	26 47	0 ♎ 29	14 39	28 16	0 ♒ 49	18 3	24 36
18	18 45	10 ♈ 35	19 48	13 ♊ 19	21 1	9 ♍ 46	12 46	26 30	10 ♑ 25	13 28	1 ♈ 48	9 ♉ 3
19	2 ♓ 31	24 59	4 ♉ 39	27 51	4 ♌ 52	22 21	24 49	8 ♐ 23	22 49	26 28	16 1	23 54
20	16 25	9 ♉ 19	19 23	11 ♋ 59	18 14	4 ♎ 36	6 ♏ 43	20 22	5 ♒ 32	9 ♓ 54	0 ♉ 42	9 ♊ 3
21	0 ♈ 23	23 32	3 ♊ 54	25 42	1 ♍ 9	16 37	18 33	2 ♑ 32	18 36	23 47	15 45	24 21
22	14 25	7 ♊ 36	18 9	8 ♌ 59	13 42	28 30	0 ♐ 24	14 56	2 ♓ 3	8 ♈ 6	1 ♊ 3	9 ♋ 37
23	28 29	21 30	2 ♋ 6	21 54	25 57	10 ♏ 19	12 22	27 36	15 52	22 47	16 24	24 39
24	12 ♉ 34	5 ♋ 13	15 43	4 ♍ 29	7 ♎ 59	22 8	24 28	10 ♒ 35	0 ♈ 2	7 ♉ 45	1 ♋ 36	9 ♌ 18
25	26 40	18 45	29 2	16 49	19 53	4 ♐ 1	6 ♑ 46	23 52	14 27	22 51	16 30	23 28
26	10 ♊ 45	2 ♌ 5	12 ♌ 4	28 57	1 ♏ 42	16 1	19 18	7 ♓ 26	29 3	7 ♊ 55	0 ♌ 59	7 ♍ 8
27	24 48	15 13	24 51	10 ♎ 57	13 30	28 11	2 ♒ 4	21 14	13 ♉ 43	22 48	14 58	20 18
28	8 ♋ 44	28 7	7 ♍ 24	22 50	25 20	10 ♑ 30	15 3	5 ♈ 14	28 21	7 ♋ 23	28 28	3 ♎ 3
29	22 31		19 45	4 ♏ 40	7 ♐ 14	23 0	28 15	19 23	12 ♊ 52	21 36	11 ♍ 31	15 27
30	6 ♌ 4		1 ♎ 56	16 30	19 14	5 ♒ 40	11 ♓ 39	3 ♉ 36	27 10	5 ♌ 25	24 11	27 35
31	19 22		13 59		1 ♑ 21		25 14	17 50		18 50		9 ♏ 32

D M	Jan.	Feb.	March	April	May	June	July	August	Sept.	Oct.	Nov.	Dec
	° ′	° ′	° ′	° ′	° ′	° ′	° ′	° ′	° ′	° ′	° ′	° ′
1	21 ♏ 24	5 ♑ 25	13 ♑ 26	28 ♒ 32	3 ♈ 1	24 ♉ 24	3 ♋ 16	26 ♌ 44	16 ♎ 37	20 ♏ 23	4 ♑ 57	6 ♒ 47
2	3 ♐ 13	17 31	25 36	11 ♓ 35	16 57	9 ♊ 32	18 33	11 ♍ 7	29 44	2 ♐ 49	16 49	18 36
3	15 4	29 47	7 ♒ 59	25 1	1 ♉ 19	24 48	3 ♌ 39	25 4	12 ♏ 29	15 1	28 38	0 ♓ 33
4	26 59	12 ♒ 15	20 36	8 ♈ 47	16 2	10 ♋ 0	18 26	8 ♎ 35	24 55	27 2	10 ♒ 30	12 41
5	8 ♑ 59	24 53	3 ♓ 31	22 53	0 ♊ 57	24 59	2 ♍ 47	21 40	7 ♐ 6	8 ♑ 55	22 30	25 7
6	21 6	7 ♓ 44	16 42	7 ♉ 14	15 57	9 ♌ 37	16 40	4 ♏ 22	19 7	20 47	4 ♓ 43	7 ♈ 56
7	3 ♒ 20	20 46	0 ♈ 8	21 45	0 ♋ 51	23 48	0 ♎ 5	16 45	1 ♑ 1	2 ♒ 42	17 13	21 12
8	15 42	4 ♈ 0	13 49	6 ♊ 18	15 33	7 ♍ 33	13 5	28 55	12 53	14 44	0 ♈ 6	4 ♉ 58
9	28 13	17 27	27 41	20 49	29 56	20 52	25 43	10 ♐ 54	24 48	26 58	13 25	19 14
10	10 ♓ 55	1 ♉ 5	11 ♉ 42	5 ♋ 13	13 ♌ 58	3 ♎ 50	8 ♏ 5	22 48	6 ♒ 50	9 ♓ 28	27 9	3 ♊ 55
11	23 50	14 56	25 50	19 25	27 38	16 29	20 14	4 ♑ 40	19 1	22 17	11 ♉ 18	18 56
12	7 ♈ 1	29 0	10 ♊ 2	3 ♌ 24	10 ♍ 58	28 53	2 ♐ 14	16 33	1 ♓ 24	5 ♈ 27	25 47	4 ♋ 6
13	20 30	13 ♊ 15	24 14	17 9	24 0	11 ♏ 6	14 9	28 31	14 1	18 57	10 ♊ 29	19 14
14	4 ♉ 19	27 40	8 ♋ 26	0 ♍ 40	6 ♎ 48	23 12	26 2	10 ♒ 35	26 53	2 ♉ 45	25 17	4 ♌ 12
15	18 29	12 ♋ 9	22 34	13 58	19 22	5 ♐ 11	7 ♑ 54	22 48	10 ♈ 0	16 48	10 ♋ 1	18 51
16	2 ♊ 59	26 39	6 ♌ 36	27 3	1 ♏ 47	17 7	19 48	5 ♓ 9	23 21	1 ♊ 1	24 36	3 ♍ 7
17	17 46	11 ♌ 2	20 30	9 ♎ 56	14 2	29 0	1 ♒ 45	17 42	6 ♉ 56	15 20	8 ♌ 55	17 0
18	2 ♋ 43	25 15	4 ♍ 13	22 37	26 11	10 ♑ 52	13 47	0 ♈ 26	20 42	29 40	22 59	0 ♎ 29
19	17 42	9 ♍ 10	17 44	5 ♏ 7	8 ♐ 13	22 45	25 56	13 24	4 ♊ 38	13 ♋ 57	6 ♍ 45	13 38
20	2 ♌ 33	22 46	1 ♎ 0	17 27	20 9	4 ♒ 41	8 ♓ 13	26 37	18 43	28 7	20 15	26 30
21	17 7	6 ♎ 0	14 0	29 37	2 ♑ 3	16 41	20 41	10 ♉ 5	2 ♋ 53	12 ♌ 10	3 ♎ 31	9 ♏ 7
22	1 ♍ 17	18 52	26 44	11 ♐ 38	13 54	28 49	3 ♈ 24	23 49	17 8	26 4	16 34	21 33
23	15 2	1 ♏ 25	9 ♏ 13	23 34	25 47	11 ♓ 9	16 24	7 ♊ 50	1 ♌ 24	9 ♍ 49	29 26	3 ♐ 49
24	28 18	13 41	21 28	5 ♑ 26	7 ♒ 44	23 46	29 44	22 7	15 30	23 24	12 ♏ 8	15 57
25	11 ♎ 10	25 45	3 ♐ 33	17 19	19 50	6 ♈ 43	13 ♉ 27	6 ♋ 36	29 49	6 ♎ 50	24 39	27 58
26	23 39	7 ♐ 40	15 30	29 17	2 ♓ 9	20 4	27 34	21 15	13 ♍ 52	20 4	7 ♐ 0	9 ♑ 54
27	5 ♏ 51	19 33	27 23	11 ♒ 24	14 46	3 ♉ 53	12 ♊ 5	5 ♌ 56	27 43	3 ♏ 6	19 12	21 45
28	17 51	1 ♑ 27	9 ♑ 17	23 46	27 46	18 11	26 54	20 34	11 ♎ 19	15 54	1 ♑ 14	3 ♒ 34
29	29 44		21 16	6 ♓ 27	11 ♈ 13	2 ♊ 55	11 ♋ 55	5 ♍ 2	24 39	28 28	13 9	15 22
30	11 ♐ 35		3 ♒ 26	19 31	25 9	18 0	27 0	19 15	7 ♏ 40	10 ♐ 49	24 59	27 13
31	23 27		15 50		9 ♉ 34		12 ♌ 0	3 ♎ 7		22 58		9 ♓ 9

THE PLACE OF THE MOON FOR THE YEARS 1868–1869

D M	Jan.	Feb.	March	April	May	June	July	August	Sept.	Oct.	Nov.	Dec.
	° ′	° ′	° ′	° ′	° ′	° ′	° ′	° ′	° ′	° ′	° ′	° ′
1	21 ♓ 17	8 ♉ 45	2 ♊ 19	24 ♋ 59	4 ♍ 8	25 ♎ 47	1 ♐ 39	17 ♑ 42	2 ♓ 1	4 ♈ 49	21 ♉ 59	28 ♊ 31
2	3 ♈ 39	22 14	16 5	9 ♌ 15	18 8	9 ♏ 0	14 11	29 35	13 55	17 11	5 ♊ 21	12 ♋ 41
3	16 23	6 ♊ 7	0 ♋ 10	23 35	2 ♎ 1	22 2	26 31	11 ♒ 25	25 54	29 45	18 55	26 55
4	29 31	20 27	14 32	7 ♍ 57	15 48	4 ♐ 52	8 ♑ 42	23 13	8 ♈ 1	12 ♉ 31	2 ♋ 38	11 ♌ 10
5	13 ♉ 8	5 ♋ 9	29 8	22 16	29 24	17 29	20 43	5 ♓ 1	20 18	25 31	16 28	25 22
6	27 15	20 9	13 ♌ 54	6 ♎ 29	12 ♏ 49	29 53	2 ♒ 38	16 52	2 ♉ 48	8 ♊ 42	0 ♌ 25	9 ♍ 31
7	11 ♊ 51	5 ♌ 19	28 43	20 29	25 58	12 ♑ 5	14 27	28 50	15 31	22 7	14 26	23 33
8	26 50	20 29	13 ♍ 28	4 ♏ 14	8 ♐ 52	24 6	26 14	10 ♈ 56	28 30	5 ♋ 44	28 31	7 ♎ 30
9	12 ♋ 5	5 ♍ 29	28 3	17 40	21 29	5 ♒ 59	8 ♓ 2	23 15	11 ♊ 47	19 35	12 ♍ 41	21 21
10	27 25	20 12	12 ♎ 20	0 ♐ 45	3 ♑ 50	17 48	19 55	5 ♉ 51	25 24	3 ♌ 40	26 53	5 ♏ 3
11	12 ♌ 38	4 ♎ 31	26 16	13 29	15 57	29 36	1 ♈ 58	18 47	9 ♋ 21	17 57	11 ♎ 5	18 36
12	27 35	18 24	9 ♏ 47	25 54	27 53	11 ♓ 28	14 14	2 ♊ 6	23 40	2 ♍ 25	25 13	1 ♐ 58
13	12 ♍ 9	1 ♏ 49	22 54	8 ♑ 3	9 ♒ 43	23 30	26 49	15 50	8 ♌ 16	17 1	9 ♏ 13	15 6
14	26 16	14 49	5 ♐ 37	20 0	21 32	5 ♈ 47	9 ♉ 47	0 ♋ 1	23 8	1 ♎ 40	23 0	27 59
15	9 ♎ 56	27 26	18 0	1 ♒ 51	3 ♓ 25	18 24	23 12	14 35	8 ♍ 7	16 14	6 ♐ 31	10 ♑ 37
16	23 10	9 ♐ 45	0 ♑ 8	13 40	15 28	1 ♉ 25	7 ♊ 5	29 29	23 6	0 ♏ 37	19 42	22 59
17	6 ♏ 2	21 50	12 4	25 33	27 45	14 53	21 25	14 ♌ 36	7 ♎ 56	14 43	2 ♑ 32	5 ♒ 7
18	18 35	3 ♑ 46	23 54	7 ♓ 35	10 ♈ 21	28 47	6 ♋ 8	29 47	22 30	28 27	15 2	17 4
19	0 ♐ 54	15 36	5 ♒ 42	19 49	23 20	13 ♊ 7	21 9	14 ♍ 53	6 ♏ 41	11 ♐ 46	27 15	28 54
20	13 1	27 24	17 34	2 ♈ 20	6 ♉ 43	27 46	6 ♌ 17	29 44	20 27	24 41	9 ♒ 14	10 ♓ 41
21	25 0	9 ♒ 14	29 32	15 10	20 30	12 ♋ 38	21 24	14 ♎ 15	3 ♐ 45	7 ♑ 13	21 5	22 30
22	6 ♑ 53	21 7	11 ♓ 40	28 19	4 ♊ 36	27 33	6 ♍ 21	28 20	16 37	19 26	2 ♓ 52	4 ♈ 27
23	18 44	3 ♓ 7	24 1	11 ♉ 46	18 57	12 ♌ 23	21 1	11 ♏ 58	29 8	1 ♒ 25	14 42	16 36
24	0 ♒ 33	15 15	6 ♈ 35	25 30	3 ♋ 28	27 2	5 ♎ 19	25 11	11 ♑ 20	13 16	26 40	29 3
25	12 23	27 33	19 24	9 ♊ 25	18 0	11 ♍ 26	19 14	8 ♐ 0	23 18	25 3	8 ♈ 51	11 ♉ 54
26	24 15	10 ♈ 1	2 ♉ 28	23 30	2 ♌ 29	25 31	2 ♏ 44	20 29	5 ♒ 9	6 ♓ 53	21 18	25 5
27	6 ♓ 12	22 43	15 45	7 ♋ 38	16 50	9 ♎ 18	15 53	2 ♑ 42	16 56	18 50	4 ♉ 6	8 ♊ 44
28	18 16	5 ♉ 38	29 15	21 49	1 ♍ 0	22 46	28 43	14 43	28 45	0 ♈ 57	17 14	22 46
29	0 ♈ 30	18 50	12 ♊ 56	5 ♌ 58	14 59	5 ♏ 59	11 ♐ 15	26 36	10 ♓ 38	13 19	0 ♊ 43	7 ♋ 7
30	12 57		26 48	20 5	28 46	18 56	23 34	8 ♒ 25	22 38	25 56	14 30	21 43
31	25 41		10 ♋ 50		12 ♎ 22		5 ♑ 42	20 12		8 ♉ 50		6 ♌ 25

D M	Jan.	Feb.	March	April	May	June	July	August	Sept.	Oct.	Nov.	Dec.
	° ′	° ′	° ′	° ′	° ′	° ′	° ′	° ′	° ′	° ′	° ′	° ′
1	21 ♌ 7	14 ♎ 17	23 ♎ 8	13 ♐ 40	17 ♑ 44	2 ♓ 10	3 ♈ 47	18 ♉ 7	5 ♋ 4	11 ♌ 18	4 ♎ 10	13 ♏ 2
2	5 ♍ 43	28 26	7 ♏ 34	26 50	0 ♒ 9	14 2	15 43	0 ♊ 41	18 43	25 41	19 13	27 41
3	20 8	12 ♏ 11	21 33	9 ♑ 33	12 17	25 52	27 47	13 35	2 ♌ 49	10 ♍ 29	4 ♏ 21	12 ♐ 9
4	4 ♎ 20	25 34	5 ♐ 3	21 56	24 13	7 ♈ 46	10 ♉ 4	26 52	17 21	25 36	19 21	26 19
5	18 16	8 ♐ 37	18 6	4 ♒ 1	6 ♓ 2	19 49	22 39	10 ♋ 35	2 ♍ 14	10 ♎ 53	4 ♐ 6	10 ♑ 7
6	1 ♏ 57	21 20	0 ♑ 47	15 55	17 50	2 ♉ 4	5 ♊ 33	24 41	17 23	26 10	18 26	23 30
7	15 23	3 ♑ 49	13 8	27 43	29 42	14 35	18 49	9 ♌ 10	2 ♎ 37	11 ♏ 15	2 ♑ 18	6 ♒ 28
8	28 35	16 4	25 15	9 ♓ 30	11 ♈ 41	27 22	2 ♋ 25	23 54	17 44	25 59	15 41	19 4
9	11 ♐ 33	28 10	7 ♒ 12	21 18	23 50	10 ♊ 27	16 21	8 ♍ 47	2 ♏ 38	10 ♐ 15	28 37	1 ♓ 22
10	24 18	10 ♒ 9	19 2	3 ♈ 12	6 ♉ 11	23 48	0 ♌ 32	23 41	17 9	24 1	11 ♒ 9	13 26
11	6 ♑ 50	22 0	0 ♓ 49	15 13	18 46	7 ♋ 24	14 54	8 ♎ 29	1 ♐ 15	7 ♑ 18	23 23	25 21
12	19 11	3 ♓ 49	12 37	27 23	1 ♊ 34	21 11	29 23	23 4	14 53	20 9	5 ♓ 24	7 ♈ 13
13	1 ♒ 21	15 37	24 26	9 ♉ 43	14 35	5 ♌ 7	13 ♍ 52	7 ♏ 21	28 6	2 ♒ 38	17 17	19 5
14	13 22	27 26	6 ♈ 20	22 13	27 47	19 10	28 18	21 19	10 ♑ 57	14 51	29 7	1 ♉ 3
15	25 15	9 ♈ 18	18 19	4 ♊ 54	11 ♋ 10	3 ♍ 17	12 ♎ 37	4 ♐ 55	23 28	26 51	10 ♈ 58	13 10
16	7 ♓ 3	21 16	0 ♉ 26	17 47	24 44	17 27	26 46	18 12	5 ♒ 45	8 ♓ 45	22 54	25 29
17	18 50	3 ♉ 24	12 42	0 ♋ 53	8 ♌ 28	1 ♎ 38	10 ♏ 43	1 ♑ 11	17 52	20 35	4 ♉ 57	8 ♊ 1
18	0 ♈ 39	15 46	25 9	14 12	22 22	15 48	24 27	13 54	29 50	2 ♈ 26	17 8	20 47
19	12 35	28 25	7 ♊ 50	27 48	6 ♍ 27	29 56	7 ♐ 58	26 23	11 ♓ 44	14 18	29 28	3 ♋ 48
20	24 42	11 ♊ 25	20 48	11 ♌ 41	20 41	13 ♏ 58	21 14	8 ♒ 42	23 36	26 15	11 ♊ 59	17 2
21	7 ♉ 5	24 50	4 ♋ 5	25 52	5 ♎ 3	27 51	4 ♑ 17	20 50	5 ♈ 27	8 ♉ 17	24 40	0 ♌ 28
22	19 48	8 ♋ 40	17 44	10 ♍ 20	19 30	11 ♐ 33	17 6	2 ♓ 52	17 19	20 25	7 ♋ 31	14 6
23	2 ♊ 56	22 58	1 ♌ 47	25 2	3 ♏ 56	25 0	29 41	14 48	29 14	2 ♊ 40	20 33	27 53
24	16 31	7 ♌ 40	16 13	9 ♎ 53	18 17	8 ♑ 11	12 ♒ 3	26 40	11 ♉ 13	15 5	3 ♌ 47	11 ♍ 48
25	0 ♋ 33	22 42	1 ♍ 0	24 44	2 ♐ 25	21 4	24 14	8 ♈ 30	23 19	27 40	17 15	25 51
26	15 0	7 ♍ 56	16 3	9 ♏ 29	16 16	3 ♒ 40	6 ♓ 16	20 22	5 ♊ 35	10 ♋ 28	0 ♍ 59	10 ♎ 0
27	29 48	23 11	1 ♎ 13	23 57	29 46	16 0	18 11	2 ♉ 17	18 3	23 32	14 58	24 13
28	14 ♌ 49	8 ♎ 18	16 22	8 ♐ 4	12 ♑ 53	28 7	0 ♈ 2	14 20	0 ♋ 48	6 ♌ 55	29 12	8 ♏ 28
29	29 55		1 ♏ 18	21 44	25 38	10 ♓ 4	11 53	26 34	13 53	20 40	13 ♎ 41	22 42
30	14 ♍ 56		15 53	4 ♑ 57	8 ♒ 3	21 56	23 48	9 ♊ 3	27 23	4 ♍ 48	28 20	6 ♐ 51
31	29 46		0 ♐ 1		20 13		5 ♉ 51	21 52		19 19		20 51

THE PLACE OF THE MOON FOR THE YEARS 1870–1871

D M	Jan.	Feb.	March	April	May	June	July	August	Sept.	Oct.	Nov.	Dec.
	° ′	° ′	° ′	° ′	° ′	° ′	° ′	° ′	° ′	° ′	° ′	° ′
1	4♑37	22♒20	1♓4	16♈7	18♉48	4♋22	9♌32	0♎53	24♏33	3♑10	22♒50	26♓59
2	18 7	4♓46	13 17	27 59	0♊46	16 55	22 52	15 6	8♐43	16 46	5♓28	9♈8
3	1♒19	17 0	25 23	9♉51	12 48	29 41	6♍25	29 21	22 38	0♒3	17 52	21 7
4	14 12	29 4	7♈23	21 44	24 58	12♌40	20 11	13♏35	6♑19	13 3	0♈5	3♉1
5	26 47	11♈1	19 17	3♊40	7♋17	25 56	4♎9	27 46	19 47	25 49	12 10	14 52
6	9♓5	22 53	1♉9	15 43	19 49	9♍29	18 17	11♐51	3♒2	8♓23	24 9	26 42
7	21 11	4♉45	13 0	27 56	2♌38	23 22	2♏35	25 50	16 6	20 48	6♉4	8♊35
8	3♈8	16 41	24 55	10♋24	15 47	7♎35	16 58	9♑39	28 58	3♈4	17 56	20 31
9	15 1	28 46	6♊57	23 11	29 19	22 5	1♐24	23 18	11♓39	15 12	29 47	2♋33
10	26 54	11♊4	19 11	6♌23	13♍17	6♏48	15 47	6♒45	24 9	27 13	11♊37	14 42
11	8♉51	23 40	1♋41	20 1	27 41	21 39	0♑4	19 58	6♈28	9♉9	23 31	27 0
12	20 59	6♋38	14 34	4♍9	12♎28	6♐29	14 9	2♓56	18 37	21 0	5♋29	9♌29
13	3♊20	20 0	27 52	18 46	27 32	21 12	27 59	15 40	0♉37	2♊49	17 36	22 13
14	15 58	3♌47	11♌38	3♎46	12♏44	5♑39	11♒31	28 8	12 31	14 39	29 56	5♍14
15	28 54	17 59	25 54	19 3	27 55	19 45	24 42	10♈23	24 21	26 34	12♌32	18 34
16	12♋11	2♍30	10♍35	4♏24	12♐53	3♒27	7♓34	22 27	6♊12	8♋38	25 30	2♎16
17	25 47	17 15	25 36	19 39	27 29	16 44	20 8	4♉24	18 8	20 56	8♍52	16 19
18	9♌40	2♎6	10♎49	4♐37	11♑40	29 37	2♈25	16 16	0♋14	3♌34	22 42	0♏44
19	23 4	16 54	26 2	19 10	25 22	12♓10	14 31	28 9	12 36	16 37	7♎1	15 27
20	8♍2	1♏34	11♏4	3♑14	8♒37	24 27	26 28	10♊7	25 19	0♍7	21 45	0♐23
21	22 23	15 58	25 47	16 48	21 26	6♈30	8♉21	22 17	8♌26	14 8	6♏50	15 23
22	6♎45	0♐4	10♐6	29 56	3♓55	18 26	20 15	4♋41	22 1	28 39	22 5	0♑19
23	21 3	13 51	23 59	12♒41	16 8	0♉19	2♊14	17 24	6♍4	13♎34	7♐21	15 4
24	5♏15	27 19	7♑27	25 7	28 10	12 12	14 23	0♌30	20 33	28 45	22 27	29 29
25	19 18	10♑31	20 31	7♓19	10♈4	24 9	26 45	13 59	5♎21	14♏3	7♑14	13♒31
26	3♐12	23 27	3♒16	19 21	21 56	6♊14	9♋22	27 51	20 21	29 15	21 36	27 6
27	16 54	6♒10	15 46	1♈17	3♉47	18 29	22 17	12♍2	5♏22	14♐11	5♒30	10♓16
28	0♑25	18 42	28 4	13 10	15 42	0♋55	5♌31	26 29	20 16	28 46	18 56	23 2
29	13 43		10♓13	25 2	27 41	13 34	19 1	11♎3	4♐54	12♑54	1♓57	5♈28
30	26 48		22 15	6♉54	9♊46	26 26	2♍47	25 40	19 13	26 36	14 37	17 38
31	9♒41		4♈13		22 0		16 45	10♏11		9♒54		29 37

D M	Jan	Feb.	March	April	May	June	July	August	Sept.	Oct.	Nov.	Dec.
	° ′	° ′	° ′	° ′	° ′	° ′	° ′	° ′	° ′	° ′	° ′	° ′
1	11♉29	25♊9	2♋55	18♌14	23♍20	15♏22	24♐5	17♒3	6♈47	10♉28	24♊43	26♋43
2	23 18	7♋18	15 6	1♍31	7♎31	0♐30	9♑10	1♓20	19 49	22 45	6♋30	8♌37
3	5♊9	19 41	27 34	15 14	22 8	15 48	24 7	15 14	2♉29	4♊48	18 18	20 40
4	17 5	2♌20	10♌23	29 23	7♏5	0♑53	8♒49	28 44	14 49	16 41	0♌10	2♍56
5	29 8	15 16	23 34	13♎54	22 12	15 50	23 9	11♈49	26 55	28 29	12 13	15 31
6	11♋21	28 30	7♍7	28 39	7♐20	0♒27	7♓4	24 31	8♊49	10♋17	24 32	28 27
7	23 46	11♍59	21 1	13♏31	22 20	14 40	20 32	6♉52	20 38	22 11	7♍11	11♎49
8	6♌22	25 41	5♎12	28 20	7♑4	28 27	3♈34	18 57	2♋27	4♌16	20 15	25 39
9	19 11	9♎33	19 32	12♐59	21 27	11♓48	16 13	0♊51	14 21	16 37	3♎45	9♏56
10	2♍14	23 33	3♏58	27 25	5♒27	24 45	28 33	12 40	26 25	29 18	17 42	24 37
11	15 30	7♏37	18 22	11♑33	19 5	7♈23	10♉38	24 28	8♌44	12♍22	2♏3	9♐37
12	29 0	21 44	2♐41	25 24	2♓20	19 43	22 32	6♋20	21 20	25 50	16 44	24 47
13	12♎44	5♐52	16 52	8♒57	15 17	1♉50	4♊21	18 20	4♍15	9♎41	1♐37	9♑59
14	26 41	20 0	0♑53	22 16	27 57	13 48	16 8	0♌31	17 29	23 51	16 33	25 2
15	10♏50	4♑6	14 45	5♓20	10♈24	25 39	27 57	12 55	1♎1	18♏14	1♑26	9♒49
16	25 11	18 9	28 26	18 12	22 39	7♊27	9♋51	25 34	14 48	22 44	16 7	24 13
17	9♐39	2♒6	11♒59	0♈52	4♉45	19 15	21 52	8♍28	28 45	7♐16	0♒33	8♓12
18	24 11	15 54	25 21	13 21	16 43	1♋4	4♌3	21 37	12♏49	21 43	14 40	21 45
19	8♑43	29 30	8♓33	25 40	28 35	12 56	16 25	4♎58	26 56	6♑3	28 27	4♈53
20	23 8	12♓51	21 33	7♉49	10♊24	24 55	28 58	18 30	11♐4	20 12	11♓55	17 40
21	7♒20	25 56	4♈21	19 49	22 11	7♌3	11♍45	2♏13	25 12	4♒11	25 5	0♉9
22	21 16	8♈42	16 55	1♊42	3♋59	19 21	24 46	16 6	9♑17	17 57	7♈59	12 24
23	4♓51	21 11	29 16	13 30	15 51	1♍54	8♎2	0♐6	23 20	1♓32	10 39	24 27
24	18 3	3♉24	11♉24	25 17	27 50	14 43	21 34	14 14	7♒20	14 56	3♉6	6♊23
25	0♈54	15 25	23 22	7♋6	10♌0	27 52	5♏22	28 29	21 14	28 8	15 22	18 13
26	30 24	27 17	5♊12	19 2	22 26	11♎22	19 26	12♑48	5♓0	11♈7	27 28	0♋2
27	25 37	9♊6	17 0	1♌10	5♍12	25 15	3♐46	27 10	18 36	23 53	9♊27	11 50
28	7♉37	20 57	28 50	13 36	18 21	9♏32	18 19	11♒29	1♈59	6♉26	21 19	23 40
29	19 29		10♋47	26 23	1♎57	24 9	3♑1	25 41	15 6	18 46	3♋8	5♌33
30	1♊19		22 56	9♍37	16 0	9♐2	17 47	9♓41	27 56	0♊55	14 55	17 33
31	13 10		5♌24		0♏30		2♒30	23 24		12 53		29 41

THE PLACE OF THE MOON FOR THE YEARS 1872–1873

D M	Jan.	Feb.	March	April	May	June	July	August	Sept.	Oct.	Nov.	Dec.
	° ′	° ′	° ′	° ′	° ′	° ′	° ′	° ′	° ′	° ′	° ′	° ′
1	12♍ 1	0♏29	24♏28	17♑16	26♒26	17♈34	22♉41	7♋51	22♌11	25♍16	12♏48	19♐19
2	24 35	13 59	8♐14	1♒25	10♓18	0♉29	4♊54	19 40	4♍15	7♎52	26 25	3♑48
3	7♎27	27 47	22 13	15 36	23 59	13 9	16 58	1♌30	16 28	20 41	10♐15	18 24
4	20 40	11♐56	6♑25	29 45	7♈28	25 37	28 54	13 21	28 49	3♏42	24 15	2♒59
5	4♏17	26 23	20 47	13♓49	20 44	7♊53	10♋47	25 18	11♎20	16 55	8♑21	17 30
6	18 19	11♑ 8	5♒18	27 44	3♉46	20 0	22 36	7♍19	24 1	0♐18	22 31	1♓51
7	2♐45	26 4	19 52	11♈26	16 33	1♋59	4♌26	19 28	6♏54	13 53	6♒43	15 59
8	17 34	11♒ 3	4♓24	24 52	29 6	13 52	16 17	1♎46	20 0	27 38	20 54	29 52
9	2♑39	25 57	18 46	7♉59	11♊25	25 42	28 12	14 14	3♐20	11♑34	5♓ 3	13♈30
10	17 52	10♓36	2♈52	20 47	23 32	7♌31	10♍13	26 56	16 57	25 41	19 7	26 54
11	3♒ 3	24 54	16 37	3♊16	5♋30	19 23	22 24	9♏54	0♑52	9♒57	3♈ 4	10♉ 3
12	18 3	8♈45	29 57	15 29	17 21	1♍22	4♎47	23 12	15 6	24 20	16 51	22 59
13	2♓42	22 7	12♉53	27 30	29 11	13 31	17 26	6♐52	29 38	8♓46	0♉27	5♊43
14	16 55	5♉ 3	25 27	9♋23	11♌ 2	25 55	0♏26	20 56	14♒23	23 11	13 48	18 16
15	0♈39	17 34	7♊41	21 12	23 1	8♎37	13 49	5♑25	29 15	7♈27	26 54	0♋37
16	13 55	29 46	19 43	3♌ 4	5♍11	21 43	27 39	20 14	14♓ 6	21 31	9♊45	12 49
17	26 44	11♊44	1♋33	15 2	17 37	5♏13	11♐55	5♒19	28 48	5♉17	22 19	24 52
18	9♉12	23 34	13 22	27 13	0♎24	19 11	26 36	20 31	13♈12	18 41	4♋39	6♌48
19	21 22	5♋20	25 12	9♍40	13 33	3♐33	11♑38	5♓39	27 13	1♊44	16 46	18 41
20	3♊20	17 9	7♌ 9	22 26	27 6	18 18	26 52	20 33	10♉47	14 26	28 45	0♍32
21	15 10	29 2	19 17	5♎32	11♏ 3	3♑18	12♒ 9	5♈ 4	23 54	26 50	10♌37	12 26
22	26 57	11♌ 5	1♍40	18 59	25 21	18 26	27 17	19 7	6♊37	8♋58	22 29	24 26
23	8♋44	23 19	14 19	2♏44	9♐55	3♒31	12♓ 8	2♉41	18 59	20 56	4♍24	6♎38
24	20 34	5♍45	27 14	16 45	24 40	18 26	26 33	15 46	1♋ 6	2♌48	16 28	19 7
25	2♌30	18 23	10♎25	0♐58	9♑27	3♓ 3	10♈31	28 26	13 2	14 40	28 44	[illegible]♏56
26	14 32	1♎13	23 50	15 17	24 11	17 17	23 59	10♊46	24 53	26 36	11♎17	15 9
27	26 44	14 15	7♏27	29 39	8♒46	1♈ 6	7♉ 0	22 50	6♌43	8♍41	24 11	28 49
28	9♍ 5	27 29	21 13	13♑59	23 6	14 31	19 38	4♋45	18 38	20 58	7♏26	12♐56
29	21 36	10♏53	5♐ 6	28 15	7♓10	27 32	1♊58	16 34	0♍40	3♎30	21 4	27 28
30	4♎20		19 5	12♒25	20 56	10♉15	14 4	28 23	12 52	16 19	5♐ 3	12♑19
31	17 17		3♑ 9		4♈23		26 0	10♌16		29 25		27 21

D M	Jan.	Feb.	March	April	May	June	July	August	Sept.	Oct.	Nov.	Dec.
	° ′	° ′	° ′	° ′	° ′	° ′	° ′	° ′	° ′	° ′	° ′	° ′
1	12♒25	5♈42	14♈ 3	3♊44	7♋18	21♌43	23♍32	8♏ 3	25♐28	2♒31	25♓52	4♉29
2	27 21	19 52	28 24	16 45	19 40	3♍37	5♎27	20 35	9♑11	16 57	10♈37	18 40
3	12♓ 2	3♉32	12♉15	29 23	1♌49	15 30	17 30	3♐29	23 25	1♓46	25 23	2♊43
4	26 22	16 46	25 37	11♋43	13 48	27 27	29 47	16 50	8♒ 6	16 49	10♉ 2	16 32
5	10♈19	29 36	8♊32	23 48	25 42	9♎33	12♏22	0♑40	23 9	1♈59	24 26	0♋ 5
6	23 52	12♊ 6	21 4	5♌45	7♍35	21 51	25 20	15 0	8♓27	17 6	8♊31	13 19
7	7♉ 4	24 22	3♋20	17 37	19 32	4♏26	8♐42	29 46	23 46	1♉59	22 14	26 13
8	19 58	6♋28	15 23	29 29	1♎37	17 20	22 31	14♒50	8♈57	16 32	5♋32	8♌48
9	2♊36	18 27	27 18	11♍25	13 53	0♐36	6♑45	0♓ 3	23 49	0♊40	18 27	21 7
10	15 1	0♌21	9♌10	23 26	26 23	14 13	21 20	15 15	8♉17	14 20	1♌ 1	3♍11
11	27 17	12 14	21 1	5♎36	9♏ 7	28 10	6♒ 9	0♈15	22 16	27 33	13 18	15 7
12	9♋25	24 6	2♍54	17 56	22 8	12♑22	21 4	14 54	5♊48	10♋23	25 21	26 57
13	21 27	6♍ 0	14 51	0♏26	5♐25	26 45	5♓56	29 10	18 54	22 52	7♍15	8♎48
14	3♌24	17 55	26 53	13 8	18 57	11♒14	20 37	13♉ 0	1♋39	5♌ 5	19 6	20 45
15	15 18	29 55	9♎ 2	26 2	2♑41	25 43	5♈ 2	26 25	14 5	17 7	0♎57	2♏52
16	27 10	12♎ 0	21 18	9♐ 9	16 37	10♓ 6	19 7	9♊29	26 19	29 1	12 53	15 13
17	9♍ 2	24 13	3♏42	22 29	0♒41	24 21	2♉53	22 14	8♌22	10♍52	24 58	27 52
18	20 57	6♏38	16 18	6♑ 2	14 51	8♈25	16 20	4♋45	20 18	22 43	7♏13	10♐51
19	2♎57	19 17	29 6	19 50	29 5	22 16	29 30	17 4	2♍11	4♎36	19 42	24 10
20	15 6	2♐17	12♐10	3♒51	13♓19	5♉55	12♊25	29 14	14 2	16 35	2♐24	7♑48
21	27 29	15 40	25 32	18 5	27 32	19 22	25 8	11♌17	25 54	28 41	15 22	21 42
22	10♏11	29 29	9♑14	2♓31	11♈40	2♊36	7♋40	23 15	7♎47	10♏55	28 33	5♒47
23	23 16	13♑46	23 19	17 2	25 41	15 38	20 2	5♍ 9	19 43	23 19	11♑58	20 0
24	6♐48	28 29	7♒45	1♈36	9♉33	28 28	2♌15	17 0	1♏45	5♐54	25 35	4♓15
25	20 49	13♒34	22 29	16 6	23 12	11♋ 5	14 21	28 50	13 55	18 42	9♒24	18 28
26	5♑19	28 50	7♓26	0♉25	6♊37	23 31	26 20	10♎41	26 15	1♑45	23 21	2♈38
27	20 14	14♓ 8	22 27	14 29	19 46	5♌45	8♍13	22 36	8♐49	15 4	7♓27	16 43
28	5♒27	29 16	7♈22	28 13	2♋38	17 50	20 4	4♏38	21 40	28 40	21 38	0♉40
29	20 48		22 3	11♊36	15 14	29 47	1♎54	16 52	4♑53	12♒34	5♈54	14 31
30	6♓ 4		6♉23	24 37	37 35	11♍40	13 48	29 22	18 29	26 45	20 12	28 15
31	21 5		20 17		9♌43		25 49	12♐12		11♓12		11♊50

THE PLACE OF THE MOON FOR THE YEARS 1874 1875

D M	Jan.	Feb.	March	April	May	June	July	August	Sept.	Oct.	Nov.	Dec.
	° ′	° ′	° ′	° ′	° ′	° ′	° ′	° ′	° ′	° ′	° ′	° ′
1	25♊14	12♌43	21♌43	6♎29	9♏0	25♐1	0♒54	23♓5	16♉33	24♊39	13♌51	17♍22
2	8♋27	25 1	3♍49	18 18	21 3	7♑57	14 40	7♈29	0♊42	8♋16	26 25	29 24
3	21 27	7♍9	15 48	0♏8	3♐16	21 6	28 36	21 48	14 33	21 31	8♍41	11♎15
4	4♌11	19 9	27 42	12 3	15 39	4♒29	12♓38	5♉59	28 8	4♌26	20 44	23 2
5	16 41	1♎1	9♎31	24 3	28 14	18 3	26 44	20 1	11♋27	17 4	2♎39	4♏48
6	28 57	12 49	21 19	6♐13	11♑4	1♓50	10♈52	3♊54	24 32	29 28	14 27	16 37
7	11♍0	24 37	3♏8	18 35	24 9	15 48	25 0	17 38	7♌23	11♍39	26 14	28 34
8	22 55	6♏30	15 2	1♑13	7♒32	29 55	9♉8	1♋11	20 1	23 42	8♏2	10♐39
9	4♎45	18 32	27 5	14 11	21 13	14♈12	23 13	14 34	2♍27	5♎37	19 52	22 54
10	16 34	0♐51	9♐22	27 32	5♓13	28 35	7♊15	27 45	14 42	17 27	1♐47	5♑20
11	28 29	13 30	21 58	11♒17	19 31	13♉2	21 11	10♌43	26 47	29 14	13 49	17 58
12	10♏34	26 34	4♑57	25 28	4♈5	27 29	4♋58	23 27	8♎44	11♏1	26 0	0♒48
13	22 56	10♑7	18 23	10♓2	18 51	11♊50	18 32	5♍57	20 34	22 50	8♑21	13 49
14	5♐38	24 9	2♒18	24 57	3♉42	26 0	1♌51	18 13	2♏20	4♐43	20 55	27 3
15	18 44	8♒38	16 42	10♈3	18 32	9♋54	14 52	0♎17	14 7	16 44	3♒44	10♓31
16	2♑16	23 28	1♓31	25 13	3♊14	23 28	27 35	12 12	25 57	28 57	16 51	24 13
17	16 13	8♓31	16 38	10♉16	17 39	6♌41	10♍0	24 0	7♐55	11♑25	0♓18	8♈10
18	0 32	23 37	1♈53	25 5	1♋44	19 31	22 10	5♏47	20 6	24 12	14 6	22 22
19	15 6	8♈35	17 6	9♊33	15 24	2♍1	4♎9	17 38	2♑36	7♒23	28 17	6♉49
20	29 47	23 19	2♉7	23 35	28 39	14 14	15 59	29 37	15 27	20 58	12♈50	21 28
21	14♓28	7♉42	16 48	9♋11	11♌29	26 13	27 48	11♐50	28 45	5♓1	27 40	6♊12
22	29 3	21 44	1♊5	20 20	23 59	8♎5	9♏39	24 22	12♒31	19 30	12♉42	20 56
23	13♈25	5♊24	14 56	3♌7	6♍11	19 54	21 39	7♑17	26 44	4♈20	27 49	5♋32
24	27 34	18 43	28 22	15 33	18 10	1♏45	3♐53	20 39	11♓22	19 27	12♊50	19 51
25	11♉26	1♋45	11♋25	27 44	0♎1	13 44	16 24	4♒26	26 18	4♉41	27 36	3♌48
26	25 4	14 32	24 7	9♍44	11 50	25 54	29 17	18 38	11♈24	19 53	12♋1	17 20
27	8♊29	27 6	6♌34	21 36	23 39	8♐19	12♑32	3♓9	26 31	4♊52	25 58	0♍26
28	21 42	9♌29	18 45	9♎25	5♏34	21 2	26 10	17 54	11♉30	19 32	9♌27	13 7
29	4♋43		0♍51	15 3	17 38	4♑2	10♒6	2♈14	26 14	3♋47	22 29	25 27
30	17 34		12 48	27 4	29 52	17 20	24 18	17 31	10♊38	17 35	5♍5	7♎30
31	0 14		24 40		12♐20		8♓40	1♉9		0♌55		19 23

D M	Jan.	Feb.	March	April	May	June	July	August	Sept.	Oct.	Nov.	Dec.
	° ′	° ′	° ′	° ′	° ′	° ′	° ′	° ′	° ′	° ′	° ′	° ′
1	1♏10	14♐46	22♐35	8♒32	14♓1	6♉6	15♊5	7♌58	26♍58	0♏15	14♐33	17♑5
2	12 57	27 5	4♑54	21 55	28 8	21 8	0♋2	21 58	9♎40	12 21	26 23	29 5
3	24 50	9♑42	17 33	5♓44	12♈42	6♊19	14 53	5♍36	22 6	24 19	8♑16	11♒13
4	6♐52	22 39	0♒34	19 58	27 36	21 30	29 29	18 50	4♏18	6♐12	20 14	23 33
5	19 6	5♒56	13 59	4♈33	12♉44	6♋30	13♌42	1♎41	16 18	18 2	2♒21	6♓8
6	1♑34	19 30	27 46	19 25	27 58	21 11	27 29	14 11	28 12	29 55	14 43	19 3
7	14 18	3♓20	11♓55	4♉26	13♊7	5♌26	10♍48	26 25	10♐3	11♑55	27 23	2♈21
8	27 17	17 20	26 19	19 26	28 2	19 12	23 41	8♏25	21 57	24 6	10♓26	16 7
9	10♒29	1♈27	10♈53	4♊18	12♋34	2♍29	6♎11	20 18	3♑58	6♒32	23 55	0♉22
10	23 53	15 37	25 31	18 55	26 41	15 19	18 23	2♐9	16 12	19 19	7♈52	15 4
11	7♓27	29 48	10♉6	3♋12	10♌20	27 47	0♏22	14 3	28 41	2♓28	22 17	0♊9
12	21 9	13♉57	24 34	17 7	23 32	9♎58	12 14	26 3	11♒28	16 2	7♉6	15 28
13	4♈58	28 3	8♊52	0♌40	6♍20	21 56	24 3	8♑15	24 36	0♈1	22 13	0♋50
14	18 54	12♊6	22 56	13 52	18 49	3♏46	5♐55	20 40	8♓4	14 22	7♊27	16 3
15	2♉57	26 3	6♋46	26 45	1♎2	15 36	17 52	3♒21	21 50	29 1	22 39	0♌57
16	17 7	9♋54	20 22	9♍22	13 4	27 25	29 57	16 17	5♈53	13♉50	7♋39	15 25
17	1♊22	23 36	3♌44	21 45	24 59	9♐17	12♑14	29 28	20 7	28 43	22 17	29 22
18	15 39	7♌7	16 51	3♎57	6♏49	21 16	24 42	12♓54	4♉29	13♊31	6♌30	12♍49
19	29 55	20 25	29 45	16 0	18 38	3♑22	7♒22	26 31	18 54	28 8	20 15	25 48
20	14♋5	3♍28	12♍25	27 56	0♐28	15 36	20 13	10♈19	3♊18	12♋29	3♍35	8♎24
21	28 4	16 15	24 53	9♏49	12 20	28 0	3♓16	24 14	17 36	26 30	16 31	20 42
22	11♌47	28 45	7♎9	21 38	24 18	10♒34	16 30	8♉16	1♋47	10♌12	29 9	2♏47
23	25 9	11♎1	19 16	3♐28	6♑21	23 19	29 56	22 24	15 49	23 34	11♎31	14 43
24	8♍11	23 4	1♏13	15 20	18 33	6♓18	13♈33	6♊35	29 38	6♍39	23 41	26 35
25	20 50	4♏58	13 5	27 16	0♒55	19 31	27 23	20 47	13♌15	19 28	5♏44	8♐25
26	3♎11	16 47	24 34	9♑22	13 30	3♈1	11♉26	5♋0	26 39	2♎3	17 41	20 16
27	15 16	28 36	6♐44	21 39	26 22	16 50	25 41	19 8	9♍49	14 27	29 34	2♑10
28	27 10	10♐30	18 38	4♒12	9♓32	0♉58	10♊6	3♌10	22 46	26 42	11♐26	14 8
29	8♏59		0♑42	17 4	23 5	15 26	24 39	17 1	5♎29	8♏48	23 17	26 11
30	20 47		12 59	0♓20	7♈2	0♊10	9♋12	0♍37	17 58	20 48	5♑10	8♒19
31	2♐41		25 35		21 23		23 41	13 56		2♐42		20 36

THE PLACE OF THE MOON FOR THE YEARS 1876–1877

D M	Jan.	Feb.	March	April	May	June	July	August	Sept.	Oct.	Nov.	Dec.
	° ′	° ′	° ′	° ′	° ′	° ′	° ′	° ′	° ′	° ′	° ′	° ′
1	3♓ 2	22♈ 3	16♉23	9♋48	18♌41	8♎42	13♏10	28♐ 6	12♒22	15♓16	3♉13	10♊15
2	15 40	5♉38	0♊23	23 56	2♍19	21 21	25 19	9♑58	24 32	28 4	17 16	25 10
3	28 34	19 31	14 31	7♌57	15 39	3♏47	7♐20	21 51	6♓52	11♈ 9	1♊36	10♋ 9
4	11♈47	3♊41	28 45	21 47	28 45	16 4	19 16	3♒48	19 23	24 31	16 5	25 3
5	25 22	18 8	13♋ 2	5♍27	11♎38	28 13	1♑ 9	15 49	2♈ 8	8♉ 8	0♋36	9♌44
6	9♉22	2♋46	27 21	18 54	24 20	10♐15	13 2	27 57	15 5	21 58	15 5	24 6
7	23 47	17 32	11♌36	2♎10	6♏51	22 13	24 54	10♓13	28 16	5♊58	29 26	8♍ 9
8	8♊34	2♌17	25 43	15 12	19 12	4♑ 7	6♒49	22 39	11♉41	20 5	13♌35	21 51
9	23 38	16 54	9♍39	28 0	1♐24	15 59	18 48	5♈17	25 19	4♋15	27 33	5♎15
10	8♋49	1♍15	23 20	10♏35	13 28	27 51	0♓53	18 9	9♊11	18 27	11♍19	18 22
11	23 58	15 15	6♎43	22 58	25 26	9♒45	13 7	1♉18	23 15	2♌37	24 53	1♏16
12	8♌53	28 51	19 47	5♐ 8	7♑20	21 45	25 33	14 45	7♋30	16 44	8♎15	13 57
13	23 25	12♎ 1	2♏32	17 10	19 12	3♓54	8♈16	28 33	21 54	0♍47	21 27	26 28
14	7♍31	24 49	15 0	29 5	1♒ 5	16 17	21 19	12♊42	6♌22	14 43	4♏28	8♐50
15	21 6	7♏16	27 13	10♑58	13 4	28 59	4♉46	27 11	20 51	28 31	17 18	21 3
16	4♎13	19 27	9♐16	22 52	25 14	12♈ 3	18 39	11♋55	5♍15	12♎ 7	29 55	3♑ 8
17	16 55	1♐26	21 11	4♒53	7♓38	25 35	2♊59	26 48	19 30	25 31	12♐21	15 5
18	29 17	13 20	3♑ 4	17 5	20 23	9♉37	17 44	11♌44	3♎30	8♏39	24 36	26 57
19	11♏23	25 11	14 59	29 33	3♈32	24 7	2♋47	26 32	17 11	21 32	6♑39	8♒46
20	23 20	7♑ 6	27 1	12♓20	17 9	9♊ 2	18 0	11♍ 7	0♏33	4♐ 8	18 35	20 33
21	5♐11	19 7	9♒14	25 31	1♉14	24 14	3♌12	25 21	13 33	16 29	0♒25	2♓24
22	17 1	1♒17	21 42	9♈ 6	15 46	9♋32	18 13	9♎11	26 13	28 37	12 13	14 22
23	28 53	13 40	4♓27	23 4	0♊38	24 46	2♍55	22 35	8♐36	10♑34	24 5	26 33
24	10♑51	26 15	17 31	7♉24	15 44	9♌45	17 11	5♏36	20 44	22 26	6♓ 6	9♈ 2
25	22 56	9♓ 5	0♈54	21 59	0♋52	24 21	0♎59	18 15	2♑43	4♒17	18 20	21 54
26	5♒ 9	22 8	14 35	6♊44	15 52	8♍30	14 20	0♐35	14 36	16 12	0♈54	5♉14
27	17 31	5♈25	28 31	21 29	0♌37	22 11	27 16	12 42	26 28	28 16	13 53	19 4
28	0♓ 2	18 53	12♉39	6♋ 8	15 0	5♎26	9♏51	24 40	8♒25	10♓34	27 19	3♊25
29	12 44	2♉33	26 55	20 35	28 59	18 18	22 9	6♑33	20 29	23 10	11♉12	18 12
30	25 37		11♊14	4♌47	12♍35	0♏51	4♐15	18 26	2♓45	6♈ 8	25 33	3♋18
31	8♈43		25 33		25 48		16 13	0♒21		19 29		18 34

D M	Jan.	Feb.	March	April	May	June	July	August	Sept.	Oct.	Nov.	Dec
	° ′	° ′	° ′	° ′	° ′	° ′	° ′	° ′	° ′	° ′	° ′	° ′
1	3♌48	26♍27	4♎20	23♏40	27♐13	11♒30	13♓20	28♈22	16♊47	24♋24	17♍32	26♎ 7
2	18 51	10♎34	18 35	6♐41	9♑32	23 18	25 15	11♉ 3	0♋33	8♌39	1♎58	10♏ 1
3	3♍33	24 13	2♏24	19 20	21 38	5♓ 7	7♈20	24 6	14 44	23 11	16 24	23 47
4	17 52	7♏27	15 47	1♑40	3♒33	17 2	19 41	7♊35	29 17	7♍55	0♏46	7♐19
5	1♎44	20 16	28 44	13 45	15 22	29 8	2♉23	21 32	14♌ 8	22 46	14 57	20 36
6	15 11	2♐46	11♐19	25 40	27 12	11♈30	15 31	5♋55	29 12	7♎36	28 52	3♑35
7	28 17	15 1	23 36	7♒29	9♓ 7	24 13	29 5	20 41	14♍20	22 19	12♐25	16 16
8	11♏ 3	27 4	5♑39	19 18	21 12	7♉21	13♊ 7	5♌44	29 23	6♏46	25 36	28 39
9	23 34	8♑59	17 32	1♓12	3♈33	20 54	27 35	20 55	14♎12	20 50	8♑24	10♒47
10	5♐52	20 49	29 21	13 14	16 13	4♊52	12♋22	6♍ 5	28 39	4♐30	20 51	22 43
11	18 1	2♒38	11♒ 9	25 29	29 13	19 10	27 22	21 4	12♏42	17 43	3♒ 0	4♓32
12	0♑ 3	14 27	23 1	7♈59	12♉35	3♋44	12♌24	5♎44	26 17	0♑30	14 57	16 20
13	11 59	26 19	4♓58	20 45	26 16	18 26	27 20	20 20	9♐25	12 56	26 46	28 11
14	23 51	8♓16	17 4	3♉48	10♊15	3♌ 8	12♍ 4	3♏55	22 10	25 4	8♓34	10♈11
15	5♒40	20 19	29 20	17 6	24 25	17 44	26 29	17 23	4♑34	7♒ 1	20 25	22 26
16	17 29	2♈31	11♈49	0♊38	8♋42	2♍ 9	10♎34	0♐27	16 42	18 50	2♈25	4♉59
17	29 19	14 54	24 29	14 22	23 0	16 21	24 18	13 10	28 39	0♓37	14 39	17 54
18	11♓13	27 30	7♉24	28 15	7♌17	0♎18	7♏42	25 36	10♒29	12 27	27 8	1♊12
19	23 14	10♉22	20 32	12♋15	21 28	14 0	20 47	7♑48	22 16	24 24	9♉56	14 52
20	5♈27	23 34	3♊54	26 19	5♍34	27 28	3♐36	19 50	4♓ 4	6♈31	23 2	28 51
21	17 54	7♊ 6	17 31	10♌28	19 32	10♏42	16 10	1♒44	15 56	18 50	6♊25	13♋ 6
22	0♉42	21 1	1♋22	24 39	3♎23	23 45	28 32	13 34	27 55	1♉23	20 2	27 30
23	13 55	5♋19	15 27	8♍50	17 5	6♐35	10♑44	25 22	10♈ 1	14 9	3♋50	11♌57
24	27 34	19 56	29 45	23 0	0♏39	19 13	22 47	7♓10	22 17	27 9	17 46	26 23
25	11♊42	4♌48	14♌13	7♎ 7	14 2	1♑39	4♒42	19 1	4♉44	10♊21	1♌49	10♍43
26	26 17	19 49	28 48	21 5	27 13	13 54	16 33	0♈57	17 23	23 44	15 50	24 56
27	11♋15	4♍51	13♍25	4♏53	10♐11	25 59	28 21	13 0	0♊16	7♋18	29 54	8♎58
28	26 28	19 44	27 58	18 25	22 53	7♒55	10♓ 8	25 14	13 23	21 1	13♍59	22 51
29	11♌45		12♎21	1♐40	5♑21	19 45	21 58	7♉40	26 46	4♌56	28 4	6♏33
30	26 57		26 28	14 36	19 35	1♓32	3♈55	20 22	10♋26	18 58	12♎ 7	20 3
31	11♍53		10♏15		29 36		16 1	3♊24		3♍11		3♐23

THE PLACE OF THE MOON FOR THE YEARS 1878–1879

DM	Jan.	Feb.	March	April	May	June	July	August	Sept.	Oct.	Nov.	Dec
	° ′	° ′	° ′	° ′	° ′	° ′	° ′	° ′	° ′	° ′	° ′	° ′
1	16♐30	3♒14	12♒44	26♓32	29♈13	15♊57	22♋2	14♍28	8♏11	15♐56	4♒14	7♓5
2	29 23	15 16	24 7	8♈24	11♉31	29 10	6♌3	29 7	22 29	29 30	16 39	19 5
3	12♑4	27 11	5♓56	20 23	24 1	12♋36	20 13	13♎40	6♐23	12♑37	28 48	0♈57
4	24 30	9♓2	17 44	2♉28	6♊42	26 11	4♍28	28 2	19 53	25 21	10♓46	12 48
5	6♒44	20 49	29 33	14 43	19 34	9♌56	18 44	12♏10	3♑1	7♒46	23 38	24 41
6	18 46	2♈37	11♈24	27 7	2♋37	23 49	3♎0	26 1	15 50	19 57	4♈28	6♉39
7	0♓40	14 28	23 30	9♊43	15 53	7♍50	17 12	9♐37	28 23	1♓58	16 19	18 46
8	12 28	26 27	5♉24	22 32	29 20	21 58	1♏19	22 56	10♒42	13 52	28 14	1♊4
9	24 15	8♉37	17 38	5♋36	13♌2	6♎11	15 18	5♑59	22 52	25 44	10♉15	13 33
10	6♈6	21 3	0♊5	18 57	26 58	20 27	29 9	18 48	4♓54	7♈35	22 23	26 14
11	18 4	3♊50	12 48	2♌39	11♍9	4♏45	12♐48	1♒25	16 51	19 27	4♊38	9♋6
12	0♉16	17 0	25 52	16 42	25 33	18 59	26 15	13 49	28 44	1♉21	17 2	22 10
13	12 47	0♋37	9♋18	1♍6	10♎9	3♐4	9♑27	26 2	10♈35	13 20	29 35	5♌25
14	25 39	14 42	23 9	15 49	24 50	16 57	22 23	8♓7	22 26	25 24	12♋19	18 51
15	8♊58	29 12	7♌27	0♎46	9♏30	0♑34	5♒5	20 5	4♉20	7♊35	25 15	2♍29
16	22 42	14♌4	22 8	15 50	24 2	13 50	17 31	1♈57	16 17	19 56	8♌26	16 19
17	6♋52	29 10	7♍9	0♏51	8♐18	26 47	29 44	13 48	28 23	2♋30	21 54	0♎21
18	21 22	14♍22	22 22	15 40	22 13	9♒23	11♓47	25 39	10♊40	15 19	5♍41	14 34
19	6♌9	29 30	7♎37	0♐8	5♑43	21 42	23 42	7♉36	23 13	28 27	19 49	28 56
20	21 2	14♎26	22 44	14 10	18 48	3♓48	5♈33	19 41	6♋4	11♌59	4♎17	13♏24
21	5♍55	29 1	7♏34	27 43	1♒29	15 44	17 25	2♊0	19 19	25 56	19 2	27 53
22	20 41	13♏11	21 58	10♑48	13 50	27 35	29 22	14 36	3♌1	10♍19	3♏57	12♐17
23	5♎14	26 56	5♐55	23 27	25 55	9♈27	11♉29	27 34	17 10	25 6	18 54	26 29
24	19 29	10♐15	19 22	5♒46	7♓49	21 24	23 50	10♋57	1♍46	10♎11	3♐44	10♑25
25	3♏25	23 11	2♑21	17 49	19 39	3♉30	6♊30	24 45	16 44	25 26	18 18	24 1
26	17 2	5♑48	14 57	29 41	1♈29	15 51	19 30	9♌0	1♎57	10♏40	2♑30	7♒15
27	0♐21	18 8	27 14	11♓29	13 24	28 29	2♋54	23 37	17 15	25 41	16 15	20 7
28	13 23	0♒16	9♒16	23 17	25 27	11♊25	16 40	8♍31	2♏27	10♐21	29 32	2♓39
29	26 9		21 9	5♈8	7♉43	24 41	0♌47	23 35	17 22	24 33	12♒24	14 54
30	8♑42		2♓57	17 6	20 13	8♋14	15 11	8♎38	1♐53	8♑15	24 53	26 57
31	21 3		14 43		2♊58		29 47	23 33		21 28		8♈52

DM	Jan.	Feb.	March	April	May	June	July	August	Sept.	Oct.	Nov.	Dec.
	° ′	° ′	° ′	° ′	° ′	° ′	° ′	° ′	° ′	° ′	° ′	° ′
1	20♈43	4♊32	12♊27	28♋39	4♍36	27♎27	6♐40	28♑41	17♓1	20♈25	4♊54	7♋35
2	2♉37	16 56	24 47	12♌1	18 47	12♏26	21 18	12♒17	29 36	2♉29	16 43	19 40
3	14 37	29 39	7♋25	25 52	3♎26	27 30	5♑46	25 37	11♈57	14 25	28 35	1♌53
4	26 48	12♋42	20 27	10♍10	18 27	12♐31	20 0	8♓39	24 7	26 16	10♋32	14 20
5	9♊12	26 8	3♌55	24 59	3♏42	27 20	3♒55	21 23	6♉7	8♊6	22 40	27 2
6	21 51	9♌56	17 50	10♎7	19 2	11♑48	17 28	3♈51	18 1	19 56	5♌2	10♍5
7	4♋47	24 3	2♍12	25 25	4♐13	25 51	0♓38	16 5	29 52	1♋53	17 44	23 32
8	18 0	8♍26	16 54	10♏43	19 7	9♒27	13 26	28 7	11♊44	14 1	0♍50	7♎24
9	1♌28	22 57	1♎52	25 48	3♑36	22 37	25 55	10♉3	23 44	26 26	14 24	21 41
10	15 10	7♎32	16 54	10♐33	17 36	5♓23	8♈9	21 55	5♋56	9♌13	28 29	6♏23
11	29 3	22 5	1♏53	24 52	1♒7	17 49	20 11	3♊50	18 24	22 6	13♎2	21 22
12	13♍4	6♏29	16 39	8♑42	14 11	0♈0	2♉6	15 51	1♌14	6♍8	28 0	6♐32
13	27 11	20 42	1♐7	22 5	26 53	12 0	13 59	28 4	14 28	20 19	13♏14	21 42
14	11♎22	4♐42	15 12	5♒5	9♓15	23 54	25 53	10♋32	28 8	4♎57	28 33	6♑43
15	25 33	18 27	28 55	17 44	21 24	5♉45	7♊54	23 18	12♍13	19 55	13♐47	21 26
16	9♏44	1♑58	12♑16	0♓8	3♈24	17 38	20 3	6♌24	26 39	5♏4	28 45	5♒45
17	23 51	15 14	25 19	12 20	15 18	29 35	2♋25	19 51	11♎20	20 13	13♑19	19 37
18	7♐52	28 18	8♒5	24 23	27 9	11♊39	15 0	3♍36	26 8	5♐13	27 27	3♓2
19	21 45	11♒10	20 38	6♈21	9♉1	23 51	27 51	17 38	10♏54	19 54	11♒8	16 1
20	5♑28	23 50	3♓0	18 15	20 54	6♋12	10♌56	1♎52	25 32	4♑14	24 23	28 38
21	18 58	6♓18	15 13	0♉8	2♊51	18 45	24 17	16 12	9♐57	18 9	7♓15	10♈58
22	2♒14	18 36	27 20	11 59	14 53	1♌29	7♍51	0♏35	24 4	1♒40	19 48	23 4
23	15 13	0♈45	9♈20	23 52	27 2	14 26	21 38	14 55	7♑54	14 51	2♈7	5♉0
24	27 57	12 46	21 16	5♊47	9♋19	27 37	5♎35	29 9	21 27	27 44	14 15	16 51
25	10♓25	24 40	3♉0	17 17	21 47	11♍4	19 40	13♐18	4♒45	10♓22	26 15	28 41
26	22 39	6♉32	15 0	29 55	4♌27	24 46	3♏52	27 12	17 49	22 48	8♉10	10♊32
27	4♈43	18 24	26 53	12♋13	17 24	8♎44	18 7	10♑59	0♓40	5♈4	20 2	22 27
28	16 38	0♊21	8♊49	24 46	0♍40	22 57	2♐23	24 35	13 22	17 13	1♊53	4♋28
29	28 31		20 53	7♌38	14 18	7♏24	16 38	8♒0	25 52	29 15	13 44	16 37
30	10♌24		3♋9	20 54	28 19	22 0	0♑48	21 13	8♈14	11♉11	25 38	28 55
31	22 23		15 43		12♎43		14 50	4♓13		23 4		11♌24

THE PLACE OF THE MOON FOR THE YEARS 1880–1881

DM	Jan.	Feb.	March	April	May	June	July	August	Sept.	Oct.	Nov.	Dec.
	° ′	° ′	° ′	° ′	° ′	° ′	° ′	° ′	° ′	° ′	° ′	° ′
1	24♌ 5	14♎14	8♏53	2♑15	10♒28	29♓51	3♉51	18♊ 8	2♌ 6	5♍13	23♎55	1♐ 2
2	6♍59	28 6	23 5	16 15	23 58	12♈25	15 53	29 55	14 25	18 19	8♏16	16 3
3	20 10	12♏ 7	7♐15	0♒ 1	7♓ 9	24 44	27 47	11♋47	26 59	1♎46	22 52	1♑ 9
4	3♎37	26 15	21 22	13 35	20 6	6♉52	9♊36	23 46	9♍50	15 32	7♐35	16 9
5	17 22	10♐29	5♑24	26 57	2♈48	18 52	21 23	5♌54	22 58	29 33	22 17	0♒58
6	1♏26	24 48	19 20	10♓ 7	15 18	0♊45	3♋11	18 14	6♎21	13♏44	6♑54	15 28
7	15 46	9♑ 7	3♒11	23 7	27 38	12 34	15 3	0♍47	19 56	28 0	21 19	29 37
8	0♐21	23 24	16 54	5♈55	9♉48	24 22	27 1	13 33	3♏41	12♐18	5♒31	13♓23
9	15 6	7♒35	0♓27	18 31	21 50	6♋ 9	9♌ 7	26 32	17 33	26 32	19 28	26 47
10	29 55	21 34	13 50	0♉55	3♊44	18 0	21 23	9♎44	1♐32	10♑42	3♓ 9	9♈50
11	14♑40	5♓18	26 58	13 7	15 34	29 56	3♍51	23 10	15 35	24 46	16 36	22 35
12	29 14	18 43	9♈52	25 10	27 21	12♌ 1	16 33	6♏48	29 42	8♒43	29 49	5♉ 5
13	13♒31	1♈48	22 29	7♊ 3	9♋ 8	24 17	29 30	20 40	13♑52	22 33	12♈48	17 22
14	27 26	14 33	4♉51	18 52	20 59	6♍50	12♎46	4♐44	28 3	6♓16	25 34	29 29
15	10♓57	26 59	17 0	0♋39	2♌59	19 42	26 21	19 1	12♒13	19 49	8♉ 8	11♊28
16	24 3	9♉ 9	28 57	12 30	15 11	2♎56	10♏16	3♑27	26 20	3♈10	20 30	23 21
17	6♈47	21 8	10♊48	24 29	27 42	16 36	24 32	18 0	10♓18	16 19	2♊41	5♋11
18	19 10	2♊59	22 36	6♌42	10♍34	0♏42	9♐ 5	2♒36	24 5	29 13	14 43	16 59
19	1♉18	14 48	4♋28	19 14	23 53	15 12	23 53	17 8	7♈36	11♉52	26 37	28 47
20	13 15	26 41	16 28	2♍10	7♎41	0♐ 3	8♑49	1♓30	20 48	24 16	8♋25	10♌38
21	25 6	8♋42	28 43	15 33	21 57	15 8	23 47	15 36	3♉40	6♊25	20 12	22 36
22	6♊56	20 56	11♌17	29 25	6♏38	0♑20	8♒37	29 21	16 12	18 24	2♌ 0	4♍43
23	18 48	3♌26	24 13	13♎43	21 38	15 27	23 12	12♈43	28 27	0♋14	13 55	17 4
24	0♋47	16 15	7♍34	28 23	6♐49	0♒22	7♓27	25 41	10♊28	12 1	26 1	29 42
25	12 56	29 24	21 20	13♏18	22 1	14 57	21 16	8♉17	22 20	23 50	8♍23	12♎41
26	25 17	12♍53	5♎27	28 18	7♑ 3	29 8	4♈39	20 34	4♋ 8	5♌45	21 5	26 5
27	7♌51	26 37	19 52	13♐15	21 49	12♓52	17 36	2♊36	15 58	17 53	4♎12	9♏55
28	20 41	10♎35	4♏26	28 1	6♒13	26 9	0♉11	14 28	27 55	0♍19	17 56	24 12
29	3♍45	24 42	19 4	12♑30	20 13	9♈ 3	12 26	26 16	10♌ 3	13 6	1♏48	8♐54
30	17 3		3♐37	26 39	3♓48	21 35	24 28	8♋ 5	22 28	26 17	16 15	23 55
31	0♎33		18 2		17 0		6♊20	20 0		9♎54		9♑ 7

DM	Jan.	Feb.	March	April	May	June	July	August	Sept.	Oct.	Nov.	Dec.
	° ′	° ′	° ′	° ′	° ′	° ′	° ′	° ′	° ′	° ′	° ′	° ′
1	24♑21	16♓54	24♓50	13♉48	16♊59	1♌ 3	3♍20	19♎ 9	8♐ 5	16♑ 9	9♓40	18♈ 9
2	9♒28	1♈ 4	8♈57	26 36	29 7	12 53	15 21	1♏53	21 48	0♒22	23 55	1♉41
3	24 18	14 45	22 41	9♊ 4	11♋ 4	24 46	27 34	14 56	5♑53	14 49	8♈ 5	15 1
4	8♓44	27 58	5♉57	21 14	22 55	6♍47	10♎ 1	28 23	20 20	29 26	22 5	28 7
5	22 43	10♉44	18 48	3♋13	4♌45	19 0	22 47	12♐15	5♒ 7	14♓ 8	5♉53	11♊ 0
6	6♈14	23 8	1♊15	15 4	16 38	1♎30	5♏56	26 32	20 7	28 47	19 24	23 39
7	19 19	5♊14	13 24	26 53	28 40	14 21	19 30	11♑15	5♓12	13♈15	2♊37	6♋ 5
8	2♉ 0	17 9	25 21	8♌45	10♍55	27 35	3♐32	26 18	20 13	27 27	15 30	18 19
9	14 23	28 57	7♋10	20 46	23 27	11♏15	17 59	11♒32	4♈59	11♉16	28 5	0♌23
10	26 31	10♋44	18 57	3♍ 0	6♎19	25 20	2♑50	26 48	19 22	24 41	10♋24	12 19
11	8♊29	22 32	0♌48	15 29	19 33	9♐47	17 56	11♓55	3♉18	7♊41	22 29	24 11
12	20 20	4♌25	12 46	28 16	3♏10	24 31	3♒10	26 43	16 45	20 19	4♌26	6♍ 3
13	2♋ 8	16 26	24 54	11♎22	17 6	9♑26	18 20	11♈ 5	29 45	2♋38	16 18	17 59
14	13 55	28 37	7♍16	24 45	1♐20	24 24	3♓19	24 58	12♊20	14 42	28 11	0♎ 3
15	25 45	10♍57	19 52	8♏24	15 46	9♒16	17 56	8♉21	24 36	26 37	10♍ 8	12 22
16	7♌38	23 28	2♎41	22 14	0♑18	23 56	2♈ 9	21 17	6♋38	8♌28	22 16	24 58
17	19 37	6♎11	15 44	6♐14	14 51	8♓19	15 54	3♊50	18 32	20 20	4♎37	7♏55
18	1♍44	19 4	28 59	20 20	29 20	22 21	29 12	16 4	0♌21	2♍17	17 15	21 17
19	14 0	2♏10	12♏25	4♑28	13♒41	6♈ 1	12♉ 7	28 6	12 11	14 24	0♏11	5♐ 4
20	26 27	15 30	26 0	18 38	27 52	19 21	24 41	9♋59	24 6	26 42	13 28	19 14
21	9♎ 8	29 4	9♐44	2♒48	11♓49	2♉22	7♊ 0	21 48	6♍ 7	9♎14	27 3	3♑43
22	22 5	12♐54	23 37	16 56	25 34	15 6	19 6	3♌37	18 17	22 0	10♐55	18 27
23	5♏21	27 1	7♑39	1♓ 0	9♈ 4	27 35	1♋ 4	15 28	0♎37	5♏ 1	25 1	3♒17
24	18 58	11♑24	21 49	14 59	22 20	9♊53	12 56	27 23	13 8	18 15	9♑16	18 5
25	2♐59	26 2	6♒ 6	28 49	5♉22	22 0	24 46	9♍24	25 49	1♐41	23 36	2♓44
26	17 22	10♒48	20 28	12♈29	18 10	4♋ 0	6♌36	21 32	8♏41	15 19	7♒56	17 9
27	2♑ 7	25 37	4♓50	25 56	0♊45	15 55	18 27	3♎48	21 45	29 5	22 14	1♈17
28	17 7	10♓20	19 8	9♉ 7	13 7	27 46	0♍21	16 13	5♐ 0	13♑ 0	6♓26	15 5
29	2♒15		3♈15	22 1	25 17	9♌35	12 19	28 49	18 28	27 3	20 31	28 35
30	17 22		17 7	4♊38	7♋19	21 25	24 25	11♏38	2♑11	11♒12	4♈25	11♉47
31	2♓18		0♉39		19 13		6♎41	24 42		25 25		24 44

THE PLACE OF THE MOON FOR THE YEARS 1882–1883

D M	Jan.	Feb.	March	April	May	June	July	August	Sept.	Oct.	Nov.	Dec.
	° ′	° ′	° ′	° ′	° ′	° ′	° ′	° ′	° ′	° ′	° ′	° ′
1	7 ♊ 27	23 ♋ 29	2 ♌ 28	16 ♍ 48	19 ♎ 30	6 ♐ 24	12 ♑ 45	6 ♓ 4	29 ♈ 44	6 ♊ 38	24 ♋ 16	26 ♌ 54
2	19 59	5 ♌ 27	14 20	28 48	1 ♏ 57	19 55	27 12	21 3	13 ♉ 57	20 7	6 ♌ 43	8 ♍ 55
3	2 ♋ 21	17 21	26 12	10 ♎ 56	14 38	3 ♑ 42	11 ♒ 50	5 ♈ 48	27 44	3 ♋ 10	18 54	20 48
4	14 34	29 14	8 ♍ 5	23 11	27 32	17 42	26 30	20 13	11 ♊ 5	15 51	0 ♍ 54	2 ♎ 39
5	26 40	11 ♍ 6	20 1	5 ♏ 25	10 ♐ 39	1 ♒ 52	11 ♓ 7	4 ♉ 16	24 4	28 14	12 46	14 31
6	8 ♌ 39	23 0	2 ♎ 0	18 10	24 0	16 7	25 35	17 57	6 ♋ 43	10 ♌ 23	24 37	26 29
7	20 34	4 ♎ 57	14 4	0 ♐ 56	7 ♑ 33	0 ♓ 25	9 ♈ 49	1 ♊ 17	19 7	22 23	6 ♎ 28	8 ♏ 38
8	2 ♍ 25	17 0	26 15	13 55	21 19	14 41	23 48	14 18	1 ♌ 20	4 ♍ 17	18 24	21 0
9	14 17	29 13	8 ♏ 35	27 8	5 ♒ 15	28 53	7 ♉ 31	27 4	13 25	16 8	0 ♏ 28	3 ♐ 38
10	26 12	11 ♏ 40	21 6	10 ♑ 39	19 22	12 ♈ 58	21 0	9 ♋ 37	25 23	27 59	12 40	16 34
11	8 ♎ 14	24 25	3 ♐ 53	24 27	3 ♓ 37	26 56	4 ♊ 14	22 0	7 ♍ 17	9 ♎ 51	25 4	29 46
12	20 27	7 ♐ 32	16 58	8 ♒ 34	17 57	10 ♉ 43	17 16	4 ♌ 14	19 9	21 48	7 ♐ 39	13 ♑ 13
13	2 ♏ 57	21 7	0 ♑ 25	22 58	2 ♈ 20	24 20	0 ♋ 6	16 21	1 ♎ 0	3 ♏ 49	20 27	26 54
14	15 48	5 ♑ 10	14 17	7 ♓ 37	16 40	7 ♊ 44	12 45	28 22	12 51	15 58	3 ♑ 29	10 ♒ 46
15	29 5	19 42	28 35	22 24	0 ♉ 55	20 55	25 12	10 ♍ 17	24 45	28 16	16 44	24 45
16	12 ♐ 49	4 ♒ 39	13 ♒ 16	7 ♈ 12	14 59	3 ♋ 52	7 ♌ 30	22 8	6 ♏ 43	10 ♐ 45	0 ♒ 13	8 ♓ 50
17	27 2	19 54	28 16	21 54	28 48	16 35	19 38	3 ♎ 58	18 50	23 28	13 56	22 58
18	11 ♑ 41	5 ♓ 16	13 ♓ 27	6 ♉ 23	12 ♊ 20	29 3	1 ♍ 39	15 48	1 ♐ 9	6 ♑ 27	27 53	7 ♈ 7
19	26 41	20 33	28 38	20 31	25 32	11 ♌ 18	13 33	27 43	13 44	19 46	12 ♓ 3	21 15
20	11 ♒ 53	5 ♈ 34	13 ♈ 38	4 ♊ 16	8 ♋ 25	23 23	25 24	9 ♏ 47	26 40	3 ♒ 27	26 24	5 ♉ 21
21	27 6	20 11	28 19	17 36	21 0	5 ♍ 20	7 ♎ 15	22 4	10 ♑ 0	17 29	10 ♈ 54	19 24
22	12 ♓ 9	4 ♉ 19	12 ♉ 34	0 ♋ 32	3 ♌ 19	17 13	19 11	4 ♐ 40	23 47	1 ♓ 54	25 27	3 ♊ 20
23	26 55	17 57	26 20	13 7	15 25	29 6	1 ♏ 16	17 39	8 ♒ 3	16 37	9 ♉ 59	17 8
24	11 ♈ 16	1 ♊ 7	9 ♊ 38	25 25	27 23	11 ♎ 4	13 36	1 ♑ 5	22 45	1 ♈ 33	24 24	0 ♋ 44
25	25 12	13 53	22 30	7 ♌ 29	9 ♍ 17	23 12	26 15	15 1	7 ♓ 48	16 33	8 ♊ 36	14 5
26	8 ♉ 41	26 19	5 ♋ 0	19 25	21 11	5 ♏ 34	9 ♐ 18	29 27	23 3	1 ♉ 30	22 32	27 9
27	21 46	8 ♋ 31	17 14	1 ♍ 18	3 ♎ 10	18 15	22 49	14 ♒ 19	8 ♈ 20	16 15	6 ♋ 6	9 ♌ 56
28	4 ♊ 32	20 33	29 15	13 11	15 18	1 ♐ 18	6 ♑ 47	29 29	23 27	0 ♊ 41	19 19	22 26
29	17 2		11 ♌ 10	25 9	27 39	14 44	21 12	14 ♓ 47	8 ♉ 17	14 43	2 ♌ 9	4 ♍ 40
30	29 19		23 1	7 ♎ 14	10 ♏ 16	28 34	5 ♒ 59	0 ♈ 2	22 41	28 19	14 40	16 42
31	11 ♋ 27		4 ♍ 53		23 11		20 59	15 4		11 ♋ 30		28 35

D M	Jan.	Feb.	March	April	May	June	July	August	Sept.	Oct.	Nov.	Dec
	° ′	° ′	° ′	° ′	° ′	° ′	° ′	° ′	° ′	° ′	° ′	° ′
1	10 ♎ 25	24 ♏ 10	2 ♐ 22	19 ♑ 21	26 ♒ 11	19 ♈ 13	28 ♉ 9	19 ♋ 38	7 ♍ 37	10 ♎ 44	24 ♏ 58	28 ♐ 0
2	22 16	6 ♐ 35	14 44	2 ♒ 51	10 ♓ 22	3 ♉ 50	12 ♊ 24	2 ♌ 59	19 57	22 36	6 ♐ 50	10 ♑ 20
3	4 ♏ 14	19 22	27 27	16 49	24 54	18 32	26 32	16 5	2 ♎ 5	4 ♏ 24	18 49	22 51
4	16 24	2 ♑ 35	10 ♑ 36	1 ♓ 14	9 ♈ 43	3 ♊ 11	10 ♋ 29	28 54	14 3	16 10	0 ♑ 56	5 ♒ 34
5	28 51	16 16	24 14	16 3	24 43	17 42	24 11	11 ♍ 28	25 54	27 58	13 15	18 31
6	11 ♐ 37	0 ♒ 24	8 ♒ 22	1 ♈ 9	9 ♉ 46	1 ♋ 57	7 ♌ 34	23 46	7 ♏ 41	9 ♐ 50	25 48	1 ♓ 43
7	24 47	14 54	22 57	16 23	24 43	15 53	20 37	5 ♎ 50	19 28	21 52	8 ♒ 40	15 13
8	8 ♑ 19	29 41	7 ♓ 53	1 ♉ 34	9 ♊ 26	29 26	3 ♍ 20	17 44	1 ♐ 19	4 ♑ 7	21 53	29 1
9	22 12	14 ♓ 34	23 1	16 35	23 49	12 ♌ 35	15 44	29 33	13 21	16 40	5 ♓ 30	13 ♈ 10
10	6 ♒ 22	29 26	8 ♈ 13	1 ♊ 15	7 ♋ 47	25 20	27 52	11 ♏ 21	25 38	29 36	19 32	27 37
11	20 43	14 ♈ 9	23 16	15 32	21 19	7 ♍ 45	9 ♎ 48	23 14	8 ♑ 14	12 ♒ 57	3 ♈ 59	12 ♉ 20
12	5 ♓ 9	28 36	8 ♉ 4	29 22	4 ♌ 25	19 54	21 38	5 ♐ 17	21 15	26 46	18 48	27 51
13	19 35	12 ♉ 46	22 30	12 ♋ 46	17 8	1 ♎ 50	3 ♏ 27	17 35	4 ♒ 43	11 ♓ 2	3 ♉ 52	12 ♊ 13
14	3 ♈ 55	26 36	6 ♊ 33	25 46	29 31	13 41	15 20	0 ♑ 14	18 38	25 43	19 4	27 7
15	18 6	10 ♊ 9	20 11	8 ♌ 25	11 ♍ 39	25 29	27 23	13 15	2 ♓ 59	10 ♈ 43	4 ♊ 15	11 ♋ 47
16	2 ♉ 8	23 27	3 ♋ 28	20 47	23 35	7 ♏ 21	9 ♐ 39	26 41	17 40	25 54	19 14	26 5
17	15 59	6 ♋ 30	16 24	2 ♍ 55	5 ♎ 25	19 20	22 13	10 ♒ 30	2 ♈ 34	11 ♉ 6	3 ♋ 53	9 ♌ 58
18	29 40	19 20	29 5	14 54	17 13	1 ♐ 30	5 ♑ 6	24 40	17 33	26 9	18 7	23 23
19	13 ♊ 11	2 ♌ 0	11 ♌ 31	26 47	29 3	13 53	18 20	9 ♓ 5	2 ♉ 28	10 ♊ 57	1 ♌ 53	6 ♍ 20
20	26 32	14 29	23 46	8 ♎ 36	10 ♏ 57	26 32	1 ♒ 52	23 39	17 12	25 23	15 10	18 53
21	9 ♋ 43	26 49	5 ♍ 53	20 25	22 58	9 ♑ 26	15 40	8 ♈ 15	1 ♊ 41	9 ♋ 23	28 2	1 ♎ 7
22	22 43	8 ♍ 59	17 53	2 ♏ 15	5 ♐ 9	22 36	29 41	22 47	15 50	22 58	10 ♍ 31	13 6
23	5 ♌ 31	21 1	29 47	14 9	17 31	5 ♒ 59	13 ♓ 49	7 ♉ 11	29 39	6 ♌ 9	22 43	24 56
24	18 6	2 ♎ 56	11 ♎ 37	26 8	0 ♑ 5	19 34	28 1	21 24	13 ♋ 9	18 58	4 ♎ 42	6 ♏ 42
25	0 ♍ 28	14 46	23 25	8 ♐ 16	12 53	3 ♓ 20	12 ♈ 14	5 ♊ 24	26 21	1 ♍ 28	16 32	18 29
26	12 38	26 33	5 ♏ 14	20 34	25 54	17 14	26 24	19 12	9 ♌ 16	13 44	28 19	0 ♐ 22
27	24 37	8 ♏ 22	17 6	3 ♑ 4	9 ♒ 10	1 ♈ 16	10 ♉ 31	2 ♋ 47	21 56	25 48	10 ♏ 5	12 23
28	6 ♎ 29	20 16	29 4	15 51	22 41	15 24	24 33	16 10	4 ♍ 24	7 ♎ 44	21 54	24 36
29	18 17		11 ♐ 13	28 57	6 ♓ 27	29 36	8 ♊ 31	29 20	16 40	19 35	3 ♐ 49	7 ♑ 0
30	0 ♏ 7		23 35	12 ♒ 23	20 29	13 ♉ 52	22 22	12 ♌ 18	28 46	1 ♏ 22	15 50	19 38
31	12 2		6 ♑ 17		4 ♈ 4		6 ♋ 5	25 4		13 10		2 ♒ 28

THE PLACE OF THE MOON FOR THE YEARS 1884–1885

D M	Jan.	Feb.	March	April	May	June	July	August	Sept.	Oct.	Nov.	Dec.
	° ′	° ′	° ′	° ′	° ′	° ′	° ′	° ′	° ′	° ′	° ′	° ′
1	15♒30	6♈21	0♉47	24♊5	2♌0	20♍38	23♎52	7♐44	22♑0	25♒18	14♈8	21♉24
2	28 44	20 20	15 8	8♋10	15 29	3♎2	5♏48	19 38	4♒31	8♓33	28 39	6♊37
3	12♓8	4♉21	29 23	21 57	28 34	15 9	17 38	1♑40	17 20	22 11	13♉29	21 57
4	25 43	18 26	13♊31	5♌26	11♍19	27 7	29 26	13 52	0♓27	6♈10	28 30	7♋15
5	9♈29	2♊33	27 31	18 38	23 47	8♏58	11♐17	26 16	13 51	20 26	13♊34	22 18
6	23 26	16 40	11♋21	1♍33	6♎2	20 47	23 14	8♒53	27 30	4♉55	28 32	6♌58
7	7♉36	0♋47	25 1	14 15	18 6	2♐36	5♑18	21 44	11♈22	19 31	13♋15	21 10
8	21 56	14 50	8♌30	26 43	0♏3	14 28	17 31	4♓47	25 23	4♊8	27 37	4♍29
9	6♊25	28 45	21 46	9♎1	11 55	26 24	29 54	18 3	9♉31	18 41	11♌36	18 5
10	20 57	12♌28	4♍49	21 8	23 45	8♑27	12♒27	1♈29	23 43	3♋4	25 12	0♎52
11	5♋29	25 56	17 38	3♏8	5♐35	20 36	25 11	15 6	7♊56	17 14	8♍26	13 30
12	19 51	9♍6	0♎12	15 2	17 26	2♒55	8♓6	28 52	22 9	1♌9	21 21	25 46
13	3♌59	21 56	12 33	26 52	29 21	15 25	21 13	12♉49	6♋18	14 50	3♎59	7♏50
14	17 46	4♎28	24 42	8♐41	11♑22	28 7	4♈34	26 54	20 22	28 15	16 25	19 48
15	1♍9	16 43	6♏41	20 33	23 32	11♓4	18 10	11♊8	4♌19	11♍25	28 39	1♐41
16	14 8	28 45	18 33	2♑30	5♒54	24 20	2♉2	25 29	18 6	24 21	10♏46	13 32
17	26 44	10♏38	0♐22	14 37	18 32	7♈56	16 12	9♋52	1♍41	7♎4	22 46	25 24
18	9♎0	22 26	12 12	26 57	1♓28	21 54	0♊37	24 13	15 2	19 35	4♐42	7♑16
19	21 1	4♐16	24 8	9♒37	14 47	6♉16	15 16	8♌28	28 7	1♏55	16 34	19 12
20	2♏52	16 13	6♑16	22 38	28 31	20 58	0♋3	22 30	10♎56	14 5	28 25	1♒11
21	14 40	28 21	18 39	6♓4	12♈40	5♊56	14 50	6♍15	23 30	26 7	10♑17	13 16
22	26 29	10♑45	1♒22	19 57	27 15	21 3	29 30	19 40	5♏49	8♐2	22 11	25 29
23	8♐24	23 29	14 28	4♈15	12♉11	6♋8	13♌54	2♎44	17 55	19 53	4♒11	7♓53
24	20 31	6♒34	27 59	18 57	27 21	21 3	27 57	15 27	29 53	1♑44	16 20	20 32
25	2♑52	20 1	11♓54	3♉55	12♊36	5♌37	11♍34	27 51	11♐45	13 37	28 44	3♈30
26	15 30	3♓47	26 12	19 3	27 45	19 45	24 45	10♏1	23 37	25 38	11♓26	16 51
27	28 25	17 50	10♈46	4♊10	12♋40	3♍25	7♎31	21 59	5♑32	7♒50	24 30	0♉38
28	11♒36	2♈4	25 32	19 7	27 11	16 36	19 57	3♐52	17 35	20 19	8♈2	14 53
29	25 2	16 25	10♉21	3♋48	11♌14	29 21	2♏5	15 43	29 51	3♓8	22 2	29 34
30	8♓40		25 7	18 7	24 49	11♎44	14 3	27 39	12♒25	16 22	6♉30	14♊37
31	22 27		9♊43		7♍56		25 54	9♑43		0♈2		29 54

D M	Jan.	Feb.	March	April	May	June	July	August	Sept.	Oct.	Nov.	Dec.
	° ′	° ′	° ′	° ′	° ′	° ′	° ′	° ′	° ′	° ′	° ′	° ′
1	15♋13	7♍29	15♍27	3♏38	6♐47	21♑11	23♒49	10♈5	29♉55	8♋45	2♍5	9♎53
2	0♌24	21 27	29 14	16 15	18 53	3♒3	5♓52	22 55	13♊48	22 58	15 56	23 5
3	15 15	4♎57	12♎40	28 38	0♑51	14 57	18 6	6♉5	27 58	7♌15	29 39	6♏4
4	29 39	18 0	25 44	10♐48	12 46	26 58	0♈33	19 38	12♋23	21 32	13♎12	18 53
5	13♍33	0♏40	8♏26	22 48	24 37	9♓10	13 20	3♊35	27 0	5♍48	26 34	1♐31
6	26 57	13 0	20 50	4♑43	6♒32	21 38	26 30	17 56	11♌44	19 58	9♏45	13 59
7	9♎53	25 5	3♐0	16 36	18 35	4♈27	10♉7	2♋39	26 27	3♎58	22 42	26 17
8	22 27	7♐1	14 59	28 32	0♓49	17 42	24 13	17 38	11♍4	17 44	5♐25	8♑25
9	4♏42	18 52	26 52	10♒36	13 20	1♉25	8♊47	2♌45	25 26	1♏15	17 54	20 24
10	16 44	0♑44	8♑45	22 53	26 13	15 37	23 44	17 50	9♎31	14 27	0♑9	2♒16
11	28 38	12 38	20 41	5♓25	9♈30	0♊16	8♋57	2♍43	23 12	27 20	12 13	14 4
12	10♐28	24 39	2♒45	18 18	23 14	15 17	24 15	17 17	6♏31	9♐55	24 8	25 52
13	22 19	6♒49	15 0	1♈31	7♉24	0♋29	9♌28	1♎27	19 26	22 13	5♒58	7♓45
14	4♑11	19 9	27 29	15 6	21 56	15 43	24 24	15 10	2♐2	4♑19	17 48	19 46
15	16 8	1♓40	10♓14	29 1	6♊44	0♌47	8♍57	28 27	14 19	16 15	29 43	2♈3
16	28 10	14 23	23 14	13♉12	21 40	15 33	23 2	11♏19	26 24	28 7	11♓49	14 41
17	10♒19	27 17	6♈31	27 36	6♋35	29 56	6♎39	23 51	8♑21	10♒0	24 10	27 44
18	22 35	10♈23	20 2	12♊6	21 21	13♍52	19 50	6♐6	20 13	21 57	6♈51	11♉15
19	5♓0	23 41	3♉46	26 36	5♌51	27 22	2♏38	18 9	2♒6	4♓5	19 57	25 16
20	17 34	7♉12	17 41	11♋2	20 2	10♎30	15 7	0♑5	14 3	16 26	3♉28	9♊45
21	0♈21	20 56	1♊44	25 19	3♍52	23 17	27 21	11 58	26 9	29 5	17 25	24 37
22	13 23	4♊54	15 52	9♌24	17 22	5♏49	9♐26	23 50	8♓24	12♈4	1♊43	9♋42
23	26 42	19 4	0♋4	23 17	0♎34	18 9	21 23	5♒45	20 53	25 22	16 18	24 51
24	10♉21	3♋26	14 17	6♍56	13 29	0♐19	3♑17	17 45	3♈36	8♉59	1♋1	9♌52
25	24 22	17 56	28 29	20 23	26 12	12 22	15 9	29 52	16 33	22 53	15 45	24 39
26	8♊44	2♌29	12♌36	3♎37	8♏43	24 20	27 2	12♓7	29 45	6♊59	0♌22	9♍5
27	23 26	16 59	26 37	16 38	21 5	6♑15	8♒57	24 32	13♉11	21 13	14 47	23 8
28	8♋22	1♍20	10♍29	29 28	3♐18	18 8	20 55	7♈9	26 49	5♋31	28 57	6♎48
29	23 23		24 9	12♏5	15 24	0♒0	2♓59	19 58	10♊39	19 47	12♍51	20 7
30	8♌21		7♎34	24 31	27 24	11 53	15 10	3♉1	24 38	3♌59	26 29	3♏8
31	23 5		20 44		9♑19		27 31	16 20		18 6		15 53

THE PLACE OF THE MOON FOR THE YEARS 1886–1887

D M	Jan.	Feb.	March	April	May	June	July	August	Sept.	Oct.	Nov.	Dec.
	° ′	° ′	° ′	° ′	° ′	° ′	° ′	° ′	° ′	° ′	° ′	° ′
1	28♏26	14♑ 5	22♑52	6♓45	9♈18	26♉51	3♋44	27♌ 9	20♎19	26♏55	14♑16	16♒30
2	10♐48	25 57	4♒41	18 47	21 58	10♊46	18 28	12♍10	4♏36	10♐26	26 37	28 25
3	23 1	7♒47	16 29	1♈ 0	4♉56	24 59	3♌20	26 57	18 27	23 30	8♒42	10♓13
4	5♑ 6	19 36	28 20	13 26	18 12	9♋22	18 11	11♎24	1♐51	6♑10	20 36	22 1
5	17 5	1♓26	10♓15	26 6	1♊45	23 51	2♍53	25 29	14 50	18 29	2♓24	3♈55
6	28 59	13 20	22 18	9♉ 0	15 33	8♌19	17 22	9♏10	27 28	0♒33	14 12	15 58
7	10♒49	25 19	4♈49	22 8	29 30	22 42	1♎35	22 29	9♑48	12 27	26 4	28 17
8	22 36	7♈26	16 50	5♊30	13♋34	6♍56	15 30	5♐28	21 54	24 15	8♈ 6	10♉54
9	4♓25	19 46	29 24	19 4	27 42	21 0	29 7	18 8	3♒51	6♓ 3	20 20	23 51
10	16 18	2♉21	12♉11	2♋50	11♌51	4♎53	12♏28	0♑34	15 41	17 53	2♉48	7♊ 9
11	28 19	15 14	25 13	16 46	25 59	18 36	25 33	12 48	27 29	29 49	15 32	20 45
12	10♈33	28 31	8♊33	0♌52	10♍ 5	2♏ 9	8♐25	24 52	9♓17	11♈53	28 32	4♋37
13	23 6	12♊13	22 11	15 6	24 9	15 31	21 4	6♒49	21 7	24 8	11♊45	18 40
14	6♉ 2	26 21	6♋ 7	29 26	8♎ 8	28 41	3♑32	18 41	3♈ 3	6♉35	25 11	2♌49
15	19 25	10♋54	20 22	13♍51	22 2	11♐39	15 48	0♓29	15 5	19 13	8♋47	17 2
16	3♊18	25 48	4♌54	28 15	5♏46	24 24	27 55	12 16	27 16	2♊ 4	22 31	1♍13
17	17 41	10♌55	19 38	12♎34	19 20	6♑56	9♒53	24 6	9♉37	15 7	6♌22	15 22
18	2♋31	26 7	4♍28	26 44	2♐40	19 15	21 45	5♈59	22 12	28 23	20 19	29 27
19	17 39	11♍14	19 19	11♏40	15 43	1♒22	3♓33	18 0	5♊ 2	11♋53	4♍23	13♎28
20	2♌58	26 7	4♎ 1	24 17	28 29	13 19	15 20	0♉12	18 9	25 36	18 31	27 23
21	18 14	10♎38	18 30	7♐33	10♑58	25 9	27 10	12 39	1♋36	9♌34	2♎44	11♏12
22	3♍19	24 43	2♏37	20 27	23 12	6♓56	9♈ 7	25 25	15 24	23 46	16 59	24 53
23	18 4	8♏21	16 21	3♑ 1	5♒13	18 46	21 16	8♊33	29 33	8♍11	1♏13	8♐23
24	2♎23	21 33	29 39	15 17	17 5	0♈43	3♉42	22 5	14♌ 3	22 46	15 21	21 40
25	16 19	4♐21	12♐34	27 20	28 54	12 53	16 29	6♋ 5	28 50	7♎28	29 18	4♑43
26	29 42	16 48	25 6	9♒13	10♓45	25 20	29 42	20 29	13♍49	21 8	13♐ 0	17 30
27	12♏45	29 0	7♑20	21 2	22 42	8♉10	13♊22	5♌16	28 51	6♏41	26 22	0♒ 1
28	25 27	11♑ 0	19 21	2♓52	4♈52	21 25	27 30	20 19	13♎49	20 58	9♑23	12 17
29	7♐53		1♒13	14 49	17 19	5♊ 7	12♋ 4	5♍30	28 33	4♐54	22 4	24 20
30	20 6		13 2	26 56	0♉ 7	19 14	26 57	20 39	12♏57	18 26	4♒25	6♓13
31	2♑ 9		24 51		13 17		12♌ 2	5♎38		1♑33		18 1

D M	Jan.	Feb.	March	April	May	June	July	August	Sept.	Oct.	Nov.	Dec.
	° ′	° ′	° ′	° ′	° ′	° ′	° ′	° ′	° ′	° ′	° ′	° ′
1	29♓49	14♉ 3	22♉42	10♋29	17♌44	10♎54	20♏ 1	10♑54	27♒56	0♈50	15♉24	18♊50
2	11♈41	26 36	5♊12	23 58	1♍48	25 22	4♐ 2	23 52	10♓ 2	12 41	27 28	1♋24
3	23 44	9♊32	18 2	7♌50	16 10	9♏53	17 53	6♒36	22 1	24 33	9♊38	14 7
4	6♉ 2	22 54	1♋14	22 7	0♎48	24 20	1♑30	19 6	3♈56	6♉26	21 56	27 1
5	18 40	6♋43	14 53	6♍46	15 39	8♐38	14 51	1♓23	15 47	18 22	4♋24	10♌ 8
6	1♊41	20 58	28 58	21 44	0♏34	22 40	27 55	13 30	27 38	0♊23	17 4	23 27
7	15 6	5♌35	13♌30	6♎54	15 25	6♑22	10♒40	25 29	9♉31	12 33	29 58	7♍ 2
8	28 56	20 29	28 23	22 6	0♐ 4	19 41	23 8	7♈22	21 29	24 54	13♌11	20 53
9	13♋ 6	5♍32	13♍33	7♏ 9	14 23	2♒37	5♓22	19 13	3♊37	7♋29	26 46	5♎ 1
10	27 33	20 35	28 48	21 55	28 16	15 11	17 23	1♉ 5	15 58	20 24	10♍43	19 25
11	12♌10	5♎29	14♎ 0	6♐16	11♑41	27 27	29 18	13 4	28 37	3♌42	25 5	4♏ 1
12	26 51	20 8	28 58	20 9	24 40	9♓30	11♈ 9	25 13	11♋38	17 25	9♎49	18 46
13	11♍28	4♏27	13♏35	3♑32	7♒15	21 24	23 2	7♊38	25 4	1♍36	24 50	3♐30
14	25 57	18 24	27 46	16 27	19 30	3♈14	5♉ 1	20 22	8♌58	16 14	9♏59	18 7
15	10♎14	1♐58	11♐29	28 58	1♓31	15 6	17 12	3♋28	23 18	1♎15	25 6	2♑28
16	24 18	15 10	24 45	11♒11	13 23	27 4	29 38	16 59	8♍ 3	16 30	10♐ 1	16 29
17	8♏ 7	28 4	7♑36	23 10	25 11	9♉13	12♊22	0♌54	23 5	1♏49	24 34	0♒ 5
18	21 41	10♑40	20 6	5♓ 1	7♈ 0	21 35	25 27	15 11	8♎17	17 1	8♑40	13 16
19	5♐ 1	23 3	2♒20	16 48	18 55	4♊13	8♋52	29 47	23 27	1♐56	22 17	26 3
20	18 8	5♒14	14 22	28 35	0♉58	17 8	22 37	14♍35	8♏27	16 25	5♒26	8♓30
21	1♑ 1	17 17	26 15	10♈26	13 13	0♋19	6♌39	29 27	23 8	0♑25	18 9	20 40
22	13 42	29 13	8♓ 4	22 22	25 40	13 45	20 54	14♎17	7♐25	13 55	0♓31	2♈39
23	26 10	11♓ 4	19 52	4♉27	8♊19	27 24	5♍17	28 56	4♑40	26 57	12 37	14 31
24	8♒26	22 52	1♈40	16 41	21 11	11♌13	19 43	13♏21	17 40	9♒36	24 33	26 23
25	20 32	4♈40	13 31	29 4	4♋15	25 10	4♎ 9	27 27	0♒21	21 55	6♈24	8♉17
26	2♓29	16 30	25 27	11♊38	17 31	9♍13	18 30	11♐13	12 45	4♓ 1	18 15	20 19
27	14 20	28 25	7♉29	24 23	0♌57	23 21	2♏43	24 39	24 57	15 58	0♉ 7	2♊31
28	26 7	10♉28	19 39	7♋20	14 34	7♎31	16 46	7♑47	7♓ 0	27 50	12 6	14 55
29	7♈55		2♊ 0	20 32	28 22	21 43	0♐38	20 39	18 57	9♈40	24 12	27 33
30	19 47		14 33	3♌59	12♍22	5♏54	14 17	3♒16		21 32	6♊26	10♋24
31	1♉48		27 22		26 33		27 42	15 41		3♉26		23 29

THE PLACE OF THE MOON FOR THE YEARS 1888–1889

D M	Jan.	Feb.	March	April	May	June	July	August	Sept.	Oct.	Nov.	Dec.
	° ′	° ′	° ′	° ′	° ′	° ′	° ′	° ′	° ′	° ′	° ′	° ′
1	6♌47	28♍13	22♎35	16♐5	23♑14	10♓56	13♈46	27♉35	11♋44	15♌5	4♎34	12♏27
2	20 16	12♎32	7♏18	0♑10	6♒34	23 16	25 45	9♊31	24 17	28 27	19 19	27 39
3	3♍56	26 51	21 48	13 49	19 29	5♈23	7♉38	21 34	7♌12	12♍16	4♏23	12♐57
4	17 46	11♏6	6♐2	27 4	2♓4	17 20	19 31	3♋49	20 29	26 33	19 39	28 9
5	1♎44	25 14	19 58	9♒59	14 23	29 13	1♊25	16 18	4♍8	11♎11	4♐54	13♑6
6	15 50	9♐13	3♑36	22 37	26 30	11♉4	13 26	29 3	18 9	26 5	19 57	27 40
7	0♏2	23 3	16 57	5♓2	8♈29	22 57	25 34	12♌6	2♎27	11♏5	4♑42	11♒47
8	14 18	6♑42	0♒2	17 16	20 24	4♊53	7♋54	25 26	16 56	26 0	19 1	25 26
9	28 35	20 8	12 53	29 23	2♉16	16 54	20 24	9♍2	1♏29	10♐44	2♒55	8♓39
10	12♐49	3♒23	25 33	11♈24	14 8	29 2	3♌8	22 52	16 1	25 10	16 23	21 29
11	26 59	16 24	8♓1	23 20	26 1	11♋18	16 5	6♎52	0♐25	9♑16	29 29	3♈59
12	10♑53	29 11	20 21	5♉14	7♊56	23 44	29 16	21 0	14 39	23 2	12♓16	16 14
13	24 33	11♓45	2♈31	17 5	19 55	6♌21	12♍40	5♏13	28 41	6♒28	24 47	28 18
14	7♒56	24 6	14 35	28 57	1♋59	19 12	26 17	19 27	12♑29	19 36	7♈6	10♉14
15	21 0	6♈16	26 32	10♊51	14 13	2♍18	10♎8	3♐40	26 5	2♓30	19 16	22 6
16	3♓45	18 17	8♉25	22 50	26 37	15 42	24 12	17 49	9♒28	15 12	1♉19	3♊56
17	16 12	0♉11	20 16	4♋57	9♌17	29 26	8♏26	1♑53	22 40	27 43	13 16	15 47
18	28 24	12 3	2♊9	17 17	22 15	13♎31	22 48	15 49	5♓40	10♈5	25 9	27 40
19	10♈25	23 57	14 7	29 55	5♍37	27 54	7♐15	29 36	18 29	22 18	7♊0	9♋38
20	22 20	5♊57	26 14	12♌54	19 23	12♏34	21 44	13♒12	1♈7	4♉23	18 50	21 42
21	4♉12	18 8	8♋36	26 20	3♎37	27 25	6♑7	26 35	13 32	16 22	0♋41	3♌54
22	16 7	0♋34	21 18	10♍15	18 15	12♐20	20 21	9♓43	25 47	28 15	12 36	16 16
23	28 9	13 21	4♌24	24 40	3♏14	27 9	4♒22	22 35	7♉52	10♊5	24 37	28 52
24	10♊22	26 31	17 57	9♎31	18 26	11♑46	18 4	5♈12	19 49	21 54	6♌50	11♍43
25	22 51	10♌5	1♍58	24 42	3♐40	26 4	1♓27	17 34	1♊40	3♋45	19 17	24 52
26	5♋37	24 4	16 28	10♏2	18 45	9♒58	14 29	29 44	13 30	15 44	2♍3	8♎23
27	18 42	8♍24	1♎20	25 21	3♑33	23 27	27 12	11♉43	25 23	27 54	15 13	22 16
28	2♌7	23 1	16 27	10♐27	17 56	6♓32	9♈37	23 37	7♋23	10♌22	28 50	6♏32
29	15 49	7♎47	1♏39	25 10	1♒51	19 14	21 48	5♊29	19 37	23 13	12♎56	21 8
30	29 47		16 45	9♑27	15 18	1♈37	3♉48	17 24	2♌10	6♍30	27 30	6♐0
31	13♍56		1♐36		28 18		15 42	29 27		20 17		21 1

D M	Jan.	Feb.	March	April	May	June	July	August	Sept.	Oct.	Nov	Dec.
	° ′	° ′	° ′	° ′	° ′	° ′	° ′	° ′	° ′	° ′	° ′	° ′
1	6♑3	27♒33	5♓53	23♈52	27♉2	11♋15	14♌6	1♎18	22♏8	1♑5	24♒3	1♈33
2	20 55	11♓20	19 25	6♉20	8♊59	23 4	26 18	14 25	6♐3	15 11	7♓45	14 36
3	5♒32	24 44	2♈39	18 35	20 49	4♌59	8♍42	27 48	20 7	29 16	21 16	27 24
4	19 46	7♈46	15 36	0♊38	2♋36	17 3	21 22	11♏28	4♑20	13♒19	4♈36	9♉59
5	3♓35	20 26	28 14	12 32	14 23	29 21	4♎21	25 25	18 39	27 18	17 44	22 21
6	16 57	2♉47	10♉35	24 21	26 16	11♍57	17 41	9♐39	3♒3	11♓12	0♉39	4♊33
7	29 55	14 53	22 41	6♋9	8♌18	24 55	1♏24	24 8	17 27	24 57	13 20	16 37
8	12♈30	26 48	4♊37	18 2	20 35	8♎19	15 31	8♑49	1♓47	8♈29	25 48	28 32
9	24 47	8♊38	16 27	0♌5	3♍12	22 10	0♐0	23 37	15 57	21 46	8♊3	10♋23
10	6♉51	20 28	28 16	12 24	16 13	6♏29	14 49	8♒25	29 51	4♉46	20 6	22 10
11	18 45	2♋22	10♋10	25 3	29 43	21 12	29 50	23 6	13♈26	17 29	2♋1	3♌58
12	0♊35	14 25	22 14	8♍7	13♎41	6♐14	14♑57	7♓33	26 39	29 53	13 49	15 48
13	12 25	26 40	4♌33	21 37	28 6	21 26	0♒0	21 39	9♉29	12♊3	25 36	27 46
14	24 17	9♌10	17 11	5♎33	12♏54	6♑38	14 50	5♈22	21 59	24 0	7♌25	9♍55
15	6♋16	21 56	0♍10	19 52	27 55	21 42	29 22	18 39	4♊11	5♋50	19 23	22 20
16	18 23	4♍59	13 31	4♏29	13♐2	6♒28	13♓29	1♉31	16 10	17 38	1♍34	5♎6
17	0♌40	18 18	27 14	19 16	28 5	20 51	27 9	14 1	28 0	29 28	14 3	18 15
18	13 8	1♎51	11♎14	4♐4	12♑55	4♓49	10♈22	26 12	9♋48	11♌27	26 54	1♏58
19	25 49	15 36	25 27	18 46	27 27	18 22	23 11	8♊11	21 39	23 40	10♎11	15 56
20	8♍43	29 30	9♏48	3♑16	11♒36	1♈30	5♉39	20 1	3♌38	6♍11	23 55	0♐26
21	21 51	13♏31	24 11	17 31	25 24	14 16	17 50	1♋49	15 49	19 4	8♏4	15 17
22	5♎12	27 36	8♐30	1♒30	8♓50	26 44	29 49	13 38	28 15	2♎20	22 35	0♑23
23	18 48	11♐44	22 44	15 12	21 56	8♉58	11♊40	25 33	11♍0	15 58	7♐21	15 35
24	2♏38	25 53	6♑50	28 39	4♈45	21 0	23 27	7♌38	24 4	29 57	22 15	0♒42
25	16 42	10♑2	20 47	11♓52	17 19	2♊54	5♋15	19 55	7♎26	14♏12	7♑8	15 37
26	0♐58	24 9	4♒35	24 52	29 40	14 44	17 5	2♍25	21 3	28 37	21 54	0♓11
27	15 25	8♒12	18 14	7♈40	11♉52	26 31	29 2	15 10	4♏52	13♐6	6♒26	14 22
28	29 58	22 8	1♓45	20 16	23 54	8♋19	11♌7	28 9	18 50	27 33	20 41	28 3
29	14♑33		15 5	2♉42	5♊50	20 9	23 22	11♎22	2♐53	11♑53	4♓37	11♈27
30	29 5		28 13	14 57	17 41	2♌4	5♍48	24 46	16 59	26 7	18 14	24 24
31	13♒27		11♈10		29 28		18 26	8♏22		10♒10		7♉2

THE PLACE OF THE MOON FOR THE YEARS 1890–1891

D M	Jan.	Feb.	March	April	May	June	July	August	Sept.	Oct.	Nov.	Dec.
	° ′	° ′	° ′	° ′	° ′	° ′	° ′	° ′	° ′	° ′	° ′	° ′
1	19 ♉ 24	4 ♋ 12	12 ♋ 39	16 ♌ 27	29 ♍ 18	17 ♏ 21	24 ♐ 13	17 ♒ 51	11 ♈ 11	17 ♉ 21	3 ♋ 56	6 ♌ 1
2	1 ♊ 33	15 59	24 26	8 ♍ 42	12 ♎ 14	1 ♐ 28	9 ♑ 6	3 ♓ 4	25 28	0 ♊ 41	16 11	17 56
3	13 32	27 47	6 ♌ 17	21 11	25 29	15 53	24 10	18 4	9 ♉ 15	13 35	28 14	29 48
4	25 26	9 ♌ 40	18 14	3 ♎ 57	9 ♏ 4	0 ♑ 31	9 ♒ 16	2 ♈ 40	22 32	26 6	10 ♌ 8	11 ♍ 41
5	7 ♋ 16	21 38	0 ♍ 22	16 58	22 55	15 15	24 15	16 50	5 ♊ 23	8 ♋ 19	22 0	23 40
6	19 4	3 ♍ 44	12 40	0 ♏ 14	7 ♐ 0	29 59	8 ♓ 59	0 ♉ 30	17 51	20 20	3 ♍ 53	5 ♎ 49
7	0 ♌ 52	15 59	25 11	13 43	21 13	14 ♒ 36	23 23	13 43	0 ♋ 2	2 ♌ 12	15 53	18 13
8	12 43	28 24	7 ♎ 53	27 21	5 ♑ 31	29 2	7 ♈ 22	26 32	12 1	14 2	28 3	0 ♏ 56
9	24 39	11 ♎ 0	20 47	11 ♐ 9	19 50	13 ♓ 13	20 58	8 ♊ 59	23 52	25 54	10 ♎ 27	14 0
10	6 ♍ 42	23 48	3 ♏ 52	25 3	4 ♒ 7	27 7	4 ♉ 10	21 12	5 ♌ 41	7 ♍ 52	23 6	27 25
11	18 55	6 ♏ 52	17 9	9 ♑ 3	18 19	10 ♈ 44	17 2	3 ♋ 12	17 31	19 58	6 ♏ 2	11 ♐ 12
12	1 ♎ 22	20 12	0 ♐ 37	23 8	2 ♓ 25	24 4	29 36	15 6	29 24	2 ♎ 15	19 15	25 19
13	14 4	3 ♐ 51	14 17	7 ♒ 18	16 23	7 ♉ 8	11 ♊ 56	26 56	11 ♍ 24	14 44	2 ♐ 43	9 ♑ 40
14	27 6	17 51	28 10	21 30	0 ♈ 12	19 57	24 5	8 ♌ 45	23 31	27 25	16 24	24 10
15	10 ♏ 31	2 ♑ 11	12 ♑ 16	5 ♓ 43	13 49	2 ♊ 32	6 ♋ 6	20 36	5 ♎ 47	10 ♏ 18	0 ♑ 17	8 ♒ 44
16	24 21	16 50	26 36	19 53	27 15	14 56	18 1	2 ♍ 29	18 11	23 22	14 17	23 16
17	8 ♐ 37	1 ♒ 44	11 ♒ 6	3 ♈ 56	10 ♉ 26	27 8	29 52	14 27	0 ♏ 45	6 ♐ 38	28 23	7 ♓ 40
18	23 17	16 45	25 42	17 48	23 22	9 ♋ 12	11 ♌ 42	26 31	13 30	20 4	12 ♒ 33	21 54
19	8 ♑ 16	1 ♓ 44	10 ♓ 19	1 ♉ 24	6 ♊ 4	21 9	23 32	8 ♎ 43	26 27	3 ♑ 42	26 45	5 ♈ 54
20	23 27	16 33	24 49	14 43	18 30	3 ♌ 0	5 ♍ 24	21 4	9 ♐ 38	17 31	10 ♓ 55	19 40
21	8 ♒ 41	1 ♈ 3	9 ♈ 6	27 41	0 ♋ 44	14 50	17 22	3 ♏ 38	23 6	1 ♒ 33	25 3	3 ♉ 12
22	23 48	15 8	23 3	10 ♊ 20	12 47	26 40	29 27	16 27	6 ♑ 52	15 45	9 ♈ 5	16 30
23	8 ♓ 38	28 44	6 ♉ 36	22 41	24 41	8 ♍ 35	11 ♎ 43	29 35	20 58	0 ♓ 7	23 0	29 35
24	23 3	11 ♉ 52	19 44	4 ♋ 47	6 ♌ 31	20 39	24 14	13 ♐ 5	5 ♒ 24	14 35	6 ♉ 44	12 ♊ 27
25	7 ♈ 1	24 34	2 ♊ 28	16 43	18 22	2 ♎ 55	7 ♏ 4	26 58	20 5	29 4	20 16	25 7
26	20 30	6 ♊ 54	14 52	28 34	0 ♍ 17	15 29	20 16	11 ♑ 17	4 ♓ 58	13 ♈ 28	3 ♊ 32	7 ♋ 36
27	3 ♉ 32	18 59	26 58	10 ♌ 24	12 21	28 23	3 ♐ 54	25 59	19 54	27 41	16 32	19 54
28	16 9	0 ♋ 52	8 ♋ 53	22 19	24 40	11 ♏ 42	17 59	11 ♒ 1	4 ♈ 44	11 ♉ 38	29 16	2 ♌ 2
29	28 27		20 42	4 ♍ 23	7 ♎ 16	25 27	2 ♑ 30	26 13	19 19	25 15	11 ♋ 44	14 2
30	10 ♊ 31		2 ♌ 31	16 42	20 14	9 ♐ 38	17 24	11 ♓ 25	3 ♉ 33	8 ♊ 30	23 58	25 57
31	22 24		14 25		3 ♏ 36		2 ♒ 34	26 28		21 23		7 ♍ 48

D M	Jan.	Feb.	March	April	May	June	July	August	Sept.	Oct.	Nov.	Dec.
	° ′	° ′	° ′	° ′	° ′	° ′	° ′	° ′	° ′	° ′	° ′	° ′
1	19 ♍ 41	4 ♏ 25	13 ♏ 29	1 ♑ 50	9 ♒ 48	3 ♈ 26	12 ♉ 8	1 ♋ 53	18 ♌ 25	21 ♍ 17	5 ♏ 46	9 ♐ 10
2	1 ♎ 37	16 57	26 0	15 23	23 57	17 39	25 43	14 32	0 ♍ 26	3 ♎ 8	17 55	21 58
3	13 43	29 50	8 ♐ 50	29 18	8 ♓ 50	1 ♉ 47	9 ♊ 6	27 1	12 22	14 59	0 ♐ 12	5 ♑ 1
4	26 3	13 ♐ 9	22 1	13 ♒ 36	22 51	15 46	22 17	9 ♌ 20	24 15	26 53	12 40	18 17
5	8 ♏ 41	26 56	5 ♑ 38	28 14	7 ♈ 27	29 35	5 ♋ 15	21 31	6 ♎ 5	8 ♏ 51	25 20	1 ♒ 46
6	21 42	11 ♑ 13	19 43	13 ♓ 8	22 3	13 ♊ 9	18 1	3 ♍ 34	17 55	20 55	8 ♑ 13	15 26
7	5 ♐ 9	25 57	4 ♒ 16	28 10	6 ♉ 30	26 28	0 ♌ 34	15 30	29 47	3 ♐ 8	21 22	29 18
8	19 2	11 ♒ 3	19 12	13 ♈ 11	20 44	9 ♋ 30	12 55	27 22	11 ♏ 45	15 34	4 ♒ 49	13 ♓ 19
9	3 ♑ 22	26 21	4 ♓ 26	28 1	4 ♊ 40	22 15	25 4	9 ♎ 11	23 52	28 16	18 34	27 28
10	18 3	11 ♓ 39	19 45	12 ♉ 32	18 15	4 ♌ 43	7 ♍ 5	21 3	6 ♐ 13	11 ♑ 17	2 ♓ 37	11 ♈ 43
11	2 ♒ 59	26 48	4 ♈ 59	26 39	1 ♋ 27	16 58	19 0	3 ♏ 0	18 53	24 42	16 58	26 2
12	18 2	11 ♈ 36	19 57	10 ♊ 19	14 17	29 1	0 ♎ 51	15 7	1 ♑ 56	8 ♒ 32	1 ♈ 34	10 ♉ 22
13	3 ♓ 1	25 58	4 ♉ 31	23 32	26 48	10 ♍ 58	12 44	27 30	15 27	22 48	16 20	24 39
14	17 48	9 ♉ 51	18 35	6 ♋ 21	9 ♌ 3	22 51	24 44	10 ♐ 13	29 28	7 ♓ 29	1 ♉ 9	8 ♊ 49
15	2 ♈ 17	23 17	2 ♊ 10	18 49	21 6	4 ♎ 46	6 ♏ 54	23 22	13 ♒ 57	22 28	15 54	22 48
16	16 24	6 ♊ 18	15 17	1 ♌ 1	3 ♍ 2	16 46	19 20	6 ♑ 59	28 52	7 ♈ 37	0 ♊ 29	6 ♋ 32
17	0 ♉ 8	18 58	28 0	13 1	14 55	28 58	2 ♐ 6	21 6	14 ♓ 5	22 48	14 46	19 57
18	13 31	1 ♋ 21	10 ♋ 23	24 55	26 50	11 ♏ 24	15 17	5 ♒ 40	29 25	7 ♉ 50	28 41	3 ♌ 3
19	26 34	13 32	22 32	6 ♍ 47	8 ♎ 50	24 9	28 53	20 36	14 ♈ 41	22 35	12 ♋ 11	15 48
20	9 ♊ 20	25 35	4 ♌ 31	18 40	21 0	7 ♐ 13	12 ♑ 55	5 ♓ 45	29 42	6 ♊ 55	25 18	28 15
21	21 53	7 ♌ 32	16 25	0 ♎ 38	3 ♏ 22	20 39	27 19	20 57	14 ♉ 21	20 48	8 ♌ 2	10 ♍ 26
22	4 ♋ 15	19 26	28 16	12 42	15 57	4 ♑ 24	12 ♒ 0	6 ♈ 2	28 33	4 ♋ 14	20 26	22 25
23	16 28	1 ♍ 19	10 ♍ 8	24 56	28 49	18 26	26 51	20 49	12 ♊ 17	17 14	2 ♍ 35	4 ♎ 17
24	28 34	13 12	22 3	7 ♏ 19	11 ♐ 55	2 ♒ 1[illegible]	11 ♓ 1[illegible]	5 ♉ 15	25 34	29 53	14 33	16 7
25	10 ♌ 35	25 6	4 ♎ 1	19 53	25 17	17 6	26 26	19 15	8 ♋ 28	12 ♌ 13	26 25	28 0
26	22 31	7 ♎ 2	16 5	2 ♐ 39	8 ♑ 53	1 ♓ 32	10 ♈ 57	2 ♊ 51	21 3	24 19	8 ♎ 15	10 ♏ 1
27	4 ♍ 24	19 3	28 10	15 37	22 41	15 57	25 10	16 4	3 ♌ 22	6 ♍ 17	20 8	22 14
28	16 16	1 ♏ 11	10 ♏ 34	28 49	6 ♒ 39	0 ♈ 15	9 ♉ 4	28 59	15 30	18 9	2 ♏ 7	4 ♐ 43
29	28 8		23 2	12 ♑ 14	20 45	14 24	22 40	11 ♋ 37	27 30	29 59	14 16	17 31
30	10 ♎ 5		5 ♐ 43	25 53	4 ♓ 56	28 22	5 ♊ 59	24 2	9 ♍ 25	11 ♎ 50	26 36	0 ♑ 39
31	22 9		18 37		19 11		19 3	6 ♌ 18		23 46		14 6

THE PLACE OF THE MOON FOR THE YEARS 1892–1893

DM	Jan.	Feb.	March	April	May	June	July	August	Sept.	Oct.	Nov.	Dec.
	° ′	° ′	° ′	° ′	° ′	° ′	° ′	° ′	° ′	° ′	° ′	° ′
1	27 ♑ 50	20 ♓ 12	14 ♈ 15	7 ♊ 9	13 ♋ 40	1 ♍ 3	3 ♎ 32	17 ♏ 0	1 ♑ 20	5 ♒ 17	25 ♓ 23	3 ♉ 20
2	11 ♒ 47	4 ♈ 48	29 4	21 11	27 1	13 22	15 27	28 55	14 4	18 50	10 ♈ 5	18 19
3	25 54	19 14	13 ♉ 36	4 ♋ 48	9 ♌ 58	25 26	27 16	11 ♐ 2	27 13	2 ♓ 50	25 6	3 ♊ 27
4	10 ♓ 6	3 ♉ 28	27 47	18 2	22 34	7 ♎ 21	9 ♏ 5	23 24	10 ♒ 48	17 17	10 ♉ 18	18 33
5	24 18	17 28	11 ♊ 37	0 ♌ 55	4 ♍ 52	19 10	21 0	6 ♑ 6	24 48	2 ♈ 5	25 32	3 ♋ 29
6	8 ♈ 29	1 ♊ 14	25 7	13 29	16 56	0 ♏ 58	3 ♐ 4	19 10	9 ♓ 9	17 6	10 ♊ 39	18 6
7	22 36	14 46	8 ♋ 18	25 50	28 52	12 50	15 21	2 ♒ 36	23 46	2 ♉ 13	25 28	2 ♌ 17
8	6 ♉ 38	28 7	21 13	7 ♍ 59	10 ♎ 42	24 48	27 54	16 22	8 ♈ 32	17 15	9 ♋ 55	16 0
9	20 34	11 ♋ 16	3 ♌ 55	19 59	22 30	6 ♐ 56	10 ♑ 44	0 ♓ 25	23 18	2 ♊ 5	23 55	29 14
10	4 ♊ 23	24 14	16 25	1 ♎ 54	4 ♏ 19	19 16	23 52	14 39	7 ♉ 58	16 38	7 ♌ 28	12 ♍ 2
11	18 5	7 ♌ 2	28 45	13 44	16 12	1 ♑ 49	7 ♒ 16	29 0	22 27	0 ♋ 48	20 35	24 27
12	1 ♋ 38	19 38	10 ♍ 56	25 33	28 10	14 36	20 54	13 ♈ 22	6 ♊ 42	14 36	3 ♍ 18	6 ♎ 25
13	15 0	2 ♍ 4	22 59	7 ♏ 22	10 ♐ 17	27 36	4 ♓ 42	27 41	20 41	28 1	15 43	18 31
14	28 8	14 18	4 ♎ 55	19 13	22 23	10 ♒ 50	18 39	11 ♉ 54	4 ♋ 24	11 ♌ 6	27 52	0 ♏ 19
15	11 ♌ 2	26 22	16 47	1 ♐ 10	5 ♑ 1	24 17	2 ♈ 41	26 0	17 51	23 52	9 ♎ 51	12 5
16	23 41	8 ♎ 17	28 35	13 14	17 42	7 ♓ 56	16 47	9 ♊ 58	1 ♌ 4	6 ♍ 23	21 42	23 52
17	6 ♍ 4	20 7	10 ♏ 23	25 29	0 ♒ 38	21 48	0 ♉ 54	23 47	14 3	18 41	3 ♏ 30	5 ♐ 45
18	18 14	1 ♏ 54	22 14	7 ♑ 58	13 52	5 ♈ 51	15 3	7 ♋ 28	26 49	0 ♎ 49	15 16	17 44
19	0 ♎ 13	13 44	4 ♐ 12	20 46	27 24	20 4	29 12	20 58	9 ♍ 23	12 48	27 5	29 53
20	12 4	25 42	16 21	3 ♒ 56	11 ♓ 15	4 ♉ 27	13 ♊ 18	4 ♌ 18	21 45	24 41	8 ♐ 57	12 ♑ 13
21	23 53	7 ♐ 52	28 48	17 30	25 26	18 55	27 21	17 25	3 ♎ 56	6 ♏ 30	20 54	24 43
22	5 ♏ 44	20 21	11 ♑ 36	1 ♓ 30	9 ♈ 55	3 ♊ 26	11 ♋ 15	0 ♍ 18	15 57	18 17	3 ♑ 0	7 ♒ 25
23	17 44	3 ♑ 13	24 49	15 55	24 38	17 53	24 59	12 57	27 51	0 ♐ 4	15 14	20 18
24	29 57	16 32	8 ♒ 31	0 ♈ 42	9 ♉ 30	2 ♋ 12	8 ♌ 28	25 21	9 ♏ 39	11 54	27 40	3 ♓ 24
25	12 ♐ 28	0 ♒ 20	22 42	15 45	24 24	16 17	21 40	7 ♎ 31	21 25	23 50	10 ♒ 21	16 43
26	25 22	14 36	7 ♓ 20	0 ♉ 55	9 ♊ 12	0 ♌ 3	4 ♍ 33	19 30	3 ♐ 12	5 ♑ 56	23 18	0 ♈ 17
27	8 ♑ 41	29 16	22 19	16 3	23 47	13 27	17 7	1 ♏ 21	15 6	18 16	6 ♓ 34	14 7
28	22 25	14 ♓ 12	7 ♈ 31	1 ♊ 0	8 ♋ 3	26 28	29 24	13 9	27 10	0 ♒ 54	20 12	28 13
29	6 ♒ 32	29 15	22 45	15 38	21 55	9 ♍ 7	11 ♎ 28	24 57	9 ♑ 31	13 52	4 ♈ 12	12 ♉ 34
30	20 57		7 ♉ 51	29 52	5 ♌ 22	21 27	23 22	6 ♐ 51	22 12	27 16	18 36	27 10
31	5 ♓ 32		22 41		18 24		5 ♏ 10	18 57		11 ♓ 6		11 ♊ 55

DM	Jan.	Feb.	March	April	May	June	July	August	Sept.	Oct.	Nov.	Dec.
	° ′	° ′	° ′	° ′	° ′	° ′	° ′	° ′	° ′	° ′	° ′	° ′
1	26 ♊ 43	18 ♌ 9	26 ♌ 56	14 ♎ 13	17 ♏ 3	1 ♑ 28	4 ♒ 56	22 ♓ 56	14 ♉ 14	23 ♊ 27	16 ♌ 24	23 ♍ 9
2	11 ♋ 26	1 ♍ 44	10 ♍ 8	26 25	28 54	13 28	17 23	6 ♈ 14	28 18	7 ♋ 41	29 55	5 ♎ 56
3	25 57	14 57	23 5	8 ♏ 27	10 ♐ 44	25 34	0 ♓ 1	19 43	12 ♊ 27	21 47	13 ♍ 9	18 25
4	10 ♌ 7	27 47	5 ♎ 44	20 22	22 34	7 ♒ 50	12 51	3 ♉ 26	26 39	5 ♌ 43	26 7	0 ♏ 42
5	23 52	10 ♎ 17	18 8	2 ♐ 13	4 ♑ 28	20 18	25 55	17 22	10 ♋ 54	19 28	8 ♎ 51	12 49
6	7 ♍ 11	22 30	0 ♏ 17	14 2	16 29	3 ♓ 1	9 ♈ 16	1 ♊ 33	25 7	3 ♍ 1	21 22	24 50
7	20 4	4 ♏ 29	12 16	25 54	28 39	16 2	22 56	15 55	9 ♌ 15	16 20	3 ♏ 43	6 ♐ 46
8	2 ♎ 33	16 19	24 7	7 ♑ 52	11 ♒ 4	29 24	6 ♉ 56	0 ♋ 28	23 14	29 26	15 54	18 39
9	14 44	28 7	5 ♐ 56	20 3	23 47	13 ♈ 10	21 17	15 5	7 ♍ 1	12 ♎ 18	27 58	0 ♑ 30
10	26 41	9 ♐ 58	17 47	2 ♒ 30	6 ♓ 52	27 21	5 ♊ 57	29 40	20 31	24 55	9 ♐ 56	12 22
11	8 ♏ 30	21 57	29 47	15 16	20 21	11 ♉ 57	20 50	14 ♌ 6	3 ♎ 43	7 ♏ 20	21 49	24 15
12	20 16	4 ♑ 9	11 ♑ 58	28 27	4 ♈ 17	26 52	5 ♋ 50	28 17	16 36	19 32	3 ♑ 39	6 ♒ 12
13	2 ♐ 6	16 36	24 27	12 ♓ 3	18 39	12 ♊ 1	20 48	12 ♍ 8	29 11	1 ♐ 35	15 30	18 15
14	14 2	29 22	7 ♒ 17	26 5	3 ♉ 24	27 15	5 ♌ 33	25 34	11 ♏ 30	13 30	27 25	0 ♓ 28
15	26 9	12 ♒ 28	20 29	10 ♈ 30	18 27	12 ♋ 22	19 59	8 ♎ 37	23 35	25 21	9 ♒ 27	12 54
16	8 ♑ 30	25 51	4 ♓ 5	25 13	3 ♊ 40	27 13	3 ♍ 59	21 17	5 ♐ 32	7 ♑ 13	21 41	25 38
17	21 5	9 ♓ 31	18 2	10 ♉ 9	18 51	11 ♌ 40	17 31	3 ♏ 37	17 24	19 9	4 ♓ 11	8 ♈ 45
18	3 ♒ 54	23 23	2 ♈ 16	25 8	3 ♋ 52	25 39	0 ♎ 35	15 43	29 16	1 ♒ 13	17 2	22 18
19	16 57	7 ♈ 25	16 44	10 ♊ 2	18 34	9 ♍ 8	13 15	27 39	11 ♑ 14	13 32	0 ♈ 19	6 ♉ 19
20	0 ♓ 13	21 31	1 ♉ 17	24 45	2 ♌ 52	22 10	25 35	9 ♐ 30	23 21	26 8	14 2	20 50
21	13 39	5 ♉ 39	15 52	9 ♋ 11	16 43	4 ♎ 48	7 ♏ 39	21 22	5 ♒ 42	9 ♓ 6	28 14	5 ♊ 46
22	27 15	19 48	0 ♊ 22	23 16	0 ♍ 7	17 6	19 34	3 ♑ 19	18 19	22 28	12 ♉ 53	21 0
23	10 ♈ 58	3 ♊ 56	14 44	7 ♌ 0	13 6	29 10	1 ♐ 23	15 25	1 ♓ 16	6 ♈ 14	27 52	6 ♋ 23
24	24 50	18 1	28 54	20 22	25 44	11 ♏ 4	13 13	27 43	14 33	20 24	13 ♊ 3	21 42
25	8 ♉ 50	2 ♋ 2	12 ♋ 52	3 ♍ 25	8 ♎ 5	22 54	25 7	10 ♒ 15	28 9	4 ♉ 53	28 16	6 ♌ 46
26	22 57	15 59	26 35	16 10	20 13	4 ♐ 42	7 ♑ 8	23 2	12 ♈ 2	19 37	13 ♋ 21	21 26
27	7 ♊ 11	29 48	10 ♌ 6	28 41	2 ♏ 11	16 33	19 18	6 ♓ 4	26 8	4 ♊ 27	28 9	5 ♍ 37
28	21 30	13 ♌ 28	23 22	10 ♎ 59	14 4	28 28	1 ♒ 39	19 20	10 ♉ 24	19 15	12 ♌ 33	19 17
29	5 ♋ 51		6 ♍ 24	23 8	25 54	10 ♑ 29	14 12	2 ♈ 49	24 46	3 ♋ 56	26 31	2 ♎ 29
30	20 8		19 13	5 ♏ 8	7 ♐ 43	22 38	26 55	16 29	9 ♊ 8	18 23	10 ♍ 2	15 16
31	4 ♌ 16		1 ♎ 49		19 34		9 ♓ 50	0 ♉ 17		2 ♌ 33		27 42

THE PLACE OF THE MOON FOR THE YEARS 1894–1895

D M	Jan.	Feb.	March	April	May	June	July	August	Sept.	Oct.	Nov.	Dec.
	° ′	° ′	° ′	° ′	° ′	° ′	° ′	° ′	° ′	° ′	° ′	° ′
1	9♏53	24♐17	2♑30	16♒22	19♓11	7♉27	14♊51	8♌56	1♎34	7♏11	23♐35	25♑51
2	21 54	6♑8	14 22	28 42	2♈10	21 46	29 57	24 5	15 37	20 22	5♑50	7♒43
3	3♐48	18 2	26 19	11♓17	15 33	6♊29	15♋14	8♍56	29 14	3♐13	17 52	19 32
4	15 39	0♒3	8♒24	24 11	29 19	21 28	0♌30	23 24	12♏26	15 44	29 46	1♓21
5	27 29	12 10	20 39	7♈23	13♉27	6♋34	15 36	7♎25	25 14	27 59	11♒37	13 17
6	9♑22	24 26	3♓7	20 53	27 53	21 37	0♍21	20 58	7♐43	10♑1	23 29	25 24
7	21 17	6♓51	15 48	4♉39	12♊31	6♌27	14 42	4♏5	19 56	21 56	5♓28	7♈48
8	3♒16	19 26	28 42	18 39	27 14	20 59	28 34	16 49	1♑57	3♒48	17 38	20 34
9	15 20	2♈11	11♈49	2♊49	11♋54	5♍8	12♎0	29 14	13 52	15 41	0♈5	3♉46
10	27 31	15 8	25 9	17 4	26 26	18 54	25 3	11♐26	25 44	27 41	12 51	17 26
11	9♓51	28 20	8♉41	1♋22	10♌44	2♎17	7♏45	23 27	7♒37	9♓51	26 0	1♊34
12	22 21	11♉46	22 25	15 38	24 46	15 21	20 11	5♑22	19 34	22 13	9♉31	16 5
13	5♈6	25 31	6♊19	29 50	8♍32	28 8	2♐25	17 14	1♓39	4♈51	23 24	0♋52
14	18 9	9♊33	20 22	13♌56	22 2	10♏42	14 30	29 7	13 52	17 46	7♊34	15 48
15	1♉33	23 54	4♋34	27 53	5♎17	23 4	26 29	11♒1	26 16	0♉58	21 56	0♌43
16	15 22	8♋29	18 52	11♍40	18 18	5♐18	8♑24	22 59	8♈53	14 25	6♋24	15 29
17	29 36	23 15	3♌13	25 17	1♏7	17 25	20 16	5♓2	21 41	28 7	20 52	29 59
18	14♊15	8♌4	17 32	8♎41	13 45	29 26	2♒9	17 12	4♉43	11♊59	5♌15	14♍10
19	29 13	22 48	1♍47	21 52	26 13	11♑22	14 2	29 31	17 59	26 1	19 29	28 1
20	14♋24	7♍19	15 52	4♏50	8♐31	23 15	25 57	12♈1	1♊29	10♋7	3♍32	11♎34
21	29 37	21 32	29 43	17 33	20 40	5♒7	7♓58	24 44	15 12	24 17	17 24	24 50
22	14♌41	5♎20	13♎17	0♐3	2♑42	16 59	20 6	7♉43	29 10	8♌28	1♎5	7♏52
23	29 26	18 44	26 32	12 20	14 38	28 55	2♈25	21 1	13♋20	22 38	14 35	20 41
24	13♍45	1♏43	9♏27	24 26	26 30	10♓59	14 59	4♊39	27 41	6♍45	27 54	3♐19
25	27 35	14 19	22 4	6♑24	8♒22	23 14	27 51	18 39	12♌10	20 47	11♏3	15 47
26	10♎55	26 37	4♐24	18 18	20 18	5♈46	11♉7	3♋0	26 42	4♎42	24 1	28 5
27	23 49	8♐42	16 32	0♒11	2♓22	18 40	24 49	17 39	11♍12	18 27	6♐47	10♑15
28	6♏20	20 38	28 30	12 8	14 39	2♉0	8♊58	2♌32	25 35	2♏0	19 21	22 17
29	18 33		10♑24	24 14	27 14	15 48	23 33	17 30	9♎45	15 19	1♑42	4♒12
30	0♐34		22 17	6♓34	10♈11	0♊6	8♋30	2♍25	23 38	28 21	13 51	16 2
31	12 27		4♒15		23 35		23 41	17 9		11♐6		27 49

D M	Jan.	Feb.	March	April	May	June	July	August	Sept.	Oct.	Nov.	Dec.
	° ′	° ′	° ′	° ′	° ′	° ′	° ′	° ′	° ′	° ′	° ′	° ′
1	9♓37	24♈44	4♉13	23♊40	2♌14	25♍32	3♏46	23♐0	8♒56	11♓20	25♈50	29♉38
2	21 30	7♉22	16 56	7♋24	16 20	9♎28	17 9	5♑30	20 49	23 10	8♉15	12♊51
3	3♈34	20 22	29 58	21 23	0♍31	23 17	0♐20	17 47	2♓37	5♈4	20 53	26 18
4	15 54	3♊48	13♊20	5♌36	14 45	6♏58	13 18	29 55	14 25	17 6	3♊43	9♋59
5	28 35	17 43	27 5	20 1	28 59	20 30	26 4	11♒55	26 14	29 16	16 47	23 48
6	11♉41	2♋7	11♋12	4♍36	13♎10	3♐50	8♑38	23 49	8♈7	11♉36	0♋2	7♌44
7	25 17	16 55	25 42	19 15	27 17	16 56	21 0	5♓38	20 5	24 7	13 28	21 44
8	9♊23	2♌3	10♌29	3♎54	11♏13	29 48	3♒10	17 25	2♉12	6♊51	27 5	5♍46
9	23 58	17 19	25 29	18 25	24 56	12♑24	15 10	29 13	14 31	19 49	10♌53	19 50
10	8♋56	2♍35	10♍33	2♏42	8♐21	24 45	27 3	11♈5	27 4	3♋3	24 51	3♎56
11	24 8	17 39	25 32	16 41	21 27	6♒53	8♓51	23 6	9♊56	16 34	9♍0	18 2
12	9♌23	2♎24	10♎19	0♐17	4♑14	18 50	20 39	5♉20	23 8	0♌23	23 19	2♏6
13	24 30	16 44	24 45	13 30	16 42	0♓40	2♈30	17 50	6♋43	14 31	7♎45	16 6
14	9♍22	0♏36	8♏47	26 19	28 53	12 28	14 29	0♊43	20 44	28 56	22 15	0♐0
15	23 51	14 1	22 22	8♑48	10♒53	24 20	26 43	14 0	5♌8	13♍37	6♏43	13 42
16	7♎54	27 2	5♐31	21 0	22 44	6♈20	9♉15	27 44	19 53	28 28	21 3	27 9
17	21 33	9♐41	18 17	2♒58	4♓33	18 34	22 10	11♋56	4♍53	13♎23	5♐9	10♑19
18	4♏49	22 3	0♑42	14 49	16 25	1♉7	5♊32	26 33	20 2	28 13	18 55	23 10
19	17 45	4♑12	12 51	26 38	28 25	14 3	19 22	11♌29	5♎9	12♏50	2♑19	5♒42
20	0♐24	16 11	24 48	8♓29	10♈38	27 23	3♋38	26 38	20 7	27 7	15 18	17 58
21	12 49	28 3	6♒39	20 26	23 7	11♊9	18 16	11♍49	4♏45	11♐0	27 55	29 59
22	25 4	9♒53	18 27	2♈34	5♉57	25 16	3♌9	26 53	19 0	24 26	10♒12	11♓52
23	7♑10	21 41	0♓16	14 55	19 7	9♋41	18 9	11♎42	3♐48	7♑25	22 14	23 39
24	19 9	3♓31	12 9	27 32	2♊37	24 17	3♍7	26 10	16 8	20 0	4♓6	5♈28
25	1♒3	15 24	24 10	10♉24	16 25	8♌57	17 55	10♏13	29 3	2♒16	15 54	17 23
26	12 54	27 23	6♈19	23 33	0♋27	23 33	2♎27	23 52	11♑36	14 17	27 43	29 31
27	24 42	9♈29	18 40	6♊56	14 38	8♍2	16 41	7♐6	23 51	26 9	9♈38	11♉54
28	6♓31	21 45	1♉13	20 31	28 53	22 18	0♏34	19 59	5♒52	7♓56	21 44	24 38
29	18 22		13 58	4♋17	13♌9	6♎21	14 7	2♑33	17 45	19 44	4♉5	7♊43
30	0♈18		26 58	18 12	27 21	20 11	27 21	14 52	29 33	1♈37	16 42	21 12
31	12 24		10♊12		11♍29		10♐18	26 58		13 38		5♋0

THE PLACE OF THE MOON FOR THE YEARS 1896–1897

D M	Jan.	Feb.	March	April	May	June	July	August	Sept.	Oct.	Nov.	Dec.
	° ′	° ′	° ′	° ′	° ′	° ′	° ′	° ′	° ′	° ′	° ′	° ′
1	19 ♋ 5	11 ♍ 35	5 ♎ 8	28 ♏ 3	4 ♑ 17	20 ♒ 58	23 ♓ 4	6 ♉ 39	21 ♊ 30	25 ♋ 48	16 ♍ 10	24 ♎ 41
2	3 ♌ 33	26 23	20 9	12 ♐ 12	17 34	3 ♓ 10	4 ♈ 57	18 40	4 ♋ 17	9 ♌ 17	0 ♎ 48	9 ♏ 34
3	17 46	11 ♎ 1	4 ♏ 53	25 52	0 ♒ 24	15 9	16 48	0 ♊ 55	17 28	23 14	15 48	24 34
4	2 ♍ 10	25 23	19 15	9 ♑ 4	12 52	27 0	28 41	13 25	1 ♌ 4	7 ♍ 38	1 ♏ 1	9 ♐ 31
5	16 31	9 ♏ 29	3 ♐ 12	21 51	25 2	8 ♈ 49	10 ♉ 43	26 15	15 7	22 28	16 18	24 16
6	0 ♎ 46	23 15	16 43	4 ♒ 16	6 ♓ 58	20 41	22 57	9 ♋ 28	29 33	7 ♎ 36	1 ♐ 28	8 ♑ 41
7	14 53	6 ♐ 44	29 50	16 25	18 48	2 ♉ 40	5 ♊ 26	23 2	14 ♍ 19	22 53	16 19	22 39
8	28 51	19 55	12 ♑ 36	28 22	0 ♈ 35	14 49	18 12	6 ♌ 58	29 18	8 ♏ 9	0 ♑ 45	6 ♒ 10
9	12 ♏ 40	2 ♑ 50	25 4	10 ♓ 12	12 24	27 11	1 ♋ 17	21 13	14 ♎ 21	23 12	14 41	19 14
10	26 18	15 31	7 ♒ 19	21 59	24 18	9 ♊ 47	14 40	5 ♍ 41	29 19	7 ♐ 54	28 7	1 ♓ 54
11	9 ♐ 45	27 59	19 22	3 ♈ 47	6 ♉ 20	22 38	28 19	20 17	14 ♏ 4	22 9	11 ♒ 5	14 14
12	23 1	10 ♒ 16	1 ♓ 19	15 37	18 32	5 ♋ 42	12 ♌ 11	4 ♎ 56	28 30	5 ♑ 56	23 39	26 19
13	6 ♑ 3	22 24	13 10	27 32	0 ♊ 54	18 58	26 14	19 30	12 ♐ 34	19 15	5 ♓ 55	8 ♈ 14
14	18 52	4 ♓ 23	24 58	9 ♉ 33	13 27	2 ♌ 26	10 ♍ 24	3 ♏ 56	26 15	2 ♒ 9	17 58	20 5
15	1 ♒ 27	16 16	6 ♈ 45	21 42	26 12	16 4	24 37	18 10	9 ♑ 33	14 43	29 52	1 ♉ 56
16	13 48	28 5	18 36	4 ♊ 0	9 ♋ 7	29 51	8 ♎ 52	2 ♐ 9	22 31	27 0	11 ♈ 43	13 51
17	25 57	9 ♈ 52	0 ♉ 29	16 28	22 15	13 ♍ 47	23 5	15 52	5 ♒ 12	9 ♓ 6	22 33	25 53
18	7 ♓ 55	21 42	12 29	29 9	5 ♌ 35	27 51	7 ♏ 15	29 20	17 39	21 3	5 ♉ 26	8 ♊ 5
19	19 46	3 ♉ 36	24 37	12 ♋ 5	19 9	12 ♎ 3	21 20	12 ♑ 33	29 55	2 ♈ 57	17 23	20 27
20	1 ♈ 34	15 40	6 ♊ 56	25 17	2 ♍ 58	26 20	5 ♐ 17	25 31	12 ♓ 2	14 48	29 27	3 ♋ 0
21	13 22	27 58	19 31	8 ♌ 49	17 3	10 ♏ 40	19 4	8 ♒ 15	24 2	26 39	11 ♊ 37	15 44
22	25 16	10 ♊ 35	2 ♋ 24	22 43	1 ♎ 23	24 59	2 ♑ 40	20 47	5 ♈ 57	8 ♉ 32	23 55	28 40
23	7 ♉ 21	23 34	15 40	6 ♍ 59	15 56	9 ♐ 13	16 2	3 ♓ 7	17 50	20 28	6 ♋ 21	11 ♌ 46
24	19 42	6 ♋ 58	29 20	21 35	0 ♏ 39	23 15	29 8	15 17	29 41	2 ♊ 29	18 57	25 5
25	2 ♊ 24	20 49	13 ♌ 26	6 ♎ 29	15 24	7 ♑ 3	11 ♒ 59	27 19	11 ♉ 32	14 35	1 ♌ 45	8 ♍ 35
26	15 29	5 ♌ 7	27 57	21 33	0 ♐ 3	20 31	24 34	9 ♈ 14	23 27	26 50	14 47	22 18
27	29 1	19 49	12 ♍ 50	6 ♏ 39	14 30	3 ♒ 38	6 ♓ 54	21 6	5 ♊ 28	9 ♋ 15	28 6	6 ♎ 13
28	12 ♋ 57	4 ♍ 49	27 59	21 36	28 37	16 25	19 2	2 ♉ 56	17 39	21 55	11 ♍ 43	20 22
29	27 17	19 58	13 ♎ 15	6 ♐ 15	12 ♑ 20	28 52	1 ♈ 1	14 50	0 ♋ 3	4 ♌ 53	25 42	4 ♏ 42
30	11 ♌ 55		28 28	20 30	25 37	11 ♓ 4	12 53	26 50	12 44	18 14	10 ♎ 2	19 10
31	26 43		13 ♏ 26		8 ♒ 28		24 44	9 ♊ 2		1 ♍ 59		3 ♐ 41

D M	Jan.	Feb.	March	April	May	June	July	August	Sept.	Oct.	Nov	Dec.
	° ′	° ′	° ′	° ′	° ′	° ′	° ′	° ′	° ′	° ′	° ′	° ′
1	18 ♐ 11	8 ♒ 45	17 ♒ 50	4 ♈ 26	7 ♉ 21	22 ♊ 1	25 ♋ 36	14 ♍ 8	6 ♏ 26	15 ♐ 49	8 ♒ 0	13 ♓ 58
2	2 ♑ 32	21 55	0 ♓ 38	16 30	19 13	4 ♋ 5	8 ♌ 12	27 46	20 46	0 ♑ 3	21 20	26 40
3	16 39	4 ♓ 48	13 14	28 29	1 ♊ 5	16 16	21 0	11 ♎ 36	5 ♐ 2	14 0	4 ♓ 22	9 ♈ 6
4	0 ♒ 27	17 25	25 39	10 ♉ 24	12 58	28 37	4 ♍ 3	25 36	19 11	27 41	17 7	21 19
5	13 53	29 47	7 ♈ 53	22 16	24 55	11 ♌ 9	17 20	9 ♏ 44	3 ♑ 13	11 ♒ 7	29 40	3 ♉ 23
6	26 57	11 ♈ 56	19 58	4 ♊ 7	6 ♋ 57	23 57	0 ♎ 53	23 58	17 6	24 19	12 ♈ 2	15 21
7	9 ♓ 39	23 55	1 ♉ 56	16 0	19 9	7 ♍ 3	14 44	8 ♐ 15	0 ♒ 50	7 ♓ 19	24 16	27 14
8	22 2	5 ♉ 49	13 49	28 0	1 ♌ 34	20 30	28 51	22 33	14 23	20 7	6 ♉ 22	9 ♊ 6
9	4 ♈ 11	17 41	25 41	10 ♋ 10	14 17	4 ♎ 22	13 ♏ 13	6 ♑ 48	27 44	2 ♈ 45	18 22	20 56
10	16 9	29 37	7 ♊ 35	22 35	27 21	18 37	27 47	20 58	10 ♓ 54	15 13	0 ♊ 17	2 ♋ 48
11	28 2	11 ♊ 41	19 36	5 ♌ 20	10 ♍ 52	3 ♏ 14	12 ♐ 29	4 ♒ 57	23 50	27 31	12 8	14 42
12	9 ♉ 54	23 57	1 ♋ 48	18 29	24 51	18 9	27 11	18 43	6 ♈ 33	9 ♉ 39	23 57	26 42
13	21 50	6 ♋ 29	14 18	2 ♍ 7	9 ♎ 18	3 ♐ 14	11 ♑ 48	2 ♓ 14	19 2	21 39	5 ♋ 47	8 ♌ 49
14	3 ♊ 55	19 22	27 8	16 [illegible]	24 11	18 20	26 12	15 26	1 ♉ 18	3 ♊ 33	17 40	21 8
15	16 11	2 ♌ 36	10 ♌ 23	0 ♎ 50	9 ♏ 22	3 ♑ 17	10 ♒ 18	28 20	13 23	15 23	29 41	3 ♍ 41
16	28 42	16 11	24 5	15 49	24 41	17 56	24 3	10 ♈ 57	25 20	27 12	11 ♌ 55	16 34
17	11 ♋ 28	0 ♍ 7	8 ♍ 13	1 ♏ 3	9 ♐ 58	2 ♒ 11	7 ♓ 24	23 17	7 ♊ 12	9 ♋ 5	24 27	29 48
18	24 31	14 20	22 45	16 21	25 1	16 0	20 23	5 ♉ 25	19 3	21 7	7 ♍ 21	13 ♎ 28
19	7 ♌ 49	28 45	7 ♎ 34	1 ♐ 31	9 ♑ 41	29 22	3 ♈ 1	17 23	0 ♋ 58	3 ♌ 23	20 42	27 34
20	21 22	13 ♎ 17	22 33	16 25	23 54	12 ♓ 18	15 21	29 16	13 3	15 59	4 ♎ 33	12 ♏ 6
21	5 ♍ 6	27 49	7 ♏ 33	0 ♑ 54	7 ♒ 38	24 53	27 28	11 ♊ 9	25 23	28 59	18 53	26 59
22	19 1	12 ♏ 16	22 23	14 57	20 53	7 ♈ 10	9 ♉ 26	23 6	8 ♌ 2	12 ♍ 27	3 ♏ 41	12 ♐ 6
23	3 ♎ 4	26 34	6 ♐ 58	28 32	3 ♓ 45	19 15	21 19	5 ♋ 13	21 4	26 25	18 49	27 19
24	17 11	10 ♐ 40	21 13	11 ♒ 43	16 16	1 ♉ 11	3 ♊ 12	17 33	4 ♍ 32	10 ♎ 50	4 ♐ 7	12 ♑ 26
25	1 ♏ 22	24 33	5 ♑ 7	24 32	28 31	13 4	15 8	0 ♌ 9	18 24	25 39	19 24	27 19
26	15 34	8 ♑ 12	18 38	7 ♓ 3	10 ♈ 35	24 55	27 13	13 4	2 ♎ 39	10 ♏ 43	4 ♑ 30	11 ♒ 51
27	29 44	21 38	1 ♒ 50	19 21	22 32	6 ♊ 50	9 ♋ 27	26 20	17 12	25 52	19 15	25 56
28	13 ♐ 50	4 ♒ 50	14 45	1 ♈ 30	4 ♉ 24	18 49	21 55	9 ♍ 54	1 ♏ 55	10 ♐ 55	3 ♒ 36	9 ♓ 34
29	27 50		27 26	13 31	16 16	0 ♋ 55	4 ♌ 36	23 46	16 40	25 44	17 29	22 45
30	11 ♑ 41		9 ♓ 55	25 28	28 8	13 11	17 32	7 ♎ 52	1 ♐ 20	10 ♑ 13	0 ♓ 55	5 ♈ 32
31	25 20		22 15		10 ♊ 2		0 ♍ 43	22 7		24 18		18 0

THE PLACE OF THE MOON FOR THE YEARS 1898–1899

D M	Jan.	Feb.	March	April	May	June	July	August	Sept.	Oct.	Nov.	Dec.
	° ′	° ′	° ′	° ′	° ′	° ′	° ′	° ′	° ′	° ′	° ′	° ′
1	0♉12	14♊13	22♊ 8	5♌49	8♍55	28♎ 4	5♐52	29♑35	21♓52	27♈29	13♊35	15♋41
2	12 13	26 3	3♋58	18 13	22 6	12♏34	20 53	14♒32	5♈50	10♉32	25 39	27 29
3	24 6	7♋58	15 54	0♍58	5♎44	27 26	6♑ 3	29 16	19 24	23 14	7♋33	9♌16
4	5♊56	20 1	28 1	14 7	19 50	12♐32	21 14	13♓42	2♉34	5♊38	19 21	21 7
5	17 46	2♌15	10♌22	27 39	4♏19	27 43	6♒16	27 43	15 20	17 45	1♌ 8	3♍ 7
6	29 38	14 41	23 1	11♎35	19 6	12♑50	21 1	11♈19	27 45	29 41	13 0	15 20
7	11♋35	27 21	5♍59	25 49	4♐ 2	27 42	5♓22	24 27	9♊53	11♋30	25 1	27 52
8	23 38	10♍16	19 16	10♏17	18 59	12♒16	19 18	7♉12	21 48	23 18	7♍18	10♎47
9	5♌50	23 25	2♎51	24 51	3♑48	26 26	2♈47	19 35	3♋38	5♌10	19 54	24 8
10	18 12	6♎46	16 40	9♐24	18 23	10♓11	15 51	1♊43	15 25	17 13	2♎53	7♏56
11	0♍45	20 20	0♏40	23 51	2♒40	23 34	28 33	13 38	27 17	29 29	16 17	22 11
12	13 31	4♏ 6	14 46	8♑ 8	16 38	6♈34	10♉56	25 27	9♌16	12♍ 4	0♏ 6	6♐49
13	26 32	18 1	28 56	22 14	0♓17	19 17	23 4	7♋14	21 28	24 59	14 17	21 43
14	9♎50	2♐ 6	13♐ 6	6♒ 7	13 38	1♉44	5♊ 2	19 3	3♍54	8♎15	28 44	6♑46
15	23 26	16 18	27 14	19 48	26 43	13 58	16 53	0♌58	16 36	21 50	13♐22	21 49
16	7♏21	0♑37	11♑19	3♓18	9♈33	26 2	28 40	13 1	29 34	5♏41	28 2	6♒42
17	21 34	14 58	25 20	16 36	22 11	7♊58	10♋27	25 14	12♎47	19 45	12♑40	21 21
18	6♐ 4	29 20	9♒16	29 44	4♉37	19 50	22 17	1♍39	26 13	3♐56	27 9	5♓39
19	20 47	13♒37	23 6	12♈40	16 53	1♋38	4♌11	20 16	9♏50	18 10	11♒26	19 35
20	5♑37	27 46	6♓48	25 24	29 0	13 25	16 12	3♎ 6	23 37	2♑24	25 30	3♈10
21	20 27	11♓40	20 19	7♉56	10♊58	25 13	28 21	16 10	7♐30	16 34	9♓19	16 23
22	5♒ 9	25 16	3♈37	20 15	22 51	7♌ 6	10♍42	29 27	21 30	0♒40	22 54	29 17
23	19 37	8♈33	16 40	2♊23	4♋39	19 5	23 15	12♏58	5♑34	14 41	6♈14	11♉55
24	3♓44	21 28	29 27	14 21	16 25	1♍15	6♎ 4	26 42	19 43	28 37	19 22	24 19
25	17 28	4♉ 4	11♉57	26 11	28 14	13 39	19 10	10♐40	3♒56	12♓25	2♉16	6♊32
26	0♈47	16 21	24 12	7♋59	10♌ 9	26 31	2♏35	24 52	18 10	26 5	14 58	18 36
27	13 41	28 24	6♊14	19 47	22 14	9♎25	16 21	9♑16	2♓22	9♈36	27 28	0♋32
28	26 14	10♊18	18 8	1♌42	4♍36	22 53	0♐28	23 49	16 28	22 54	9♊45	12 24
29	8♉29		29 57	13 48	17 18	6♏48	14 55	8♒27	0♈24	5♉57	21 52	24 13
30	20 31		11♋46	26 11	0♎25	21 8	29 39	23 5	14 6	18 45	3♋50	6♌ 0
31	2♊24		23 42		14 0		14♑35	7♓35		1♊18		17 50

D M	Jan.	Feb.	March	April	May	June	July	August	Sept.	Oct.	Nov.	Dec.
	° ′	° ′	° ′	° ′	° ′	° ′	° ′	° ′	° ′	° ′	° ′	° ′
1	29♌44	15♎49	25♎38	15♐49	24♑31	17♓52	25♈47	13♊59	29♋ 4	1♍20	16♎ 9	20♏ 0
2	11♍46	28 37	8♏36	29 36	8♒40	1♈44	8♉57	26 12	10♌53	13 18	28 47	3♐24
3	23 59	11♏43	21 48	13♑33	22 49	15 22	21 50	8♋14	22 43	25 23	11♏39	17 6
4	6♎28	25 10	5♐14	27 40	6♓57	28 48	4♊28	20 10	4♍36	7♎37	24 44	1♑ 3
5	19 16	9♐ 0	18 56	11♒56	21 1	11♉59	16 52	2♌ 1	16 33	20 1	8♐ 2	15 11
6	2♏28	23 13	2♑55	26 19	4♈59	24 55	29 6	13 51	28 37	2♏35	21 31	29 26
7	16 5	7♑50	17 13	10♓45	18 48	7♊39	11♋11	25 41	10♎47	15 19	5♑10	13♒45
8	0♐10	22 45	1♒46	25 9	2♉24	20 8	23 9	7♍33	23 6	28 14	18 59	28 3
9	14 40	7♒52	16 32	9♈25	15 45	2♋26	5♌ 2	19 29	5♏34	11♐21	2♒57	12♓17
10	29 33	23 2	1♓23	23 27	28 49	14 32	16 52	1♎30	18 15	24 41	17 2	26 25
11	14♑41	8♓ 6	16 13	7♉10	11♊36	26 30	28 42	13 40	1♐10	8♑15	1♓14	10♈26
12	29 56	22 53	0♈52	20 32	24 5	8♌22	10♍33	26 0	14 23	22 6	15 30	24 16
13	15♒ 7	7♈16	15 12	3♊31	6♋20	20 12	22 31	8♏36	27 56	6♒12	29 47	7♉56
14	0♓ 6	21 11	29 8	16 8	18 22	2♍ 3	4♎37	21 29	11♑51	20 35	14♈ 2	21 25
15	14 43	4♉37	12♉38	28 27	0♌16	14 0	16 57	4♐45	26 10	5♓10	28 11	4♊40
16	28 55	17 34	25 40	10♋30	12 6	26 7	29 34	18 25	10♒50	19 53	12♉ 8	17 42
17	12♈39	0♊ 8	8♊18	22 24	23 57	8♎29	12♏32	2♑32	25 47	4♈37	25 50	0♋30
18	25 50	12 22	20 35	4♌14	5♍55	21 0	25 55	17 5	10♓54	19 14	9♊14	13 4
19	8♉48	24 23	2♋37	16 4	18 3	4♏13	9♐44	2♒ 1	26 0	3♉37	22 18	25 25
20	21 20	6♋14	14 29	28 1	0♎26	17 41	24 0	17 12	10♈56	17 39	5♋ 3	7♌34
21	3♊35	18 0	26 17	10♍ 7	13 8	1♐33	8♑41	2♓30	25 31	1♊17	17 30	19 34
22	15 38	29 47	8♌ 5	22 29	26 12	15 49	23 41	17 43	9♉41	14 30	29 43	1♍28
23	27 32	11♌38	19 59	5♎ 6	9♏36	0♑25	8♒52	2♈41	23 22	27 18	11♌43	13 20
24	9♋22	23 34	2♍ 2	18 2	23 22	15 14	24 4	17 15	6♊31	9♋46	23 37	25 13
25	21 9	5♍39	14 16	1♏14	7♐26	0♒ 9	9♓ 8	1♉21	19 20	21 56	5♍29	7♎13
26	2♌57	17 53	26 43	14 43	21 43	15 2	23 54	14 57	1♋44	3♌55	17 24	19 24
27	14 48	0♎17	9♎24	28 25	6♑10	29 47	8♈18	28 4	13 52	15 48	29 26	1♏51
28	26 44	12 52	22 18	12♐17	20 40	14♓16	22 14	10♊47	25 49	27 39	11♎39	14 37
29	8♍46		5♏25	26 17	5♒ 9	28 27	5♉44	23 9	7♌39	9♍33	24 8	27 46
30	20 56		18 43	10♑23	19 33	12♈17	18 49	5♋16	19 29	21 34	6♏54	11♐20
31	3♎16		2♐11		3♓48		1♊33	17 13		3♎45		25 18

THE PLACE OF THE MOON FOR THE YEARS 1900–1901

D M	Jan.	Feb.	March	April	May	June	July	August	Sept.	Oct.	Nov.	Dec.
	° ′	° ′	° ′	° ′	° ′	° ′	° ′	° ′	° ′	° ′	° ′	° ′
1	9♑37	2♓40	10♓49	4♉17	10♊43	28♋2	0♍39	14♎33	29♏4	3♑15	23♒27	2♈10
2	24 13	17 48	26 10	18 45	24 16	10♌29	12 39	26 26	11♐30	16 23	7♓42	16 38
3	8♒58	2♈41	11♈19	2♊44	7♋23	22 41	24 34	8♏27	24 18	29 58	22 19	1♉12
4	23 46	17 13	26 7	16 15	20 8	4♍42	6♎26	20 39	7♑31	14♒1	7♈11	15 48
5	8♓28	1♉20	10♉28	29 19	2♌33	16 37	18 21	3♐9	21 14	28 32	22 13	0♊20
6	22 59	15 1	24 19	11♋59	14 43	28 31	0♏24	16 0	5♒27	13♓28	7♉15	14 42
7	7♈14	28 18	7♊42	24 20	26 43	10♎27	12 39	29 18	20 8	28 40	22 8	28 48
8	21 11	11♊13	20 39	6♌27	8♍37	22 30	25 10	13♑3	5♓11	13♈58	6♊45	12♋35
9	4♉50	23 51	3♋14	18 24	20 29	4♏44	8♐2	27 16	20 26	29 12	21 0	25 59
10	18 11	6♋15	15 33	0♍17	2♎24	17 12	21 16	11♒53	5♈43	14♉11	4♋49	9♌1
11	1♊17	18 29	27 40	12 8	14 25	29 57	4♑50	26 46	20 51	28 47	18 12	21 42
12	14 9	0♌35	9♌39	24 1	26 35	12♐59	18 53	11♓48	5♉40	12♊57	1♌10	4♍3
13	26 48	12 36	21 33	5♎58	8♏55	26 20	3♒11	26 48	20 5	26 38	13 46	16 10
14	9♋17	24 32	3♍25	18 1	21 27	9♑56	17 42	11♈38	4♊3	9♋52	26 3	28 7
15	21 36	6♍26	15 18	0♏11	4♐12	23 48	2♓19	26 10	17 35	22 43	8♍8	9♎57
16	3♌47	18 19	27 11	12 29	17 11	7♒50	16 55	10♉22	0♋43	5♌14	20 3	21 48
17	15 50	0♎11	9♎8	24 57	0♑22	22 1	1♈25	24 12	13 32	17 30	1♎54	3♏42
18	27 47	12 6	21 8	7♐35	13 47	6♓16	15 45	7♊42	26 3	29 34	13 44	15 45
19	9♍40	24 5	3♏15	20 25	27 25	20 32	29 50	20 52	8♌22	11♍30	25 37	27 59
20	21 32	6♏12	15 29	3♑30	11♒15	4♈46	13♉41	3♋46	20 31	23 23	7♏36	10♐28
21	3♎24	18 32	27 53	16 52	25 16	18 56	27 18	16 27	2♍33	5♎13	19 42	23 13
22	15 22	1♐7	10♐31	0♒31	9♓28	2♉59	10♊41	28 56	14 30	17 4	1♐59	6♑15
23	27 29	14 3	23 26	14 30	23 47	16 54	23 51	11♌16	26 23	28 58	14 26	19 33
24	9♏51	27 25	6♑43	28 48	8♈11	0♊39	6♋49	2 28	8♎14	10♏56	27 6	3♒5
25	22 31	11♑15	20 23	13♓22	22 36	14 12	19 35	5♍33	20 4	22 59	9♑59	16 49
26	5♐35	25 34	4♒30	28 9	6♉57	27 33	2♌11	17 31	1♏56	5♐11	23 5	0♓43
27	19 5	10♒21	19 2	13♈0	21 10	10♋39	14 35	29 24	13 51	17 32	6♒25	14 43
28	3♑4	25 29	3♓56	27 49	5♊9	23 30	26 49	11♎14	25 52	0♑7	20 0	28 48
29	17 31		19 5	12♉26	18 52	6♌6	8♍53	23 3	8♐4	12 56	3♓50	12♈56
30	2♒21		4♈18	26 46	2♋15	18 29	20 51	4♏55	20 30	26 5	17 54	27 6
31	17 28		19 26		15 18		2♎43	16 54		9♒34		11♉15

D M	Jan.	Feb.	March	April	May	June	July	August	Sept.	Oct.	Nov.	Dec.
	° ′	° ′	° ′	° ′	° ′	° ′	° ′	° ′	° ′	° ′	° ′	° ′
1	25♉23	16♋13	25♋59	12♍59	15♎52	0♐8	3♑24	21♒57	14♈6	23♉1	15♋35	21♌47
2	9♊25	29 21	8♌46	25 2	27 41	12 13	16 9	5♓49	28 38	7♊35	29 21	4♍50
3	23 20	12♌17	21 23	6♎59	9♏30	24 28	29 9	19 51	13♉3	21 53	12♌43	17 29
4	7♋5	25 1	3♍49	18 52	21 21	6♑55	12♒23	3♈58	27 20	5♋51	25 42	29 48
5	20 36	7♍30	16 5	0♏41	3♐16	19 34	25 50	18 8	11♊25	19 30	8♍21	11♎53
6	3♌51	19 47	28 12	12 29	15 18	2♒26	9♓29	2♉18	25 19	2♌50	20 44	23 47
7	16 48	1♎52	10♎10	24 19	27 30	15 33	23 17	16 26	9♋1	15 54	2♎54	5♏35
8	29 27	13 47	22 2	6♐13	9♑53	28 56	7♈14	0♊31	22 32	28 42	14 55	17 21
9	11♍49	25 37	3♏50	18 15	22 31	12♓34	21 18	14 33	5♌50	11♍17	26 48	29 9
10	23 57	7♏25	15 38	0♑30	5♒27	26 29	5♉29	28 29	18 57	23 40	8♏37	11♐0
11	5♎54	19 17	27 29	13 2	18 43	10♈39	19 46	12♋19	1♍51	5♎52	20 24	22 57
12	17 45	1♐18	9♐29	25 56	2♓21	25 4	4♊5	26 1	14 32	17 55	2♐12	5♑2
13	29 34	13 34	21 43	9♒14	16 23	9♉40	18 25	9♌31	27 0	29 51	14 2	17 15
14	11♏28	26 10	4♑16	22 59	0♈47	24 23	2♋40	22 47	9♎14	11♏41	25 56	29 39
15	23 32	9♑11	17 12	7♓13	15 30	9♊6	16 46	5♍46	21 18	23 27	7♑58	12♒14
16	5♐49	22 38	0♒37	21 52	0♉28	23 45	0♌38	18 29	3♏13	5♐14	20 10	25 2
17	18 25	6♒32	14 30	6♈51	15 32	8♋10	14 13	0♎55	15 1	17 3	2♒35	8♓5
18	1♑23	20 50	28 52	22 2	0♊34	22 18	27 27	13 6	26 47	29 0	15 17	21 26
19	14 42	5♓28	13♓39	7♉16	15 25	6♌2	10♍20	25 5	8♎36	11♑7	28 19	5♈5
20	28 24	20 16	28 41	22 22	29 59	19 23	22 52	6♏55	20 32	23 31	11♓44	19 4
21	12♒23	5♈7	13♈51	7♊12	14♋9	2♍19	5♎7	18 43	2♑42	6♒16	25 35	3♉23
22	26 37	19 52	28 57	21 39	27 53	14 53	17 9	0♐33	15 9	19 25	9♈51	18 1
23	10♓58	4♉25	13♉51	5♋41	11♌11	27 8	29 1	12 31	27 58	3♓1	25 30	2♊54
24	25 22	18 42	28 26	19 17	24 4	9♎9	10♏50	24 42	11♒13	17 5	9♉29	17 54
25	9♈43	2♊41	12♊39	2♌28	6♍35	21 2	22 40	7♑10	24 55	1♈35	24 40	2♋53
26	23 58	16 23	26 28	15 17	18 50	2♏51	4♐38	20 0	9♓4	16 27	9♊54	17 42
27	8♉3	29 49	9♋55	27 47	0♎51	14 40	16 47	3♒14	23 35	1♉33	25 0	2♌13
28	22 0	13♋0	23 2	10♍2	12 44	26 35	29 12	16 51	8♈22	16 45	9♋50	16 20
29	5♊47		5♌51	22 6	24 32	8♐39	11♑55	0♓50	23 17	1♊53	24 17	29 58
30	19 25		18 25	4♎1	6♏20	20 55	24 57	15 6	8♉13	16 48	8♌16	13♍9
31	2♋54		0♍47		18 12		8♒18	29 34		1♋23		25 53

THE PLACE OF THE MOON FOR THE YEARS 1902–1903

DM	Jan.	Feb.	March	April	May	June	July	August	Sept.	Oct.	Nov.	Dec.
	° ′	° ′	° ′	° ′	° ′	° ′	° ′	° ′	° ′	° ′	° ′	° ′
1	8♎15	22♏ 0	29♏47	13♑26	16♒29	4♈48	12♉12	5♋50	28♌43	4♎46	21♏12	23♐48
2	20 20	3♐48	11♐36	25 41	29 19	18 47	26 47	20 41	12♍39	17 46	3♐19	5♑40
3	2♏13	15 40	23 29	8♒14	12♓34	3♉11	11♊41	5♌28	26 16	0♏28	15 17	17 31
4	14 1	27 40	5♑31	21 9	26 14	17 59	26 47	20 3	9♎32	12 55	27 11	29 23
5	25 47	9♑53	17 47	4♓27	10♈21	3♊ 4	11♋56	4♍18	22 25	25 8	9♑ 1	11♒19
6	7♐36	22 22	0♒21	18 10	24 51	18 18	26 58	18 8	4♏59	7♐11	20 53	23 23
7	19 32	5♒ 7	13 15	2♈16	9♉42	3♋31	11♌43	1♎31	17 15	19 5	2♒49	5♓39
8	1♑38	18 8	26 30	16 41	24 45	18 33	26 4	14 29	29 18	0♑57	14 55	18 11
9	13 56	1♓25	10♓ 5	1♉20	9♊52	3♌15	9♍57	27 4	11♐13	12 50	27 16	1♈ 4
10	26 26	14 54	23 57	16 6	24 53	17 30	23 20	9♏19	23 4	24 48	9♓54	14 22
11	9♒ 8	28 34	8♈ 3	0♊52	9♋41	1♍18	6♎16	21 21	4♑58	6♒58	22 56	28 9
12	22 2	12♈22	22 18	15 31	24 9	14 36	18 49	3♐15	16 57	19 22	6♈23	12♉24
13	5♓ 7	26 16	6♉37	29 58	8♌13	27 30	1♏ 3	15 5	29 7	2♓ 5	20 16	27 7
14	18 23	10♉15	20 57	14♋11	21 53	10♎ 2	13 4	26 57	11♒31	15 9	4♉35	12♊12
15	1♈51	24 18	5♊13	28 7	5♍10	22 17	24 56	8♑54	24 10	28 35	19 16	27 30
16	15 30	8♊25	19♊24	11♌45	18 4	4♏19	6♐45	21 0	7♓ 7	12♈23	4♊11	12♋50
17	29 22	22 34	3♋29	25 6	0♎41	16 13	18 35	3♒17	20 21	26 29	19 14	28 0
18	13♉26	6♋44	17 25	8♍11	13 3	28 3	0♑28	15 47	3♈50	10♉50	4♋13	12♌51
19	27 43	20 52	1♌12	21 1	25 13	9♐52	12 28	28 29	17 33	25 21	19 2	27 16
20	12♊10	4♌54	14 49	3♎37	7♏14	21 42	24 35	11♓24	1♉27	9♊56	3♌33	11♍12
21	26 45	18 46	28 14	16 2	19 9	3♑36	6♒52	24 31	15 29	24 29	17 42	24 40
22	11♋21	2♍25	11♍26	28 15	1♐ 1	15 35	19 18	7♈49	29 37	8♋55	1♍29	7♎41
23	25 51	15 45	24 24	10♏20	12 50	27 40	1♓55	21 18	13♊48	23 10	14 53	20 22
24	10♌ 9	28 47	7♎ 8	22 17	24 41	9♒53	14 42	4♉58	28 1	7♌12	27 58	2♏45
25	24 8	11♎29	19 36	4♐ 9	6♑33	22 16	27 41	18 48	12♋12	21 0	10♎44	14 55
26	7♍45	23 52	1♏52	15 59	18 31	4♓50	10♈53	2♊49	26 20	4♍34	23 17	26 56
27	20 56	6♏ 0	13 56	27 49	0♒36	17 39	24 21	16 59	10♌22	17 53	5♏38	8♐52
28	3♎43	17 57	25 51	9♑43	12 51	0♈45	8♉ 5	1♋19	24 17	0♎58	17 50	20 45
29	16 8		7♐41	21 45	25 21	14 11	22 7	15 43	8♍ 0	13 50	29 55	2♑37
30	28 16		19 31	3♒58	8♓ 8	28 0	6♊27	0♌ 9	21 31	26 29	11♐53	14 29
31	10♏12		1♑24		21 16		21 3	14 31		8♏56		26 22

DM	Jan.	Feb.	March	April	May	June	July	August	Sept.	Oct.	Nov.	Dec.
	° ′	° ′	° ′	° ′	° ′	° ′	° ′	° ′	° ′	° ′	° ′	° ′
1	8♒18	24♓18	3♈53	23♉44	2♋24	26♌ 2	3♎47	22♏ 4	7♑22	9♒25	23♓29	26♈36
2	20 19	6♈57	16 50	7♊41	16 50	10♍ 1	17 5	4♐26	19 15	21 19	5♈58	9♉54
3	2♓27	19 50	0♉ 0	21 45	1♌10	23 41	0♏ 2	16 35	1♒ 7	3♓19	18 46	23 37
4	14 44	3♉ 0	13 23	5♋55	15 21	7♎ 2	12 41	28 36	13 0	15 29	1♉53	7♊44
5	27 14	16 29	27 0	20 8	29 21	20 6	25 7	10♑32	24 57	27 50	15 20	22 9
6	10♈ 2	0♊20	10♊50	4♌22	13♍ 8	2♏57	7♐23	22 25	6♓59	10♈24	29 3	6♋47
7	23 11	14 33	24 56	18 33	26 43	15 36	19 31	4♒17	19 9	23 12	13♊ 1	21 28
8	6♉46	29 8	9♋14	2♍40	10♎ 6	28 4	1♑32	16 10	1♈27	6♉15	27 9	6♌ 7
9	20 48	14♋ 0	23 43	16 40	23 16	10♐23	13 29	28 6	13 56	19 31	11♋22	20 36
10	5♊19	29 2	8♌17	0♎28	6♏14	22 34	25 23	10♓ 5	26 36	3♊ 1	25 37	4♍52
11	20 13	14♌ 5	22 52	14 4	18 59	4♑37	7♒15	22 11	9♉30	16 43	9♌50	18 53
12	5♋26	28 58	7♍21	27 24	1♐33	16 35	19 6	4♈26	22 40	0♋35	23 59	2♎39
13	20 47	13♍34	21 38	10♏27	13 55	28 29	1♓ 0	16 52	6♊ 6	14 38	8♍ 2	16 11
14	6♌ 4	27 45	5♎37	23 14	26 6	10♒20	12 59	29 33	19 50	28 48	21 59	29 30
15	21 6	11♎29	19 15	5♐45	8♑ 8	22 12	25 6	12♉32	3♋52	13♌ 4	5♎48	12♏37
16	5♍43	24♎46	2♏30	18 1	20♑ 4	4♓ 9	7♈26	25 54	18 12	27 23	19 28	25 34
17	19 52	7♏36	15 23	0♑ 6	1♒57	16 15	20 3	9♊40	2♌45	11♍43	2♏59	8♐20
18	3♎29	20 5	27 56	12 3	13 50	28 35	3♉ 2	23 51	17 29	25 58	16 18	20 55
19	16 38	2♐17	10♐12	23 56	25 48	11♈14	16 27	8♋26	2♍16	10♎ 7	29 25	3♑19
20	29 22	14 17	22 16	5♒50	7♓56	24 17	0♊20	23 20	16 59	24 3	12♐17	15 33
21	11♏45	26 10	4♑12	17 50	20 19	7♉47	14 43	8♌27	1♎32	7♏44	24 54	27 37
22	23 53	8♑ 1	16 4	0♓ 0	3♈ 1	21 46	29 31	23 36	15 47	21 8	7♑17	9♒32
23	5♐51	19 53	27 58	12 24	16 7	6♊14	14♋39	8♍37	29 42	4♐11	19 27	21 22
24	17 43	1♒50	9♒57	25 6	29 38	21 5	29 57	23 22	13♏10	16 56	1♒20	3♓10
25	29 33	13 55	22 6	8♈ 8	13♉34	6♋12	15♌13	7♎44	26 19	29 23	13 17	14 59
26	11♑24	26 8	4♓27	21 31	27 55	21 25	0♍18	21 40	9♐ 4	11♑34	25 7	26 55
27	23 18	8♓32	17 3	5♉14	12♊34	6♌33	15 1	5♏ 8	21 29	23 34	6♓59	9♈ 4
28	5♒17	21 7	29 54	19 16	27 25	21 27	29 18	18 11	3♑40	5♒28	18 59	21 31
29	17 21		13♈ 0	3♊31	12♋19	5♍58	13♎ 7	0♐52	15 39	17 19	1♈11	4♉22
30	29 32		26 22	17 56	27 8	20 5	26 29	13 14	27 33	29 13	13 43	17 39
31	11♓51		9♉57		11♌44		9♏27	25 23		11♓15		1♊26

THE PLACE OF THE MOON FOR THE YEARS 1904–1905

D M	Jan.	Feb.	March	April	May	June	July	August	Sept.	Oct.	Nov.	Deo.
	' °	° '	° '	° '	° '	° '	° '	° '	° '	° '	° '	° '
1	15♊42	8♌31	1♍45	24♎34	0♐48	18♑ 3	20♒36	4♈27	19♉32	24♊37	15♌31	24♍22
2	0♋22	23 49	16 56	8♏53	14 15	0♒24	2♓30	16 20	2♊ 8	7♋53	29 37	8♎34
3	15 21	9♍ 0	1♎57	22 49	27 21	12 31	14 18	28 22	15 5	21 31	13♍58	22 51
4	0♌27	23 54	16 39	6♐20	10♑ 5	24 27	26 6	10♉40	28 26	5♌31	28 31	7♏ 9
5	15 31	8♎25	0♏57	19 25	22 29	6♓17	7♈59	23 17	12♋13	19 53	13♎13	21 23
6	0♍24	22 29	14 48	2♑ 8	4♒37	18 6	20 2	6♊18	26 27	4♍34	27 58	5♐30
7	14 58	6♏ 8	28 12	14 30	16 34	29 59	2♉21	19 46	11♌ 5	19 30	12♏38	19 22
8	29 11	19 22	11♐11	26 36	28 24	12♈ 3	15 0	3♋41	26 2	4♎34	27 6	2♑56
9	13♎ 1	2♐14	23 47	8♒32	10♓13	24 21	28 3	18 3	11♍12	19 37	11♐15	16 9
10	26 31	14 48	6♑ 6	20 21	22 5	6♉59	11♊32	2♌48	26 23	4♏30	25 0	29 1
11	9♏41	27 7	18 11	2♓ 9	4♈ 7	19 58	25 28	17 47	11♎29	19 5	8♑19	11♒31
12	22 34	9♑16	0♒ 7	14 0	16 21	3♊20	9♋46	2♍54	26 18	3♐16	21 13	23 44
13	5♐14	21 16	11 57	25 57	28 51	17 3	24 23	17 57	10♏46	17 0	3♒44	5♓43
14	17 43	3♒10	23 45	8♈ 4	11♉39	1♋ 5	9♌ 9	2♎50	24 49	0♑16	15 56	17 34
15	0♑ 2	15 1	5♓34	20 22	24 44	15 21	23 59	17 25	8♐24	13 7	27 55	29 22
16	12 12	26 50	17 26	2♉53	8♊ 7	29 45	8♍43	1♏39	21 35	25 35	9♓44	11♈12
17	24 15	8♓39	29 24	15 39	21 45	14♌11	23 16	15 30	4♑22	7♒46	21 32	23 10
18	6♒12	20 30	11♈29	28 38	5♋35	28 33	7♎35	28 59	16 50	19 44	3♈21	5♉20
19	18 3	2♈25	23 44	11♊51	19 34	12♍50	21 37	12♐ 7	29 2	1♓34	15 17	17 48
20	29 51	14 27	6♉10	25 17	3♌38	26 58	5♏23	24 57	11♒ 3	13 21	27 24	0♊34
21	11♓39	26 39	18 49	8♋55	17 45	10♎57	18 52	7♑30	22 57	25 9	9♉44	13 40
22	23 29	9♉ 6	1♊42	22 45	1♍53	24 47	2♐ 6	19 51	4♓45	7♈ 1	22 19	27 6
23	5♈25	21 50	14 52	6♌47	16 1	8♏26	15 6	2♒ 0	16 33	19 1	5♊10	10♋48
24	17 32	4♊55	28 21	20 58	0♎ 7	21 56	27 53	14 1	28 22	1♉ 9	18 14	24 43
25	29 55	18 25	12♋ 9	5♍17	14 12	5♐15	10♑28	25 55	10♈14	13 29	1♋31	8♌46
26	12♉40	2♋22	26 16	19 43	28 11	18 21	22 51	7♓45	22 12	25 59	15 0	22 55
27	25 50	16 44	10♌42	4♎11	12♏ 4	1♑15	5♒ 4	19 33	4♉17	8♊42	28 37	7♍ 5
28	9♊29	1♌30	25 22	18 36	25 47	13 55	17 7	1♈21	16 32	21 37	12♌23	21 14
29	23 39	16 33	10♍13	2♏55	9♐16	26 22	29 2	13 11	28 58	4♋44	26 15	5♎20
30	8♋16		25 7	17 0	22 29	8♒35	10♓52	25 7	11♊39	18 5	10♍15	19 23
31	23 17		9 56		5♑25		22 39	7♉13		1♌41		3♏23

D M	Jan.	Feb.	March	April	May	June	July	August	Sept.	Oct.	Nov.	Dec.
	° '	° '	° '	° '	° '	° '	°	° '	° '	° '	° '	° '
1	17♏17	7♑40	17♑27	3♓27	5♈53	20♉18	23♊55	12♌51	5♎14	14♏13	6♑41	12♒ 8
2	1♐ 4	20 28	29 58	15 19	17 41	2♊38	6♋56	26 57	20 4	29 3	20 25	25 3
3	14 43	3♒ 4	12♒16	27 7	29 34	15 10	20 13	11♍14	4♏46	13♐30	3♒39	7♓34
4	28 10	15 28	24 24	8♈55	11♉34	27 53	3♌42	25 36	19 16	27 31	16 28	19 47
5	11♑22	27 40	6♓24	20 44	23 42	10♋49	17 23	10♎ 0	3♐30	11♑ 7	28 56	1♈48
6	24 19	9♓42	18 17	2♉37	5♊59	23 56	1♍14	24 22	17 25	24 18	11♓ 8	13 41
7	6♒59	21 36	0♈ 7	14 35	18 26	7♌15	15 12	8♏38	1♑ 1	7♒ 8	23 9	25 31
8	19 23	3♈25	11 56	26 40	1♋ 4	20 44	29 16	22 46	14 18	19 40	5♈ 4	7♉22
9	1♓33	15 13	23 44	8♊55	13 53	4♍26	13♎24	6♐44	27 19	1♓58	16 55	19 17
10	13 31	27 2	5♉36	21 20	26 56	18 20	27 36	20 31	10♒ 4	14 6	28 45	1♊19
11	25 21	8♉58	17 34	4♋ 1	10♌15	2♎26	11♏49	4♑ 5	22 37	26 7	10♉38	13 28
12	7♈ 8	21 6	29 42	16 59	23 52	16 45	26 1	17 26	4♓58	8♈ 2	22 34	25 45
13	18 58	3♊30	12♊ 4	0♌17	7♍47	1♏13	10♐ 8	0♒33	17 9	19 55	4♊34	8♋12
14	0♉55	16 15	24 44	13 59	22 2	15 46	24 7	13 25	29 13	1♉47	16 40	20 48
15	13 5	29 24	7♋46	28 5	6♎36	0♐19	7♑54	26 4	11♈10	13 39	28 52	3♌35
16	25 33	13♋ 0	21 12	12♍36	21 24	14 45	21 26	8♓29	23 3	25 32	11♋13	16 33
17	8♊22	27 2	5♌ 5	27 27	6♏21	28 58	4♒40	20 42	4♉54	7♊30	23 45	29 44
18	21 35	11♌28	19 25	12♎34	21 18	12♑52	17 36	2♈45	16 46	19 35	6♌31	13♍10
19	5♋12	26 14	4♍ 9	27 48	6♐ 6	26 23	0♓13	14 41	28 41	1♋49	19 34	26 52
20	19 11	11♍12	19 12	12♏57	20 36	9♒30	12 34	26 32	10♊43	14 16	2♍57	10♎53
21	3♌28	26 14	4♎25	27 53	4♑42	22 15	24 41	8♉24	22 57	27 1	16 44	25 10
22	17 59	11♎11	19 39	12♐26	18 21	4♓39	6♈39	20 19	5♋27	10♌ 7	0♎55	9♏43
23	2♍35	25 56	4♏44	26 32	1♒32	16 48	18 31	2♊23	18 17	23 38	15 31	24 27
24	17 12	10♏24	19 31	10♑ 8	14 17	28 45	0♉22	14 40	1♌32	7♍37	0♏27	9♐15
25	1♎43	24 31	3♐54	23 15	26 40	10♈36	12 18	27 14	15 12	22 3	15 35	23 59
26	16 5	8♐16	17 50	5♒57	8♓47	22 26	24 23	10♋10	29 21	6♎55	0♐46	8♑31
27	0♏15	21 39	1♑18	18 18	20 42	4♉21	6♊42	23 28	13♍54	22 6	15 50	22 44
28	14 11	4♑42	14 20	0♓23	2♈31	16 24	19 17	7♌12	28 49	7♏25	0♑35	6♒34
29	27 54		27 0	12 17	14 20	28 40	2♋11	21 18	13♎57	22 43	14 55	19 58
30	11♐23		9♒22	24 6	26 11	11♊ 9	15 25	5♍44	29 9	7♐47	28 47	2♓57
31	24 38		21 30		8♉10		28 59	20 25		22 28		15 33

THE PLACE OF THE MOON FOR THE YEARS 1906-1907.

DM	Jan.	Feb.	March	April	May	June	July	August	Sept.	Oct.	Nov.	Dec.
	° ′	° ′	° ′	° ′	° ′	° ′	° ′	° ′	° ′	° ′	° ′	° ′
1	27♓51	11♉31	19♉22	3♋22	6♌44	25♍35	3♏47	27♐36	19♒34	25♓14	11♉31	14♊13
2	9♈55	23 24	1♊14	15 37	19 33	9♎38	18 22	12♑6	3♓6	7♈59	23 34	26 3
3	21 50	5♊22	13 11	28 9	2♍46	24 7	3♐11	26 28	16 24	20 33	5♊30	7♋53
4	3♉41	17 29	25 16	11♌3	16 29	8♏59	18 7	10♒38	29 26	2♉54	17 21	19 45
5	15 33	29 49	7♋34	24 23	0♎41	24 8	3♑3	24 32	12♈12	15 5	29 10	1♌42
6	27 31	12♋26	20 11	8♍11	15 21	9♐23	17 48	8♓6	24 42	27 5	10♋59	13 48
7	9♊37	25 20	3♌8	22 27	0♏24	24 35	2♒17	21 19	6♉57	8♊59	22 53	26 6
8	21 54	8♌34	16 30	7♎8	15 41	9♑32	16 23	4♈12	19 1	20 49	4♌57	8♍42
9	4♋23	22 5	0♍16	22 8	1♐1	24 7	0♓5	16 45	0♊57	2♋40	17 16	21 41
10	17 6	5♍53	14 24	7♏17	16 13	8♒14	13 21	29 2	12 49	14 36	29 55	5♎5
11	0♌2	19 54	28 52	22 25	1♑7	21 53	26 13	11♉7	24 42	26 42	12♍59	18 58
12	13 11	4♎5	13♎32	7♐22	15 35	5♓5	8♈45	23 3	6♋41	9♌5	26 32	3♏20
13	26 32	18 21	28 17	22 0	29 35	17 53	21 0	4♊56	18 50	21 49	10♎36	18 7
14	10♍4	2♏39	13♏1	6♑15	13♒6	0♈21	3♉3	16 50	1♌15	4♍58	25 8	3♐14
15	23 47	16 55	27 36	20 6	26 12	12 33	14 58	28 49	13 59	18 34	10♏4	18 31
16	7♎40	1♐6	11♐57	3♒32	8♓56	24 35	26 50	10♋57	27 4	2♎38	25 15	3♑48
17	21 47	15 11	26 1	16 37	21 23	6♉30	8♊43	23 18	10♍32	17 6	10♐30	18 53
18	5♏51	29 7	9♑48	29 24	3♈36	18 21	20 40	5♌54	24 21	1♏52	25 39	3♒38
19	20 6	12♑54	23 18	11♓56	15 40	0♊13	2♋43	18 47	8♎29	16 47	10♑32	17 58
20	4♐25	26 29	6♒32	24 16	27 37	12 6	14 56	1♍56	22 51	1♐43	25 2	1♓50
21	18 44	9♒52	19 32	6♈28	9♉31	24 4	27 19	15 22	7♏19	16 31	9♒7	15 15
22	2♑58	23 2	2♓19	18 33	21 23	6♋7	9♌55	29 3	21 50	1♑4	22 47	28 15
23	17 3	5♓59	14 55	0♉32	3♊15	18 18	22 43	12♎56	6♐16	15 18	6♓3	10♈55
24	0♒54	18 41	27 21	12 28	15 8	0♌37	5♍44	26 58	20 33	29 12	18 59	23 17
25	14 28	1♈10	9♈37	24 20	27 4	13 6	19 0	11♏7	4♑40	12♒47	1♈38	5♉26
26	27 43	13 26	21 46	6♊12	9♋4	25 49	2♎29	25 19	18 35	26 5	14 4	17 25
27	10♓38	25 32	3♉46	18 4	21 12	8♍46	16 12	9♐32	2♒18	9♓7	26 19	29 19
28	23 15	7♉29	15 41	29 59	3♌30	22 1	0♏9	23 44	15 49	21 56	8♉26	11♊10
29	5♈34		27 33	12♋2	16 1	5♎35	14 18	7♑52	29 9	4♈34	20 26	23 0
30	17 41		9♊25	24 15	28 50	19 30	28 38	21 55	12♓17	17 2	2♊21	4♋52
31	29 38		21 20		12♍0		13♐5	5♒49		29 21		16 46

DM	Jan.	Feb.	March	April	May	June	July	August	Sept.	Oct.	Nov.	Dec.
	° ′	° ′	′ ′	° ′	° ′	° ′	° ′	° ′	° ′	° ′	° ′	° ′
1	28♋46	15♍18	24♍43	15♏42	24♐32	17♒41	24♓50	12♉41	27♊22	28♋59	13♍9	16♎44
2	10♌52	28 17	8♎7	0♐1	9♑6	1♓38	8♈9	25 0	9♋10	10♌53	25 51	0♏15
3	23 8	11♎29	21 44	14 20	23 27	15 14	21 5	7♊3	20 57	22 57	8♎55	14 11
4	5♍35	24 57	5♏32	28 35	7♒32	28 30	3♉41	18 58	2♌49	5♍16	22 21	28 31
5	18 17	8♏39	19 27	12♑44	21 23	11♈27	16 2	0♋46	14 48	17 51	6♏9	13♐9
6	1♎16	22 36	3♐29	26 46	4♓58	24 10	28 10	12 33	26 58	0♎44	20 15	27 58
7	14 36	6♐48	17 35	10♒40	18 19	6♉38	10♊8	24 21	9♍21	13 55	4♐33	12♑50
8	28 19	21 11	1♑45	24 26	1♈27	18 56	22 0	6♌14	21 57	27 23	18 57	27 38
9	12♏25	5♑44	15 56	8♓4	14 23	1♊3	3♋48	18 14	4♎47	11♏4	3♑22	12♒15
10	26 53	20 21	0♒7	21 32	27 8	13 3	15 35	0♍23	17 50	24 55	17 44	26 37
11	11♐40	4♒58	14 15	4♈49	9♉40	24 57	27 24	12 41	1♏6	8♐52	2♒0	10♓42
12	26 39	19 28	28 18	17 54	22 2	6♋45	9♌15	25 12	14 34	22 54	16 7	24 28
13	11♑43	3♓45	12♓12	0♉45	4♊13	18 32	21 13	7♎56	28 13	6♑59	0♓5	7♈57
14	26 42	17 43	25 53	13 22	16 14	0♌20	3♍18	20 54	12♐2	21 4	13 53	21 8
15	11♒29	1♈20	9♈18	25 44	28 7	12 11	15 36	4♏7	26 2	5♒10	27 32	4♉5
16	25 55	14 33	22 25	7♊53	9♋55	24 10	28 7	17 38	10♑11	19 16	10♈59	16 47
17	9♓57	27 24	5♉13	19 51	21 42	6♍20	10♎56	1♐27	24 29	3♓19	24 15	29 17
18	23 32	9♉54	17 42	1♋42	3♌32	18 47	24 5	15 33	8♒54	17 19	7♉19	11♊35
19	6♈42	22 6	29 55	13 30	15 28	1♎35	7♏38	29 57	23 22	1♈11	20 9	23 44
20	19 27	4♊6	11♊56	25 20	27 38	14 47	21 35	14♑35	7♓48	14 53	2♊46	5♋44
21	1♉53	15 58	23 48	7♌18	10♍6	28 26	5♐55	29 24	22 6	28 21	15 8	17 37
22	14 2	27 47	5♋37	19 29	22 56	12♏33	20 37	14♒15	6♈11	11♉32	27 18	29 26
23	26 1	9♋38	17 28	1♍58	6♎12	27 7	5♑35	29 4	19 58	24 24	9♋17	11♌13
24	7♊52	21 36	29 27	14 49	19 57	12♐1	20 42	13♓40	3♉23	6♊58	21 8	23 2
25	19 41	3♌44	11♌38	28 7	4♏10	27 10	3♒49	27 50	16 24	19 15	2♌55	4♍56
26	1♋31	16 5	24 6	11♎50	18 47	12♑22	20 47	11♈53	29 4	1♋18	14 43	16 59
27	13 26	28 41	6♍53	25 57	3♐42	27 30	5♓29	25 23	11♊24	13 11	26 36	29 15
28	25 28	11♍34	20 3	10♏24	18 46	12♒24	19 47	8♉26	23 28	24 59	8♍40	11♎50
29	7♌38		3♎33	25 4	3♑49	26 58	3♈40	21 5	5♋22	6♌47	20 59	24 48
30	19 59		17 23	9♐49	18 44	11♓7	17 5	3♊25	17 10	18 42	3♎40	8♏121
31	2♍32		1♏27		3♒23		0♉4	15 28		0♒47		22

THE PLACE OF THE MOON FOR THE YEARS 1908-1909.

DM	Jan.	Feb.	March	April	May	June	July	August	Sept.	Oct.	Nov.	Dec.
	° ′	° ′	° ′	° ′	° ′	° ′	° ′	° ′	° ′	° ′	° ′	° ′
1	6 ♐ 20	29 ♑ 2	22 ♒ 25	15 ♈ 15	21 ♉ 21	7 ♋ 53	10 ♌ 18	24 ♍ 33	10 ♏ 25	16 ♐ 1	7 ♒ 27	16 ♓ 46
2	21 2	14 ♒ 17	7 ♓ 29	29 23	4 ♊ 30	20 2	22 8	6 ♎ 34	23 6	29 20	21 35	0 ♈ 56
3	6 ♑ 1	29 29	22 26	13 ♉ 9	17 19	2 ♌ 0	3 ♍ 58	18 44	6 ♐ 4	12 ♑ 57	5 ♓ 53	15 3
4	21 11	14 ♓ 28	7 ♈ 6	26 30	29 49	13 52	15 51	1 ♏ 7	19 22	26 54	20 21	29 4
5	6 ♒ 20	29 6	21 24	9 ♊ 26	12 ♋ 2	25 42	27 50	13 47	3 ♑ 5	11 ♒ 12	4 ♈ 53	12 ♉ 56
6	21 21	13 ♈ 17	5 ♉ 14	21 58	24 3	7 ♍ 35	10 ♎ 0	26 49	17 14	25 48	19 23	26 37
7	6 ♓ 4	26 59	18 35	4 ♋ 12	5 ♌ 56	19 35	22 25	10 ♐ 15	1 ♒ 47	10 ♓ 39	3 ♉ 45	10 ♊ 3
8	20 26	10 ♉ 13	1 ♊ 29	16 12	17 45	1 ♎ 46	5 ♏ 9	24 7	16 42	25 38	17 54	23 14
9	4 ♈ 23	23 2	13 59	28 3	29 38	14 14	18 17	8 ♑ 27	1 ♓ 52	10 ♈ 34	1 ♊ 43	6 ♋ 7
10	17 55	5 ♊ 29	26 10	9 ♌ 52	11 ♍ 37	27 2	1 ♐ 50	23 12	17 8	25 20	15 10	18 44
11	1 ♉ 3	17 39	8 ♋ 8	21 42	23 49	10 ♏ 11	15 49	8 ♒ 17	2 ♈ 18	9 ♉ 46	28 14	1 ♌ 6
12	13 50	29 37	19 58	3 ♍ 40	6 ♎ 16	23 45	0 ♑ 13	23 32	17 12	23 47	10 ♋ 57	13 14
13	26 20	11 ♋ 27	1 ♌ 44	15 48	19 1	7 ♐ 40	14 57	8 ♓ 49	1 ♉ 41	7 ♊ 21	23 21	25 13
14	8 ♊ 35	23 15	13 33	28 9	2 ♏ 6	21 55	29 56	23 55	15 42	20 27	5 ♌ 29	7 ♍ 7
15	20 40	5 ♌ 2	25 26	10 ♎ 46	15 30	6 ♑ 26	15 ♒ 0	8 ♈ 42	29 12	3 ♋ 9	17 27	18 59
16	2 ♋ 37	16 52	7 ♍ 28	23 38	29 11	21 5	0 ♓ 2	23 3	12 ♊ 15	15 30	29 19	0 ♎ 54
17	14 29	28 47	19 40	6 ♏ 44	13 ♐ 7	5 ♒ 47	14 52	6 ♉ 56	24 52	27 35	11 ♍ 11	12 58
18	26 18	10 ♍ 48	2 ♎ 3	20 4	27 13	20 25	29 24	20 21	7 ♋ 10	9 ♌ 31	23 7	25 14
19	8 ♌ 6	22 57	14 38	3 ♐ 35	11 ♑ 26	4 ♓ 55	13 ♈ 33	3 ♊ 20	19 14	21 21	5 ♎ 11	7 ♏ 47
20	19 55	5 ♎ 15	27 24	17 15	25 42	19 12	27 19	15 56	1 ♌ 9	3 ♍ 12	17 28	20 39
21	1 ♍ 48	17 44	10 ♏ 21	1 ♑ 4	9 ♒ 58	3 ♈ 14	10 ♉ 42	28 16	12 58	15 6	29 58	3 ♐ 53
22	13 47	0 ♏ 25	23 30	15 0	24 12	17 0	23 43	10 ♋ 22	24 47	27 7	12 ♏ 45	17 28
23	25 54	13 20	6 ♐ 51	29 2	8 ♓ 22	0 ♉ 29	6 ♊ 26	22 19	6 ♍ 39	9 ♎ 18	25 48	1 ♑ 24
24	8 ♎ 13	26 31	20 24	13 ♒ 10	22 25	13 42	18 54	4 ♌ 11	18 35	21 40	9 ♐ 6	15 36
25	20 46	10 ♐ 1	4 ♑ 10	27 23	6 ♈ 20	26 40	1 ♋ 9	16 1	0 ♎ 37	4 ♏ 13	22 38	0 ♒ 0
26	3 ♏ 38	23 51	18 11	11 ♓ 39	20 6	9 ♊ 24	13 15	27 51	12 47	16 58	6 ♑ 23	14 30
27	16 52	8 ♑ 3	2 ♒ 26	25 54	3 ♉ 40	21 55	25 14	9 ♍ 42	25 6	29 54	20 17	29 1
28	0 ♐ 30	22 35	16 53	10 ♈ 4	17 1	4 ♋ 14	7 ♌ 7	21 37	7 ♏ 33	13 ♐ 1	4 ♒ 18	13 ♓ 28
29	14 34	7 ♒ 25	1 ♓ 30	24 5	0 ♊ 7	16 23	18 58	3 ♎ 37	20 10	26 20	18 25	27 46
30	29 4		16 11	7 ♉ 52	12 57	28 24	0 ♍ 48	15 44	2 ♐ 59	9 ♑ 50	2 ♓ 34	11 ♈ 52
31	13 ♑ 55		0 ♈ 48		25 33		12 39	27 59		23 32		25 46

DM	Jan.	Feb.	March	April	May	June	July	August	Sept.	Oct.	Nov.	Dec.
	° ′	° ′	° ′	° ′	° ′	° ′	° ′	° ′	° ′	° ′	° ′	° ′
1	9 ♉ 26	28 ♊ 41	8 ♋ 16	23 ♌ 39	25 ♍ 57	10 ♏ 25	13 ♐ 56	3 ♒ 23	26 ♓ 39	5 ♉ 31	27 ♊ 10	2 ♌ 3
2	22 53	11 ♋ 10	20 33	5 ♍ 31	7 ♎ 52	22 53	27 10	17 55	11 ♈ 46	20 20	10 ♋ 48	14 58
3	6 ♊ 6	23 28	2 ♌ 41	17 23	19 52	5 ♐ 35	10 ♑ 44	2 ♓ 40	26 40	4 ♊ 43	24 0	27 31
4	19 7	5 ♌ 39	14 42	29 15	2 ♏ 0	18 32	24 36	17 29	11 ♉ 15	18 39	6 ♌ 48	9 ♍ 47
5	1 ♋ 55	17 44	26 38	11 ♎ 11	14 17	1 ♑ 44	8 ♒ 44	2 ♈ 14	25 25	2 ♋ 8	19 17	21 49
6	14 31	29 43	8 ♍ 32	23 12	26 44	15 10	23 1	16 49	9 ♊ 12	15 13	1 ♍ 29	3 ♎ 43
7	26 56	11 ♍ 38	20 25	5 ♏ 17	9 ♐ 29	28 50	7 ♓ 24	1 ♉ 9	22 35	27 56	13 30	15 33
8	9 ♌ 10	23 30	2 ♎ 18	17 30	22 11	12 ♒ 41	21 47	15 11	5 ♋ 38	10 ♌ 23	25 24	27 24
9	21 15	5 ♎ 22	14 12	29 52	5 ♑ 14	26 41	6 ♈ 7	28 56	18 24	22 36	7 ♎ 15	9 ♏ 19
10	3 ♍ 12	17 16	26 10	12 ♐ 24	18 31	10 ♓ 49	20 20	12 ♊ 23	0 ♌ 57	4 ♍ 40	19 5	21 22
11	15 5	29 15	8 ♏ 13	25 11	2 ♒ 2	25 3	4 ♉ 24	25 35	13 18	16 38	0 ♏ 58	3 ♐ 35
12	26 57	11 ♏ 25	20 25	8 ♑ 14	15 49	9 ♈ 19	18 17	8 ♋ 34	25 31	28 31	12 55	16 1
13	8 ♎ 51	23 48	2 ♐ 49	21 36	29 52	23 35	2 ♊ 0	21 20	7 ♍ 36	10 ♎ 22	24 8	28 40
14	20 51	6 ♐ 31	15 28	5 ♒ 22	14 ♓ 10	7 ♉ 48	15 31	3 ♌ 56	19 35	22 13	7 ♐ 9	11 ♑ 33
15	3 ♏ 4	19 37	28 29	19 30	28 40	21 55	28 50	16 22	1 ♎ 29	4 ♏ 5	19 30	24 40
16	15 32	3 ♑ 11	11 ♑ 54	4 ♓ 1	13 ♈ 17	5 ♊ 52	11 ♋ 57	28 38	13 21	15 59	2 ♑ 2	8 ♒ 1
17	28 22	17 14	25 47	18 51	27 56	19 36	24 52	10 ♍ 46	25 10	27 59	14 47	21 34
18	11 ♐ 35	1 ♒ 46	10 ♒ 8	3 ♈ 52	12 ♉ 31	3 ♋ 5	7 ♌ 33	22 45	7 ♏ 0	10 ♐ 6	27 46	5 ♓ 18
19	25 16	16 42	24 55	18 57	26 55	16 17	20 1	4 ♎ 39	18 54	22 24	11 ♒ 3	19 13
20	9 ♑ 22	1 ♓ 55	10 ♓ 3	3 ♉ 55	11 ♊ 2	29 12	2 ♍ 17	16 30	0 ♐ 55	4 ♑ 56	24 38	3 ♈ 18
21	23 52	17 14	25 21	18 37	24 48	11 ♌ 49	14 22	28 20	13 8	17 47	8 ♓ 33	17 31
22	8 ♒ 41	2 ♈ 27	10 ♈ 40	2 ♊ 56	8 ♋ 12	24 10	26 20	10 ♏ 13	25 39	1 ♒ 0	22 46	1 ♉ 50
23	23 39	17 24	25 46	16 49	21 13	6 ♍ 19	8 ♎ 12	22 15	8 ♑ 31	14 39	7 ♈ 17	16 12
24	8 ♓ 39	1 ♉ 58	10 ♉ 31	0 ♋ 15	3 ♌ 53	18 18	20 4	4 ♐ 29	21 49	28 44	22 0	0 ♊ 34
25	23 31	16 4	24 49	13 14	16 15	0 ♎ 12	1 ♏ 59	17 3	5 ♒ 36	13 ♓ 14	6 ♉ 51	14 51
26	8 ♈ 8	29 42	8 ♊ 37	25 51	28 23	12 6	14 4	0 ♑ 0	19 53	28 7	21 42	28 59
27	22 24	12 ♊ 54	21 57	8 ♌ 10	10 ♍ 22	24 3	26 22	13 24	4 ♓ 38	13 ♈ 14	6 ♊ 25	12 ♋ 53
28	6 ♉ 19	25 44	4 ♋ 50	20 16	22 16	6 ♏ 9	8 ♐ 58	27 17	19 45	28 28	20 53	26 30
29	19 52		17 23	2 ♍ 13	4 ♎ 9	18 28	21 57	11 ♒ 39	5 ♈ 3	13 ♉ 36	5 ♋ 0	9 ♌ 47
30	3 ♊ 5		29 38	14 5	16 6	1 ♐ 2	5 ♑ 21	26 25	20 22	28 31	18 44	22 43
31	16 0		11 ♌ 42		28 10		19 10	11 ♓ 29		13 ♊ 3		5 ♍ 19

THE PLACE OF THE MOON FOR THE YEARS 1910-1911.

D M	Jan.	Feb.	Mar.	April	May	June	July	August	Sept.	Oct.	Nov.	Dec.
	° ′	° ′	° ′	° ′	° ′	° ′	° ′	° ′	° ′	° ′	° ′	° ′
1	17♍37	1♏13	9♏13	23♐25	27♑27	17♓22	25♈58	19♊18	10♌45	16♍14	1♏53	4♐18
2	29 41	13 2	21 1	5♑43	10♒26	1♈24	10♉18	3♋26	24 2	28 44	13 44	16 8
3	11♎36	24 57	2♐54	18 20	23 49	15 47	24 47	17 28	7♍4	11♎1	25 32	28 2
4	23 26	7♐3	14 58	1♒21	7♓38	0♉25	9♊20	1♌20	19 52	23 8	7♐19	10♑2
5	5♏17	19 24	27 17	14 50	21 52	15 16	23 53	15 0	2♎24	5♏6	19 7	22 11
6	17 13	2♑7	9♑58	28 49	6♈31	0♊12	8♋19	28 22	14 42	16 56	0♑59	4♒30
7	29 19	15 13	23 4	13♓15	21 28	15 6	22 34	11♍26	26 46	28 43	13 0	17 2
8	11♐40	28 44	6♒38	28 4	6♉37	29 50	6♌31	24 10	8♏41	10♐29	25 12	29 49
9	24 17	12♒38	20 40	13♈11	21 47	14♋17	20 7	6♎35	20 30	22 19	7♒40	12♓55
10	7♑14	26 52	5♓8	28 24	6♊51	28 21	3♍19	18 45	2♐17	4♑18	20 28	26 22
11	20 29	11♓21	19 56	13♉33	21 38	12♌0	16 9	0♏43	14 8	16 30	3♓39	10♈12
12	4♒3	25 56	4♈54	28 30	6♋4	25 13	28 37	12 33	26 8	29 1	17 17	24 26
13	17 51	10♈32	19 54	13♊7	20 4	8♍2	10♎49	24 21	8♑22	11♒55	1♈22	9♉2
14	1♓51	25 1	4♉47	27 21	3♌37	20 30	22 47	6♐13	20 56	25 15	15 53	23 56
15	15 58	9♉20	19 26	11♋9	16 45	2♎40	4♏38	18 14	3♒53	9♓2	0♉46	9♊3
16	0♈8	23 26	3♊46	24 34	29 30	14 39	16 27	0♑29	17 15	23 17	15 54	24 13
17	14 19	7♊19	17 45	7♌36	11♍55	26 30	28 18	13 1	1♓3	7♈55	1♊9	9♋16
18	28 27	20 59	1♋24	20 20	24 6	8♏18	10♐17	25 53	15 13	22 50	16 20	24 4
19	12♉32	4♋27	14 45	2♍48	6♎6	20 7	22 27	9♒8	29 42	7♉54	1♋19	8♌28
20	26 32	17 44	27 49	15 3	17 58	2♐1	4♑51	22 43	14♈22	22 57	15 56	22 25
21	10♊27	0♌50	10♌39	27 8	29 47	14 4	17 32	6♓35	29 6	7♊52	0♌9	5♍53
22	24 16	13 45	23 16	9♎6	11♏35	26 17	0♒30	20 42	13♉47	22 32	13 54	18 53
23	7♋56	26 29	5♍43	20 59	23 25	8♑42	13 43	4♈57	28 19	6♋52	27 13	1♎28
24	21 27	9♍2	17 59	2♏48	5♐20	21 20	27 12	19 15	12♊39	20 50	10♍7	13 44
25	4♌45	21 23	0♎7	14 36	17 21	4♒11	10♓52	3♉33	26 44	4♌25	22 40	25 44
26	17 48	3♎33	12 8	26 26	29 31	17 16	24 42	17 47	10♋35	17 40	4♎56	7♏36
27	0♍36	15 32	24 2	8♐19	11♑52	0♓34	8♈40	1♊56	24 10	0♍35	17 0	19 22
28	13 8	27 25	5♏51	20 18	24 25	14 6	22 42	15 58	7♌31	13 14	28 55	1♐8
29	25 25		17 39	2♑27	7♒12	27 51	6♉48	29 52	20 39	25 39	10♏44	12 57
30	7♎29		29 27	14 48	20 16	11♈48	20 57	13♋39	3♍33	7♎53	22 31	24 53
31	19 23		11♐21		3♓39		5♊7	27 17		19 57		6♑56

D M	Jan.	Feb.	Mar.	April	May	June	July	August	Sept.	Oct.	Nov.	Dec.
	° ′	° ′	° ′	° ′	° ′	° ′	° ′	° ′	° ′	° ′	° ′	° ′
1	19♑9	6♓38	15♓49	7♉7	15♊46	8♌59	15♍42	2♏43	16♐52	18♑31	3♓3	6♈49
2	1♒33	19 57	29 32	21 39	0♋33	23 1	28 56	14 53	28 43	0♒33	15 50	20 19
3	14 7	3♈25	13♈26	6♊9	15 6	6♍37	11♎44	26 52	10♑37	12 46	28 59	4♉18
4	26 53	17 3	27 27	20 34	29 20	19 47	24 10	8♐43	22 37	25 15	12♈33	18 44
5	9♓50	0♉49	11♉33	4♋49	13♌14	2♎35	6♏20	20 33	4♒49	8♓2	26 31	3♊33
6	23 1	14 44	25 40	18 53	26 46	15 4	18 19	2♑24	17 13	21 8	10♉50	18 39
7	6♈27	28 48	9♊48	2♌44	9♍59	27 18	0♐11	14 21	29 51	4♈33	25 25	3♋52
8	20 8	13♊1	23 54	16 23	22 54	9♏22	12 0	26 26	12♓44	18 16	10♊11	19 1
9	4♉6	27 20	7♋59	29 48	5♎33	21 18	23 49	8♒41	25 51	2♉14	24 59	3♌56
10	18 22	11♋43	22 1	12♍59	17 58	3♐9	5♑42	21 6	9♈11	16 23	9♋42	18 30
11	2♊53	26 6	5♌57	25 57	0♏13	14 59	17 39	3♓42	22 43	0♊39	24 14	2♍40
12	17 37	10♌22	19 44	8♎41	12 18	26 49	29 43	16 29	6♉24	14 59	8♌31	16 23
13	2♋27	24 26	3♍21	21 13	24 17	8♑41	11♒55	29 27	20 15	29 18	22 31	29 41
14	17 16	8♍12	16 44	3♏31	6♐10	20 37	24 16	12♈36	4♊14	13♋33	6♍11	12♎37
15	1♌56	21 37	29 50	15 39	18 1	2♒40	6♓46	25 58	18 19	27 43	19 34	25 16
16	16 18	4♎39	12♎40	27 38	29 50	14 50	19 29	9♉33	2♋30	11♌45	2♎41	7♏39
17	0♍17	17 20	25 12	9♐31	11♑42	27 11	2♈25	23 22	16 45	25 36	15 33	19 52
18	13 50	29 40	7♏29	21 21	23 39	9♓45	15 37	7♊26	1♌1	9♍17	28 12	1♐57
19	26 55	11♏45	19 32	3♑11	5♒44	22 37	29 7	21 45	15 15	22 45	10♏40	13 56
20	9♎35	23 40	1♐27	15 6	18 2	5♈49	12♉58	6♋15	29 22	6♎0	22 57	25 51
21	21 54	5♐28	13 17	27 11	0♓36	19 24	27 11	20 54	13♍18	19 1	5♐6	7♑43
22	3♏57	17 17	25 7	9♒30	13 30	3♉25	11♊45	5♌34	27 0	1♏48	17 8	19 35
23	15 49	29 12	7♑2	22 7	26 48	17 50	26 35	20 9	10♎23	14 21	29 3	1♒27
24	27 36	11♑16	19 7	5♓6	10♈32	2♊39	11♋36	4♍30	23 27	26 40	10♑55	13 21
25	9♐23	23 35	1♒27	18 30	24 42	17 44	26 38	18 33	6♏12	8♐48	22 46	25 20
26	21 16	6♒12	14 7	2♈19	9♉18	2♋58	11♌32	2♎12	18 39	20 47	4♒38	7♓27
27	3♑17	19 6	27 7	16 32	24 13	18 11	26 5	15 27	0♐50	2♑40	16 36	19 45
28	15 30	2♓19	10♓31	1♉6	9♊22	3♌10	10♍22	28 17	12 51	14 31	28 43	2♈20
29	27 56		24 16	15 55	24 34	17 49	24 7	10♏47	24 45	26 24	11♓5	15 15
30	10♒37		8♈20	0♊51	9♋40	2♍0	7♎24	22 59	6♑36	8♒24	23 45	28 35
31	23 31		22 39		24 30		20 15	4♐59		20 36		12♉23

THE PLACE OF THE MOON FOR THE YEARS 1912-13.

DM	Jan.	Feb.	Mar.	April	May	June	July	August	Sept.	Oct.	Nov.	Dec.
	° ′	° ′	° ′	° ′	° ′	° ′	° ′	° ′	° ′	° ′	° ′	° ′
1	26 ♉ 41	19 ♋ 59	13 ♌ 48	6 ♎ 1	11 ♏ 35	27 ♐ 50	0 ♒ 31	15 ♓ 6	1 ♉ 25	7 ♊ 43	0 ♌ 9	9 ♍ 28
2	11 ♊ 26	5 ♌ 14	28 38	19 46	24 27	9 ♑ 56	12 23	27 9	14 15	21 18	14 19	23 25
3	26 34	20 24	13 ♍ 19	3 ♏ 12	7 ♐ 5	21 55	24 14	9 ♈ 21	27 22	5 ♋ 8	28 29	7 ♎ 12
4	11 ♋ 54	5 ♍ 20	27 42	16 18	19 29	3 ♒ 49	6 ♓ 8	21 46	10 ♊ 50	19 12	12 ♍ 39	20 49
5	27 17	19 52	11 ♎ 44	29 4	1 ♑ 40	15 40	18 7	4 ♉ 29	24 40	3 ♌ 29	26 46	4 ♏ 16
6	12 ♌ 29	3 ♎ 56	25 20	11 ♐ 33	13 42	27 34	0 ♈ 16	17 34	8 ♋ 52	17 56	10 ♎ 48	17 33
7	27 20	17 31	8 ♏ 31	23 46	25 38	9 ♓ 33	12 39	1 ♊ 4	23 25	2 ♍ 30	24 41	0 ♐ 39
8	11 ♍ 45	0 ♏ 36	21 18	5 ♑ 48	7 ♒ 31	21 43	25 23	15 1	8 ♌ 15	17 4	8 ♏ 23	13 34
9	25 39	13 18	3 ♐ 45	17 44	19 26	4 ♈ 10	8 ♉ 31	29 26	23 13	1 ♎ 34	21 52	26 16
10	9 ♎ 4	25 39	15 56	29 37	1 ♓ 27	16 56	22 6	14 ♋ 15	8 ♍ 13	15 54	5 ♐ 5	8 ♑ 44
11	22 2	7 ♐ 45	27 55	11 ♒ 32	13 40	0 ♉ 8	6 ♊ 12	29 23	23 5	29 58	18 0	21 1
12	4 ♏ 38	19 42	9 ♑ 48	23 34	26 8	13 47	20 45	14 ♌ 38	7 ♎ 42	13 ♏ 43	0 ♑ 38	3 ♒ 5
13	16 56	1 ♑ 33	21 40	5 ♓ 47	8 ♈ 56	27 53	5 ♋ 43	29 52	21 57	27 6	13 0	15 1
14	29 2	13 23	3 ♒ 34	18 13	22 6	12 ♊ 25	20 55	14 ♍ 52	5 ♏ 47	10 ♐ 7	25 8	26 51
15	10 ♐ 59	25 16	15 34	0 ♈ 57	5 ♉ 40	27 16	6 ♌ 13	29 32	19 10	22 47	7 ♒ 6	8 ♓ 39
16	22 52	7 ♒ 12	27 43	13 58	19 36	12 ♋ 18	21 23	13 ♎ 45	2 ♐ 10	5 ♑ 10	18 57	20 31
17	4 ♑ 43	19 15	10 ♓ 4	27 17	3 ♊ 52	27 21	6 ♍ 17	27 30	14 47	17 18	0 ♓ 48	2 ♈ 32
18	16 34	1 ♓ 25	22 36	10 ♉ 53	18 23	12 ♌ 15	20 48	10 ♏ 48	27 7	29 16	12 42	14 47
19	28 27	13 44	5 ♈ 21	24 44	3 ♋ 1	26 54	4 ♎ 52	23 42	9 ♑ 13	11 ♒ 8	24 46	27 22
20	10 ♒ 24	26 12	18 20	8 ♊ 47	17 41	11 ♍ 13	18 30	6 ♐ 16	21 10	23 0	7 ♈ 4	10 ♉ 21
21	22 24	8 ♈ 50	1 ♉ 31	22 57	2 ♌ 15	25 8	1 ♏ 43	18 33	3 ♒ 2	4 ♓ 56	19 40	23 47
22	4 ♓ 31	21 39	14 55	7 ♋ 12	16 38	8 ♎ 42	14 34	0 ♑ 39	14 54	16 59	2 ♉ 37	7 ♊ 41
23	16 44	4 ♉ 42	28 31	21 29	0 ♍ 47	21 55	27 8	12 37	26 49	29 14	15 56	22 0
24	29 8	18 0	12 ♊ 18	6 ♌ 43	14 41	4 ♏ 51	9 ♐ 28	24 31	8 ♓ 49	11 ♈ 44	29 37	6 ♋ 38
25	11 ♈ 44	1 ♊ 35	26 17	19 52	28 19	17 32	21 37	6 ♒ 23	20 56	24 29	13 ♊ 37	21 29
26	24 37	15 29	10 ♋ 25	3 ♍ 55	11 ♎ 43	0 ♐ 1	3 ♑ 40	18 15	3 ♈ 14	7 ♉ 30	27 51	6 ♌ 23
27	7 ♉ 50	29 43	24 41	17 50	24 53	12 21	15 37	0 ♓ 10	15 42	20 48	12 ♋ 14	21 11
28	21 27	14 ♋ 13	9 ♌ 3	1 ♎ 34	7 ♏ 50	24 33	27 31	12 10	28 22	4 ♊ 20	26 40	5 ♍ 47
29	5 ♊ 30	28 57	23 26	15 8	20 36	6 ♑ 38	9 ♒ 24	24 15	11 ♉ 15	18 5	11 ♌ 3	20 6
30	19 59		7 ♍ 47	28 28	3 ♐ 11	18 37	21 16	6 ♈ 28	24 22	2 ♋ 0	25 20	4 ♎ 6
31	4 ♋ 51		22 0		15 36		3 ♓ 9	18 50		16 2		17 48

DM	Jan.	Feb.	March	April	May	June	July	Aug.	Sept.	Oct.	Nov.	Dec.
	° ′	° ′	° ′	° ′	° ′	° ′	° ′	° ′	° ′	° ′	° ′	° ′
1	1 ♏ 12	19 ♐ 42	29 ♐ 2	13 ♒ 56	15 ♓ 48	0 ♉ 7	3 ♊ 59	24 ♋ 14	17 ♍ 31	25 ♎ 57	17 ♐ 23	22 ♑ 7
2	14 22	2 ♑ 3	11 ♑ 17	25 45	27 41	12 46	17 32	9 ♌ 0	2 ♎ 39	10 ♏ 45	1 ♑ 2	4 ♒ 54
3	27 19	14 14	23 21	7 ♓ 32	9 ♈ 43	25 45	1 ♋ 28	23 56	17 35	25 12	14 14	17 21
4	10 ♐ 4	26 18	5 ♒ 16	19 23	21 56	9 ♊ 4	15 43	8 ♍ 53	2 ♏ 12	9 ♐ 12	27 0	29 30
5	22 39	8 ♒ 15	17 7	1 ♈ 19	4 ♉ 24	22 42	0 ♌ 12	23 44	16 26	22 45	9 ♒ 25	11 ♓ 26
6	5 ♑ 4	20 7	28 56	13 23	17 7	6 ♋ 35	14 48	8 ♎ 23	0 ♐ 16	5 ♑ 51	21 32	23 14
7	17 20	1 ♓ 57	10 ♓ 45	25 36	0 ♊ 6	20 38	29 23	22 43	13 41	18 34	3 ♓ 27	5 ♈ 2
8	29 26	13 44	22 35	8 ♉ 1	13 19	4 ♌ 49	13 ♍ 53	6 ♏ 45	26 44	0 ♒ 56	15 15	16 53
9	11 ♒ 25	25 33	4 ♈ 30	20 39	26 46	19 2	28 13	20 27	9 ♑ 26	13 4	27 2	28 53
10	23 17	7 ♈ 26	16 31	3 ♊ 30	10 ♋ 25	3 ♍ 14	12 ♎ 22	3 ♐ 50	21 52	25 0	8 ♈ 52	11 ♉ 6
11	5 ♓ 5	19 27	28 41	16 35	24 13	17 24	26 18	16 56	4 ♒ 5	6 ♓ 50	20 48	23 35
12	16 52	1 ♉ 39	11 ♉ 1	29 55	8 ♌ 11	1 ♎ 29	10 ♏ 1	29 47	16 7	18 37	2 ♉ 54	6 ♊ 20
13	28 42	14 7	23 36	13 ♋ 30	22 14	15 30	23 32	12 ♑ 24	28 2	0 ♈ 25	15 11	19 22
14	10 ♈ 41	26 56	6 ♊ 28	27 22	6 ♍ 24	29 25	6 ♐ 50	24 48	9 ♓ 53	12 17	27 41	2 ♋ 41
15	22 52	10 ♊ 10	19 40	11 ♌ 29	20 38	13 ♏ 13	19 57	7 ♒ 2	21 41	24 13	10 ♊ 24	16 12
16	5 ♉ 22	23 52	3 ♋ 14	25 51	4 ♎ 55	26 53	2 ♑ 51	19 6	3 ♈ 29	6 ♉ 18	23 19	29 55
17	18 16	8 ♋ 3	17 11	10 ♍ 24	19 11	10 ♐ 22	15 33	1 ♓ 3	15 19	18 32	6 ♋ 26	13 ♌ 45
18	1 ♊ 38	22 40	1 ♌ 32	25 4	3 ♏ 24	23 38	28 2	12 55	27 13	0 ♊ 56	19 44	27 40
19	15 30	7 ♌ 40	16 13	9 ♎ 47	17 29	6 ♑ 39	10 ♒ 19	24 42	9 ♉ 15	13 31	3 ♌ 13	11 ♍ 40
20	29 51	22 54	1 ♍ 10	24 25	1 ♐ 21	19 24	22 25	6 ♈ 29	21 27	26 21	16 54	25 42
21	14 ♋ 38	8 ♍ 11	16 14	8 ♏ 51	14 57	1 ♒ 53	4 ♓ 21	18 19	3 ♊ 52	9 ♋ 25	0 ♍ 46	9 ♎ 47
22	29 44	23 22	1 ♎ 18	23 1	28 15	14 7	16 11	0 ♉ 15	16 34	22 47	14 51	23 54
23	14 ♌ 57	8 ♎ 16	16 13	6 ♐ 50	11 ♑ 11	26 9	27 59	12 21	29 35	6 ♌ 26	29 6	8 ♏ 2
24	0 ♍ 8	22 47	0 ♏ 50	20 14	23 48	8 ♓ 2	9 ♈ 47	24 44	12 ♋ 59	20 26	13 ♎ 31	22 7
25	15 6	6 ♏ 52	15 4	3 ♑ 15	6 ♒ 7	19 50	21 42	7 ♊ 25	26 48	4 ♍ 44	28 3	6 ♐ 8
26	29 44	20 30	28 52	15 53	18 12	1 ♈ 40	3 ♉ 49	20 31	11 ♌ 2	19 20	12 ♏ 36	19 59
27	13 ♎ 59	3 ♐ 43	12 ♐ 14	28 12	0 ♓ 6	13 35	16 12	4 ♋ 3	25 39	4 ♎ 10	27 4	3 ♑ 37
28	27 50	16 32	25 10	10 ♒ 16	11 56	25 42	28 56	18 3	10 ♍ 35	19 6	11 ♐ 20	16 58
29	11 ♏ 16		7 ♑ 44	22 10	23 45	8 ♉ 6	12 ♊ 6	2 ♌ 29	25 42	4 ♏ 2	25 18	29 59
30	24 22		20 0	3 ♓ 59	5 ♈ 41	20 51	25 43	17 17	10 ♎ 53	18 48	8 ♑ 55	12 ♒ 42
31	7 ♐ 10		2 ♒ 3		17 47		9 ♋ 47	2 ♍ 21		3 ♐ 18		25 6

THE PLACE OF THE MOON FOR THE YEARS 1914-1915

DM	Jan.	Feb.	March	April	May	June	July	August	Sept.	Oct.	Nov.	Dec.
	° '	° '	° '	° '	° '	° '	° '	° '	° '	° '	° '	° '
1	7 ♓ 15	20 ♈ 41	28 ♈ 58	13 ♊ 53	18 ♋ 40	9 ♍ 3	17 ♎ 56	11 ♐ 22	2 ♒ 9	6 ♓ 55	22 ♈ 2	24 ♉ 35
2	19 11	2 ♉ 32	10 ♉ 49	26 20	1 ♌ 43	23 1	2 ♏ 12	25 16	15 2	19 7	3 ♉ 53	6 ♊ 34
3	1 ♈ 1	14 31	22 48	9 ♋ 4	15 6	7 ♎ 15	16 34	9 ♑ 1	27 41	1 ♈ 12	15 46	18 40
4	12 48	26 44	4 ♊ 59	22 9	28 50	21 46	0 ♐ 57	22 32	10 ♓ 9	13 10	27 39	0 ♋ 52
5	24 40	9 ♊ 16	17 27	5 ♌ 37	12 ♍ 56	6 ♏ 28	15 17	5 ♒ 49	22 25	25 5	9 ♊ 37	13 12
6	6 ♉ 41	22 9	0 ♋ 14	19 32	27 25	21 15	29 29	18 49	4 ♈ 32	6 ♉ 56	21 39	25 42
7	18 56	5 ♋ 27	13 26	3 ♍ 52	12 ♎ 14	6 ♐ 1	13 ♑ 27	1 ♓ 33	16 31	18 47	3 ♋ 48	8 ♌ 22
8	1 ♊ 29	19 11	27 5	18 37	27 17	20 37	27 6	14 2	28 24	0 ♊ 40	16 6	21 15
9	14 23	3 ♌ 19	11 ♌ 10	3 ♎ 40	12 ♏ 25	4 ♑ 56	10 ♒ 25	26 16	10 ♉ 15	12 37	28 38	4 ♍ 24
10	27 39	17 46	25 41	18 55	27 29	18 52	23 22	8 ♈ 19	22 7	24 42	11 ♌ 26	17 51
11	11 ♋ 16	2 ♍ 28	10 ♍ 32	4 ♏ 10	12 ♐ 18	2 ♒ 21	5 ♓ 59	20 14	4 ♊ 3	6 ♋ 59	24 35	1 ♎ 40
12	25 11	17 17	25 37	19 16	26 45	15 25	18 18	2 ♉ 6	16 9	19 31	8 ♍ 8	15 51
13	9 ♌ 20	2 ♎ 5	10 ♎ 47	4 ♐ 3	10 ♑ 45	28 4	0 ♈ 23	13 58	28 29	2 ♌ 24	22 8	0 ♏ 23
14	23 38	16 47	25 52	18 25	24 16	10 ♓ 23	12 19	25 56	11 ♋ 6	15 40	6 ♎ 35	15 13
15	8 ♍ 0	1 ♏ 15	10 ♏ 43	2 ♑ 18	7 ♒ 18	22 28	24 10	8 ♊ 4	24 6	29 24	21 27	0 ♐ 13
16	22 20	15 29	25 15	15 43	19 55	4 ♈ 22	6 ♉ 2	20 26	7 ♌ 30	13 ♍ 37	6 ♏ 36	15 15
17	6 ♎ 37	29 24	9 ♐ 23	28 40	2 ♓ 12	16 11	18 0	3 ♋ 7	21 20	28 16	21 55	0 ♑ 9
18	20 47	13 ♐ 2	23 6	11 ♒ 15	14 15	28 1	0 ♊ 7	16 8	5 ♍ 35	13 ♎ 16	7 ♐ 10	14 45
19	4 ♏ 50	26 22	6 ♑ 24	23 31	26 7	9 ♉ 56	12 28	29 31	20 12	28 31	22 12	28 58
20	18 44	9 ♑ 27	19 20	5 ♓ 34	7 ♈ 55	22 0	25 6	13 ♌ 16	5 ♎ 4	13 ♏ 48	6 ♑ 51	12 ♒ 43
21	2 ♐ 29	22 16	1 ♒ 58	17 28	19 43	4 ♊ 15	8 ♋ 0	27 20	20 5	28 58	21 1	26 0
22	16 4	4 ♒ 52	14 19	29 16	1 ♉ 34	16 43	21 13	11 ♍ 40	5 ♏ 4	13 ♐ 50	4 ♒ 40	8 ♓ 51
23	29 28	17 16	26 29	11 ♈ 3	13 31	29 25	4 ♌ 42	26 11	19 54	28 17	17 51	21 19
24	12 ♑ 40	29 30	8 ♓ 29	22 52	25 37	12 ♋ 20	18 25	10 ♎ 46	4 ♐ 28	12 ♑ 16	0 ♓ 36	3 ♈ 31
25	25 38	11 ♓ 34	20 23	4 ♉ 44	7 ♊ 53	25 28	2 ♍ 20	25 20	18 41	25 47	13 0	15 31
26	8 ♒ 21	23 30	2 ♈ 14	16 41	20 19	8 ♌ 47	16 24	9 ♏ 49	2 ♑ 32	8 ♒ 52	25 8	27 23
27	20 50	5 ♈ 21	14 2	28 45	2 ♋ 56	22 17	0 ♎ 33	24 7	16 1	21 35	7 ♈ 6	9 ♉ 14
28	3 ♓ 6	17 10	25 51	10 ♊ 57	15 44	5 ♍ 58	14 45	8 ♐ 13	29 8	4 ♓ 0	18 59	21 6
29	15 10		7 ♉ 42	23 19	28 43	19 48	28 58	22 4	11 ♒ 58	16 11	0 ♉ 49	3 ♊ 4
30	27 4		19 37	5 ♋ 52	11 ♌ 55	3 ♎ 47	13 ♏ 10	5 ♑ 40	24 33	28 13	12 40	15 10
31	8 ♈ 53		1 ♊ 40		25 21		27 19	19 2		10 ♈ 9		27 25

DM	Jan.	Feb.	March	April	May	June	July	August	Sept.	Oct.	Nov.	Dec.
	° '	° '	° '	° '	° '	° '	° '	° '	° '	° '	° '	° '
1	9 ♋ 50	27 ♌ 39	6 ♍ 18	28 ♎ 15	7 ♐ 12	0 ♒ 6	6 ♓ 1	22 ♈ 31	6 ♊ 37	8 ♋ 15	22 ♌ 51	27 ♍ 7
2	22 27	11 ♍ 15	20 21	13 ♏ 13	22 13	14 3	19 9	4 ♉ 43	18 29	20 15	5 ♍ 39	10 ♎ 44
3	5 ♌ 15	25 3	4 ♎ 38	28 6	6 ♑ 53	27 30	1 ♈ 53	16 45	0 ♋ 24	2 ♌ 27	18 53	24 51
4	18 13	9 ♎ 0	19 4	12 ♐ 47	21 7	10 ♓ 32	14 18	28 39	12 25	14 56	2 ♎ 37	9 ♏ 27
5	1 ♍ 24	23 3	3 ♏ 34	27 10	4 ♒ 54	23 13	26 28	10 ♊ 31	24 38	27 47	16 50	24 26
6	14 46	7 ♏ 12	18 2	11 ♑ 13	18 15	5 ♈ 35	8 ♉ 28	22 25	7 ♌ 5	11 ♍ 1	1 ♏ 28	9 ♐ 41
7	28 21	21 23	2 ♐ 24	24 55	1 ♓ 14	17 44	20 22	4 ♋ 25	19 50	24 41	16 25	24 59
8	12 ♎ 10	5 ♐ 35	16 35	8 ♒ 17	13 55	29 45	2 ♊ 13	16 34	2 ♍ 55	8 ♎ 44	1 ♐ 31	10 ♑ 11
9	26 12	19 45	0 ♑ 35	21 21	26 20	11 ♉ 39	14 6	28 54	16 18	23 7	16 36	25 6
10	10 ♏ 28	3 ♑ 51	14 22	4 ♓ 10	8 ♈ 34	23 31	26 2	11 ♌ 26	0 ♎ 0	7 ♏ 44	1 ♑ 30	9 ♒ 38
11	24 54	17 49	27 56	16 47	20 39	5 ♊ 23	8 ♋ 4	24 13	13 57	22 26	16 7	23 43
12	9 ♐ 27	1 ♒ 37	11 ♒ 18	29 13	2 ♉ 39	17 16	20 13	7 ♍ 15	28 5	7 ♐ 7	0 ♒ 22	7 ♓ 22
13	24 2	15 12	24 26	11 ♈ 30	14 35	29 11	2 ♌ 31	20 30	12 ♏ 19	21 39	14 14	20 35
14	8 ♑ 31	28 32	7 ♓ 22	23 39	26 28	11 ♋ 11	15 0	4 ♎ 0	26 37	5 ♑ 58	27 44	3 ♈ 27
15	22 48	11 ♓ 35	20 6	5 ♉ 41	8 ♊ 19	23 17	27 40	17 42	10 ♐ 53	20 3	10 ♓ 55	16 1
16	6 ♒ 47	24 21	2 ♈ 38	17 39	20 11	5 ♌ 31	10 ♍ 33	1 ♏ 35	25 5	3 ♒ 52	23 49	28 21
17	20 26	6 ♈ 51	14 59	29 32	2 ♋ 5	17 56	23 42	15 38	9 ♑ 11	17 25	6 ♈ 29	10 ♉ 30
18	3 ♓ 42	19 7	27 10	11 ♊ 23	14 4	0 ♍ 35	7 ♎ 6	29 49	23 10	0 ♓ 45	18 58	22 31
19	16 35	1 ♉ 11	9 ♉ 11	23 15	26 10	13 32	20 48	14 ♐ 6	7 ♒ 0	13 53	1 ♉ 17	4 ♊ 27
20	29 7	13 8	21 7	5 ♋ 11	8 ♌ 28	26 49	4 ♏ 47	28 26	20 41	26 49	13 28	16 19
21	11 ♈ 23	25 0	2 ♊ 59	17 15	21 1	10 ♎ 29	19 4	12 ♑ 45	4 ♓ 11	9 ♈ 34	25 32	28 9
22	23 26	6 ♊ 54	14 51	29 32	3 ♍ 55	24 35	3 ♐ 35	27 1	17 29	22 9	7 ♊ 30	10 ♋ 0
23	5 ♉ 21	18 53	26 48	12 ♌ 7	17 14	9 ♏ 4	18 16	11 ♒ 8	0 ♈ 35	4 ♉ 33	19 22	21 52
24	17 12	1 ♋ 2	8 ♋ 55	25 5	1 ♎ 0	23 54	3 ♑ 2	25 4	13 26	16 48	1 ♋ 12	3 ♌ 47
25	29 6	13 26	21 16	8 ♍ 30	15 16	8 ♐ 58	17 45	8 ♓ 45	26 4	28 52	13 0	15 50
26	11 ♊ 6	26 8	3 ♌ 55	22 24	29 59	24 6	2 ♒ 18	22 8	8 ♉ 27	10 ♊ 49	24 51	28 1
27	23 15	9 ♌ 10	16 58	6 ♎ 47	15 ♏ 3	9 ♑ 10	16 35	5 ♈ 13	20 38	22 40	6 ♌ 47	10 ♍ 26
28	5 ♋ 38	22 34	0 ♍ 27	21 35	0 ♐ 21	23 59	0 ♓ 32	17 59	2 ♊ 38	4 ♋ 29	18 54	23 9
29	18 15		14 22	6 ♏ 43	15 41	8 ♒ 26	14 5	0 ♉ 27	14 32	16 19	1 ♍ 16	6 ♎ 12
30	1 ♌ 8		28 41	21 59	0 ♑ 51	22 28	27 15	12 40	26 22	28 16	13 59	19 39
31	14 16		13 ♎ 21		15 41		10 ♈ 3	24 42		10 ♌ 25		3 ♏ 34

THE PLACE OF THE MOON FOR THE YEARS 1916-1917

DM	Jan.	Feb.	March	April	May	June	July	August	Sept.	Oct.	Nov.	Dec.
	° ′	° ′	° ′	° ′	° ′	° ′	° ′	° ′	° ′	° ′	° ′	° ′
1	17♏54	11♑18	5♒14	26♓43	2♉14	18♊11	20♋42	5♍24	22♎41	29♏44	22♑26	1♓28
2	2♐39	26 11	19 37	10♈11	14 53	0♋7	2♌29	17 37	5♏50	13♐32	6♒34	15 24
3	17 42	11♒0	3♓53	23 24	27 20	11 57	14 18	0♎3	19 12	27 26	20 37	29 6
4	2♑54	25 38	17 57	6♉20	9♊34	23 43	26 13	12 43	2♐48	11♑28	4♓36	12♈35
5	18 6	9♓57	1♈44	18 59	21 37	5♌31	8♍17	25 39	16 39	25 35	18 30	25 51
6	3♒7	23 53	15 12	1♊22	3♋31	17 22	20 34	8♏55	0♑45	9♒47	2♈17	8♉54
7	17 50	7♈25	28 19	13 20	15 19	29 22	3♎7	22 31	15 5	24 3	15 56	21 44
8	2♓8	20 31	11♉4	25 28	27 7	11♍36	16 0	6♐29	29 36	8♓19	29 23	4♊21
9	15 59	3♉14	23 30	7♋18	8♌58	24 8	29 17	20 48	14♒16	22 32	12♉36	16 46
10	29 23	15 37	5♊40	19 7	20 58	7♎4	13♏0	5♑26	28 58	6♈37	25 34	28 59
11	12♈22	27 45	17 38	0♌59	3♍13	20 26	27 10	20 19	13♓35	20 29	8♊16	11♋2
12	24 59	9♊41	29 29	13 0	15 47	4♏17	11♐44	5♒21	28 2	4♉4	20 41	22 57
13	7♉18	21 32	11♋18	25 16	28 45	18 35	26 39	20 22	12♈11	17 18	2♋52	4♌46
14	19 24	3♋20	23 10	7♍50	12♎11	3♐18	11♑47	5♓15	25 58	0♊12	14 50	16 33
15	1♊20	15 12	5♌11	20 46	26 3	18 18	26 59	19 51	9♉20	12 44	26 41	28 22
16	13 11	27 10	17 24	4♎7	10♏20	3♑27	12♒6	4♈5	22 17	24 59	8♌28	10♍17
17	25 1	9♌17	29 53	17 50	24 58	18 35	26 59	17 53	4♊52	7♋0	20 17	22 23
18	6♋51	21 36	12♍40	1♏53	9♐49	3♒33	11♓32	1♉14	17 7	18 51	2♍13	4♎46
19	18 45	4♍7	25 46	16 13	24 43	18 14	25 39	14 9	29 8	0♌39	14 22	17 29
20	0♌44	16 53	9♎10	0♐41	9♑34	2♓34	9♈20	26 41	10♋59	12 29	26 48	0♏37
21	12 50	29 52	22 50	15 12	24 14	16 30	22 35	8♊55	22 46	24 26	9♎36	14 12
22	25 6	13♎6	6♏42	29 39	8♒38	0♈3	5♉26	20 55	4♌35	6♍35	22 47	28 14
23	7♍30	26 32	20 43	14♑0	22 44	13 13	17 57	2♋47	16 30	19 0	6♏24	12♐41
24	20 8	10♏10	4♐49	28 10	6♓31	26 5	0♊12	14 34	28 35	1♎44	20 23	27 27
25	3♎0	23 59	18 59	12♒9	20 1	8♉39	12 15	26 21	10♍53	14 49	4♐40	12♑25
26	16 9	7♐59	3♑6	25 58	3♈15	21 0	24 9	8♌12	23 26	28 13	19 11	27 27
27	29 35	22 9	17 13	9♓35	16 14	3♊10	5♋57	20 10	6♎14	11♏55	3♑49	12♒24
28	13♏21	6♑26	1♒18	23 1	29 0	15 11	17 44	2♍17	19 18	25 50	18 26	27 9
29	27 26	20 49	15 19	6♈17	11♉33	27 5	29 32	14 35	2♏35	9♐55	2♒57	11♓36
30	11♐50		29 15	19 21	23 56	8♋54	11♌23	27 4	16 5	24 5	17 19	25 43
31	26 29		13♓4		6♊8		23 20	9♎46		8♑16		9♈27

DM	Jan.	Feb.	March	April	May	June	July	August	Sept.	Oct.	Nov.	Dec.
	° ′	° ′	° ′	° ′	° ′	° ′	° ′	° ′	° ′	° ′	° ′	° ′
1	22♈51	10♊36	19♊28	3♌37	5♍18	20♎4	24♏13	14♑37	8♓10	16♈47	7♊47	11♋57
2	5♉55	22 44	1♋34	15 24	17 19	2♏56	7♐54	29 29	23 28	1♉34	21 12	24 33
3	18 41	4♋43	13 29	27 15	29 33	16 10	21 58	14♒35	8♈34	15 57	4♋12	6♌53
4	1♊13	16 35	25 17	9♍13	12♎2	29 44	6♑24	29 47	23 19	29 52	16 50	18 59
5	13 32	28 24	7♌4	21 20	24 47	13♐37	21 5	14♓55	7♉38	13♊17	29 8	0♍56
6	25 41	10♌11	18 52	3♎40	7♏50	27 46	5♒56	29 49	21 26	26 15	11♌12	12 48
7	7♋42	22 1	0♍45	16 13	21 8	12♑6	20 49	14♈22	4♊46	8♋48	23 7	24 41
8	19 37	3♍53	12 45	28 58	4♐41	26 32	5♓36	28 29	17 39	21 3	4♍58	6♎39
9	1♌27	15 51	24 53	11♏57	18 26	10♒59	20 11	12♉11	0♋10	3♌4	16 50	18 46
10	13 15	27 56	7♎11	25 6	2♑20	25 24	4♈29	25 27	12 24	14 57	28 47	1♏6
11	25 3	10♎10	19 39	8♐27	16 20	9♓42	18 28	8♊20	24 26	26 47	10♎52	13 43
12	6♍55	22 35	2♏17	21 58	0♒25	23 51	2♉8	20 55	6♌19	8♍37	23 9	26 38
13	18 52	5♏15	15 8	5♑39	14 33	7♈50	15 28	3♋14	18 9	20 31	5♏38	9♐51
14	0♎59	18 11	28 11	19 31	28 43	21 36	28 30	15 22	29 59	2♎31	18 21	23 22
15	13 19	1♐28	11♐29	3♒34	12♓53	5♉10	11♊16	27 21	11♍50	14 40	1♐18	7♑10
16	25 58	15 7	25 3	17 47	27 1	18 30	23 48	9♌15	23 44	26 57	14 27	21 10
17	8♏58	29 10	8♑54	2♓9	11♈5	1♊36	6♋9	21 6	5♎44	9♏24	27 48	5♒19
18	22 23	13♑37	23 4	16 37	25 1	14 28	18 19	2♍56	17 49	22 1	11♑20	19 34
19	6♐14	28 25	7♒32	1♈6	8♉47	27 6	0♌21	14 47	0♏2	4♐49	25 2	3♓51
20	20 33	13♒29	22 15	15 30	22 18	9♋31	12 17	26 40	12 24	17 47	8♒53	18 6
21	5♑16	28 40	7♓8	29 42	5♊33	21 44	24 9	8♎38	24 57	0♑59	22 54	2♈18
22	20 18	13♓49	22 2	13♉37	18 29	3♌46	5♍59	20 42	7♐43	14 24	7♓3	16 22
23	5♒31	28 46	6♈49	27 11	1♋8	15 41	17 49	2♏56	20 46	28 6	21 18	0♉19
24	20 44	13♈21	21 21	10♊21	13 30	27 32	29 44	15 24	4♑9	12♒5	5♈37	14 7
25	5♓49	27 30	5♉30	23 9	25 38	9♍22	11♎45	28 8	17 54	26 22	19 56	27 43
26	20 37	11♉9	19 13	5♋36	7♌36	21 16	23 58	11♐12	2♒3	10♓53	4♉11	11♊8
27	5♈1	24 20	2♊28	17 46	19 28	3♎18	6♏26	24 41	16 35	25 36	18 17	24 19
28	18 58	7♊5	15 17	29 44	1♍18	15 33	19 14	8♑37	1♓28	10♈23	2♊10	7♋16
29	2♉27		27 43	11♌35	13 13	28 5	2♐25	22 59	16 34	25 8	15 45	19 58
30	15 31		9♋51	23 25	25 15	10♏57	16 3	7♒46	1♈44	9♉41	29 1	2♌27
31	28 13		21 48		7♎31		0♑7	22 53		23 55		14 43

THE PLACE OF THE MOON FOR THE YEARS 1918-1919

DM	Jan.	Feb.	March	April	May	June	July	August	Sept.	Oct.	Nov.	Dec.
	° ′	° ′	° ′	° ′	° ′	° ′	° ′	° ′	° ′	° ′	° ′	° ′
1	26♌48	10♎39	19♎17	4♐44	9♑58	1♓14	10♈38	3♊32	23♋12	27♌35	12♎28	14♏26
2	8♍45	22 34	1♏14	17 14	23 10	15 21	24 51	17 3	5♌49	9♍41	24 18	26 48
3	20 38	4♏36	13 16	0♑0	6♒41	29 38	8♉59	0♋21	18 15	21 41	6♏10	8♐58
4	2♎30	16 50	25 28	13 6	20 31	14♈2	23 0	13 27	0♍32	3♎36	18 5	21 18
5	14 26	29 20	7♐55	26 36	4♓41	28 30	6♊53	26 22	12 42	15 28	0♐4	3♑50
6	26 31	12♐12	20 41	10♒31	19 10	12♉56	20 35	9♌5	24 43	27 18	12 10	16 34
7	8♏49	25 30	3♑50	24 53	3♈54	27 16	4♋5	21 36	6♎39	9♏8	24 25	29 32
8	21 25	9♑15	17 27	9♓39	18 46	11♊25	17 20	3♍57	18 31	21 0	6♑51	12♒43
9	4♐23	23 28	1♒33	24 44	3♉40	25 18	0♌21	16 7	0♏20	2♐57	19 32	26 9
10	17 44	8♒7	16 8	9♈58	18 26	8♋53	13 6	28 8	12 10	15 3	2♒30	9♓50
11	1♑29	23 6	1♓8	25 10	2♊56	22 7	25 36	10♎2	24 4	27 21	15 48	23 47
12	15 36	8♓15	16 24	10♉11	17 5	5♌1	7♍52	21 53	6♐8	9♑56	29 30	7♈59
13	0♒3	23 24	1♈45	24 50	0♋50	17 36	19 57	3♏44	18 25	22 52	13♓35	22 23
14	14 42	8♈24	17 0	9♊3	14 10	29 55	1♎54	15 40	1♑3	6♒14	28 3	6♉56
15	29 27	23 5	1♉58	22 47	27 5	12♍1	13 47	27 46	14 4	20 5	12♈50	21 34
16	14♓10	7♉23	16 31	6♋2	9♌39	23 58	25 41	10♐7	27 33	4♓24	27 50	6♊12
17	28 45	21 16	0♊36	18 53	21 56	5♎52	7♏39	22 48	11♒33	19 10	12♉55	20 42
18	13♈7	4♊44	14 11	1♌23	4♍0	17 46	19 48	5♑54	26 2	4♈17	27 56	4♋59
19	27 13	17 50	27 20	13 36	15 56	29 45	2♐11	19 26	10♓56	19 34	12♊43	18 57
20	11♉1	0♋37	10♋5	25 38	27 48	11♏53	14 52	3♒26	26 6	4♉52	27 10	2♌34
21	24 31	13 8	22 32	7♍33	9♎42	24 13	27 55	17 51	11♈23	19 59	11♋13	15 48
22	7♊46	25 28	4♌45	19 25	21 39	6♐49	11♑20	2♓36	26 35	4♊47	24 48	28 39
23	20 46	7♌40	16 48	1♎17	3♏43	19 41	25 8	17 33	11♉32	19 9	7♌58	11♍10
24	3♋33	19 44	28 45	13 11	15 57	2♑51	9♒26	2♈32	26 7	3♋3	20 44	23 23
25	16 9	1♍43	10♍39	25 10	28 21	16 17	23 38	17 25	10♊16	16 29	3♍10	5♎24
26	28 35	13 39	22 31	7♏15	10♐58	29 59	8♓10	2♉4	23 59	29 31	15 20	17 17
27	10♌51	25 32	4♎24	19 27	23 48	13♒54	22 44	16 24	7♋18	12♌11	27 19	29 6
28	22 59	7♎24	16 18	1♐48	6♑51	27 58	7♈15	0♊23	20 16	24 33	9♎11	10♏58
29	5♍0		28 16	14 19	20 7	12♓9	21 38	14 2	2♌55	6♍43	21 1	22 55
30	16 55		10♏18	27 2	3♒36	26 24	5♉49	27 21	15 21	18 43	2♏51	5♐3
31	28 48		22 27		17 18		19 47	10♋24		0♎37		17 23

DM	Jan.	Feb.	March	April	May	June	July	August	Sept.	Oct.	Nov.	Dec.
	° ′	° ′	° ′	° ′	° ′	° ′	° ′	° ′	° ′	° ′	° ′	° ′
1	29♐59	18♒30	26♒52	19♈30	28♉7	20♋24	26♌4	12♎20	26♏5	27♐46	13♒1	18♓4
2	12♑51	2♓35	11♓19	4♉36	13♊4	4♌21	9♍12	24 27	7♐53	9♑49	25 58	1♈42
3	25 59	16 50	26 1	19 35	27 42	17 50	21 55	6♏23	19 47	22 7	9♓21	15 46
4	9♒21	1♈10	10♈49	4♊18	11♋55	0♍54	4♎19	18 12	1♑51	4♒45	23 12	0♉16
5	22 57	15 31	25 34	18 40	25 42	13 35	16 26	0♐1	14 11	17 48	7♈30	15 8
6	6♓44	29 47	10♉11	2♋40	9♌4	25 57	28 22	11 55	26 50	1♓17	22 12	0♊15
7	20 39	13♉56	24 34	16 17	22 3	8♎4	10♏11	23 57	9♒52	15 13	7♉12	15 29
8	4♈41	27 57	8♊41	29 34	4♍42	20 0	22 0	6♑14	23 17	29 33	22 22	0♋41
9	18 47	11♊50	22 32	12♌32	17 4	1♏50	3♐51	18 47	7♓5	14♈12	7♊32	15 40
10	2♉56	25 35	6♋6	25 14	29 14	13 38	15 50	1♒39	21 11	29 2	22 33	0♌19
11	17 7	9♋11	19 26	7♍43	11♎13	25 27	27 59	14 50	5♈31	13♉57	7♋18	14 31
12	1♊17	22 37	2♌33	20 1	23 7	7♐20	10♑21	28 18	19 59	28 47	21 40	28 15
13	15 25	5♌54	15 28	2♎9	4♏56	19 20	22 57	12♓1	4♉28	13♊26	5♌38	11♍31
14	29 27	18 59	28 12	14 11	16 45	1♑29	5♒47	25 56	18 54	27 50	19 11	24 21
15	13♋21	1♍51	10♍45	26 5	28 34	13 48	18 52	9♈58	3♊13	11♋56	2♍20	6♎49
16	27 2	14 29	23 7	7♏56	10♐26	26 19	2♓10	24 4	17 23	25 44	15 9	19 0
17	10♌27	26 53	5♎20	19 44	22 24	9♒3	15 41	8♉12	1♋22	9♌13	27 40	0♏59
18	23 35	9♎4	17 23	1♐32	4♑30	22 2	29 22	22 19	15 10	22 26	9♎56	12 50
19	6♍24	21 3	29 18	13 24	16 46	5♓15	13♈13	6♊26	28 48	5♍23	22 2	24 37
20	18 55	2♏55	11♏8	25 21	29 16	18 45	27 14	20 31	12♌15	18 5	3♏59	6♐23
21	1♎9	14 44	22 55	7♑30	12♒2	2♈32	11♉22	4♋32	25 30	0♎36	15 50	18 12
22	13 11	26 33	4♐44	19 53	25 8	16 35	25 38	18 28	8♍32	12 54	27 39	0♑5
23	25 4	8♐30	16 39	2♒36	8♓36	0♉55	9♊58	2♌18	21 22	25 3	9♐26	12 5
24	6♏54	20 38	28 46	15 42	22 27	15 28	24 21	15 57	3♎58	7♏3	21 14	24 13
25	18 45	3♑4	11♑9	29 15	6♈42	0♊11	8♋43	29 22	16 20	18 56	3♑5	6♒30
26	0♐42	15 52	23 54	13♓17	21 19	14 58	22 57	12♍37	28 30	0♐44	15 1	18 58
27	12 52	29 6	7♒6	27 45	6♉12	29 43	6♌59	25 25	10♏29	12 30	27 8	1♓38
28	25 18	12♒46	20 46	12♈36	21 16	14♋17	20 45	7♎59	22 20	24 17	9♒26	14 32
29	8♑4		4♓54	27 43	6♊21	28 35	4♏10	20 18	4♐7	6♑9	21 59	27 43
30	21 12		19 29	12♉57	21 20	12♌32	17 14	2♏22	15 54	18 11	4♓50	11♈12
31	4♒41		4♈24		6♋3		29 57	14 16		0♒27		25 2

TABLE OF HOUSES FOR LONDON. LATITUDE 51°32'N.

Sidereal Time H.	M.	S.	10 ♈ °	11 ♉ °	12 ♊ °	ASC. ♋ °	'	2 ♌ °	3 ♍ °
0	0	0	0	9	22	26	36	12	3
0	3	40	1	10	23	27	17	13	3
0	7	20	2	11	24	27	56	14	4
0	11	0	3	12	25	28	42	15	5
0	14	41	4	13	25	29	17	15	6
0	18	21	5	14	26	29	55	16	7
0	22	2	6	15	27	0 ♌	34	17	8
0	25	42	7	16	28	1	14	18	8
0	29	23	8	17	29	1	55	18	9
0	33	4	9	18	♋	2	33	19	10
0	36	45	10	19	1	3	14	20	11
0	40	26	11	20	1	3	54	20	12
0	44	8	12	21	2	4	33	21	13
0	47	50	13	22	3	5	12	22	14
0	51	32	14	23	4	5	52	23	15
0	55	14	15	24	5	6	30	23	15
0	58	57	16	25	6	7	9	24	16
1	2	40	17	26	6	7	50	25	17
1	6	23	18	27	7	8	30	26	18
1	10	7	19	28	8	9	9	26	19
1	13	51	20	29	9	9	48	27	19
1	17	35	21	♊	10	10	28	28	20
1	21	20	22	1	10	11	8	28	21
1	25	6	23	2	11	11	48	29	22
1	28	52	24	3	12	12	28	♍	23
1	32	38	25	4	13	13	8	1	24
1	36	25	26	5	14	13	48	1	25
1	40	12	27	6	14	14	28	2	25
1	44	0	28	7	15	15	8	3	26
1	47	48	29	8	16	15	48	4	27
1	51	37	30	9	17	16	28	4	28

Sidereal Time H.	M.	S.	10 ♉ °	11 ♊ °	12 ♋ °	ASC. ♌ °	'	2 ♍ °	3 ♍ '
1	51	37	0	9	17	16	28	4	28
1	55	27	1	10	18	17	8	5	29
1	59	17	2	11	19	17	48	6	♎
2	3	8	3	12	19	18	28	7	1
2	6	59	4	13	20	19	9	8	2
2	10	51	5	14	21	19	49	9	2
2	14	44	6	15	22	20	29	9	3
2	18	37	7	16	22	21	10	10	4
2	22	31	8	17	23	21	51	11	5
2	26	25	9	18	24	22	32	11	6
2	30	20	10	19	25	23	14	12	7
2	34	16	11	20	25	23	55	13	8
2	38	13	12	21	26	24	36	14	9
2	42	10	13	22	27	25	17	15	10
2	46	8	14	23	28	25	58	15	11
2	50	7	15	24	29	26	40	16	12
2	54	7	16	25	29	27	22	17	12
2	58	7	17	26	♌	28	4	18	13
3	2	8	18	27	1	28	46	18	14
3	6	9	19	27	2	29	28	19	15
3	10	12	20	28	3	0 ♍	12	20	16
3	14	15	21	29	3	0	54	21	17
3	18	19	22	♋	4	1	36	22	18
3	22	23	23	1	5	2	20	22	19
3	26	29	24	2	6	3	2	23	20
3	30	35	25	3	7	3	45	24	21
3	34	41	26	4	7	4	28	25	22
3	38	49	27	5	8	5	11	26	23
3	42	57	28	6	9	5	54	27	24
3	47	6	29	7	10	6	38	27	25
3	51	15	30	8	11	7	21	28	25

Sidereal Time H.	M.	S	10 ♊ °	11 ♋ °	12 ♌ °	ASC. ♍ °	'	2 ♍ °	3 ♎ °
3	51	15	0	8	11	7	21	28	25
3	55	25	1	9	12	8	5	29	26
3	59	36	2	10	12	8	49	♎	27
4	3	48	3	10	13	9	33	1	28
4	8	0	4	11	14	10	17	2	29
4	12	13	5	12	15	11	2	2	♏
4	16	26	6	13	16	11	46	3	1
4	20	40	7	14	17	12	30	4	2
4	24	55	8	15	17	13	15	5	3
4	29	10	9	16	18	14	0	6	4
4	33	26	10	17	19	14	45	7	5
4	37	42	11	18	20	15	30	8	6
4	41	59	12	19	21	16	15	8	7
4	46	16	13	20	21	17	0	9	8
4	50	34	14	21	22	17	45	10	9
4	54	52	15	22	23	18	30	11	10
4	59	10	16	23	24	19	16	12	11
5	3	29	17	24	25	20	3	13	12
5	7	49	18	25	26	20	49	14	13
5	12	9	19	25	27	21	35	14	14
5	16	29	20	26	28	22	20	15	14
5	20	49	21	27	28	23	6	16	15
5	25	9	22	28	29	23	51	17	16
5	29	30	23	29	♍	24	37	18	17
5	33	51	24	♌	1	25	23	19	18
5	38	12	25	1	2	26	9	20	19
5	42	34	26	2	3	26	55	21	20
5	46	55	27	3	4	27	41	21	21
5	51	17	28	4	4	28	27	22	22
5	55	38	29	5	5	29	13	23	23
6	0	0	30	6	6	30	0	24	24

TABLE OF HOUSES FOR LONDON. LATITUDE 51°32'N.

Sidereal Time			10 ♋	11 ♌	12 ♍	ASC. ♎		2 ♎	3 ♏	Sidereal Time			10 ♌	11 ♍	12 ♎	ASC. ♎		2 ♏	3 ♐	Sidereal Time			10 ♍	11 ♎	12 ♎	ASC. ♏		2 ♐	3 ♑
H.	M.	S.	°	°	°	°	'	°	°	H.	M.	S.	°	°	°	°	'	°	°	H.	M.	S.	°	°	°	°	'	°	°
6	0	0	0	6	6	0	0	24	24	8	8	45	0	5	2	22	40	19	22	10	8	23	0	2	26	13	33	13	20
6	4	22	1	7	7	0	47	25	25	8	12	54	1	5	3	23	24	20	23	10	12	12	1	3	26	14	13	14	21
6	8	43	2	8	8	1	33	26	26	8	17	3	2	6	3	24	7	21	24	10	16	0	2	4	27	14	53	15	22
6	13	5	3	9	9	2	19	27	27	8	21	11	3	7	4	24	50	22	25	10	19	48	3	5	28	15	33	15	23
6	17	26	4	10	10	3	5	27	28	8	25	19	4	8	5	25	34	23	26	10	23	35	4	5	29	16	13	16	24
6	21	48	5	11	10	3	51	28	29	8	29	26	5	9	6	26	18	23	27	10	27	22	5	6	29	16	52	17	25
6	26	9	6	12	11	4	37	29	♐	8	33	31	6	10	7	27	1	24	28	10	31	8	6	7	♏	17	32	18	26
6	30	30	7	13	12	5	23	♏	1	8	37	37	7	11	8	27	44	25	29	10	34	54	7	8	1	18	13	19	27
6	34	51	8	14	13	6	9	1	2	8	41	41	8	12	8	28	26	26	♑	10	38	40	8	9	2	18	52	20	28
6	39	11	9	15	14	6	55	2	3	8	45	45	9	13	9	29	8	27	1	10	42	25	9	10	2	19	31	20	29
6	43	31	10	16	15	7	40	2	4	8	49	48	10	14	10	29	50	27	2	10	46	9	10	11	3	20	11	21	♒
6	47	51	11	16	16	8	26	3	4	8	53	51	11	15	11	0 ♏	32	28	3	10	49	53	11	11	4	20	50	22	1
6	52	11	12	17	16	9	12	4	5	8	57	52	12	16	12	1	15	29	4	10	53	37	12	12	4	21	30	23	2
6	56	31	13	18	17	9	58	5	6	9	1	53	13	17	12	1	58	♐	4	10	57	20	13	13	5	22	9	24	3
7	0	50	14	19	18	10	43	6	7	9	5	53	14	18	13	2	39	1	5	11	1	3	14	14	6	22	49	24	4
7	5	8	15	20	19	11	28	7	8	9	9	53	15	18	14	3	21	1	6	11	4	46	15	15	7	23	28	25	5
7	9	26	16	21	20	12	14	8	9	9	13	52	16	19	15	4	3	2	7	11	8	28	16	16	7	24	8	26	6
7	13	44	17	22	21	12	59	8	10	9	17	50	17	20	16	4	44	3	8	11	12	10	17	17	8	24	47	27	8
7	18	1	18	23	22	13	45	9	11	9	21	47	18	21	16	5	26	3	9	11	15	52	18	17	9	25	27	28	9
7	22	18	19	24	23	14	30	10	12	9	25	44	19	22	17	6	7	4	10	11	19	34	19	18	10	26	6	29	10
7	26	34	20	25	24	15	15	11	13	9	29	40	20	23	18	6	48	5	11	11	23	15	20	19	10	26	45	♑	11
7	30	50	21	26	25	16	0	12	14	9	33	35	21	24	18	7	29	5	12	11	26	56	21	20	11	27	25	0	12
7	35	5	22	27	25	16	45	13	15	9	37	29	22	25	19	8	9	6	13	11	30	37	22	21	12	28	5	1	13
7	39	20	23	28	26	17	30	13	16	9	41	23	23	26	20	8	50	7	14	11	34	18	23	22	13	28	44	2	14
7	43	34	24	29	27	18	15	14	17	9	45	16	24	27	21	9	31	8	15	11	37	58	24	23	13	29	24	3	15
7	47	47	25	♍	28	18	59	15	18	9	49	9	25	28	22	10	11	9	16	11	41	39	25	23	14	0 ♐	3	4	16
7	52	0	26	1	29	19	43	16	19	9	53	1	26	28	23	10	51	9	17	11	45	19	26	24	15	0	43	5	17
7	56	12	27	2	29	20	27	17	20	9	56	52	27	29	23	11	32	10	18	11	49	0	27	25	15	1	23	6	18
8	0	24	28	3	♎	21	11	18	20	10	0	43	28	♎	24	12	12	11	19	11	52	40	28	26	16	2	3	6	19
8	4	35	29	4	1	21	56	18	21	10	4	33	29	1	25	12	53	12	20	11	56	20	29	27	17	2	43	7	20
8	8	45	30	5	2	22	40	19	22	10	8	23	30	2	26	13	33	13	20	12	0	0	30	27	17	3	23	8	21

TABLE OF HOUSES FOR LONDON. LATITUDE 51°32′N

Sidereal Time H.	M.	S.	10 ♎ °	11 ♎ °	12 ♏ °	ASC. ♐ °	′	2 ♑ °	3 ♒ °
12	0	0	0	27	17	3	23	8	21
12	3	40	1	28	18	4	4	9	23
12	7	20	2	29	19	4	45	10	24
12	11	0	3	♏	20	5	26	11	25
12	14	41	4	1	20	6	7	12	26
12	18	21	5	1	21	6	48	13	27
12	22	2	6	2	22	7	29	14	28
12	25	42	7	3	23	8	10	15	29
12	29	23	8	4	23	8	51	16	♓
12	33	4	9	5	24	9	33	17	2
12	36	45	10	6	25	10	15	18	3
12	40	26	11	6	25	10	57	19	4
12	44	8	12	7	26	11	40	20	5
12	47	50	13	8	27	12	22	21	6
12	51	32	14	9	28	13	4	22	7
12	55	14	15	10	28	13	47	23	9
12	58	57	16	11	29	14	30	24	10
13	2	40	17	11	♐	15	14	25	11
13	6	23	18	12	1	15	59	26	12
13	10	7	19	13	1	16	44	27	13
13	13	51	20	14	2	17	29	28	15
13	17	35	21	15	3	18	14	29	16
13	21	20	22	16	4	19	0	♒	17
13	25	6	23	16	4	19	45	1	18
13	28	52	24	17	5	20	31	2	20
13	32	38	25	18	6	21	18	4	21
13	36	25	26	19	7	22	6	5	22
13	40	12	27	20	7	22	54	6	23
13	44	0	28	21	8	23	42	7	25
13	47	48	29	21	9	24	31	8	26
13	51	37	30	22	10	25	20	10	27

Sidereal Time H.	M.	S.	10 ♏ °	11 ♏ °	12 ♐ °	ASC. ♐ °	′	2 ♒ °	3 ♓ °
13	51	37	0	22	10	25	20	10	27
13	55	27	1	23	11	26	10	11	28
13	59	17	2	24	11	27	2	12	♈
14	3	8	3	25	12	27	53	14	1
14	6	59	4	26	13	28	45	15	2
14	10	51	5	26	14	29	36	16	4
14	14	44	6	27	15	0 ♑	29	18	5
14	18	37	7	28	15	1	23	19	6
14	22	31	8	29	16	2	18	20	8
14	26	25	9	♐	17	3	14	22	9
14	30	20	10	1	18	4	11	23	10
14	34	16	11	2	19	5	9	25	11
14	38	13	12	2	20	6	7	26	13
14	42	10	13	3	20	7	6	28	14
14	46	8	14	4	21	8	6	29	15
14	50	7	15	5	22	9	8	♓	17
14	54	7	16	6	23	10	11	2	18
14	58	7	17	7	24	11	15	4	19
15	2	8	18	8	25	12	20	6	21
15	6	9	19	9	26	13	27	8	22
15	10	12	20	9	27	14	35	9	23
15	14	15	21	10	27	15	43	11	24
15	18	19	22	11	28	16	52	13	26
15	22	23	23	12	29	18	3	14	27
15	26	29	24	13	♑	19	16	16	28
15	30	35	25	14	1	20	32	17	29
15	34	41	26	15	2	21	48	19	♉
15	38	49	27	16	3	23	8	21	2
15	42	57	28	17	4	24	29	22	3
15	47	6	29	18	5	25	51	24	5
15	51	15	30	18	6	27	15	26	6

Sidereal Time H.	M.	S.	10 ♐ °	11 ♐ °	12 ♑ °	ASC. ♑ °	′	2 ♓ °	3 ♉ °
15	51	15	0	18	6	27	15	26	6
15	55	25	1	19	7	28	42	28	7
15	59	36	2	20	8	0 ♒	11	♈	9
16	3	48	3	21	9	1	42	2	10
16	8	0	4	22	10	3	16	3	11
16	12	13	5	23	11	4	53	5	12
16	16	26	6	24	12	6	32	7	14
16	20	40	7	25	13	8	13	9	15
16	24	55	8	26	14	9	57	11	16
16	29	10	9	27	16	11	44	12	17
16	33	26	10	28	17	13	34	14	18
16	37	42	11	29	18	15	26	16	20
16	41	59	12	♑	19	17	20	18	21
16	46	16	13	1	20	19	18	20	22
16	50	34	14	2	21	21	22	21	23
16	54	52	15	3	22	23	29	23	25
16	59	10	16	4	24	25	36	25	26
17	3	29	17	5	25	27	46	27	27
17	7	49	18	6	26	0 ♓	0	28	28
17	12	9	19	7	27	2	19	♉	29
17	16	29	20	8	29	4	40	2	♊
17	20	49	21	9	♒	7	2	3	1
17	25	9	22	10	1	9	26	5	2
17	29	30	23	11	3	11	54	7	3
17	33	51	24	12	4	14	24	8	5
17	38	12	25	13	5	17	0	10	6
17	42	34	26	14	7	19	33	11	7
17	46	55	27	15	8	22	6	13	8
17	51	17	28	16	10	24	40	14	9
17	55	38	29	17	11	27	20	16	10
18	0	0	30	18	13	30	0	17	11

TABLE OF HOUSES FOR LONDON. LATITUDE 51°32′N.

Sidereal Time H.	M.	S.	10 ♑ °	11 ♑ °	12 ♒ °	ASC. ♈ °	′	2 ♉ °	3 ♊ °
18	0	0	0	18	13	0	0	17	11
18	4	22	1	20	14	2	39	19	13
18	8	43	2	21	16	5	19	20	14
18	13	5	3	22	17	7	55	22	15
18	17	26	4	23	19	10	29	23	16
18	21	48	5	24	20	13	2	25	17
18	26	9	6	25	22	15	36	26	18
18	30	30	7	26	23	18	6	28	19
18	34	51	8	27	25	20	34	29	20
18	39	11	9	29	27	22	59	♊	21
18	43	31	10	♒	28	25	22	1	22
18	47	51	11	1	♓	27	42	2	23
18	52	11	12	2	2	29	58	4	24
18	56	31	13	3	3	2 ♉	13	5	25
19	0	50	14	4	5	4	24	6	26
19	5	8	15	6	7	6	30	8	27
19	9	26	16	7	9	8	36	9	28
19	13	44	17	8	10	10	40	10	29
19	18	1	18	9	12	12	39	11	♋
19	22	18	19	10	14	14	35	12	1
19	26	34	20	12	16	16	28	13	2
19	30	50	21	13	18	18	17	14	3
19	35	5	22	14	19	20	3	16	4
19	39	20	23	15	21	21	48	17	5
19	43	34	24	16	23	23	29	18	6
19	47	47	25	18	25	25	9	19	7
19	52	0	26	19	27	26	45	20	8
19	56	12	27	20	28	28	18	21	9
20	0	24	28	21	♈	29	49	22	10
20	4	35	29	23	2	1 ♊	19	23	11
20	8	45	30	24	4	2	45	24	12

Sidereal Time H.	M.	S.	10 ♒ °	11 ♒ °	12 ♈ °	ASC. ♊ °	′	2 ♊ °	3 ♋ °
20	8	45	0	24	4	2	45	24	12
20	12	54	1	25	6	4	9	25	12
20	17	3	2	27	7	5	32	26	13
20	21	11	3	28	9	6	53	27	14
20	25	19	4	29	11	8	12	28	15
20	29	26	5	♓	13	9	27	29	16
20	33	31	6	2	14	10	43	♋	17
20	37	37	7	3	16	11	58	1	18
20	41	41	8	4	18	13	9	2	19
20	45	45	9	6	19	14	18	3	20
20	49	48	10	7	21	15	25	3	21
20	53	51	11	8	23	16	32	4	21
20	57	52	12	9	24	17	39	5	22
21	1	53	13	11	26	18	44	6	23
21	5	53	14	12	28	19	48	7	24
21	9	53	15	13	29	20	51	8	25
21	13	52	16	15	♉	21	53	9	26
21	17	50	17	16	2	22	53	10	27
21	21	47	18	17	4	23	52	10	28
21	25	44	19	19	5	24	51	11	28
21	29	40	20	20	7	25	48	12	29
21	33	35	21	22	8	26	44	13	♌
21	37	29	22	23	10	27	40	14	1
21	41	23	23	24	11	28	34	15	2
21	45	16	24	25	13	29	29	15	3
21	49	9	25	26	14	0 ♋	22	16	4
21	53	1	26	28	15	1	15	17	4
21	56	52	27	29	16	2	7	18	5
22	0	43	28	♈	18	2	57	19	6
22	4	33	29	2	19	3	48	19	7
22	8	23	30	3	20	4	38	20	8

Sidereal Time H.	M.	S.	10 ♓ °	11 ♈ °	12 ♉ °	ASC. ♋ °	′	2 ♋ °	3 ♌ °
22	8	23	0	3	20	4	38	20	8
22	12	12	1	4	21	5	28	21	8
22	16	0	2	6	23	6	17	22	9
22	19	48	3	7	24	7	5	23	10
22	23	35	4	8	25	7	53	23	11
22	27	22	5	9	26	8	42	24	12
22	31	8	6	10	28	9	29	25	13
22	34	54	7	12	29	10	16	26	14
22	38	40	8	13	♊	11	2	26	14
22	42	25	9	14	1	11	47	27	15
22	46	9	10	15	2	12	31	28	16
22	49	53	11	17	3	13	16	29	17
22	53	37	12	18	4	14	1	29	18
22	57	20	13	19	5	14	45	♌	19
23	1	3	14	20	6	15	28	1	19
23	4	46	15	21	7	16	11	2	20
23	8	28	16	23	8	16	54	2	21
23	12	10	17	24	9	17	37	3	22
23	15	52	18	25	10	18	20	4	23
23	19	34	19	26	11	19	3	5	24
23	23	15	20	27	12	19	45	5	24
23	26	56	21	29	13	20	26	6	25
23	30	37	22	♉	14	21	8	7	26
23	34	18	23	1	15	21	50	7	27
23	37	58	24	2	16	22	31	8	28
23	41	39	25	3	17	23	12	9	28
23	45	19	26	4	18	23	53	9	29
23	49	0	27	5	19	24	32	10	♍
23	52	40	28	6	20	25	15	11	1
23	56	20	29	8	21	25	56	12	2
24	0	0	30	9	22	26	36	13	3

Syllabus of Lectures.

I.—The Zodiac—the nature of the twelve Signs—their influence on humanity—the "rising sign" and "ruling planet"—rulers of nations—the *kâma rûpa.* Illustrations.

II.—The Planets, their apparent influence upon nations and individuals—Mercury, Venus, Mars, Jupiter, Saturn—colours and the human aura—the growth of individuals—the "individual star"—Uranus and Neptune.

III.—The Sun and its rays—individual characteristics—the Moon as receiver and collector—personal characteristics—the Moon and Saturn—the Sun and Saturn—the polarities—character and destiny—Fate and Freewill.

IV.—The horoscope—the rationale of the twelve mansions—the three main influences—elements—Fire, Air, Earth, Water—how we make our future horoscope—how the wise man can rule his stars—summary and conclusion.

Appendix to ASTROLOGY FOR ALL.

ASTROLOGY:
Exoteric and Esoteric.

A SERIES OF FOUR LECTURES DELIVERED BEFORE THE THEOSOPHICAL SOCIETY, LONDON, IN MAY AND JUNE, 1900

BY

ALAN LEO.

REVISED AND CONSIDERABLY AMPLIFIED.

PUBLISHER'S NOTE.

It may perhaps be wondered why these Four Lectures should be published as an Appendix to this book rather than issued separately, in which form they have already passed through a First Edition. The reason is briefly as follows :

When first delivered these Lectures attracted a good deal of attention especially among members of the Theosophical Society, and a large issue, in paper covers, was immediately struck off from a shorthand reporter's unrevised notes to meet the immediate demand for propaganda purposes. When it was realised how imperfect in many respects this issue was, (as may readily be surmised when it is borne in mind that each lecture was delivered without notes and was rather of the nature of an informal talk than a set discourse), some regret was felt by the Author that it had ever been allowed to go forth at all, and it was decided not to republish it when the first issue was sold out. However, the little book proved to have so much life, and met with so favourable a reception on all hands, in spite of its shortcomings, that when M. Miéville, our French representative, suggested making a translation the question was reconsidered, and finally the translation was made from the present revised and amplified arrangement.

Meantime the " Astrology for All " Series had gradually grown into being, and when the original large stock of the " Four Lectures " was exhausted, and the advisability of reissue became once more a matter for consideration, it was found that although much they contained was not to be found elsewhere, yet a place for it could not be found either in the " Astrology for All " Series or in the series of Shilling Manuals ; it belonged to neither series exactly, but was " betwixt and between," as folks say. On the other hand it was hardly suited for separate issue to the general public, from the fact—inevitable under the circumstances of its production—that a certain amount of familiarity with elementary theosophical ideas was taken for granted throughout, and that technical theosophical terms were (naturally) freely used without explanation.

This being so, it is probable that in spite of the urging of many readers who spoke enthusiastically of the help they had gained from them, these Four Lectures would have gone " out of print " altogether, had not the happy expedient been hit upon of adding them as an Appendix to this book, thereby bringing its bulk into uniformity with the remaining books of the same Series as well as adding very considerably to its value as an introduction to the study of Modern Astrology.

No attempt has been made to alter the style from that of a lecture to that of a book, as that could have robbed it of much of its freshness if not of its simplicity. For the rest, the occasional restatement of what has by this time become all too familiar to the reader will, it is hoped, be excused.

ASTROLOGY—EXOTERIC AND ESOTERIC.

LECTURE I.

BEFORE commencing this series of lectures I should like to make one remark, by way of clearing the ground of a possible source of misconception. The idea seems to be prevalent that Astrology teaches *Fatalism*. Those, however, who have studied the subject from the deeper standpoint know that it does *not* teach (absolute) fatalism. We are not utterly bound : neither, on the other hand, are we entirely free. We are limited and restrained by——*ignorance*.

All our misfortunes are the result of imperfect knowledge : had we complete knowledge, " fate " would have no power over us. Had we but a little more knowledge even, there would be so much the less misfortune. Hence I contend that by a knowledge of Astrology—which is a Science of Life—we may avoid many of our troubles. It will be my object in the ensuing lectures to indicate how this may be done.

The word ASTRO-LOGY means " The Wisdom " or " the Message of the Stars." There are two aspects of this Science : the *exoteric* and the *esoteric*. That side of Astrology which we call exoteric may be styled fatalism, fortune-telling, charlatanry—what you will : but the esoteric Astrology is that which reveals the soul of the Science, its divine aspect ; and the whole of *that* can never be expressed in words. Those who attempt to explain its inner meaning in writing must ever fail ; but those whose minds are intuitive enough to catch the hidden significance of the esoteric side of Astrology know that it is part of THE MYSTERIES.

The subject of Astrology comprises many branches. Thus we have :

1. Natal Astrology, or Life and Character as revealed by the horoscope of birth.

2. Horary Astrology, the art of interpreting the influences operating at any given moment, and the final issue of those influences relative to any work that may have been then started, any struggle then impending, any question then sought to be answered, etc., etc.

3. Mundane Astrology, or the destiny of nations and the world at large, as revealed by the stars.

4. Atmospheric or Meteorological.

5. Medical. And lastly,
6. Esoteric or Metaphysical Astrology.

In these lectures I shall deal principally with Natal Astrology, following the course outlined in the syllabus.

The Zodiac is a belt of the heavens in the neighbourhood of the celestial equator and extending some 8 degrees on either side of the *Ecliptic*, which is the Sun's annual path through the heavens.*

Since the Earth revolves on its axis once in twenty-four hours, the twelve Signs may be considered as passing over any given spot on the earth in regular succession, each Sign occupying two hours in transit. The circle of the Zodiac is divided into 360 degrees, each Sign thus comprising 30 degrees. There are further and more subtle divisions, which, however, I shall not treat of in these lectures.

Each Sign, moreover, little as one might suppose it, is found to have an influence totally distinct from and entirely at variance with that of every other Sign. Each has *its own* purpose and influence; and when we can understand the significance of each Sign, we shall obtain a glimpse of the great mystery that is hidden in the Zodiac.

The subject may be considered in this way:—Each of us has a physical body, and a psychic atmosphere around it which we call the 'astral aura.' Certain subtle influences playing on humanity are deflected by the Zodiac, (being filtered, as it were, through these twelve Signs); *and these forces affect the psychic body.* So that it is important for us to understand the nature of these influences, and the particular quality which each Sign transmits to us.

It is therefore desirable that we should start with clear ideas, and that we should, in continuing our studies, group these ideas together with due regard to their relative importance in the scheme of things. The relation of the Zodiac and the Planets to mankind may be briefly expressed in this way:

I. Think of the Earth as representing the Physical Body:
II. The Twelve Signs as representing the desire-nature, or Astral Body (kama):
III. The Planets as governing the Mind: and

* Really the path of the Earth round the Sun: I shall, however, for the sake of clearness here deal with the Zodiac and Planets entirely from the *geocentric* standpoint. This matter has been already explained in the earlier part of this book but is gone into more fully in Chapter XVI. of *Astrology for All, Part II.*

IV. The Sun as symbolical of the Spiritual Part of man. These are the four grand divisions, corresponding to the Four Elements of the ancients and of the mediæval alchemists, EARTH, WATER, AIR, and FIRE.

The Zodiac will, all through life, influence *the desires.*

The *nature* of the desires will be in accordance with the Sign 'rising' at the moment of birth (*i.e.*, occupying the position which the Sun has at dawn).

This desire-nature is synonymous with what Western psychologists term "The Feelings": it is conditioned—inflamed or repressed—by these Twelve Signs; it is their influence that lies behind our sensations, and in accordance with their nature shall we experience sensation or 'feeling.' Those who are dominated entirely or chiefly by the Zodiacal influence are those in whom the Mind is not yet fully acting apart from the Senses and the lower Feelings, but who, like the animals, are almost wholly swayed by the latter.

To get a clear idea of the nature of these Signs of the Zodiac we must deal with each one separately, bearing in mind that the revolution of the Earth brings the whole twelve successively into influence each day we live. The Signs stand as follows:

Related to PRESENT	E.						
	Fire	Cardinal (or movable)	I.	ARIES	ruling the	Head	INTELLECTUAL TRINITY
	Earth	Fixed	II.	TAURUS	„	Neck and Throat	
	Air	Common	III.	GEMINI	„	Lungs, Shoulders, and Arms	
	N.						
	Water	Cardinal	IV.	CANCER	„	Breast and Stomach	MATERNAL TRINITY
Related to PAST	Fire	Fixed	V.	LEO	„	Heart and Back	
	Earth	Common	VI.	VIRGO	„	Solar Plexus	
	W.						
	Air	Cardinal	VII.	LIBRA	„	Loins	REPRODUCTIVE TRINITY
	Water	Fixed	VIII.	SCORPIO	„	Generative System	
Related to FUTURE	Fire	Common	IX.	SAGITTARIUS	„	Thighs	
	S.						
	Earth	Cardinal	X.	CAPRICORN	„	Knees	SERVING TRINITY
	Air	Fixed	XI.	AQUARIUS	„	Legs and Ankles	
	Water	Common	XII.	PISCES	„	Feet	

It is important to know just the part of the body these Signs govern, as all accidents that may occur to us injure the particular part of the body indicated by the sign whence the 'affliction' proceeds.

But the point that I wish especially to impress upon you is that the Zodiacal Signs control or influence certain vital centres in our bodies, both 'astral' and 'physical.' These centres of consciousness we are continually forming and strengthening through experience; and according to that Sign that we are working through, so shall we be making the corresponding centre stronger or weaker as the case may be.

The Moon may be considered as governing the Twelve Signs in the aggregate: it is, as it were, the synthetic expression of the total forces of the Zodiac. The mode of operation of the Moon's influence, as distinct from that of the rising sign, may be understood in this way:

Suppose a soul is born into manifested life to express itself through some one of these Signs, the Moon being at the same time posited in another: it would express as many of the attributes of the said Sign as it was able to, until the Moon began to have an influence over the life, whereupon the qualities of the Sign through which the Moon was functioning would begin to make themselves apparent: we should then say that Fate—or rather Destiny—was beginning to act.

Every one of the Signs of the Zodiac controls or influences the fate of each one of us. We are fated to go through that particular class of experiences represented by the several Zodiacal Signs: and the Moon is the representative of the complete Zodiac. While, however, the Signs of the Zodiac show the fate of the *past*, the destiny of the *future* is indicated by the Moon. This I shall treat of later.

When a child is born, some one of the Twelve Signs will be rising upon the Eastern Horizon: *this gives it a peculiar and distinctive prominence in the life.*

You will see later on that the functions of the Signs are further intensified, restrained, or modified, by the presence of Planets therein at the time of birth, or by the passage of planets through them during the life-time.

The influence of the Signs will be experienced by the native in accordance with their *mundane positions; i.e.*, their elevation or depression above or below the eastern and western horizon respectively: these relative angular positions denoting the twelve "Houses" of the horoscope, and having sympathy with the twelve Signs taken in the same order :—thus, the First House is in sympathy with the first Sign, Aries; the Second House with the Sign Taurus, and so on.

THE 'DHARMA' OF THE SIGNS

♈ ♉ ♊ *The Intellectual Trinity* ♈ ♉ ♊

Each Sign, has, however, its own special meaning, irrespective of its position in the nativity.

Thus, as I said, ARIES governs the Head—but it governs a great deal more than the mere bone-and-blood structure: you may regard it from the physical, mental, or spiritual standpoint:—Aries governs (1) *that part of the body called the head;* (2) the *directive energies* generally, and (3) the *beginnings* of all things, personal, national, or cosmic: it is the commencement of the circle.

In humanity, however, these Signs express themselves either in vices, or virtues. Those born under Aries, for instance, may express that Sign as deception, lying, and roguery; but its internal meaning is TRUTH: clear thinking, intuition,* pure reason, and so forth. Any person under the Aries influence who had not extracted the virtue of this Sign would display great impulse, and be very independent, always seeking freedom and liberty: so that this Sign produces pioneers and investigators, men desirous of taking the lead, and who are also capable of maintaining a prominent position; for they always refer everything to the intellect, working from *the head* first.

Before proceeding further I should say that the Signs, beginning with Aries, are successively *positive* and *negative* (male . . . female), thus showing a constant alternation of the two aspects of Life and Form: the forceful, imperious, life-giving energy flowing through the Positive Signs, while the Negative Signs receive, hold, and retain this energy.

Aries, then, will typically represent the *positive* force, while

TAURUS, on the other hand, is a *negative* Sign, possessing all the Aries qualities in latency, but tending always towards expression through the solid, practical, matter-of-fact side of life: thus, while Aries would be eager and energetic, quick and enterprising but incontinent and changeful; Taurus would be dubious and lethargic, slow and stolid, but patient and enduring: so entirely different, in fact, are the attributes of these two Signs that the contrast is startling. The virtue of Taurus is

* Intuition: enlightenment from within.

endurance, its vice obstinacy: the internal quality, however, or *dharma* of this Sign is OBEDIENCE.

Aries represents the Father, so to speak, while Taurus typifies the Mother. Their Offspring, then, is seen in

GEMINI, The Twins. All that is involved in Aries and Taurus finds expression in Gemini, a positive (hermaphrodite) Sign, typical of true genius. Whatever was latent or concealed in Aries and Taurus will be shown in Gemini; so that if you can conceive the attributes of the first two Signs, and can balance these together in your mind, you will see what Gemini really expresses. The Zodiac, indeed, is a kind of Alphabet, and these three Signs its ABC. If you can read these letters and can put them together, you will have the Key to this profound yet simple Language of the Cosmos.

Taurus represents those who are slow, plodding and methodical, rather executing than initiating, whereas Gemini, having the life and form together, will always have some motive-power behind its expression, and will manifest *intellect*. Aries represents the energising or thought side of life; Taurus the solid, practical, 'bread-and-butter' side of existence; and Gemini, the synthesiser, manifests the combination of the two—adaptability, and intellect. As you have ardent, impulsive, progressive souls in Aries; stubborn, dogmatic, conservative people in Taurus; so Gemini produces enthusiastic, impressionable, sympathetic, and versatile men and women.

In those who have not yet realised the meaning of this Sign, Gemini represents *diffusiveness;* but they are always fond of details, and love to go into minutiæ. The *dharma* of Gemini is MOTIVE.

♋ ♌ ♍ *The Maternal Trinity.* ♋ ♌ ♍

The next Sign, Cancer, is totally different to any of the first three, starting as it were a fresh round: the Maternal Trinity inaugurating an entirely new phase of experience.

Cancer is a Cardinal Sign, a leading Sign, a 'head' Sign, occupying a similar position to that of Aries: but you see another quality in course of evolution here; the crab-like faculty of *holding on* at all costs. Hence we find in this Sign, as its virtue, tenacity of purpose; as its vice, indolence and love of ease.

The weakness of Cancer is its extreme sensitiveness, and those who are born under its influence feel very keenly on the emotional side of life: they are, in fact, exceptionally sensitive. But they have the qualities of *attachment* and *perseverance* and, like the crab, who will rather lose a claw than forego his hold, so they will rather witness the destruction of their hopes than relinquish their purposes: they love position and influence, and will hold on quietly and steadily till they can gain their ends. The *dharma* of this Sign is POWER.

LEO. I trust you will constantly bear in mind the *alternating polarities* of the Signs: thus Cancer, just alluded to, is negative, and receptive —ruling the stomach; while the fifth Sign, LEO, is positive and energic —ruling the heart.

These two Signs are, from one standpoint, the most important in the Zodiac, being the chosen vehicles for the expression of The Luminaries: the Sun ☉ being lord of Leo, and the Moon ☽ lady of Cancer; corresponding to the Individuality and Personality respectively.* Here we note that Cancer is a movable, receptive, watery Sign, inconstant and changeable as the Moon herself, ever in quest of fresh sensation and experience; while the royal Leo, like the Sun, fixed, positive, and fiery, of inexhaustible energy, is yet life-giver, as it were, to the fickle Cancer, furnishing the very life-currents that maintain its mobility: even as it is from the Sun (primarily) that the sea derives its motion—or as the heart is the source of the digestive and assimilative power of the stomach (which nevertheless nourishes the heart). So is the deathless *Individuality* the informing and directing power of the ephemeral *Personality*; the experiences of the latter being, notwithstanding, of permanent value to the former.

It is in this sense that these two signs, Cancer and Leo, may be said to be the most important of the twelve.

Leo represents all that has to do with the heart, and the love nature: in its lowest expression we find passion and ferocity, but its final manifestation is Perfect Love. The *dharma* of this sign is HARMONY.

The next sign, VIRGO, is negative, representing as its vice great selfishness, as its virtue, knowledge and purity. Perhaps the most selfish of all people are born under the Virgo influence, and they are most exacting and critical. The reason of this is that the purpose of their evolution is to acquire the power of distinguishing between good and evil, and the natural attitude engendered at first is to see only the

* For the distinction between *individuality* and *personality* see any Theosophical text-book. There is also a special Essay on this subject in *Rays of Truth*, by B. Leo.

shortcomings of others. Nevertheless, the virtues of modesty, purity and industry are acquired through this sign, the *dharma* of which is DISCRIMINATION.

♎ ♏ ♐ *The Reproductive Trinity.* ♎ ♏ ♐

LIBRA, the sign of the balance, is opposite to Aries, and serves to evolve those qualities of justice and discernment that are needed to "balance" the impulse and energy of the first sign. The vice of this sign is separateness, a desire to isolate one's self from others, and to stand apart from the rest of one's fellows. Nevertheless, a balanced state will finally be reached, for the *dharma* of this sign is EQUILIBRIUM.

SCORPIO represents on the one hand the greatest ignorance, and on the other, the greatest wisdom; for in this sign we have the widest extremes possible, and much time should be given to its study if we would understand it properly. It gives us many vices—pride, jealousy, maliciousness, envy; and yet under this same sign are born the very strongest characters also, those who have the power of regeneration, those who have wonderful power in the world and who do great things. Transmutation is said to be its special quality, or in other words "the sting has to be extracted from the scorpion" in this sign, which is supposed to represent death, but which really means in its highest phase the passing from this physical plane into another world. The *dharma* of this sign is REGENERATION.

SAGITTARIUS has two qualities, the vice of rebellion, and the virtue of law and order. Religious people come under this sign. There are few persons who live up to all the qualities that can be manifested in Sagittarius. Thought transference, prophecy and clear vision manifest through the qualities conferred by this sign. The *dharma* of this sign is LAW.

We have now completed the third trinity of the zodiacal signs, the Reproductive Trinity as it is called, consisting of Libra, Scorpio, and Sagittarius. These reproduce that which is expressed in the intellectual and maternal trinities.

♑ ♒ ♓ *The Serving Trinity.* ♑ ♒ ♓

CAPRICORN is the most wonderful sign of the twelve, indicating the quality of climbing, climbing to the highest point we can reach. Service is the virtue, and slavery, submission and servility the vices. The virtues of this sign are what are called the self-perfecting qualities. The moral virtues come through it. The *dharma* of this sign is PERFECTION.

AQUARIUS, the eleventh sign, represents the man, the perfected thinker, possessing the power of judgment *par excellence*. It seems as though when all the experience of the other signs has been gathered, souls are born under the sign Aquarius, and exhibit all the qualities of the perfected man. The *dharma* of this sign is UNIVERSAL SERVICE. Finally we have:

PISCES, through which descend those who are about to commence the cycle once more. It is impossible to convey an adequate idea of this sign, the true meaning of which is far beyond us at present. But its *dharma* may be said to be UNIVERSAL LOVE.

What I wish most particularly to impress upon you is that you can look on these twelve signs as governing the physical body; and the object of evolution seems to be to make certain vital centres of consciousness of feeling.

If you study it from that standpoint you will be astounded at the wonderful centres that may be formed. Persons born under Cancer, for instance, with that quality which renders them very sensitive to everything affecting them from without, may, by turning that sensitiveness inwards, awaken the occult centre at the breast and so become sensitive to psychic impressions. They would then sense the conditions of rooms, or of those around them, and in general have a peculiar "feeling" of surrounding conditions. In Virgo, again, you have the psychic quality of intuitively 'sensing' mental conditions; while if you concentrated your thought on the *throat* (Taurus) you would awaken that particular centre, and so on with each of the signs.

The next point with regard to the signs is their influence on humanity. From the very lowest feelings and sensations, up to the highest we can think of as intellect working through the brain, these signs have their influence on humanity, and affect them in accordance with the nature of the sign. But before proceeding further I think I must give you another idea.

The signs are divided into what we call triplicities, of which there are *four*, named after the four "elements," and known as the Fiery, Watery, Airy and Earthy triplicities. If the twelve Signs are arranged in a circle, the cardinal signs ♈ (fire) ♋ (water) ♎ (air) ♑ (earth) marking the East, North, West and South points, each will then be the apex of a triangle, or triplicity. The diagram on p. 48 will make this clear.

These triplicities form distinct classes; for instance, Aries is a *Fiery* sign, and everything to do with Aries is of a fiery nature, the fiery Will expressing itself throngh this sign. We get intellect and everything representing the fiery will working through Aries; in the next fiery sign, Leo, the heart and emotions are active; while in the last fiery sign, Sagittarius, we have the combination of Aries and Leo. Thus in Sagittarius you would have all the qualities necessary for science, philosophy and religion, wrought out of the other two fiery signs. But whereas the Fiery signs represent everything connected with the ideal world—all that we think of as spiritual, or idealistic—the Earthy signs, which are Taurus, Virgo and Capricorn, represent everything solid and objective, everything on the level as it were, not idealistic in any way, but thorough and practical. Through Taurus you get the expression of slow, patient working, a steady, plodding patience; in Virgo the formation of ideas and feelings; and the final expression in Capricorn, the Man who has climbed to the summit (as far as the physical world is concerned). The *Airy* signs, Gemini, Libra and Aquarius, represent all that has to do with the mind proper, the mental conditions; so that refinement of mind will be acquired through the Airy signs. Cancer, Scorpio and Pisces, the *Watery* signs, represent the passional nature, the animal soul, everything connected with the feelings and passions. These divisions give us a clear idea as to how the signs will work out in life; for many planets in Earthy signs indicate a practical, sober, but perhaps somewhat sensual nature, while in Airy signs, the life will be chiefly mental; and so on.

There is a further division of the signs into *three* groups of four signs each, known as the Qualities; *Cardinal*, *Fixed* and *Mutable*; Aries, Taurus and Gemini are typical of these respectively. I shall have more to say regarding this division later on, but for the present this must suffice.

Now with regard to the "rising sign" or *Ascendant*. At birth, one of the signs will be rising. Broadly speaking, you may take the sign the Sun is in as the rising sign till about two hours after dawn; then, the next sign; two hours later, the next—and so on. (This, however, is only a very rough approximation.)

The Rising Sign is a most important part of Astrology, because its influence stamps itself on the life. When a child is born, the magnetic currents set in motion by the particular sign rising stamp themselves on the child, and throughout the whole life the qualities of that sign will be seeking expression. You will find people look out of that particular window, as it were; thus, an Aries person will look on the world from the standpoint of alertness and will always want to be leading and active whereas the Taurus person will be slow, reserved and steady. In fact, so important is the rising sign that in many cases it takes a lifetime before one can entirely work through the influence thus prominently indicated at the time of birth.

So you will now see how important it is to know the nature of the signs. You must study the whole of the twelve signs, working up from the physical base into the mental, until you can get some idea as to how the person born under any sign looks out on the world. Suppose Gemini were rising, for instance, the Airy triplicity would be evident, and the person born under that sign would be very intellectual. Cancer rising, we should find one who is very receptive and tenacious; all the feelings would be at work, the person would be attached to home and family, desiring to feel through them satisfaction; never without sensation of some sort, but could give sympathy too, and be very affectionate. In one born under Leo there would be seen all the qualities that have to do with the heart, the nature never being satisfied unless the affections were engaged, always seeking harmony, peace and love: but, in the unregenerate, much passion would be working. In Virgo people you would find much selfishness and criticism, or else much discrimination; they are persons who are very clever and wide awake, the combination of Cancer and Leo working through this sign. Libra persons would be harmonious, very kind and sympathetic, but very approbative and fond of praise. I shall explain these different signs when dealing with the planets, because each planet has a sign as its house. Scorpio persons manifest much jealousy and personal pride, until they get to the higher side of this sign, when they study all occult matters. Sagittarius persons, while working on purely physical lines, would be fond of sport, but as they rose to the highest point they would become philosophical, scientific or religious, because philosophy and religion would be evolved. Capricorn persons would be inclined towards politics, seeking to be practical and looking at the world from a very acute standpoint; all the practical virtues would be worked out there. Very few people express the last two signs, Aquarius and Pisces, which might almost be termed super-human signs. People born under Aquarius, however, are original and versatile, and somewhat inclined to Socialism. Pisces persons are marked by extreme sympathy and impressionability.

Thus persons born under any particular sign look at the world from that particular standpoint. It is their way of looking at things; if could understand the nature of the sign someone else was born under, they would see things as he saw them, and not be so bound down to their own particular view. We find many people who may be said to cling to their particular rising sign, feeling that it is the only way of looking on life. These are people who are practically under the dominion of fate, under the thraldom of the particular sign rising at birth.

I will add that not only will you find the whole description of the person indicated by the rising sign, but also the health and disposition. In a general way you can read the whole character and life, and even the events that will happen, from the rising sign,* because that particular influence is prominent, and until the person has worked his way through it, he will be continually under its power. For instance, Aries persons would be under the Aries influence; their health would be affected through the head, and they would always be independent and impulsive, and desirous of being at the head of things.

When we come to the Ruling Planet, however, we have something totally different. Nearly everyone who is progressing in any way passes as it were through the rising sign to the ruling planet. Suppose some one took up the study of Astrology with the idea of developing himself, and thought that there were higher goals to be attained than that for which he had been striving. His first business would be to find out his Ruling Planet. (I may say that the ruling planet is the lord of the sign rising, as a rule, but sometimes the planet in the ascendant, if there is one; thus we find cases of persons who have worked through the planet ruling the sign ascending and taken up the planet rising.) Each of the twelve signs has a planet as its ruler: Mars governs Aries; Venus, Taurus; Mercury, Gemini; the Moon, Cancer; the Sun, Leo; and so on. This is shown in the accompanying table.

* *See* pp. 164 to 184.

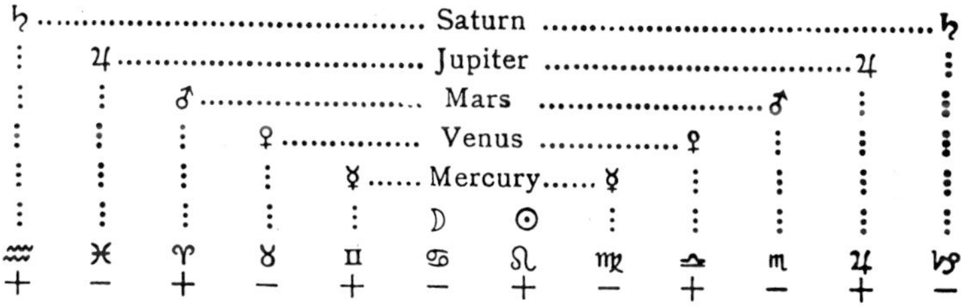

(*Aquarius is the positive and Capricorn the negative 'house' or sign of Saturn Pisces the negative house of Jupiter, and so on.*)

By 'ruling planet' is meant that these particular planets find their best expression through these particular signs. Thus, the influence of Mars can express itself best through Aries and Scorpio, positively or negatively as the case may be. This is a very important point. The planets have each a positive and negative sign, and you get the real quality of the two houses expressed in the one planet; *i.e.*, the planet itself has the internal quality. And that seems to be the quality we are to evolve, because we are to progress, first out of the signs of the Zodiac, then beyond the ruling planets, and finally into the particular planet governing the whole world for the time. Thus we see how important it is to know what one's ruling planet is; for when one has worked through the rising sign, overcoming its different vices and tendencies, the ruling planet's influence must be taken up, and that affects the life. It is as though one rises from the purely psychic into the higher intellectual conditions; as though one rises to the point where he can see more clearly and is less biased by the sign the planet has previously worked through. It is as though he has extracted the whole of the virtue of the sign and found its completer expression in the planet.

With regard to the next point, the rulers of nations, we have some very interesting points for consideration. There are certain signs that rise more rapidly in some countries than in others. Each sign governs a race or nation. The history of the whole world is contained in these twelve signs, but we are now looking at it merely from the national standpoint. Aries governs England, and Mars is the ruler. You will find if you study the nature of Aries that the Britons are rather impulsive people, always independent and free; their ruling planet being Mars, it is the warlike qualities which are to the fore. Those born under Aries are particularly courageous persons, evolving strength. It is very strange that the three signs following Aries govern the other three countries of the United Kingdom, Ireland, Wales and Scotland, and we find the racial tendencies of these signs in those born in these countries. Thus we find all the beauty of Taurus in the women of Ireland, while its power of stubborn resistance is well shown in the Irish peasantry. We have the qualities of Gemini coming out in the Welsh people, and the tenacious, clannish qualities of Cancer manifesting in the Scotch. The generosity and freedom of Aries is seen in the English people.

The United States also is governed by Gemini; and Africa by Cancer. There is a strange thing to be noted in connection with the late Transvaal War. I mentioned that Mars rules England. Every planet has its 'exaltation' and 'fall' in some appropriate sign. Now Mars has its 'fall' in Cancer, and you see what trouble Britain has had in Africa, whose ruling sign is Cancer, our then enemies showing just those tenacious characteristics typical of the sign; and all the trouble and difficulty arose from no other reason than that Mars has no dignity in Cancer. On the other hand in India England holds sway because Mars is 'exalted' in Capricorn (the sign ruling India). The whole history of the nations is shown by their ruling planets and signs. France is governed by Leo, and the French are very emotional and easily affected through their feelings; Virgo governs Turkey, and Libra China and Japan. Scorpio governs Barbary; Sagittarius, Spain; Capricorn, India; Aquarius, Russia; and Pisces, Portugal. So that by watching the different planets governing these signs, you may predict just how a given nation will act. When what are called the malefic planets pass through the signs governing these nations, they "stir them up." Mars passing through Leo always stirs up the French, for instance, and similarly planets passing through Aries affect the British. In 1916 and 1917, Jupiter will pass through Aries and England will be benefited. Each nation gains by the benefic planets, as they are called, passing through the sign that governs it, while when the malefic planets pass through they are afflicted.

I wish now to say a few words about the twelve signs and the animals they are supposed to represent, what may be termed the *Kâma rûpa*.

Aries, the Ram, governs all Aries people. If you study the different zodiacal types, you will find a marked Ram feature in the Aries people. This resemblance is most marked in races that are comparatively pure, where there is no mixture of blood like we have in Great Britain and America. Yet, even amongst us, if you find a person born under Aries with no planets rising, purely under the sign, he will have the Ram features. In the same way persons purely under Taurus have a distinct bull-like tendency which comes out in the face, and in many cases is very striking.

But we must know just what these signs mean, apart from the animals they correspond to; because there are special characteristics belonging to each sign. For instance, Gemini the twins. It is difficult to trace an animal resemblance in this case, because it is what is called a refined, human sign. But the Gemini people who are undeveloped will show all the cunning and even some of the facial peculiarities of the monkey, which is the animal type of the sign.

Cancer persons are characterised by the short nose and crab face, telling of their tenacity; but there are some natives of Cancer who resemble the cat. Then Leo, the lion, gives a very leonine face, fierce and aggressive. Virgo gives a foxy tendency; but I must remind you that in all these cases they are *undeveloped* persons, because as soon as they get the humane attributes they break away from the animal tendencies.

I have not been able to get a pure representative of Libra; but as a rule the Librans are very human, rarely having any marked animal tendency. Scorpio, the scorpion, and the eagle, are two distinct symbols, and in the natives of Scorpio we find resemblances to both scorpions and eagles. The likeness to the eagle can be readily traced in the evenly developed Scorpio person. Many of you may have seen persons like the horse, Sagittarius; or like the goat, Capricorn. Aquarius is another "human sign," and there appear to be very few who at all express the sign Aquarius. We cannot easily represent the Pisces people, but I find such people very much like the parrot, chatterboxes; in some cases there is in the face a distinct fish-like, or more rarely a seal-like, look.

The reason I have introduced this part of the subject is, that we are all more or less influenced by the animal part of the sign we are born under; but those born under the "human" signs (♊ ♎ ♒) have most nearly exterminated the animal nature.

I must now conclude this first lecture, which is intended as a kind of introduction to the deeper part that will follow. The Signs of the Zodiac affect us all; there is *no one* who has entirely broken away from their influence. When I come to deal with The Moon you will see how we make our fate, and how we can dominate it: but no one I know living to-day has completely broken away from the signs and lives entirely in the planetary conditions; for that would mean he had dominated his stars to such an extent that he had perfect control over the *mind*. To get rid of the influence of the Signs of the Zodiac would mean controlled *feelings and emotions*.

When we come to study the planets, which are the correlatives of the forces of the mind, we shall recognise the necessity for extracting from them their essence, which, translated into ordinary terms of consciousness, means the obtaining of perfect mental control. And as, beyond this, subduing even the planets to its mighty will, is the radiant orb of the Sun, so must man learn to rise till, having conquered passion, and having subdued the mind, he comes forth free and untrammelled, in purity perfect, in wisdom radiant, and in love supreme.

LECTURE II.

To-night I shall deal with the planets and their influence. The Zodiac will represent to us the sounding board of a vast musical instrument, of which the Planets are the strings. If you think of that you will be able to understand what part the planets play in their relation to the Zodiac. You will understand, of course, that each string is tight or loose in accordance with our particular constitution. Nevertheless quite apart from the signs of the zodiac, the planets also have a special influence over us, and this is not theory only, for we have after very long practice and study found that there are distinctive types of persons who manifest the characteristic qualities ascribed to the planets. You are all familiar with the "Martial," "Saturnine," "Jovial," and "Mercurial" types of persons, and know their distinctive features. If you understood the influence which each planet exerts on those born under its particular dominion, you would quickly recognise the unconscious response of the majority of people to the planetary influences.

I mentioned last week that each sign has a lord or ruler, and also that there were positive and negative signs, the planets standing between and behind each pair as the neutral point on which both positive and negative attributes are founded. I said that Aries ruled England: therefore Mars is the ruling planet, the English people being a martial race. Saturn governs India (Capricorn being its rising sign), and the Indians are totally different to the British: cold, thoughtful, meditative, slow, and in a way lethargic; while the Britisher is active and energetic, with the martial influence manifesting. There are four distinct nations, under four of the principal planets: *Great Britain* under Mars (♂); *India* under Saturn (♄); *China and Japan* under Venus (♀); and *Africa* under the Moon (☽). You will remember I mentioned that England was bound to suffer, while fighting in South Africa, owing to her ruling planet having its fall in Cancer.

With regard to individuals, when they have worked through the rising sign, then the planetary ruler has its greatest influence over the native. It is as though they had risen above the form and taken more of the life;

as though they had broken away from the crystallised conditions of the sign on the ascendant, so that the ruling planet was beginning to energise through them. Although there are 360 totally distinct varieties of persons born each day, you have only seven great types coming under the planets.

Before saying exactly what the influence of each planet is on the native, I had better mention just how the nature of the planets may be understood; because all we know about these planets has been handed down to us *through their symbols.* In looking at the symbol we know exactly what the planet means; and if you carefully watch how the symbols are made up, you will grasp something of a beautiful principle.

The *circle* has always stood as the symbol for Spirit or Life; without beginning and without end, containing the whole. It represents the Sun. The *half circle* represents the soul or mind, and is the symbol of the Moon; while the *cross* is the symbol of the body, earth, matter. These three together make up Mercury; and from these three symbols, representing body, soul, and spirit, or Sun, Moon, and Earth, you have the whole basis of astrological symbology, so far as the planets are concerned.

This is an easy way to remember the symbols. For when you see the circle in the signature of a planet you know that life or spirit operates largely throughout that planet; and when you see the crescent or half circle, you know that the soul or mind is more prominent than the spirit or life; and in accordance with the position of the cross you will know the nature of the planet, whether tending chiefly towards matter or spirit. Now Mercury (☿) adapts itself to whatever planet it is in aspect with, so that it acts as a temporary channel, so to speak, for the planet which it aspects.

To enable you to understand this, I must touch upon another side of astrological symbology. In the old books gold always stands as a symbol for the Sun; silver for the Moon; copper, Venus; iron, Mars; lead, Saturn; tin, Jupiter; quicksilver, Mercury. Thus you have seven primary metals:

Gold	☉	Sun	Copper	♀	Venus	Lead	♄	Saturn
Silver	☽	Moon	Iron	♂	Mars	Tin	♃	Jupiter
			Quicksilver	☿	Mercury			

The signature of *Mars* is made up of the circle and the cross, the circle beneath the cross representing life or spirit dominated by material desires; and so you see a constant stream of energy passing through this circle into the cross, a constant welling up of force, showing the energetic nature of Mars. Quite the reverse is the case with *Venus*, the circle being over the cross; and here life or spirit is above matter. The truths here conveyed are borne out by study. Any person having Mars prominently situated in his horoscope will be determined, energetic and fiery; whereas Venus people are totally different, being gentle, soft, loving and sympathetic, almost complete opposites. The circle and cross are complements, as it were, one to the other. Nevertheless—and this is *a most important point*—the influence of the planets Mars and Venus is identically the same in essence, though the Mars influence shows itself as force, and the Venus influence simply as love.

Now we come to *Saturn* and *Jupiter*. In Saturn, the crescent (half-circle) or soul is beneath the cross or body; and you find it gives a cold, earthy nature, because the soul or mind is fastened by the weight of the earthy nature. In Jupiter we find just the reverse, the half-circle or soul over the cross or body. As in the case of Mars and Venus, these two planets are positive and negative to each other, Jupiter being positive and Saturn negative. This is very simple and beautiful, looked at from the standpoint of astrological symbology.

Mercury on the other hand represents, as I have said, body, soul and spirit in one, or father, mother, child; the paternal positive influence, the maternal negative influence, and the child born of the two. When judging any one's life astrologically, the Sun will represent the individual character, while the mental qualifications will be represented by Mercury. Now the planets Mars and Venus and Saturn and Jupiter, affect Mercury; and the Sun and Moon have also an influence over this planet. Upon an understanding of this symbology, a correct view of the whole science of Astrology depends.

Now, in the physical world, Mars represents *heat*. If you have Mars in aspect with Jupiter on any day, you will notice that there will be thunder, if it be summer. (You can easily verify this by looking at an Ephemeris.) Saturn, the reverse of Mars, is a cold planet, and whenever Mercury or the Sun come to an aspect with Saturn, or when Mercury comes to the conjunction, it is always very cold for the time of the year.

Mars and Saturn are called the great malefics—Mars 'the devil'; Saturn, 'Satan.' They are really extremes of heat and extremes of cold; or, translated into terms of the emotions, impulse and selfishness.

As a matter of fact, these two planets are *not* evil; they are, rightly understood, two of the very best planets you can be born under. Many people think that if born under Mars they must be very bad characters (or rather, they generally think this with regard to other people). Not at all: without Mars there would be no courage, strength or endurance. We need the martial influence to give us energy, push and go; and therefore the martial person may be a very excellent person, if he but "rule his stars." Saturn appears just as evil, in a way, as Mars, in that it seems to constrict the character, making one reserved, self-centred and selfish. But however that may be, once that extreme selfishness is overcome, the Saturnians are among the finest people in the world; they are thoughtful, meditative, contemplative and reflective, steady, economical and cautious; and just as the good influence of Mars gives courage, strength and energy, so Saturn gives that calmness, thoughtfulness and steadiness which makes the character reliable. Therefore, if Mercury is in aspect with Mars in a horoscope, it will tend to make the mind impulsive, full, buoyant and expansive; but if in aspect with Saturn, it will be thoughtful, contemplative and restricted. But just as you would expect to find, this influence can act either for good or evil. You may find someone under the influence of an aspect of Mercury to Mars, who is considered untruthful simply because he exaggerates, or over-estimates, —seeing things bigger than they really are. In the same way you may have Mercury in aspect with Saturn, which would make persons thoughtful and scheming, perhaps covetous even, and thievish; and so on. So that these influences will make for evil only in those persons who cannot extract the bad and get to the good; nevertheless, both Mars and Saturn are, in themselves, two very good and necessary influences.

Under another symbology, but conveying identical truths, the mediæval alchemists referred to the transmutation of these astral influences. The transmutation of iron and lead into gold, and so on, meant simply the converting of force from a gross to a finer influence. Let us see how that would act astrologically. Mars, as I said, is the positive side of Venus; the force from these two planets being one, but acting in different ways, showing the same kind of influence in different forms. Now, all that the martial person has to do is to transmute Force into Love; that is to say, instead of constantly scattering his forces and wasting his energy, he should try to soften his nature and let this force work inwardly instead of outwardly, so that it ultimately comes forth as sympathy and love. In that way he would come under the Venus influence; the same applies to the influence of Saturn. The Saturnian person should transmute his tendencies to suspicion, repining and sloth, into thoughtfulness, carefulness and steadiness.

Most people we see to-day are under the martial influence; English people in particular, for they have Mars as their ruler. The particular planet one is born under will, of course, most strongly influence the life; but, as individuals composing the English nation, we are all more or less tinctured with the influence of Mars, since we must all partake in a measure of the dominant characteristics of the national soul.

Now we find also that the planets have an influence on the physical plane as well as on the mental and emotional planes. Thus Saturn governs minerals and crystals; it represents the crystallising principle in the physical world. Mars is an expanding, out-rushing force, and controls the animal kingdom in general. Jupiter governs the whole of the vegetable kingdom. And thus we can see how those born under Saturn are cold, heavy, and slow, whereas Martial people are energetic and combative, possessing much vital force; for you will observe that in the symbol of Saturn there is only the half-circle, whereas the whole circle appears in that of Mars, and the circle represents "spirit" and "life." The Jupiterians are orthodox religionists, with a tendency to pride and arrogance, while Venus people are very fond of pleasure and love the sensuous delights of the physical plane. Mercurial people are fond of light literature, are very talkative and so on. But we are not interested so much in the lower tendencies of the planets, for we are coming more and more under their mental influence.

Mentally these planets act in quite a different way, although you can trace the gradual growth of the influence from the physical to the mental condition. Mentally, then, the Martial man has much quickness, alertness and shrewdness, is always ready to perceive things—he is wide-awake; while Venus people are fond of music, the arts, and everything beautiful and lovely, and have a very quick appreciation of all that is refined and beautiful, for Venus makes the mind appreciate beauty. The Saturnine person differs totally from either of these, and I will take up Saturn particularly, Saturn being the planet we are all of us looking to, as students of the profound and occult.

We are all more or less coming into touch with the Saturnine influence; *i.e.*, becoming more thoughtful, meditative, steady, and contemplative. Saturn, acting in the mental world, stimulates thought. So you see this is the next higher stage for us, because instead of perceiving merely, we are to reflect, instead of perceiving only, to meditate on what we have perceived; and this is the Saturnine stage of growth.

Finally, it will lead us to the Jupiterian stage. When the mind is steady, and we begin to grow more thoughtful, more serious, we shall have this upturning of the half-circle—the soul rising over matter. Thus we have the half-circle above the cross in the symbol of Jupiter, whose influence is to draw out the religious tendencies and widen the sympathies. In the mental sphere, this Jupiterian influence, acting on the mind, makes it more religious and philosophical, expanding into a glad and full activity all the virtues that we have found in Saturn. Under Mars we have the senses always very active (persons under Mars and Venus always lean more towards the senses than the mind), but as the Saturnine influence gains the ascendancy, we have economy, frugality, and chastity developed. So that between the extremes of Mars and Saturn we have these two moderating influences, Venus and Jupiter, Venus softening and Jupiter making things temperate.

It will be observed, consequently, that Mars and Saturn are not malefics, and we should always recollect that *any* planetary influence is only 'evil' in the sense that while it dominates us we are to some extent subject to its passional or lower influence; for as soon as we realise that these planets have their own special virtue, and that we have a part of this influence working through us, we shall endeavour to live in that influence, and thus we shall in time be able to "rule our stars."

Now with regard to colours. In the human aura there are certain colours vibrating, and these colours will be dominant or otherwise according to the strength in the nativity of the planets that they represent. This has been tested. Those who are clairvoyant have told us of certain colours seen in the aura of certain persons, and we have found that the planets represented by these colours are strongly posited. Some very remarkable cases of this kind have come under our notice. Now do not for a moment think that the planets *are* the colours that I am now going to mention—they are not; but the vibration set up by them in the astral 'elemental essence' (some of which enters into the human astral body) is, we are taught, the primary cause of these colours. No one could very well say that Saturn was green or Mars red, but they are without doubt represented by these colours. Those who come under the influence of Mars have a decidedly red aura, for instance, and those under Saturn green. The whole of the colours are represented in the Sun and split up through these different planets. Some very strange predictions are sometimes made by astrologers who study this subject minutely in its relation to the physical plane, that is to say, the influence of colour in ordinary everyday affairs. This is a branch of what is called "horary astrology." Thus, if Mercury were rising at the time a question was asked, it would indicate the colour of any particular article; if, for instance, a horse were stolen it would show the colour of the animal; and so on. Without doubt this can be done, though it is bringing the science down to the lowest physical standpoint. Even in connection with the physical body these colours possess some influence, for persons born under Mars have a red complexion; persons under Saturn have a greenish-yellow appearance, and so on. This is the complete list:

		☿	Yellow		
♄	Green	♀	Blue	☽	(White)
♃	Indigo	♂	Red	☉	(Orange)

With regard to the Moon, she is practically colourless, while the Sun, considered separately, is said to be orange. But these are not so important to us in this connection as are the other planets. It will now be easily understood why we speak of Mars as representing heat, and Saturn cold.

There are many points in connection with this that you can work out for yourselves. Anyone born with Mercury rising, for example, would have much yellow in his aura, because the mind would be active. Now the sub-shade, as it were, of that yellow, would be in accordance with the planet aspecting Mercury; greenish-yellow would show Saturn to be operating, and so on. Those who study Music would be especially interested in these different vibrations, because we have different notes in the scale allotted to each of these planets. Moreover you find that people under Mercury have shrill voices, as a rule, at least when excited, while Mars gives a strong but sharp voice, Saturn a weak and unmusical one; Jupiter on the other hand gives a round full tone rather deep, and Venus a voice of a soft, rich quality. Indeed, devotees of this particular muse might, with a little attention, learn their planetary ruler from the conversational pitch of the voice.

Now I wish to say something about the "exaltation" and "trans mutation" of these planets. The planets have certain signs of the zodiac in which they are exalted, showing that they progress to a certain situation in which their whole nature is transmuted; for instance, a person born under Mars, with that planet in Cancer or Libra, would have that planet in its 'fall' or 'detriment,' as it is called—he would not be so strongly imbued with the martial influence; but if Mars were in a fiery sign, all the fiery characteristics would be strengthened. For instance, Mars in Aries, Sagittarius, or Leo, would be a good influence, because the nature of Mars would manifest in its true light; but Mars in Cancer, the sign of its fall, would be bad.

When Mars has risen to its highest point—Capricorn—it is said to be exalted, and it should be noted that the highest point Mars can reach is a calm, cool, contemplative spirit. Not that its fire and energy is *lost*, but the whole of the martial tendency is elevated by this position, and made more temperate, cooler, and able to act quite dispassionately; so that people with Mars in Capricorn have much influence, because their force and strength will be used tactfully and diplomatically. Mars exalted in Capricorn then, may be metaphorically said to have the gross iron of its nature transmuted into steel. The martial influence in Capricorn is as fine steel compared with the raw iron; all the rough and gross particles of the iron are changed into the fine grain of the steel.

Saturn is exalted in Libra, the house of Venus. Now it is said that those born under Saturn cannot love. Saturnine people are certainly undemonstrative, are very thoughtful and have not much feeling or expansiveness; but when Saturn occupies Libra it takes on the Venus quality and with it the expansive nature, so that in the glyph you have, as it were, the half-circle extended into the circle. Thus it is said, and with truth, that these two planets are enemies when working separately, but when their influences blend the better qualities of each seek expression. Saturn in Libra is balanced, so to speak, and you have all its cold and hardening influence softened down.

The other exaltations are also very remarkable, but the only one I shall deal with now is that of the Sun. The Sun is exalted in Aries, and the whole of the iron typifying Aries in the mineral world is thus said to be transmuted into gold. When the Sun is in Aries we have the highest vibration it is possible to have, because the heart influence has been taken into the head. The Sun governs Leo, the heart, and when one has the Sun in Aries at birth the whole of the thought is illuminated by love, and the nature is extremely idealistic, ardent, yet sympathetic and thoughtful. People with the Sun in Aries have splendid natures.

The next point on the syllabus is the "growth of individuals." In regard to this you must not think that when people are born under a particular planet, evil or otherwise, it is inevitably their dominant influence. It is only so for this particular life. Moreover, as I mentioned just now, the planet itself is not evil, nor its influence evil *per se*; for one person born under Mercury may have the brilliant mind of a great thinker, and you may also find a thievish and degraded person, so petty that nothing is too small or mean for him, also under the Mercurial influence. And a further point to be remembered is, that it is not only the ruling planet which has to be considered, but also its aspects; for as Mercury may in one case represent a magnificent person, a splendid individual, and in another case represent a very low type of person indeed, the question of the aspects received by the ruling planet assumes considerable importance.

I will mention a few of these aspects, so that you can understand what they mean. MERCURY in conjunction or good aspect with *Venus* assists the mind and makes the person love knowledge, because Venus is the planet of love and Mercury the planet of knowledge; so the inclinations of that person would be in the direction of gaining knowledge. In aspect with *Mars*, Mercury will expand the whole mind, and if the aspect is good, we shall find courage and strength of character, the mental outlook being clear and decisive, and the perceptions ready and keen. Mercury in aspect with *Saturn* will cool and tone down the Mercurial influence, giving in an undeveloped person a very sordid intellect; but when the higher Saturnine virtues are reached we have a calm, contemplative, thoughtful mind. When in aspect with *Jupiter* we have knowledge turned into wisdom; we have here the finest intuition, reflection, and reason, the best mental influence we can possibly get, for the Jupiterian influence always acts on Mercury in the very highest manner.

So you can quite see how one might grow by absorbing the nature of the planet with which Mercury was in aspect and also by absorbing the influence of the sign Mercury was in. Again, a person born under Mars would have the martial influence liberated in his nature according to the sign, house and aspect the planet was in, and he would rise above the lower side of Mars by stimulating his courage, endurance and energy; while as he worked out the lower side of Mars, its impulse, rashness, and recklessness, he would begin to acquire the martial virtues, and would grow to a high point. The Venus persons, by seeing that all they loved was only of the purest and most beautiful, would refine their natures, so that they would become true sons and daughters of Venus, possessing an admiration for beauty, art and poetry. Similarly, Saturnian people may rise to the highest meditation or contemplation, growing by study, thoughtfulness, and so forth, or, on the other hand, they may fall back and look at the world from a hopeless, gloomy standpoint; their individual *status* and growth being shown in the horoscope by the aspects of that planet. The Jupiterian persons on the other hand grow by becoming more religious and more devout, Jupiter being the planet of devotion.

With regard to the "individual star," we have learnt that individuals grow by getting to the virtuous side of the planet, if I may be allowed the phrase. When we think that the whole of humanity to-day is gradually passing out of the martial into the saturnine influence, into a more thoughtful state generally, you can see how Saturn and Jupiter would be the Individual Star for the whole of humanity; not Saturn alone, not Jupiter alone, but the two blended. For we cannot possibly get to the wisdom of Jupiter at once; we must come through the emotions and feelings into this thoughtful steadiness, and then, getting first of all our meditation, contemplation and reflection from Saturn, expand that into the loftier and more beneficent Jupiter, sinking the positive material side and always leaning to the spiritual and receptive side. Just as once we were always leaning to the positive side of Mars, now we are trying to expand into the positive side of Jupiter. Practically, Saturn may be said to be the individual star for each one of us. It is the star operating on all of us to-day who are thinking at all, particularly those who are studying metaphysical or occult subjects. Esoterically it is the most mystical of all the planets, the planet that makes one turn towards the occult and deeper side of life, and try to understand that which is operating upon us. So that as we raise the consciousness, bringing it to a steady concentrated condition where the mind is brought, one-pointed, to a focus, we shall find that from this condition (which means for it expansion) spring joy and a true appreciation of the religious aspect of life.

There are just one or two things I wish to touch upon before closing this lecture, namely the planets Uranus and Neptune. Without going fully into the subject I may say they are, as it were, the higher octaves of Saturn and Jupiter.

Uranus is operating on but few to-day; yet it is said that those who take up a study of occultism, in any form, are coming under this planet's influence. Having come through the best Saturnine influences, the Jupiterian are flowing through them, and later on they will come under the Uranian. The evil side of Uranus is extreme Bohemianism and recklessness. The colours of Uranus are curious, such as all striped colours and tartans.

Neptune is esoterically said to represent those who are endeavouring to realise what is called the Platonic life. In the world to-day, strangely enough, its evil side shows in frauds, cheats, charlatanry, illusions and deceptions gigantic swindles come under Neptune.

Nevertheless, a study of Planetary Influence helps us to realise that out of *all* evil good is eventually to follow.

LECTURE III.

In our last two lectures we separately dealt with the Signs of the Zodiac, and the Planets and their influence upon humanity.

I now wish to deal with a very important point. There is much confusion, amongst those who take up Astrology casually, with regard to the *Sun in the Sign* and the *Rising Sign*. In America about four or five years ago some of the principal newspapers took up the subject of the Sun in the sign, giving the character of those persons born during a particular month; and there were several books written on this subject. In the horoscopes of people, the Sun and the sign it is in will govern the Individual characteristics. In fact, when I first gave my rendering of that in *Modern Astrology*, many people wrote to me to say how marvellously true the descriptions were. Yet if you were to ask a person in what month he was born, and gave him a reading of the character from the Sun in the sign, he might not altogether recognise it as accurate. To-night I wish to explain the reason of this.

At the commencement then, I may say that the Sun's place in your horoscope will undoubtedly describe your individual characteristics, that is, the characteristics of the *individual*, the most real and permanent part of you. Now I will try to give you some idea of these characteristics for the various months. The earth as a planet revolving round the Sun will receive from the Sun a specialised ray, as it were, during each month. The whole of that month the earth will be vitalised by the Sun-ray passing through a particular sign of the zodiac. All persons born in that month will have the characteristics of that sign strongly marked in their individual character. (Remember, by the way, that the sign commences about the 21st of each month; for the true astronomical year commences March 21st, when the Sun enters Aries.) In beginning to go into the sign its influence is weak, but as it advances, the character becomes stronger, till in those born about the first week of the month you find very strong characters indeed. Those born during the first three weeks of April have their Sun in Aries—not really the Sun *in* that sign, but the ray from the Sun *permeated by* its influence.

The Sun in Aries will govern all persons born from the 21st of March to the 21st of April, and they will all be leaders, fiery, impulsive persons, always wanting to control others mentally; because Aries, governing the head, makes the consciousness more active in the head than elsewhere. You will find them all very progressive people, always wanting to be in the front, very loyal, but very independent. You will see that the vices of the signs do not come in at all in the descriptions, because the Sun in the sign should not manifest any of the vices. It would be easy to continue, but indeed one might continue explaining the characteristics of a person born with the Sun in Aries all the evening; for so much does the Sun in the sign mean, that it is really a horoscope in itself.

The Sun in Taurus will have a different effect altogether. Aries is idealistic, but Taurus is practical. All persons born from April 21st to May 21st are marked with one special feature—obstinacy; they are dogmatic and determined, with much affection and warm-heartedness, but very firm and often obstinate.

Gemini, governing from May 21st to June 21st, has a totally different expression. These people are very dualistic, wanting to be in two places at one time, as it were; they have much motive behind them, but are very diffusive, yet at the same time are fond of things intellectual, refined and artistic.

Persons born between June 21st and July 21st with the Sun in Cancer are very negative and sensitive, but possess much tenacity or power to hold. When these people can overcome indolence, they have great power, and become very strong in these qualities. Cancer is a watery sign, and very marked traits are economy, thrift and carefulness—indeed, we often find misers born with the Sun in Cancer. But Cancer persons in this life have to display a certain amount of selfishness to protect themselves. They are so sensitive that if they were not a little selfish and conservative, they would lay themselves open to much injury from attack.

Those born from July 21st to August 21st with the Sun in Leo are very warm-hearted, affectionate, kind and generous, and very high spirited; but often the heart leads them astray, because the Sun working through that sign vivifies the heart more than any other part. But it is a very good sign for those who strive to live that high-minded, spiritual life where love is the principal expression of the soul.

The next sign, Virgo, through which the Sun's ray passes from August

21st to September 21st, gives us very discriminative persons, those who are exceedingly critical and also practical. There again you have, in a certain way, selfishness showing itself. This time, however, it is chiefly a mental selfishness, and if they have to doubt and be sceptical, it is because the quality of discrimination is to be worked out in their character.

The next sign, Libra, governing those born from September 21st to October 21st, is the sign of the balance. You have here expressed great separateness, and yet a making for unity, a love of harmony and peace, yet oftentimes persons who are too pleasure-loving and fond of ease; for this sign brings out the Venus quality strongly. But harmony and unity is their highest goal.

The next sign, Scorpio, governing from October 21st to November 21st, produces perhaps some of the strongest characters of all the twelve signs, and they nearly always have dignity or pride strongly marked. They are very reserved, cautious and secretive. They are frequently inclined towards mysticism and magic, and possess a strong liking for all those things termed occult. Oftentimes they are fond of scheming. They are very critical, and have marvellous judgment, which is generally used in a condemnatory sense. But, when the "sting" of the Scorpion is extracted, some of the finest characters are found with the Sun in Scorpio. Some of the most wicked and also some of the most exalted characters are born with Sun in this sign, which is in every sense a critical one.

Sagittarius governs those born from November 21st to December 21st, and gives us demonstrative persons, who however nearly always waste their forces by over-activity or over-excitement; they are very enthusiastic. A marked feature of the Sagittarius nature is rebelliousness. But those who have begun to recognise the working of great laws develope splendid qualities. These more advanced ones are always strongly inclined towards philosophy and religious thought.

The next sign, Capricorn, governing those born from December 21st to January 21st, gives a grave, steady, studious nature, thoughtful, careful, prudent, always seeking to attain some ideal, but withal practical in their ideals, yet liking grand surroundings. Nothing is too majestic for them; but they are wonderfully earnest and sober characters when they manifest all that the Sun in Capricorn can give. Tact, diplomacy, careful forethought, steadiness, perseverance, and all the higher and nobler of the Saturnine qualities are expressed through this sign.

Of those born from January 21st to February 21st with the Sun in the sign Aquarius, scarcely any live up to their heritage, the influence of this sign of The Man, *the* human sign. They are, however, always splendid judges of human nature. They are not emotional, but faithful and sincere. You can always rely upon them, and where they give their affection and devotion, it is lasting and binding. They are fond of science and all that is steady, generally also loving everything refined and humanitarian.

Pisces governs all persons born from February 21st to March 21st, this sign giving some very strange characters. Their best features are hospitality, love of dumb animals, kindness, softness and gentleness. Yet they are strange characters, nearly always unfortunate. They are indecisive, although kind. You will find many spiritualists have the Sun in Pisces; it is the beginning of occultism, in a sense, the beginning of the search for truth. Certainly, as a rule, they make the finest mediums.

You see, then, that there is a great deal to be learnt from a study of these signs, and that they stamp the individual character. If mankind could but rise to a full expression of all that these signs mean, the human race would be crowned with a glory which is unfortunately still far in the future.

Now I want to explain to you why you do not find people expressing all that the "Sun in the sign" indicates. When I first studied Astrology the science was in a most chaotic condition, and each student had to discover for himself what the planets in the signs meant and what the signs themselves meant. I set to work, therefore, to classify the whole and I found the Sun really indicated the individual character, that is, the character that is at the root of us, behind our personality; that which, on self analysis, would be found to express the individual part of us. But in ordinary everyday life, the Moon or lunar characteristics only are apparent. Practically, if we allowed the spiritual nature to act more frequently in our common life, it might be said we were living up to the expression of the Sun in the sign, and we should be acting beyond the limitations of our personality. We are all subjected to limitations caused by the planets and the signs of the zodiac, and we identify ourselves with these different influences—sometimes with each in turn; but the true life is hid, as it were, in the Sun. Therefore it is well to study the characteristics of the month, to which I have recently alluded, that we may know what our individual, our *real*, character is. If we could concentrate the whole of our mind and turn it in towards the diviner part of our nature, we should find that that in itself was a veritable spiritual Sun, a ray from which, penetrating our personal Self, constituted its very life and being. And it is with this *personal* ray that we identify ourselves. Not one person in a thousand ever lives up to what the Sun in the sign indicates.

The Sun is positive, the Moon negative; therefore the Moon receives the whole of the influence from the Sun and the planets. The Sun is symbolical of the heart, and the Moon of the head. If you watched your own consciousness, you might discover from the quality of your thinking and feeling the position the Moon occupied among the zodiacal signs. Further, if you could locate your consciousness in the heart you would know exactly the nature of the sign that the Sun was in at your birth.

Thus, suppose you had the Moon in Aries, you would find yourself doing things hastily and upon impulse, and speech would be rapid and fluent. (The Sun represents the creative thought, or that which is to become speech or action, the Moon speech, and the Rising Sign the activities.) The Moon in Aries would show all the characteristics of the Sun in that sign, but reduced, if I may be permitted the expression, to the plane of the personal. Nearly the whole of the characteristics we manifest are tinctured with the personality, and this personal element is considerably accentuated by the position of the Moon. Briefly, the Moon in Aries in your horoscope would make you impulsive, reckless, independent, brusque, and irritable, all of which is an indication, in this connection, of too much force in the brain.

The Moon in Taurus—the place of its exaltation—would make one practical, steady, and calm, but personally sensitive and affectionate, though obstinate and determined. In fact, all these positions of the Moon give the individual characteristics of the Sun expressed as personal characteristics; this I have studied most minutely in thousands of cases, and have found it to be correct. In whatever sign you find the Moon you will find the key to the nature of the personality.

The Moon receives and collects the influence of the other planets. Without some such distributive or radiating energy as the Sun, and some collective or focussing centre like the Moon, it is doubtful whether we could answer to the vibrations of any planet or sign of the zodiac, because we should have nothing to respond through. The Sun has for its spiritual expression Mars on the one hand and Venus on the other. The life-giving properties of the Sun express themselves through Mars as force, energy, courage, pluck, and so on; for which reason the circle is under the cross in the symbol of Mars—representing spirit seeking to burst through matter. The very opposite is shown through Venus, which represents everything gentle, loving, kind, sympathetic and beautiful. In Venus you have love of beauty, art and refinement, everything that goes to maintain a harmonious whole, whereas in Mars you have love of military glory and fame, everything that goes to destroy and break up. In the Sun we have constructive power; in Venus everything that holds together; in Mars everything that seeks to break up: these three planets thus representing a trinity of powers—construction, preservation and destruction. These are essentially the spiritual forces. The Moon in aspect with Venus will give a gentle and kind disposition, because the personality will be refined, but in aspect with Mars it will give a forceful personality, with much desire and energy. Here you have the Moon collecting all the red rays of Mars and distributing them as force, aggression and destruction; but the Moon receiving the rays from Venus gives us worshippers of beauty.

The individual characteristics are, of course, shown more strongly by the nature of the planet in aspect with the Sun; and exactly the same occurs in regard to the personality, when the Moon is in aspect with the planets. The Moon has on the one side Saturn, and on the other Jupiter. Just as the Sun found its two outlets in Mars and Venus, so the Moon finds its chief channels in Jupiter and Saturn. That which we think of as selfish and binding and limiting is represented by Saturn; while that which we regard as hopeful and expanding may be associated with Jupiter.

Having these three symbols—circle, half-circle and cross, representing the Sun, Moon and Earth, or father, mother and son, we find them all synthesised in Mercury. Suppose someone coming into life for the first time from the animal kingdom; over such a life the Moon would at first have the greatest influence, and, step by step, as in the course of evolution the instincts were called out, you would find they corresponded to the influence of the planets as the Moon received their rays; and stage by stage that life would advance until it could respond to the spiritual energies of the Sun.

When, at length, we have extracted all the virtues from the planets, we have reached up to Mercury. Here we have the real mind, the combination of spirit, soul and body, or man working with the whole of these three in perfect harmony. That is the individual characteristic; but, when evilly aspected, Mercury manifests as cunning, trickery and theft. So that much depends on Mercury, just as much depends on the Sun and Moon. You could write up a whole horoscope by knowing the positions of the three planets, the Sun, Moon and Mercury.

In a previous lecture I mentioned that Saturn represents the principle of crystallisation—in both the mental and physical worlds. For this reason, Saturn is the planet most usually associated with the idea of fate, or *Karma*, as the bringer of evil, the power that precipitates in this life the results of past thoughts and deeds. Saturn represents the outermost ring of limitation in the life. Beyond that, there is freedom. The power of Saturn must be broken ere the soul can express to the full its gains from previous lives. Astrologically, the symbol of this lofty liberation is a beneficent aspect of Saturn with the Sun. The Moon in affliction with Saturn gives the most sorrowful life you can imagine, and if you have persons with this in their horoscope, you will find the fate is most melancholy. They have permeated themselves to such an extent with this Saturnine influence that they invariably look at the dark side of things and as a result become melancholic, desponding, doubtful, fearful of results and consequences. When, however, you have the Sun in good aspect to Saturn, you have the fire of the Sun melting the coldness of Saturn.

These two planets may easily represent St. George and the dragon; for here you have the beginning of the great fight between the higher and lower mind, and the gradual breaking up of selfishness. Then you have sorrow, for the self that loves itself yields only after suffering has softened the nature. All the lunar instincts are crystallised in Saturn, the lower mind. So it is said that Saturn is evil. But let me correct any misconception. There is no such thing as evil *per se*. As I have said before, some of the finest characters in the world are under Saturn's influence, because they have contemplated and meditated and brought all their instinctual consciousness to a focus; they can steadily weigh up things. But Saturn is useless without Jupiter. Cold justice is no good without mercy. It is not till the personal begin to seek through religion (represented by Jupiter) for the truth they now feel to exist, that they overcome the personality. Thus it is that the Moon is shown in the symbol of Saturn to be under the cross, and in Jupiter to be over the cross—the instinctual consciousness risen above matter, no longer bound or limited by it.

With regard to the polarities, as I term them, we have a wonderful number of combinations. The Sun in any sign must have something wherewith to focus its influence; that focus is the Moon. I do not know what sort of a person you would have if you suppose the lunar influence to be entirely unrepresented in a horoscope, probably an idiot, or one very simple-minded. It does not matter what aspect the Moon has to Mercury or the Sun, it is good, because Mercury is a means by which the Sun expresses itself; *i.e.*, it allows the individuality to be manifested. These 'polarities' are known by the position of the Sun and Moon in the nativity, they being positive and negative to each other.

The Sun in each sign represents the individual character, and will find its expression in the personality in accordance with the Moon's position at birth. You can overcome that lunar position altogether and rise to the full possibilities of the solar position, but you cannot in one incarnation overcome *that* position, because it represents many lives of work. But your personal character may rise above all that the Moon indicates and you may pass on. I cannot possibly tell you about the 144 polarities as there is not time to do so.* But you will find that when the Sun is in one sign and the Moon in another, your outlook on the world is coloured by what we term the lunar consciousness. What I want to show you is that the personality expresses the individuality in accordance with the sign the Moon is in at birth, and that they are positive and negative the one to the other.

There is a point that may be interesting; it is this: the Sun is like a telescope to you. You are always looking at things on a far larger scale from the Sun standpoint; but the Moon is like a microscope magnifying the personal side of life. The Sun represents the ideal, the Moon the details. You have the ideal character shown by the Sun, the personal character by the Moon. There is another strange thing about this. The luminaries govern the eyes—the Sun the right eye, and the Moon the left eye, while Mercury governs the tongue. Where the luminaries are much afflicted you sometimes find blindness.

* These polarities have been given in Chapter XVIII., p 71.

On the vast subject of character and destiny I cannot, of course, say much here. You will, I think, see that all our destiny is the result of our character. I do not say our final destiny, because that is mapped out for us by the great Logos of our system. We have all to reach that point indicated by the Sun in our horoscope, but our present fate is really the result of our character. If we continue to identify ourselves with the limitations imposed by the Moon, we shall be fettered and hampered, because the Moon is not yet able to express the higher virtues. Unfortunately we are always instinctually limiting our consciousness. If you study the horoscope of anyone you will find that their characteristics are in harmony with their environment. Their whole outer condition of life seems to arise from their character.

In the horoscope, while our measure of freewill is shown by the Sun, our fate is represented by Saturn and Mars, the two so-called malefics. Practically, therefore, the Moon as the synthesis of these two planets represents one's ordinary fate, and the aspects that the Moon forms show the limitations of the soul, and how far it has evolved. Now the limitation of this freewill is found in the sign the Sun is in at birth. You may try as hard as you can to rise above that, but you will not be able. Try to think what it would mean to extract all the virtues from Aries. It means absolute truthfulness. The vice of this sign is deception. If one sought to be always truthful, and attained that ideal, how long would he be under his horoscopical delineation? We are limited to the extent our Sun indicates; and we are fated to the extent the Moon indicates, fated to work out the destiny made by ourselves. But, having this solar ray in us, we can, if we resolutely seek to unite ourselves with it, break up this lunar or personal side, and show forth in our lives the more beautiful and noble characteristics represented in the horoscope by the radiant solar orb.

LECTURE IV.

To-NIGHT we shall consider, not the idea of the zodiac and planets in general, but the horoscope itself; for although you may know all about the various influences of the signs and planets, until you can read the horoscope itself and combine the different influences represented therein, your knowledge will not be very valuable. You may know the general theory connected with the planets and the signs, but the whole must be put together and judged. It is not sufficient to know the general influence of the signs and of the planets, or how to erect the horoscope; this preliminary knowledge is, indeed necessary, but it is in the ability to combine into a synthetic whole the different qualities signified by the signs and planets that lies the secret of an accurate judgment of the nativity.

First, then, the basic structure of the horoscope is in the form of a cross. When the Sun rises in the morning, his rays will shoot straight across the earth, from East to West, and at noon, when the Sun reaches the mid-heaven, his rays will pour downwards through the earth, from South to North. These two lines or positive and negative rays are the axes upon which we build the horoscope, and from these the whole of the twelve houses have sprung.

There is an objection raised by many people to the apparently arbitrary arrangement of the twelve houses, but these twelve houses represent what may be termed our fate. In one respect they have a similar function to the twelve signs, the houses representing a certain portion of our fate, just as the twelve signs represent the various parts ot the body.

There are 360 distinct types of persons born each day of twenty-four hours, because every four minutes of time brings a fresh degree of the zodiac upon the ascendant; and each of these 360 types of persons has a totally different nativity. Then if you will take into consideration the different sign over which the Sun rules each month, you will see that during the course of a year there will be born many thousands of persons whose horoscopes will be totally different. For a considerable number of years there can be no two persons with even approximately the same nativity, because the Sun, Moon and planets are constantly altering their positions in the heavens.

The nativity is a map of the heavens representing the position of the zodiac and planets at the time of a child's birth, and it is interesting to trace out the whole life and future of the person in that particular map. A babe at the moment of its emergence on to the physical plane draws in its first breath, and at the same time is stamped, as it were, with the prevailing astral influences, this condition of things having already been selected for it as the meet and fitting environment for the initial stages of its terrestrial career.

Now a word as to how these houses come to have their special influences. They work in what are called "triplicities," a point I have already touched upon in a previous lecture. The primary influence comes from the apex of the triplicity, which is invariably one of the four angular points.

The First House, which is known as the "Ascendant," affects the whole nativity very powerfully; its bases are in the fifth and ninth houses, these being off-shoots of the first house. The ascendant symbolises the life of the personality, and springing from that are the two rays, one leading to the fifth house representing the creative and constructive properties, and the other to the ninth house, which is concerned with the creation of thoughts. The chief influence of the triplicity is centred in the first house. The Hindu Astrologers consider the fifth house (which is ruled by the Sun) to represent the Karma of our past birth—probably because its root is in the ascendant—and from it the whole of our past must be worked out before we can effectually and consciously build for the future through the ninth house. In the ninth house, which Hindu astrologers assert indicates our future birth, we have the Sagittarius principle. Here the animal part of our nature, the senses, is being left behind as the influence of the human life comes to have its greatest activity in this house. These three houses, starting from the eastern angle, are termed the Fiery triplicity, and their influence works itself out normally either as physical creation, making ties and links through desire, or as devotion either to scientific study, philosophy, some religious teacher, or to religion itself. A man at birth has either of these two lines of development awaiting him.

Apart from this particular triangle of the first, fifth, and ninth houses, the whole of the twelve divisions appear to be purely fatalistic in their influence, and I shall endeavour to show upon what this opinion is based. That which a man brings with him into his physical life is signified by the first house; that over which he has little or no control.

The Earthy triplicity starting from the mid-heaven, is called the physical triangle, and runs down from the tenth house to the second, and the sixth; from this meridianal point, which indicates the man's credit, honour or fame, we have action, which works out as acquisitiveness and is denoted by finance, the second house; while sickness, resulting from his actions in the past, is shown in the sixth house.

The Airy triplicity arises in the Western angle, the seventh house, running to the eleventh and third houses. The seventh house has to do with partners and the influence of others coming into the life; and this affects the third house, which signifies relatives and brethren, and the eleventh house, which is concerned with friends and acquaintances resulting from association with others.

All psychic and astral conditions have their root in the fourth house, the apex of the Watery triplicity, From the fourth house a ray passes to the eighth house, and another to the twelfth house, and these are called the occult houses. The fourth house is practically the house of occultism; but it has two off-shoots. the eighth house, the house of death, and the twelfth house, the house of misfortune. The eighth house seems to be concerned with the awakening of the astral consciousness, because it represents the death of the physical and the reaching up to the house of the new birth—the ninth house, the house of science, philosophy and religion. People with planets in the eighth house, if they have no occult tendencies, will be drawn a as rule to Masonic or Secret Societies. The twelfth house is the house of self-undoing, the house where one brings trouble and misfortune on oneself by taking one's own life in hand and seeking to alter it. The majority of persons with their planets in angles, however, and not in the occult houses, are not in the least concerned with things occult. The Watery triplicity represents the psychic nature, and those who have their planets in these cadent houses nearly always have what the world calls an unfortunate life. They have no real desire for fame, and always appear to be kept backward in life; and by looking at the cadent houses you can see at once the reason for the lack of opportunity to shine in the world. On the other hand, those who have their planets in angles are strongly desirous to enter into the world and to be active, and are always ready to take advantage of opportunities presented to them. It is as though that which had been crystallised in the past had worked its way from the inner houses to the external points, where it had to be manifested or broken up in the life of that person.

It is important for us to note that these triangles of houses correspond to the Fiery, Airy, Earthy and Watery triplicities of the signs; but of these four groups the Fiery and Airy are the principal influences affecting the life. Before considering these, however, we may condense what I have just said into the symbol of two triangles; the Sun governing the upper triangle, symbolising the spiritual qualities, and the Moon the lower triangle, symbolising the psychic qualities.

The whole of the twelve signs are divided into seven groups: *i.e.*, Cardinal, Fixed and Mutable, the three primary influences; and the four triplicities: Fire, Air, Water and Earth. Bearing in mind these seven divisions, we may know fairly accurately the type of person we are dealing with.

The status or quality of a person is shown by the number of planets found at birth in Fixed, Cardinal and Mutable or Common signs. People with the majority of planets in fixed signs are very determined, plodding and self-reliant. Those born with the majority of planets in cardinal signs are totally different. They will seek to become famous, or well-known in their own sphere, and it is essential for them to be at the head of things; they must be leaders, this arising from the fact that the cardinal signs are the heads of the triplicities. Persons born with the majority of planets in common signs are generally weak and indecisive, always indifferent, loving peace at any price, and liking to take things easily without stress or strain; the majority are very inert and lethargic. These three groups correspond to the Hindu "Gunas," Tamas, Rajas, and Sattva, representing Stability, Activity and Pliability.

Those persons who are born with the majority of their planets in Fiery signs have much fire and energy, and an active or passional nature. Those who have the majority of planets in Airy signs are intellectual, refined, and artistic; they cannot tolerate or submit to anything coarse or unrefined. The Watery signs indicate those who are chiefly more or less sensational, or those who are psychic and emotional. People with most of their planets in Fiery signs are emotional also, but it is a different phase of emotion to that of the Watery signs the Fiery signs representing the higher emotions, the Watery signs the lower.

The Earthy signs indicate persons who are practical, stolid, and matter-of-fact.

In a general sense, all persons born between 6 o'clock in the morning and noon have the best opportunities for worldly success, because they have more of what is called the "Electric" force in them. The whole of the eastern portion of the heavens, between the ascendant and the mid-heaven, is Electric; when the Sun has turned at noon, the influence becomes "Magnetic." Persons born between noon and sunset have this magnetic quality; they are not the propellers, but the receivers, the attractors. The positive portion of the nativity is that above the earth, while the negative portion is below.

Again, the position of the Moon at the time of "Epoch" as it is called, has a great influence upon the character. It is a singular fact that the character and life of the native will be according to the nature of the sign in which the Moon is at this time of "Epoch." When two persons who are united come together, a magnetic vortex is created between them, and from this auric sphere arise sound and colour which attract the incoming Ego, and out of this springs all that is to be in the future. The Moon at the moment of epoch will indicate the sign of the zodiac that is to make the ascendant or descendant of the nativity; and you could predict from that lunar position the whole of the horoscope and say what kind of child would be manifesting about nine months hence, its fate, disposition and character; for in that moment its whole future history seems to be concerned. And it is impossible for any birth to take place before the Moon reaches this particular position, before the appointed time, as it were. This fact it was that led me to the idea of reincarnation. I could come to no other conclusion but that since each Ego was to be born into a special set of conditions there must be some inherent necessity in that soul which linked it to those conditions; this necessity could be nothing but a state of development, and this development must have been attained in some previous existence.

I will now illustrate some of my previous remarks with the horoscope of Napoleon I.

Napoleon was born under the sign Libra, and Venus was his ruling planet, together with the planet Saturn in the sign Cancer, a sign of power. Venus elevated in the meridianal sign of Cancer, raised him to the highest position it was possible for him to attain. The military instinct which is very characteristic of his whole life, is indicated by the position of the planet Mars in the eleventh house in the sign Virgo. Any one taking his horoscope for study could see at once that he was destined to rise to a high position in life. His ruling planet being placed in this cardinal sign Cancer, he was bound to rise. Had he been born with Venus beneath the earth, afflicted, or in a cadent house, he could not have risen. The planet Uranus, whose influence causes sudden and unexpected events, falls in his seventh house, and as you know, Napoleon was divorced, and his love affairs were remarkable, being affected by the Sun in the sign Leo. Napoleon was born with the Moon in opposition to Saturn, and he had much selfishness in his nature. Saturn, the crystallised selfishness, had risen to the highest point in his nativity, and the ruling planet and Saturn were in the same sign, side by side. He had brought his whole selfishness to a culminating point; he had one great ambition and desire; and he had the power given him to work it out.

Let us now consider for a moment how we make our future horoscope. The whole of our thoughts during this life remain at our death and have a large share in shaping our next horoscope. You may ask: "Why are we born under this particular horoscope? Why do we answer to these particular vibrations? Is it blind fate or did we make it ourselves?" I would say emphatically: "We make it for ourselves." For this reason we can rule our stars. In other words, we may rise superior to the directions of the horoscope. I am quite positive that any one who takes himself in hand and tries to eradicate any part of the "evil" in his horoscope may do so. If you saw that you were born with a particular evil in your nature, you could set to work to eradicate it. Let me take, for example, an aspect of the Moon square Mars, which produces irritability, hasty speech, and an inclination to anger. Recognising this, one would try to eradicate it. If he did not do so, he would have the same aspect again in the horoscope of the next life. I believe that there is not one single thought, though trivial and unimportant, which does not finally crystallise into an act. We go on thinking and thinking in a certain groove, until the whole of these thoughts form a habit, and once a habit is set up, actions must follow. That is what I mean by thought becoming crystallised. All inevitable actions are under Saturn, therefore I have called him the great producer of fate. When Mars is in conjunction with Saturn, in mundane affairs, you will find many warring influences in the world. We may say that the majority of earth's inhabitants are more or less under the influence of Mars all their lives, but as life advances the Saturnine vibrations begin to play their part, and the working out of fate becomes inevitable.

To summarise the whole of my remarks on this subject of Astrology, I might say that so far as I can see there is no better course to pursue, in ruling our stars, than the development of character. We have made our character what it is; the horoscope represents us as we have made ourselves, and we have the task before us of evolving higher qualities. The different vibrations indicated by the planets constantly affect our natures; but once we know this, we may use these vibrations as a skilled gardener uses his tools—for the cultivation of the garden of the soul. To do this, we must rise to the occasion when opportunities present, otherwise we shall tend to drift downward and fall more deeply under the sway of the planetary influences. We possess within us a streak, as it were, of God's own free-will, and this we may use for growth. We should make a careful study of our individual nature, which Astrology helps us to understand; we should try to understand the strength and weakness of our personality, which the Moon represents, and then by giving allegiance to the Higher Self symbolised by the Sun, we shall be able by perseverance to break down the influence of Fate. We each have different horoscopes, and it is no use to expect others to see things as we see them. Thus, those who study astrology must in time become exceedingly tolerant, because they know that each individual is fettered by his own nativity, and it is the duty of the astrologer to help him to unfetter himself.

There is a Law governing us which is harmonious and beautiful, yet if we go against it, we come under malefic influences; but if we work in harmony with the Law, we come under the all-wise and ever-lasting benefic influences. Finally we cannot too strongly impress upon ourselves that "The stars incline, they do not compel." Essentially we are rays from the One Eternal White Light—sons of our Father in Heaven; a ray from the spiritual solar orb manifesting through many different sheaths for the purpose of making permanent and realisable the latent potentialities of the God within us. With any one of us, the time may be long or short ere the Christ is born within, and we "reverse our spheres"; but two things we know—that we shall in future have that special horoscope that we have made for ourselves, and that to tarry in our efforts to win the supreme perfection is but to delay the joy and peace that must come when, wearied of the earthy illusion, we set our face toward that spiritual Sun whose splendour never sets.